Handbook of Pain Syndromes
Biopsychosocial Perspectives

Handbook of Pain Syndromes
Biopsychosocial Perspectives

Edited by

Andrew R. Block
The WellBeing Group

Edwin F. Kremer
Mary Free Bed Hospital and Rehabilitation Center

Ephrem Fernandez
Southern Methodist University

LEA

LAWRENCE ERLBAUM ASSOCIATES, PUBLISHERS
1999   Mahwah, New Jersey   London

Lawrence Erlbaum Associates, Inc., Publishers
10 Industrial Avenue
Mahwah, NJ 07430

Cover design by Kathryn Houghtaling Lacey

Library of Congress Cataloging-in-Publication Data

Handbook of pain syndromes : biopsychosocial perspec-
tives / edited by Andrew R. Block, Edwin F. Kremer, Ephrem
Fernandez.
   p. cm.
Includes bibliographical references and indexes.
ISBN 0-8058-2680-7 (alk. paper)
   1. Chronic pain—Psychological aspects.   2. Chronic
pain—Social aspects. I. Block, Andrew. II. Kremer, Edwin F.
III. Fernandez, Ephrem.
   [DNLM: 1. Pain—etiology.   2. Chronic Disease.   3.
Pain—therapy.   4. Pain—psychology.   WL 704H2438
1998]
   RB127.H358   1998
   616'.0472—dc21
   DNLM/DLC   98-36687
   for Library of Congress   CIP

Books published by Lawrence Erlbaum Associates are printed
on acid-free paper, and their bindings are chosen for strength
and durability.

Printed in the United States of America
10 9 8 7 6 5 4 3 2 1

Dedication

*This volume is dedicated to our families
for their support, understanding, and tolerance.*

Debbie, Aaron, and Stefan (Block)

*Ann Margaret, Sara, Emily, Tim, Jeff,
& Kirstin Marie (Kremer)*

*My parents, Martin and Irene,
and to Emily (Fernandez)*

*We would also like to thank the many
mentors and colleagues who have influenced us
along the way, especially the following individuals:*

Doug Heath, Rogers Elliott, Frank Keefe (Block)

Leon Kamin (Kremer)

Dennis Turk, C. Richard Chapman (Fernandez)

Contents

Part II: Specific Pain Syndromes

Section A: Orthopedic and Rheumatologic Conditions

Section B: Neurological Conditions

Preface

Pain is both a curse and a blessing. At its best, pain serves to warn of real or impending tissue damage. Through its motivational and aversive aspects, pain compels individuals to take action, avoiding a worsening of damage, and/or beginning the process of restoration of damaged tissues. Unfortunately, pain's value as a warning signal is limited, and it may have exceedingly negative consequences. There are many situations, such as cancers, in which an individual can experience extreme and even life-threatening pathophysiology, without the perception of pain. An opposite problem may occur. Some individuals experience pain in the absence of any pathophysiological process, as in the case of somatoform pain disorder. Finally, many patients with tissue damage or a disease process may experience protracted disabling pain, leading to a downward spiral of emotional malaise, decreased physical function, and psychosocial upheaval.

Pain is ubiquitous. As the chapter by LeResche and VonKorff in the present volume demonstrates, pain can strike almost any organ system, and afflicts the young and old alike. The universal and aversive nature of pain has led to rapid development of the field of pain management.

Pain is complex. As discussed in the chapter by Riley and Robinson, pain is no longer considered a simple sensory occurrence. Rather, the most widely accepted current framework for the understanding of pain is now the biopsychosocial model. According to this model, nociception serves as a starting point for a series of events that culminate in the patient's perception of pain and overt pain behaviors. In the process, the pain experience is influenced by a) physical factors involved in pain signal transmission, b) psychological and emotional factors involved in the interpretation of pain signals, and c) environmental factors that provide incentives or disincentives for recovery.

The biopsychosocial model serves as a guide for the current volume. Part I of this volume provides in-depth coverage of some of the major psychosocial factors influencing pain syndromes. Financial and economic factors influencing pain syndromes are discussed in the chapter by Hadjistavropolous. Craig, Hill, and McMurtry both discuss how pain patients may be influenced to be deceptive or to malinger as a result of these incentives, and provide guidelines for caution in the judgment of deceptive behavior. The chapter by Okifuji, Turk, and Kalkuokalani discusses both the economic impact of chronic pain and the cost savings that result from a treatment approach based on the biopsychosocial model. Kerns discusses the motivation of the patient to engage in pain treatment, and proposes a stage model for matching treatment approach to the patient's motivational level. Fernandez, Clark, and Ruddick-Davis take an indepth look at the role of affect in the experience of chronic pain. This section of the volume concludes with Merskey's insightful and critical examination into the use of narcotics, antidepressants, and other medication in chronic pain.

Part II, comprising the bulk of this volume, examines 14 pain syndromes from a biopsychosocial perspective. Most of the chapters in this section are cowritten by a physician and a psychologist, in order to provide a truly integrated approach to evaluation and treatment of the syndrome. Section A examines orthopedic and rheumatological conditions. Chronic back pain, on which the largest body of research has been conducted, is examined in two chapters, one by Geisser and Colwell, and the second by Block and Callewart. The other chapters in this section provide insight into the physical and psychological factors associated with temporomandibular joint dysfunction (Massoth), whiplash (Teasell & Shapiro), and rheumatological disorders (Bradley).

Section B of Part II examines seven chronic pain conditions having a strong neurological basis. In many of these syndromes specific elements of nociception and pain transmission have been examined, in such a way that they provide insight into the interplay of pathophysiology and psychology. Of particular interest in this regard is the discussion of "pain memory" in phantom limb pain, in the chapter by Katz. However, for some syndromes, such as trigeminal neuralgia (as discussed by Eliav & Gracely) and muscular dystrophy (as reviewed by Perkins, Moxley, & Papciak), it will be noted that research into psychosocial factors is in its infancy. Other syndromes discussed within this section are general headaches (Kremer & Hudson), posttraumatic headache (Duckro & Chibnal), postherpetic neuralgia (Dworkin & Johnson), and complex regional pain syndromes (Steger, Bruehl, & Hardin).

Section C of Part II examines abdominal (Crowell & Barofsky) and pelvic pain (Reiter) syndromes, two conditions that are becoming increasingly frequent as complaints, and which are associated with significant medical costs. As noted in these chapters, physicians have long recognized that there is an interplay of medical and psychological factors in these conditions, but recent research is fleshing out many of the details of this complexity.

The current volume concludes with a discussion of pain syndromes in six special populations. These chapters demonstrate that chronic pain can affect the elderly (Roy, Thomas, & Cook) and young (McAlpine & McGrath) alike. Pain can occur in the context of the life-threatening disease of cancer (Roth & DeRosayro), which makes it especially difficult to handle. The disfigurement and intense hospitalization associated with burn pain (Patterson, Doctor, & Sharar) present special challenges to patients and their health care team. Along with the systemic problems caused by sickle-cell disease (Wilson, Gil, & Porter) pain creates it own difficulties, especially in children so afflicted. The final chapter, by Lautenbacher and Rollman, examines the pain that can occur in the complete absence of identifiable pathophysiology.

The current volume illustrates the challenge of pain syndromes. These chapters demonstrate that pain is almost inevitable, very expensive and extremely difficult to adequately evaluate and treat. It is our hope that the volume underscores the value and importance of considering pain from a biopsychosocial perspective, in order to provide for the most effective management of patients who suffer from such protracted, noxious conditions.

This volume is the culmination of 3 years of work. We would like to thank several individuals who have provided significant assistance with this manuscript. Sam Signoretta and Joan Davis have provided much appreciated help with organizing the chapters, phone calls, and the general office support necessary to produce this volume. Susan Milmoe at Lawrence Erlbaum Associates has been very helpful and supportive, and has provided important guidance in our efforts.

—Andrew R. Block
—Edwin F. Kremer
—Ephrem Fernandez

GENERAL CONSIDERATIONS

Chapter 1

Epidemiology of Chronic Pain

Linda LeResche
University of Washington

Michael Von Korff
Center for Health Studies—
Group Health Cooperative of Puget Sound

EPIDEMIOLOGIC PERSPECTIVES

Epidemiology is defined as the study of distribution, determinants, and natural history of disease in populations (Lillienfeld & Lillienfeld, 1980). This definition embodies the three important perspectives of epidemiology: the population perspective, the environmental perspective, and the developmental perspective. We have elaborated the implications of these perspectives for research and treatment of chronic pain elsewhere (Dworkin, Von Korff, & LeResche, 1992). Here we provide a brief review.

Population Perspective

Much of this book is written from the perspective of clinicians who treat patients with chronic pain. Such pain patients, often seen in tertiary care centers, certainly experience a great deal of suffering and interference with social roles associated with their pain; they also account for significant health care costs and disability. However, as a group these patients represent only a small fraction of persons in the population who experience pain, or even persistent pain. Thus, inferences about pain generated from the study of this highly selected group of patients may not be useful, and may even be misleading, in terms of developing an understanding of the etiology and natural history of acute, recurrent, and chronic pain conditions (Fields, 1987).

3

In contrast, study of pain in populations allows for the documentation of the full spectrum of pain severity. For example, we can determine the extent to which pain of a particular type, persistence, or intensity is associated with interference with work, social, or family activities. In addition, the population perspective provides data for defining or delineating disease and illness from the range of normal variation. Because pain is such a prevalent human experience, in order to develop an understanding of when "pain" becomes a "pain problem" either for the individual or society, it is essential to study the full range of persons with pain—both in and outside treatment settings. Examination of pain in the population (as opposed to exclusively in treatment settings) also allows for investigation of etiologic and risk factors for pain, as distinct from factors that may be associated with seeking treatment. Finally, only studies in the population can provide data on the full burden of pain in society.

Ecological Perspective

The ecological perspective of epidemiology implies that diseases are a product of the dynamic interaction of disease agents, host factors that increase disease susceptibility, and environmental factors that influence exposure to the agent or increase its virulence. Environmental factors are viewed broadly, and include both physical and social factors. Although this perspective was initially developed in the investigation of acute, infectious disease, it holds equally well for chronic diseases and conditions. In fact, the ecological perspective of epidemiology is quite similar to the biopsychosocial model of illness first elaborated by Engel (1960) and now espoused by most clinicians and researchers as the most useful model for the investigation of chronic pain conditions.

Developmental/Temporal Perspective

The developmental perspective suggests that diseases have specific temporal characteristics within an individual, and have a natural history within the population as a whole that is a product of the individual patterns. Within the individual, important temporal characteristics include age of onset, duration of the condition, temporal patterning (e.g., episodic vs. constant), and staging or course of the illness. Within the population, important elements of natural history include the predictability of temporal patterning, as well as the typical course of the condition. In the area of chronic pain, important issues of natural history include the rates with which people make transitions between acute, recurrent and chronic pain states, what the typical course or prognosis of a pain condition is, and how the course is affected by host and environmental factors.

A Dynamic Population Model of Pain

Incorporating the perspectives of epidemiology outlined previously, epidemiologic research on chronic pain aims to investigate pain in populations as a dynamic process characterized by the interactions of agent, host, and environmental factors. One possible approach to characterizing change in pain status over time is the dynamic population model we have presented elsewhere (Von Korff, 1992). This model suggests that at any given point in time, persons may be pain free or may be experiencing acute, recurrent, or persistent pain with or without dysfunction. In terms of this dynamic model, some of the aims of epidemiologic research involve characterizing and defining pain states across this spectrum of severity. Because pain is dynamic, transitions among these states over time are to be expected. Thus, additional aims of epidemiology are to estimate the probability of being in a particular state during a given time period, to estimate the probability of transition among states over time, and to identify factors predicting or controlling the probabilities of transition.

Epidemiologic Measures

The basic measures employed by epidemiologists to describe the distribution, determinants and natural history of disease in populations include prevalence, incidence, duration, and risk. These measures are defined as follows.

Prevalence. This is defined as the proportion of persons in the population with a disease or condition at a particular time. Thus, both the number of persons with the condition and the total population at risk of having the condition (i.e., the numerator and denominator, respectively) have to be known in order to calculate a prevalence rate. If the enumeration is done at a single point in time (or approximates this kind of measure), the prevalence rate is called a *point prevalence* rate. Other commonly reported kinds of prevalence rates include *period prevalence* (e.g., number of cases in the population over a 3- or 6-month time period) or *lifetime prevalence* (number of persons who experience the condition over the course of their lifetime). Period prevalence is probably the most appropriate type of prevalence measure for chronic pain conditions, since it better captures significant pain problems that may be frequent or persistent, but may not be present at the exact time of the survey.

Incidence is defined as the rate of onset of the condition over a defined time period (usually 1 year). Calculation of incidence requires knowledge of the number of new cases appearing in a population over the time period (numerator of the incidence rate) as well as the number of persons at risk of developing the condition (the denominator). Note that persons at risk include all those capable of developing the condition (e.g., men in the case of prostate cancer) who do not already have the condition, or who have no history of the condition.

Duration is simply the length of time the condition lasts. For conditions that are episodic or recurrent, the total duration would be equivalent to the sum of the durations of each episode.

Prevalence, incidence, and duration are related, by a steady-state equation, such that (under steady-state conditions):

$$Point\ Prevalence = Incidence \times Mean\ Duration$$

For recurrent conditions, in a steady-state population,

$$Point\ Prevalence = Incidence \times Mean\ Episode\ Duration \times Mean\ No.$$
$$Episodes\ \text{(Von Korff, 1992; Von Korff & Parker, 1980)}.$$

Risk is defined as the likelihood that persons who do not have a specific condition (but who have particular attributes or are exposed to certain "risk factors") will develop the condition.

Most of the epidemiologic literature in the field of pain involves reporting of prevalence rates. There are some studies aimed at identifying risk factors, a few that specifically examine the temporal course of pain, and only a handful of studies of the incidence, or rates of onset of specific pain conditions.

PREVALENCE DATA

An exhaustive review of the literature on the prevalence of particular pain conditions is beyond the scope of this chapter. However, the following sections present age- and gender-specific prevalence rates for those pain conditions that are most common in the adult population. In addition, data are presented on a few less common conditions (e.g., fibromyalgia) that may be of particular interest to researchers and pain clinicians. Only studies investigating entire populations are reviewed (e.g., studies of a particular occupational group are excluded). Although absolute prevalence rates of specific pain conditions may vary from study to study depending on the definitions used and the population studied, the age- and gender-specific *patterns* of prevalence for particular pain conditions are of interest because they can potentially shed light on biologic, psychologic, and social factors that might influence rates of onset or duration of these pain conditions in a given age-gender group. Thus we selectively review those studies that have examined age by gender-specific prevalence. This chapter focuses on pain in adults; for a review of the epidemiology of pain in children and adolescents, see Goodman and McGrath (1991).

Back Pain

Given the public health importance of back pain, there are numerous epidemiologic studies of the condition; however, data are not always presented in such a way that it is possible to calculate age by gender-specific prevalence rates. Figure 1.1 shows prevalence rates for back pain in several studies of the adult population, where age- by gender-specific prevalence

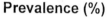

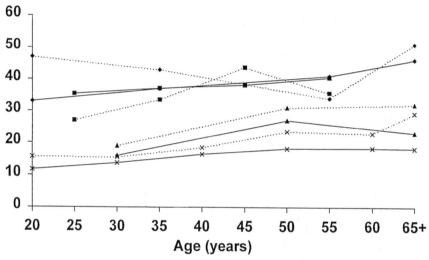

FIG. 1.1. Patterns of age- and gender-specific prevalence rates of back pain from four population-based studies. Solid lines indicate rates for men, dotted lines for women. Study sites were: Seattle (Von Korff et al., 1988); rural Great Britain (Walsh et al., 1992); Northwest England (Wright et al., 1995); and a national sample of the population of Great Britain (Croft et al., 1994). Data for each age group are plotted at the approximate midpoint of the age interval. Detailed age- and gender-specific prevalence rates (e.g., for 32-year-old men) cannot be inferred, due to the form of the original data. See text for specific age groupings and definitions of prevalence used in these studies.

rates could be determined. The studies employed a range of definitions of back pain, and a variety of study methods and populations.

Von Korff, Dworkin, LeResche, and Kruger (1988) conducted an epidemiologic study of five common pain conditions in a stratified random sample of 1,016 enrollees of a large HMO in Seattle. Respondents were asked to report pains occurring in the last six months that had lasted at least a day and were not fleeting or minor. Prevalence rates for back pain among men increased with age, with the 6-month prevalence being 33% among 18–24 year-olds, 37% in those 25–44, 41% in the 45–64 year-olds and 46% among men 65 and older. In contrast, the prevalence of back pain declined with age in women, at least up to the age of 65. (Rates were 47% in women 18–24, 43% in 25–44 year-olds, 34% in 45–64 year-olds, and 51% in women over 65.)

In contrast to the findings of the Seattle study, data from a study of back pain in a sample of 2,667 persons from small towns and rural areas in Great Britain (Walsh, Cruddas, & Coggon, 1992) indicate 1-year prevalence rates that are higher in young men than in young women (i.e., 35% in men vs. 27% in women 20–29 years of age) and increase only slightly for men with increasing age (rates of 37% among men in their 30s, 38% of those in their 40s and 40% of those in their 50s). For women, rates increased to 34% in those 30–39, 44% in those 40–49 and then dropped to 36% among women 50–59 years old, so that in the oldest group, back pain prevalence was again higher for men than for women.

Two other population-based studies in Great Britain have found back pain to be somewhat more prevalent in women than in men at all ages. Croft and Rigby (1994) used data from the Health and Lifestyle Survey of 9,003 adults from a representative sample of households in Great Britain to assess the 1-month prevalence of "trouble with a bad back." Given the shorter time frame and the wording of the question used to identify back pain in this study, it is perhaps not surprising that the rates of pain observed were lower than in the studies described previously. Rates for men ranged from 11.8% in those 18–25 to 17.4% in those 65–74, with a rather gradual rise with age. For women, rates ranged from 15.7% in those 18–25 to 27.9% in those 65–74, however rates did not rise continuously with age; for example, the rate for women aged 45–54 (23.5%) was almost identical to that for those 55–64 (22.9%).

Finally, Wright, Barrow, Fisher, Horsley, and Jayson (1995) surveyed over 34,000 persons in 19 health districts in the Northwest of England. Subjects were asked about the presence, in the past year, of "sciatica, lumbago or recurring backache." Sixteen percent of the men and 19% of the women aged 18–39 reported experiencing back pain in the prior year. For those 40–64, rates were 27% for men and 31% for women, whereas 23% of the men and 32% of the women over 65 reported back pain.

Although there are other epidemiologic studies of back pain, many are confined to persons working in specific industries. In those population-based back pain studies reviewed here, the absolute differences in prevalence levels may be largely explainable by the differences in case definition. However, a more important concern is that the *pattern* of prevalence varies from study to study shown in Fig. 1.1 (i.e., the lines are not parallel). Thus, the data on age- and sex-specific prevalence appear contradictory, and no clear inferences can be drawn concerning age and gender influences, other than that back pain prevalence appears to rise in men up to age 50. Occupational (Walsh et al., 1992), socioeconomic (Croft & Rigby, 1994), psychosocial (Foppa & Noack, 1996; Wright et al., 1995), and possibly geographic, cultural, and cohort differences, as well as differences in life-style risk factors such as smoking (Foppa & Noack, 1996; Wright et al., 1995) may be so powerful for back pain that the influences of age and gender are difficult to discern.

Headache

Migraine. Stewart, Schechter, and Rasmussen (1994) have recently reviewed population-based prevalence studies of migraine. Twenty-four population-based studies were identified. Prevalence rates varied widely for studies using different case definitions. However, the four recent studies that employed International Headache Society (IHS) criteria for migraine (Headache Classification Committee of the International Headache Society, 1988) produced very consistent prevalence estimates. One-year prevalence rates for women ranged from 12.9% to 17.6%; those for men ranged from 3.4% to 6.1%. The lowest rates were found in the one study that surveyed only 21–30 year-olds (Breslau, Davis, & Andreski, 1991). Overall prevalence rates in the remaining three studies, conducted in the United States, France, and Denmark (Henry et al., 1992; Rasmussen, R. Jensen, Schroll, & Olesen, 1991; Stewart, Lipton, Celentano, & Reed, 1992) varied very little: 15%–17.6% for women, and 5.7%–6.1% for men. Age patterns for migraine prevalence follow a bell-shaped curve, with age. For example, in the American study (Stewart et al., 1992) the highest prevalence for both men and women was among those 35 to 45 years old. Rates for women are higher than for men at all ages, although the gender ratio is not consistent over the life span. The female:male ratio appears to increase with age from menarche to about age 42 and to decline thereafter, although the ratio remains about 2:1 in those over age 60. Thus, it has been suggested that although hormonal factors may account for much of the difference in prevalence rates of migraine for men and women, undoubtedly other factors operate as well. In addition to addressing age- and gender-specific prevalence, the U.S. survey examined prevalence rates by race and socioeconomic status. After adjusting for other factors, White men had higher migraine rates than Black men, but rates for women did not differ by race. Prevalence decreased with increasing household income for both genders.

Tension-Type Headache. Although there are numerous population-based studies of headache, few have specifically differentiated tension-type headache. Among four recent prevalence studies using the IHS criteria for various types of headache (Alders, Hentzen, & Tan, 1996; Gobel, Petersen-Braun, & Soyka, 1994; Jabbar & Ogunniyi, 1997; Rasmussen et al., 1991), only one provided estimates of period prevalence of tension-type headache broken down by age and gender. In a study of 740 persons in the County of Copenhagen, Denmark, Rasmussen et al. found the 1-year prevalence rates of tension-type headache to decline with age in women. Rates were 93% for women aged 25–34, 92% for those 35–44, 82% in 45–54 year-olds and 74% in those 55–64 years of age. For men, rates were highest in the 45–54 year age group (70%). Estimated prevalence for men 25–34 years old was 68%; for 35–44 year-olds, the rate was 63%. Prevalence dropped to 49% in the 55–64 year age group. Thus, prevalence of tension-type headache was higher for women than for men in each of the age groups studied. The vast majority of those with tension-type headache had episodic headache, whereas approximately 3% of the total population met criteria for chronic daily headache (i.e., headache 180 days per year or more).

Other studies have used similar criteria to estimate the prevalence of tension-type headache in different populations, including both industrialized (Gobel et al., 1994) and Third World countries (Alders et al., 1996; Jabbar & Ogunniyi, 1997). These studies either identified a primary headache (i.e., a subject was assigned a diagnosis of migraine *or* tension-type headache, but not both), or used a hierarchical system (i.e., assigned all those with both types of headaches to the migraine group). Because most persons with migraine have tension-type headache as well, the actual prevalence rates of tension-type headache in these populations are likely to be much higher than those reported. In addition, some studies reported only lifetime prevalence rates. Thus, it is not possible at this time to compare prevalence patterns in different countries that might illuminate cultural variability in the rates of tension-type headache.

Joint Pain

Although a number of epidemiologic studies of rheumatoid arthritis (RA) and osteoarthritis (OA) have been conducted, these studies frequently define cases based on radiologic joint changes or level of rheumatoid factor, rather than on the presence of pain. The total prevalence of RA in the population has been estimated to be approximately 1% (McDuffie,

1985; Wolfe, 1994). Presuming that almost all active cases of RA are associated with pain, this estimate is probably an accurate reflection of RA-associated pain in the population. Onset of RA is rare before age 40. The prevalence of RA increases with age in both genders, with overall prevalence in women about three times that in men (Wolfe, 1994).

In contrast to the situation with RA, osteoarthritic changes are frequently present in the absence of pain. From a large epidemiologic survey conducted in Northern England (Lawrence, Bremner, & Bier, 1966), it is possible to calculate age- and gender-specific prevalence rates for pain in specific joints. It should be noted that it is possible that these rates include some persons with RA, as well as OA. The following are prevalence rates for pain, not objectively assessed arthritic changes in joints. In a sample of 1,098 men and 1,198 women over age 15, rates of pain in the joints of the fingers (proximal interphalangeal joints) increased with age in both genders (with the exception that rates were similar in men 25–34 and 35–44). Rates for men and women were similar up to age 34 (around 2% in those 15–24 and 6%–7% in those 25–34). Thereafter, pain prevalence in women was approximately twice that of men the same age. Prevalence rose to 31% in women and 15% in men over age 65.

Pain in the knees was more prevalent than pain in the joints of the fingers, and showed less of a gender difference. However, prevalence of knee pain also increased with age in both genders. Rates in men were 20% for those 35–44 years old, 29% in those 45–54, 33% in those 55–64 and 39% in those 65 or older. In women, rates were 19% for 35–44 year-olds, 30% in those 45–54, 45% in those 55–64, and 50% in those 65 or older.

The age-specific prevalence of joint pain certainly reflects the degenerative changes that occur with age; the reason for the higher rates in women appears to be related to a higher rate of degenerative changes in women, because the rates of pain complaint among those with changes was similar for men and women (Lawrence et al., 1966).

Chest Pain

Chest pain is a common symptom that can be caused by a wide range of diseases and disorders (Psaty, 1995), including not only coronary heart disease, but also mitral valve problems, disorders of esophageal motility, and panic disorder, among others. In a population-based study of more than 19,000 persons over age 20 in Copenhagen, Denmark, G. Jensen (1984) assessed the lifetime prevalence of chest pain, asking, "Have you ever had any pain or oppression (discomfort) in the chest?" Prevalence rates for chest pain were almost comparable for men and women, and varied little with age. Prevalence in men varied from 32%–38% and rates for women varied from 32% to 35%.

In contrast, some smaller studies assessing period prevalence have detected gender and age differences. For example, in our survey of approximately 1,000 persons in Seattle (Von Korff et al., 1988), 6-month prevalence rates were highest for both men and women in the 45–64 year old age group (17% for men and 15% for women). Rates were fairly comparable for men and women 25–44 years old (11% for men, 10% for women) and in those 65 and older (14% for men, 13% for women). However, in the 18–24 year-olds, the rate for women (13%) was almost twice that for men (7%).

In the Danish study (G. Jensen, 1984), in addition to overall chest pain, specific angina-like pain was assessed according to the Rose Questionnaire. This questionnaire follows up on the initial, "Have you ever had any pain or oppression (discomfort) in the chest?" with specific questions about the pain, worded in the present tense (e.g., "Do you get it when you walk uphill in a hurry?"); the questionnaire yields an algorithm diagnosis of angina. Rates for chest pain meeting the criteria for angina in the Danish study rose with age in both men and women, rising from 2% in those 20–29 to 13% for those 80 and above for men, and from 2% for those 20–29 to 10% for those 80 and older among women.

Another study that used the Rose criteria for angina-like pain in a population of 2,085 White women and 2,348 White men in the United States, found that the reliability of symptom report was lower for women than for men (Harris & Weissfeld, 1991). Prevalence rates, based on meeting Rose criteria on two occasions several months apart, indicated a rising rate of angina for men with age (from 0.6% at age 30–39, to 5.4% for those 70 years of age and older), similar to the Danish study. However, rates showed no clear age pattern for women, varying between 1.5% and 3.2%. Interestingly, in this U.S. study, the prevalence rate for women in the youngest age group (30–39 year-olds) was much higher than the rate for men of similar age (0.6% for men vs. 2.2% for women).

Thus, there may be some cultural differences operating, such that young women in the U.S. appear to report both more chest pain and more angina-like pain than their male counterparts, whereas these gender differences do not seem to occur in Denmark.

Facial Pain

The vast majority of facial pain is pain in the muscles of the face and/or the temporomandibular joint (i.e., the musculoskeletal pain of temporomandibular disorders, or TMD). We have recently reviewed the epidemiology of TMD in some detail (LeResche, 1997). Although the literature on prevalence of TMD per se is somewhat confusing because a variety of signs and symptoms may be assessed and case definitions are highly variable, prevalence rates of TMD *pain* are, in fact, relatively consistent (Goulet, Lavigne, & Lund, 1995; Helkimo, 1974; Locker & Slade, 1988; Mohlin, 1983; Szentpetery, Huhn, & Fazekas, 1986; Von Korff et al., 1988). Prevalence rates for pain in the temporomandibular region (pain in the jaw joint and/or muscles of mastication) range from 3% to 10% for men, and from 6% to 15% for women, depending on the specific question asked. These studies reported either a 6-month period prevalence, or no specific time frame was specified, although the question was worded in the present tense (e.g., "Do you have pain in the muscles of your face or the joint in front of the ear?"). TMD pain prevalence presents an age-gender distribution similar to that of migraine headache, i.e., overall prevalence rates are about twice as high for women as for men, and prevalence rises with age in women until the mid-40s; rates are low in those over age 65. This pattern of age- and gender-specific prevalence again suggests that hormonal factors may play a role in these pain conditions, although they are unlikely to be the only risk factors influencing the onset or duration of pain (LeResche, Saunders, Von Korff, Barlow, & Dworkin, 1997).

Abdominal Pain

Abdominal pain can be attributable to a number of specific bacterial and viral infections, as well as to less well defined causes. Several studies recently conducted in Europe and North America have attempted to assess the prevalence in the population of abdominal pain, as a pain complaint per se (Adelman, Revicki, Magaziner, & Hebel, 1995; Agreus, Svardsudd, Nyren, & Tibblin, 1994; Kay, Jorgensen, & K. H. Jensen, 1994; Von Korff et al., 1988). Some of these studies have also attended to possible specific causes of the reported pain. Although prevalence rates of abdominal pain in the general population vary widely from study to study, probably because of the differing time frames and criteria used to define a case, the age- and gender-specific *patterns* for abdominal pain are highly consistent across studies. All of the recent population-based studies reviewed indicate that abdominal pain is more prevalent in women than in men, and that the prevalence declines with age.

Our own study of a sample 1,016 persons in an HMO population in Seattle (Von Korff et al., 1988) found that 6-month prevalence of abdominal pain in men declined from 14% in 18–24 year-olds to 7% in men aged 65 and older. The decline was not totally linear, as the highest prevalence rate (17%) was for men 45–64 years old. In women, rates declined in a regular manner from 31% in those 18–24 years old to 12% among those 65 years of age and older. Our definition of pain included pains that had lasted a whole day or more or that had recurred several times in a year. Subjects were asked not to report "fleeting" or "minor" pain. It is possible that women reported pain related to menstruation, as this type of pain was not specifically excluded.

Kay et al. (1994) studied abdominal pain in 3,608 residents of the western part of Copenhagen County, Denmark. Subjects were selected randomly from those aged 30, 40, 50, or 60 in 1982. One year prevalence rates were assessed for abdominal pain, with no exclusion of particular types of pain, and no severity criteria. Prevalence rates for men were 47.8% in the 30 year-olds, 41.6% in the 40 year-olds, 32.7% in the 50 year-olds and 30.4% in men aged 60. In women, rates were higher and the age-specific rates showed a general, but not totally consistent decline: prevalence for 30 year-olds was 52.1%; for 40 year-olds, 55.2%; for 50 year-olds 45.6% and for 60 year-olds, 42.5%.

Another Scandinavian study (Agreus et al., 1994) assessed the 3-month period prevalence of any abdominal pain or discomfort by region (upper abdomen, central abdomen, lower abdomen) among a representative sample of persons 20–79 years old in the municipality of Östhammar, Sweden. Among the final sample of 582 men, rates for upper abdominal pain declined from 16.8% in the 20–34 year-olds to 6.7% in those 64–79 years old. A similar pattern was seen for central abdominal pain (24.2% in the youngest group and 8.9% in the oldest). For lower abdominal pain, rates declined from 12.8% in the youngest group to 6.2% in 35–49 year-olds and 5.9% in 50–64 year-olds, but rose again to 11.2% in those aged 65–79. For the 572 women who completed the questionnaire, rates for pain at all three locations showed a steady decline with increasing age. The prevalence of upper abdominal pain declined from 26.3% in the 20–34 year-olds to 13.6% in those aged 64–79; central abdominal pain declined from 35.3% in the youngest group to 17.3% in the oldest group; and lower abdominal pain declined from 36.1% in the youngest group to 13.3% in the oldest group.

Finally, Adelman et al. (1995) conducted a study of abdominal pain among a random sample of persons aged 17 and older enrolled in an HMO in Howard County, Maryland. Pregnant women were excluded, and women were specifically asked not to report menstrually-related pain. The final sample size was 6,199. As in other studies, a decline in prevalence with age was seen in both genders, and rates were higher for women than for men at all ages. One-year prevalence for men aged 18–44 was 24%, and for men 65 years of age and older, prevalence was 17%. For women, prevalence rates declined from 31% among those 18–44 to 23% in those 65 and older. About 20% of all persons with pain attributed their pain to a specific cause. The most common causes mentioned were reflux esophagitis/heartburn, urinary tract infections, gastric ulcer, duodenal ulcer and gallstones/cholelithiasis. Although rates of pain were lowest in the elderly, both the percentage of subjects attributing pain to a particular cause, and the percentage of subjects seeking care for pain increased with age.

Interestingly, the single population-based study we identified that presented age- and gender-specific prevalence rates for irritable bowel syndrome, defined according to the Manning criteria (Jones & Lydeard, 1990), also found higher rates in women than in men in all the age groups where sample sizes were 100 or more, that is, among persons 30–79 years of age. (In 20–29 year-olds, where sample sizes were around 90, rates were similar for men and women; in those over age 80, the sample size for men was only 25, so rates are probably unreliable.) Again, overall prevalence rates declined with age.

Chronic Widespread Pain/Fibromyalgia

We identified only two population-based studies of widespread pain and/or fibromyalgia that presented age- by gender-specific prevalence rates. Croft, Rigby, Boswell, Schollum, and Silman (1993) drew an age-stratified random sample of persons enrolled in two general practices in Cheshire, England. The area covered included both a rural town and a suburb of Manchester. Questionnaires were returned by 1,340 persons. Chronic widespread pain was defined as pain of longer than 3 months duration in two contralateral quadrants of the body—that is, by the definition of the American College of Rheumatology (Wolfe et al., 1990). (This definition constitutes part of the ACR criteria for fibromyalgia; in addition, 11 of 18 specific sites must be tender to palpation in order for a subject to qualify for a diagnosis of fibromyalgia.) For men, rates of chronic widespread pain rose with age up to age 65. The prevalence in men younger than 34 years old was 4.7%; for those 35–44 the rate was 4.8%; for those 45–54, 9.3%; and for those 55–64, 17.2%. The prevalence in men 65–74 years old dropped to 7.2%, and then rose to 19.9% in those 75 and older. However, the number of subjects in the two oldest age groups was small, so these estimates may be unreliable. For women the picture was similar, although the age of peak prevalence was slightly younger. For women less than 34 and those between 35 and 44 years old, prevalence of chronic widespread pain was 9.3%. The rate jumped to 25.0% in women 45–54, and dropped to 17.4% in those 55–64. The prevalence rate for women aged 65–74 was 20.0%, and for those 75 and older, 26.3%. Again, sample size is somewhat limited for women 65 and older. Thus, from this single study, the prevalence of chronic widespread pain is higher for women than for men. Prevalence rises steeply for both sexes into middle age, and then drops, possibly with a secondary peak in the very elderly population.

Wolfe, Ross, Anderson, Russell, and Hebert (1995) found a similar pattern for chronic widespread pain in their community survey of fibromyalgia and its components. The study was conducted in a sample of 3,006 persons in randomly selected households in Wichita, Kansas. Subjects completed mail or telephone surveys, and a subsample of those with and without widespread pain were invited for a follow up clinical examination of tender points to ascertain the prevalence of fibromyalgia. Rates obtained from the sample were weighted based on the age-gender distribution of the Wichita population, and the crude weighted rates were smoothed using a logistic model. Using these methods, chronic widespread pain rose with age from age 18–29 years, peaking in the 60–69 year age group for both men and women, and then dropping off in the oldest age groups (70–79 year-olds and those 80 and older). Rates for men aged 18–29 were approximately 3%, and for women around 6%; at age 60–69, rates were about 13% for men and 22.5% for women. In the very oldest subjects, 80 years of age and older, rates were around 8% for men and 15% for women.

The prevalence of fibromyalgia was, of course, lower, but followed roughly the same age pattern as widespread pain for women. However, for men, the age-related rise in prevalence was much less dramatic for fibromyalgia than for widespread pain. Estimated fibromyalgia prevalence rates in men rose from 0.1% in 18–29 year-olds to 1.2% in 70–79 year-olds, dropping slightly in men 80 years of age and older. Rates in women rose from 0.9% in those 18–29 to 7.4% of those 70–79, again falling slightly (to 5.9%) in women 80 years of age and older.

Thus, based on the two available studies, both widespread pain and fibromyalgia demonstrate significantly higher prevalence rates in women than in men and prevalence rises with age from young adulthood in both genders. The prevalence of widespread pain appears to peak at somewhat younger ages (i.e., in the 50s or 60s) than the full-blown diagnosis of fibromyalgia, which has its highest prevalence in persons in their 70s. Although the patterns presented appear relatively consistent, any conclusions about the prevalence of widespread pain and fibromyalgia in the general population should be considered tentative, as they are based on only two studies.

INCIDENCE DATA

In contrast to the abundant literature on pain prevalence, there are virtually no studies examining rates of onset of pain in the general population, or risk factors associated with pain onset. (There are a number of prospective studies specifically focusing on predictors of back pain complaints in industrial workers; however, because these studies usually measure requests for workers compensation or sick leave, rather than pain per se, they are not covered here.) The few studies conducted in the general population are reviewed next.

Kay et al. (1994), in the study of abdominal pain described earlier, conducted a 5-year follow up of 2,987 of the subjects in the original sample.

One-year incidence rates were estimated, with incident cases defined as persons who reported abdominal pain in the 1-year period prior to follow up, but who reported no abdominal pain in the year prior to the baseline measure. As the authors acknowledge, this is not truly a measure of incidence, as recurrent cases whose prior pain episodes had occurred at some time other than the year prior to the baseline interview would also be included. The incidence/recurrence rates found, like prevalence rates for this pain condition, were higher in women than in men, and declined with age. (Overall rates were 15.3% for men and 20.7% for women.) Unfortunately, Kay and colleagues do not appear to have taken advantage of their prospective study design to identify baseline characteristics that might predict the onset or recurrence of pain at the 5-year follow up.

In contrast, Magni, Moreschi, Rigatti-Luchini, and Merskey (1994), using population-based data from the U.S. National Center for Health Statistics, specifically set out to examine whether depression at baseline predicts the presence of chronic musculoskeletal pain conditions (neck, back, hip, or knee pain or significant swelling or pain in other joints) at follow up, and whether chronic musculoskeletal pain at baseline predicts later depression. Data were obtained for a representative sample of 2,324 subjects who had baseline and follow-up data an average of 8 years apart, although 209 of these subjects had "uncertain" chronic pain status at baseline, follow up, or both, and were not included in the analysis. Again, the investigators did not inquire into chronic pain occurring prior to the baseline measurement and did not assess onsets and offsets during the years between baseline and follow up. Thus, the cases with pain present at follow up who did not have pain at baseline likely include a significant number of recurrent cases, as well as first-onset cases. Four hundred forty-one persons, or about 19% of the sample, had chronic musculoskeletal pain at follow up, but not at baseline. In logistic regression analyses that included demographic factors, baseline depression was a statistically significant, but very weak, predictor of the presence of pain at follow up.

In a prospective study of an HMO population (Von Korff, LeResche, & Dworkin, 1993), we assessed 3-year pain onset rates and predictors of pain onset for five common pain conditions. Only persons who reported no history of the pain condition of interest prior to the baseline survey were included, that is, the focus was on first-onset cases. The probability of first onset of back pain over the 3-year period between baseline and follow up was 17.7%; onset probabilities for other pains were: TMD pain, 6.5%; severe headache, 4.2%; abdominal pain, 3.1%; and chest pain, 3.0%. Demographic factors, depression, and number of existing pain conditions at baseline were assessed for their relationship to pain onset. The most consistent predictor of onset of a new pain condition was having an existing pain condition at baseline. Presence of baseline pain was a significant predictor of onset for four of the five pain conditions (all except chest pain). There were not significant differences in onset rates of back pain, abdominal pain, or TMD pain by severity or chronicity of depressive symptoms. However, relative to the nondepressed, persons with moderate to severe depression were more likely to develop severe headache and chest pain, with onset risks highest among the chronically depressed. Although a few significant relationships between demographic factors and pain onset were found, none of the demographic factors measured (age, gender, and education) was associated with pain onset for more than one of the pain conditions. Because of the focus on first onsets of pain in this study, persons with a prior history were excluded and some of the sample sizes are relatively small (e.g., only 271 persons had no prior history of back pain).

Thus, there are only a handful of studies of pain onset and possible risk factors for pain onset in the general population. Clearly, more prospective studies to assess pain incidence and risk factors for first onset of pain are needed. In addition, studies are needed of pain recurrence, but ideally recurrent and first-onset cases should be distinguished, as different risk factors may affect initial onsets and pain recurrences. Prospective study designs are particularly important for identifying risk factors for pain, as many factors hypothesized to be associated with pain onset are psychological factors. Because these factors are not static, they can change with the presence of pain, and thus in studies comparing existing pain cases with control groups (i.e., case-control studies) it is difficult to determine whether any differences observed are a cause or an effect of the pain problem.

DURATION

Most of the pain conditions associated with significant suffering, disability, and health care costs are not one-time, acute pain conditions, but rather chronic or recurrent pains. Studying duration for such conditions is tricky. Chronic pain is frequently characterized by insidious onset, such that the subject cannot identify when the pain began, even if pain started in the recent past. Problems of recall for pain conditions beginning some time in the past further complicate the dating of onset. Even if an accurate onset date is available, chronic pain is frequently episodic. Thus, although one can easily calculate "pain duration" by subtracting the onset date from the date of interview, persons with identical durations, by this definition, could, in fact, have experienced significantly different numbers of days, weeks, or months in pain. Retrospective assessment of number and duration of pain episodes may not be accurate. For these reasons, much basic information on pain duration and the natural history of pain episodes is lacking. Prospective studies with frequent measurement points appear to be the best approach to obtaining this information.

IMPLICATIONS FOR EVALUATION AND TREATMENT

Perhaps the most obvious use of epidemiology for clinical practice is what Morris (1975) termed the assessment of individual chances and risks—that is, assessment of risks of pain onset, risks of pain recurrence, or risks of transition from nondysfunctional to dysfunctional pain states. Although, as we have pointed out in this chapter, epidemiologic data on pain are currently incomplete in a number of areas, epidemiology can potentially provide answers to such questions as, "What are the risks of disabling back pain among workers who participate in a program that teaches body mechanics and lifting techniques relative to comparable workers who do not receive such instruction?" (Daltroy et al., 1997). Use of epidemiology to evaluate preventive or health services interventions for chronic pain may identify effective interventions to reduce the burden of chronic pain, and may also reduce health care expenditures on ineffective interventions (Fletcher, Fletcher, & Wagner, 1988).

In terms of prognosis, natural history data for back pain developed using the dynamic model described above have recently provided a much more thorough picture of the prognosis of back pain seen in primary-care populations than earlier studies that relied only on return to the clinic to assess back pain outcomes (Von Korff & Saunders, 1996). Because back pain patients identify receiving information on prognosis as an important goal of their health care visits (Turner, LeResche, Von Korff, & Ehrlich, 1998), the ability to provide accurate, albeit probabilistic information on prognosis is likely to decrease patient anxiety and increase patient satisfaction.

Finally, if epidemiologic methods are successful in identifying risk factors for pain, modification of those risk factors can lead to new strategies for prevention as well as treatment of chronic pain.

ACKNOWLEDGMENTS

During the preparation of this work, the first author was supported by Grants DE08773 and DE10766 from the National Institutes of Health. The second author was supported by National Institutes of Health Grant DE08773.

REFERENCES

Adelman, A. M., Revicki, D. A., Magaziner, J., & Hebel, R. (1995). Abdominal pain in an HMO. *Family Medicine, 27,* 321–325.

Agreus, L., Svardsudd, K., Nyren, O., & Tibblin, G. (1994). The epidemiology of abdominal symptoms: Prevalence and demographic characteristics in a Swedish adult population. *Scandinavian Journal of Gastroenterology, 29,* 102–109.

Alders, E. E. A., Hentzen, A., & Tan, C. T. (1996). A community-based prevalence study on headache in Malaysia. *Headache, 36,* 379–384.

Breslau, N., Davis, G. C., & Andreski, P. (1991). Migraine, psychiatric disorders, and suicide attempts: An epidemiologic study of young adults. *Psychiatry Research, 37,* 11–23.

Croft, P. R., & Rigby, A. S. (1994). Socioeconomic influences on back problems in the community in Britain. *Journal of Epidemiology and Community Health, 48,* 166–170.

Croft, P., Rigby, A. S., Boswell, R., Schollum, J., & Silman, A. (1993). The prevalence of chronic widespread pain in the general population. *Journal of Rheumatology, 20,* 710–713.

Daltroy, L. H., Iversen, M. D., Larson, M. G., Lew, R., Wright, E., Ryan, J., Zwerling, C., Fossell, A. H., & Liang, M. H. A controlled trial of an educational program to prevent low back injuries. *New England Journal of Medicine, 337,* 322–328.

Dworkin, S. F., Von Korff, M., & LeResche, L. (1992). Epidemiologic studies of chronic pain: A dynamic-ecologic perspective. *Annals of Behavioral Medicine, 14,* 3–11.

Engel, G. (1960). A unified concept of health and disease. *Perspectives in Biology and Medicine, 3,* 459–485.

Fields, H. (1987). *Pain.* New York: McGraw-Hill.

Fletcher, R. H., Fletcher, S. W., & Wagner, E. H. (1988). *Clinical epidemiology: The essentials* (2nd ed.). Baltimore: Williams & Wilkins.

Foppa, I., & Noack, R. H. (1996). The relation of self-reported back pain to psychosocial, behavioral, and health-related factors in a working population in Switzerland. *Social Science and Medicine, 43,* 1119–1126.

Gobel, H., Petersen-Braun, M., & Soyka, D. (1994). The epidemiology of headache in Germany: A nationwide survey of a representative sample on the basis of the headache classification of the International Headache Society. *Cephalalgia, 14,* 97–106.

Goodman, J. E., & McGrath, P. J. (1991). The epidemiology of pain in children and adolescents: A review. *Pain, 46,* 247–264.

Goulet, J.-P., Lavigne, G. J., & Lund, J. P. (1995). Jaw pain prevalence among French-speaking Canadians in Quebec and related symptoms of temporomandibular disorders. *Journal of Dental Research, 74,* 1738–1744.

Harris, R. B., & Weissfeld, L. A. (1991). Gender differences in the reliability of reporting symptoms of angina pectoris. *Journal of Clinical Epidemiology, 44,* 1071–1078.

Headache Classification Committee of the International Headache Society. (1988). Classification and diagnostic criteria for headache disorders, cranial neuralgias, and facial pain. *Cephalalgia, 8*(Suppl. 7), 1–96.

Helkimo, M. (1974). Studies on function and dysfunction of the masticatory system. *Acta Odontologica Scandinavica, 32,* 255–267.

Henry, P., Michel, P., Brochet, B., Dartigues, J. F., Tison, S., Salamon, R., & GRIM (Groupe de Recherche Interdisciplinaire sur la Migraine). (1992). A nationwide survey of migraine in France: Prevalence and clinical features in adults. *Cephalalgia, 12,* 229–237.

Jabbar, M. A., & Ogunniyi, A. (1997). Sociodemographic factors and primary headache syndromes in a Saudi community. *Neuroepidemiology, 16,* 48–52.

Jensen, G. (1984). Epidemiology of chest pain and angina pectoris: With special reference to treatment needs. *Acta Medica Scandinavica, Suppl. 682,* 1–120.

Jones, R., & Lydeard, S. (1990). Irritable bowel syndrome in the general population. *British Medical Journal, 304,* 87–90.

Kay, L., Jorgensen, T., & Jensen, K. H. (1994). Epidemiology of abdominal symptoms in a random population: Prevalence, incidence, and natural history. *European Journal of Epidemiology, 10,* 559–566.

Lawrence, J. S., Bremner, J. M., & Bier, F. (1966). Osteo-arthrosis: Prevalence in the population and relationship between symptom and x-ray changes. *Annals of the Rheumatic Diseases, 25,* 1–23.

LeResche, L. (1997). Epidemiology of temporomandibular disorders: Implications for the investigation of etiologic factors. *Critical Reviews in Oral Biology and Medicine, 8,* 291–305.

LeResche, L., Saunders, K., Von Korff, M., Barlow, W., & Dworkin, S. F. (1997). Use of exogenous hormones and risk of temporomandibular disorder pain. *Pain, 69,* 153–160.

Lillienfeld, A. M., & Lillienfeld, D. E. (1980). *Foundations of epidemiology* (2nd ed.). New York: Oxford University Press.

Locker, D., & Slade, G. (1988). Prevalence of symptoms associated with temporomandibular disorders in a Canadian population. *Community Dentistry and Oral Epidemiology, 16,* 310–313.

Magni, G., Moreschi, C., Rigatti-Luchini, S., & Merskey, H. (1994). Prospective study on the relationship between depressive symptoms and chronic musculoskeletal pain. *Pain, 56,* 289–297.

McDuffie, F. C. (1985). Morbidity impact of rheumatoid arthritis on society. *American Journal of Medicine, 78*(Suppl. 1a), 1–5.

Mohlin, B. (1983). Prevalence of mandibular dysfunction and relation between malocclusion and mandibular dysfunction in a group of women in Sweden. *European Journal of Orthodontics, 4,* 115–123.

Morris, J. N. (1975). *Uses of epidemiology* (3rd ed.). Edinburgh: Churchill Livingstone.

Psaty, B. M. (1995). Chest pain: Prevalence and mortality. *APS Bulletin, 5* (March/April), 13–14.

Rasmussen, B. K., Jensen, R., Schroll, M., & Olesen, J. (1991). Epidemiology of headache in a general population—A prevalence study. *Journal of Clinical Epidemiology, 44,* 1147–1157.

Stewart, W. F., Lipton, R. B., Celentano, D. D., & Reed, M. L. (1992). Prevalence of migraine headache in the United States. Relation to age, income, race and other sociodemographic factors. *Journal of the American Medical Association, 267,* 64–69.

Stewart, W. F., Shechter, A., & Rasmussen, B. K. (1994). Migraine prevalence: A review of population-based studies. *Neurology, 44*(Suppl. 4), S17–S23.

Szentpetery, A., Huhn, E., & Fazekas, A. (1986). Prevalence of mandibular dysfunction in an urban population in Hungary. *Community Dentistry and Oral Epidemiology, 14,* 177–180.

Turner, J. A., LeResche, L., Von Korff, M., & Ehrlich, K. (1998). Back pain in primary care: Patient characteristics, content of initial visit, and short-term outcomes. *Spine, 23,* 463–469.

Von Korff, M. (1992). Epidemiologic and survey methods: Chronic pain assessment. In D. C. Turk & R. Melzack (Eds.), *Handbook of pain assessment* (pp. 391–408). New York: Guilford Press.

Von Korff, M., Dworkin, S. F., LeResche, L., & Kruger, A. (1988). An epidemiologic comparison of pain complaints. *Pain, 32,* 173–183.

Von Korff, M., LeResche, L., & Dworkin, S. F. (1993). First onset of common pain symptoms: A prospective study of depression as a risk factor. *Pain, 55,* 251–258.

Von Korff, M., & Parker, R. D. (1980). The dynamics of the prevalence of chronic episodic disease. *Journal of Chronic Disease, 33,* 79–85.

Von Korff, M., & Saunders, K. (1996). The course of back pain in primary care. *Spine, 21,* 2833–2839.

Walsh, K., Cruddas, M., & Coggon, D. (1992). Low back pain in eight areas of Britain. *Journal of Epidemiology and Community Health, 46,* 227–230.

Wolfe, F. (1994). Rheumatoid arthritis and osteoarthritis. *APS Bulletin, 4* (April/May), 15–22.

Wolfe, F., Ross, K., Anderson, J., Russell, I. J., & Herbert, L. (1995). The prevalence and characteristics of fibromyalgia in the general population. *Arthritis and Rheumatism, 38,* 19–28.

Wolfe, F., Smythe, H. A., Yunus, M. B., Bennett, R. M., Bombardier, C., Goldenberg, D. L., Tugwell, P., Campbell, S. M., & Abeles, M. (1990). The American College of Rheumatology 1990 criteria for the classification of fibromyalgia. *Arthritis and Rheumatism, 33*, 160–172.

Wright, D., Barrow, S., Fisher, A. D., Horsley, S. D., & Jayson, M. I. V. (1995). Influence of physical, psychological and behavioural factors on consultations for back pain. *British Journal of Rheumatology, 34*, 156–161.

Chapter 2

Models of Pain

Michael E. Robinson
Department of Clinical and Health Psychology,
University of Florida

Joseph L. Riley, III
Claude Pepper Center for Research of Oral Health in Aging,
College of Dentistry, University of Florida

CHAPTER OVERVIEW

Understanding chronic pain requires the clinician or researcher to organize a vast amount of clinical and experimental information about a given patient or problem. A number of conceptual models have arisen from the need to integrate this information and serve as heuristic guides to planning treatment or research projects. These have ranged from simple models of sensory transduction to more complex models involving physiological, psychological, and environmental components. As the knowledge base has increased, models have attempted to incorporate new findings and have, in general, become more complex. All models, however, represent simplifications of what are likely to be the real interrelationships between a person's physiology, his or her psychological make-up, history, environment, and treatments. A model serves as a conceptual framework from which a clinician or scientist can address a problem in an orderly fashion and have some level of confidence in treatment or scientific results.

The purpose of this chapter is to survey several models of pain with particular emphasis on chronic pain. The intention is to present the models from a conceptual viewpoint and then review empirical literature that pertains to each model. Other chapters within this book are directed at specific types of chronic pain conditions. In most cases, more than one of the models described in this chapter may have some application to a given pain condition. We offer these models as conceptual frameworks for clinician-scientists to organize their thinking about the specific pain conditions elucidated in the other chapters.

EARLY MODELS

Before discussing theories or models of chronic pain as a syndrome, some discussion of general pain models will help shed light on the historical development of theories about pain. Early models (19th and early 20th centuries) of pain were primarily physiologically based, with an emphasis on the peripheral structures of pain sensation and a direct relationship between pain report and stimulus intensity. These theories roughly follow the development of physiological and anatomical studies of both human and nonhuman animals. The first of these theories to reach significant popularity was the specificity theory advocated by Descartes, Galen, and others (Bonica, 1990).

The specificity theory stated that pain was a unique sensation separate from the other senses. This assertion was supported primarily by the finding that when the spinal cord of test animals was lesioned, pain and touch were found to be independent from each other and dependent on the portion of the cord lesioned. Lesioning the cord gray matter resulted in pain cessation, whereas lesioning the posterior white matter resulted in touch being lost, but sparing of pain sensation. Follow-up studies in the late 19th century demonstrated cutaneous areas differentially sensitive to touch, warm, cold, and pain (von Frey, cited in Bonica, 1990).

The main competitive theory of the early part of this period was the summation theory, which was endorsed by a number of leading scientists of the time, including Darwin, Wundt, Titchener, and Goldsheider (Bonica, 1990). It stated that pain was the result of intense stimulation of the sense of touch or temperature. Pathological pain states were thus described as the result of excessively long periods of summation in normally non-nociceptive pathways.

Theories of pain continued to become more complex as the 20th century began. These include the pattern theory, which suggested that all receptor fiber types could code pain depending on the temporal and spatial patterns of innervation (Sinclair, 1955; Wedell, 1955). The central summation theory also developed more as additional anatomical evidence and understanding of the nervous system progressed. This theory included references to higher brain centers and incorporated the effects of emotional states on pain perception (Bonica, 1990).

Hardy, Wolff, and Goodell (1952) presented a dualist theory, which distinguished between the perception of pain and the reaction to pain. The perception of pain was proposed to be served by relatively simple neurophysiology, whereas the reaction to pain included the higher cognitive processes.

GATE CONTROL MODEL

Taking into account the empirical support for various pain theories (primarily the central summation and specificity theories) while recognizing the shortcomings of each, Melzack and Wall (1965) developed the gate control theory of pain. This theory has undergone its own revisions as new anatomical and physiological evidence has arisen, although its basic heuristic premise has remained intact. Its essence is the existence of a "spinal gate," located in the dorsal horn of the spinal cord, which modulates spinal cord T (transmission) cells. The T cells are influenced by the relative firing of large-diameter (inhibitory) and small-diameter (facilitative) fibers. The relative summation of these different fiber types either opens or closes the gate, activating the T cells and transmitting the pain impulse. Also influencing the gate are descending fibers presumably related to cognitive and affective brain systems that can either inhibit or facilitate the action of the gate. This theory is the most inclusive and was probably the first to incorporate all the existing physiologic and psychological/behavioral data.

The gate control model has become arguably the most influential model in the pain field. Numerous studies have been undertaken to investigate components of the original model and have resulted in significant revisions (Wall, 1996). The original model was based on incomplete data and technological limitations precluded testing certain aspects of the model. More recent studies have confirmed that cells in the substantia gelatinosa are the likely candidates for the moniker "T" cell (Bennett, Abdelmoumene, Hayashi, & Dubner, 1980). Other studies using technologies (i.e., positron-emission tomography [PET] scan) unavailable to Melzack and Wall in 1965 have shown that the central processing of pain is distributed, involving a large number of structures in complex patterns of interaction to code pain (Coghill, 1996). Other studies have demonstrated that primary afferents are also dynamically influenced by processes such as inflammation (Reichling & Gold, 1996), suggesting that "gating" occurs at multiple sites along the pain axis. These newer iterations of the model reflect the increasing sophistication of the researchers and the tools available to them much as the history of pain study reflects. The essence of the model has remained unchanged: (a) Pain is not a "hard-wired" single circuit, (b) differential stimulation of two fiber types influences subsequent transmission of a pain signal farther along the spinal cord, (c) descending control mechanisms affect the transmission at the spinal gate. Although the anatomical location and structures of the gate have been controversial, the model has had powerful heuristic value and is consistent with a considerable body of experimental and clinical data (Wall, 1996).

The aforementioned theories represent a progression in the conceptualizations of pain from the physiology of receptors to models attempting to incorporate higher brain function and cognition. They also represent more global attempts to organize the data available at the time. None of them was formulated with chronic pain conditions specifically in mind. What follows are explications of models of chronic pain that have been proposed in the past few decades.

PSYCHOLOGICAL MODELS

Psychoanalytic

The psychodynamic view of chronic pain could be considered the first psychological model of pain because of its emphasis on psychological etiology. Freud stressed the subjective nature of pain, which shifted the focus from organic factors to the psychological domain. His perspective on pain differed from the traditional medical model of his day in that the underlying problem was conceptualized as emotional. What differentiates psychoanalytic models from other models of pain is the emphasis on unconscious process as a major determinate. Freud generally considered pain to manifest itself as a consequence or symptomatic expression of an unconscious emotional conflict seeking awareness.

More recent analytic theories have expanded on Freud's views. An adaptational approach emphasizes coping and defense strategies used by the individual in adjusting to environmental demands. Of particular importance is the defense of somatization, where emotional pain, often experienced in childhood through the association of pain with important formative emotional experiences, is displaced into the body as somatic pain, where it is more acceptable (Kellner, 1991). Thus, pain helps to avoid even more unpleasant feelings, and is thought to be an expression of repressed hostility, defense against loss or threatened loss, aggression, guilt, or resentment.

Engle (1959) emphasized the role of pain as a depressive equivalent. In pain patients characterized by developmental histories where pain, punishment, and affection became linked, pain serves as reconciliation for guilt and is reinforced by attention from the family. Pain is more likely to serve as a depressive equivalent in families where illness models are present and the family does not define distress in psychological terms (Katon, Kleinman, & Rosen, 1982). Blumer and Heilbronn (1981, 1982) expanded on Engle's model to describe the "pain prone personality" characterized by dependency, denial of emotional and interpersonal problems, lack of initiative, inability to enjoy recreational or social life, depressed mood, and a family history of depression and chronic pain. According to this formulation, these patients are a homogenous and diagnostically unique group, which can be considered part of the depressive spectrum.

Empirical Evidence for Psychodynamic Models. The psychodynamic literature has attempted to show that emotional difficulties were associated with chronic pain. The variables generally studied were (a) family size and birth order, (b) early family relationship problems, (c) socioeconomic status of the family, (d) marital adjustment, (e) personality disorders, and (f) depression. Pilowsky (1986) reported that symptomatic studies of psychodynamic theories of pain have been scarce and reports in the literature are based on clinical studies of small numbers of patients. Gamsa (1994), in her review, concluded that the psychodynamic literature fails to provide support for the hypothesis that childhood emotional problems generate and perpetuate chronic pain, although others disagree (Grzesiak & Ciccone, 1994). Recent psychodynamic models are integrating cognitive constructs such as irrational beliefs, catastrophic thinking, appraisal of a situation, and coping skills as variables in their model.

Behavioral/Social Learning Models

Learning models of pain have several commonalities. A major difference between learning models and the traditional medical disease model is the distinction between nociception and pain behavior. Learning models consider pain to be a behavior like any other. As such, pain behavior is subject to influences from both within the individual (including nociception) and from the environment surrounding the individual. This implies that there is not a one-to-one relationship between tissue damage, nociceptive input, and pain behavior. This is a well-accepted conceptualization as suggested by the most recent definition of pain provided by the International Association for the Study of Pain (IASP, 1979). Pain as exhibited by a patient with a chronic pain syndrome in many cases does not have a direct relationship to the demonstrable tissue pathology. Even given the limitations of medical imaging and diagnostics, the learning history and current environmental influences on a patient's pain behavior are likely to explain, at least in part, why the relationship between measurable tissue damage and pain report is not perfectly correlated.

Both classical conditioning and operant conditioning contribute to the behavioral expression of pain. Of the two, operant conditioning has received far greater attention and study in the chronic pain field (Fordyce, 1976). Fordyce was the first to articulate what we now consider a learning model of chronic pain (Fordyce, Fowler, Lehmann, & DeLateur, 1968), focusing primarily on an operant conceptualization of pain behavior (Fordyce, 1990). Reinforcers from the patient's environment can include social reinforcement from family and friends, medications from physicians, avoidance of unpleasant activities, or financial incentives, to name a few. Fordyce made a valuable distinction between "respondent pain behavior" and "operant pain behavior," the former being pain behavior occurring as a result of ongoing nociception, whereas operant pain behaviors require the presence of reinforcing environmental contingencies. One plausible scenario of this model is that in the initial stages of an injury, where nociception is present, operant pain behaviors become learned through well-established principles of reinforcement. The model does not preclude the possibility of pain behaviors in the absence of nociception, the minimum requirements simply being that reinforcement must be contingent on the expression of pain behavior.

A final component to learning models involves the social context and social modeling influences in the expression of pain. The expression of pain occurs in a context that is rich with the aforementioned learning influences, both internal and external, but also in a rich social milieu. How we learn to express pain is in part due to how we have seen others express pain. The context of learning can also be very specific to the situation in which pain behavior is modeled. Dramatic examples of pain modeling can be found in number of religious or ritualistic procedures that involve flaggelation, body piercing, or mutilation, all without the expression of pain. Similarly, athletic events often encourage "playing with pain." The individuals undergoing these activities must learn how to behave in those circumstances (Craig, 1986). Those contexts apparently include rules on what is socially acceptable with regard to the expression of pain.

Empirical Evidence for Learning Models.   The operant model of pain has received considerable empirical support in the last two decades. The scope of this chapter does not allow for an exhaustive review of that literature. However, a few representative studies serve to illustrate the general conclusions from the body of literature. The preponderance of studies related to learning models of chronic pain are in the area of treatment outcome from behavioral interventions or multidisciplinary interventions, including a behavioral component based on learning principles. Much more exhaustive reviews of the outcome research in this area can be found in Block (1982) and Flor, Fydrich, and Turk (1992). These reviews attest to the strong influence of behavioral interventions on chronic pain treatment outcome. A lesser literature exists examining more isolated behavioral interventions (not part of a multidisciplinary pain program). For example, Doleys, Crocker, and Patton (1982) and Schmidt (1985a, 1985b) have shown that patients with chronic pain respond to operant methods of increasing exercise tolerance. Other studies have shown that chronic pain patients' social environment, specifically spouse reinforcement of pain behavior, affects patients' pain reports (Flor, Kerns, & Turk, 1987; Williamson, Robinson, & Melamed, 1997). Models of successful coping with pain have also suggested a strong learning component to pain behavior (Melamed, Hawes, Heiby, & Blick, 1975). The data are overwhelmingly in support of a learning contribution to the expression of pain. It is clear that social influences, particularly significant others' reinforcement or modeling of pain, can influence patients' pain report and other pain behavior in both directions. It is also evident from the literature that selectively reinforcing well behaviors can increase pain patients' responses to treatment.

Cognitive-Behavioral Models

The interest in cognitive models in psychology grew out of behavioral models that tended to focus exclusively on target behaviors, while largely ignoring cognitive processes in the development, maintenance, and modification of behavior. Increased emphasis on cognitive theories and techniques had broad clinical influences on a variety of psychological problems (Beck, 1976; Ellis, 1962; Meichenbaum, 1977). In applying cognitive models, there are two ways in which cognition could affect behavior. First, it can mediate behavior. In the classical conditioning paradigm, the cognitive process can intervene between the stimulus and response. In operant conditioning terms, the definition of consequences as punishing or rewarding is a function of cognition (e.g., personal goals). The second way cognition can affect behavior is directly, by enhancing or impairing physiological responses. Therefore, an individual's perceptions, beliefs, attitudes, feelings, thoughts, and goals have the potential to affect physiological responses.

In the context of chronic pain, cognitive processes are broadly defined as thoughts, self-statements, or evaluations about their pain, beliefs, interpretations, or attributions regarding their pain and medical condition (Turk & Rudy, 1986). Cognitive theories of pain then emphasize the influences of these variables on the interaction between sensory, affective, motivational, and evaluative components of the experience of chronic pain and related dysfunction. Developments in cognitive-behavioral models of chronic pain are reflected in the current definition of pain by the IASP as "an unpleasant sensory and emotional experience associated with actual or potential tissue damage, or described in terms of such damage" (IASP, 1979). This definition implies that pain is a subjective psychological experience that is associated with the perception of somatic sensation.

Ciccone and Grzesiak (1984) outlined a strict cognitive model that hypothesized that specific patterns of thinking account for the problems of chronic pain patients. They suggested that humans draw the meaning of sensation from the knowledge of past sensory experience, particularly painful stimuli, which form a knowledge structure or schema. These schemata frequently contain incorrect beliefs based on cognitive errors, and these cognitive patterns are the primary cause of dysfunction in chronic pain patients. Their support for cognition as the central component in the chronic pain experience comes indirectly from cognitive treatment studies. These studies generally focus on reducing and controlling pain resulting from increased physiological arousal, somatic focus, and physical deconditioning associated with fear of pain or additional injury. Criticism of this article frequently involves the restrictiveness of the model in suggesting that cognitive events alone account for treatment efficacy (Novy, Nelson, Frances, & Turk, 1995). Turk and Flor (1984) warned that cognitive processes should not be considered in isolation from other aspects of the experience of pain. Gamsa (1994) pointed out that although cognitive theory may be "mentalistic" and seemingly incompatible with behavioral philosophy, they complement each other in cognitive-behavioral models of pain.

Turk and Rudy (1989) have written extensively on cognitive-behavioral models of pain and have proposed five general assumptions that characterize the cognitive-behavioral model:

1. Individuals are active processors of information. They attempt to interpret information from their environment by processing information through organized schemata, which are a function of their learning history. Consequently, their responses are based on their appraisals and expectations rather than being contingent exclusively on the consequences of their behavior.

2. Thoughts can evoke or influence emotions and physiology and can serve as the motivation for behavior. Conversely, emotions, physiology, and behavior can initiate or influence thoughts. The experience of pain is a reciprocal interaction of thoughts, feelings, physiology, and behavior.

3. Behavior is reciprocally determined by the individual and the environment. Unlike operant-behavioral models, reciprocal effects of the individual and the environment are proposed as well as the unidirectional influence of environment on behavior.

4. Individuals have learned maladaptive ways of behaving, thinking, and feeling and treatment interventions should be designed to modify these factors.

5. Patients play a role in the development and maintenance of their maladaptive behaviors and cognition and are capable of and should be involved as active agents in change.

The cognitive-behavioral model of pain does not make the linear causation assumptions of the sensory-physiological or operant-behavioral models. The cognitive-behavioral model also provides a theoretical framework, emphasizing the multidetermined dynamic nature of the patient's response to pain. Consequently, from this integrated perspective, coping with pain is viewed as a process wherein an individual's beliefs, attitudes, and thinking style mediate emotional and behavioral responses. It describes pain perception as a complex interpretive process, rather than transmission and registration of impulses from physically defined stimuli. Turk and Rudy (1986) argued that "an important contribution of the cognitive-behavioral model is the increased attention given to the attitudes and beliefs of patients regarding their understanding of their plights, of the health care system, of appropriate behavioral responses to disease, of their own capacities, and of their responses to stress" (p. 762).

Empirical Evidence for Cognitive-Behavioral Models. Research supporting cognitive-behavioral models has frequently demonstrated that an individual's cognition relates to psychosocial distress and dysfunction. Cognitive factors that have received the most attention have included coping strategies and beliefs or appraisals (see M. P. Jensen, Turner, & Romano, 1991, for review). Pain coping is defined as purposeful attempts to manage or negate the impact of pain. Stress-pain-coping models are often used to explain the considerable variability in adjustment observed in pain patients, with pain identified as the source of stress. Coping has frequently been conceptualized as active and passive (G. K. Brown & Nicassio, 1987). Active coping implies some instrumental action to control pain, whereas passive coping involves surrendering control to an external source. Active coping has typically been found to be positively associated with measures of psychological and physical functioning (G. K. Brown, Nicassio, & Wallston, 1989; Snow-Turek, Norris, & Tan, 1996). Passive coping, however, is linked to increased pain and depression (Holmes & Stevenson, 1990; Snow-Turek et al., 1996).

Self-efficacy beliefs, a judgment regarding the ability to perform a particular behavior, are thought to play a role in pain coping by influencing the use of pain-coping strategies (M. P. Jensen, Turner, & Romano, 1991). Greater belief in the ability to manage pain has been shown to be related to activity level and well-being (M. P. Jensen & Karoly, 1991). Negative appraisals, such as catastrophizing, are thought to mediate the relationship between pain and depression (Geisser, Robinson, Keefe, & Weiner, 1994) and have been shown to be associated with increased pain and reduced functioning (Keefe, G. K. Brown, Wallston, & Caldwell, 1989).

There is evidence to support cognitive-behavioral therapy's association with improvements in patient report of pain, depression, and disability

(Kerns, Turk, Holzman, & Rudy, 1985; Nicholas, Wilson, & Goyen, 1992; Turner & M. P. Jensen, 1993). Cognitive-behavioral-based treatment programs focus on providing patients with skills to enhance their sense of control over the effects of pain. Relaxation training, imagery, biofeedback, and hypnosis can be used to modify attention focus as well as to enhance the sense of mastery. Cognitive techniques are used to help place affective, behavioral, cognitive, and sensory responses under patients' control, the assumption being that long-term behavioral changes are more likely to be maintained when the patient attributes success to his or her efforts (Dolce, 1987). Social modeling is also useful in teaching coping self-statements, problem solving, and goal setting. Treatment can result in changes in beliefs about pain, coping strategies, reported pain severity, as well as direct behavioral changes (M. P. Jensen et al., 1994; Turk & Rudy, 1986).

Additional support for a cognitive-behavioral model of pain comes from a number of treatment outcome studies that have compared cognitive-behavioral treatment packages to controls. For example, Phillips (1987) compared a treatment package consisting of relaxation, exercise, activity pacing, and cognitive interventions with a wait-list control condition. The patients in the cognitive-behavioral treatment group showed significant improvements in mood, affective reaction to pain, self-efficacy, medication use, and exercise capacity, whereas the control condition did not. Therapeutic gains were maintained at 12-month follow-up. Keefe et al. (1990) compared a cognitive-behavioral pain-coping skills-training program with an educational informational intervention. After 10 weeks of treatment, patients in the cognitive-behavioral group reported significantly lower levels of pain and physical disability than those receiving the educational intervention. Engstrom (1983) conducted a study comparing a cognitive-behavioral treatment package with a placebo medication condition. Chronic back patients in the treatment group had significant reductions in pain and increases in locus of control in contrast to those receiving the placebo medication, who failed to show any treatment gains during the study period.

At least one study suggests that cognitive-behavioral treatment can play a role in preventing chronic pain. Linton, Bradley, I. Jensen, Spangfort, and Sundell (1989) tested the efficacy of a secondary prevention program for nurses who were at risk for back pain. The prevention program consisted of (a) training in cognitive-behavioral strategies for managing pain and maintaining healthy habits, (b) physical therapy to increase conditioning and bodily awareness, and (c) training in ways to avoid reinjury. Nurses receiving the treatment showed significant improvement over and above the wait-list control group on measures of pain, pain behavior, emotional distress, or fatigue. A significant change was also found in the rate of work absenteeism. Overall, treatment of chronic pain patients using cognitive-behavioral principles appear to be efficacious and, as a result, the American Psychological Association has endorsed the use of cognitive-behavioral intervention for chronic pain as an empirically supported intervention.

PSYCHOPHYSIOLOGICAL MODEL

Historically there has been a distinction between mind and body with respect to the etiology and expression of pain disorders. Psychogenic versus organic distinctions have been proposed for a variety of pain conditions. The psychophysiological model explicitly attempts to incorporate mind into body. This model states that through activation of primarily the autonomic nervous system (but also the muscle efferents) disregulation of muscle and organ systems can lead to pain. Variants of this model have been described as the "stress-hyperactivity-pain theory" (Ohrbach & McCall, 1996). The source or proposed cause of this overactivation is thought to be the organism's reaction to either external or internal stressors. These stressors can include environmental conditions (e.g., loud workplace), or inter- and intrapersonal conflicts. Our language attests to the ubiquity of the belief that stressors result in physiological reactions. For example, we "blush with excitement," "tremble in fear," get "butterflies in our stomachs," and "get cold feet." Muscle tension and vascular headaches, Raynaud's phenomena, irritable bowel and colitis, chest pain, back pain, and temporomandibular disorders (TMD), among others, are common disorders believed to have a stress component either as part of their etiology or as a factor in the maintenance and exacerbation of the condition.

Empirical Support for the Psychophysiological Model. Although the assessment of the psychophysiology of pain remains problematic with respect to the cutpoints for levels of physiological activation necessary for symptom production, good empirical support exists for the relationship of psychological stress and physiological activation and symptom presentation in some disorders, but not others. For instance, the mechanisms of migraine headache are relatively well understood to be triggered at least in part by vasoconstriction resulting from chronic stress (Oleson & Bonica, 1990). This is contrasted with the studies investigating the surface electromyographic (EMG) studies of chronic low back pain (CLBP), which have shown virtually every conceivable relationship between muscle tension and pain. Some studies have shown that CLBP patients have higher levels of surface EMG, whereas others have shown lower levels of surface EMG (Schmidt & Arntz, 1987). Orbach and McCall (1996), Rudy and Greco (1996), Clark (1996), and Flor and Turk (1996) have reviewed the literature extensively on this hypothesis with respect to muscular pain conditions and have noted a number of methodological and conceptual difficulties, particularly stemming from the reliance on surface EMG. Other problems noted by these authors include the lack of support for a link between autonomic hyperactivity and pain (Clark, 1996) and the presumed homogeneity of the model that ignores a number of studies indicating the heterogeneity of pain patient populations (Rudy & Greco, 1996).

EMPIRICAL MODELING APPROACHES

Over the past few decades, theories of pain have grown increasingly complex as earlier perspectives have proven to be unsuccessful in consistently predicting observable evidence. Beginning with the gate control theory and followed by operant-behavioral and cognitive-behavioral models, all have combined physiological and psychological processes in an attempt to provide a comprehensive, theoretical framework that would be useful in the conceptualization and treatment of the chronic pain patient. Many different relationships between variables are implied, the most complex of which is the reciprocal determinism of the cognitive-behavioral perspective. However, as Novy et al. (1995) pointed out, explicit explanations are lacking for the posited interrelationships among sensory-physical, affective, behavioral, and cognitive processes.

Several researchers have suggested that structural equation modeling (SEM) provides an appropriate research methodology within which specific hypothesized relationships can be tested (Bentler & Stein, 1992; Hoyle & Smith, 1994; Novy et al., 1995). This technique is appropriate for testing a priori multivariate models in addition to testing for homogeneity in the chronic pain experience across subpopulations. As these relationships are determined, SEM can be a useful tool to test additional hypothesized models. Theory development through model testing will lead to better understanding of the chronic pain experience and, ultimately, improve clinical prediction.

Several authors have tested empirical models using the SEM methodology in the chronic pain literature. Although none has tested what could be considered comprehensive models, each has examined a subset of variables, consistent with cognitive-behavioral theory. The first such example was that of Rudy, Kerns, and Turk (1988), who tested a model with life interference and perception of self-control as mediators of the relationship between pain perception and depression. They tested this model using SEM in a sample of chronic pain outpatients. This model was based on the theory that it is only after the chronic pain patient experiences lifestyle disruption, or interference in instrumental activities, that he or she experiences depression, anxiety, or anger. Their results indicated there was not a direct path between pain to depression. However, increases in pain severity predicted increases in life interference and self-control. As a result, this study supports a model of chronic pain in which life interference and self-control mediate the relationship between pain and depression.

G. K. Brown (1991), citing a theoretically controversial literature regarding a causal relationship between pain and depression, examined the temporal relationship between depression and pain with a 3½ year cross-legged design using SEM. Data were collected on 243 patients suffering from rheumatoid arthritis. Pain and depression were found to predict each other across time, even when controlling somatic symptoms, although the relationships were modest. Zautra et al. (1995) attempted to improve on the methodology of Brown by distinguishing between state (fluctuating) and trait (stable) distress and pain. They used SEM to analyze longitudinal data collected monthly on a sample of 110 women suffering from myofascial facial pain. This model suggested that fluctuating states of pain and distress share a common affective basis that is not stable. A time lag relationship was found between the two state variables in that monthly increases in psychological distress were followed the next month with elevations in report of pain, even while controlling for major life events and medication usage.

Parker and associates (1992) used SEM to test a model predicting pain and depression with disease activity (number of joints involved), immune activation (HLA-DR+ cells), and a measure of helplessness in a sample of rheumatoid arthritis patients. Immune activation and disease activity were related as expected, as was the positive relationship between disease activity and both helplessness and depression. The most interesting finding was that depression predicted pain; however, the reciprocal relationship was not found. The authors stated their results suggest mood is involved in modulation of rheumatoid arthritis pain and is consistent with gate control theory of reticulolimbic involvement in pain.

In our laboratory, we have performed several studies testing a priori theoretical models (Brown, Robinson, Riley, & Gremillion, 1996; Geisser, Gaskin, Robinson, & Greene, 1993; Geisser et al., 1994; Holzberg, Robinson, Geisser, & Gremillion, 1996; Riley & Robinson, 1997). For example (Brown et al., 1996), 104 TMD patients were studied in which we examined the relationships among negative affect (depression, anxiety, and anger), daily microstressors, pain severity, and their ability to predict instrumental activity, using SEM. We had hypothesized that minor daily irritations, or microstressors, would account for significant variability in reduced functioning over and above that of pain severity and negative mood. The results were consistent with a learning model of chronic pain and showed that life interference was predicted directly by pain severity and this relationship was mediated by negative affect. Microstressors were not a significant predictor and may not be a relevant issue in the TMD population. The results suggest that the impact of chronic pain conditions is influenced by both pain and negative affect and inconsistent with a sensory model of pain in which tissue damage is directly related to both sensory and affective components of illness behavior.

In the most recent study (Riley & Robinson, 1998), a hierarchical clustering procedure performed on 569 CLBP patients resulted in four cluster profiles (within normal limits, V-type, neurotic triad, and depressed-pathological) similar to those identified in previous work (Riley, Robinson, Geisser, & Wittmer, 1993). We proposed a three-variable model using pain severity and depression to predict changes in activity level. We performed two analyses on each subgroup using SEM, testing cognitive coping strategies and then somatization, separately, as mediator variables. A number of interesting multivariate differences were found between several of the chronic pain subgroups. For example, somatization mediated the relationship between depression and activity level for the neurotic triad group but not the other three groups. Cognitive coping strategies mediated the relationship between depression and activity level only for the within normal limits group. In addition, cognitive coping was predictive of activity level for the within normal limits, V-type, and neurotic triad groups but not for the depressed-pathological group. The most intriguing result of this study was the directional differences in the linear relationship between somatization and depression in that there was a positive linear relationship for the within normal limits, neurotic triad, and depressed-pathological groups, whereas the association was negative for the V-type group.

SUMMARY

The models described in this chapter lead to a natural confluence best described as a "biopsychosocial" model that recognizes biological/physiological, psychological/behavioral, and environmental influences (Schwartz, 1982; Turk & Flor, 1984). In many ways such a conceptualization is quite daunting. It at times seems too inclusive, too unwieldy, difficult to define, perhaps untestable, and impossible to operationalize. Although considerable data exist to support various models described earlier, none of the models is likely to explain all patients. Testing a given model tends to imply that the individuals that comprise the particular sample under study are homogeneous relative to a number of important variables. Empirical clustering studies have repeatedly shown that the chronic pain population has considerable heterogeneity with the possibility of distinct subgroups (Riley & Robinson, 1998). It may be presumptuous to conclude that any one model is the "best." There may be room for a better matching of models to particular types of patients or disorders. Although the moniker biopsychosocial may seem unwieldy, the models taken as a whole clearly lead to the conclusion that all the factors of such a definition contribute to the experience of chronic pain.

We propose that future research attempts to test competing models with recognition of the heterogeneity of the population of patients with chronic pain. This is very likely to necessitate large-sample, multivariate designs that are costly. Given the complexity of the psychological, environmental, and to a lesser extent physiological contributions to these disorders, it may be possible that many of these models thought to be exclusive of each other may only be so with respect to whom they are applied. Similarly, treatment validation studies pitting treatments based on various models need to be conducted with respect to the potential subgroups in the population.

REFERENCES

Beck, A. T. (1976). *Cognitive therapy and the emotional disorders.* New York: International Universities Press.

Bennett, G. J., Abdelmoumene, M., Hayashi, H., & Dubner, R. (1980). Physiology and morphology of substantia gelatinosa neurons intracellularly stained with horseradish peroxidase. *Journal of Comparative Neurology, 194,* 809–827.

Bentler, P. M., & Stein, J. A. (1992). Structural equation models in medical research. *Statistical Methods in Medical Research, 1,* 159–181.

Block, A. R. (1982). Multidisciplinary treatment of low back pain: A review. *Rehabilitation Psychology, 27,* 51–63.

Blumer, D., & Heilbronn, M. (1981). The pain prone patient: A clinical and psychological profile. *Psychosomatics, 22,* 395–402.

Blumer, D., & Heilbronn, M. (1982). Chronic pain as a variant of depressive disease: The pain-prone disorder. *Journal of Nervous and Mental Disease, 170,* 381–389.

Bonica, J. J. (1990). *The management of pain.* Philadelphia: Lea & Febiger.

Brown, G. K. (1991). A causal analysis of chronic pain and depression. *Journal of Abnormal Psychology, 99,* 123–137.

Brown, G. K., & Nicassio, P. M. (1987). The development of a questionnaire for the assessment of active and passive coping strategies in chronic pain patients. *Pain, 31,* 53–65.

Brown, G. K., Nicassio, P. M., & Wallston, K. A. (1989). Pain coping strategies, and depression in rheumatoid arthritis. *Journal of Consulting and Clinical Psychology, 57,* 652–657.

Brown, F. F., Robinson, M. E., Riley, J. L., & Gremillion, H. A. (1996). Pain severity, negative affect, and microstressors as predictors of life interference in TMD patients. *Cranio, 14,* 63–70.

Ciccone, D., & Grzesiak, R. C. (1984). Cognitive dimensions of chronic pain. *Social Science and Medicine, 19,* 1339–1345.

Clark, G. T. (1996). A critique of the stress-hyperactivity-pain theory of myogenic pain. *Pain Forum, 5*(1), 70–73.

Coghill, R. C. (1996). Gate control theory and beyond. *Pain Forum, 5*(1), 40–44.

Craig, K. D. (1986). Social modeling influences: Pain in context. In R. S. Sternbach (Ed.), *The psychology of pain* (pp. 67–95). New York: Raven.

Dolce, J. J. (1987). Self-efficacy and disability beliefs in behavioral treatment of pain. *Behavior Research and Therapy, 25,* 289–299.

Doleys, D., Crocker, M., & Patton, D. (1982). Responses of patients with chronic pain to exercise quotas. *Journal of the American Physical Therapy Association, 62,* 1111–1114.

Ellis, A. (1962). *Reason and emotion in psychotherapy.* New York: Lyle Stuart.

Engle, G. L. (1959). "Psychogenic" pain and the pain-prone patient. *American Journal of Medicine, 26,* 899–918.

Engstrom, D. (1983). Cognitive behavioral therapy methods in chronic pain treatment. In J. J. Bonica (Ed.), *Advances in pain research and therapy* (Vol. 5, pp. 829–838). New York: Raven.

Flor, H., Fydrich, T., & Turk, D. C. (1992). Efficacy of multidisciplinary pain treatment centers: A meta-analytic review. *Pain, 49,* 221–230.

Flor, H., Kerns, R. D., & Turk, D. C. (1987). The role of spouse reinforcement, perceived pain, and activity levels of chronic pain patients. *Journal of Psychosomatic Research, 31,* 251–259.

Flor, H., & Turk, D. C. (1996). Integrating central and peripheral mechanism in chronic muscular pain. *Pain Forum, 5*(1), 74–76.

Fordyce, W. E. (1976). *Behavioral methods in chronic pain and illness.* St. Louis, MO: Mosby.

Fordyce, W. E. (1990). Learned pain: Pain as behavior. In J. J. Bonica (Ed.), *The management of pain* (pp. 291–299). Philadelphia: Lea & Febiger.

Fordyce, W., Fowler, R., Lehmann, J., & DeLateur, B. (1968). Some implications of learning in problems of chronic pain. *Journal of Chronic Diseases, 21,* 179.

Gamsa, A. (1994). The role of psychological factors in chronic pain: I. A half century of study. *Pain, 57,* 5–15.

Geisser, M. E., Gaskin, M. E., Robinson, M. E., & Greene, A. F. (1993). The relationship of depression and somatic focus to experimental and clinical pain in chronic pain patients. *Psychology and Health, 8,* 405–415.

Geisser, M. E., Robinson, M. E., Keefe, F. J., & Weiner, M. L. (1994). Catastrophizing, depression and the sensory, affective and evaluative aspects of chronic pain. *Pain, 59,* 79–83.

Grzesiak, R. C., & Ciccone, D. C. (1994). *Psychological vulnerability to chronic pain.* New York: Springer.

Holmes, J. A., & Stevenson, C. A. Z. (1990). Differential effects of avoidant and attentional coping strategies on adaptation to chronic and recent-onset pain. *Health Psychology, 9,* 577–584.

Holzberg, A. D., Robinson, M. E., Geisser, M. E., & Gremillion, H. A. (1996). The effects of depression and chronic pain on psychosocial and physical functioning. *The Clinical Journal of Pain, 12,* 118–125.

Hoyle, R. H., & Smith, G. T. (1994). Formulating clinical research hypothesis as structural equation models: A conceptual overview. *Journal of Consulting and Clinical Psychology, 62,* 429–440.

Hardy, J. D., Wolff, H. G., & Goodell, H. (1952). *Pain sensations and reactions.* Baltimore: Williams & Wilkins.

International Association for the Study of Pain. (1979). Pain terms: A list with definitions and notes on usage. *Pain, 6,* 249.

Jensen, M. P., & Karoly, P. (1991). Control beliefs, coping efforts, and adjustment to chronic pain. *Journal of Consulting and Clinical Psychology, 59,* 431–438.

Jensen, M. P., Turner, J. A., & Romano, J. M. (1991). Self-efficacy and outcome expectancies: Relationship to chronic pain coping strategies and adjustment. *Pain, 44,* 263–269.

Jensen, M. P., Turner, J. A., & Romano, J. M. (1994). Correlations of improvement in multidisciplinary treatments of chronic pain. *Journal of Consulting and Clinical Psychology, 62,* 172–179.

Katon, W., Kleinman, A., & Rosen, G. (1982). Depression and somatization: A review. *The American Journal of Medicine, 72,* 127–135.

Keefe, F. J., Brown, G. K., Wallston, K. A., & Caldwell, D. S. (1989). Coping with rheumatoid arthritis pain: Catastrophizing as a maladaptive strategy. *Pain, 37*, 51–56.

Keefe, F. J., Caldwell, D. S., Williams, D. A., Gil, K. M., Mitchell, D., Martinez, S., Nunley, J., Beckham, J. C., Crisson, J. E., & Helms, M. (1990). Pain coping skills training in the management of osteoarthritic knee pain: A comparative study. *Behavior Therapy, 21*, 49–62.

Kellner, R. (1991). *Psychosomatic syndromes and somatic symptoms.* Washington, DC: American Psychiatric Press.

Kerns, R. D., Turk, D. C., Holzman, A. D., & Rudy, T. E. (1985). Comparison of cognitive-behavioral and behavioral approaches to the outpatient treatment of chronic pain. *Clinical Journal of Pain, 1*, 195–204.

Linton, S. J., Bradley, L. A., Jensen, I., Spangfort, E., & Sundell, L. (1989). The secondary prevention of low back pain: A controlled study with follow-up. *Pain, 36*, 197–207.

Meichenbaum, D. (1973). *Cognitive behavior modification.* New York: Plenum.

Meichenbaum, D. (1977). *Cognitive behavioral modification: An integrated approach.* New York: Plenum.

Melamed, B. G., Hawes, R., Heiby, E., & Blick, J. (1975). Use of filmed modeling to reduce unco-operative behavior of children during dental treatment. *Journal of Dental Research, 54*, 797–801.

Melzack, R., & Wall, P. D. (1965). Pain mechanisms: A new theory. *Science, 150*, 971–979.

Nicholas, M. K., Wilson, P. H., & Goyen, J. (1992). Comparison of cognitive-behavioral group treatment and an alternative non-psychological treatment for chronic low-back pain. *Pain, 48*, 339–347.

Novy, D. M., Nelson, D. V., Frances, D. J., & Turk, D. C. (1995). Perspectives of chronic pain: An evaluative comparison of restrictive and comprehensive models. *Psychological Bulletin, 118*, 238–247.

Ohrbach, R., & McCall, W. D. (1996). The stress-hyperactivity-pain theory of myogenic pain. *Pain Forum, 5*(1), 51–66.

Oleson, J., & Bonica, J. (1990). Headache. In J. Bonica (Ed.), *The management of pain* (pp. 687–726). Philadelphia: Lea & Febiger.

Parker, J. C., Smarr, K. L., Angelone, E. O., Mothersead, P. K., Lee, B. S., Walker, S. E., Bridges, A. J., & Caldwell, C. W. (1992). Psychological factors, immunologic activation, and disease activity in rheumatoid arthritis. *Arthritis Care Research, 5*, 196–201.

Phillips, H. C. (1987). The effects of behavioral treatment on chronic pain. *Behavioral Research and Therapy, 25*, 365–377.

Pilowsky, I. (1986). Psychodynamic aspects of the pain experience. In R. A. Sternbach (Ed.), *The psychology of pain* (pp. 203–217). New York: Raven.

Reichling, D. B., & Gold, M. S. (1996). Gate control begins in the primary afferent. *Pain Forum, 5*(1), 45–50.

Riley, J. L., & Robinson, M. E. (1998). *Validity of MMPI–2 profiles in chronic pain patients: Differences in path models of coping and somatization.* Manuscript submitted for publication.

Riley, J. L., Robinson, M. E., Geisser, M. E., & Wittmer, V. (1993). Multivariate cluster analysis of the MMPI–2 in chronic low-back pain patients. *The Clinical Journal of Pain, 9*, 248–252.

Riley, J. L., Robinson, M. E., Geisser, M. E., Wittmer, V. T., & Graham-Smith, A. (1995). The relationship between MMPI–2 cluster profiles and surgical outcome in chronic low-back pain patients. *Journal of Spinal Disorders, 8*, 213–219.

Rudy, T. E., & Greco, C. M. (1996). Stretching psychophysiological models of TMD. *Pain Forum, 5*(1), 67–69.

Rudy, T. E., Kerns, R. D., & Turk, D. C. (1988). Chronic pain and depression: Towards a cognitive-behavioral mediation model. *Pain, 35*, 129–140.

Schmidt, A. J. (1985a). Cognitive factors in the performance level of chronic low back pain patients. *Journal of Psychosomatic Research, 2*, 183–189.

Schmidt, A. J. (1985b). Performance level of chronic low back pain patients on different treadmill test conditions. *Journal of Psychosomatic Research, 29,* 639–645.

Schmidt, A. M., & Arntz, A. (1987). Psychological research and chronic low back pain: A standstill or breakthrough? *Social Science and Medicine, 25,* 1095–1104.

Schwartz, G. E. (1982). Testing the biopsychosocial model: The ultimate challenge facing behavioral medicine. *Journal of Consulting and Clinical Psychology, 50,* 1040–1050.

Sinclair, D. C. (1955). Cutaneous sensation in the doctrine of specific nerve energy. *Brain, 78,* 584.

Snow-Turek, A. L., Norris, M. P., & Tan, G. (1996). Active and passing coping strategies in chronic pain patients. *Pain, 64,* 455–462.

Turk, D. C., & Flor, H. (1984). Etiological theories and treatments for chronic back pain: II. Psychological models-interventions. *Pain, 19,* 209–223.

Turk, D. C., & Rudy, T. E. (1986). Assessment of cognitive factors in chronic pain: A worthwhile enterprise? *Journal of Consulting and Clinical Psychology, 54,* 760–768.

Turk, D. C., & Rudy, T. E. (1989). A cognitive-behavioral perspective on chronic pain: Beyond the scalpel and syringe. In C. D. Tollison (Ed.), *Handbook of chronic pain management* (pp. 222–235). Baltimore: Williams & Wilkins.

Turner, J. A., & Jensen, M. P. (1993). Efficacy of cognitive therapy for chronic low back pain. *Pain, 52,* 169–177.

Wall, P. D. (1996). Comments after 30 years of the gate control theory of pain. *Pain Forum, 5*(1), 12–22.

Wedell, G. (1955). Somesthesis in chemical senses. *Annual Review of Psychology, 6,* 119.

Williamson, D. J., Robinson, M. E., & Melamed, B. (1997). Pain behavior, spouse responsiveness, and marital satisfaction in patients with rheumatoid arthritis. *Behavior Modification, 21,* 97–118.

Zautra, A. J., Marbach, J. J., Raphael, K. G., Dohrenwend, B. P., Lennon, M. C., & Kenney, D. A. (1995). The examination of myofascial face pain and its relationship to psychological distress among women. *Health Psychology, 14,* 223–231.

Chapter 3

Detecting Deception and Malingering

Kenneth D. Craig
Marilyn L. Hill
Bruce W. McMurtry
University of British Columbia

Ideally, this chapter would identify features of pain representations known to discriminate between subjective experiences of pain and claims that are falsified. Regrettably, it is too soon to promise strategies capable of producing an absolute differentiation. Definitive, empirically validated procedures for distinguishing genuine and deceptive pain report are not available and current approaches to the detection of deception remain to some degree intuitive. Fortunately, recent research provides evidence that (a) genuine presentations of pain differ from deceptive presentations, (b) informed and careful observers, clinicians as well as others, can discriminate genuine and deceptive presentations, and (c) empirically informed assessment approaches can be developed.

There are numerous incentives for duplicitous pain reports. The person may fake or exaggerate a display of pain to enhance the likelihood of desired outcomes, including financial payoffs, in the form of compensation payments, litigation awards, or long-term disability income, access to controlled drugs for illicit use, or other less tangible payoffs, including manipulation of others and avoidance of work, domestic, or social responsibilities. Alternatively, pain displays may be suppressed to avoid adverse consequences of others recognizing pain, including imposing the illness role on the individual, the prescription of feared medications, delivery of analgesics via needles, or deprivation of work.

Concerns about the prospects of deception and malingering of chronic pain and other medical and psychological conditions are commonplace

(Rogers, 1997). Purposeful exaggeration of pain is usually treated with alarm and even anger by health care providers and institutions. In contrast, suppression of pain complaints has received less attention from health care practitioners or institutions, although failure to engage in early identification or misdiagnosis can have unfortunate long-term consequences, as disease progression cannot be checked.

Base rates for deception and malingering generally are believed to be quite low (Chapman & Brena, 1990; Fordyce, 1995; Jensen, 1997; Leavitt & Sweet, 1986; Mendelson, 1992), although individual clinician estimates based on clinical impressions can be high (Leavitt & Sweet, 1986). Of course, the real incidence is difficult to establish, because of the secretive nature of the actions, the challenge in distinguishing between conscious and unconscious motivation, and the skills that people exercise to succeed with their lies. There also can be incentives for overstating the actual incidence and costs of deception and malingering. Frequent media coverage of fraudulent accidents or injuries and corporate publicity devoted to the importance of cracking down on fraud may overplay the true incidence by focusing on dishonest claims.

DEFINITION

Deception refers to an attempt to induce in a perceiver a false judgment or belief by deliberately providing false information. Malingering concerns adopting a role to deceive others for a recognizable goal. The essential feature of malingering, according to the American Psychiatric Association's *Diagnostic and Statistical Manual of Mental Disorders* (4th ed. [*DSM–IV*], 1994), is "the intentional production of false or grossly exaggerated physical or psychological symptoms, motivated by external incentives" (p. 683).

Key to these definitions would be the requirement that the individual's actions were intentional, purposeful, deliberate, or voluntary. If an observer detects behavior inconsistent with subjective states of pain, the challenge then becomes one of deciding whether conscious choice to dissemble was present. No theory of human behavior rejects the possibility that people can adopt or become engaged in complex patterns of behavior without awareness. From the perspective of the operant model of pain behavior, symptomatic complaints, guarded actions, limping, facial expression, and more complex behaviors such as physician visits can come under the control of social reinforcement without conscious mediation (Fordyce, 1976). Similarly, current cognitive-behavioral formulations (Turk, 1996) and ecological models of chronic pain (Dworkin, Von Korff, & LeResche, 1992), theories of somatic amplification (Ciccone, Just, & Bandilla, 1996), and psychiatric accounts of exaggerated illness behavior (Ellard, 1970; Miller,

1961) provide for the possibility of cognitive facilitation of pain, but they do not require awareness or purposeful intent to deceive.

The issue of intentionality is further complicated by the potential for self-deception. Individuals may come to deceive themselves about the severity of their problems (Paulhus & Suedfeld, 1988), thereby justifying an overly dramatic pain or illness presentation. Feedback mechanisms also have been proposed whereby exaggerating behavior in excess of the actual experience could lead to amplification of the actual experience of pain (Bayer, 1984).

Further confusion can be contributed by examiners who fail to recognize or acknowledge the distinction between purposeful and nonintentional overrepresentation of pain. Certain language may imply intentionality on the part of the patient, even though that may not be the intended effect. Stating that a patient is exaggerating complaints, engaging in symptom magnification, or displaying amplified pain behavior is often inferred as signaling a conclusion the patient was engaged in willing and base manipulation of the situation when that was not the speaker's intent.

There is of course a risk of harm when self-interested motives are imputed to account for pain behavior. The decision, accusation, or even an unspoken assumption of deception or malingering can lead to underestimation of pain (Poole & Craig, 1992), denial of treatment, or adversely affect treatment, because successful treatment is largely based on the development of a trusting relationship between the practitioner and patient.

THE NATURE OF DECEPTION

Dissembling chronic pain behavior should be recognized as having continuity with acts of deception that become commonplace in childhood to control life demands. Common forms of deception deemed quite acceptable in good company include "white lies," not allowing the truth to ruin a good story, and the deceptive trickery of a practical joke. Lies concerning one's health also may be socially sanctioned. One example would be exercising the perceived right to take "earned sick days," despite good health. Similarly, when insurance policies cover physical but not psychological health, medical complaints can be used to provide access to health care.

The inevitability of deception and its counterpart, the capacity to detect deception, suggest an inherent capacity for both deception and the detection of deception. There is evidence for biological dispositions to sensitivity to deception in others (Fridlund, 1994) and indications that our human ancestral history may leave us adept at identifying cheating (Cosmides & Tooby, 1989).

A biological perspective on voluntary and involuntary behavior provides theoretical grounds to expect differences between spontaneous and purposively controlled social displays of pain, confirming that facial expression provides a key source of information about the credibility of displays of distress. Separate neural systems are responsible for voluntary and involuntary facial movements (Rinn, 1984). The pyramidal system, which descends from cortical areas, plays a primary role in voluntary movement, as lesions lead to deficits in the ability to produce certain facial actions on demand, whereas the individual retains the ability to exhibit the same expression spontaneously. Involuntary facial movements depend more on the subcortical, extrapyramidal system. Lesions in this area may result in deficits in spontaneous facial expressions of emotion, although leaving unaffected the ability to deliberately produce these movements (Rinn, 1984). Thus, different neurophysiological systems should yield identifiable differences in the topography of genuine and deliberate actions.

Further insights into the nature of deception are evident in the emergence of deceptive interpersonal behavior and the capacity to detect it early in life (Chandler & Afifi, 1996). Children acquire skills in impression management, learn that other people operate on their understanding of others, rather than their real attributes (Olson, 1993), and learn to play many roles in life (e.g., friend, worker, family member, healthy person, sick person, chronic pain patient). Practice in assuming different roles could make children and the adults they become masters of pretense.

ASSESSMENT OF DECEPTION AND MALINGERING

Success in detecting misrepresentations about pain and related disability will depend on characteristics of the examiner, the nature of the deception, and the instruments used to evaluate the credibility of claims. Knowledge and experience in pain assessment will enhance skills, as will a good understanding of the many modes and psychological, behavioral, and social correlates of deception and the use of instruments developed for this purpose.

The challenge of detecting deceptive messages about pain relates to a long-standing and as yet unresolved general problem in the field of pain assessment—distinguishing qualities of the perceptual experience of pain from its behavioral manifestations. As a subjective experience, pain is not available to independent, direct scrutiny. All forms of assessment are inferential, whether one is using self-report, nonverbal, or physiological measures.

The observer may access diverse sources of information, including archival searches, unobtrusive surveillance, solicitation of reports of informed others, and direct examination (see Table 3.1). The emphasis here is on the latter, how a clinician in the course of an examination might access information indicative of dishonest representations about health. Multidis-

TABLE 3.1
Information Sources Useful in Discriminating Felt and Falsified Pain

Context of Assessment
1. Medicolegal issues, including compensation, litigation, or criminal charges.
2. Evidence of physical pathology, lack of response to treatment.
3. Pain behavior payoffs and aversive disincentives.

Characteristics of the Individual
1. Personal background.
• Accessible through self-report, archival searches, informed others.
2. Verbal behavior.
• Through interview and nonobtrusive observation; content, quality, and clarity.
• Through interview; nonpainful complaints and symptoms.
3. Psychometric assessment.
• Personality tests evaluating trait dispositions.
• Specialized scales evaluating credibility.
• Consistency measures.
4. Nonverbal expression.
• Clinic observations, obtrusive or nonobtrusive.
• Assessment of medically incongruent pain behavior.
• Unobtrusive surveillance.

ciplinary assessments are most likely to include a broad range of perspectives and types of information

Clinicians should distinguish indices of deception that have been empirically validated from those that remain untested and, therefore, have the potential to be misleading (Leavitt & Sweet, 1986). Strategically, it is advisable to use progressively more refined techniques when evaluating credibility. A general assessment should screen for possible credibility problems, with more specific tools and strategies employed when suspicions arise until the possibility can be confirmed or excluded or remains indeterminate. Decisions are likely to be made on the basis of consistencies among information sources and progressive exclusion of the possibility of deception on available evidence, with confirmatory evidence highly desirable. Collateral information is most likely to demonstrate inconsistencies or contradictions (Faust, 1995).

Context of the Assessment. Deception and malingering are more probable in certain situations than others. Clinicians have been encouraged to consider malingering when medicolegal issues arise, there is a marked discrepancy between claims of distress or disability and objective findings, there is a lack of cooperation during assessment or in compliance with the prescribed treatment regimen, or antisocial personality features are present (American Psychiatric Association, 1994). These rough guidelines are overdrawn and could provoke suspicion unwarranted by our current understanding of chronic pain. These will be observed far more often in honest than dishonest people. For example, the base rate for treatment compliance among people even with life-threatening diseases is distressingly low.

Suspicion of lying tends to be particularly severe when complaints and pain behavior are nonspecific or vague and there is no concrete evidence of physical pathology. The presence of organic pathology weighs very heavily in decisions about deception and malingering (Leavitt & Sweet, 1986), even though a large proportion of chronic pain complaints has little or no relationship to detectable organic pathology (Waddell, 1991), substantial pathology can often be demonstrated in asymptomatic people (Turk, 1996), and ongoing research can disclose new pathophysiological sources of pain (Teasell & Merskey, 1997). However, lies are likely to be more successful if there is some element of truth to the claims. If some organic pathology were to be associated with a substantial accident, it would be easier to convince judges of the veracity of one's claims to being in severe pain. People not informed about the complexities of pain have difficulty imagining how there can be tissue damage without pain and how pain can be present when there is no identifiable injury.

When there is no adequate evidence of physical pathology, yet symptoms persist, clinicians will probe further. The usual practice is to search for "secondary gain" or apparent benefits that could promote or maintain pain and illness behavior. Their presence need not necessarily signal intentional manipulation of the situation, but they represent grounds for further search. Consideration also must be given to the substantial disincentives, or "secondary punishers" to a life of chronic pain. Patients readily point out the hardships they suffer in the form of financial losses, deprivation of work, recreational, and social opportunities, increased family stress, grievous loss of self-esteem, and unhappy, isolated lifestyles.

The potential for financial and other benefits deriving from chronic pain presentations cannot be presumed to lead inevitably to conscious motivation to dissemble. Some studies indicate increased pain, distress, or disability when financial compensation is available (Guest & Drummond, 1992; Hayes, Solyom, Wing, & Berkowitz, 1993; Phillips & Grant, 1991a, 1991b; Sanders & Meyers, 1986). Others have failed to find such over-representation of problems (Melzack, Katz, & Jeans, 1985), or have found that they exist for only certain diagnostic groups (Dworkin, Handlin, Richlin, Brand, & Vanucci, 1985), or that they can be accounted for by a third variable (Leavitt, Garron, McNeill, & Whisler, 1982). The complexity of the relationship between financial compensation and pain (Mendelson, 1992, 1994) argues against simplistic attributions of malingering based only on the availability of compensation.

It also has been suggested that pain-related disabilities, including utilization of health care resources and time off work, will resolve upon settlement of compensation issues (Miller, 1961), but anecdotal impressions often dictate the conclusion and sweeping generalizations are unwarranted. Nevertheless, the impact of financial benefits on pain disabilities can be considerable. Although compensation programs and disability insurance policies vary, it is not unusual for people on disability to have a more substantial income than prior to the termination of work. Nachemson (1983) observed that when compensation for injury rises above 55% of net income the number of claims increases dramatically. Although the potential for financial gain could motivate dishonest behavior, lower levels of income also can compel workers to remain on the job, despite costs to health, if financial necessity dictates same.

The role of contingent payoffs for pain behavior may be more obvious when individual cases are examined. Treatment settings sometimes set the circumstances for more dramatic displays of pain than would ordinarily be expected by making opportunities for relief from pain contingent upon demonstrations of high levels of distress. For example, patients with chronic pain often must struggle to convince health care practitioners of the legitimacy of their pain, which encourages forceful displays that are not necessarily purposefully exaggerated.

Suspicion of deception can also be provoked when patients fail to work toward recovery. People who are ill are expected to attempt to overcome their problems, either alone, through "willpower," or by adhering to treatment regimens. Does failure to actively pursue treatment represent a form of moral dereliction or deception?

Characteristics of the Individual.   Direct contact with the person through interview or unobtrusive behavioral observation may provide valuable information (DePaulo, Stone, & Lassiter, 1985; DePaulo, 1994). Although currently available data do not suggest malingering of chronic pain is more likely in groups varying by age (excluding issues of competency), gender, education, employment, or social and cultural backgrounds, personal biases may influence an observer's decision making. A more relevant source of information would be the individual's life history. A history of dishonesty would be particularly informative, if available, but not definitive, signaling a need for more information. Physical appearance, including dress, stature, and information relating to demographic characteristics, often assumes a role in judgments of others, perhaps providing a context for other information or leading to errors because of stereotypes and biases.

Verbal Behavior.   It can be argued that self-report comes closest to direct correspondence to the actual experience of pain (Jensen, 1997), but even here there is room for distortion (Chapman & Brena, 1990; Craig, 1992), not necessarily willful. Subjective experiences are extremely complex compounds and synergies of sensations, feelings, images, memories, and thoughts. The complexities often defy the use of language; hence the individual must summarize or select specific features to report. The production of descriptive language depends on the individual's capabilities and willingness to characterize experiences. Despite these constraints, pain report does provide caretakers with important information concerning the nature, origins, and impact of diseases or injuries and allows detailed analysis of the effects of analgesics and other palliatives. As Jensen observed, "the clinician who trusts that a patient's self-report reflects his or her pain experience will be correct much more often than not" (p. 654). It is the potential for the individual to be incompetent or not motivated to provide an honest report that leads us to recognize uncritical acceptance of self-report could lead to faulty conclusions.

Clinicians' judgments regarding the possibility of deception are influenced by the content, quality, and clarity of the individual's self-report of symptoms, with insufficient or inconsistent details often suggesting deception (Chapman & Brena, 1990). It is ordinarily advantageous to be honest about feelings of pain, but if the individual wants to misrepresent private states, self-report will reflect this intent rather than the real state of the individual. Bias is both less likely and more likely to be observed on systematic measures than on casual queries. For example, healthy volunteers voluntarily faking disabling low back pain tend to use words indicative of more intense pain and affective distress and fewer words focusing upon sensory features of painful experience (Leavitt, 1987). Although generality of this finding to a clinical population must be questioned, it was less likely to have been observed on casual inquiry.

Though provoking suspicion, it should be recognized that a lack of clarity in self-report could be the product of deficiencies in verbal facility, depression, concentration problems, or an absence of prior experience with pain. Lack of definition may also be a quality of the medical condition. Variability in reports of symptom location, duration, and intensity is typical of fibromyalgia. Structured interviews have been used successfully for detecting deception with respect to many medical conditions (cf. Rogers, 1997), but to date no such instrument has been developed to detect malingering in chronic pain patients.

Pain is not alone as a so-called subjective complaint. People suffering from chronic pain may also present with vague and ill-defined complaints of depression, sleep difficulties, fatigue, sensory dysfunction, memory loss, difficulties with concentration, or inability to engage in various activities. Unlike complaints of pain, some of these could be verified (Pankratz & Binder, 1997), if clinicians could commit time or resources to doing so, but often these are not available and trust in patient claims becomes necessary.

Clinicians are also capable of becoming suspicious of patients who complain about treatment or the demands of referral agencies (e.g., insurance companies, courts), or who are not generally compliant or cooperative. Although this could represent an evasive pattern, the incidence of irritability among people at large, and in patients suffering chronic pain in particular (Fernandez & Turk, 1995), as well as the possibility that the feelings of grievance are legitimate, should lead the examiner to question the usefulness of this information.

Psychometric Assessment. Formal psychological testing can be construed as complementary to self-report interviews, but as taking place under standardized conditions permitting normative comparisons. Scales may be able to contribute information regarding the credibility of an individual's general self-presentation (Greene, 1997), but this may only reflect indirectly the validity of declarations concerning pain. The MMPI-2 (Minnesota Multiphasic Personality Inventory, 2nd ed.; Butcher & Williams, 1992), for example, provides validity scales that assess whether an individual's overall presentation is forthright. The nonobvious nature of these scales contributes to their usefulness because test takers cannot anticipate their use. They must not be used indiscriminately as indexes of malingering, however, given their ambiguous meaning. For example, one of the most useful scales on the MMPI-2, the F scale, indicates whether the person answers in an atypical and deviant manner. This could mean malingering, but it also could reflect a high level of psychopathology, or high levels of distress provoked by tragic or disastrous personal circumstances.

Efforts to find personality profiles of people engaged in deception or malingering have not led to consistent findings (e.g., Chapman & Brena, 1990), indicating that a capacity to lie is not restricted to particular personality types. The replicability of a test may provide additional information concerning the veracity of self-report. Inconsistencies in responding to psychological tests on repeated administrations (Hayes, Solyom, Wing, & Berkowitz, 1993) have been found to be related to the receipt or expectation of financial compensation. Patients who were receiving or pursuing compensation showed significantly more inconsistency in their responses, although, again, deliberate deception cannot be implied.

Nonverbal Behavior. Nonverbal communications also provide considerable information to observers, both in combination with self-report or as an exclusive source of information for people who are nonverbal. Considerable information can be extracted from posture, body and limb movements, paralinguistic vocalizations, and facial expression. Facial expression is particularly informative because of its plasticity and dynamic range (Craig, 1992; Ekman & Friesen, 1978; Prkachin & Craig, 1995). Although clinicians are often charged to believe what patients say, the usefulness of nonverbal information makes it inevitable that their judgments will represent a compound of nonverbal and verbal input. Poole and Craig (1992) found that judgments about another's pain were more heavily weighted by facial expression when both self-report and facial displays were available. Clinicians also assign greater weight to nonverbal expression than to patient self-reports when judging the location and severity of pain experienced (Johnson, 1977).

It should be recognized that nonverbal behavior is subject to voluntary control, but it does not appear to be self-monitored to as great an extent as verbal behavior. Nonverbal expression seems to be closer to a spontaneous manifestation of felt states than an attempt to represent the public persona the individual wishes to project at a particular point in time. However, no public behavioral display, verbal or nonverbal, should be construed as exclusively expressive of emotional or motivational states or judged to be independent of the individual's appraisal of his or her best interests. Virtually all social behavior is predicated upon the actor's intent to have an impact on others (Fridlund, 1994).

Nonverbal expression adds context, qualification, and meaning to speech. Astute examiners usually look for a behavioral display consistent with alleged physical impairment, with departures and inconsistencies over time triggering questions about credibility. A common example would be the clinician's appraisal of a patient's physical movements as he or she moves into the examining room. Various behavioral cues have been associated with deception, including indifference to severe pain, higher voice pitch, shorter answers, speech errors, eye blinking, and language repetitions, but these are suggestive rather than specific to deception.

People's feelings about engaging in a deception may also provide nonverbal cues. Fear of discovery and severe adverse consequences, or feelings of shame or guilt, could produce physiological or visible emotional distress. A "shifty" appearance or averted gaze, although usually complex and fleeting, again are often suggestive, but there is no reason to believe they are conclusive. Deception can be confused with patient nervousness, indecision, self-doubt, or extreme defensiveness. The adversarial nature of disputes about the legitimacy of pain complaints can provoke or exacerbate these states in both guilty and innocent people and lead to greater difficulty in making the distinction.

Also of interest are patterns of pain behavior inconsistent with expectations derived from the current understanding of normal anatomy and physiology. Medically incongruent pain (H. D. Hadjistavropoulos & Craig, 1994; Reesor & Craig, 1988) or abnormal illness behavior (Waddell, Pilowsky, & Bond, 1989) often gives rise to suspicions of deceptive behavior, but current evidence does not support this interpretation. The "nonorganic signs" identified by Waddell and associates (Waddell, McCulloch, Kummel, & Venner, 1980) are important because they are not uncommon in acute and chronic pain patients, particularly in patients receiving financial compensation (H. D. Hadjistavropoulos & Craig, 1994; Hayes et al., 1993). Similarly significant are incongruent pain complaints, for example, checklists of inappropriate or nonorganic symptoms (Waddell, Main, Morris, DiPaolo, & Gray, 1984), because they are related to the likelihood of emergency admissions for pain (Waddell et al., 1984) and poor response to a variety of treatment modalities (Dzioba & Doxey, 1984; Lehmann, Russell, & Spratt, 1983). Waddell et al. (1984) suggested elevation on these measures should be construed as "the clinical equivalent of psychologic distress" (p. 211). People high on these measures display dysfunctional cognitions, high levels of anxiety, higher reported pain intensity (Reesor & Craig, 1988), and elevations on scales of the MMPI indicating dysfunctional personality traits (McCulloch, 1977; Waddell et al., 1980; Wiltse & Rochio, 1975). Thus, medically incongruent pain should be recognized as having multiple origins, with deception only one of many possibilities.

Research on duplicity in facial displays of emotion is instructive when considering deceptive displays of pain (Ekman, 1985; Ekman & Friesen, 1969). For example, faking a smile is a considerable challenge. Posed smiles differ from felt smiles in subtle but detectable ways, with, most often, an absence of the raised cheeks that give "little crow's-feet" at the edges of the eyes (Ekman, Friesen, & O'Sullivan, 1988; LeResche, Ehrlick, & Dworkin, 1990). In addition, Hager and Ekman (1985) found that a deliberately produced startle expression contained more facial actions not prototypical of a startle response than during a genuine startle response.

These observations provide a basis for detailed empirical study of attempts to deceive observers about pain experiences. People experiencing acute pain tend to exhibit a facial grimace that may include lowered brow, raised cheeks, tightened eyelids, a raised upper lip or opened mouth, and narrowed or closed eyes (Craig, Hyde, & Patrick, 1991; LeResche & Dworkin, 1988; Prkachin, 1992; Prkachin & Mercer, 1989), with some elements of moderate muscular tension (H. D. Hadjistavropoulos & Craig, 1994). There also is considerable individual variability, associated with the type and severity of pain experienced, prior experience with the painful event, and situational and individual difference variables (Craig, Prkachin, & Grunau, 1992). Patients voluntarily faking pain expressions replicate rather well the pattern observed in the usual display, with no specific facial actions indicative of purposeful misrepresentation, indicating that even people not trained as actors can fabricate a pain display (Craig et al., 1991; H. D. Hadjistavropoulos & Craig, 1994; Hill, 1996). However, the faked displays are not wholly successful, as a number of pain-related facial actions have been observed in research investigations (H. D. Hadjistavropoulos & Craig, 1994; Hill, 1996) to occur with greater frequency (i.e., brow lowering and mouth opening) and intensity (brow lowering). Some actions that more often occur during faked pain (lip corner pull, lip stretch, inner or outer brow raise), relative to the usual spontaneous display, tend to be associated with people's efforts to cope with pain rather than the spontaneous display. As well, in the falsified display, the component facial actions present themselves in a more sequential rather than contiguous manner observed during genuine pain (Hill, 1996). Finally, when expressions are faked, the duration of peak intensity and the overall duration of the facial expression increase (Hill, 1996). The general pattern during faked displays is more of a "caricature" of the spontaneous display. Even though people can be fooled by the faked displays (Poole & Craig, 1992), judges can make subtle distinctions (H. D. Hadjistavropoulos, Craig, T. Hadjistavropoulos, & Poole, 1996; Hill, 1996).

TRAINING TO IMPROVE DETECTION

The few investigations of training to improve detection of any form of lying have been largely unsuccessful (Kohnken, 1987; Zuckerman, Koestner, & Alton, 1984; Zuckerman, Koestner, & Colella, 1985). Usually the training involves provision of feedback rather than instruction in cue utilization or strategy deployment. One exception (Ekman & Friesen, 1974) found a cue utilization–training approach did assist coders to correctly classify honest and deceptive emotional expressions.

Two studies have found training to improve detection of simulated facial displays of pain. Galin and Thorn (1993) found that training and corrective feedback led to limited improvements in detecting deceptive pain, but a constrained description of the facial display of pain and delayed feedback were used, limiting the generality of the findings. Hill (1996) contrasted corrective feedback with a training program designed to increase the breadth and acuity of judges' decision-making procedures, but only immediate corrective feedback improved accuracy in identifying deception of pain displays. It is noteworthy that in neither the Hill study nor in other investigations (DePaulo & Pfeifer, 1986; Kohnken, 1987) was confidence in judgments related to detection accuracy. Indeed, judges generally tended to be overconfident in their ability to make discriminations, even when their judgments were erroneous. In conclusion, there is limited evidence indicating that it is possible to improve through training the detection of misrepresentations about pain.

DECISION MAKING AND JUDGMENTAL PROCESSES

The decision processes judges use to evaluate the credibility of information require further study. As described here, detection of deception and malingering is a dynamic process involving a continuing evaluation of information and a progressive search for validating or disconfirming information. The end product of decision making often seems to be a matter of "does it ring true," with observers unable to explicate fully their decisions. The potential for error is considerable and it would be advantageous if there were statistical algorithms that could be applied (Dawes, Faust, & Meehl, 1989). A major impediment is the lack of definitive criteria for deception or malingering.

In the absence of empirically validated strategies, judgments are vulnerable to bias. Characteristics of individuals being judged and attributes of those doing the judging that ordinarily would be seen as irrelevant could have an impact. For example, attractiveness of patients (H. D. Hadjistavropoulos, Ross, & von Baeyer, 1990; T. Hadjistavropoulos, McMurtry, & Craig, 1996) was associated with lower pain attributions. In contrast, prior but spurious knowledge that people were hypersensitive to painful events (Prkachin & Craig, 1985) and high levels of judge succorance (von Baeyer, Johnson, & McMillan, 1984) led to attributions of greater levels of pain when judges were observing nonverbal displays. It is possible that information that compensation is pending, or that the individual is involved in litigation, or that the self-report is incongruent with the severity of tissue damage would have an impact on judgments. Awareness that one is evaluating another person's credibility could also have an impact on decisions. Questioning another's moral integrity is likely to be seen as a confrontational or even aggressive challenge that may provoke counteraggression. The possibility of legal challenges, the demands of due process, and the potential for appeals can make clinicians reluctant to conclude they have detected deception or malingering.

Does suspicion of high base rates of deception improve detection? Poole and Craig (1992) advised judges that a number of the facial displays they were judging in fact were either faked expressions or were attempts to suppress the display of pain. Relative to others who were not so informed, this did not improve detection of faked or suppressed displays, but it did lead to a consistent reduction in the severity of pain attributed to the patients, irrespective of whether the displays were spontaneous, faked, or suppressed. The judges were less willing in general to believe other people were experiencing pain. Others have noted that increasing the base rate expectation of deception has little effect on success in detecting deception (Faust, Hart, Guilmette, & Arkes, 1988).

Individual differences in detection skill have been observed. In a study examining the ability to detect deception in facial displays of pain, Hill (1996) reported variation in judgment accuracy, ranging from accuracy levels well below chance (18%) to a 63% accuracy level (an impressive 4 *SD*s [standard deviations] above the mean) when the base rate probability was 25%. This perhaps could be the product of greater interpersonal sensitivity, in the first instance, although Hill found that a multidimensional measure of empathy, including a scale of social acuity, was not related to judgment accuracy, more experience in successfully identifying fabrication, or specific training in the art. Ekman and O'Sullivan (1991) found that, among professionals with experience in lie detection, those who were better discriminators of deception of emotional states paid greater attention to nonverbal cues, reported they found a broader variety of cues to be of value, and seemed more attentive to microexpressions, even though these people could not articulate use of these strategies. Hill found that, even with substantial differences within genders, women were more accurate in identifying deception of pain, an outcome consistent with stereotypes that women are more sensitive, more understanding, and more aware of others' feelings than men, and findings that women are better able to decode nonverbal cues of emotion (Hall, 1984).

CONCLUSION

Clinicians must be alert to the possibility of dishonest attempts to fake pain or associated disability, because of the numerous incentives for misrepresentation, even though the base rate appears low. The challenge of identifying malingering is complicated by (a) the requirement for evidence of conscious intent, given that current formulations of pain provide for nonintentional amplification of pain behavior, (b) the complexities of assessing subjective experiences of pain and deceptive intent, (c) the considerable opportunities most people have throughout their life span to practice role playing, and (d) the absence of single or unique markers for deception and malingering, requiring clinicians and others to attend to the complex patterns of information available to them. Numerous cautions one must attend to when assessing deception and malingering are summarized in Table 3.2. Counterbalancing these are (a) judges' inherent and acquired decision-making skills requisite to problem solving of all types, including judgments of deception, (b) considerable opportunity to practice the judgmental skills given the ubiquity of marginal and flagrant deception in everyday lives, (c) evidence for discontinuities and inconsistencies in the behavior of people misrepresenting pain, and (d) a developing understanding of various sources of information available to discriminate deceptive from honest behavior, including contextual information concerning the individual's life history and current circumstances, self-report measures, psychometric measures, and nonverbal behavior. Clinicians who engage in a progressive search for disconfirming or confirmative information will improve detection rates. Although the task of detecting deception and malingering continues to depend on clinical judgment, data are becoming available that could lead to evidence-based practice.

TABLE 3.2
Cautions Concerning Judgments of Deception or Malingering Pain

1. No specific markers identified; the task requires judgment of the pattern of evidence.
2. The true incidence appears quite low (contrary to some inflated estimates).
3. People can be successful in both exaggerating and suppressing evidence of pain.
4. Life histories and current circumstances can provide expert training in deception.
5. Theories of illness behavior permit both conscious and nonattended facilitation.
6. Judgments of deception require a judgment of conscious intent.
7. Consequences of false positive and false negative judgments need consideration.
8. Specific signs usually associated with deception often are observed in honest people.
9. Absence of physical pathology consistent with representations is only suggestive.
10. Lack of treatment adherence is commonplace among honest people.
11. Self-report is vulnerable to purposeful and unwitting bias.
12. Nonverbal behavior can be dissimulated, but self-monitoring is less rigorous.
13. Distinction between evidence-based and speculative observations needs to be recognized.
14. Financial compensation is not invariably linked to facilitated pain-related disability.
15. Neither demographic nor broad-band personality characteristics predict pain deception.
16. Unclear symptom presentation typifies some painful conditions and some honest people.
17. Psychometric scales addressing credibility are not specific to lying about pain.
18. Inconsistencies during assessment are not unique to those engaged in deception.
19. Medically incongruent pain behavior (e.g., "nonorganic signs") is not specific to deception.
20. Confidence in complex interpersonal judgments is usually unrelated to detection accuracy.

REFERENCES

American Psychiatric Association. (1994). *Diagnostic and statistical manual of mental disorders* (4th ed.). Washington, DC: Author.

Bayer, T. (1984). Weaving a tangled web: The psychology of deception in psychogenic pain. *Social Science and Medicine, 20,* 517–527.

Butcher, J. N., & Williams, C. L. (1992). *Essentials of MMPI–2 and MMPI–A interpretation.* Minneapolis: University of Minnesota Press.

Chandler, M. J., & Afifi, J. (1996). On making a virtue out of telling lies. *Social Research, 63,* 731–762.

Chapman, S. L., & Brena, S. F. (1990). Patterns of conscious failure to provide accurate self-report data in patients with low back pain. *Clinical Journal of Pain, 6,* 178–190.

Ciccone, D. S., Just, J., & Bandilla, E. G. (1996). Non-organic symptom reporting in patients with chronic non-malignant pain. *Pain, 68,* 329–341.

Cosmides, L., & Tooby, J. (1989). Evolutionary psychology and the generation of culture: Part II. *Ethology and Sociobiology, 10,* 51–97.

Craig, K. D. (1992). The facial expression of pain: Better than a thousand words? *American Pain Society Journal, 1,* 153–162.

Craig, K. D. (1994). Emotional aspects of pain. In P. D. Wall & R. Melzack (Eds.), *Textbook of pain* (3rd ed., pp. 261–274). Edinburgh: Churchill Livingstone.

Craig, K. D., Hyde, S., & Patrick, C. J. (1991). Genuine, suppressed, and faked facial behavior during exacerbation of chronic low back pain. *Pain, 46,* 161–172.

Craig, K. D., Prkachin, K. M., & Grunau, R. V. E. (1992). The facial expression of pain. In D. C. Turk & R. Melzack (Eds.), *Handbook of pain assessment* (pp. 257–274). Amsterdam: Elsevier Science.

Dawes, R. M., Faust, D., & Meehl, R. E. (1989). Clinical versus actuarial judgment. *Science, 243,* 1668–1673.

DePaulo, B. M. (1994). Spotting lies: Can humans learn to do better? *Current Directions in Psychological Science, 3,* 83–97.

DePaulo, B. M., & Pfeifer, R. L. (1986). On the job experience and skill at detecting deception. *Journal of Applied Social Psychology, 16,* 249–267.

DePaulo, B., Stone, J. I., & Lassiter, G. D. (1985). Deceiving and detecting deception. In B. R. Schlenker (Ed.), *The self and social power* (pp. 323–370). New York: McGraw-Hill.

Dworkin, R. H., Handlin, D. S., Richlin, D. M., Brand, L., & Vanucci, C. (1985). Unravelling the effects of compensation, litigation, and employment on treatment response in chronic pain. *Pain, 23,* 49–59.

Dworkin, S. F., Von Korff, M. R., & LeResche, L. (1992). Epidemiologic studies of chronic pain: A dynamic-ecologic perspective. *Annals of Behavioral Medicine, 14,* 3–11.

Dzioba, R. B., & Doxey, N. C. (1984). A prospective investigation into the orthopaedic and psychological predictors of outcome of first lumbar surgery following industrial injury. *Spine, 9,* 614–623.

Ekman, P. (1985). *Telling lies: Clues to deceit in the marketplace, marriage and politics.* New York: Norton.

Ekman, P., & Friesen, W. V. (1969). Nonverbal leakage and clues to deception. *Psychiatry, 32,* 88–105.

Ekman, P., & Friesen, W. V. (1974). Detecting deception from the body or face. *Journal of Personality and Social Psychology, 29,* 288–298.

Ekman, P., & Freisen, W. V. (1978). *Facial action coding system, investigator's guide.* Palo Alto, CA: Consulting Psychologists Press.

Ekman, P., Friesen, W. V., & O'Sullivan, M. (1988). Smiles when lying. *Journal of Personality and Social Psychology, 54,* 414–420.

Ekman, P., & O'Sullivan, M. (1991). Who can catch a liar? *American Psychologist, 9,* 913–920.

Ellard, J. (1970). Psychological reactions to ostensible injury. *The Medical Journal of Australia, 2,* 349–355.

Faust, D. (1995). The detection of deception. *Neurologic Clinics, 13,* 255–265.

Faust, D., Hart, K. J., Guilmette, T. J., & Arkes, H. R. (1988). Neuropsychologists' capacity to detect adolescent malingerers. *Professional Psychology: Research and Practice, 19,* 508–515.

Fernandez, E., & Turk, D. C. (1995). The scope and significance of anger in the experience of chronic pain. *Pain, 6,* 165–172.

Fordyce, W. (1976). *Behavioral methods in chronic pain and illness.* St. Louis, MO: Mosby.

Fordyce, W. E. (Ed.). (1995). *Back pain in the workplace.* Seattle: IASP Press.

Fridlund, A. J. (1994). *Human facial expression: An evolutionary view.* Santa Barbara, CA: Academic Press.

Galin, K. E., & Thorn, B. E. (1993). Unmasking pain: Detection of deception in facial expressions. *Journal of Social and Clinical Psychology, 12,* 182–197.

Greene, R. L. (1997). Assessment of malingering and defensiveness. In R. Rogers (Ed.), *Clinical assessment of malingering and deception* (pp. 169–207). New York: Guilford.

Guest, G. H., & Drummond, P. D. (1992). Effect of compensation on emotional state and disability in chronic back pain. *Pain, 48,* 125–130.

Hadjistavropoulos, H. D., & Craig, K. D. (1994). Acute and chronic low back pain: Cognitive, affective and behavioral dimensions. *Journal of Consulting and Clinical Psychology, 62,* 341–349.

Hadjistavropoulos, H. D., Craig, K. D., Hadjistavropoulos, T., & Poole, G. D. (1996). Subjective judgments of deception in pain expression: Accuracy and errors. *Pain, 65,* 247–254.

Hadjistavropoulos, H. D., Ross, M. M., & von Baeyer, C. (1990). Are physicians' ratings affected by patients' physical attractiveness? *Social Science and Medicine, 31,* 69–72.

Hadjistavropoulos, T., McMurtry, B., & Craig, K. D. (1996). Beautiful faces in pain: Biases and accuracy in the perception of pain. *Psychology and Health, 11,* 411–420.

Hager, J. C., & Ekman, P. (1985). The asymmetry of facial actions is inconsistent with models of hemispheric specialisation. *Psychophysiology, 22,* 307–318.

Hall, J. A. (1984). *Nonverbal sex differences: Communication accuracy and expressive style.* Baltimore: Johns Hopkins University Press.

Hayes, B., Solyom, C. A. E., Wing, P. C., & Berkowitz, J. (1993). Use of psychometric measures and nonorganic signs testing in detecting nomogenic disorders in low back pain patients. *Spine, 18,* 1254–1262.

Hill, M. L. (1996). *Deception in facial expressions of pain: Strategies to improve detection.* Unpublished doctoral dissertation, University of British Columbia, Vancouver.

Jamison, R. N., Matt, D. A., & Parris, W. C. V. (1988). Effects of time limited vs. unlimited compensation on pain behaviors and treatment outcome in low back pain patients. *Journal of Psychosomatic Research, 32,* 277–283.

Jensen, M. P. (1997). Validity of self-report and observation measures. In T. S. Jensen, J. A. Turner, & Z. Weisenfeld-Hallen (Eds.), *Proceedings of the 8th World Congress on Pain* (pp. 637–661). Seattle: IASP Press.

Johnson, M. (1977). Assessment of clinical pain. In A. K. Jacox (Ed.), *Pain: A sourcebook for nurses and other health professionals* (pp. 130–166). Boston: Little, Brown.

Kohnken, G. (1987). Training police officers to detect deceptive eyewitness statements: Does it work? *Social Behavior, 2,* 1–17.

Leavitt, F. (1987). A linguistic signature in simulated low back pain. *Journal of Pain and Symptom Management, 2,* 83–88.

Leavitt, F., Garron, D. C., McNeill, T. W., & Whisler, W. W. (1982). Organic status, psychological disturbance, and pain report characteristics in low back pain patients in compensation. *Spine, 7,* 398–402.

Leavitt, F., & Sweet, J. J. (1986). Characteristics and frequency of malingering among patients with low back pain. *Pain, 25,* 357–364.

Lehmann, T. R., Russell, D. W., & Spratt, K. F. (1983). The impact of patients with nonorganic physical findings on a controlled trial of transcutaneous electrical nerve stimulation and electroacupuncture. *Spine, 8,* 625–634.

LeResche, L., & Dworkin, S. F. (1988). Facial expression of pain and emotions in chronic TMD patients. *Pain, 35,* 71–78.

LeResche, L., Ehrlick, K. J., & Dworkin, S. (1990). Facial expressions of pain and masking smiles: Is "grin and bear it" a pain behavior? *Pain* (Suppl. 5), S286.

McCulloch, J. A. (1977). Chemoneucleolosis. *Journal of Bone and Joint Surgery, 59,* 45–52.

Melzack, R., Katz, J., & Jeans, M. E. (1985). The role of compensation in chronic pain: Analysis using a new method of scoring the McGill Pain Questionnaire. *Pain, 23,* 101–112.

Mendelson, G. (1992). Compensation and pain. *Pain, 48,* 121–123.

Mendelson, G. (1994). Chronic pain and compensation issues. In P. D. Wall & R. Melzack (Eds.), *Textbook of pain* (pp. 1387–1400). Edinburgh: Churchill Livingstone.

Miller, H. (1961). Accident neurosis. *British Medical Journal, 1,* 919–925.

Nachemson, A. (1983). Work for all–for those with low back pain as well. *Clinical Orthopaedics, 179,* 77–85.

Olson, D. R. (1993). The development of representations: The origins of mental life. *Canadian Psychology, 34,* 293–306.

Pankratz, L., & Binder, L. M. (1997). Malingering on intellectual and neuropsychological measures. In R. Rogers (Ed.), *Clinical assessment of malingering and deception* (2nd ed., pp. 223–236). New York: Guilford.

Paulhus, D. L., & Suedfeld, P. (1988). A dynamic complexity model of self-deception. In J. S. Lockand & D. L. Paulhus (Eds.), *Self deception: An adaptive mechanism?* (pp. 132–145). Englewood Cliffs, NJ: Prentice-Hall.

Phillips, H. C., & Grant, L. (1991a). Acute back pain: A psychological analysis. *Behavior Research and Therapy, 29,* 429–434.

Phillips, H. C., & Grant, L. (1991b). The evolution of chronic back pain problems: A longitudinal study. *Behavior Research and Therapy, 29,* 435–441.

Poole, G. D., & Craig, K. D. (1992). Judgments of genuine, suppressed, and faked facial expressions of pain. *Journal of Personality and Social Psychology, 63,* 797–805.

Prkachin, K. M. (1992). Dissociating spontaneous and deliberate expressions of pain: Signal detection analyses. *Pain, 51,* 57–65.

Prkachin, K. M., & Craig, K. D. (1985). Influencing non-verbal expressions of pain: Signal detection analysis. *Pain, 21,* 399–409.

Prkachin, K. M., & Craig, K. D. (1995). Expressing pain: The communication and interpretation of facial pain signals. *Journal of Nonverbal Behavior, 19,* 191–205.

Prkachin, K. M., & Mercer, S. R. (1989). Pain expression in patients with shoulder pathology: Validity, properties and relationship to sickness impact. *Pain, 39,* 257–265.

Reesor, K. A., & Craig, K. D. (1988). Medically incongruent back pain: Physical limitations, suffering and ineffective coping. *Pain, 32,* 35–45.

Rinn, W. E. (1984). The neuropsychology of facial expression: A review of the neurological and psychological mechanisms for producing facial expression. *Psychological Bulletin, 95,* 52–77.

Rogers, R. (Ed.). (1997). *Clinical assessment of malingering and deception* (2nd ed.). New York: Guilford.

Sander, R. A., & Meyers, J. E. (1986). The relationship of disability to compensation status in railroad workers. *Spine, 11,* 141–143.

Teasell, R. W., & Merskey, H. (1997). Chronic pain disability in the workplace. *Pain Research and Management, 2,* 197–205.

Turk, D. C. (1996). Cognitive factors in chronic pain and disability. In K. S. Dobson & K. D. Craig (Eds.), *Advances in cognitive behavioral therapy* (pp. 83–115). Thousand Oaks, CA: Sage.

von Baeyer, C. L., Johnson, M. E., & McMillan, M. J. (1984). Consequences of nonverbal expressions of pain: Patient distress and observer concern. *Social Science and Medicine, 19,* 1319–1324.

Waddell, G. (1991). Low back disability: A syndrome of Western civilisation. *Neurosurgery Clinics of North America, 2,* 719–738.

Waddell, G., Main, C. J., Morris, E. W., DiPaolo, M., & Gray, I. C. M. (1984). Chronic low back pain, psychological distress and illness behavior. *Spine, 9,* 209–213.

Waddell, G., McCulloch, J. A., Kummel, E., & Venner, R. M. (1980). Non-organic physical signs in low back pain. *Spine, 5,* 117–125.

Waddell, G., Pilowsky, I., & Bond, M. R. (1989). Clinical assessment and interpretation of abnormal illness behaviour in low back pain. *Pain, 39,* 41–53.

Wiltse, L. L., & Rochio, P. D. (1975). Preoperative psychological tests as predictors of success of chemoneucleolosis in the treatment of low-back syndrome. *Journal of Bone and Joint Surgery, 57*(A1), 478–483.

Zuckerman, M., Koestner, R., & Alton, A. O. (1984). Learning to detect deception. *Journal of Personality and Social Psychology, 46,* 519–528.

Zuckerman, M., Koestner, R., & Colella, M. J. (1985). Learning to communicate deception from three communication channels. *Journal of Nonverbal Behavior, 9,* 188–194.

Chapter 4

Chronic Pain on Trial:
The Influence of Litigation
and Compensation on
Chronic Pain Syndromes

Thomas Hadjistavropoulos
University of Regina

Recently, I became aware of a disability claimant who was placed under surveillance by an insurance company.[1] The claim was for a chronic pain problem and the surveillance was undertaken for an approximate total of 7 different days. During one of these occasions, the claimant was videotaped driving from his residence to a psychological assessment appointment. There was no evidence of apparent pain on the video. Once he arrived to a parking lot on the way to the psychologist's office he was described (in the surveillance report) as putting on a neck collar and then proceeding to continue the drive to the office. Following the appointment, the claimant was described as taking off the neck collar near the parking lot and driving home with no apparent pain. The only other surveillance occasion during which he was seen with a neck collar was as he was leaving from a medical appointment on a different day (on that occasion, the surveillance commenced only following the medical appointment and it is not known at what point the claimant put the collar on). In no instance was he recorded while displaying any overt signs of pain. Furthermore, he was depicted on several occasions turning his head to the side with no apparent difficulty, laughing and conversing with others.

Independent of the aforementioned, the psychologist's assessment conclusion suggested this claimant as having a high degree of pain severity

---

[1]Some of the details of this case were altered for illustration purposes and to disguise the identity of the claimant.

and life interference. These were indicated during the interview and on the Multi-Dimensional Pain Inventory. The claimant's MMPI–2 (Minnesota Multiphasic Personality Inventory, 2nd ed.) profile was assessed as valid and as being indicative of conversion/somatization characteristics. The psychologist also concluded that there was no evidence of cognitive impairment such as concentration difficulties relating to the pain syndrome.

After submitting reports to the insurance company, the psychologist as well as a medical specialist were made aware of the findings of the surveillance tape. The medical specialist concluded that the behavior depicted on the videotape was not congruent with the pain syndrome reported by the patient and that there was no disability. The psychologist concluded that "to the extent that the patient's pain report is valid" it is possible that his pain fluctuates depending on the degree to which he focuses on his pain; thus, further comments or determinations as to whether or not the claimant was disabled were avoided.

The preceding scenario underscores many of the practical difficulties that are encountered when assessing legal influences on chronic pain. These practical difficulties stem largely from the absence of direct and objective measures of pain. The difficulties also relate to evidence that pain can occur in the absence of detectable tissue damage and from suspicion that some patients may be malingering. To some extent, the case also illustrates some differences in the philosophies of different health specialists. Medical residents, for example, are often trained to base their expert opinions primarily on interview information. Predoctoral psychology interns are often trained to recognize that interview-based opinions have serious limitations (e.g., Lopez, 1989) and that their conclusions must be, as much as possible, based on more objective and/or actuarial information.

The scenario also illustrates a number of ethical dilemmas. What obligation does a professional have to a claimant he or she assessed if he or she revises his or her conclusions as a result of evidence that became available after the original assessment report was completed? How can a professional shift readily from his or her traditional role of being a helper to (and often an advocate for) the patient to one who assesses (and often challenges) the degree to which the patient's symptoms are genuine?

In this chapter I attempt to address many of the issues that emerge when considering claimants such as the one just described. More specifically, the impact of compensation/litigation on chronic pain is examined. In order to accomplish this, I discuss (a) theoretical formulations that can be used to support the notion that legal influences can affect chronic pain syndromes, (b) malingering, (c) cross-cultural research examining information from countries differing in their approach to compensation, and (d) empirical research contrasting compensation and noncompensation patients. Finally, some relevant ethical issues that may trouble professionals who work in the field are also discussed and some practical solutions are proposed.

THEORETICAL FORMULATIONS
AND CONTROVERSIAL PROPOSALS

In attempting to determine whether there is theoretical grounding for the view that litigation and compensation affect the course of chronic pain syndromes, some theoretical propositions are reviewed. These are derived from the biopsychosocial model (e.g., Waddell, Newton, Henderson, Somerville, & Main, 1993) and the learning theory (e.g., Fordyce, 1976) of pain, and are compatible with Melzack and Wall's (1982) gate control theory.

The biopsychosocial model of chronic pain accepts the original physical basis of pain even when the anatomical site or pathological basis for nociception cannot be identified. It also recognizes that the social environment as well as affective (e.g., anger and other emotional responses to an adversarial litigation system) and cognitive factors (e.g., beliefs about the importance of convincing insurance carriers of one's disability) can impact on chronic illness behavior (Waddell et al., 1993). Such beliefs, for example, could lead to avoidance of activity that could, in turn, exacerbate one's physiological impairment. On the other hand, it could also be argued that negative emotional responses could potentially be reduced as a result of compensation because compensation provides some financial stability and could reduce stress (e.g., Melzack, Katz, & Jeans, 1985). Evidence exists in support of biopsychosocial views, in that chronic pain outcomes relate to belief systems and affect (e.g., Jensen & Karoly, 1991; Mikail, D'Eon, & De Gagne, 1996). The ideas of the biopsychosocial model are also compatible with Melzack and Wall's (1982) gate control theory of pain, which recognizes the role of affective and cognitive factors in pain modulation.

Another relevant formulation is operant conditioning. It has been argued that immediate consequences of pain behaviors may exert a powerful influence on the future probability of occurrence of these behaviors. Thus, pain behaviors that are followed by positive consequences (e.g., elicitation of attention and sympathy) are expected to increase in frequency (e.g., Fordyce, 1976). Within an operant framework, it could also be suggested that rewards for pain and disability could prolong and extend such states. Similarly, pain behavior may persist because it allows one to avoid aversive responsibilities. Likewise, investigators have recently suggested that pain behavior may persist as a result of social rewards (e.g., reduced social anxiety resulting from reduced social responsibility) (Asmundson, Norton, & Jacobson, 1996), and the reduction of anxiety associated with the anticipation of further aversive pain-related experiences (McCracken, Zayfert, & Gross, 1993).

Drawing largely on such operant formulations of pain, the Task Force on Pain in the Workplace of the International Association for the Study of Pain (IASP) recently released a report (Fordyce, 1995). In this report, it is suggested that disability claims pertinent to low back pain have shown rapid increases in the absence of evidence that back injuries are becoming more frequent or severe. Benefits are awarded increasingly frequently for back pain occurring in the absence of evidence of specific back injury. Robertson and Keeve (1983) studied work site efforts to prevent industrial accidents by minimizing physical hazards. Although objectively verifiable injuries were reduced, subjective injury complaints such as back strains were unaffected. The task force also argued that assignment of disability status for chronic low back pain may expose workers to potentially debilitating circumstances that include excessive rest, well-intentioned but harmful treatments, and overprotection by family members. The conclusion was that existing disability programs contribute to the explosion in disability ascribed to nonspecific low back pain. The report characterized workers with nonspecific low back pain as "activity intolerant" and recommended limiting the wage replacement benefits for a maximum of 6 weeks unless credible diagnostic evidence indicates a disabling condition other than nonspecific low back pain.

This report has led to a great deal of controversy (e.g., Block, 1997; Craig, 1996; Fordyce, 1996; Loeser, 1996; Merskey, 1996a, 1996b). The Canadian chapter of IASP, for example, has dissociated itself from both the document and its policy proposal after it characterized the report's literature review as incomplete and as representing the opinion of a limited number of individuals. Moreover, the policy recommendations from the report were described as not following from the knowledge base informing our understanding of chronic pain. Merskey (1996a) argued, for example, that the recommendations of the task force's report will likely increase the suffering of a large number of honest individuals, especially injured workers with nonspecific low back pain (i.e., soft-tissue or mechanical back pain). Merskey's assertion is supported by the literature. Giles and Crawford (1997), for example, reviewed histopathological findings that can be associated with pain but cannot be seen in imaging due to device limitations. It is important to mention that the task force report did not imply that those with nonspecific low back pain are malingering. It merely suggested that social factors play a potent role in the maintenance of nonspecific low back pain.

The task force report carries the operant model of pain to its extreme and may be taken to imply that extended disability following nonspecific low back pain is primarily the result of operant and societal factors. Although operant factors may be responsible in many cases, there are likely to be marked individual differences in the extent to which learning plays a role in the maintenance of nonspecific low back pain. The following sections examine evidence for the presence of such individual differences as well as for the overall effects of compensation/litigation on chronic pain. The inconsistencies that exist in the literature, as well as the lack of a clear and full understanding of many chronic pain syndromes, are largely responsible for the controversy that has arisen as a result of the task force report.

HOW FREQUENT IS MALINGERING?

Leavitt and Sweet (1986) surveyed orthopedic surgeons and neurosurgeons in the United States and concluded that 60% of surgeons were in agreement that malingering is an infrequent condition occurring in less than 5% of low back pain patients. Others also agree that base rates for deception and malingering are quite low (Craig, Hill, & McMurtry, chap. 3, this volume; Fordyce, 1995). The real incidence is difficult to establish because of the secretive nature of action and difficulties in distinguishing between conscious and unconscious motivation (Craig et al., chap. 3, this volume). Media presentations emphasizing cases of malingering may serve to create the public perception of an inflated incidence in the population.

Health professionals frequently try to identify those who dissimulate chronic pain syndromes. Our existing methods include, among others, the MMPI–2 validity scales, the examination of nonverbal pain behaviors, and consistency of effort tests (e.g., Young & Doyle, 1997). These methods, however, are less than perfect. Studies have also found some differences between injury patients and those asked to simulate the psychological profiles of such patients (Dush, Simons, Platt, Nation, & Ayres, 1994; Leavitt, 1985); yet simulations of malingering may be quite different from actual malingering. Furthermore, it would be premature to stringently use the criteria derived from these studies in clinical practice because the probability of error would be high.

CROSS-CULTURAL RESEARCH

As many have argued that the litigious nature of North American society can have an impact on the symptoms reported by patients, cross-cultural research has focused on examining the pain syndromes of patients in several different parts of the world. Balla (1982) studied an Australian sample of 300 patients with "late whiplash syndrome" and found that it occurred more often in upper-middle occupational groups, men 30–50 years of age, and women 20–40 years of age. Nonetheless, the car accident statistics suggested that these involve primarily younger age groups. Furthermore, migrants of Northern European ancestry were overrepresented among the patients. Balla contrasted these results to those derived from Singapore patients and reported that late whiplash was extremely rare in

Singapore and when it occurred it tended to involve patients of European background.

Another study involved comparing U.S. patients to patients from New Zealand (Carron, DeGood, & Tait, 1985). New Zealand has a nonadversarial system that compensates all victims regardless of fault and without the need to prove injury at work. Whereas 49% of the U.S. sample were receiving pain-related compensation, only 17% of the New Zealand sample were. Despite initially similar reports of pain frequency and intensity, U.S. patients were found to experience greater emotional and behavioral disruption as a result of chronic low back pain. On follow-up, the researchers found some differential effects linked to compensation status in the United States (e.g., pain intensity and frequency differences); on the other hand, such effects were almost nonexistent in the New Zealand sample. Carron et al. concluded that the absence of an adversarial system in New Zealand contributes to the cross-cultural difference.

A more recent study was conducted in Lithuania where few car drivers are covered by insurance and there is little public awareness of the effects of late whiplash injury (Schrader et al., 1996). The authors of this retrospective study identified and interviewed 202 persons 1 to 3 years after rear-end collisions. The names of the participants were derived from police records. The researchers concluded that nobody in the study had disabling symptoms as a result of a car accident. Thus, they argued that the late whiplash syndrome has little validity. They also compared related pain complaints in the accident sample to a gender- and age-matched group of uninjured individuals selected randomly from the population. No differences were found between the accident and control groups. Merskey (1997) criticized the study because of its retrospective nature and on other methodological grounds.

Despite some limitations of the cross-cultural research (retrospective research, unequal sample sizes), there are indications that the type of compensation system plays some role in the course of chronic pain syndromes. Although the answer to the question concerning the magnitude of any cross cultural differences on pain syndromes cannot be given in very specific terms, any differences that do exist could be explained best by considering cross-cultural differences in social attitudes and operant factors.

PSYCHOLOGICAL AND SOCIAL CHARACTERISTICS OF LITIGATION/COMPENSATION PATIENTS

Several studies have examined the psychological profiles of litigation/compensation patients. In an extensive review of the literature, Kolbison, Epstein, and Burgess (1996) indicated that there are inconsistent conclusions regarding differences between litigating and nonlitigating patients. They attributed the inconsistencies to the heterogeneity of populations used in various studies (e.g., resolved vs. unresolved claims, those in adversarial vs. nonadversarial systems). Mendelson (1986) argued that, despite such inconsistencies, there does not appear to be strong support for the notion that compensation patients are more emotionally disturbed than noncompensation ones.

Several studies involving the MMPI or MMPI–2 exist. Harness and Chase (1994), for instance, studied 111 chronic facial pain patients, 18% of whom were in litigation at the time of their initial visit. Forty-five percent of the litigation patients had four or more clinical scales elevated, whereas only 18% of the patients not in litigation had four or more significant MMPI elevations. The authors concluded that those in litigation are more likely to present with symptoms of psychological disturbance than those who are not. Nonetheless, no information on the subjects' responses on the MMPI validity scales was provided. Such information could help determine whether there are differences with respect to the validity of profiles of those who were in litigation versus those who were not. In a related study involving the MMPI–2, a group of litigating pain patients (of diverse pain conditions and etiologies) was compared to nonlitigating ones (Dush et al., 1994). It was found that litigators were more distinct in endorsing more obvious and fewer subtle symptoms. Furthermore, a conversion profile was salient for litigators once the obvious versus subtle differences were taken into account. Trabin, Rader, and Cummings (1987) studied 75 men with chronic low back pain and concluded that MMPI profiles did not differ as a function of compensation benefits. It is possible, however, that compensation patients have different MMPI profiles from those who are in litigation. Melzack et al. (1985) also failed to find differences between compensation and noncompensation patients on the MMPI pain triad (depression, hysteria, and hypochondriasis). The inconsistencies among the various studies likely relate to factors such as sample characteristics.

Other researchers have found evidence of increased depression in compensation patients (Pilowsky & Spence, 1975). Along similar lines, Blanchard et al. (1996) identified the initiation of litigation as a significant predictor of posttraumatic stress symptoms among motor vehicle accident victims. It also appears that any emotional distress experienced by litigation patients continues after claims are settled (Guest & Drummond, 1992). This may be taken to suggest that compensation encourages not working which, in turn, contributes to increased emotional distress.

With respect to other differences, Moldofsky, Wong, and Lue (1993), studied 16 patients who had unresolved medical claims and 8 who had resolved ones. They found no significant differences with respect to demographics, nature of the accident, polysomnographic findings, and disability. Furthermore, the medicolegal status of these patients did not differentiate the outcome of their symptoms. Nonetheless, the small sample size could have obscured significant effects. Overall, the literature concerning differences in the characteristics of compensation and noncompensation patients is not conclusive.

PAIN SEVERITY AND TREATMENT RESPONSE

There are also inconsistent findings regarding the question of whether compensation patients report more pain than do noncompensation ones. It has been suggested that the monetary secondary gain, which is often the outcome of litigation involving chronic pain patients, prolongs their disability. Melzack et al. (1985) concluded that the financial security provided by compensation decreases anxiety, which is reflected in lower afffective or evaluative ratings on the McGill Pain Questionnaire but not the sensory or total McGill scores.

Leavitt, Garron, McNeill, and Whisler (1982) compared compensation and noncompensation patients. They concluded that compensation patients who had objective evidence of injury but showed no significant psychological disturbance reported more intense sensory discomfort. The findings of Melzack et al. (1985) and Leavitt et al. (1982) are not necessarily contradictory because in the Melzack et al. study, data from patients with objective evidence of injury were not examined separately. Clearer differences may exist with respect to pain measures focusing on dimensions other than intensity. Guest and Drummond (1992), for example, concluded that compensation recipients reported that pain disrupted aspects of their lives to a greater degree than did those who had settled their claims. The inconsistencies in the literature are likely due to sample and measurement differences. Despite these inconsistencies there are several studies that identified pain differences between compensation and noncompensation patients.

Although compensation and noncompensation patients may be similar in at least some dimensions, it has been suggested that those who are on compensation are less responsive to treatment. In a widely cited study, Miller (1961) implied that the "compensation neurosis" syndrome is a reflection of malingered attempts at freeloading. He followed 200 cases and concluded that severity was inversely proportional to the original severity of the injury. When he examined 50 cases more closely, he concluded that 45 persons returned to work within 2 years following the settlement of the claims. Thus, he argued that symptoms improved after financial gain was secured. This is, however, a conclusion that has been criticized. Another plausible hypothesis is that the impoverished workers returned to work despite persistent symptoms (Cullien, 1988). The study has also been criticized for being uncontrolled, nonrandomized, and as having employed a biased patient sample (Kolbison et al., 1996). In fact, the majority of studies have led to entirely different conclusions (Kolbison et al., 1996).

Schofferman and Wasserman (1994) examined the treatment response of 39 low back or neck pain patients with pain litigation. They concluded, based on responses on the McGill Pain Questionnaire and the Oswestry Low Back Disability Questionnaire, that the patients improved despite litigation. The conclusions that can be drawn from their study are limited by the absence of a control group of nonlitigating patients.

Norris and Watt (1983) found that there was no statistically significant change in the symptoms of litigating patients after their claims were settled. Many others have drawn similar conclusions (see Mendelson, 1995, for a review). Thus, there seems to be a fair degree of consensus that, for most claimants, disability from injury does not resolve following the settlement of litigation (Kolbison et al., 1996; Mendelson, 1995). Such findings do not rule out the possibility that litigation affects the course of chronic pain. It is possible that social influences continue to impact on chronic pain after the settlement of litigation. Quick and dramatic improvements, even when occurring after the conclusion of litigation, might be viewed with some suspicion by former coworkers. Consistent with this idea, Bellamy (1997) suggested that adversarial administrative and legal systems challenge claimants to prove repeatedly that they are ill and, thus, harden the conviction of illness. Bellamy also argued that improvements in the claimants' health condition after the resolution of disability may result in denial of disability status in the future. This may compel claimants to guard against getting well. For such individuals, there may not be an honorable way to recover from the illness.

In a related meta-analytic investigation, Rohling, Binder and Langhinrichen-Rohling (1995) found only 32 relevant studies that contained quantifiable data for treatment and control groups. Based on these studies, they concluded that compensation is related to increased reports of pain and reduced treatment efficacy. They also suggested that the relation between compensation and the identified effects is probably causal because the studies of the meta-analysis had either matched or comparable control groups of patients who were not being compensated. When pretreatment group differences in health status were controlled for, the analyses did not substantiate that another factor (e.g., employment) could better account for the results. Nonetheless, the researchers did not rule out the possibility of third-factor influences (e.g., the treating/assessing professionals' knowledge of the compensation status of the patients). Using binomial effect size displays, Rohling et al. found that if compensation was to be eliminated as a variable, the experience of chronic pain would decrease by an average of 24%. Unlike the Fordyce (1995) report, they stopped short of recommending that our current compensation systems be eliminated because such an action could leave some truly disabled patients without necessary resources. They suggested, rather, that if we were able to identify patient subtypes who are the most affected by the presence of compensation (e.g., possibly patients with poor coping skills and no physical findings), we might be able to intervene. Treatment programs offering early intervention in a well-planned and organized manner were judged to have more encouraging results. The findings of Rohling et al. concerning treatment responsiveness are consistent with those of others who reviewed the literature (e.g., Mendelson, 1986; Walsh & Dumitru, 1988). Along similar lines, Kolbison et al. (1996) concluded that compensation patients with temporomandibular joint problems may be less responsive to treatment.

Burns, Sherman, Devine, Mahoney, and Pawl (1995) attempted to identify specific characteristics of compensation patients that affect treatment responsiveness. They showed that the relationship between treatment outcome and compensation was mediated by a pessimistic belief regarding return to former occupation. Compensation recipients with high initial pain and pain-related surgery did worse. Those compensation recipients not characterized by high pain and a history of surgery responded as well as noncompensation patients. The investigators concluded that compensation recipients should not be considered to be at high risk for poor treatment responsiveness solely on the basis of compensation status. Multifaceted assessments are needed to identify those who are at such risk in order to make appropriate adjustments in treatment regiments.

Although results such as those of Rohling et al. (1995) are supportive of operant models of pain, they do not necessarily imply that compensated patients exaggerate their problems at a conscious level. It could be that such patients are hypersensitive to nociception as a result of the cognitive dissonance that could result if they felt well while on compensation (Rohling et al., 1995). A complicating factor in the examination of the relationship between length of disability and compensation/litigation is that there are referral delays that are built into the compensation system (e.g., compensation-related bureaucracy and insurer authorizations for assessment). Such delays are both costly and can result in the prolongation of the disability period, as prognosis is poorer for those who are disabled for longer periods (Gallagher & Myers, 1996). These factors may be contributing to the prolongation of painful conditions in compensation patients.

In conclusion, although the effects of compensation on recovery and severity of pain are still controversial, it appears that compensation factors may contribute to delay in recovery and reinforce the sick role (Turk, 1997). There also appear to be more studies that found wage replacement and compensation as being predictive of chronicity than studies that failed to find such relationships (see Turk, 1997). Existing inconsistencies in the literature can be accounted by a number of methodological factors. These include, but are not necessarily limited to, sample composition (i.e., recruitment procedures, sample sizes), the limited attention that is often paid to quantifying and considering the nature or severity of injury, differences in measures, and outcome criteria (Turk, 1997). It has also been found that the nature of the job to which an injured worker is expected to return to may have an influence on whether he or she is able to return to work. Those on compensation (especially injured workers) may be more likely to have jobs with higher physical demands than do noncompensation patients and may be less likely to return to work because of the physical demands that are involved. Finally, job satisfaction has also been found to relate to return to work and the prevention of chronicity (see Turk, 1997, for a review of these factors).

IS THERE ANOTHER WAY?

The solution and policy changes that were proposed in the IASP Task Force on Pain in the Workplace report (Fordyce, 1995) were radical, controversial, and, despite good intentions, could result in the unfair treatment of some individuals. This section examines whether there is another way to reduce compensation costs for chronic pain while at the same time reducing patient suffering. The following strategies may prove helpful:

1. *Health professionals can do more to encourage compensated and other insured patients to return to work.* There are many health professionals today who still prescribe prolonged time off work for a substantial portion of their musculoskeletal pain patients. Cathclove and Cohen (1982) concluded that compensation patients who were directed to return to work during treatment were more likely to do so than did patients in another group who were treated similarly but for whom return to work was not a component of therapy. According to follow-up results at approximately 9.6 months, 90% of the patients in the group directed to return to work were still working. Similarly, McGill (1968) found that the longer a person is off work because of low back pain, the lower his or her chances of return to work.

2. *Employers can do more to address job dissatisfaction issues in the workplace.* As many studies have shown job dissatisfaction to be a predictor of chronicity (see Turk, 1997), improvements in work conditions and environment could go a long way in facilitating the recovery of many injured workers.

3. *More can be done to enhance diagnostic accuracy.* Findings suggest that there is a serious risk of overlooking diagnoses in patients who are involved

in litigation. Specifically, Hendler and Kozikowski (1993) studied patients in a pain diagnostic center and found that the most common referral "diagnoses" were really descriptors or vague explanations such as "chronic pain" and "psychogenic pain." The authors concluded that the overall rate of inaccurate or incomplete diagnosis at referral was 66.7% and that the most frequently missed diagnoses were myofascial disease, facet disease, peripheral nerve entrapment, radiculopathy, and thoracic outlet syndrome.

4. *Research on the clinical assessment of malingering should continue.* Detection of dissimulation is difficult. Although some promising initial attempts have been made, more research is needed before the sensitivity and specificity of such procedures in medicolegal contexts can be estimated with confidence (see Main & Spanswick, 1995, for a review). Similarly, questions have been raised about the validity of measures of power and force in the detection of dissimulation (Main & Spanswick, 1995).

5. *Patient subtypes that are especially susceptible to the effects of compensation and litigation should be identified.* There is evidence suggesting that there are specific patient characteristic that mediate the relation between treatment responsiveness and compensation status (Burns et al., 1995). Further investigating relevant interactions and identifying such characteristics during assessment could allow for appropriate adjustments in treatment regiment. These adjustments could lead to improved outcomes.

6. *Some modifications in the adversarial nature of North American litigation/compensation systems are worth considering.* Countries such as New Zealand provide different incentives than those offered in the United States and appear to accomplish better outcomes and recovery rates. The New Zealand system, for instance, removes the adversarial relationship between the employer, the claimant, and the insurer by allowing income compensation for accidental injury without the need to prove the injury at work and by allowing rapid rehabilitation intervention (Walsh & Dumitru, 1988).

SOME ETHICAL MATTERS

Most organizations of health professionals in North America have codes of ethics that include standards and principles that are relevant to the assessment of those with disabilities (e.g., Canadian Psychological Association, 1991; Council on Ethical and Judicial Affairs of the American Medical Association, 1994; National Association of Social Workers, 1993). There are many ethical issues that apply to these assessments as well as to a wide variety of other assessment situations. The vulnerabilities involved, for instance, should be considered (i.e, the potential impact that a report could have for a vulnerable party). Although there are numerous ethical issues pertinent to assessment in general, a few selected ones are reviewed here because they have special relevance to medicolegal assessments of chronic pain patients.

Selected Issues Pertaining to Competence

Keith-Spiegel and Koocher (1985) outlined a series of important issues that are relevant to assessment in general. To be competent, practitioners must have had specialized training and experience in the type of population with whom they work (e.g., chronic pain patients). If psychological tests are being used, users must have adequate familiarity with measurement theory and issues pertaining to test reliability and validity. They should also be aware of the limitations associated with the use of computerized interpretation systems for psychological tests (e.g., the MMPI–2 is used frequently to detect dissimulation); specifically, these should not be accepted at face value as they are often simulations of clinical decision making and may be of limited validity (Matarazzo, 1986). In all cases, computer-generated interpretations should be checked against other psychological tests and/or interview and chart information, and it is very important to ensure that manuals accompanying computerized interpretive systems include evidence on the validity of the reports that they generate.

Divided Loyalties

The most complex general issue in disability assessments relates to potential for divided loyalties to the client, the legal system, and/or the insurance company. The adversarial nature of the system may force the client to be viewed with suspicion as insurance companies may specifically request an assessment of how genuine a claimant's symptoms are. At the same time, the claimant may approach the assessment situation with defensiveness and fear (especially when seeing a psychologist or psychiatrist). The claimant may, thus, avoid giving responses that relate to psychological factors as he or she might feel that revelation of these could have a negative impact on his or her claim.

The adversarial system of litigation invites health professionals and especially those who engage in independent assessments for third-party payers to be suspicious of the patient. This can disrupt the trust that traditionally exists in such relationships and affect patient disclosure. Furthermore, it is conceivable that some third-party payers may favor (i.e., send more referrals) to professionals who are the least sympathetic of patient complaints. Bellamy (1997) also asserted that the role of the health professional is one of a helper and advocate for the patient. The health professional who is perceived as functioning in any other capacity will not be well received by the patient. Some of these issues can be dealt with, at least to some extent, by clarifying and discussing loyalties, limits of confidentiality, and ethical obligations to the patient and third parties ahead of time. A professional who emphasizes honesty and integrity during all interactions is most likely to be received well by the majority of claimants and third-party payers.

Self-Interest

Unquestionably accepting a patient's self-report at face value, when agreeing to conduct an independent assessment for the purposes of determining the degree to which symptoms are genuine, could be construed as being unethical. Health professionals are often worried about being sued or complained against by a patient if they deem that the patient is not disabled. It would be unheard of, although not impossible, for a professional to be sued by an insurance company for deciding that a nondisabled patient is disabled. Thus, the risk for the professional is far greater when he or she certifies that, in his or her professional opinion, a patient is not disabled than if he or she certifies the opposite. Letting one's conclusions be affected primarily by the need to protect one's self from a complaint (as opposed to acting with integrity) is unethical.

Assessment Feedback

An important but often neglected area in the disability assessments pertains to the issue of feedback to the patient. The fact that an assessor may be hired by an insurance provider does not diminish that provider's ethical responsibility to the patient nor the obligation to provide the patient with feedback about the assessment. It is useful to release a copy of the report to the patient's general practitioner. The patient can be informed that he or she can go over the report with the general practitioner and that the assessor will be available to provide clarifications. A feedback session with the patient is also useful. At times, some insurance companies request assessments on the condition that the report will be their property and that it will only be released to them. Such conditions should be clarified with all parties at the outset and, under these circumstances, the patient should be given the opportunity to consent prior to the assessment to waive his or her right to a copy of the report.

Issues pertaining to purpose of the assessment and access to results should be clarified in advance. The use of a clear consent form is highly recommended. The independent assessor will need to obtain consent to communicate with the insurance company about all pertinent aspects of the assessment and to provide any clarifications about his or her report.

The client should also be informed that if the assessor is provided with additional information (e.g., new medical reports) after he or she completes his or her report, he or she may have to revise his or her conclusions and make this known to all parties concerned.

Consider the scenario discussed in the beginning of this chapter. Let us assume that the medical specialist who was hired by the insurance company had informed all parties concerned that she would send a copy of her report to the insurance company and another to the claimant's general practitioner. She also informed the claimant that he should feel free to contact her if he needs any clarifications about the report. Initially, she concluded that the symptoms of the claimant appeared to be supported by the findings of the assessment and that the claimant was disabled. A few weeks after she completed her final report, she received a copy of the surveillance information and video that was sent to her by the insurance company. As indicated in the beginning of this chapter, the video led her to conclude that the claimant was not disabled and that he was successful in deceiving her. The insurance company asked the physician if she would be willing to change her written conclusions given the new information. What is the ethical responsibility of the assessor to the insurance company and the claimant?

The author of this chapter is of the opinion that anybody who is assessed by a health professional is entitled to feedback about the results of the assessment. If the results change, for whatever reason, the client is entitled to feedback. An appropriate course of action would be to write an addendum to the report and send it to all parties who received the original report. Nonetheless, it is vital to clarify issues pertaining to feedback with all parties ahead of time.

CONCLUSIONS

Psychosocial factors affect chronic pain outcomes. Despite some controversy, evidence suggests that compensation/litigation can prolong the duration of disability from pain. Although a small portion of compensation/litigation patients may be malingering, most authorities agree that malingerers (including those who consciously exaggerate the severity of their symptoms) represent a very small percentage of claimants. There are many other ways, however, through which compensation can affect outcomes. Some compensation/litigation patients, for example, may reduce their activity level fearing that activity could jeopardize their claim. The countertherapeutic effects of such inactivity (e.g., deconditioning) could prolong their disability. Other factors that could be having a negative impact on compensation/litigation patients relate to referral delays due to insurance company red tape.

It is important to recognize that if compensation systems contribute to the prolongation of disability, marked individual differences among patients are likely to exist. Some nonspecific low back pain patients' disability may be quite unaffected by the presence or absence of compensation. Thus, deciding to eliminate our existing disability systems in the hopes that this will make everyone better could have disastrous consequences for some injured persons. Our challenge is to identify the individual difference variables and intervene in order to reduce the likelihood that compensation will have a negative consequence on one's disability. Several other factors that could affect outcomes (e.g., referral delays due to insurance company red tape) can also be modified.

In the context of this work, ethical problems are likely to arise. When matters are clarified in advance, with all parties concerned, the potential for ethical violations is much reduced.

ACKNOWLEDGMENTS

The author thanks Drs. Gord Asmundson and Heather Hadjistavropoulos for their helpful comments. The preparation of this chapter was supported, in part, by a Health Services Utilization and Research Commission grant.

REFERENCES

Asmundson, G. J. G., Norton, R., & Jacobson, S. (1996). Social, blood/injury and agoraphobic fears in patients with physically unexplained chronic pain: Are they clinically significant? *Anxiety, 2,* 28–33.

Balla, J. I. (1982). The late whiplash syndrome: A study of an illness in Australia and Singapore. *Culture Medicine and Psychiatry, 6,* 191–210.

Bellamy, R. (1997). Compensation neurosis. *Clinical Orthopedics and Related Research, 336,* 94–106.

Blanchard, E. B., Hickling, E. J., Taylor, A. E., Loos, W. R., Forneris, C. A., & Jaccard, J. (1996). Who develops PTSD from motor vehicle accidents? *Behaviour Research and Therapy, 34,* 1–10.

Block, A. (1997). Controlling the costs of pain-related disability. *Journal of Pain and Symptom Management, 13,* 1–3.

Burns, J. W., Sherman, M. L., Devine, J., Mahoney, N., & Pawl, R. (1995). Association between workers' compensation and outcome following multidisciplinary treatment for chronic pain: Roles of mediators and moderators. *Clinical Journal of Pain, 11,* 94–102.

Canadian Psychological Association. (1991). *Canadian code of ethics for psychologists.* Ottawa: Author.

Carron, H., DeGood, D. E., & Tait, R. A. (1985). A comparison of low back pain patients in the United States and New Zealand: Psychosocial and economic factors affecting severity of disability. *Pain, 21,* 77–89.

Catchlove, R., & Cohen, K. (1982). Effects of a directive return to work approach in the treatment of workman's compensation patients with chronic pain. *Pain, 14,* 181–191.

Council on Ethical and Judicial Affairs. (1994). *Code of medical ethics: Current opinions with annotations.* Chicago: American Medical Association.

Craig, K. D. (1996). The back pain controversy—Reply. *Pain Research and Management, 1,* 183.

Cullien, A. J. (1988). Psychiatric and medical syndromes associated with deception. In R. Rogers (Ed.), *Clinical assessment of malingering and deception* (pp. 13–33). New York: Guilford.

Dush, D. M., Simons, L. E., Platt, M., Nation, P. C., & Ayres, S. Y. (1994). Psychological profiles distinguishing litigating and nonlitigating pain patients: Subtle, and not so subtle. *Journal of Personality Assessment, 62,* 299–313.

Fordyce, W. E. (1976). *Behavioral methods for chronic pain and illness.* St. Louis, MO: Mosby.

Fordyce, W. E. (1995). *Back pain in the workplace.* Seattle: IASP Press.

Fordyce, W. E. (1996). Response to Thompson/Merskey/Teasell. *Pain, 65,* 112–114.

Gallagher, R. M., & Myers, P. (1996). Referral delay in back pain patients on worker's compensation: Costs and policy implications. *Psychosomatics, 37,* 270–284.

Giles, L. G., & Crawford, C. M. (1997). Shadows of truth in patients with spinal pain: A review. *Canadian Journal of Psychiatry, 42,* 44–48.

Guest, G. H., & Drummond, P. D. (1992). Effect of compensation on emotional state and disability in chronic back pain. *Pain, 48,* 125–130.

Harness, D. M., & Chase, P. F. (1994). Litigation and chronic facial pain. *Journal of Orofacial Pain, 8,* 289–292.

Hendler, N. H., & Kozikowski, J. G. (1993). Overlooked physical diagnoses in chronic pain patients involved in litigation. *Psychosomatics, 34,* 494–501.

Jensen, M. P., & Karoly, P. (1991). Control beliefs, coping efforts and adjustment to chronic pain. *Journal of Consulting and Clinical Psychology, 59,* 431–438.

Keith-Spiegel, P., & Koocher, G. P. (1985). *Ethics in psychology: Professional standards and cases.* New York: McGraw-Hill.

Kolbison, D. A., Epstein, J. B., & Burgess, J. A. (1996). Temporomandibular disorders, headaches, and neck pain following motor vehicle accidents and the effects of litigation: Review of the literature. *Journal of Orofacial Pain, 10,* 101–125.

Leavitt, F. (1985). Pain and deception: Use of verbal pain measurement as a diagnostic aid in differentiating between clinical and simulated low-back pain. *Journal of Psychosomatic Research, 29,* 495–505.

Leavitt, F., Garron, D. C., McNeil, T. W., & Whisler, W. W. (1982). Organic status, psychological disturbance and pain report characteristics in low back pain patients on compensation. *Spine, 7,* 398–402.

Leavitt, F., & Sweet, J. J. (1986). Characteristics and frequency of malingering among patients with low back pain. *Pain, 25,* 357–364.

Loeser, J. D. (1996). The IASP report on back pain in the work place. *Pain Research and Management, 1,* 180.

Lopez, S. R. (1989). Patient variable biases in clinical judgement: Conceptual overview and methodological considerations. *Psychological Bulletin, 106,* 184–203.

Main, C. J., & Spanswick, C. C. (1995). "Functional overlay", and illness behaviour in chronic pain: Distress or malingering? Conceptual difficulties in medicolegal assessment of personal injury claims. *Journal of Psychosomatic Research, 39,* 737–753.

Matarazzo, J. D. (1986). Computerized test interpretations. *American Psychologist, 41,* 14–24.

McCracken, L. M., Zayfert, C., & Gross, R. T. (1993). The pain anxiety symptoms scale (PASS): A multi-modal measure of pain specific anxiety symptoms. *Behaviour Research and Therapy, 31,* 647–652.

McGill, G. M. (1968). Industrial back programmes: A control program. *Journal of Occupational Medicine, 10,* 174–178.

Melzack, R., Katz, J., & Jeans, M. E. (1985). The role of compensation in chronic pain: Analysis using a new method of scoring the McGill Pain Questionnaire. *Pain, 23,* 101–112.

Melzack, R., & Wall, P. (1982). *The challenge of pain.* London: Penguin.

Mendelson, G. (1986). Chronic pain and compensation: A review. *Journal of Pain and Symptom Management, 1*, 135–144.

Mendelson, G. (1995). Compensation neurosis revisited: Outcome studies of the effects of litigation. *Journal of Psychosomatic Research, 39*, 695–706.

Merskey, H. (1996a). Back pain, psychology and money. *Pain Research and Management, 1*, 13.

Merskey, H. (1996b). Re: Back pain in the work place (W. E. Fordyce, Ed.). *Pain, 65*, 111–112.

Merskey, H. (1997). Whiplash in Lithuania. *Pain Research and Management, 2*, 13–14.

Mikail, S. F., D'Eon, J. L., & De Gagne, T. A. (1996). Validation of the Pain Beliefs and Perceptions Inventory. *Pain Research and Management, 1*, 31–38.

Miller, H. (1961). Accident neurosis. *British Medical Journal, 1*, 919–925.

Moldofsky, H., Wong, M. T., & Lue, F. A. (1993). Litigation, sleep, symptoms and disabilities in postaccident pain. *Journal of Rheumatology, 20*, 1935–1940.

National Association of Social Workers. (1993). *Code of ethics of the National Association of Social Workers*. Washington, DC: Author.

Norris, S. H., & Watt, I. (1983). The prognosis of neck injuries resulting from rear-end vehicle collisions. *Journal of Bone and Joint Surgery [British volume], 65*, 608–611.

Pilowsky, I., & Spence, N. D. (1975). Patterns of illness behaviour in patients with intractable pain. *Journal of Psychosomatic Research, 19*, 279–287.

Robertson, L., & Keeve, J. (1983). Worker injuries: The effects of workers compensation and OSHA inspections. *Journal of Health Politics Policy and Law, 8*, 581–597.

Rohling, M. L., Binder, L. M., & Langhinrichsen-Rohling, J. (1995). Money matters: A meta-analytic review of the association between financial compensation and the experience and treatment of chronic pain. *Health Psychology, 14*, 537–547.

Schofferman, J., & Wasserman, S. (1994). Successful treatment of low back pain and neck pain after a motor vehicle accident despite litigation. *Spine, 19*, 1007–1010.

Schrader, H., Obelieniene, D., Boivim, G., Surkiene, D., Mickeviciene, I., & Sand, T. (1996). Natural evolution of late whiplash syndrome outside the medicolegal context. *Lancet, 347*, 1207–1211.

Trabin, T., Rader, C., & Cummings, C. (1987). A comparison of pain management outcomes for disability compensation and non-compensation patients. *Psychology and Health, 1*, 341–351.

Turk, D. (1997). The role of demographic and psychosocial factors in transition from acute to chronic pain. In T. S. Jensen, J. A. Turner, & Z. Wiesenfeld-Hallin (Eds.), *Proceedings of the 8th World Congress on Pain: Progress in pain research and management* (pp. 185–213). Seattle: IASP Press.

Waddell, G., Newton, M., Henderson, I., Somerville, D., & Main, C. J. (1993). A fear-avoidance beliefs questionnaire (FABQ) and the role of fear avoidance beliefs in chronic low back pain and disability. *Pain, 52*, 157–168.

Walsh, N. E., & Dumitru, D. (1988). The influence of compensation on recovery from low back pain. *Occupational Medicine: State of the Art Reviews, 3*, 109–120.

Young, D., & Doyle, C. (1997, February). Detecting malingering: A psychological and medical view. *Canadian Underwriter*, pp. 34–35.

Chapter 5

Clinical Outcome and Economic Evaluation of Multidisciplinary Pain Centers

Akiko Okifuji
Dennis C. Turk
Donna Kalauokalani
University of Washington

Chronic pain is one of the most prevalent conditions in Western society. It has been estimated that over 90 million Americans suffer from some form of persistent or recurrent pain (Marketdata Enterprises, 1995). Chronic pain is also a costly condition for society due to health care expenditures and indirect costs associated with disability compensations and loss of productivity resulting from absenteeism. Updating Bonica's (1986) figures and using Frymoyer and Durett's (1997) data on changes in medical and hospital charges, we can estimate that over $125 billion are expended annually on health care to treat chronic pain sufferers.

Not only does chronic pain adversely affect patients' physical well-being, but it also leads to substantial declines in familial, emotional, social, and occupational functioning. Patients and their families feel progressively more distressed as medical costs escalate and disability increases. Health care providers frequently become frustrated as treatment options are exhausted while reports of pain and disability persist.

PERSPECTIVE ON CHRONIC PAIN

In general, pain experience results from acute tissue damage that resolves spontaneously or with treatment, rarely causing significant disability. In these instances, pain serves as a warning sign of underlying pathology. In the case of acute pain, there appears to be a close relationship between pain and physical pathology. This association forms the basis for the somatogenic hypothesis (Turk & Stacey, 1997).

Despite tremendous advances in our understanding of physiology, anatomy, biochemistry, and biomedical technologies, the persistence and extent of pain among many chronic pain patients cannot be explained solely by somatic factors. The inability of the somatogenic perspective to explain the recalcitrance of chronic pain has led to several alternative hypotheses suggesting that chronic pain may be caused or maintained primarily due to psychological factors (Turk & Stacey, 1997). In the classic psychogenic view, chronic pain is conceptualized as a hysteric condition resulting from unresolved psychological conflict expressed through somatic channels.

An alternative psychogenic hypothesis views reports of pain in the absence of or disproportionate to object pathology as motivationally determined. This view considers reports of pain to be consciously motivated with the intent to obtain financial or other benefits. In another model, although not usually viewed as a psychogenic model, the operant conditioning perspective (Fordyce, 1976) tends to view persistent pain in the absence of a physical basis as being maintained by environmental contingencies of reinforcement (i.e., behavioral influences). Thus, the consequence of behavior determines the likelihood of that behavior occurring again. Each of these hypotheses is a unidimensional model with the erroneous assumption that pain complaints are either physically based or psychologically based. Moreover, the unidimensional models fail to consider pain as a subjective, perceptual experience.

A growing body of research has provided evidence substantiating the view of pain as a complex, multifactorial phenomenon, involving sensory, cognitive, affective, and behavioral components (Turk, Meichenbaum, & Genest, 1983). Given the multifactorial nature of the problem, the importance of interventions that address the synergistic features that comprise the chronic pain experience has been advocated.

MULTIDISCIPLINARY PAIN CENTERS

A multidisciplinary pain center (MPC) is a facility in which comprehensive treatment is provided by a team consisting of health care professionals from various specialties including physicians, physical therapists, occupational therapists, nurses, and psychologists (Turk & Stacey, 1997). Since the first comprehensive MPC was founded in 1961 at the University of Washington, the number of MPCs and single-modality pain treatment clinics has grown exponentially. By the mid-1970s, there were 327 pain clinics worldwide (Modell, 1977). A recent report by the American Pain Society (APS) compiled information about 352 MPCs in the United States (APS, 1996).

Although there is variability in treatment approaches, the basic treatment at an MPC typically includes: (a) medication management (especially opioid medications), (b) graded physical exercises, and (c) cognitive and behavioral techniques for pain and stress management (e.g., relaxation). It is evident that MPCs attempt to treat both physical and psychological factors that comprise the experience of pain and disability.

Despite the growing acceptance of the mutidisciplinary practice of chronic pain treatment among health care providers, skepticism among third-party payers regarding the efficacy and cost-effectiveness of MPC treatment persists. Many third-party payers continue to adhere to the inappropriate somatogenic-psychogenic dichotomy, potentially contributing to refusal of coverage for MPC treatment. In this chapter, we challenge this skepticism by reviewing empirical evidence for the efficacy of MPC treatment and estimating the cost savings of the MPC, compared to conventional, medical and surgical treatment of chronic pain.

EVALUATION OF THE EFFICACY OF MPC TREATMENT

What may at first seem a simple question, whether MPC treatment is effective, cannot be answered easily. It is essential to consider the set of different criteria that can be used to evaluate the outcomes of MPC.

Effective for Whom

There is abundant evidence indicating that patients who are referred to MPCs are not representative of the chronic pain population. Generally, there are several factors that differentiate MPC-referred patients from other chronic pain patients. MPC-referred patients tend to have injuries that are work related, consume greater quantities of opioid medication, have had a greater number of previous treatments (e.g., surgery), and report high levels of emotional distress (Crook, Tunks, Rideout, & Bowne, 1986; Crook, Weir, & Tunks, 1989). Thus, MPCs tend to treat patients with highly complex problems. An MPC is often the treatment of last resort for a very challenging sample of chronic pain patients whose options have been exhausted.

Criteria of Success

When a patient is evaluated following treatment, how can we establish whether the treatment program is a "success"? Various constituent groups will have different criteria on which they base the answer to this question. Patients generally seek treatment to reduce pain and suffering, referring physicians may be most concerned about managing opioid medications, managed care organizations are most interested in reducing health care utilization, and worker's compensation carriers are primarily interested in closure of disability claims and reduction in disability payments. Thus, the outcome of treatment (success) must be considered in light of whose perspective it reflects. Moreover, an improvement in one outcome criterion does not infer improvement in any other. The lack of concordance among clinical outcomes in various domains seems to reflect the multifactorial nature of chronic pain problems. It has been suggested that impairment, disability, and disease activity are only weakly correlated, and should be measured separately (Bostrom, 1995).

Not only is it important to ask whether MPC treatments are effective on diverse outcome criteria, but we also need to ask "effective compared to what alternative?". For example, surgical interventions seem to be considered as a gold standard for back pain treatment. Third-party payers rarely refuse to approve payment for surgical interventions for back pain. Many other patients may receive "conventional" medical treatment, generally including some combination of medication and physical therapy. Thus, the efficacy of MPC treatments can be contrasted with the efficacy of surgical and conventional medical treatments for chronic pain. Conventional medical treatments include nonsurgical, pharmacological or physical therapies that are provided in a unimodal fashion (e.g., medical trials, physical therapy).

Pain Reduction

A wide range of rates of pain reduction following MPC treatment has been reported in the literature. On average, the rates of pain reduction range from 0% (Deardorff, Rubin, & Scott, 1991; Sturgis, Schaefer, & Sikora, 1984) to 60% (Moore, Berk, & Nypaver, 1984; Tollison, Kriegel, & Downie, 1985). A meta-analysis of 65 studies evaluating MPC treatments ($N = 3,089$ patients) reports an average pain reduction of 20% following treatment at MPCs (Flor, Fydrich, & Turk, 1992). These rates can be compared with the rates of pain reduction following surgical treatment. The surgical literature indicates that approximately 57% to 70% of patients who have undergone lumbar surgeries continue to report significant levels of pain following treatment (Dvorak, Gauchat, & Valach, 1988; North et al., 1991; Wilkinson, 1993).

When comparing the outcome of surgeries to MPC treatments, we need to recall the characteristics of patients treated at MPCs. The majority of MPC patients already had unsuccessful surgical interventions. The meta-analysis of MPCs (Flor et al., 1992) estimated that MPC patients had on average 1.7 surgeries prior to being referred to an MPC. Given the challenging nature of patients, the rates of pain reduction reported following treatment at MPCs are quite impressive, even when compared to surgery.

Management of Opioid Medications

Opioid medications are commonly prescribed for chronic pain patients referred for treatment at MPCs. Approximately 50% of chronic pain patients are consuming opioid medications at the time of initial evaluation at MPCs (Flor et al., 1992).

The long-term use of opioid medication for chronic pain of nonmalignant origin continues to be controversial (Turk, 1996). Although opioid medication may be helpful in some patients, the high prevalence rates of opioid prescriptions among the patients referred to MPCs suggest that a large number of patients do not benefit from these medications. Concerns regarding physical dependency and tolerance are commonly expressed by physicians (Turk, Brody, & Okifuji, 1994). In one survey (Deathe & Helmes, 1993), the primary reason physicians referred patients to MPCs was concerns about "excessive" use of opioids.

In addition to the potentially serious side-effects, opioid prescriptions may promote psychological distress (Taylor, Zlutnick, Corley, & Flora, 1980). Furthermore, elimination or reduction of opioid medications is desirable because opioids may reinforce passive attitudes toward rehabilitation thereby interfering with one of the primary goals of MPC treatment—promotion of self-management of pain and disability (Turk et al., 1983).

Outcome studies for MPC treatments generally report substantial reduction in opioid use. Tollison (1991), for example, compared the opioid use of chronic pain patients who underwent MPC treatment with others who were not able to attend due to denial by insurance companies. The difference was substantial at 1-year follow-up. MPC treatment reduced the opioid use from 69% to 22%, whereas the opioid consumption of untreated patients remained approximately the same (81% to 75%). Other studies (Seres, 1993; Tollison et al., 1985) report that over 65% of MPC-treated patients maintain their opioid-free status at 1-year follow-up. It is worth noting, however, that the controversy surrounding the efficacy and ethical concerns of opioid therapy for chronic pain suggests that we exercise caution to determine the value of elimination or reduction of opioid as an outcome criterion (Turk, 1996).

Functional Restoration: Activity and Return-to-Work

It is, unfortunately, a common practice to report pain severity as the sole outcome criterion. This is especially evident in studies evaluating the efficacy of surgical and pharmacological interventions. Yet, functional restoration is also a highly desirable goal in light of severe disability experienced by many chronic pain patients. The improvement in physical functioning could be a driving factor in chronic pain rehabilitation because it provides patients an opportunity to feel a sense of accomplishment, leading to a better quality of life even in the absence of significant pain reduction. Therefore, reduction in pain in the absence of improvement in physical functioning seems inadequate.

Flor and colleagues (1992) indicate that MPC treatments appear to be effective in increasing activity levels of chronic pain patients. They estimated that MPC-treated patients average a 65% increase in physical activity compared to 35% in conventionally treated patients. In contrast, change in physical activity following surgery or prolonged use of opioid medication is rarely evaluated. Even when assessed, improvement in function is rarely observed (North et al., 1991; Turk, 1996).

Evaluation of return-to-work is extremely complex. A number of factors influence return-to-work in chronic pain patients including (a) physical demands of the job, (b) regional variation in the job market, (c) availability of job accommodations, (d) marketability of patients' skills, (e) extent of wage replacement, and (f) financial incentives. Finding employment may be particularly difficult for patients who have long histories of chronic pain and job skills that are dependent on high degrees of physical exertion. Given two applicants for a job requiring physical labor, who is more likely to be offered the job, the individual with a history of long-term disability for back pain or the candidate who has no history of previous disability associated with back pain?

Furthermore, not only are patients much older than they were at the onset of their pain problems (7 years on the average: Flor et al., 1992), but also years of unemployment might have resulted in considerable mismatch between patients' job skills and skills that are required for today's jobs. Depreciation of job skills is likely to be accelerated by rapid advancements in technology. Thus, the difficulties in regaining employment may arise from the lack of opportunity for MPC patients to acquire job skills needed for today's job market because of long-term unemployment.

In light of the multiple factors adversely affecting the chances of patients to be employed it should not be surprising that, if untreated, only 25% of patients return to work (Flor et al., 1992). Figure 5.1 summarizes the results from 12 studies comparing the rates of return-to-work between MPC-treated patients and patients receiving conventional, nonsurgical treatments. Examination of the figure reveals that the average return-to-work rate for MPC-treated patients is 67%, substantially higher than 24% rate achieved by patients who receive conventional medical treatment.

The willingness among third-party payers to provide payment for surgery despite the expense implies a belief that surgery is particularly effective in returning people to work. The return-to-work rates among back pain patients who have undergone surgery, however, are not as good as those

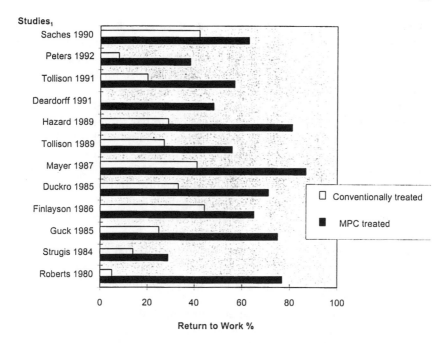

FIG. 5.1. Return-to-work rates for MPC and surgically treated patients. Study references are included in the References section.

reported for MPC-treated patients. Studies have shown that only from 36% (Beals & Hickman, 1972) to 50% (Wiesel, Feffer, & Rothman, 1984) return to work following surgery for back pain. Improved techniques and innovative technologies have not increased these rates. For example, North and his colleagues (1991) reported that only 20% of repeat back surgery patients return to work and only 25% of those who had spinal cord stimulators implanted to control pain return to work.

Given that a large proportion of patients referred to MPC programs have undergone at least one surgical procedure without success (Flor et al., 1992), the return-to-work rate following MPC treatments appears to be impressive. This is especially true considering the recalcitrant nature of pain problems MPC patients present.

Health Care Utilization

There is no question that treatment of chronic pain is costly. Simmons et al. (1988) reported that the health care costs of chronic pain patients for the 1 year preceding referral to MPC to ranged from $500 to $35,400, with the average of $13,284, excluding the costs for surgical procedures. In many cases, surgical procedures will add substantially to health care expenses.

Wiesel et al. (1984) estimated the cost of surgery for back pain was approximately $40,000; however, more recent data suggest that the cost for lumbar surgery (including surgery, anesthesiology, and hospitalization) is approximately $15,000 (Frymoyer & Durett, 1997). Costs for MPC treatment vary depending on the settings and level of extensiveness. The average outpatient MPC rehabilitation program is estimated to cost $8,100 (Marketdata Enterprises, 1995), one-half of the cost of lumbar surgery.

MPC-treated patients are less likely to have additional hospitalization or surgery following treatment, compared to the patients who receive conventional medical treatments. On the average, 17% and 16% of MPC-treated patients required additional hospitalization and surgery, respectively, whereas 47% and 28% of conventionally treated patients required those treatments, respectively (Cassisi, Sypert, Salamon, & Kapel, 1989; Tollison, 1991; Tollison, Kriegel, Satterthwaite, & Turner, 1989). Serious complications following surgery that require additional surgery are relatively common. For example, Long et al. (1988) noted that up to 35% of repeat back surgeries were performed to treat problems associated with previous surgeries.

In contrast to conventional medical and surgical interventions, health care utilization can be expected to decrease following MPC treatment. One study conducted in a health maintenance organization reported a 36% reduction in pain-related clinic visits in the first year following MPC treatment (Caudill et al., 1991). Subsequent pain-related visits occurred at half the frequency compared with untreated patients at 2-year follow-up (Mayer et al., 1987). These results imply the potential for substantial savings in health care expenditures in the years following MPC treatment.

Closure of Disability Claims

Between $11 billion and $43 billion are spent annually for disability compensation for back pain alone (Frymoyer & Durett, 1997). Needless to say, development of rehabilitation programs to reduce the disability claims has been of considerable interest. Outcome studies evaluating MPC treatments (Fey, Williamson-Kirkland, & Fraugione, 1987; Mayer et al., 1985; Seres & Newman, 1976) consistently report that substaintial percentages of claims (68% to 89%) are settled within 3 months following MPC treatment. No comparable data have been presented from studies evaluating surgery or conventional medical treatment for chronic pain.

Although rarely discussed, the procedure by which claims are processed may have a confounding effect on the outcome of MPC treatment. Claims closure for many chronic pain patients will, given the nature of the symptom manifestations, be dependent on subjective reports rather than objective findings. The extent and quality of the training for claim adjusters have not been systematically examined. To our knowledge, there are no published data on reliability of decisions regarding claim closures by case managers. Societal and organizational pressures to facilitate closures may be growing as available financial resources decline. Thus, the value of the closures of disability claims, wage loss, and return-to-work should be interpreted with caution. Such outcome criteria may tell us more about the zeal of claims managers and fiscal policies than about treatment efficacy. Until the reliability of the claims process is established, the equability of the decisions remains an open question.

Evaluation of "Significance"

In evaluation of treatment efficacy, one looks for "significant" improvement. Most studies use "statistical" significance to demonstrate difference between pretreatment and posttreatment and difference between MPC-treated patients and control patients. With inferential statistics, the p value of .05 or less is conventionally used as the basis for statistical significance. When $p < .05$, there is less than a 5% chance (1 case in 20) that the observed difference occurred by chance.

There are several concerns with the statistical method of significance testing. First, the inferential statistics do not allow identification of patients who benefit from the treatment. F tests and t tests are the tests that are used most frequently to compare group means on a basis of group differences. Second, significant p values are conventionally and arbitrarily driven with no scientific rationale. P values are also misinterpreted; small p values are often mistaken as a sign of strong effects although p values are simply an indication of the probability of the difference happening by chance.

Third, and most important, the meaning of statistical significance is often unclear. For example, assume an analysis reveals a statistically significant difference ($p < .05$) in depressed mood of MPC-treated patients between pretreatment score of 25 and posttreatment score of 20, using a commonly used measure of depression, the Center for Epidemiological Study of Depression Scale (CES–D; Radloff, 1977). The result indicates that the reduction of scores from 25 to 20 is statistically different; however, the posttreatment score of 20 is still above the cutoff point of 19 recommended for chronic pain patients (Turk & Okifuji, 1994), indicating that on the average patients continue to express significant levels of depressed mood.

Instead of relying on p values to determine the efficacy of treatment programs, one may wish to develop a set of criteria based on clinical observations and conventions such as an increase in achievement of individually established goals. However, the validity of "homemade" criteria is difficult to evaluate, and some degrees of consistency in the variability of quality and values across studies are needed in order to evaluate outcome.

Another alternative way to determine treatment responses is to use the Reliable Change (RC) Index. The RC Index was originally developed by Jacobson, Follette, and Revenstorf (1984) in an attempt to quantitatively define clinical significance with an assumption that clinically improved patients move from a distribution of "dysfunctional" to a distribution of "functional." Several variations of their formula have been developed (see Speer, 1992). Calculation of the RC Index requires information on the means and standard deviations of target variables and the test–retest reliability of the measurements that one uses to obtain those means. An RC Index greater than 1.96 is considered as clinically significant improvement. The RC Index has been used in several chronic pain treatment outcome studies (Harkapaa, Melin, Jarvikoski, & Hurri, 1989; Rudy, Turk, Kubinski, & Zaki, 1995; Turk, Okifuji, Sinclair, & Starz, 1998).

ECONOMIC EVALUATION OF MPC TREATMENT

Cost containment in the managed health care environment has increased the importance of establishing economic advantages of therapeutic interventions. Two types of analytic methods to evaluate economic consequences of interventions are cost-benefit analysis and cost-effective analysis. The two terms are often mislabeled and are frequently used interchangeably (Provenzale & Lipscomb, 1996). The confusion in the current literature in the economic analysis of health care delivery seems to result largely from confusion in the definition and the use of the terms.

Definitions

Both cost-benefit and cost-effective analyses are methods to compare the relationships between cost and clinical outcomes across different interventions. The two methods, however, differ in the expressions of effectiveness.

Cost-benefit analysis evaluates the costs and effects of the intervention in a same, usually monetary, unit. The standardization of unit has an advantage because it permits comparisons across dissimilar intervention programs. On the other hand, the conversion of treatment effects to monetary unit may not always be feasible.

In a cost-effective analysis, treatment outcomes are measured by criteria other than monetary terms, such as lives saved or return to work. The cost to outcome ratio can be estimated, and comparisons can be made between any interventions using the ratios with common denominators.

An intervention is considered as cost-effective when the intervention satisfies one of the following conditions: (a) It is more effective than alternative modality at same cost, (b) it is less costly and at least as effective as an alternative modality, (c) it is more effective and more costly than an alternative treatment, but the benefit exceeds the added cost, or (d) it is less effective and less costly, but the added benefit of the alternative is not worth the added cost (Doubilet, Weinstein, & McNeil, 1986). Examples meeting each of these criteria are depicted in Table 5.1.

Cost Savings of MPC Treatment

As noted earlier, there seems to be a persistent view among third-party payers that MPC treatment is expensive and not cost-effective. The problem may be more one of dissemination than availability of the outcome data. In order to evaluate whether the criticisms are justified, we discuss and estimate the extent of MPC treatments in saving medical and disability costs. The estimates of savings we use are based on calculations for a hypothetical 17,600 patients. This figure was derived from the conservative assumption that each MPC in the United States treats at least 50 patients annually. There are 352 MPCs listed in the APS directory, hence, the estimated number of patients ($352 \times 50 = 17,600$).

TABLE 5.1
Hypothetical Examples of Cost-Effective Analyses

	Treatment 1	Treatment 2
CASE 1:		
Cost	$500	$250
Improvement	50%	50%

Treatment 2 is less expensive with equivalent effectiveness.

Cost-effectiveness Treatment 1 < Treatment 2

	Treatment 1	Treatment 2
CASE 2:		
Cost	$500	$250
Improvement	50%	10%

Treatment 1 is more costly and more effective, but the added benefit is worth the added cost.

Cost-effectiveness Treatment 1 > Treatment 2

	Treatment 1	Treatment 2
CASE 3:		
Cost	$500	$250
Improvement	50%	40%

Treatment 2 is less costly and less effective, but the 10% difference in improvement is not worth the added cost of Treatment 1.

Cost-effectiveness Treatment 1 < Treatment 2

Treatment Costs

Using published figures, we can estimate treatment costs for different treatment procedures. The recent report (Marketdata Enterprises, 1995) estimated that outpatient MPC treatment on the average costs $8,100 per patient. Back surgery is estimated to cost $15,000 (Frymoyer & Durett, 1997). Conventional, nonsurgical medical cost in the year prior to treatment at MPCs was estimated as $13,000 in 1987 (Simmons et al., 1988). The mean medical price index change from 1985 to 1994 was 7.22% (Frymoyer & Durett, 1997); thus, the present cost of conventional, nonsurgical medical treatment of chronic pain is estimated as $26,000 per year.

Back pain is the most common problem seen at MPCs. Approximately 60% of pain problems are back pain (Marketdata Enterprises, 1995). Thus, in our attempt to estimate the cost-effectiveness for MPC treatment, we compare the outcomes for MPCs with surgical treatments for back pain problems. We focus on surgical costs for 60% of the patients with back pain (Marketdata Enterprises, 1995). The costs of the three types of treatments for an annual cohort of 17,600 patients are:

- If treated at MPC: 17,600 patients × $8,100 = $142,560,000.
- If treated with conventional modalities: 17,600 patients × $26,000 = $457,600,000.
- If treated with surgery: 60% × 17,600 patients × $15,000 = $158,400,000.

Surgical and Medical Costs

MPC Treated Versus Conventionally (Nonsurgically) Treated. As described earlier in this chapter, 28% of conventionally treated patients and 16% of MPC-treated patients later require additional surgery. Thus:

- MPC: 60% of 17,600 patients × 16% require additional surgery × $15,000 = $25,344,000.
- Conservative: 60% of 17,600 patients × 28% require additional surgery × $15,000 = $44,352,000.

Posttreatment surgical costs in patients undergoing conventional, nonsurgical medical treatment are substantially higher than that of MPC-treated patients, with the saving of *approximately $20 million.*

For nonsurgical medical costs, Simmons et al. (1988) reported that on the average patients spent $5,596 for nonsurgical medical cost in 1 year following MPC-treatment. Using the average medical price index change of 7.22%, we estimate the post-MPC treatment medical cost to be approximately $11,200. No change in cost is expected for the conventional treat-

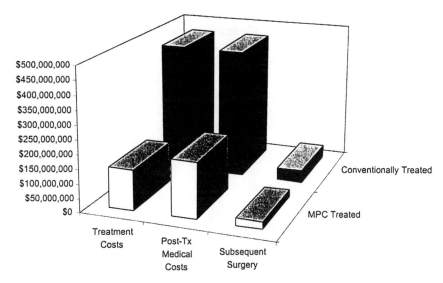

FIG. 5.2. Treatment costs and subsequent surgical and medical costs of MPC treatment and conventional medical treatment.

ment. Thus, for a year following treatment, medical costs are estimated to be (see Fig. 5.2):

- If treated at MPC: 17,600 patients × $11,200 = $197,120,000.
- If treated with conventional medical (excluding surgery): 17,600 × $26,000 = $457,600,000.

Based on these analyses, MPCs would save over $260 million in nonsurgical medical costs. Altogether, MPC-treated patients would spend *$280 million* less in medical costs in the following year and additional surgery than would patients who are treated with the conventional approach.

MPC Treated Versus Surgically Treated.   Prevalence of additional surgery required at posttreatment for MPC-treated patients is 16% and for surgically treated patients is 56% (North et al., 1991). Thus the saving of MPC treatment will be:

- MPC: 60% of 17,600 patients × 16% need additional surgery × $15,000 = 25,344,000.
- Surgery: 60% of 17,600 patients × 56% need additional surgery × $15,000 = $88,704,000.

Annual saving for the surgical costs of MPC programs relative to surgical treatment is thus approximately *$63 million*. Data on the medical costs following surgical intervention are not available; thus cost savings in medical (nonsurgical) costs of MPC relative to surgery following treatment cannot be estimated.

In summary, MPC treatment would save close to $280 million in surgical and medical costs when compared to conventional, nonsurgical medical treatments. Similarly, MPC-treated patients would spend $63 million less for surgery compared to surgically treated patients. These savings are likely to continue in subsequent years. Moreover, the estimate is only for an annual cohort. Every year, a new cohort of patients is treated. The potential savings in the medical expenditures that MPCs can achieve therefore are tremendous.

Disability Payments

It has been estimated that over 5 million individuals in the United States are permanently disabled due to chronic back pain (Frymoyer & Durett, 1997). Approximately $250,000 were paid for permanent disability for each compensation-covered man with a back injury on the job (Stieg & Williams, 1983).

In 1988, the average amount of disability compensation per year was estimated as $15,171 (Turk, Rudy, & Stieg, 1988). Using the annual increase rate of 3.55% based on the annual changes of consumer price index (Frymoyer & Durett, 1997) as a basis, we estimate the annual average disability payment as $20,766 in 1997 dollars.

It was reported that 50% of chronic pain patients who are referred to MPCs are receiving long-term disability compensation (Flor et al., 1992). Thus, 17,600 patients × 50% = 8,800 patients/year receive disability. As described in Fig. 5.1, the average return-to-work rates are 67% and 24% for MPC treatment and conservative, nonsurgical treatment, respectively. Thus, we anticipate that for MPC treatment, 67% of 8,800 patients = 5,896 patients, and for conservative treatment, 24% of 8,800 patients = 2,112 patients. These patients will resume their occupational lives and be no longer in need for disability payments. Using our estimate, we can consider the lifetime disability expenditure. Based on available research (Steig & Turk, 1988), the annual cost of disability is estimated at $20,766. Because the average age of MPC-treated patients is 45 years old (Flor et al., 1992), assuming that they would need the disability payments until the age of 65 (20 years) and taking the annual increment of 3.55% into consideration, lifetime costs of disability can be estimated at approximately $632,000. Following the MPC treatment, 67% of the patients return to work (Fig. 5.1). Thus:

- MPC treatment: 2,904 patients (8,800 − 5,896) × $632,000 = $1,835,328,000.

TABLE 5.2
Cost Comparisons Among MPC, Surgical Treatment, and Conventional
Medical Treatment for an Annual Cohort of 17,600 Patients

Tx	Initial Tx Costs	Subsequent Surgery	1-yr Post-Tx Medical[a]	Lifetime Disability	Total Costs
MPC	$142,560,000	$25,344,400	$197,120,000	$1,835,328,000	**$2,200,352,400**
Surgical	$158,400,000	$88,704,000	—[b]	—[b]	
Conventional	$457,600,000	$44,352,000	$457,600,000	$4,226,816,000	**$5,186,368,000**

[a]Medical treatment excludes surgical procedures. [b]Data not available for estimates.

- Conservative treatment: 6,688 patients (8,800 − 2,112) × $632,000 = $4,226,816,000.

The saving by the MPC treatment for an annual cohort of chronic pain patients approaches *$2.5 billion* over a period of 20 years.

A summary of the initial and subsequent medical and disability costs for the MPC, conventional, and surgical treatments is presented in Table 5.2.

Return-to-Work: Gainful Employment

As noted earlier, the loss of gainful employment is one of the most serious socioeconomic concerns associated with chronic pain. The importance of return-to-work as an outcome criterion has been discussed. A related issue is relative cost-effectiveness of the treatment to achieve success in this criterion. In order to evaluate the cost-effectiveness of MPC, surgical, and conservative treatments, we use a cost-effectiveness index as:

$$\text{Cost} - \text{Effectiveness Index} = \frac{\text{Improvement}}{\text{Cost of Treatment}} \times 100$$

From Fig. 5.1, the return-to-work is achieved by 67% of MPC-treated patients and 24% of conventionally treated patients. For surgically treated patients, the average of two studies (Beals & Hickman, 1972; Wiesel et al., 1984) is 43%. Treatment costs for MPC, conservative, and surgical treatments are estimated as $8,100, $26,000, and $15,000, respectively. Using the return-to-work rate as the improvement score, the Cost-Effective Index score for each treatment modality is reported in Fig. 5.3. The Cost-Effective Index score of the MPC treatment far exceeds surgical and medical treatments. Indeed, based on the index scores, MPC treatment can be considered as nine times more cost-effective than conservative treatment and 3.6

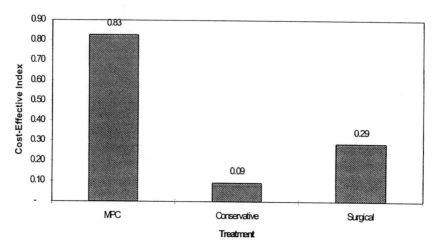

FIG. 5.3. Cost-effective index scores for MPC, surgical, and conventional medical treatments.

times more cost-effective than surgical treatment in helping patients return-to-work.

PREVENTIVE TREATMENT

The amount of human suffering and socioeconomic impact associated with chronic pain is enormous. Increasingly more and more attention has been paid to prevention of chronicity (Turk, 1997). Prevention may be primary (prevention of the initial injury that may become chronic subsequently) or secondary involving early intervention following the acute injury thereby preventing chronicity. The assumptions that prevention can spare long-term disability and facilitate reduction in health care and disability costs are intuitively appealing. However, one must ask whether there is evidence that preventive treatments are clinically effective and cost-effective?

Despite the growing interest among industries, third-party payers, and disability agencies, only a handful of studies have actually estimated monetary savings achieved with preventive interventions. Those studies generally demonstrate that the preventive approach helps reduce medical and disability expenditures.

One review (Lahad, Malter, Berg, & Deyo, 1994) strongly suggests that educational sessions for adaptive body mechanics and coping are not sufficient to reduce risk of back pain episodes and disability. Versloot, Rozenman, van Son, and van Akkerveeken (1992), however, evaluated a relatively brief, psychoeducational program for primary prevention of back pain among bus drivers. They reported that the program reduced absenteeism by 6.5 days per year per employee, which were translated to savings of $900 per treated employee.

Other studies employed various combinations of therapies. For example, Brown, Sirles, Hillyer, and Thomas (1992) evaluated education and exercise therapy for individuals with acute back pain. Compared to the no-treatment group, the intervention saved $9,700 in medical cost for their 70 subjects in 6 months following the treatment, despite greater wage loss and medical costs were associated with the assignment to the treatment group at pretreatment. Linton and Bradley (1992) provided a combination of exercise therapy, ergometric education, and behavioral therapy for nurses with back pain. A comparison of sick days due to pain between 18 months prior to and 18 months following the treatment revealed that the nurses averaged 6.7 fewer posttreatment sick days due to pain. The authors did not estimate the savings in lost wages for their subjects, but listed hypothesized savings for various occupations based on their daily wages. (e.g., postal worker, rubber industry worker).

Cost savings have also been observed when more intensive treatment programs are used. McElligott, Miskovich, and Fielding (1989) implemented a three-phase program involving education, physical exercise, and work simulation for individuals with back injuries. All 273 participants returned to work within 60 days, and none received disability payments. Savings in the medical costs, wage loss, and litigation fees were approximately $1,300 per employee for a total of $354,900. Finally, Michell and Carmen (1994) evaluated an intensive 8-week daily treatment program for 271 injured workers who had not returned to work within 90 days. The program was multidiciplinary, comprised of exercise, education, cognitive-behavioral approach for pain and anxiety management, and counseling. Based on the costs for treatment, wage loss, and disability payment, the savings of the program were estimated in comparison with the costs incurred by control subjects who continued conventional treatments. Although the program was more costly than the conventional treatment ($6,400 vs. $3,900 per subject), medical and disability costs were lower in the treatment group ($36,400) than in the control group ($41,000) at 24-month follow-up. By 30-month follow-up, the cost saving of the program, controlling for the treatment cost, approached $5,000 per subject, a total of $1.36 million for this project.

Cost estimates of these studies, however, are limited in the short term. No studies have attempted to estimate whether and to what extent these prevention programs would reduce costs by preventing chronicity of pain. Approximately 5% to 10% of acute pain patients develop into chronic pain patients (Liebenson, 1992). Longitudinal research is needed to determine the cost-effectiveness of providing treatment to acute pain patients for preventing chronicity when 90% to 95% of those patients will remit on their own.

Cost savings that can be achieved by preventing chronic pain are likely to be enormous. A typical patient who is referred to an MPC is, in addition to experiencing incalculable suffering and distress, unemployed for an average of 7 years and has had at least one unsuccessful surgery (Flor et al., 1992). Thus, the estimated costs for this patient by the time he or she is referred to an MPC are $182,800 ($26,000/yr + inflation) for conventional treatment, $25,500 for surgery (1.7 surgeries/patient), and if receiving disability compensation, $145,362 ($20,766/yr + inflation) for disability payment. Approximately $354,000 could be saved by preventing chronicity of pain problem per unemployed patient and $208,300 for employed patients. If prevention is perfectly effective in preventing chronicity, all 17,600 patients whom we estimate to be treated at MPC would resume productive lives in a reasonable period, turning into the *cost saving of $5 billion per year*. The savings would be far greater if the comparison is made to patients who are treated only by surgical and conventional medical treatments.

CONCLUDING COMMENTS

MPC treatments have been more rigorously examined than most other treatment modalities used with chronic pain patients. More data are available for the efficacy of MPC than for any surgical procedures or conventional medical treatment for chronic pain. The comparisons further suggest that MPC treatments result in greater clinical effectiveness and cost saving than the alternatives. It is essential that those who work in MPCs communicate more effectively with the public and third-party payers on this matter in order to avoid patients being denied treatment from which they could otherwise benefit greatly.

Greater attention needs to be given to prevention of chronicity. The few studies available provide support for the contention that preventive efforts might save billions of dollars in medical expenditures and indemnity costs. This estimate, of course, does not take into account the reduction in human misery observed in chronic pain patients.

REFERENCES

American Pain Society. (1996). *1996 pain facilities directory.* Glenview, IL: Author.
Beals, P. K., & Hickman, N. W. (1972). Industrial injuries of the back and extremities. *Journal of Bone and Joint Surgery, 54B,* 1593–1611.
Bonica, J. J. (1986). Past and current status of pain research and therapy. *Seminars in Anesthesiology, 5,* 82–99.

Bostrom, J. M. (1995). Multiple health care contracts: Changing the rules for hospital staff and systems. *Nursing Economics, 13,* 99–103.

Brown, K. C., Sirles, A. T., Hilyer, J. C., & Thomas, M. J. (1992). Cost-effectiveness of a back school intervention for municipal employees. *Spine, 17,* 1224–1228.

Cassisi, J. E., Sypert, G. W., Salamon, A., & Kapel, L. (1989). Independent evaluation of a multidisciplinary rehabilitation program for chronic low back pain. *Neurosurgery, 25,* 877–883.

Caudill, M., Schnabble, R., Zuttermeister, P., Benson, H., & Friedman, R. (1991). Decreased clinic use by chronic pain patients: Responsive to behavioral medical intervention. *Clinical Journal of Pain, 7,* 305–310.

Crook, J., Tunks, E., Rideout, E., & Bowne, G. (1986). Epidemiologic consideration of persistent pain sufferers in speciality pain clinic and the community. *Archives of Physical Medicine and Rehabilitation, 67,* 451–455.

Crook, J., Weir, R., & Tunks, E. (1989). An epidemiological follow-up survey of persistent pain sufferers in a group family practice and specialty pain clinic. *Pain, 36,* 49–61.

Deardorff, W. W., Rubin, H. S., & Scott, D. W. (1991). Comprehensive multidisciplinary treatment of chronic pain: A follow-up study of treated and non-treated groups. *Pain, 45,* 35–43.

Deathe, A. B., & Helmes, E. (1993). Evaluation of a chronic pain programme by referring physicians. *Pain, 52,* 113–121.

Doubilet, P., Weinstein, M. G., & McNeil, B. J. (1986). Use and misuse of the term "cost effective" in medicine. *New England Journal of Medicine, 314,* 253–256.

Duckro, P. N., Margolis, R. B., Tait, R. C., & Korytnyk, N. (1985). Long-term follow-up of chronic pain patients: A preliminary study. *International Journal of Psychiatry in Medicine, 15,* 283–292.

Dvorak, J., Gauchat, M. H., & Valach, L. (1988). The outcomes of surgery for lumbar disc herniation: I. 4–17 years follow-up with emphasis on somatic aspects. *Spine, 13,* 1418–1422.

Fey, S. G., Williamson-Kirkland, T. E., & Fraugione, R. (1987). Vocational restoration in injured workers with chronic pain. *Pain* (Suppl. 4), S379.

Finlayson, R. E., Maruta, T., Morse, R. M., & Martin, M. A. (1986). Substance dependence and chronic pain: Experience with treatment and follow-up results. *Pain, 26,* 175–180.

Flor, H., Fydrich, T., & Turk, D. C. (1992). Efficacy of multidisciplinary pain treatment centers: A meta-analytic review. *Pain, 49,* 221–230.

Fordyce, W. E. (1976). *Behavioral methods in chronic pain and illness.* St. Louis, MO: Mosby.

Frymoyer, J. W., & Durett, C. L. (1997). The economics of spinal disorders. In J. W. Frymoyer, T. B. Ducker, N. M. Hadler, J. P. Kostuik, J. N. Weinstein, & T. S. Whitecloud, III (Eds.), *The adult spine* (2nd ed., pp 143–150). Philadelphia: Lippincott-Raven.

Guck, T. P., Skultety, F. M., Meilman, P. W., & Dowd, E. T. (1985). Multidisciplinary pain center follow-up study: Evaluation with a no-treatment control group. *Pain, 21,* 295–306.

Harkapaa, K., Melin, G., Jarvikoski, A., & Hurri, H. (1989). A controlled study on the outcome of impatient and outpatient treatment of low back pain: Part I. Pain disability, compliance, and reported treatment benefits three months after treatment. *Scandinavian Journal of Rehabilitation Medicine, 21,* 81–89.

Jacobson, N. S., Follette, W. C., & Revenstorf, D. (1984). Psychotherapy outcome research: Methods for reporting variability and evaluating clinical significance. *Behavior Therapy, 15,* 336–352.

Lahad, A., Malter, A. D., Berg, A. O., & Deyo, R. A. (1994). The effectiveness of four interventions for the prevention of low back pain. *Journal of the American Medical Association, 272,* 1286–1291.

Liebenson, C. S. (1992). Pathogenesis of chronic back pain. *Journal of Manipulative and Physiological Therapy, 15,* 299–308.

Linton, S. J., & Bradley, L. A. (1992). An 18-month follow-up of a secondary prevention program for back pain: Help and hindrance factors related to outcome maintenance. *Clinical Journal of Pain, 8,* 227–236.

Long, D. M., Filtzer, D. L., Ben Debba, M., & Hendler, N. M. (1988). Clinical features of the failed-back syndrome. *Journal of Neurosurgery, 69,* 61–71.

Marketdata Enterprises. (1995). *Chronic pain management programs: A market analysis.* Valley Stream, NY: Author.

Mayer, T. G., Gatchel, R. J., Kishino, N., Keeley, J., Capra, P., Mayer, H., Barnett, J., & Mooney, V. (1985). Objective assessment of spine function following industrial injury: A prospective study with comparison group and one-year follow-up. *Spine, 10,* 484–493.

Mayer, T. G., Gatchel, R. J., Mayer, H., Kishino, N. D., Keeley, J., & Mooney, V. (1987). A prospective two-year study of functional restoration in industrial low back injury: An objective assessment procedure. *Journal of the American Medical Association, 258,* 1763–1767.

McElligott, J., Miscovich, S. J., & Fielding, L. P. (1989). Low back injury in industry: The value of a recovery program. *Connecticut Medicine, 53,* 711–714.

Michell, R. I., & Carmen, G. M. (1994). The functional restoration approach to the treatment of chronic pain in patients with soft tissue and back injuries. *Spine, 19,* 633–642.

Modell, J. (1977). *Dietary of pain clinics.* Oak Ridge, TN: American Society of Anesthesiologists.

Moore, M. E., Berk, S. N., & Nypaver, A. (1984). Chronic pain: Inpatient treatment with small group effects. *Archive of Physical Medicine and Rehabilitation, 65,* 356–361.

North, R. B., Campbell, J. N., James, C. S., Conover-Walker, M. K., Wang, H., Piantadosi, S., Rybock, J. D., & Long, D. M. (1991). Failed back surgery syndrome: 5-year follow-up in 102 patients undergoing repeated operation. *Neurosurgery, 28,* 685–691.

Peters, J., Large, R. G., & Elkind, G. (1992). Follow-up results from a randomized controlled trial evaluating in- and outpatient pain management programmes. *Pain, 50,* 41–50.

Provenzale, D., & Lipscomb, J. (1996). Cost-effectiveness: Definitions and use in the gastroenterology literature. *American Journal of Gastroenterology, 91,* 1488–1493.

Radloff, L. S. (1977). A self-report depression scale for research in the general population. *Applied Psychological Measurement, 1,* 385–392.

Roberts, A. H., & Reinhardt, L. (1980). The behavioral management of chronic pain: Long-term follow-up with comparison groups. *Pain, 8,* 151–162.

Romano, J., & Turner, J. A. (1985). Chronic pain and depression: Does the evidence support a relationship? *Psychological Bulletin, 97,* 18–34.

Rudy, T. E., Turk, D. C., Kubinski, J., & Zaki, H. S. (1995). Differential treatment responses of TMD patients as a function of psychological characteristics. *Pain, 61,* 103–112.

Sachs, B. L., David, J. A. F., Olimpio, D., Scala, A. D., & Lacroix, M. (1990). Spinal rehabilitation by work tolerance based on objective physical capacity assessment of dysfunction: A prospective study with central subjects and 12 month review. *Spine, 15,* 1325–1332.

Seres, J. L. (1993). The neurosurgical management of pain: A critical review. *Clinical Journal of Pain, 9,* 289–290.

Seres, J. L., & Newman, R. I. (1976). Results of treatment of chronic low-back pain at the Portland Pain Center. *Journal of Neurosurgery, 45,* 32–36.

Simmons, J. W., Avant, W. S., Demski, J., & Parisher, D. (1988). Determining successful pain clinic treatment trough validation of cost effectiveness. *Spine, 12,* 342–344.

Speer, D. C. (1992). Clinically significant change: Jacobson and Truax (1991) revisited. *Journal of Consulting and Clinical Psychology, 60,* 402–408.

Stieg, R. L., & Turk, D. C. (1988). Chronic pain syndrome: The necessity of demonstrating the cost-benefit of treatment. *Pain Management, 1,* 58–63.

Stieg, R. K., & Williams, R. C. (1983). Chronic pain as a biosociocultual phenomenon: Implications for treatment. *Seminars in Neurology, 3,* 370–376.

Sturgis, E. T., Schaefer, C. A., & Sikora, T. L. (1984). Pain center follow-up study of treated and untreated patients. *Archives of Physical Medicine and Rehabilitation, 65,* 301–303.

Taylor, C. M. B., Zlutnick, S. I., Corley, M. J., & Flora, J. (1980). The effects of detoxification, relaxation, and brief supportive therapy on chronic pain. *Pain, 8,* 319–329.

Tollison, C. D. (1991). Comprehensive treatment approach for lower back workers' compensation injuries. *Journal of Occupational Rehabilitation, 1,* 281–287.

Tollison, C. D., Kriegel, M. L., & Downie, G. R. (1985). Chronic low back pain: Results of treatment at the pain therapy center. *Southern Medical Journal, 78,* 1291–1295.

Tollison, C. D., Kriegel, M. L., Satterthwaite, J. R., Hinnant, D. W., & Turner, K. P. (1989). Comprehensive pain center treatment of low back workers' compensation injuries. *Orthopaedic Review, 18,* 1115–1126.

Turk, D. C. (1996). Clinician attitudes about prolonged use of opioids and the issue of patient heterogeneity. *Journal of Pain and Symptom Management, 11,* 218–230.

Turk, D. C. (1997). Transition from acute to chronic pain: Role of demographic and psychosocial factors. In T. S. Jensen, J. A. Turner, & Z. Weisenberg-Halling (Eds.), *Proceedings of the 8th World Congress on Pain: Progress in pain research and management* (pp. 185–213). Seattle: IASP Press.

Turk, D. C., Brody, M. C., & Okifuji, A. (1994). Physicians' attitudes and practices regarding the long-term prescribing of opioids for non-cancer pain. *Pain, 59,* 201–208.

Turk, D. C., Meichenbaum, D., & Genest, M. (1983). *Pain and behavioral medicine: A cognitive-behavioral approach.* New York: Guilford.

Turk, D. C., & Okifuji, A. (1994). Detecting depression in chronic pain patients: Adequacy of self-reports. *Behaviour Research and Therapy, 32,* 9–16.

Turk, D. C., Okifuji, A., Sinclair, J. C., & Starz, T. W. (in press). Interdisciplinary treatment for fibromyalgia: Clinical and statistical significance. *Arthritis Care & Research.*

Turk, D. C., Rudy, T. E., & Stieg, R. L. (1988). The disability determination dilemma: Toward a multiaxial solution. *Pain, 34,* 217–229.

Turk, D. C., & Stacey, B. R. (1997). Multidisciplinary pain centers in the treatment of chronic pain. In J. W. Frymoyer, T. B. Ducker, N. M. Hadler, J. P. Kostuik, J. N. Weinstein, & T. S. Whitecloud, III (Eds.), *The adult spine: Principles and practice* (2nd ed., pp. 253–274). New York: Raven.

Versloot, J. M., Rozenman, A., van Son, A. M., & van Akkerveeken, P. F. (1992). The cost-effectiveness of a back school program in industry: A longitudinal controlled field study. *Spine, 17,* 22–27.

Wiesel, S. W., Feffer, H. L., & Rothman, R. H. (1984). Industrial low-back pain: A prospective evaluation of a standardized diagnostic and treatment protocol. *Spine, 9,* 199–206.

Wilkinson, G. A. (1983). The role of improper surgery in the etiology of failed back syndrome. In H. A. Wilkinson (Ed.), *The failed back syndrome* (pp. 15–16). Philadelphia: Lippincott.

Chapter 6

Motivation and Adherence in the Management of Chronic Pain

Robert D. Kerns
VA Connecticut Healthcare System and Yale University

Laura A. Bayer
Yale University

James C. Findley
Yale University

The past 20 years have seen significant advances in the development of effective medical, psychological, rehabilitative, and multimodal approaches to the management of chronic pain (cf. Cohen & Campbell, 1996). In the psychological domain alone, well-controlled studies have demonstrated the effectiveness of a broad array of treatment approaches (Gatchel & Turk, 1996). Despite a growing body of research that encourages optimism in the ability to provide relief for individuals suffering from chronic pain and associated disability and distress, it is also clear that there are many individuals who fail to be successfully engaged in these treatments, or who relapse (Turk & Rudy, 1991). Jensen (1996), in particular, has noted that there are many possible explanations for these shortcomings. Motivation to engage in treatment and adherence to treatment recommendations and prescriptions are factors that have been particularly highlighted in discussions of this issue (Turk, Meichenbaum, & Genest, 1983).

Implicit in the belief that any treatment is effective is an assumption that the individuals receiving the treatment are motivated to engage in the treatment and will follow the specific recommendations of the health care provider. However, available data regarding patients' adherence to treatment prescriptions indicate that up to 80% of patients may be nonadherent at some point during their treatment (Dunbar-Jacob, Burke, & Puczynksi, 1995). Problems with adherence have been particularly noted for prescriptions for medication, exercise, smoking cessation, and diet for patients with a wide range of chronic medical conditions such as diabetes, hypertension, asthma, and rheumatoid arthritis. Frequently, patients are unable to reach therapeutic levels, whether with pharmacological or psychological treatments, because of difficulties with adherence (Turk & Rudy, 1991). With this in mind, judgments by health care providers about the efficacy of treatment, the contributions of a specific treatment to outcomes, prescriptive decisions, and patients' satisfaction with treatment may all be suspect. Further, it may be reasonable to hold in reserve some conclusions about the efficacy of treatments supported by even the most rigorous outcome studies when they fail to assess and consider adherence rates.

In this chapter we have employed the term *adherence* to emphasize a collaborative and active process involving both the health care provider and the patient. This is in contrast to the term *compliance,* which often connotes physician control and a passive role for the patient (Turk & Rudy, 1991). Adherence has been further defined as following recommendations closely as the health care professional intended (DiMatteo & Tavanta, 1979). Emphasis is on the degree of behavioral approximation to some ideal rather than on an absolute. It considers the intent of the health care provider rather than what is either spoken by the provider or understood by the patient. Implicit in this definition is something about the complexity and range of issues that influence adherence, as well as some of the challenges posed in efforts to promote adherence.

Motivation is conceptualized in this chapter as a cognitive and affective aspect of adherence defined as "the probability that a person will enter into, continue, and adhere to a specific change strategy" (Miller & Rollnick, 1991, p. 19). Thus, in discussing adherence we refer to motivation not as a separate entity, but rather as an inherent aspect to the initiation, adoption, and long-term maintenance of health behaviors.

Optimal management of most chronic illnesses typically requires a complex array of behavioral responsibilities, including lifestyle changes, use of medication, monitoring of symptoms and/or signs of the illness, among others. Often these behaviors interact with one another and involve judgments on the part of the patient (e.g., the diabetic patient's need to monitor blood glucose and make diet and medication adjustments). Adherence to such complex behavioral regimens is likely to be influenced by an array of variables. In this chapter these factors are discussed under the headings of patient factors (e.g., knowledge, beliefs, values), practitioner and treatment factors (e.g., patient education, complexity and intensity of the prescription), and systems and patient–practitioner interaction factors (e.g., family/cultural factors, relationships with third-party payers, practitioner–patient communication).

Adherence issues related to chronic pain management appear to be similarly complex and multidimensional. Practice guidelines for pain management increasingly emphasize the multidimensional, multidisciplinary, and multimodal nature of treatment (Cohen & Campbell, 1996). Although many practitioners continue to administer treatments that place the chronic pain patient in a relatively passive role (e.g., anesthesiological procedures, physical therapy procedures other than exercise), the standard of care is shifting toward interventions emphasizing a proactive and self-management approach (Gatchel & Turk, 1996). Given these trends, issues of motivation and adherence are likely to be particularly important in evaluation of the efficacy of these treatments and determination of their applicability to the diverse population of individuals suffering from pain. Ultimately, development of new methods to promote motivation and adherence to these treatments, refinement of existing methods, and systematic application of these methods stand to significantly improve current rates of effectiveness and promote broader applicability.

This chapter begins by describing in more detail the range of adherence issues relevant to chronic pain treatment. Factors hypothesized to influence motivation and adherence and empirical evidence supporting their role are then discussed. The cognitive-behavioral perspective on chronic pain is offered as an important framework for considering these issues. The transtheoretical model of behavior change is also discussed, as well as the relevance of one particular component of this model, stages of change, to the field of chronic pain management. A method for evaluating a patient's readiness to adopt a self-management approach to their chronic pain condition is offered and the potential utility of this method is discussed. Clinical and research implications of the stages of change model for promoting motivation and adherence conclude the chapter.

MOTIVATION AND ADHERENCE ISSUES ACROSS STAGES OF PAIN TREATMENT

Engagement in Treatment

Lack of adherence is not a singular problem behavior, but rather encompasses a spectrum of therapeutic issues across the course of chronic pain treatment. Successful initiation and engagement in treatment are crucial, particularly in light of reports that initial level of treatment adherence is the *best predictor* of long-term adherence (up to 2 years) to medical regimens (Berndt, Maier, & Schutz, 1993; Sherbourne, Hays, Ordway, DiMatteo, & Kravitz, 1992). Initially, engagement of a chronic pain patient in a non-pharmacological protocol may be difficult. Successful engagement is predicated on acceptance of a self-management approach, which is frequently at odds with patients' explanatory models of chronic pain. Typically, patients frame their pain in a traditional dualistic model suggesting *either* a pathophysiological *or* a psychological etiology (Schulz & Masek, 1996). As a result, although many pain complaints are not linked to specific, measurable biological insults, patients generally search for a biomedical explanation and treatment of pain (Turk, 1996). Continued pursuit of a medical solution to their pain problem is generally inconsistent with a self-management approach. Adoption of psychologically based interventions and self-management techniques may threaten patients, implying that they are weak, histrionic, or malingering, or that others (including health care providers) do not believe their pain is "real" (Schulz & Masek, 1996). To foster engagement, health care providers need to be clear when educating patients that pain is complex and multifaceted. Within this perspective, the potential benefit of psychological interventions can be emphasized regardless of the etiology of their pain complaints.

Another barrier to engagement concerns disability identity and/or secondary gain issues. Patients who have adopted a disability identity, particularly those seeking compensation through litigation, may be ambivalent regarding treatment (DeGood & Dane, 1996). If these issues are not recognized and addressed openly by the health care provider, they may undermine engagement in treatment (Jensen, 1996).

Additionally, actual or perceived costs to the patient for treatment (e.g., patient expenses incurred because of limitations on payment for "mental health" interventions imposed by third-party payers) may further discourage engagement in psychological treatments. Finally, psychological treatments most often require frequent visits to the treatment site. Actual or perceived mobility limitations, coordination of travel arrangements with others, transportation costs, and other associated factors may also interfere with engagement and reliable participation in treatment (Cohen & Campbell, 1996).

Adoption of Pain Management Techniques

During the course of treatment, practitioner expectations that patients practice skills such as relaxation exercises or employ specific techniques such as self-monitoring may not be met (Turk & Rudy, 1991). It is not surprising that adherence may be difficult given the complex, multimodal approach of chronic pain treatment requiring several behavioral adaptations. As regimens become more complex, they demand more effort and planning. Turk and Rudy suggested that patients may conclude that certain treatment elements may not yield sufficient clinical improvement to warrant the effort required, particularly when daily practice is prescribed. The sporadic nature of pain complaints also may lead to poor adherence. In the absence of symptoms, patients assume that self-management techniques are no longer needed. Conversely, if they experience pain while experimenting with behavioral techniques, such as exercise or increased activity, they may assume that the intervention is ineffective and/or detrimental. Finally, cognitive-behavioral techniques do not typically yield immediate intrinsic reinforcement, which can lead to both nonadherence and premature termination from treatment in the absence of additional sources of reinforcement (Turk & Rudy, 1991).

Maintenance Issues

Ultimately, treatment needs to address issues of maintenance and continued use of pain management techniques. Long-term adherence rates of rheumatoid arthritis patients to pain management techniques falls to 50%, underscoring the difficulty of maintaining versus initiating adaptive self-management techniques (Daltroy & Liang, 1993). The nature of chronic pain calls for a permanent lifestyle adoption of cognitive coping skills and behaviors that continues beyond a brief, intensive period of therapeutic intervention. However, maintaining self-management behaviors, particularly in the absence of pain, is more difficult than adoption of new skills (Epstein & Cluss, 1982). Relapse prevention and self-reinforcement are critical in maintaining self-management behaviors and progress. As Turk and Rudy (1991) suggested, generalization of coping skills and wellness behaviors beyond the treatment setting is important in maintaining treatment gains. Relapse prevention efforts need to include patient education about the likelihood that sporadic exacerbations of pain may occur even with utilization of self-management techniques.

FACTORS INFLUENCING MOTIVATION AND ADHERENCE

Patient Barriers

Patients often develop misconceptions about pain management techniques that can interfere with adherence. For example, patients commonly are reluctant to engage in exercise for fear that it will exacerbate pain intensity and/or provoke further injury. Similarly, a study of medication utilization among cancer pain patients reported that patient beliefs and concerns were a significant factor among the 42% of patients who were underutilizing pain medication (Ward et al., 1993).

Self-efficacy and/or beliefs about a treatment's efficacy are also crucial in initiating and maintaining self-management approaches to chronic pain. In one study of a multidisciplinary rehabilitation program, perceived disability and lower expectations of return to work predicted premature termination, whereas objective baseline measures of physical impairment did not differ between chronic pain patients who dropped out or completed treatment (Carosella, Lackner, & Feuerstein, 1994). Lowered self-efficacy and treatment expectations frequently reflect an extended history of treatment failures. Duration of pain and/or disability are also predictors in early termination, as is continued pain severity (Carosella et al., 1994). Thus, the chronicity of pain complaints coupled with prior treatment failures may contribute to learned helplessness. In this way patients are less motivated to try new treatment approaches, particularly self-management techniques requiring a moderate amount of effort (Turk & Rudy, 1991).

Age also appears to be emerging as an important predictor of treatment adherence. Younger patients have been reported to have poorer adherence to medication recommendations (Berndt et al., 1993) and to be more likely to drop out of a chronic pain rehabilitation program (Carosella et al., 1994). In general, studies suggest that younger patients are more likely to have adherence difficulties in the treatment of a wide range of chronic illnesses (Sherbourne et al., 1992). It is unclear at this time what underlies this age effect. It is possible that younger patients are not as immersed in the health care system and do not as readily accept the patient role as older patients who are more likely to have multiple chronic complaints. Thus, further exploration of denial processes and patient identity development among younger patients may be beneficial in enhancing their care. In contrast, the influence of age upon adherence may be a cohort effect. Younger patients may be much less likely to passively accept and follow health care prescriptions in part because of the growing consumerism movement in health care over the past 20 years. In this case, younger patients may benefit from more collaborative relationships with health care providers where the patient's sense of control and responsibility for health maintenance is emphasized.

Treatment Factors

Although poor adherence has historically been attributed to the "bad patient," it is important to acknowledge that characteristics of treatment regimens generally have a greater influence upon adherence than patient personality or coping styles. It is well documented that as treatment regimens become more complex, intense, and long term, adherence is more problematic. It is also important to note that adherence typically varies across treatment elements. Difficulty in achieving one set of behavioral goals does *not* necessarily predict global nonadherence. Identifying primary and secondary intervention goals based, in part, on patient self-efficacy may be particularly important with chronic pain patients, because of the typical history of treatment failures and ensuing learned helplessness. Interventions that proceed in a step-wise fashion that encourage graduated skill attainment may reinforce patient success. Tailoring interventions to specific patient characteristics and needs also may strengthen the therapeutic relationship conveying a sense that the patient is being treated as a unique individual.

Adopting a progressive approach to behavioral interventions not only enhances patient self-efficacy, it also minimizes information overload associated with complex regimens (Meichenbaum & Turk, 1987). Information overload can be a common problem in chronic pain treatment that often involves several concurrent cognitive and behavioral interventions. Health care practitioners need to focus on a few points per visit, categorizing and organizing information to assist patient encoding and retention. About half of orally presented information is typically forgotten, suggesting that written materials are a helpful aid, particularly in treatment protocols enlisting multiple, simultaneous interventions (Cramer & Spilker, 1991). However, written materials are not a substitute for one-on-one patient education. Many patients do not read materials and frequently they are too difficult for patients with poor literacy skills (Meichenbaum & Turk, 1987). For a review of patient education techniques please see Meichenbaum and Turk (1987) and Falvo (1994).

Self-reinforcement is a critical aspect of pain management treatment. Incorporation of self-reinforcement training techniques in standard treatment regimens may be expected to contribute to enhanced adherence. A study of burn patients found that including patient-identified goals and self-reinforcement training significantly enhanced patients' adherence to physical therapy (Hegel, Ayllon, VanderPlate, & Spiro-Hawkins, 1986). In this study, self-reinforcing patients were more likely to increase intensity of physical rehabilitation exercises resulting in increased range of motion and flexibility. As discussed, the nature of chronic pain interventions does not generally lead to immediate reinforcement, and recurrences of acute pain episodes may lead patients to believe that a treatment element is not efficacious despite long-term benefit. Therefore, self-reinforcement is crucial for successful long-term self-management of chronic pain complaints (Turk & Rudy, 1991).

The Provider–Patient Relationship

One of the most consistent predictors of adherence is satisfaction and/or perceived support from health care providers (Fontana, Kerns, Rosenberg, Marcus, & Colonese, 1986; Nagy & Wolfe, 1984; Sherbourne et al., 1992). The unique challenge in chronic pain treatment is to recognize and address the tension and discordance between patient and provider expectations. As discussed earlier, chronic pain patients may be particularly passive or reluctant to invest energy in proactive treatments because of the episodic nature of pain complaints and the history of treatment failures. In contrast, health care providers recognize that improvement rests largely on patients maintaining behavioral and cognitive changes. Thus, it becomes particularly important for practitioners to recognize verbal and nonverbal signs of patient disagreement and disengagement, such as frequent interruption to ask questions, lack of eye contact, and body language (Lepper, Martin, & DiMatteo, 1995).

Although tensions in the patient–provider relationship need to be negotiated, it is also important to recognize that a strong rapport can also pose hidden obstacles. For example, patients may believe that "good" patients do not report pain or that requests for pain treatment may actually result in a decrease in overall treatment efforts (Ward et al., 1993). These beliefs regarding treatment elements are often not discussed unless the health care provider encourages an open dialogue with their patients.

Whereas there is consistent evidence that the patient–provider relationship is a potent avenue for adherence enhancement, the full potential of the relationship is frequently not utilized. One study of juvenile rheumatoid arthritis found that although health care providers discussed how often to employ prescribed activities, they rarely employed other adherence-promoting strategies including addressing patient beliefs, treatment barriers, or reinforcement strategies (Thompson, Dahlquist, Koenning, & Bartholomew, 1995). Nonetheless, health care providers have a powerful effect in communicating the importance of behavioral interventions. One study of back pain patients found that written materials with physician-related credibility cues was associated with 92% adherence rates to exercise protocols compared to 50% adherence rates among control patients (Jackson, 1994).

Jackson (1994) suggested that provider cues enhance adherence by normalizing difficulties in adopting and maintaining behavioral changes. In normalizing adherence difficulties, health care providers open it up as a legitimate issue for discussion and problem solving. Instead of nonadherence being indicative of a "bad" patient, it becomes reframed as a frequent "side effect" of behavioral regimens that can be resolved in much the same manner as side effects to pharmacological interventions. In some cases, the issue is normalized as a temporary side effect that tends to improve (i.e., some discomfort when initiating an exercise regimen), and in others problem solving takes place (i.e., difficulty in scheduling or forgetfulness).

System Factors

Multiple social systems have been identified and investigated for their roles in the development and perpetuation of pain and disability, and it reasonable to hypothesize that these same factors may influence motivation to engage in treatment or adherence to treatment recommendations. The operant conditioning model of chronic pain (Fordyce, 1976) provides a broad framework in which to consider these factors. According to this model, pain and disability may be maintained by powerful social contingencies. These contingencies may include solicitous responding to pain complaints and pain behaviors (e.g., lying down, nonverbal expressions of pain, taking pain medication) by family members and friends, attention and aggressive treatment on the part of physicians, and financial compensation and disability determinations. Continued pain complaints during treatment frequently reflect the lack of immediate reinforcement from self-management techniques, but they may also sabotage treatment by eliciting counterproductive responses, such as undue solicitousness from family members and physicians (Turk & Rudy, 1991). An increasingly large body of empirical evidence supports this model, particularly related to data that document reliable relationships between measures of pain and disability and solicitous responding by significant others, particularly spouses (e.g., Kerns et al., 1991; Romano et al., 1991, 1996; Turk, Kerns, & Rosenberg, 1992). Support also comes from studies demonstrating the efficacy of pain treatment and rehabilitation approaches that specifically target these social relationships.

These observations encourage additional efforts that may promote engagement and active participation in self-management therapies. Direct involvement of physicians in promoting the relevance of self-management, as an alternative to more aggressive medical interventions, is one avenue for improvement. In this context, physician endorsement of the importance and safety of specific exercise or other treatment approaches may encourage engagement and adherence to these approaches. Evidence of active communication among providers, especially involving the physician, over the course of active treatment may similarly enhance patient adherence. Education of family members and/or significant others about the treatment components is also important to treatment success. Specific efforts to promote significant other reinforcement of patients' efforts at learning and practicing self-management skills and/or engagement in rehabilitation efforts is indicated by this model.

It is apparent to many in the field that the availability of financial compensation for pain and disability is a "double-edged sword." In contrast to the obvious benefit to impaired and disabled individuals of disability determinations and financial compensation, it is reasonable to assume that these powerful contingencies may serve to promote unnecessary disability in some instances (Weintraub, 1992). Active participation of pain specialists in social policy discussions regarding disability determinations and compensation models is strongly encouraged.

THE COGNITIVE-BEHAVIORAL PERSPECTIVE

The cognitive-behavioral perspective as advanced by Turk (Turk et al., 1983) and his colleagues, among others, incorporates specific attention to many of the factors just reviewed in an effort to promote patients' adoption of a self-management approach to chronic pain. Informed by cognitive-social learning theory and behavior modification, this perspective emphasizes active collaboration between the provider and patient in assessment, conceptualization of problem domains, treatment planning, and treatment delivery. Central to the model is the notion that patients' idiosyncratic beliefs, attitudes, and other cognitive aspects determine their experience of pain and disability. Further, it is hypothesized that their beliefs about their pain, particularly those related to responsibility for pain and pain management, may determine their interest and pursuit of different treatment approaches, expectations about the efficacy of treatment, and adherence to treatment prescriptions.

Models of treatment based on the cognitive-behavioral perspective specifically encourage targeting patients' beliefs about pain and pain management from the point of initial contact in order to promote successful engagement in treatment through establishment of a strong therapuetic relationship (Turk et al., 1983). Active listening and accurate reflection of patients' descriptions of their experience of pain and related beliefs serves as the foundation for development of the therapeutic relationship. Specific efforts to demonstrate empathy and validation of the patients' experience and beliefs enhance this process. A process of increasingly selective reflection and reinforcement of statements more consistent with a self-management approach, essentially a process of behavioral shaping, is subsequently systematically introduced. In other words, only after the basis for a therapeutic relationship is secured, and patients believe that their experiences and beliefs about pain and pain management have been heard and validated are efforts to promote change initiated. Even then, the therapist should proceed carefully and systematically.

A variety of additional cognitive and behavioral assessment (Turk & Melzack, 1992) and treatment strategies (Bradley, 1996) have been articulated that are designed to enhance this process of engagement and active participation in treatment. These include such strategies as self-monitoring and diary methods, cognitive restructuring and positive reframing of patients' experiences, contingency management, the use of homework assignments, and patient education strategies including provision of written materials and emphasizing the personal relevance of the information.

TRANSTHEORETICAL MODEL OF BEHAVIOR CHANGE

Prochaska and DiClemente (Prochaska, 1979; Prochaska & DiClemente, 1984) have elaborated a transtheoretical model of behavior change that incorporates the notion that behavior modification involves two interrelated dimensions. The first dimension is labeled *stages of change* and is based on the observation that individuals vary to the extent that they are "prepared" or motivated to make changes in a specifically targeted behavior. The second dimension, called *processes of change*, focuses on activities and events that contribute to successful behavior modification. Among developments based on this model is an elaboration of a framework for considering stages of change and the development of reliable strategies for assessing an individual's "stage." Four or five stages have been identified across multiple studies in several areas of health behavior change such as tobacco use, exercise, and diet (Clark, Pera, Goldstein, Thebarge, & Guise, 1996; Marcus, Rossi, Selby, Niaura, & Abrams, 1992; Prochaska, Velicer, DiClemente, & Fava, 1988). These stages are generally labeled: *precontemplation*, referring to individuals who report a low interest in, or consideration of, changing their behavior; *contemplation*, describing individuals who are thinking about behavior change, but appear unlikely to change in the near future; individuals in the *preparation* stage are those who are actively considering attempts to change their behavior and are likely to do so in the next month; individuals who are currently taking *action* to change their behavior; and finally, those individuals who are engaged in *maintenance* of their already changed health behavior. Identification of these groups of individuals has been demonstrated to have value in predicting success in treatment efforts designed to modify behavior as well as maintenance of treatment effects. It has also been demonstrated that stage of change is associated with differing processes of change (e.g., consciousness raising, self-reevaluation, counterconditioning) (Prochaska & DiClemente, 1983).

Integration of concepts based on the cognitive-behavioral perspective on chronic pain and the transtheoretical model of behavior change has led to the speculation that individuals experiencing chronic pain may vary in their readiness to adopt a self-management approach. Further, it has be reasoned that this variable may influence patients' engagement in self-management therapies, their adherence to recommendations for skills acquisition and practice during treatment, and ultimately dropout and relapse rates. It has been hypothesized that individuals who are resistant to self-management approaches are less likely to be successfully engaged in any active psychological treatment program such as cognitive-behavior therapy than patients who are more prepared for such an approach.

Pain Stages of Change Questionnaire

Informed by both the cognitive-behavioral perspective on chronic pain and the transtheoretical model of behavior change, Kerns and colleagues have developed a reliable measure of patients' beliefs about the responsibility for pain management (i.e., physician vs. personal responsibility), especially their readiness to adopt a self-management approach to their chronic pain (Kerns, Rosenberg, Jamison, Caudill, & Haythornthwaite, 1997). The Pain Stages of Change Questionnaire (PSOCQ; Fig. 6.1) is a 30-item self-report measure with four reliable scales that assess stage of readiness as identified by Prochaska and others. Development of the scales proceeded through a sophisticated process of item development and testing, evaluation of reliability of the scales and the factor structure of the entire measure, evaluation of the stability of the scales, and examination

---

This questionnaire is to help us better understand the way you view your pain problem. Each statement describes how you *may* feel about this particular problem. Please indicate the extent to which you tend to agree or disagree with each statement. In each example, please make your choice based on how you feel right now, not how you have felt in the past or how you would like to feel.

Circle the response that best describes how much you agree or disagree with each statement.	Strongly Disagree	Disagree	Undecided or Unsure	Agree	Strongly Agree
1. I have been thinking that the way I cope with my pain could improve.	1	2	3	4	5
2. I am developing new ways to cope with my pain.	1	2	3	4	5
3. I have learned some good ways to keep my pain problem from interfering with my life.	1	2	3	4	5
4. When my pain flares up, I find myself automatically using coping strategies that have worked in the past, such as a relaxation exercise or mental distraction technique.	1	2	3	4	5
5. I am using some strategies that help me better deal with my pain problem on a day to day basis.	1	2	3	4	5
6. I have started to come up with strategies to help myself control my pain.	1	2	3	4	5
7. I have recently realized that there is no medical cure for my pain condition, so I want to learn some ways to cope with it.	1	2	3	4	5
8. Even if my pain doesn't go away, I am ready to start changing how I deal with it.	1	2	3	4	5
9. I realize now that it's time for me to come up with a better plan to cope with my pain problem.	1	2	3	4	5
10. I use what I have learned to help keep my pain under control.	1	2	3	4	5
11. I have tried everything that people have recommended to manage my pain and nothing helps.	1	2	3	4	5
12. My pain is a medical problem and I should be dealing with physicians about it.	1	2	3	4	5

FIG. 6.1.   *(Continued)*

Circle the response that best describes how much you agree or disagree with each statement.	Strongly Disagree	Disagree	Undecided or Unsure	Agree	Strongly Agree
13. I am currently using some suggestions people have made about how to live with my pain problem.	1	2	3	4	5
14. I am beginning to wonder if I need to get some help to develop skills for dealing with my pain.	1	2	3	4	5
15. I have recently figured out that it's up to me to deal better with my pain.	1	2	3	4	5
16. Everybody I speak with tells me that I have to learn to live with my pain, but I don't see why I should have to.	1	2	3	4	5
17. I have incorporated strategies for dealing with my pain into my everyday life.	1	2	3	4	5
18. I have made a lot of progress in coping with my pain.	1	2	3	4	5
19. I have recently come to the conclusion that it's time for me to change how I cope with my pain.	1	2	3	4	5
20. I'm getting help learning some strategies for coping better with my pain.	1	2	3	4	5
21. I'm starting to wonder whether it's up to me to manage my pain rather than relying on physicians.	1	2	3	4	5
22. I still think despite what doctors tell me, there must be some surgical procedure or medication that would get rid of my pain.	1	2	3	4	5
23. I have been thinking that doctors can only help so much in managing my pain and that the rest is up to me.	1	2	3	4	5
24. The best thing I can do is find a doctor who can figure out how to get rid of my pain once and for all.	1	2	3	4	5
25. Why can't someone just do something to take away my pain?	1	2	3	4	5
26. I am learning to help myself control my pain without doctors.	1	2	3	4	5
27. I am testing out some coping skills to manage my pain better.	1	2	3	4	5
28. I have been wondering if there is something I could do to manage my pain better.	1	2	3	4	5
29. All of this talk about how to cope better is a waste of my time.	1	2	3	4	5
30. I am learning ways to control my pain other than with medications or surgery.	1	2	3	4	5

FIG. 6.1. The Pain Stages of Change Questionnaire. Precontemplation: Sum(11,12,16,22,24,25,29) / 7; Contemplation / Preparation: Sum(1,7,8, 9,14,15,19,21,23,28) / 10; Action: Sum(2,6,20,26,27,30) / 6; Maintenance: Sum(3,4,5,10,13,17,18) / 7. To account for sporadic missing data, sums should be divided by the number of nonmissing items. Any scale with more than 25% of its items missing should be considered missing.

of their criterion-related and discriminant validity. Results of these analyses support the application of the PSOCQ in future research and its potential applicability in clinical settings.

Each of the four scales of the PSOCQ appears to measure discrete sets of beliefs consistent with the stages of change model with specific relevance to the management of chronic pain. *Precontemplation* refers to beliefs that pain is a medical problem, that it is the responsibility of physicians to provide pain relief, and that personal efforts to manage pain are largely irrelevant and ineffective. *Contemplation* assesses patients' beliefs that there may be limits to the effectiveness of medical approaches to pain management and that it may be useful to assume some degree of personal responsibility for pain management. *Action* refers to an acceptance of the importance of learning self-management approaches and active participation in pain management skills acquisition and practice. *Maintenance* refers to attitudes and beliefs consistent with personal responsibility for pain management, a high degree of self-efficacy with regard to successful self-management, and continued learning and use of self-management skills.

Despite the strong psychometric basis of the PSOCQ reported by Kerns and his colleagues (Kerns, Rosenberg, Jamison et al., 1997) the clinical value of the measure will likely hinge on the measure's predictive validity with regard to psychological treatment. For example, key questions remain about the ability of the measure to predict engagement and participation in self-management therapies. Results of ongoing clinical research addressing this issue have just begun to be reported.

In one study (Kerns & Rosenberg, 1997), 88 chronic pain patients who initially agreed to participate in cognitive-behavioral or operant-behavioral treatment were administered the PSOCQ prior to treatment. Of these individuals, the 37 patients who dropped out of treatment prematurely reported significantly higher scores on the Precontemplation scale, and significantly lower Contemplation scores prior to treatment than those patients who completed treatment. Interestingly, among those patients completing treatment, pretreatment PSOCQ scale scores did not predict outcome. For example, patients who were high on the Precontemplation scale prior to treatment, that is—"not ready to change"—but who were apparently successfully engaged in treatment, were no less likely to improve over the course of treatment than those who were initially more "ready to change."

Change in PSOCQ scores as a function of treatment was also examined for 37 patients who completed posttreatment evaluations. Analyses revealed a significant decline in Contemplation scores and significant increases in both Action and Maintenance scores at the end of treatment. Furthermore, change scores on the PSOCQ scales were significantly correlated with change scores on several of the measures of pain severity, disability, and depressive symptom severity (Kerns & Rosenberg, 1997).

In a second recent study, five reliable clusters or subgroups of chronic pain patients were identified based on their "profile" of scores on the four PSOCQ scales (Kerns, Rosenberg, Haythornthwaite, Jamison, & Caudill, 1997). These clusters were labeled *Precontemplators, Contemplators, Ambivalent, Strivers,* and *Maintainers* based on descriptions offered by Prochaska and DiClemente informed by analyses of data from other groups of patients (e.g., participants in alcohol treatment; DiClemente & Hughes, 1990). Examination of the predictive validity of these subgroups using methods similar to that described earlier revealed almost identical results (Kerns, 1997). For example, patients identified as Strivers were significantly more likely to complete a 10-week cognitive-behavioral treatment program than patients in the Precontemplation and Ambivalent groups.

Taken together, results of these studies provide preliminary support for the predictive validity of the PSOCQ. Individuals endorsing items consistent with a relative lack of interest in considering a self-management approach to their pain problem and a continued reliance on the medical profession appear to be more likely to drop out of treatment emphasizing a self-management approach. Results further suggest that the PSOCQ scales may be sensitive to change in beliefs about the relevance of self-management and interest in learning improved pain-coping skills. The significant relationships between change in beliefs about self-management and several measures of the experience of chronic pain (i.e., pain severity, disability, and depression) provided support for the cognitive-behavioral perspective on chronic pain management that hypothesizes that changes in beliefs about the relevance or benefits of self-management and associated self-efficacy beliefs may underlie improvements in pain management.

Clinical Implications of the Pain Stages of Change Model

As just noted, the pain stages of change model is entirely consistent with the cognitive-behavioral perspective on chronic pain and a process of cognitive-behavioral treatment. According to Turk (Turk et al., 1983), therapy proceeds through three interrelated phases. The first phase emphasizes "reconceptualization" of pain as subject to personal control and manageable. Subsequent phases focus on "skills acquisition" and "skills practice" that promote behavior change and reinforce developing perceptions of self-control and self-efficacy. Availability of the PSOCQ may prove to be useful to clinicians in identifying patients' current stage in this therapeutic process. This information may contribute to the clinician's overall conceptualization of the patient and encourage the clinician to be more "prescriptive" in planning treatment.

Further drawing on the transtheoretical model of behavior change (Prochaska & DiClemente, 1983), application of the pain stages of change model suggests that differing processes of change (i.e., therapeutic techniques) may be more appropriately applied or "matched" to patients depending on their degree of readiness or stage. For example, treatment of individuals who are not seriously contemplating a self-management approach should initially involve an approach described as "consciousness raising." Cognitive restructuring strategies described by Turk and others might be hypothesized to be an effective supplement to such approaches for individuals who acknowledge a willingness to contemplate the relevance of self-management. Alternatively, behavioral strategies (e.g., relaxation skills, exercise) that presume a commitment to skill acquisition and practice may be appropriate only for those individuals who are already reporting acceptance of a personal responsibility for pain management and an active interest in learning such skills. Such a prescriptive approach or tailoring of treatment options to match patients' stage of readiness for change appears to hold promise as a method for improving the engagement of patients, enhancing adherence to skill acquisition and practice recommendations and expectations, and ultimately, improve outcomes.

Education about the pain stages of change model and explicit feedback to patients about their current stage may be expected to further enhance patients' readiness for, and commitment to, self-management treatment, especially in the early phase of treatment. Feedback about their apparent beliefs about self-management, for example, may promote discussion and consideration of a self-management approach. Incorporation of motivational interviewing techniques as described by Miller and Rollnick (1991) that emphasize more explicit consideration of the pros and cons of continuing to pursue medical interventions, on the one hand, or self-management training, on the other, may additionally be helpful. These strategies may be particularly enhanced through physician messages that encourage self-management. Goldstein and his colleagues have recently outlined a "patient-centered" approach to health risk behavior change that integrates aspects of the stages of change model, motivational interviewing methods, and guidelines for physician advice (Goldstein, Ruggiero, & Guise, 1994). Jensen (1996) has outlined a similar clinical approach designed to promote motivation for psychological treatment for chronic pain.

Finally, brief assessment of pain stages of change during the course of treatment may assist the clinician in treatment planning (e.g., determining when and to what extent to begin explicit coping-skills training). This information may similarly be useful in specifying homework (e.g., home practice of relaxation) and other intersession goals. Explicit feedback to patients, especially when change is evident, may further reinforce changing beliefs and encourage motivation and adherence.

CLINICAL EXAMPLES

Following are excerpts from four pain treatment sessions. Each vignette represents one of the PSOCQ scales with explicit statements by both patient and therapist to demonstrate typical cognitive-behavioral interactions at a particular level of readiness to change.

Precontemplation

Patient: I don't know why they sent me to a psychologist. I'm not crazy.

Therapist: Nobody thinks you are crazy. Your pain is real. I specialize in the problems encountered by people who have medical problems and things that people can do to improve the management of their problems. Problems like your back pain.

Patient: Well, if you're not a physician, I don't see what you can do about my pain.

Therapist: Would you agree that we can examine your situation? Not change anything at this point, but to maybe work with me to get a fresh perspective on things.

Patient: That would be fine, but I've been to five doctors and had three operations. The medicine they give me only helps for a little while, and they won't even give me a new prescription for that. They say they can't do anything more for me. I can't do anything I used to.

Therapist: So medical interventions alone haven't provided you the relief you want and pain is interfering in your life a lot. Are there things you can do to manage you pain?

Patient: I want a doctor to make this pain go away so things are like they were before.

Therapist: It sounds like you don't think you can do anything to influence your pain right now. To make things like they were before? Can you give me an example of something that you don't do because of pain?

Patient: I can't work in my shop anymore. If I work for more than 15 minutes at a time, I'm laid up for 3 days. I've always started working on something and kept after it until I finished.

Therapist: What would happen if you only worked for 10 minutes at a time, then took a break?

Patient: That would be ridiculous. I'd never get anything done.

Therapist: But you don't get anything done if you're laid up for 3 days. Just suppose you did that, worked for 10 minutes then stopped. Would that make your back hurt more?

Patient: It would probably be okay.

Therapist: See, you already know ways to do things without aggravating your back. We know that there are many, many things that can influence pain. Would you be willing to work with me, your physicians, and other people like physical therapists to see if we can find some things that you can do yourself to help manage your back pain?

Patient: Yeah, sure. I'm still not sure what this is going to do for my back, but I'll do that.

Contemplation

Patient: Well, I talked to another specialist. That doctor won't operate on me or give me any medicine to help me.

Therapist: You've told me about all the physicians you've seen, the procedures performed, the medications. Is it possible that they have done all they can?

Patient: I can't believe that. That would mean I have to live with this pain and I can't do that. It's ruining my life. My wife is tired of me being grouchy all the time. I can't do anything around the house, I can't play with the kids, I'm just worthless. I get all tense and that just makes it worse. My family is the most important thing in the world to me. I just don't know what I can do, but something has got to be done.

Therapist: The interference in your life has become intolerable and you'd like that to change. Have you given any thought to the idea that there may be things that you can do, in addition to what your doctor is doing, to help manage your pain better?

Patient: Oh, doc, I try to ignore it, but it just takes control and there's nothing I can do.

Therapist: Wait a minute, you said that there are times when you can ignore it. Right? You say you're able to ignore it at those times. How do you do that?

Patient: I don't follow you.

Therapist: It's very hard to just ignore something that is so obviously there. Do you do something else apart from just trying not to think about the pain?

Patient: Well, you know, I try to think of something else or do something like read.

Therapist: So there's another example of things you do to deal with the pain better. See, learning to live with chronic pain doesn't mean white-knuckling your way through it. As you've just told me, there are specific things you *do* to live with something. There's probably no single thing you can do, but If we work together, we can systematically use things you're already doing in combination with some new things that will help make your life better. What do you think about that?

Patient: I would rather have the pain go away.

Therapist: Sure you would. That's understandable. But what would it mean if the doctors had done all they could and you still want your life to be better, especially with your family?

Patient: I guess I'm going to have to try to do something about it myself. I'm not sure how this is going to work, but maybe I should try something else.

Action

Therapist: Okay. You're feeling like pain is keeping you from doing things you want to do and it's interfering in your life a great deal. What are you thinking might help at this point?

Patient: Nobody seems to be able to do anything more for me. I have to try to do things to help the pain, stop feeling so miserable all the time, and try to get my life back. If the things you're talking about have helped other people, I'll give you chance.

Therapist: Give me a chance?

Patient: I mean I want to work with you to try to find things to make it better. I want to see how I can take the bull by the horns and help manage pain myself.

Therapist: Good. Let's decide what you want to accomplish as a result of working on this together. You don't have to accomplish all that we set out to do in the first week. In fact, that would be impossible. Let's talk about some small things you could do to get started.

Patient: I'd like to be able to throw the football with my son. That would be a great thing.

Therapist: You don't have to reach that goal this week. What would be something that you need to do to prepare to reach that goal? Be patient. You've been inactive for a long time and you'll need to work up to that goal.

Patient: Alright, let's see. I could walk over to the park where we used to throw the football.

Therapist: Can you walk that far now without making your back worse?

Patient: No. But I could probably walk to the end of our block toward the park without making it worse.

Therapist: Perfect. You get the idea. How often could you do this? Twice daily? Three times? And what about that walk would you find enjoyable?

Patient: Yeah. I could probably do it at least twice. I'd like it if my son could go with me.

Therapist: Could he?

Patient: Sure he could.

Therapist: Great. That gives us a good place to start. Now I'd like to show you something called progressive muscle relaxation that many people find helpful in coping with pain.

Patient: Okay. I want to start doing anything.

Maintenance

Therapist: How are you dealing with your pain at this point?

Patient: I still hurt a lot sometimes, but it seems like I have a life again.
Therapist: How so?
Patient: I'm doing things again. I still can't do things for very long. Like a few tosses of the football, no more than 10 yards mind you, and that's it for me. But it's better than not doing anything. Besides, it feels good just to go to the park with my son. I have to watch it though.
Therapist: Watch it?
Patient: Yeah, sometimes I'll tell myself I don't really need to go to the park, or sometimes just the opposite, I'm going to throw the football for a long time. If I do either, I'll make my back worse.
Therapist: Do you watch for muscle tension, too?
Patient: I really try to watch that. There are times when I feel my back tensing up and I have to concentrate on relaxing. I keep telling myself not to let the tension build up, because that will make my back worse. It's getting to be more automatic.
Therapist: Do you think things are better with your wife?
Patient: That part is really better. Like when we go to the movies, we sit in back on the aisle so I can get up and walk to the lobby every now and then. I hate missing parts of the movie, but it's what I need to do to go to the movies at all.
Therapist: So you can't do things exactly the way you used to, but you can do things that are important to you.
Patient: Right. And when I try to talk myself out of doing things, I start listing reasons why I should do things. Otherwise, I know I'm prone to just sit around and think about the pain, and that makes it worse.
Therapist: That's great. These are all things you need to do to maintain the great progress you've made. What do you think you'll do in the future during episodes when the pain is worse?
Patient: I'm going to try to pay attention to the situation. I have to look at what I might have done to cause a flare-up and figure out a different way to approach it in the future. I'm sure I'm going to run into new problems that we haven't worked on. I just have to keep looking for better ways to do things, and not just be miserable while I hope for something to happen. I have to do it.

SUMMARY AND CONCLUSIONS

Many individuals experiencing chronic pain continue to pursue solely medical solutions to their condition despite long histories of treatment failure. Yet many of these same individuals may achieve clinical improvements in their experience of pain, disability, and suffering through psychological interventions that promote self-management. Spurred by these observation, attention has turned to the problem of successfully engaging these individuals and promoting their active participation in self-management treatments. Informed by theory, clinical observation, and empirical research in other areas of medical and psychological treatment, as well as by an evolving literature specifically related to chronic pain management, this chapter has proposed an integrative model for the assessment of patients' readiness to adopt a self-management approach. Furthermore, suggestions were made for refinement to the therapeutic process designed to promote motivation, adherence, and outcomes.

The literature on adherence and chronic pain suggests that enhancing specific aspects of chronic pain treatment and provider rapport may significantly enhance adherence. Particular attention needs to be paid to engagement to treatment, as adherence in the initial phases of treatment predicts long-term adherence and maintenance of progress. Tailoring treatment to patient's readiness for change and developing a strong patient–provider relationship are two potentially significant interventions. Specifically, providers need to open up a dialogue of patient beliefs about pain and treatment options in order to disavow misconceptions and provide opportunities for cognitive restructuring. Difficulties with adherence need to be normalized by providers and addressed as a potential side effect that can be effectively managed. Given the sporadic nature of pain complaints and the delayed benefit of self-management techniques, treatment needs to include self-reinforcement and assist patients in the transition from behavior change to maintenance and relapse prevention.

Clearly additional research is indicated to evaluate the value or utility of these suggestions. Regardless of the ultimate value of the proposed approach, it is hoped that by more explicit acknowledgment of the problems of motivation and adherence to pain management therapies, and by encouraging refinements in treatment specifically designed to address these problems, a larger proportion of individuals experiencing chronic pain may find relief from their suffering.

REFERENCES

Berndt, S., Maier, C., & Schutz, H. (1993). Polymedication and medication compliance in patients with chronic non-malignant pain. *Pain, 52,* 331–339.

Bradley, L. A. (1996). Cognitive-behavioral therapy for chronic pain. In R. J. Gatchel & D. C. Turk (Eds.), *Psychological approaches to pain management: A practitioner's handbook* (pp. 131–147). New York: Guilford.

Carosella, A. M., Lackner, J. M., & Feuerstein, M. (1994). Factors associated with early discharge from a multidisciplinary work rehabilitation program for chronic low back pain. *Pain, 57,* 69–76.

Clark, M. M., Pera, V., Goldstein, M. G., Thebarge, R. R., & Guise, B. A. (1996). Counseling strategies for obese patients. *American Journal of Preventative Medicine, 12,* 266–270.

Cohen, M. J. M., & Campbell, J. N. (1996). *Pain treatment centers at a crossroads: A practical and conceptual reappraisal.* Seattle: IASP Press.

Cramer, J. A., & Spilker, B. (1991). *Patient compliance in medical practice and clinical trials.* New York: Raven.

Daltroy, L. H., & Liang, M. H. (1993). Arthritis education: Opportunities and state of the art. *Health Education Quarterly, 20,* 3–16.

DeGood, D. E., & Dane, J. R. (1996). The psychologist as a pain consultant in outpatient, inpatient and workplace settings. In R. J. Gatchel & D. C. Turk (Eds.), *Psychological approaches to pain management* (pp. 403–437). New York: Guilford.

DiClemente, C. C., & Hughes, S. O. (1990). Stages of change profiles in outpatient alcoholism treatment. *Journal of Substance Abuse, 2,* 217–235.

DiMatteo, M. R., & Tavanta, A. (1979). Nonverbal communication and physician–patient rapport: Toward a science of the art of medicine. *Journal of Social Issues, 10,* 540–547.

Dunbar-Jacob, J., Burke, L. A., & Puczynski, S. (1995). Clinical assessment and management of adherence in medical regimens. In P. M. Nicassio & T. W. Smith (Eds.), *Managing chronic illness: A biopsychosocial perspective* (pp. 315–350). Washington, DC: American Psychological Association.

Epstein, L. H., & Cluss, P. A. (1982). A behavioral medicine perspective on adherence to long-term medical regimens. *Journal of Consulting and Clinical Psychology, 50,* 950–971.

Falvo, D. R. (1994). *Effective patient education: A guide to increased compliance.* Gaithersburg, MD: Aspen Publishers, Inc.

Fontana, A. F., Kerns, R. D., Rosenberg, R. L., Marcus, J. L., & Colonese, K. L. (1986). Exercise training for cardiac patients: Adherence, fitness and benefits. *Journal of Cardiopulmonary Rehabilitation, 6,* 4–15.

Fordyce, W. E. (1976). *Behavioral methods for chronic pain and illness.* St. Louis, MO: Mosby.

Gatchel, R. J., & Turk, D. C. (1996). *Psychological approaches to pain management.* New York: Guilford.

Goldstein, M. G., Ruggiero, L., & Guise, B. A. (1994). Behavioral medicine strategies for medical patients. In A. Stoudemire (Ed.), *Clinical psychiatry for medical students* (2nd ed., pp. 671–693). New York: Lippincott.

Hegel, M. T., Ayllon, T., VanderPlate, C., & Spiro-Hawkins, H. (1986). A behavioral procedure for increasing compliance with self-exercise regimens in severely burn-injured patients. *Behaviour Research and Therapy, 24,* 521–528.

Jackson, L. D. (1994). Maximizing treatment adherence among back-pain patients: An experimental study of the effects of physician-related cues in written medical messages. *Health Communication, 6,* 173–191.

Jensen, M. P. (1996). Enhancing motivation to change in pain treatment. In R. J. Gatchel & D. C. Turk (Eds.), *Psychological approaches to pain management* (pp. 78–111). New York: Guilford.

Kerns, R. D. (1997, October). *Can matching chronic pain patients to psychological treatments improve outcomes?* Paper presented at the annual meeting of the American Pain Society, New Orleans.

Kerns, R. D., & Rosenberg, R. (1997, August). *Pain stages of change as predictors of pain treatment outcome.* Paper presented at the annual meeting of the American Psychological Association, Chicago.

Kerns, R. D., Rosenberg, R., Haythornthwaite, J., Jamison, R. N., & Caudill, M. A. (1997, March). *Stage determination using the Pain Stages of Change Questionnaire.* Paper presented at the annual meeting of the Society of Behavioral Medicine, San Francisco.

Kerns, R. D., Rosenberg, R., Jamison, R. N., Caudill, M. A., & Haythornthwaite, J. (1997). Readiness to adopt a self-management approach to chronic pain: The Pain Stages of Change Questionnaire (PSOCQ). *Pain, 72,* 227–234.

Kerns, R. D., Southwick, S., Giller, E. L., Haythornthwaite, J., Jacob, M. C., & Rosenberg, R. (1991). The relationship between reports of pain-relevant social interactions and expressions of pain and affective distress. *Behavior Therapy, 22,* 101–111.

Lepper, H. S., Martin, L. R., & DiMatteo, M. R. (1995). A model of nonverbal exchange in physician–patient expectations for patient involvement. *Journal of Nonverbal Behavior, 19,* 207–222.

Marcus, B. H., Rossi, J. S., Selby, V. C., Niaura, R. S., & Abrams, D. B. (1992). The stages and processes of exercise adoption and maintenance in a worksite sample. *Health Psychology, 11,* 386–395.

Meichenbaum, D., & Turk, D. C. (1987). *Facilitating treating adherence: A practitioner's guidebook.* New York: Plenum.

Miller, W. R., & Rollnick, S. (1991). *Motivational interviewing: Preparing people to change addictive behavior.* New York: Guilford.

Nagy, V. T., & Wolfe, G. R. (1984). Cognitive predictors of compliance in chronic disease patients. *Medical Care, 22,* 912–921.

Prochaska, J. O. (1979). *Systems of psychotherapy: A transtheoretical analysis.* Homewood, IL: Dorsey.

Prochaska, J. O., & DiClemente, C. C. (1983). Stages and processes of self-change of smoking: Toward an integrative model of change. *Journal of Consulting and Clinical Psychology, 51,* 390–395.

Prochaska, J. O., & DiClemente, C. C. (1984). *The transtheoretical approach: Crossing traditional boundaries of change.* Homewood, IL: Dow Jones/Irwin.

Prochaska, J. O., Velicer, W., DiClemente, C. C., & Fava, J. (1988). Measuring processes of change: Applications to cessation of smoking. *Journal of Consulting and Clinical Psychology, 56,* 520–528.

Romano, J. M., Turner, J. A., Friedman, L., Bulcroft, R. A., Jensen, M. P., & Hops, H. (1991). Observational assessment of chronic pain patient-spouse behavioral interactions. *Behavior Therapy, 22,* 549–567.

Romano, J. M., Turner, J. A., Jensen, M. P., Friedman, L., Bulcroft, R. A., Hops, H., & Wright, S. F. (1996). Chronic pain patient-spouse behavioral interactions predict patient disability. *Pain, 63,* 353–360.

Schulz, M. S., & Masek, B. J. (1996). Medical crisis intervention with children and adolescents with chronic pain. *Professional Psychology: Research and Practice, 27,* 121–129.

Sherbourne, C. D., Hays, R. D., Ordway, L., DiMatteo, M. R., & Kravitz, R. L. (1992). Antecedents of adherence to medical recommendations: Results from the medical outcomes study. *Journal of Behavioral Medicine, 15,* 447–468.

Thompson, S. M., Dahlquist, L. M., Koenning, G. M., & Bartholomew, L. K. (1995). Brief report: Adherence-facilitating behaviors of a multidisciplinary pediatric rheumatology staff. *Journal of Pediatric Psychology, 20,* 291–297.

Turk, D. C. (1996). Biopsychosocial perspective on chronic pain. In R. J. Gatchel & D. C. Turk (Eds.), *Psychological approaches to pain management* (pp. 3–32). New York: Guilford.

Turk, D. C., Kerns, R. D., & Rosenberg, R. (1992). Effects of marital interaction on chronic pain and disability: Examining the down side of social support. *Rehabilitation Psychology, 37,* 259–274.

Turk, D. C., Meichenbaum, D., & Genest, M. (1983). *Pain and behavioral medicine: A cognitive-behavioral perspective.* New York: Guilford.

Turk, D. C., & Melzack, R. (Eds.). (1992). *Handbook of pain assessment.* New York: Guilford.

Turk, D. C., & Rudy, T. E. (1991). Neglected topics in the treatment of chronic pain patients—Relapse, noncompliance, and adherence enhancement. *Pain, 44,* 5–28.

Ward, S. E., Goldberg, N., Miller-McCauley, V., Mueller, C., Nolan, A., Pawlik-Plank, D., Robbins, A., Stormoen, D., & Weissman, D. E. (1993). Patient-related barriers to management of cancer pain. *Pain, 52,* 319–342.

Weintraub, M. I. (1992). Litigation-chronic pain syndrome, a distinct entity: Analysis of 210 cases. *American Journal of Pain Management, 2,* 198–204.

Chapter 7

A Framework for Conceptualization and Assessment of Affective Disturbance in Pain

Ephrem Fernandez
Southern Methodist University

Timothy S. Clark
Baylor Center for Pain Management

David Rudick-Davis
Psychologist in Private Practice—Dallas, Texas

Though pain is commonly described in terms of its physical properties (such as location, depth, and sensation), it also encompasses an emotional quality, all pain being intrinsically aversive. The Aristotelian position placed pain outside the senses and among the passions of the soul. In recent times, pain has continued to be equated with affect (Szasz, 1957). Von Frey (1895), on the other hand, considered affect as a secondary reaction to pain. Beecher (1957) was inclined to place affect under the reactive component of pain. Today, there is little dispute about the co-occurrence of affect and pain, and the International Association for the Study of Pain has formalized this into a definition of pain as always sensory and emotional. These dual defining features are depicted in Fig. 7.1 (Fernandez, 1997). As shown, the boundaries between these two components are not rigid but fluid, thus reflecting reciprocal determinism; sensation influences affect and vice versa, and not necessarily in a proportional fashion. Furthermore, they function like parts of a whole: Reducing one has the capacity to reduce the whole directly or else indirectly through its effect on the countercomponent.

Surprisingly, little research has appeared on the affective as compared to the sensory aspects of pain. Yet, it is the affective component that is proximally responsible for help-seeking behavior and other attempts at adaptation (Chapman, 1993). Besides, an adequate explanation of pain depends on an adequate theory of human emotions, said Buytendyck (as cited in Price, 1988). For an adequate theory of human emotions, we turn

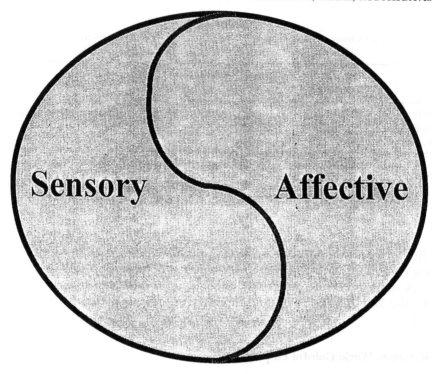

FIG. 7.1. The dual defining features of pain. From Fernandez (1997).

to the science of affect, a field that has attracted much attention within psychology.

This chapter introduces a variety of affective phenomena, and explains the relevance of some of these to the experience of pain. The dynamic interaction between affect and pain is elaborated on. Data on emotions are drawn from a recent survey of pain sufferers, and case examples of affective disturbances in pain patients are provided. Finally, avenues for the assessment of affective disturbance in this population are outlined.

THE SCIENCE OF AFFECT

An important starting point is some basic terminology in the science of affect. First of all, affect is a general category encompassing emotions, moods, and temperaments. What is common to these phenomena is the subjective feeling beyond mere physiological arousal, somewhat vague in comparison to the precision of cognitive appraisals, and essentially private in contrast to motor behavior. At the same time, affect is itself linked to certain cognitive appraisals, action tendencies, and patterns of physiological arousal.

Emotions

Like cognitions, emotions are private events but they are subjective (often described ostensively or by example) whereas cognitions (appraisals, in particular) are statements communicated with less ambiguity. Emotions are valenced, whereas cognitions in and of themselves do not possess intrinsic pleasantness/unpleasantness; emotions vary in intensity but cognitions do not (even though the latter may occur with varying degrees of certainty).

There have been numerous postulations about basic or primary emotions. Some are based on cross-linguistic similarities in the description of emotion, others on facial expressions, patterns of autonomic activity, and central nervous system mediation. None of these models, however, has produced a comprehensive taxonomy of emotions that is also universal. Due to disagreements, some scholars have lately chosen to sidestep the question of basic emotions. Scherer (1994), for example, has suggested the term *modal emotions,* which are not fundamental but merely based on the frequency with which certain synchronized changes occur in all organismic subsystems involved in emotions. Meanwhile, the demands of clinical practice have subordinated the abstract idea of basic emotions to the reality of common emotions—common not only in terms of their ubiquity and frequency in human experience (Paanksep, 1994) but also with regard to their appearance across most typologies of emotion (Skiffington, Fernandez, & McFarland, 1996). Thus, joy, and a number of negative emotions, namely, anger, fear, sadness, shame, guilt, and envy have come to be regarded as the common emotions of clinical interest.

Moods

Whereas emotions are discrete events, moods are relatively continuous processes. Emotions tend to rise and fall sharply in intensity thus having a phasic quality, whereas moods tend to fluctuate within a small margin of intensity over a longer period of time thus taking on a tonic quality. Such temporal and intensity differences aside, emotions are more clearly attributable to specific stimuli, whereas moods are more obscure in their origins; emotions are more likely to be linked to appraisals than are moods; similarly, the maintaining and terminating factors in moods are less apparent than those in emotions, thus giving the former a spontaneous and transient quality.

Temperaments and Affective Style

Davidson (1994) used the term *temperament* to refer to the entire domain of individual differences modulating a person's reactivity to emotional events. In other words, temperament disposes one to experience particular emotions with a high frequency or particular moods for extended periods of time. It represents a kind of affective style or affective bias. What is the origin of temperaments? They are partly heritable and partly learned, and they crystallize into schemata that govern the future appraisal of events.

State Versus Trait Affect

This is a potentially misleading distinction because *state* refers to the momentary feelings reported by an individual at a point in time (e.g., "right now"); *trait* refers to a more enduring disposition or proneness to certain feelings. In the current framework of concepts, state could refer to either an emotional episode or an ongoing mood; saying that I am sad right now says nothing about whether this sadness began 2 days ago or if it began 2 minutes ago. Trait, on the other hand, is usually assessed by asking someone to say "how often" she or he feels a particular way. Thus, trait may tap into the frequency or the persistence of a particular affective experience. If a person says that she feels angry very often, it could indicate that her anger is recurrent or that it is unremitting; in the former case, there is the added uncertainty about whether her anger is dispositional or situational.

Affective Disorders

Based on the definition of psychopathology used in the *Diagnostic and Statistical Manual of Mental Disorders* (4th ed.; American Psychiatric Association, 1994), an affective phenomenon becomes a disorder when it is intense, frequent, or enduring enough to produce dysfunction or concern/complaint in the person concerned, his or her significant others, responsible parties, or society at large. Thus, anger can become an affective disorder if it intensifies into rage that is typically destructive, and if it recurs or persists long enough as to be disruptive or incapacitating; should it not qualify as a "disorder," angry behavior might nevertheless appear "abnormal" if it occurs in a manner that is uncharacteristic of most people. Inevitably, this demands an understanding of statistical representations of modal behavior and a keen appreciation of sociocultural norms of what is appropriate versus inappropriate.

In short, any dysfunction due to an emotional aberration should qualify as an affective disturbance. Depression, anxiety, and anger-related disorders are especially relevant to the pain population in view of the misfortune, threat, and frustration that they elicit (Pilowsky, 1988) and the maladaptive responses produced, for example, anhedonia, avoidance, and destructiveness, respectively. But this is not to ignore guilt, shame, envy, and other emotions that, if intensified, prolonged, or recurrent, would be likely to produce dysfunction and thereby qualify as affective disorders too.

Unpleasantness, Suffering, Distress

All types of negative emotions may be grouped under the general term, *negative affect* or *negaffect*. In this chapter, the focus is on such forms of dysphoria rather than positive affect, because pain is essentially an aversive experience. Clarification should also be made of the terms *suffering, unpleasantness*, and *distress* because they are often used interchangeably. The term unpleasantness is reserved for the instant negatively valenced quality of pain; it needs little/no cognitive appraisal. Distress is the affective reaction to pain and is governed by cognitive appraisals that give it further differentiation, for example, guilt, shame, jealousy. Suffering connotes long, drawn-out distress or anguish that frequently attends chronic intractable pain or chronic illness. Like distress, suffering can take the form of one/more qualities of negative affect except that it approaches the point of unbearability.

Action Tendencies

All affect is accompanied by some action tendency. For example, social communication needs abound with most emotions (Rime, Mesquita, Philippot, & Boca, 1991). Davidson (1992) made a simple distinction between approach and avoidance behaviors that accompany emotion. These can be further differentiated into a host of action tendencies each unique to a particular emotion (Frijda, 1987). In fact, emotions are virtually definable in terms of action tendencies, and this fits with the Latin root of emotion, *ex movere*, which means "to move out." In other words, affect motivates the organism to act in certain (putatively adaptive) ways. This finds support in the context of pain, too, which has an affective-motivational system (Melzack & Casey, 1968). The concept of action tendency, therefore, is part of a functional perspective in which behavior is linked to affect through the intervening process of motivation.

Action Fantasies

The action one is propelled toward may not be the action that eventuates or the action one would *like* to take. The last of these, the action fantasy, is the response considered by the individual when constraints on behavior are hypothetically absent/minimal. This is, of course, an idealized scenario and, hence, the subject of imagination. Nevertheless, it is highly informative about the individual's emotional experience. Readers may note the resemblance of action fantasy to the Freudian concept of id, which centers around certain urges that do not necessarily come to fruition. Analogous to the id, the action fantasy seldom materializes but undergoes transformation into a more realistic tendency toward a practical course of action (action eventuality). In contrast to the id, however, the action fantasy is spared any psychodynamic theorizing. It is intended to merely serve as a reminder of the potential for discrepancies between the covert and the overt, between what is imagined and what is acted out, in the experience of emotion; this distinction is especially useful in understanding emotions like anger that are highly susceptible to social desirabilty factors.

Cognitive Appraisal

All emotion is preceded by some cognitive appraisal or interpretation that may be conscious and controlled or else automatic and below the threshold of awareness. The precise appraisal may be somewhat obscure in the case of moods, but it is safe to argue that at least basic encoding of events as approved or disapproved is a sine qua non for the experience of affect (Clore, 1994; Lazarus, 1984). Ortony, Clore, and Collins (1988) have gone further to identify the precise appraisals that are unique to each of 22 emotions. These appraisals go beyond approval/disapproval to interpretations of the actions of agents, the expectations of the recipient, and so on.

A MODEL OF AFFECTIVE PHENOMENA IN RELATION TO PAIN

The foregoing concepts are all relevant to pain, which, as emphasized earlier, is undeniably affective in experience. Figure 7.2 (Fernandez, 1997) outlines an integrative model of how cognition, affect, motivation, and behavior are intimately linked in the response sequence to pain. The event in this case is a nociceptive stimulus that is sensed and perceived as painful. Accompanying cognitive appraisals ascribe meaning to the pain; these can range from attributions about the cause of pain to expectations of its consequences. It is these interpretations that govern the type of affect that emerges: As noted by Fernandez (1989), there is a strong probability that viewing pain as an overpowering danger would produce fear, thinking of the same pain as a discouraging setback would lead to sadness/depression, pain viewed as an enemy to be fought against would produce anger, pain connoting disgrace would lead to shame, and pain viewed as punishment from God would trigger guilt. As in Fernandez (1989), each affective quality

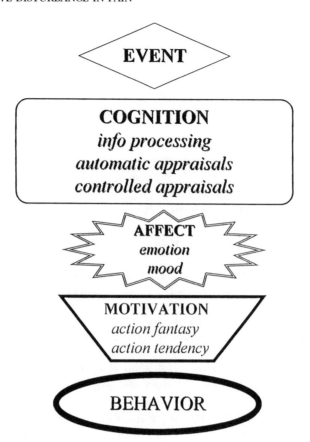

FIG. 7.2. A model of affective phenomena in relation to pain. From Fernandez (1997).

also entails a unique motivational process: Anger is to aggressiveness, as fear is to help seeking, sadness/depression is to withdrawal, shame is to concealment, and guilt is to penance or sacrifice. In each of these cases, what the individual ends up doing depends on his or her action fantasy and action tendency; recognizing that what one would *like to do* in the absence of constraints could be discordant with what is the most practical course of action. The final behavior that results represents a resolution of these two motivational forces and a culmination of the processes that unfolded with the onset of pain.

It must be pointed out that what is outlined in Fig. 7.2 is one important sequence relating cognition, affect, motivation, and behavior. Alternate sequences can be drawn to reflect bidirectional relationships among some of the variables. The present model is further premised on the common conceptualization of pain as an antecedent event. As is explained next, pain can occur in other temporal relationships with affect in which case variations of the present model would be in order.

DYNAMIC INTERACTIONS BETWEEN PAIN AND AFFECT

The interaction between pain and affect is dynamic and multifarious. Six principal relationships between affect and pain have been modeled (Fernandez, 1998). Each relationship represents a different temporal ordering of the two variables as well as a different mechanism by which one variable influences or is influenced by the other.

Affect as Predisposing Factor in Pain

Affect can be a predisposing factor when embedded within a personality trait that increases the likelihood of certain stimuli being perceived as painful. Engel's (1959) notion of a pain-prone personality was one of the earliest documented examples of how personality traits might account for individual differences in pain perception; similarly, Blumer and Heilbronn (1982) presented a profile of traits predisposing one to chronic pain. Though the notion of psychogenic pain is seldom voiced among pain scholars, the search for dispositional traits in pain patients continues unabated with the aid of various personality assessment tools. Accordingly, Polatin, Kinney, Gatchel, Lillo and Mayer (1993) discovered that 51% of pain patients in a functional restoration program met criteria for at least one personality disorder.

Affective disturbance can be a distal cause of pain, as in the case of conversion reaction (Ford, 1995). Here, psychological conflicts or past trauma lead to pain and other physical symptoms that often defy pure neurological explanations. The origin of the trauma can range from mental health crises (Chaturvedi & Albert, 1986) to work-related injury (Allodi & Goldstein, 1995). The delay between trauma and physical symptoms varies, but posttraumatic stress *is* generally associated with increased pain (Geisser, Roth, Bachman, & Eckert, 1996).

Affect as Precipitating Factor in Pain

Affect can also trigger pain with much greater immediacy than do predisposing factors. This may be difficult to demonstrate on the basis of correlational research, but the few experimental and prospective studies on this issue have supported this hypothesis (e.g., Affleck, Tennen, Urrows, & Higgins, 1992; Stalling, 1992). Of specific interest here is anxiety, which has been shown to produce pain (Weisenberg, Aviram, Wolf, & Raphaeli, 1984) as well as promote pain-avoidance behavior (Cipher & Fernandez, 1997). A dramatic illustration of this effect is often witnessed in needle phobics who report pain and withdraw from the stimulus even before contact between needle and flesh. It has been suggested that the mechanism here may simply be one of heightened attention (Arntz, Dreessen, & Merckelbach, 1991).

Affect as Correlate of Pain

Pain is inherently aversive and hence negative affect co-occurs with pain. This very component that makes a sensation aversive is best referred to as unpleasantness. It is instantaneous and needs minimal appraisal, as in the case of nausea, suffocation, and other aversive reactions. It is to be differentiated from the various forms of emotional distress that accompany pain after additional cognitive mediation. This is consistent with Price's (1988) biological accounts of first and second stages of pain-related affect. It should be noted that unpleasantness is concurrent with all pain and highly correlated with the magnitude of the sensory component of pain (Holroyd et al., 1996; Turk, Rudy, & Salovey, 1985). Yet it is separable from its sensory counterpart under the dynamic conditions of experimental manipulation or clinical intervention (Fernandez & Turk, 1992, 1994; Gracely, 1992).

Affect as Exacerbating Factor in Pain

Even if not the cause of pain, affect may aggravate existing pain. The affect may have its origins in interpersonal conflict and non-pain-related circumstances and yet end up intensifying the pain. The mechanism here may be one of physiological reactivity as proposed by Flor, Birbaumer, Schugens, and Lutzenberger (1992). One specific emotional aggravator of pain is anger, especially when it is suppressed (Kerns, Rosenberg, & Jacob, 1994), but this is further moderated by personality and gender as well (Burns, Johnson, Mahoney, Devine, & Pawl, 1996). The possibility must be considered that negative affect could be an offshoot of the pain itself and exert influence on that pain, thus becoming part of a vicious cycle in which affect compounds pain which begets more affective disturbance which further amplifies the pain, and so on.

Affect as Consequence of Pain

The emotional consequence of pain or what Price (1988) called the second stage of pain-related affect, may be termed distress as opposed to basic unpleasantness. Distress can take the form of fear, guilt, shame, or any emotion that emerges out of relatively complex cognitive mediation. Depression has received the most attention in this regard, although anger is equally likely (Fernandez & Turk, 1995). Recent research by Gamsa (1990) has confirmed that depression and other negative affective states are more often consequences than precursors of pain. This does not necessitate, however, a proportional relationship between pain and distress. For instance, Fernandez, Moon, Urrutia, Johnson, and Salinas (1995) found that more pain does not imply more anger; in fact, the correlation between pain intensity and anger approaches zero. As in studies of depression, anger in pain patients may be moderated by the degree of goal frustration and life interference.

Affect as Perpetuating Factor in Pain

In some instances, pain behavior is reinforced by consequences that can be assumed to be pleasing to the pain patient. Numerous behavior-analytic studies (Block, Kremer, & Gaylor, 1980; Fernandez & McDowell, 1995; Gil, Keefe, Grisson, & Van Dalfsen, 1987) have demonstrated that pain behaviors persist when accompanied by attention and solicitude that are obviously positive in the affect generated. In extreme cases, the pain behaviors may culminate in a sick role that is seemingly characterized by perpetual suffering and disability when in actual fact the patient derives secondary gain and positive affect from this condition.

To summarize this section, affect is diverse and dynamic in its relationship to pain. Though often concurrent with or consequent upon pain, affect can also potentiate, precipitate, exacerbate, and/or perpetuate pain. Each of these has a different implication for pain management. Therefore, it is important to identify which model applies to each patient before attempting to treat the affective disturbance in pain. This can be achieved through a combination of elaborate history taking, self-monitoring beyond the clinical context, and longitudinal measurements of both pain and affect.

COMPOSITION AND ATTRIBUTION OF NEGATIVE AFFECT IN CHRONIC PAIN

To answer the question of what emotions make up the experience of chronic pain, Fernandez and Milburn (1994) obtained visual analogue ratings of 10 emotions (comprising Izard's 1991 taxonomy of emotions) as experienced by pain patients. Patients reported moderate to high levels of anger, fear, and sadness, moderate to low levels of guilt, shame, disgust, and contempt, and minimal levels of joy, surprise, and interest. Thus, positive emotions were relatively inconspicuous in the self-report of this sample of 40 inpatient chronic pain patients. Negative emotions prevailed, and of these a subset comprising anger, fear, and sadness accounted for the bulk of the variance in the affective component of pain.

Focusing solely on the negative spectrum of emotion in chronic pain patients and to further separate affect due to pain from other sources of negaffect, a survey was undertaken of 110 chronic pain patients presenting at a multidisciplinary pain clinic in Dallas, Texas. Participants voluntarily answered a set of six questions about anger, fear, sadness, shame, guilt, and envy, respectively; these six emotions, which feature commonly in typologies of affect, have been alluded to by many chronic pain sufferers and are hence viewed as relevant to pain. Participants provided a 0–10 point rating of how often they had experienced each of the six emotions during the preceding 30 days, 0 designating "never," and 10 designating "always"; additionally, they made an attribution of the degree to which each affective state was due to pain using a 10-point scale anchored at 0 for "not at all" and 10 for "totally."

Figure 7.3 displays a stacked graph of the percentage of time taken up by each affective state over a month-long period and the proportion of each state that was directly attributed to pain. As can be seen, anger was the most dominant emotion, occupying the patients about 70% of the time, and two thirds of it was attributed to pain itself. This was followed by fear and then sadness, which prevailed about 60% of the time. The

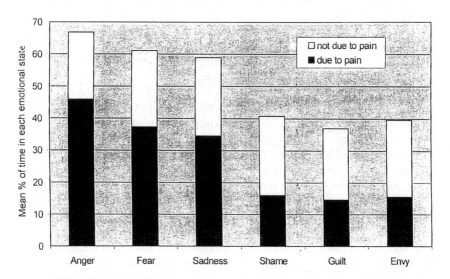

FIG. 7.3. The percentage of time taken up by each affective state over a month-long period and the proportion of each state that was directly attributed to pain.

profile shows a marked drop thereafter, with shame, guilt, and envy reportedly occurring about 40% of the time and being primarily due to non-pain-related factors. Inferential tests (Table 7.1) revealed the most significant differences for pairwise comparisons between the first three and the last three emotions; pairwise comparisons in the latter subset were all nonsignificant. These results are consistent with the intercorrelation matrix depicted in Table 7.2. As shown, correlations were generally significant, but highest within the anger, fear, and sadness subset and within the shame, guilt, and envy subset. These findings lend support for anger, fear, and sadness as constituting a core of negative affect in chronic pain; guilt, shame, and envy are not only less prevalent but, evidently, related to extraneous factors more so than to pain.

Indeed, the two most studied affective states in the context of pain are depression and to a lesser extent anxiety. Anger has been conspicuously neglected in this endeavor (Fernandez & Turk, 1993) but needs to be incorporated as part of a triad of negaffective states that co-occur with chronic pain and also share comorbidity with one another. Identification of this triadic core allows for greater focus and efficiency in the assessment and treatment of pain.

TABLE 7.1
Pairwise T Tests

	Anger	Fear	Sadness	Shame	Guilt
Fear	3.12				
Sadness	4.13	.72			
Shame	8.64	6.72	5.32		
Guilt	8.68	6.63	6.11	.25	
Envy	8.51	6.00	5.27	.03	.06

Note. At alpha = .05, t crit = 1.98 (2-tailed), df = 109; at alpha = .01, t crit = 2.62 (2-tailed), df = 109.

TABLE 7.2
Intercorrelation Matrix

	Anger	Fear	Sadness	Shame	Guilt
Fear	.58				
Sadness	.67	.67			
Shame	.42	.58	.47		
Guilt	.45	.57	.61	.70	
Envy	.41	.47	.48	.71	.65

Note. At alpha = .05, r crit = .195 (2-tailed), df = 109; at alpha = .01, r crit = .25 (2-tailed), df = 109.

CASE STUDIES OF NEGAFFECTIVE PAIN PATIENTS

The following anecdotes illustrate each of the three core negaffective states prominent among pain patients along with some associated appraisals, motivations, and behaviors. There is always the possibility of other emotions predominating in some individuals and this in turn may be related to peculiarities in the origin and consequence of the pain. The possibility of mixed emotions must also be acknowledged: As in the last vignette, one may experience multiple emotions from different appraisals and leading to multiple action tendencies.

Anger

Joe was a 39-year-old man who had been employed as a foreman in a factory. On the job, he had a fall that resulted in a broken leg. Despite initial improvement following surgery, he had to return for repeated interventions and was later diagnosed with reflex sympathetic dystrophy. He underwent a variety of interventions for this condition but the pain remained, his mobility declined, and he was unable to return to his job. With increasing confinement to his house, he missed the high level of energy that he had been accustomed to, grew increasingly restless, and irritable toward his wife and three sons. Even during therapy sessions, he would occasionally get annoyed with his wife's interjections and dismiss them with the remark "I know what's best for me."

He harbored much anger toward one of the physicians who had operated on him. He blamed that physician for the deterioration in his condition. It was this failed surgery that, in Joe's opinion, had left him in unrelenting pain, with reduced mobility, and without his job. Frustrated from his goals, he remarked in a tone of ridicule and bitterness, "You know, they can build all kinds of bridges and towers, connect millions of computers by the Internet, repair anything from a car to an airplane, but they can't get it right when it comes to working on the human body—Beats me!"

The bulk of Joe's anger was expressed quite openly to his workers' compensation insurance carrier and the various personnel at the carrier: "They're just flunkies; they're not getting their hands dirtied; they don't know half of what it takes to do the job and they wanna be in charge of running the show. Must be that they're just in it for the money; we've heard it before: the insurance industry never loses, the government never loses; so who loses?—us, the consumers, the citizens!". This attitude soon led Joe to episodes of shouting and expressing contempt at the carrier until the receptionists at the carrier would simply hang up on him when he became offensive. This frustrated Joe even more sometimes to the point of banging on the table and yelling out loud within his own house; his wife and eldest son would go through much effort to calm him down. Disinclined to apologize for his outbursts (because he viewed his anger as simply a reaction to the denial of proper medical treatment and pain relief that he felt entitled to) Joe would ultimately regain his composure until the next time he felt he had to "fight for my well-being."

Sadness/Depression

John was a 50-year-old man who sustained a spinal injury while water-skiing with friends. Surgery was successful for the most part, but pain persisted in his neck and shoulders, sometimes reaching such intensity that he would find a solitary place to sob and moan in private. The most disconcerting result of the injury, however, was John's decline in functioning at work and at home. He had risen from the ranks of supervisors in an advertising firm and become the acting vice-president. During his 2-month absence from work, his acting position had been reassigned to another employee, a friend of John's. Upon resuming work, John found himself heading a division with which he had little familiarity and, even though he continued to be treated with respect, he felt undervalued in his new job. Moreover, he felt that although his coworkers were polite, they really did not understand the limitations posed by his pain, which would strike unpredictably and force him to take a break from his work. As he put it, "They haven't been through what I have and I can't expect them to feel my pain, and I mean not just the physical pain but the disappointments I have had to come back to . . . but they should know at least in the back of their minds that it is very easy to lose everything you've worked for—just like that and for no good reason!"

John's exwife kept in touch with him during his hospitalization. His daughter visited him every weekend. One of his brothers offered him financial help. But "at the end of the day, you're still alone and nobody can really be there for you all the time," John said. He took to drinking alcohol "partly to numb the pain and partly to escape from the loss and loneliness." After the failure of his marriage, he had invested most of his time and effort in professional advancement, and now even that was in question. His self-esteem, which had been largely tied to his success at work, declined to the level of feelings of inadequacy. As the pain and impaired function continued, loss of hope set in. He saw little chance of ever returning to the high point in his life when he had been acting vice-president of the firm.

Some vegetative symptoms of depression emerged, for example, insomnia, loss of appetite, and decreased energy. John was aware of depression as a health problem and sought psychotherapy to help him adjust to his new life circumstances. When prompted about suicide, he said he was adamantly opposed to it:

> Being Christian, that's just not an option, but I tell you I can understand why some people do it. I can put up with the pain most of the time but when it gets really bad, that's when I wonder what else there is to do, especially when the medication doesn't work. How many years of this can I take, I don't know. But the worst part, as I said, is that this whole mess cost me my chance for a better life. I guess, now I'll just have to settle for what I can get. Sure, I'm not suicidal, but I am not excited about the life I see ahead of me, you know what I mean?

Fear/Anxiety

Angela was a 27-year-old schoolteacher who had been in an automobile accident that left her with recurrent headaches. The only headaches she had ever experienced before the injury were brief and mild hangovers, which she had managed to shrug off. However, the postinjury headaches she now suffered were prolonged and excruciating. Above all, they made her nervous to the point of heart palpitations and sweating. She described the typical episode of headache as one in which "I don't know how long it's going to go on for and how severe it's going to get, and so I'm never sure how to get through it; at least if I knew what to expect, that would not be so bad, but I never know and that's what makes it so terrifying." She had undergone a range of diagnostic tests (including magnetic resonance imaging [MRI]), all of which indicated no pathology. Angela's response to this was, "That's supposed to be good news when the doc tells you there's nothing abnormal, but then the headache is real and abnormal for me. My conclusion is that there's something really weird going on and they can't figure out what it is, and that's no consolation, is it?".

Angela returned to work, but in the absence of a satisfactory explantion for her headaches, her fears soon broadened in scope. Not only was she afraid that the headache might be a signal of undetectable head injury, but she also worried that the injury might be spreading like a disease. She began to have intrusive images of bruised brain tissue, ruptured blood vessels, seizures, tumors, and almost anything she had heard about that could go wrong with the brain. She was concerned about her decline in concentration, which she also viewed as a symptom of her deterioration.

Angela's fears generalized to a host of situations associated with head pain. These included physical stimuli such as bright light and loud noise to physical activities like sport and household chores, which she had previously tolerated if not enjoyed. She began to avoid any activity that she felt might aggravate the pain, thus leading her to a state of inertia and bringing on excessive sleep. Driving was frightening because it reminded her of the auto accident that triggered the headaches, but even being away from the familiarity of her home later became unnerving because of the fear that so many things could go wrong as to further threaten her health.

Angela summarized her own state: "I realize all this sounds a bit irrational, but I really feel vulnerable and I can't risk hurting myself again or getting worse than I already am. I feel OK when I'm around my parents but most of the time I'm around new people in new situations and that's a worry. Even if nothing goes wrong, what if I get one of these bad headaches and I lose control? And all the while, I have to deal with the possibility that I have a condition that is a mystery to even the expert doctors who have tried to help me. I'll just take each day at a time, more like each minute at a time, small steps, safe and secure."

Mixed Emotions: Guilt, Shame, Envy

The following is a transcript of a patient, Hank, diagnosed with AIDS-Related Complex. His physical symptoms included joint pain, headache, shortness of breath, fatigue, and diarrhea. His psychological state was characterized by a mixture of guilt, shame, and envy stemming from his view of his condition and how he was perceived by others:

> I hurt no one; I just wanted a happy life. What did I do wrong to deserve this? Sure I tried intravenous drugs but that was 15 years ago; isn't it a bit late to be punished for that? Sex I could not do without and some of it was what they now call "risky stuff"; how could I know? All of a sudden, here are the eighties, and everything I'd learned to enjoy and depend on was suddenly dangerous; I was doomed. I suppose I should have had the discipline to abstain from the pleasures of life, eh? But I'm human and therefore prone to sin, so I'm told, but God is merciful, so I'm also told, so can't I get another chance? I crossed over into the never never land, and it's not for me; if I get another chance, I can straighten myself out and maybe help a few others too.
>
> I always prided myself at being different but now I'm out in the fringe of society—like an outcast. The few people I confided in didn't want to know me anymore; they felt sorry, I could see, but I didn't want pity, I just wanted them to be there for me as I would for them; not one of them stuck around. That was some lesson, I tell you. Now I keep it to myself, except when the pain gets really bad, and when someone asks me what's wrong—in my mind I say "you don't want to know" but out of politeness, I reply "it's just stress and the aging process." And that's all it really is: AIDS makes you feel old real fast and you just can't do the same things without getting worn out.
>
> When I look at other healthy people, I see how much they have going for them and some of them don't even know it. If only they could trade places with me for a day, they'd come out better. Like I said, I never hurt

anyone, and I know there are people who're out there doing all kinds of cruel things and getting away with it. I'd be happy with just a roof over my head and a few good friends, I'll even take hard labor and old age—as long as I can have my health back—just that immune system, you know. Is that asking for too much?

Though the patient's headache and joint pain were evidently of moderate intensity, this was one in a constellation of symptoms contributing to his disfigurement and disability, and portending his death. As in cancer (Turk & Fernandez, 1990), the pain and related symptoms had also come to be interpreted as progression of disease: The cumulative effect of these connotations was a high level of distress in the patient.

The patient's disclosures can be analyzed using the framework provided in Fig. 7.2. Because the precipitating event was not an accident and the patient assumed some agency in it, guilt predominated over anger. The event was also appraised as possible punishment from God for "sins" or "transgressions" such as illicit drugs and risky sex. These were juxtaposed with controlled appraisals about deserving forgiveness. Another emotional consequence was shame, which in this instance stemmed from appraisals about being abandoned and treated as an outcast. Third, the patient revealed a combination of envy and resentment toward others who had been spared his hardship. He engaged in the action fantasy of coveting others' good health even though he was somewhat inclined to bitter resignation about his fate.

STANDARDIZED ASSESSMENT OF AFFECT IN PAIN SUFFERERS

Despite the richness of the kind of qualitative data reported earlier, measurement and hypothesis testing in this area depends largely on standardized tests. There are a few such instruments that attempt to measure affective disturbance associated with pain. The McGill Pain Questionnaire (MPQ) was a pioneering effort in this respect, and its reliance on the vocabulary of pain and affect attracted much interest (Kremer, Atkinson, & Kremer, 1983; Morley & Pallin, 1995). Measures of the affective component are computed on the basis of intensity values of words selected to describe pain. Unfortunately, the interpretability of this measure has come under some question because of inconsistencies in the categorization of MPQ pain descriptors—inconsistencies that blur the distinction among types of pain sensation and affect (Fernandez & Boyle, in press; Fernandez & Towery, 1996; Towery & Fernandez, 1996).

Clark, Fletcher, Janal, and Carroll (1995) has empirically derived an alternate classification of pain descriptors on the basis of which a new instrument called the Multidimensional Affect and Pain Survey (MAPS) has been constructed (Clark, Janal, Fletcher, Wharton, & Carroll, 1997). The MAPS comprises a list of 101 pain-related words that (among other things) provides an index of suffering and its component variables of anger, anxiety, fear, depressed mood, and self-blame. It is an improvement on the MPQ in terms of the sampling of words to describe affect, the use of an interval scale for rating each word, and the breakdown of affect into different subcategories. Independent psychometric evaluation is expected in the near future.

Because the majority of pain assessment instruments are not designed with affect as the principal object of interest, it is useful to incorporate other standardized tests developed specially for the purpose of measuring affect. Most of these tests have been developed within a body of literature remote from pain research; however, they have the capacity to measure affect in its diversity and complexity. Following are examples of the more commonly documented affect assessment instruments along with some implications for their adaptation to the pain population.

Multiple Affect Adjective Checklist

The Multiple Affect Adjective Checklist or MAACL (Zuckerman & Lubin, 1965) is an inventory of 132 adjectives with boxes to be checked or left unchecked, and pertaining to what the authors referred to as the three clinically relevant negative affects: anxiety, depression, and hostility. Psychometric evaluations of the MAACL have revealed adequate reliability and validity. The revised MAACL-R (Zuckerman & Lubin, 1985) is only moderately correlated with its forerunner and represents a marginal improvement. The recurrence of a two-factor solution (positive and negative affect) in factor analytic studies of the MAACL and MAACL-R (Gotlib & Meyer, 1986; Hunsley, 1990) suggests that scores for anxiety, hostility, and depression must be interpreted with caution when using this instrument. Though one of the oldest instruments of its genre, the MAACL appears to be declining in use.

Profile of Mood States

Widely used in health research, the Profile of Mood States or POMS (McNair, Lorr, & Droppleman, 1981) lists 65 mood-related adjectives to be rated on a 4-point scale of amount/frequency. It yields scores for tension-anxiety, depression-dejection, anger-hostility, as well as vigor-activity, fatigue-inertia, and confusion-bewilderment; these can be arithmetically combined into a total mood disturbance score. Despite some interpretive variations in multivariate studies of the POMS (Boyle, 1987; Tunis, Golbus,

Copeland, & Fine, 1990), its factor structure has been largely confirmed. Reliability and validity coefficients have remained high notwithstanding abridged versions of the instrument. One problem that has emerged, however, is that POMS single estimates of mood over time are not always in agreement with mood scores averaged over multiple points in time (Rasmussen & Jeffrey, 1995; Rasmussen, Jeffrey, Willingham, & Glover, 1994). Hence, a correction factor might be in order when calculating POMS scores based on the stipulated 1-week time frame.

Positive Affect Negative Affect Schedule

Another set of single-word items was recently put together to form the Positive Affect and Negative Affect Schedule (Watson, Clark, & Tellegen, 1988). Two sets of 10 affect words are rated on 5-point scales of the extent to which they have been experienced over a specified time frame. What should be clear, however, is that the two scores thus obtained do not relate purely to positive or negative emotion/mood but to a host of features: Positive affect, for instance, is defined as high energy, full concentration, and pleasurable engagement, whereas negative affect is defined as subjective distress and unpleasurable engagement. Furthermore, these dimensions supposedly correspond to independent traits founded in psychobiological and psychodynamic ideas. The independence of these dimensions has been a matter of debate and there is some concern about insufficient word items for lower levels of positive and negative affect (Nemanick & Munz, 1994). Yet, this test remains unique in its attempt to explore affect at the level of traits.

Differential Emotions Scale–IV

The Differential Emotions Scale (DES) departs from the aforementioned instruments in an important way. Although early versions consisted of single-word descriptors of affect, the DES–IV (Izard, Dougherty, Bloxom, & Kotsch, 1974) is a set of succinct statements about the experience of particular emotions; for example, one of the items for fear reads "feel scared, uneasy, like something might harm you," thus not only consisting of synonyms of fear but also conveying the concept of potential harm. A total of 36 statements are rated on a 5-point scale of frequency over a specified time period. These yield separate scores for the 11 affect types specified in differential emotions theory (Izard, 1991): interest, joy, surprise, sadness, anger, disgust, contempt, hostility, fear, shame, shyness, and guilt; in addition, scores for positive and negative emotionality can be derived by summation of scores for the appropriate subsets of discrete emotions. Factor analyses have by and large confirmed the construct validity of the DES–III but also raise the possibility of higher order factors in the DES–IV (Boyle, 1986).

Further Considerations

Single-emotion words are limited in the information they convey, besides begging the question about what is meant by the emotion construct. They are also subject to varied interpretations more so than are statements that describe the very experience of emotion. On this count, the DES–IV is a sound choice for the assessment of emotion. However, whereas some of the items in the DES–IV describe by example, others are simply phrases interspersed with synonyms. This shortcoming can be remedied if the precise defining characteristics of each emotion are articulated. Fortunately, this is now possible because Ortony et al. (1988) have laid out the appraisal structure for numerous emotions. Furthermore, Frijda (1987) has identified different action tendencies that are definitive of different emotions. Based on these models, a new instrument has been developed to assess discrete negative emotions, particularly, anger, fear, and sadness. Known as the Emotional Distress Questionnaire or EDQ (Fernandez, 1991), this instrument meets psychometric criteria for validity and reliability (Skiffington, Fernandez, & McFarland, 1996, in press) and is in the process of cross-validation across various clinical populations including chronic pain patients.

So far, the discussion of affect assessment has been directed mainly at self-report measures of discrete negative emotion. When scores on these negative states reach a magnitude suggestive of affective disorders, an additional battery of standardized tests might be called for: the State Trait Anxiety Inventory (Spielberger, Gorsuch, & Lushene, 1970) for anxiety, the Beck Depression Inventory (Beck, Ward, Mendelson, Mock, & Erbaugh, 1961) for depression, and the State Trait Anger Expression Inventory (Spielberger, 1988) for anger. These three tests are the most frequent choices in the assessment of these three affective disorders, respectively.

The preceding discussion has also been restricted to self-report methods of assessing affect. Needless to say, data thus obtained may be corroborated by interviews and further qualified by behavioral observations. Wherever feasible, physiological data may also reveal important patterns of synchrony or desynchrony with the emotions under investigation. These can be of special import in uncovering the mechanisms by which affect influences health and illness.

Finally, affect data collection can be extended beyond the clinical or laboratory encounter. If the data are going to be representative of the individual's functioning, they must be obtained over a larger window in time and must not be context specific. The technique of self-monitoring offers one approach toward this goal. Checklists, rating scales, diaries, graphs, and brief questionnaires too can be self-administered repeatedly at set points in time or else on an event-related basis. This self-monitoring of affective states can proceed in parallel with self-monitoring of pain so as to provide a picture of the ongoing interplay between the two variables within the individual's home, work, and other environments. Such concurrent and repeated measures in naturalistic settings (now termed ecological momentary assessment; Stone & Shiffman, 1994) have the potential to test out various models of the relationship between pain and affect outlined earlier.

CONCLUSION

This chapter emphasized the centrality of affect in pain. Accordingly, ideas were imported from the new field of affective science, which differentiates emotion from mood, temperaments, and affective disorders. An integrative model linking affect to cognitive appraisals, motivational processes, and behaviors was presented. This offers a framework for making sense of the experience of pain. Furthermore, a set of six dynamic relationships between affect and pain were specified: Not only is affect concurrent with pain, it is also a likely consequence of pain, and it can also potentiate, precipitate, exacerbate, or perpetuate pain. Anecdotal reports were provided to illustrate this diversity of relationships; nomothetic data from pain patients were analyzed to reveal a profile of affect dominated by anger, fear, and sadness. Finally, the methodology of assessing these emotions and affect in general was outlined and considerations for further research were discussed. With a theoretical framework and the available assessment technology, the affective component of pain can be demystified and ultimately brought under control with a view to managing the pain as a whole.

ACKNOWLEDGMENTS

We wish to thank Dr. Carl Noe of the Baylor Center for Pain Management for assistance in the empirical portion of this study. This chapter was funded in part by a grant to the first author from the National Institute of Mental Health (MH54678-01).

REFERENCES

Affleck, G., Tennen, H., Urrows, S., & Higgins, P. (1992). Neuroticism and the pain-mood relation in rheumatoid arthritis: Insights from a prospective daily study. *Journal of Consulting and Clinical Psychology, 60,* 119–126.

Allodi, F., & Goldstein, R. (1995). Posttraumatic somatoform disorders among immigrant workers. *Journal of Nervous and Mental Disease, 183*, 604–607.

American Psychiatric Association. (1994). *Diagnostic and Statistical Manual of Mental Disorders* (4th ed.). Washington, DC: Author.

Arntz, A., Dreessen, L., & Merckelbach, H. (1991). Attention, not anxiety, influences pain. *Behaviour Research and Therapy, 29*, 41–50.

Beck, A. T., Ward, C. H., Mendelson, M., Mock, J., & Erbaugh, J. (1961). An inventory for measuring depression. *Archives of General Psychiatry, 4*, 561–571.

Beecher, H. K. (1957). The measurement of pain: Prototype for the quantitative study of subjective responses. *Pharmacological Review, 9*, 59–209.

Block, A. R. (1996). *Presurgical psychological screening in chronic pain syndromes: A guide for the behavioral health practitioner.* Mahwah, NJ: Lawrence Erlbaum Associates.

Block, A. R., Kremer, E. F., & Gaylor, M. (1980). Behavioral treatment of chronic pain: The spouse as a discriminative cue for pain behavior. *Pain, 9*, 243–252.

Blumer, D., & Heilbronn, M. (1982). Chronic pain as a variant of depressive disease: The pain prone disorder. *Journal of Nervous and Mental Disease, 170*, 381–406.

Boyle, G. J. (1986). Higher-order factors in the Differential Emotions Scale (DES–III). *Personality and Individual Differences, 7*, 305–310.

Boyle, G. J. (1987). A cross-validation of the factor structure of the Profile of Mood States: Were the factors correctly identified in the first instance? *Psychological Reports, 60*, 343–354.

Burns, J. W., Johnson, B. J., Mahoney, N., Devine, J., & Pawl, R. (1996). Anger management style, hostility and spouse responses: Gender differences in predictors of adjustment among chronic pain patients. *Pain, 64*, 445–453.

Chapman, C. R. (1993). The emotional aspect of pain. In C. R. Chapman & K. M. Foley (Eds.), *Current and emerging issues in cancer pain: Research and practice* (pp. 83–98). New York: Raven.

Chaturvedi, S. K., & Albert, M. (1986). Chronic pain patients in a psychiatric population. *NIMHANS Journal, 4*, 19–24.

Cipher, D. J., & Fernandez, E. (1997). Expectancy variables predicting tolerance and avoidance of pain in chronic pain patients. *Behaviour Research and Therapy, 35*, 437–444.

Clark, W. C., Fletcher, J. D., Janal, M. N., & Carroll, J. D. (1995). Hierarchical clustering of pain and emotion descriptors: Toward a revision of the McGill Pain Questionnaire. In B. Bromm & J. Desmedt (Eds.), *Advances in pain research and therapy* (Vol. 22, pp. 319–330). New York: Raven.

Clark, W. C., Janal, M. N., Fletcher, D., Wharton, R. N., & Carroll, J. D. (1997). *Introducing the Multidimensional Affect and Pain Survey (MAPS).* Unpublished manuscript, Columbia University, New York.

Clore, G. L. (1994). Why emotions require cognition. In P. Ekman & R. J. Davidson (Eds.), *The nature of emotion: Fundamental questions* (pp. 181–191). New York: Oxford University Press.

Davidson, R. J. (1992). Emotion and affective style: Hemispheric substrates. *Psychological Science, 3*, 39–43.

Davidson, R. J. (1994). On emotion, mood, and related affective constructs. In P. Ekman & R. J. Davidson (Eds.), *The nature of emotion: Fundamental questions* (pp. 51–55). New York: Oxford University Press.

Engel, G. L. (1959). "Psychogenic" pain and the pain prone patient. *American Journal of Medicine, 26*, 899–918.

Fernandez, E. (1989). Primary emotions in the affective contribution to chronic pain (Doctoral dissertation, The Ohio State University, 1990). *Dissertation Abstracts International, 50*, B-5313.

Fernandez, E. (1991). *Theoretical specification of variables and items for an Emotional Distress Questionnaire.* Unpublished manuscript, The University of Queensland, Australia.

Fernandez, E. (1997, October). *The psychology of affect and its relevance to physical symptoms* (Symposium on negative affect, arousal, and emotions intrinsic to pain). Paper presented at the Sixteenth Annual Scientific Meeting of the American Pain Society, New Orleans.

Fernandez, E. (1998). The role of affect in somatoform and factitious disorders. *Current Review of Pain, 2,* 106–111.

Fernandez, E., & Boyle, G. J. (in press). Affective and evaluative descriptors in the McGill Pain Questionnaire: Category variations and intensity invariance. *European Journal of Pain.*

Fernandez, E., & McDowell, J. J. (1995). Response-reinforcement relationships in chronic pain syndrome: Applicability of Herrnstein's law. *Behaviour Research and Therapy, 33,* 855–863.

Fernandez, E., & Milburn, T. E. (1994). Sensory and affective predictors of overall pain, and emotions associated with affective pain. *The Clinical Journal of Pain, 10,* 3–9.

Fernandez, E., Moon, C., Urrutia, M., Johnson, T., & Salinas, N. (1996). Correlates of anger in chronic pain. *Annals of Behavioral Medicine, 18*(Suppl.), S200.

Fernandez, E., & Towery, S. (1996). A parsimonious set of verbal descriptors of pain sensation derived from the McGill Pain Questionnaire. *Pain, 66,* 31–37.

Fernandez, E., & Turk, D. C. (1992). Sensory and affective components of pain: Separation and synthesis. *Psychological Bulletin, 112,* 205–217.

Fernandez, E., & Turk, D. C. (1993). Anger in chronic pain patients: A neglected target of attention. *American Pain Society Bulletin, 3*(4), 5–7.

Fernandez, E., & Turk, D. C. (1994). Demand characteristics underlying differential ratings of sensory versus affective components of pain. *Journal of Behavioral Medicine, 17,* 375–389.

Fernandez, E., & Turk, D. C. (1995). The scope and significance of anger in the experience of chronic pain. *Pain, 61,* 165–175.

Flor, H., Birbaumer, N., Schugens, M. M., & Lutzenberger, W. (1992). Symptom-specific psychophysiological responses in chronic pain patients. *Psychophysiology, 29,* 452–460.

Ford, C. V. (1995). Dimensions of somatization and hypochondriasis [Special issue: Malingering and conversion reactions]. *Neurologic Clinics, 13,* 241–253.

Frijda, N. (1987). Emotions, cognitive structure, and action tendency. *Cognition and Emotion, 1,* 115–143.

Gamsa, A. (1990). Is emotional disturbance a precipitator or a consequence of chronic pain? *Pain, 42,* 183–195.

Geisser, M. E., Roth, R. S., Bachman, J. E., & Eckert, T. A. (1996). The relationship between symptoms of post-traumatic stress disorder and pain, affective disturbance and disability among patients with accident and non-accident related pain. *Pain, 66,* 207–214.

Gil, K. M., Keefe, F. J., Crisson, J. E., & Van Dalfsen, P. J. (1987). Social support and pain behavior. *Pain, 29,* 209–217.

Gotlib, I. H., & Meyer, J. P. (1986). Factor analysis of the Multiple Affect Adjective Check List: A separation of positive and negative affect. *Journal of Personality and Social Psychology, 50,* 1161–1165.

Gracely, R. H. (1992). Evaluation of multi-dimensional pain scales. *Pain, 48,* 297–300.

Holroyd, K. A., Talbot, F., Holm, J. E., Pingel, J. D., Lake, A. E., & Saper, J. R. (1996). Asssessing the dimensions of pain: A multitrait-multimethod evaluation of seven measures. *Pain, 67,* 259–265.

Hunsley, J. (1990). Dimensionality of the Multiple Affect Adjective Check List–Revised: A comparison of factor analytic procedures. *Journal of Psychopathology and Behavioral Assessment, 12,* 81–91.

Izard, C. E. (1991). *The psychology of emotions.* New York: Plenum.

Izard, C. E., Dougherty, F. E., Bloxom, B. M., & Kotsch, W. E. (1974). *The differential emotions scale: A method of measuring the subjective experience of discrete emotions.* Unpublished manuscript, Vanderbilt University, Nashville, TN.

Kerns, R. D., Rosenberg, R., & Jacob, M. C. (1994). Anger expression and chronic pain. *Journal of Behavioral Medicine, 17*, 57–67.

Kremer, E. F., Atkinson, J. H., & Kremer, A. M. (1983). The language of pain: Affective descriptors of pain are a better predictor of psychological disturbance than pattern of sensory and affective descriptors. *Pain, 16*, 185–192.

Lazarus, R. S. (1984). On the primacy of cognition. *American Psychologist, 39*, 124–129.

McNair, D. M., Lorr, M., & Droppleman, L. F. (1981). *Profile of Mood States.* San Diego, CA: Educational and Industrial Testing Service.

Melzack, R., & Casey, K. L. (1968). Sensory, motivational, and central control determinants of pain: A new conceptual model. In D. Kenshalo (Ed.), *The skin senses* (pp. 423–443). Springfield, IL: Thomas.

Morley, S., & Pallin, V. (1995). Scaling the affective domain of pain: A study of the dimensionality of verbal descriptors. *Pain, 62*, 39–49.

Nemanick, R. C., & Munz, D. C. (1994). Measuring the poles of negative and positive mood using the Positive Affect Negative Affect schedule. *Psychological Reports, 74*, 195–199.

Ortony, A., Clore, G. L., & Collins, A. (1988). *The cognitive structure of emotions.* New York: Cambridge University Press.

Paanksep, J. (1994). The basics of basic emotion. In P. Ekman & R. J. Davidson (Eds.), *The nature of emotion: Fundamental questions* (pp. 20–24). New York: Oxford University Press.

Pilowsky, I. (1988). Affective disorders and pain. In R. Dubner, G. F. Gebhart, & M. R. Bond (Eds.), *Proceedings of the 5th World Congress on Pain* (pp. 263–275). Amsterdam: Elsevier.

Polatin, P. B., Kinney, R. K., Gatchel, R., Lillo, E., & Mayer, T. G. (1993). Psychiatric illness and chronic low-back pain: The mind and the spine—Which goes first? *Spine, 18*, 66–71.

Price, D. D. (1988). *Psychological and neural mechanisms of pain.* New York: Raven.

Rasmussen, P. R., & Jeffrey, A. C. (1995). Assessment of mood states: Biases in single-administration assessments. *Journal of Psychopathology and Behavioral Assessment, 17*, 177–184.

Rasmussen, P. R., Jeffrey, A. C., Willingham, J. K., & Glover, T. L. (1994). Implications of the true score model in assessment of mood state. *Journal of Social Behavior and Personality, 9*, 107–118.

Rime, B., Mesquita, B., Philippot, P., & Boca, S. (1991). Beyond the emotional event: Six studies in the social sharing of emotion. *Cognition and Emotion, 5*, 435–465.

Scherer, K. (1994). Toward a concept of "modal emotions." In P. Ekman & R. J. Davidson (Eds.), *The nature of emotion: Fundamental questions* (pp. 25–31). New York: Oxford University Press.

Skiffington, S., Fernandez, E., & McFarland, K. (1996, August). *Multicomponential differentiation of negative emotions.* Paper presented at the One Hundred and Fourth Annual Convention of the American Psychological Association, Toronto.

Skiffington, S., Fernandez, E., & McFarland, K. A. (in press). Towards the validation of multiple features in the assessment of emotions. *European Journal of Psychological Assessment.*

Spielberger, C. D. (1988). *State-Trait Anger Expression Inventory professional manual.* Odessa, FL: Psychological Assessment Resources.

Spielberger, C. D., Gorsuch, S. L., & Lushene, R. E. (1970). Manual for the State-Trait Anxiety Inventory (self-evaluation questionnaire). Palo Alto, CA.: Consulting Psychologists Press.

Stalling, R. B. (1992). Mood and pain: The influence of positive and negative affect on reported body aches. *Journal of Social Behavior and Personality, 7*, 323–334.

Stone, A. A., & Shiffman, S. S. (1994). Ecological momentary assessment (EMA) in behavioral medicine. *Annals of Behavioral Medicine, 16*, 199–202.

Towery, S., & Fernandez, E. (1996). Reclassification and rescaling of McGill Pain Questionnaire verbal descriptors of pain sensation: A replication. *The Clinical Journal of Pain, 12*, 270–276.

Tunis, S. L., Golbus, M. S., Copeland, K. L., & Fine, B. A. (1990). Normative scores and factor structure of the Profile of Mood States for women seeking prenatal diagnosis for advanced maternal age. *Educational and Psychological Measurement, 50*, 309–324.

Turk, D. C., & Fernandez, E. (1990). On the putative uniqueness of cancer pain: Do psychological principles apply? *Behaviour Research and Therapy, 28*, 1–13.

Turk, D. C., Rudy, T. E., & Salovey, P. (1985). The McGill Pain Questionnaire reconsidered: Confirming the factor structure and examining appropriate uses. *Pain, 21*, 386–397.

Von Frey, M. (1895). Beitrage sur Sinnesphysiologie der Haut. *Sitzungsberichte sachs Gesamte Weissenschaft, 47*, 181.

Watson, D., Clark, L. A., & Tellegen, A. (1988). Development and validation of brief measures of positive and negative affect: The PANAS scales. *Journal of Personality and Social Psychology, 54*, 1063–1070.

Weisenberg, M., Aviram, O., Wolf, Y., & Raphaeli, N. (1984). Relevant and irrelevant anxiety in the reaction to pain. *Pain, 20*, 371–383.

Zuckerman, M., & Lubin, B. (1965). *Manual for the Multiple Affect Adjective Check List.* San Diego, CA: Educational and Industrial Testing Service.

Zuckerman, M., & Lubin, B. (1985). *Manual for the MAACL-R: The Multiple Affect Adjective Check List Revised.* San Diego, CA: Educational and Industrial Testing Service.

Chapter 8

Pharmacological Treatment in Chronic Pain

Harold Merskey
London Health Sciences Centre

Dwight Moulin
London Health Sciences Centre

As in many books on pain, the contents list of this volume and the range of disciplines of contributors bear witness to the need for a comprehensive approach to the management of chronic pain. The psychological causes and consequences of chronic pain—the latter probably being more important than the former—occur in practice cheek by jowl with both physical and psychological treatments. Among the physical treatments, and especially so with the common diagnoses of musculoskeletal disorders, general and specific exercises take pride of place for moral and (dare we say it?) politically correct reasons. Which is not to say that exercise is unimportant but only that it should not become a shibboleth.

Another shibboleth holds that drug treatments are bad and morally suspect, and the more psychotropic or more narcotic the drug, the more this is the case. These attitudes reflect concerns that should be taken into account, but not to the extent of disturbing the standard balanced view, which is that a combination of psychological techniques, exercise, other physical measures, and medication is required to provide the best available pattern of treatment for patients seeking help in the care of chronic pain. The purpose of this chapter is, of course, to provide information on pharmacological matters. In doing so we regard the importance of the other treatments as established, and not requiring discussion here because it is provided elsewhere in this volume.

As the contents list also makes clear there are many taxonomic categories of pain. Pain is arranged there both by system (gastrointestinal disorders and rheumatologic disorders), by anatomy (back pain, pelvic pain, regional pain), and by etiology. It is also linked specifically in one chapter (chap. 28, this volume) with psychological causes, as well as with many physical causes.

The pharmacological treatment of chronic pain has to take account of the type of pain as grouped by taxonomy, for example, migraine as compared with gastrointestinal disorders and with etiology, for example, the neuropathic compared with the arthritic or soft tissue pain syndromes. It also has to take account of the pattern of pain irrespective of known etiology, particularly with regard to stabbing versus steady pains. These considerations cut across diagnostic groups, but particular preferences in treatment may relate to more specific features of a given illness; for example, trigeminal neuralgia will be more often treated with the type of drug that is used for stabbing pains, and some of the musculoskeletal disorders attract the use of muscle relaxants more readily than does herpes zoster. In this chapter we are concerned most with the different types of drug available for chronic pain, and specific applications are mentioned largely by way of illustration, because more specific issues are tackled in individual chapters in Part II of the volume.

TYPES OF ANALGESIC MEDICATION

Besides the diversity of painful illnesses and their causes there is also a considerable diversity among drugs. The medications available can be grouped conveniently overall into seven main types: (a) nonnarcotic analgesics, especially acetylsalicylic acid (aspirin), acetaminophen (paracetamol, Tylenol, Panadol), and nonsteroidal anti-inflammatory drugs (NSAIDs). (It is quite common practice to use histamine-2 blockers, e.g., ranitidine, as remedies for peptic ulceration in conjunction with nonsteroidal anti-inflammatory drugs, and cytoprotective agents are also employed, e.g., misoprostol. Obviously, it is always more desirable to try and find a medication that works without side effects than to prescribe one with side effects and then something else to counteract the side effects.); (b) muscle relaxants; (c) anticonvulsant drugs—used in trigeminal neuralgia and certain other types of stabbing pains; (d) psychotropic medication; (e) specific remedies, e.g., ergotamine preparations, sumatriptan (Imitrex) for migraine (these are simply listed here for completeness); (f) opioid analgesics; (g) topical analgesic agents including capsaicin (Zovax), local anaesthetic creams, and patch forms of application of some opioids.

The use of psychotropic medication for pain that is due to psychiatric illness, e.g., headache with depression when the depression is the primary problem, is not reviewed. In essence, the treatment of pain in such a case is usually the treatment of the primary condition whether it be depression, anxiety, or hypochondriasis (to name the most common causes for pain of psychological origin). We are concerned here more with the use or choice of psychotropic drugs that have analgesic actions.

Throughout it also has to be noted that mild and intermittent pain is unlikely to need the use of the more potent pharmacological measures and will most often be handled by self-treatment by patients with over-the-counter preparations. Our discussion therefore deals with pain that is usually moderately severe or worse, frequently present if not continuous, and intractable.

NONSTEROIDAL ANTI-INFLAMMATORY DRUGS

The most common of these is ibuprofen (Motrin, Advil), which is now available as an over-the-counter preparation in many countries. As the name implies the drugs both abate inflammation and relieve pain and these are independent but additive actions. NSAIDs are almost invariably taken with food. They tend to cause stomach problems. Their analgesic action is linked with the inhibition of cyclooxygenase (COX) and thus the inhibition of prostaglandins throughout the body. This includes the stomach wall where the effect on prostaglandins promotes gastric irritation, dyspepsia, and even peptic ulceration. The frequency of peptic ulceration is high in individuals who take NSAIDs regularly. They often also irritate the gastrointestinal tract to produce diarrhea. More recently, the varying anti-inflammatory/analgesic effects of different NSAIDs have been attributed to a different affinity to isoforms of COX, COX–1, and COX–2 (Mitchell et al., 1993). Although most NSAIDS are nonspecific COX inhibitors, certain newer NSAIDs such as nabumetone (Relafen) are relatively specific for COX–2 inhibition, which imparts less gastrointestinal toxicity but still potent analgesia. However, even nabumetone is not free from undesirable gastric side effects.

It is important to mention these problems because many patients with chronic pain present with abdominal pain in addition say to neck pain or back pain. The abdominal pain is frequently found to be due to treatment. It is well recognized that aspirin and NSAIDs can cause these problems. It is much less well known that acetaminophen (officially paracetamol in the United Kingdom; Tylenol, Panadol) can have the same effect especially if taken on a regular basis. Because patients with chronic pain often are advised to take their drugs on a time-contingent regular basis, this is frequently a recipe for producing, at a minimum, gastric discomfort and more often significant dyspepsia, if not ulceration.

The effect on the stomach wall may occur whether or not the drug is taken by mouth. If suppositories are used, for example, indomethacin, ulceration is still liable to develop when the drug reaches the stomach via the circulation. Other effects of the NSAIDs may include some fluid retention.

After all these awful warnings it is still important to note that many patients do get useful relief from these drugs. However, practitioners in pain clinics should be actively aware that although NSAIDs (aspirin and acetaminophen) are frequently the drugs of choice in treating patients with mild to moderate chronic pain, their regular use should be reviewed very strictly and very carefully.

Acetaminophen often is given in combination with codeine and caffeine, for example, Tylenol–2, a very popular compound preparation in North America, contains acetaminophen 325 mg, caffeine 60 mg, and codeine 15 mg. The acetaminophen and codeine are expected to have analgesic actions and the caffeine is intended to counteract the sedative effects of codeine. However, caffeine itself can have some disadvantages by increasing anxiety or causing dependence, and patients seeking to get the benefit of codeine frequently raise the dose of Tylenol–2 or Tylenol–3 (which contains the same amounts of acetaminophen and caffeine but twice the amount of codeine that is in Tylenol–2). When this happens Tylenol–2 or Tylenol–3, like acetaminophen, also produce gastrointestinal difficulties. The gastrointestinal difficulties where codeine preparations are used will include a risk of constipation.

Treatment with antibiotics to eradicate Helicobacter pylori is also beginning to be considered for patients with chronic peptic ulceration or dyspepsia following the use of NSAIDs.

The aforementioned drugs are often used in slightly different ways. For example, apart from being given three to four times a day on a time-contingent basis, ibuprofen or naproxen or most other NSAIDs may be taken p.r.n. (as occasion rises) when pain is troublesome and omitted at other times. This is an acceptable approach with illnesses where the level of pain fluctuates from mild to severe. On the other hand, nabumetone, which is long-acting, should only be taken twice or, at most, three times a day, in order to maintain analgesia and it is of less advantage to take it on an urgent p.r.n. basis with the expectation of immediate relief.

The foregoing drugs are generally "virtuous" because they rarely involve addiction problems. Occasional excessive use of acetominophen, however, may damage the renal tubules, and apparently may occur through addiction to a subjective effect of acetaminophen. This appears to be more common with aspirin or with the now-abandoned drug phenacetin and is probably rare. It should be noted however that the dose of aspirin that is used for the prophylaxis of coronary artery thrombosis, embolism, and stroke is much smaller than the dose normally used for analgesia.

MUSCLE RELAXANTS

Five drugs are usually available in North America and elsewhere as muscle relaxants. They are cyclobenzaprine (Flexeril), methocarbamol (Robaxin), carisoprodol (Soma), baclofen (Lioresal), and orphenadrine (Disipal or in combination with acetaminophen and caffeine-Norgesic). It should also be noted that carisoprodol breaks down to meprobamate and that this occasionally causes leucocytopenia or affects hepatic function. Hence, with this drug the white cell count and liver function should be monitored.

All these drugs are quite likely to be effective, particularly with musculoskeletal pain. They may be given sometimes just to help with pain that occurs through the night, or they may be given on a regular time-contingent basis through the day, or on an "as needed" basis. Typical doses are as follows: cyclobenzaprine 10 mg t.i.d. (three times a day), methocarbamol 1,000–1,500 mg t.i.d., carisoprodol 350 mg t.i.d., orphenadrine 50–100 mg t.i.d., or baclofen 10–20 mg q.i.d. (four times a day). Most of these drugs are better accredited for acute relief of muscle pain than chronic relief as well. All of them may cause some sedation. The first three tend to lose some of their effect after being used for a little while. Cyclobenzaprine, which has a molecular structure very similar to that of amitriptyline, sometimes seems to be linked to weight gain also. In order to avoid loss of effect or dependence emerging with cyclobenzaprine, methocarbamol, or carisoprodol, it may be desirable to rotate their use, substituting different prescriptions in alternate months. It probably would be inappropriate to use two of these drugs simultaneously.

Orphenadrine, is an anticholinergic anti-Parkinsonian preparation and also has some muscle relaxant action. It seems to cause less dependence but more side effects in terms of dry mouth, constipation, and so forth.

Baclofen, like orphenadrine, is a drug with significant central nervous effects. It influences both monosynaptic and polysynaptic reflexes at the spinal level and, because it is an analogue of the putative inhibitory neurotransmitter gama-amino butyric acid (GABA), it is thought that it may have a similar action but there is no conclusive evidence of this. It is used for muscle relaxation, the relief of spasticity and pain. Besides the common side effects of most drugs, which include nausea, diarrhea, and skin rashes, centrally active drugs often tend to cause drowsiness. Baclofen is more troublesome in this respect than some of the other medications (but this can be put to some advantage if it is given only at night). However, it seems to have a much higher rate of other side effects, including dysphoria, confusion, and cognitive slowing. Only a minority of our patients seem to benefit from it, but those that do find it extremely helpful and it does not appear to develop significant problems of addiction. It may be used for both pain of neuropathic origin and pain of musculoskeletal type, as well perhaps as others.

Although these muscle relaxant drugs are not so prominent in the relief of pain as the others discussed earlier, they often play a useful role in reducing the overall level of pain from which patients with chronic musculoskeletal disorders may suffer.

PSYCHOTROPIC MEDICATION

Almost since their inception in psychiatry, antidepressants and neuroleptic drugs have been used in the relief of pain (Monks, 1994; Sigwald, Henne, Bouttier, Raymondeaud, & Quétin, 1956). With antidepressants the question that arose immediately was whether their effect in relieving pain occurred secondary to the relief of depression or whether it was an independent analgesic phenomenon. In view of the involvement of serotonin in some nerve pathways, there was a tendency to favor the idea that they might have an independent analgesic effect through a serotoninergic mechanism. Watson et al. (1982) were probably the first to demonstrate in a double-blind placebo-controlled trial that an antidepressant, in this case amitriptyline, was more effective than placebo in relieving pain in individuals who were not depressed. Depression was measured with the Beck Depression Scale. A series of subsequent studies (Max, 1994) has confirmed this for amitriptyline. Other antidepressants that are thought likely to be analgesic include nortriptyline, imipramine, clomipramine, doxepin, and maprotiline.

The two most favored are probably amitriptyline as a relatively serotoninergic drug and maprotiline as a relatively monaminergic antidepressant of the first generation. However, we state personal preferences here except for amitriptyline, which is generally recognized as the best accredited analgesic antidepressant. It has become well recognized that other drugs with a stronger serotoninergic effect than amitriptyline appear to be less analgesic, and unfortunately the second-generation antidepressants do not appear to carry significant analgesic benefits, whether they are serotoninergic as with fluoxetine, fluvoxamine, nefazadone, paroxetine, and sertraline or broad spectrum as with venlafaxine. This is a pity because amitriptyline has so many more side effects than the serotonin selective reuptake inhibitors and is so much harder for some patients to tolerate.

The effect of amitriptyline is best obtained by very careful initial adjustment of dosage. Watson et al. (1982) found that satisfactory doses of amitriptyline might be around 75 mg per diem for patients with postherpetic neuralgia but higher doses are sometimes needed, and lower doses are sometimes both effective and all that can be tolerated. Perhaps no drug in medicine exemplifies more than amitriptyline the position that treatment with drugs should be "tailor-made." It cannot be given to the best effect as a treatment either for depression or pain without careful adjustment of the dosage. The range of absorption of amitriptyline between different individuals is of the order of 2,000%. Some cannot tolerate 10 mg daily; others accept 300 mg and ask if the dose can be raised because the good effects are not quite complete. Amitriptyline also has a relatively long half-life and therefore has a slow onset of action even for single dosage. It is best given at night but not at bedtime. Patients should be instructed to take it 2, 3, or even 4 hours before bedtime. In this way, by the time the amitriptyline is beginning to be sedative it will be close to their normal hour of retiring and the sedative effect will not last unduly long into the next day.

Patients should be told to increase the dose by one tablet every night until they reach a level that is reasonably effective in securing sleep but does not leave them with lingering disadvantageous sedation the next morning. A few patients find the drug frankly dysphoric and this is true of all psychotropic medication. They should not be pressed to continue in that case. However, for those who can take it, adjustment of the dose is important, with attention to whether enough sleep—but not too much—is produced, whether constipation occurs and if so how it is to be managed. Attention to the common hazards of hypotensive episodes and somewhat more frequently difficulty in micturition is essential, because it will not be good practice to cure the patient's pain or to relieve it at the price of producing kidney failure from the hydrostatic back pressure of a poorly emptying bladder.

As mentioned, the common starting dose should be 10 mg for outpatients (much higher doses may be used for inpatients) and it is often helpful to tell patients that larger sized tablets are available and can be used in each of the 25-, 50-, or even 75-mg size, but that one begins cautiously. We cannot emphasize too strongly the importance of discussing carefully with the patient how to take amitriptyline and similar medication. If necessary the dose to be given day by day, and the way it is to be increased, should be tabulated and written down for the patient.

As indicated, the common side effects of amitriptyline and similar drugs are drowsiness, dry mouth, constipation, and retention of urine. There are other hazards as well with which the practicing physician needs to be familiar, including glaucoma and hypotensive fainting attacks. Patients taking amitriptyline and other first-generation antidepressants often gain weight, and this can be particularly embarrassing to those with chronic pain. Weight gain is common in patients with chronic nonmalignant pain, because although they may reduce their activities, they do not necessarily reduce their intake, and amitriptyline also causes an increased appetite and a tendency to eat, sometimes almost in a bulimic fashion.

If amitriptyline is being given, the best method to handle this problem is by anticipation. Once it is decided that the drug will be continued, patients should be told of the possibility that they will gain weight and advised to take preventive measures *ab initio*. This includes dietary advice and may also include the use of another antidepressant concomitantly with amitriptyline in the hope that the latter will reduce weight gain. Although the effects are not always predictable and are sometimes opposite to those intended, fluvoxamine (Luvox), sertraline (Zoloft), fluoxetine (Prozac), and venlafaxine (Effexor) all have a tendency in some patients to reduce appetite. The first two can usually be given quite easily with amitriptyline without problems. Fluoxetine tends to inhibit the breakdown of amitriptyline and nortriptyline so that it pushes up the serum level and makes the amitriptyline more effective, and sometimes the serum level rises too high. This can be managed by reducing the dose of amitriptyline if fluoxetine is prescribed and monitoring the serum level. Frequently a reduction of about one third in the amitriptyline dose is sufficient.

Phenothiazines are also believed to have analgesic effects, although the proof that this occurs is mostly from parenteral administration. Good double-blind evidence of analgesic efficacy for most phenothiazines is lacking (Monks, 1994). However, a good deal of other inferential evidence supports the use of methotrimeprazine (Lasagna & DeKornfeld, 1961) or other phenothiazines such as chlorpromazine, fluphenazine, perphenazine, or trifluoperazine. Like amitriptyline, methotrimeprazine (levomepromazine, Nozinan, Veractil) may provoke dysphoria, in which case it should be discontinued. If it proves helpful, the dose may be within the range of anywhere from 2 mg to 100 mg a day and it then becomes important to warn the patient about the risk of tardive dyskinesia with long-term use. We make it a practice to warn not only the patient but also the spouse. The first signs of tardive dyskinesia often do not trouble the patient, and even when the problem is pointed out to patients they may be reluctant to discontinue the medication if it has proved effective. However, if medication causing tardive dyskinesia is stopped at the early stage when the first signs of the dyskinesia appear, it can ordinarily be expected to remit over a few weeks or months. It is therefore important to warn both the patient and the spouse to be on the lookout for these side effects.

Like amitriptyline, methotrimeprazine can be associated with weight gain, perhaps in part through an action upon appetite mechanisms in the upper brain stem or hypothalamus.

MANAGEMENT OF NEUROPATHIC PAIN

Neuropathic pain represents a special category of chronic pain because the pain is not physiologic; that is, it is not generated by nociceptors. Neuropathic pain is generated by injury to the peripheral or central nervous system or both and is characterized by constant burning pain, superimposed lancinating pain, and touch-evoked pain or allodynia. A number of adjuvant analgesic agents are available for the management of neuropathic pain and they are listed in Table 8.1. Although psychotropic medication such as amitriptyline provides first-line treatment, it is important to note that the usual response to any of these agents is pain relief in only a portion of the treated population. For instance, a recent systematic review of antidepressants in neuropathic pain revealed that only 30% of patients will obtain more than 50% pain relief (McQuay et al., 1996). In addition to the use of psychotropic medications for neuropathic pain, a number of other analgesic agents have been found to be helpful in randomized controlled trials or appear promising in anecdotal reports and they are reviewed briefly.

TABLE 8.1
Pharmacologic Agents Used for Neuropathic Pain

Class	Examples
Antidepressants	Amitriptyline
	Desipramine
	Paroxetine
Phenothiazines	Methotrimeprazine
Anticonvulsants	Carbamazepine
	Phenytoin
	Valproate
	Gabapentin
Muscle Relaxants	Baclofen
Local Anesthetics	Lidocaine
	Mexilitene
	Flecainide
Sympathetic Blockers	Clonidine
	Phenoxybenzamine
Topical Agents	Capsaicin
	EMLA cream
	Lidocaine gel
NMDA Antagonists	Ketamine
	Dextromethorphan
Opioid Analgesics	Morphine
	Fentanyl
	Methadone

Anticonvulsants and Baclofen

The anticonvulsants have their greatest value in the management of lancinating neuropathic pain. Carbamazepine is the drug of first choice for
trigeminal neuralgia. Carbamazepine is given in gradually increasing doses
to 200–400 mg t.i.d. Although baclofen is marketed for spasticity, it has
efficacy in trigeminal neuralgia and is sometimes useful for other neuropathic pain syndromes in doses titrated up to 10–20 mg q.i.d. Clonazepam and
valproic acid appear useful in isolated reports, but their use has not been
substantiated in randomized controlled trials.

Newer anticonvulsants such as gabapentin appear promising in the management of neuropathic pain and, in fact, a recent randomized control
trial of gabapentin showed significant reduction of pain in patients with
painful diabetic neuropathy (Backonja et al., 1997).

Local Anesthetics

Systemic and oral local anaesthetics suppress neuronal excitability at lower
concentrations than are required for conduction block along the nerve
and may therefore have a prolonged duration of action. This has been
the rationale for using oral local anaesthetic agents such as mexilitene in
the management of neuropathic pain. Mexiletine has established efficacy
in the treatment of painful diabetic neuropathy (Dejgard, Petersen, &
Kastrup, 1988). The usual starting dose is 100 mg once or twice daily to
a maintenance dose of 200 mg t.i.d.

Sympathetic Blockers

Clonidine is an alpha-2-adrenergic agonist with analgesic properties.
Transdermal clonidine has been shown to be modestly useful for painful
diabetic neuropathy with a 20% reduction in pain relative to placebo
(Byas-Smith et al., 1995). The starting dose of clonidine is 0.1 mg per day
with the usual maintenance dose of 0.1 mg orally t.i.d. or 0.3 mg per day
administered as a transdermal patch. Phenoxybenzamine may be efficacious for causalgia, although postural hypotension can be a significant
problem with either of these drugs.

Topical Agents

Drugs that have a local site of action are attractive because there may be
minimal or no systemic side effects. Capsaicin cream has the potential to
relieve neuropathic pain by depleting local tissues of substance P. However,
clinical experience with capsaicin has been disappointing. Some patients
with postherpetic neuralgia respond to a eutectic mixture of local
anaesthetics (EMLA cream) or 5% lidocaine gel.

NMDA Antagonists

N-methyl-D-aspartate (NMDA) agonists and receptors play a major role in the generation of neuronal hyperexcitability of the dorsal horn that has been associated with neuropathic pain. Ketamine is a commonly used intravenous anaesthetic agent with NMDA receptor-blocking activity. Small randomized controlled trials of subanesthetic doses of intravenous ketamine have reported pain relief in postherpetic neuralgia and other neuropathic pain syndromes, although psychotomimetic side effects can be intolerable (Backonja et al., 1994).

Dextromethorphan, a common cough suppressant, is another NMDA receptor antagonist that has been studied in neuropathic pain states. Although a randomized controlled trial of oral dextromethorphan in a variety of central and peripheral pain syndromes did not show any benefit (McQuay et al., 1994), there are isolated reports of efficacy. Effective doses of dextromethorphan may not normally be achieved by prescribing it on its own, but doses of 15–30 mg t.i.d. or q.i.d. may become effective if given with an agent that blocks the cytochrome P450 enzyme system. One such drug that has been used in this way is quinidine and another that might have some effect (although more weakly) is fluoxetine. We have found that one patient with allodynia in an area related to repeated fractures of the tibia due to osteogenesis imperfecta did get an impressive dose-related reduction of pain with a combination of quinidine and dextromethorphan. However, patients with musculoskeletal pain seem to not find quinidine plus dextromethorphan tolerable or effective in our experience.

Opioid Analgesics

Considerable controversy surrounds the use of opioid analgesics for chronic neuropathic pain. Most clinical surveys suggest that neuropathic pain does respond to opioid analgesics, but at higher doses than are required for nociceptive pain. This increases the risk of side effects that may have a negative impact on quality of life. A recent randomized controlled trial showed that patients with neuropathic pain obtain significant pain relief from intravenous fentanyl relative to diazepam and saline (Dellemijn & Vanneste, 1997). Methadone may be a useful agent for neuropathic pain and this may relate in part to its NMDA antagonist properties.

OPIOID ANALGESICS IN THE MANAGEMENT
OF CHRONIC NONMALIGNANT PAIN

Despite the unquestionable value of opioid drugs in the management of cancer pain, the opioid literature on chronic nonmalignant pain presents conflicting data largely due to uncontrolled retrospective studies. Some surveys report significant pain relief in response to long-term opioid therapy (Portenoy & Foley, 1986), whereas others describe the additional benefit of improvement in performance status (Zenz, Strumpf, & Tryba, 1992). In contrast, surveys originating in multidisciplinary pain programs with highly selected samples suggest that chronic opioid therapy leads to greater psychological distress, impaired cognition, and poor outcomes (McNairy et al., 1984).

The role of opioid analgesics in the management of chronic nonmalignant pain is further clouded by the perceived risk of psychological dependence or addiction. However, survey data accumulated over the past 20 years do not support this view. In several studies involving almost 25,000 patients without a history of drug dependence, there were only 7 cases of iatrogenic addiction (Portenoy, 1994). These data strongly suggest that the overall risk of addiction among patients with no prior history of drug abuse is actually quite low.

Differentiating between physical and psychological dependence is crucial in understanding the role of opioid analgesics in the management of nonmalignant pain. Physical dependence is a physiologic phenomenon characterized by the development of withdrawal symptoms following abrupt discontinuation of treatment, substantial dose reduction, or antagonist drug administration. Abstinence symptoms are self-limiting and can be avoided entirely through 50% dose reductions of an opioid analgesic every 2–3 days. On the other hand, psychological dependence or addiction can be defined as compulsive drug use despite harm, an overwhelming preoccupation with securing a good supply, and the tendency to relapse after withdrawal. Addiction is a behavioral pattern of drug use in which medication is taken for its psychic effects rather than for its pain-relieving properties. As suggested by survey data, addiction is uncommon if there is no prior history of substance abuse.

Perceived government interference may discourage physicians from using opioid drugs even when medical judgment clearly supports a therapeutic trial. Regulatory bodies have a responsibility to prevent the inappropriate use of medications such as the selling of controlled drugs, but should also support the legitimate use of opioid analgesics when the primary goal is pain relief.

There are only two published randomized controlled trials that address the issue of efficacy of oral opioid analgesics in chronic nonmalignant pain, but they illustrate the limitations of pharmacologic management of chronic musculoskeletal pain. One group reported on 30 patients with predominantly musculoskeletal pain who were treated for 1 week with sustained-release codeine or placebo in a crossover study (Arkinstall et al., 1995). Using a mean daily codeine dose of 273 mg, there was an overall reduction in pain intensity of 29% and a reduction in the Pain Disability

Index of an identical 29%. However, virtually all of these patients had previously been treated with codeine, and the mean duration of opioid use prior to the study was 6 years. Another group conducted a double-blind crossover trial where 46 patients with chronic musculoskeletal pain who had not responded to codeine, anti-inflammatory agents, or antidepressants were randomized to sustained-release morphine or active placebo (benztropine) for 9 weeks (Moulin et al., 1996). The mean daily dose of morphine was 83.5 mg. The morphine group showed a significant reduction in pain intensity relative to placebo, but the benefit was modest. The reduction in pain intensity relative to placebo was in the range of 15% to 20%. There were no significant differences in psychological features, disability status, or cognition between morphine and active placebo, and there was no evidence of psychological dependence or addiction. The modest reduction to morphine in this study may be related in part to the fact that the depression scores of the participants on standard psychological tests were almost 2 *SD*s above the mean of a control population, although apparently representative of patients attending other multidisciplinary pain clinics (Flor, Fydrich, & Turk, 1992).

Given the limitation of opioid treatment, what priority should be assigned to pain relief relative to functional restoration in the management of chronic nonmalignant pain? Clinical experience suggests that a treatment program that focuses on analgesics without incorporating psychosocial and behavioral approaches can reinforce pain-related behavior and undermine a rehabilitative program targeted to functional restoration (Turk & Meichenbaum, 1994). On the other hand, numerous reviews of multidisciplinary pain treatment programs show significant improvements in physical and psychological function and reduced medication use but limited pain relief (Large & Peters, 1991).

Extensive survey data and limited controlled trials provide some guidance regarding the long-term administration of opioid drugs for chronic nonmalignant pain. There is a low risk of psychological dependence or addiction in the absence of a history of substance abuse, and cognitive impairment is unlikely to compromise the treatment program with individualized dose titration. Other side effects are usually controllable with pharmacologic measures such as antiemetics and bowel stimulants. Finally, opioid treatment probably provides modest but significant pain relief in selected patients and may in fact facilitate rehabilitative goals. If one accepts these guidelines, compatibility between opioid therapy and multidisciplinary pain management programs could be facilitated by making analgesic use purely time contingent and not pain contingent after initial dose titration. An exception to this model would be the elderly or very disabled patient where the primary goal is clearly pain relief and not functional restoration.

TABLE 8.2
Guidelines for Opioid Therapy of Chronic Nonmalignant Pain

1. Consider after other reasonable therapies have failed.
2. Perform a complete pain and psychological history and physical examination. A history of isolated tension-type headaches, substance abuse, major personality disorder, or social disruption is a relative contraindication to opioid therapy.
3. A single physician who sets up a contract with the patient should be responsible for opioid prescriptions. The agreement should specify the drug regimen, the goals of treatment, possible side effects, the functional restoration program, and violations that will result in the abrupt termination of opioid therapy.
4. The opioid analgesic of choice (preferably a sustained-release preparation) should be administered around the clock with an initial titration phase of 3–6 weeks to minimize side effects. Dosing should generally be time contingent rather than pain contingent except during the titration phase, where rescue doses for breakthrough pain should be used to help determine the maintenance dose.
5. Incremental dosing during the titration phase should result in a graded analgesic response or at least partial pain relief. Failure to realize at least partial analgesia at initial doses may mean that the pain syndrome is unresponsive to opioid treatment.
6. The patient should be seen monthly for the first 6 months and every 2 to 3 months thereafter. At each visit, the patient should be assessed for analgesia, opioid-related side effects, compliance with functional goals, and presence of aberrant drug-related behavior, and all of this should be documented in the medical record.
7. The patient should be reminded that the goal of opioid therapy is to make the pain tolerable and perhaps to improve function as part of a comprehensive treatment program.

Guidelines for Opioid Therapy in Chronic Nonmalignant Pain

Guidelines for opioid maintenance therapy in patients with chronic nonmalignant pain are provided in Table 8.2. These guidelines are based on the premise that functional restoration is at least as important a goal as pain relief. The goals of chronic opioid therapy are to make the pain tolerable and perhaps improve function. For some patients even modest pain relief can make the difference between bearable and unbearable pain.

REFERENCES

Arkinstall, W., Sandler, E., Goughnour, B., Babul, N., Harsanyi, Z., & Darke, A. C. (1995). Efficacy of control-release codeine in chronic non-malignant pain: A randomized, placebo-controlled clinical trial. *Pain, 62*, 169–178.
Backonja, M., Arndt, G., Gombar, K. A., Check, B., & Zimmerman, M. (1994). Response of chronic neuropathic pain syndromes to ketamine: A preliminary study. *Pain, 56*, 51–57.
Backonja, M., Hes, M. S., & LaMoreaux, L. K. (1997, November). *Gabapentin reduces pain in diabetics with painful peripheral neuropathy: Results of a double-blind placebo-controlled clinical trial.* Paper presented at the American Pain Society 16th Annual Scientific Meeting, New Orleans.

Byas-Smith, M. G., Max, M. B., Muir, J., & Kingman, A. (1995). Transdermal clonidine compared to placebo in painful diabetic neuropathy using a two-stage "enriched enrollment" design. *Pain, 60*, 267–274.

Dejgard, A., Petersen, P., & Kastrup, J. (1988). Mexiletine for treatment of chronic painful diabetic neuropathy. *Lancet, 1*, 9–11.

Dellemijn, P. L. I., & Vanneste, J. A. L. (1997). Randomized double-blind active-placebo-controlled crossover trial of intravenous fentanyl in neuropathic pain. *Lancet, 349*, 753–758.

Flor, H., Fydrich, T., & Turk, D. C. (1992). Efficacy of multi-disciplinary pain treatment centres: A meta-analytic review. *Pain, 49*, 221–230.

Large, R., & Peters, J. (1991). A critical appraisal of outcome of multi-disciplinary pain clinic treatments. In M. R. Bond, J. E. Charlton, & C. J. Woolf (Eds.), *Proceedings of 6th World Congress on Pain* (pp. 417–427). Amsterdam: Elsevier Science Publishers.

Lasagna, L., & DeKornfeld, T. J. (1961). Methotrimeprazine: A new phenothiazine derivative with analgesic properties. *Journal of the American Medical Association, 178*, 887–890.

Max, M. (1994). Antidepressants as analgesics. In H. L. Fields & J. G. Liebeskind (Eds.), *Pharmacological approaches to the treatment of chronic pain: New concepts and critical issues* (pp. 229–246). Seattle: IASP Press.

McNairy, S. L., Maruta, T., Ivnik, R. J., Swanson, D. W., & Ilstrup, D. M. (1984). Prescription medication dependence and neuropsychological function. *Pain, 18*, 169–177.

McQuay, H. J., Carroll, D., Jadad, A. R., Glynn, C. J., Jack, T., Moore, R. A., & Wiffen, P. J. (1994). Dextromethorphan for the treatment of neuropathic pain: A double-blind randomized controlled crossover trial with integral n-of-1 design. *Pain, 59*, 127–133.

McQuay, H. J., Tramer, M., Nye, B. A., Carroll, D., Wiffen, P. J., & Moore, R. A. (1996). A systematic review of anti-depressants in neuropathic pain. *Pain, 68*, 217–227.

Mitchell, J. A., Akarasereenont, P., Thiemermann, C., Flower, R. J., & Vane, J. R. (1993). Selectivity of non-steroidal anti-inflammatory drugs as inhibitors of constitutive and inducible cyclooxygenase. In *Proceedings of the National Academy of Science, 90*, 11693–11697.

Monks, R. (1994). Psychotropic drugs. In P. D. Wall & R. Melzak (Eds.), *Textbook of pain* (3rd ed., pp. 963–989). Edinburgh: Churchill Livingstone.

Moulin, D. E., Iezzi, A., Amireah, R., Sharpe, W. K. J., Boyd, D., & Merskey, H. (1996). Randomized trial of oral morphine for chronic non-cancer pain. *Lancet, 347*, 143–147.

Portenoy, R. K. (1994). Opioid therapy for chronic non-malignant pain: Current status. In H. L. Fields & J. C. Liebeskind (Eds.), *Progress in pain research and therapy* (Vol. 1, pp. 247–287). Seattle: IASP Press.

Portenoy, R. K., & Foley, K. M. (1986). Chronic use of opioid analgesics in non-malignant pain: Report of 38 cases. *Pain, 25*, 171–186.

Sigwald, J., Henne, M., Bouttier, D., Raymondeaud, E., & Quétin, A. (1956). Activité d'une nouvelle phénothiazine en psychiatrie et en neurologie. Propriétés thérapeutiques maleate acide de levomethoxy - 2 (dimethylamino-3-methyl-2 propyl) 10 phenothiazine [Action of a new phenothiazine in psychiatry and in neurology. Therapeutic properties of the malic acid of levomethoxy - 2 (dimethylamino-3-methyl-2 propyl) 10 phenothiazine]. *Presse Médicale, 64*, 2011.

Turk, D. C., & Meichenbaum, D. (1994). A cognitive-behavioural approach to pain management. In P. D. Wall & E. Melzak (Eds.), *Textbook of pain* (3rd ed., pp. 1337–1348). Edinburgh: Churchill Livingstone.

Watson, C. P., Evans, R. J., Reed, K., Merskey, H., Goldsmith, L., & Warsh, J. (1982). Amitriptyline versus placebo in postherpetic neuralgia. *Neurology, 32*, 671–673.

Zenz, M., Strumpf, M., & Tryba, M. (1992). Long-term oral opioid therapy in patients with chronic non-malignant pain. *Journal of Pain Symptom Management, 7*, 69–77.

SPECIFIC PAIN SYNDROMES

Orthopedic and Rheumatologic Conditions

Chapter 9

Chronic Back Pain: Conservative Approaches

Michael E. Geisser
Miles O. Colwell
University of Michigan Medical Center

Chronic back pain (CBP), and in particular chronic low back pain (CLBP), is a growing "epidemic" in the United States (Aronoff, 1991). It has been estimated that 70% to 80% of the costs for work-related low back claims are accounted for by 7% to 10% of patients who develop CLBP (Fast, 1977; Spengler et al., 1986). Annual costs of low back disability in the United States have been estimated to be approximately $50 billion, with the average cost of a single case of work-related back pain exceeding $8,000 (Hazard, Haugh, Reid, Preble, & MacDonald, 1996). Its prevalence also appears to be on the rise, as 31.8% of disability claims in 1990 were due to back pain, compared to 29.2% in 1981 (Deyo, 1993).

The pathophysiological causes of CBP vary, but in general, remain undetermined. Some causes include degenerative changes in the spine, disk abnormalities including ruptures, spinal stenosis, and spondylolisthesis. However, it is difficult to assess the degree to which pathology found in radiographic and other diagnostic studies contribute to CBP, as many asymptomatic persons display abnormal findings on these studies, including disk herniations (Deyo, 1996). In addition, some report that the vast majority of chronic pain patients have no observable underlying organic pathology. For example, White and Gordon (1982) indicated that as many as 85% of patients with low back pain have no identifiable organic pathology. Fordyce (1979) cited an unpublished study by Johnson indicating that 93.1% of injury back pain claimants in the State of Washington lacked physical findings to account for their pain, excluding cases where disk disease was ultimately documented. Many of these patients are given non-specific diagnoses, such as "chronic intractable benign pain syndrome" (Crue, 1985, p. 33) or "non-specific low back pain" (Coste, Paolaggi, & Spira, 1992, p. 1030).

In such cases, what then is the cause of CBP? The exact cause of CBP without explanatory physical findings is unknown or unclear. Traditional medical differential diagnosis would suggest that the cause must then be primarily psychogenic, and this is often inferred (Sanders, 1985; Weintraub, 1988). However, it unlikely that such a large proportion of CBP is primarily psychogenic, although this is not to say that psychosocial factors do not influence the experience of CBP. It is proposed that other potential pathophysiological factors in chronic pain often tend to go unnoticed or undetected, particularly musculoskeletal causes of pain. Although there are no validated "objective" tests that precisely identify musculoskeletal conditions such as myofascial pain, the neuroanatomical basis for musculoskeletal pain has been described in the literature (Gilliar, Kuchera, & Giulianetti, 1996; Mense, 1993). Lewit (1990) reported that over 90% of patients with "nonspecific pain" are affected by myofascial pain syndromes and dysfunctional joints. Rosomoff, Fishbain, Goldberg, Santana, and Rosomoff (1989) found that 43% of patients evaluated in a 1-year period fulfilled the diagnostic criteria for chronic intractable benign pain. Of these patients, all had at least one physical finding suggestive of musculoskeletal dysfunction, such as tender nodules, trigger points, decreased ranges of motion in the back or neck, and rigid musculature. Educating patients about musculoskeletal causes of pain, in addition to providing specific interventions for musculoskeletal dysfunctions, may have important benefits and is discussed later.

Current conservative treatments for CBP can be divided into interventions that attempt to "normalize" the physical causes of pain and those that do not necessarily "treat the underlying pathology," but are designed to decrease the experience of pain. Given that many contend conventional treatments for pain have been unsuccessful (Aronoff, 1991; Loeser & Sullivan, 1995; T. G. Mayer et al., 1995), functional restoration treatments have emerged where the goal of treatment is not to "treat" the etiology of pain or guide treatment by pain reports; rather, the focus is on increasing the daily functioning of the patient despite the fact that they have pain. Individual treatments, which include medications, injections, electrical stimulation, nontraditional treatments, cognitive/behavioral interventions, and work hardening, are described next. A discussion of multidisciplinary treatment ensues, followed by a summary of conservative treatment approaches for CBP.

INDIVIDUAL TREATMENTS

Drug Therapy

Drug therapies provide symptomatic relief for pain, but ususally do not alter the underlying physiologic cause of pain (Deyo, 1996). Nevertheless, drug therapies are frequently administered to CBP patients, although there are very few standardized guidelines pertaining to the types of medications that should be administered for specific pain problems. The use of narcotic and psychotropic medications for chronic pain is reviewed in chapter 8 (this volume), and therefore is not repeated here. Nonsteroidal anti-inflammatory drugs (NSAIDs) are frequently used to treat CBP, and as a group appear to be superior to placebo and have moderate treatment efficacy (Deyo, 1996). However, these medications have been found to have little effect on pain due to sciatica (Deyo, 1996). Deyo reported that muscle relaxants also appear to be superior to placebo for treating low back pain, but their effectiveness for treating CBP pain has rarely been studied. Their mechanism of action is generally unknown. One consideration in prescribing these medications for chronic pain is that nonbenzodiazapine medications (e.g., cyclobenzaprine hydrochloride [Flexeril], methocarbamol [Robaxin], carisoprodol [Soma], and baclofen may be more appropriate for long-term usage as these medications have lower potential to produce dependence/tolerance. Cyclobenzaprine hydrochloride is very similar in structure to the tricyclic antidepressants, and produces similar side effects. Thus, administering this medication along with a tricyclic antidepressant may produce an undesirable amount of anticholinergic side effects.

Special consideration may need to be given to patients with both CBP and depression. This is important as the analgesic effects of the tricyclic antidepressants are produced at dosage levels approximately one fifth to one third of the dosages recommended for effective treatment of depression (Sullivan, Reesor, Mikail, & Fisher, 1992). When treating patients with both disorders, a primary objective in prescribing antidepressants may be to decrease pain rather than treat depression. Consequently, the dosages administered for pain control are generally below the therapeutic level for effective treatment of depression (Sullivan et al., 1992). This bias in treatment may stem from the belief that, in most cases, depression develops as a consequence of pain and that treating the pain will then relieve the patient's depression (Gamsa, 1990; Sullivan et al., 1992). However, treatment strategies aimed specifically at treating depression among chronic pain patients appear to be effective in reducing symptoms of both pain and depression (Hameroff, Cork et al., 1982; Hameroff, Weiss et al., 1984;

Max et al., 1992; Ward et al., 1984). The efficacy of various dosages of antidepressants in chronic pain patients, or combinations of antidepressants, deserves further study as a large proportion of patients with chronic pain also suffer from depression (France & Krishnan, 1988; Kremer & Atkinson, 1983; Romano & Turner, 1985).

Transcutaneous Electrical Nerve Stimulation

Transcutaneous electrical nerve stimulation (TENS) is believed to treat or interrupt pain by stimulating large-diameter afferent fibers that modulate pain transmission at spinal or higher levels, thus "closing the gate" on pain transmission (Melzack, 1975). Two studies suggest that TENS is superior to placebo in reducing experimental cold-induced pain (Johnson, Ashton, Bousfield, & Thompson, 1989) and acute oro-facial pain (Hansson & Ekblom, 1983). Many types of chronic pain seem to respond to TENS including peripheral nerve injury, phantom limb pain, shoulder-arm pain, low back pain, and degenerative musculoskeletal disease (Melzack, 1975; Meyler, de Jongste, & Rolf, 1994). Meyler et al. reported that TENS was not as effective among persons with a high degree of psychological and social distress, and for persons with pain caused by central and autonomic dysfunction. However, among persons with an initial favorable response, some studies suggest that TENS continues to provide long-term benefits (Fried, Johnson, & McCracken, 1984; Meyler et al., 1994).

TENS can be varied on several parameters, including the electrode placement and frequency and intensity of stimulation. There is no apparent consensus in the literature on the optimal parameters for pain control, and anecdotally, ultimately pain control appears to rely on trial and error giving way to patient preference. Wolf, Gersh, and Rao (1981) found that the location of electrode placement did not appear to influence pain relief. High-frequency/low-intensity TENS is believed to stimulate A-delta fibers and blocks pain in the spinal cord, whereas low-frequency/high-intensity TENS is believed to stimulate beta-endorphin production as the effect of this type of TENS is blocked by naloxone (Hughes, Lichstein, Whitlock, & Harker, 1984). However, some studies have demonstrated that neither type of TENS influences beta-endorphin levels in humans (Hughes et al., 1984; O'Brien, Rutan, Sanborn, & Omer, 1984). Some studies have suggested that higher frequency TENS is somewhat superior to lower frequency TENS in terms of reducing both clinical and experimental pain (Johnson et al., 1989; Nash, Williams, & Machin, 1990; Tulgar, McGlone, Bowsher, & Miles, 1991b; Wolf et al., 1981). Three studies report no difference in pain relief produced by high and low frequency TENS (Fox & Melzack, 1976). Tulgar, McGlone, Bowsher, and Miles (1991a) found that pain patients preferred frequency modulation and burst stimulation in contrast to conventional continuous stimulation, whereas Nash et al. found no difference between pulsed and continuous stimulation. Melzack (1975) reported that the duration of pain relief can outlast the period of stimulation by several hours, and on occasion, for days to weeks. Thus, TENS may be beneficial even if the stimulation time is limited.

In summary, various studies find TENS to be beneficial in treating several chronic pain conditions, and it appears to have long-lasting effects in persons who initially respond to the device. A trial period is usually recommended before purchase of the unit. There appears to be a trend for more pronounced benefits produced by higher frequency TENS, and some studies suggest that pain patients prefer burst or frequency modulated stimulation compared to conventional continuous stimulation.

Neural Blockade

Nerve blocks and other types of injections for CBP have been used both diagnostically and therapeutically for years (Gregg, 1991), but have not been extensively investigated in terms of their efficacy in pain diagnosis and treatment (Hogan & Abram, 1997). Typically, these procedures involve injection of corticosteroids and/or anesthetic substances. Epidural steroid injections are often used in patients with signs and symptoms of radiculopathy, with the belief that steroids will reduce nerve root inflammation, which accompanies the disorder (Deyo, 1996). A recent review of studies examining the efficacy of epidural injections indicated that the results of different studies were inconsistent, and the benefits of these injections, if any, seemed to be short-lived (Koes, Scholten, Mens, & Bouter, 1995). Deyo reported that the average clinical effect of epidural steroids is small (10% to 15%). However, even small benefits may be enough to help patients through the acute radicular phase and avoid surgery (Deyo, 1996). Small benefits may also help patients progress more quickly in physical therapy or other treatments if employed simultaneously.

Trigger point and tender nodule injections involve infiltration of steroids, anesthetics, or a combination of both into the hypertonic muscle and surrounding tissues. These injections are often used in the diagnosis and treatment of myofascial pain syndrome (Hogan & Abram, 1997), however, their efficacy has not been demonstrated as less specific techniques (such as needle insertion without injection) have shown results comparable to actual injections (Lewit, 1979). Other anesthetic techniques for CBP include sacroiliac injection and facet blocks (Hogan & Abram, 1997).

Although these techniques are frequently employed to treat chronic pain, there are few studies examining their efficacy for this (Gregg, 1991; Hogan & Abram, 1997). Most recommend that these procedures be administered within the context of a more comprehensive rehabilitation program to address both the physical and psychosocial aspects of the patient's pain (Gregg, 1991). In addition, injections may exacerbate the patient's pain, and substances such as steroids can have undesirable side effects, such as immunosuppression and weight gain (Gregg, 1991). Abram and O'Conner (1996) indicated that central nervous system infections may be a complication of repeated epidural injections. Further studies appear to be warranted examining the effectiveness of specific types of injections in distinctive subsets of chronic pain syndromes. Deyo (1996) suggested that it may also be helpful to compare the effectiveness of corticosteroids administered both locally and systemically.

Exercise

Exercise is frequently employed in the treatment of CBP. Exercise may be an important component in the treatment of chronic pain because muscles may become weak and atrophied through disuse (Rodriquez, Bilkey, & Agre, 1992) and lead to deconditioning, which then may contribute to disability (Mayer et al., 1995). Although it is difficult to tell whether decreased muscle strength among patients with chronic pain is a cause or a consequence of their pain (Rodriquez et al., 1992), several studies have suggested that decreased strength in the abdominal and spine extensor musculature is associated with the recurrence of persistence of low back pain (Biering-Sorensen, 1984; Cady, Bischoff, O'Connell, Thomas, & Allan, 1979; Troup, Martin, & Lloyd, 1981). Diminished cardiovascular fitness has also been found to be associated with a higher incidence of back pain disability as well as more frequent episodes of low back pain (Cady et al., 1979).

In their review of the role of exercise in the treatment of chronic neck and back pain, Rodriquez et al. (1992) concluded that nonspecific, general exercise such as nonspecific strengthening and aerobic conditioning appears to decrease the intensity of CLBP, and protect against recurrence. They indicated that little research has been done on the effectiveness of specific types of exercises, for example, whether improvements are related to stretching, strengthening, increased endurance, and/or improved coordination. The optimal frequency and duration of exercise is unknown. In addition, little work has been done to address the issue of compliance with prescribed home exercise programs. Previous studies have demonstrated that compliance with prescribed exercise regimens is poor. Studies indicate that more than 50% of patients in an exercise therapy program will drop out in the first 6 months (Dishman, 1982; Martin & Dubbert, 1985). Linton, Helsing, and Bergstrom (1996) examined the effect of an intervention designed to increase exercise compliance or exercise adherence among patients with musculoskeletal pain. They found a higher rate of adherence in the exercise compliance group compared to a control group, and patients who were compliant with their exercise showed greater increases in aerobic capacity compared to noncompliers, although their pain ratings were not significantly different from controls.

Clinically, many therapists often prescribe complex regimens that include stretching, strengthening, and aerobic exercise. Studies addressing the effectiveness of each of these components as well as their combination are warranted, because decreasing the complexity of the regimen may help to increase compliance. Furthermore, it may also be important to examine the effect of general aerobic exercise versus specific adjuvant stretching and strengthening exercises for musculoskeletal dysfunctions.

Education

Although there are little data regarding the effectiveness of educating patients about the physical nature of their pain condition, existing data suggest that accurate knowledge of the physical etiology of pain, if it can be identified and conveyed to the patient, may be an important determinant of several aspects of the pain experience. Geisser and Roth (1998) found that only 32.8 % of persons in a chronic pain sample (predominantly musculoskeletal pain) were able to accurately articulate the cause of their pain, and patients who were unsure of their diagnosis or who disagreed with their actual diagnosis tended to report more dysfunctional pain beliefs, greater psychological distress, higher intensities of chronic pain, and more pain-related disability. A path analytic model suggested that lack of knowledge about the etiology of pain was related to greater beliefs that pain is a signal of harm, and that this variable, in addition to affective distress, were significantly related to disability due to pain. Pain intensity was not significantly related to disability. Similar findings have been observed by Lacroix et al. (1990) and Roth, Horowitz, and Bachman (in press).

Another popular educational intervention for CBP is back school. Back school is based in part on the work of Nachemson (1981), who assessed differences in disk pressure among normals during different functional tasks and found that the highest disk pressures took place while leaning forward or during forward flexion and rotation. Thus, back school in part emphasizes body mechanics during functional tasks that decrease disk pressure. Several reviews of the effectiveness of back schools have indicated that many of the studies suffer major methodological flaws, and outcome results have been mixed (Turner, 1996). In addition, offloading pressure on the spine may place additional stress on other joints, and potentially may promote back weakness. Although certainly one should be careful not to overstress the spine, a recent study found that CLBP patients who were prescribed light, normal activity, including bending, actually displayed better outcomes compared to a group of patients who received conservative medical treatment (Indahl, Velund, & Reikerass, 1995).

Manual Therapy

Manual therapy involves the application of specific interventions, such as muscle energy techniques, myofascial release, and thrust techniques to minimize or eliminate musculoskeletal dysfunctions. The mechanism of action is yet unproven, but some authors propose that it involves releasing chronically tight or restricted innervated tissues, thus improving microcirculation, minimizing the corresponding inflammatory response, and decreasing nociception (Mein, 1996). Specific interventions for musculoskeletal conditions have received little empirical attention, but include (a) spray and stretch techniques for myofascial pain syndrome (Simons, 1987), (b) various manual therapy techniques such as joint mobilization and articulartory techniques, (c) muscle energy techniques for specific musculoskeletal dysfunctions, such as hypomobility of spine movement, vertebral malrotation(s), sacroiliac dysfunctions, or innominate dysfunctions (e.g., pelvic asymmetry or torsion; Greenman, 1989), and (d) high-velocity thrust techniques typically employed by chiropractors. In addition to manipulation, Bookhout (1996) indicated that instruction on exercises specifically tailored for the patient with chronic musculoskeletal pain and musculoskeletal dysfunction is an important part of treatment. These might include specific stretching exercises for shortened muscles, education on proper body mechanics and posture, and self-mobilization exercises. Ideally, these techniques can be used by the patient as specific pain management tools to improve function and decrease the patient's dependence on ongoing medical care.

Unfortunately, few empirical studies have been conducted on the efficacy of manual therapy and/or specific adjuvant exercises for musculoskeletal dysfunctions. In reviewing the research on manual therapy for chronic pain, Mein (1996) indicated that three studies demonstrated positive results (Evans, Burke, Lloyd, E. E. Roberts, & G. M. Roberts, 1978; Ongley, Klein, Dorman, Eek, & Hubert, 1987; Waagen, Haldeman, Cook, Lopez, & Deboer, 1986), whereas one produced negative results (Timm, 1994). However, the Timm study examined the effectiveness of manual therapy in postlaminectomy patients, who may have had neurological as well as musculoskeletal dysfunctions contributing to their pain. In addition, all of the studies tended to recruit relatively high functioning patients, which leaves the question regarding the effectiveness of manual therapy for more chronic and severe disabling back pain unanswered. For example, Waagen et al. described a typical individual in their study as "a young adult with mild chronic low back pain," Ongley et al. excluded persons with an unsettled worker's compensation claim or persons on disability pay, and patients in the Timm study were employed. In addition, it would be helpful to examine the effectiveness of specific adjuvant exercise in addition to manual therapy among patients with CBP due to musculoskeletal dysfunction.

Acupuncture

Acupuncture for pain relief has become increasingly popular in the United States. In terms of providing pain relief, acupuncture is believed to stimulate the production of endogenous opioids. Lewith and Vincent (1995) indicated that research regarding the effectiveness of traditional acupuncture for chronic pain, where the needles are placed at classical sites that give rise to a set of sensations referred to as "Teh Chi," is somewhat inconclusive. In fact, acupuncture is somewhat difficult to study empirically, as many control or placebo treatments (e.g., needle insertion at nontraditional sties) may not necessarily be inert (Thomas & Lundeberg, 1996). Acupuncture also frequently involves electrical stimulation of the needles, thus producing effects similar to TENS. Lewith and Vincent reported that in 12 studies comparing classical acupuncture to placebo, 5 demonstrate a significant advantage of acupuncture over placebo, and several others show a nonsignificant trend of acupuncture over placebo. In addition, the authors reported a slight advantage in terms of response rate of classical acupuncture (60%) over sham acupuncture (40% to 50%) and placebo acupuncture (30%) for chronic pain. Thomas and Lundeberg stated that acupuncture with low-frequency electrical stimulation appears to be effective in treating chronic nociceptive musculoskeletal pain.

Although there is some evidence that acupuncture may help relieve chronic pain, most studies have employed small samples, and the different parameters of acupuncture that may be particularly effective, such as needle placement and depth of insertion, are not well known. Thomas and Lundeberg (1995) suggested that a combination of local and distal needles inserted deeply is optimal, but this needs to be investigated further.

Biofeedback and Relaxation Training

These techniques are frequently employed in treating chronic pain. Although some studies indicate that biofeedback and relaxation training produce roughly similar outcomes (DeGood, 1993), biofeedback may be beneficial among patients with chronic musculoskeletal pain as these patients have been found to be poor discriminators of levels of muscle tension (Flor, Schugans, & Birbaumer, 1992). Typically, the goal in biofeedback is to decrease levels of muscle tension in the affected areas. Several studies have suggested that this approach is beneficial in terms of treating back pain (Flor, Haag, & Turk, 1986; Keefe, Schapira, Williams, Brown, & Surwit, 1981; Nigl & Fisher-Williams, 1980; Nouwen & Solinger, 1979). Flor and Birbaumer (1993) found biofeedback to be superior to cognitive-behavioral therapy and conservative medical treatment (primarily physical therapy) among patients with musculoskeletal back pain. One study found that patients with the highest electromyographic (EMG) levels responded best to biofeedback (Nouwen & Solinger, 1979), whereas Flor and Birbaumer reported that they obtained the best response in patients with the lowest initial EMG levels.

Both increased and decreased muscle tension may contribute to chronic pain (Arena, Sherman, Bruno, & Young, 1989). A recent study by Lofland, Cassisi, and Blonsky (1996) suggests that CLBP patients with high levels of somatization tended to display higher than normal levels of muscle tension, whereas patients low on somatization tend to have lower than normal levels. Thus, studies evaluating muscle EMG in chronic pain patients may need to avoid collapsing data across subjects or even across time if EMG is measured repeatedly (Rudy & Greco, 1996). Studies examining individual subjects suggest that only some patients with chronic pain appear to respond to stress with increased muscle tension (Geisser, Robinson, & Richardson, 1995; Hazlett & Haynes, 1992; Kohler & Haimerl, 1990). This suggests that specific recommendations regarding biofeedback may need to be based on an individualized assessment of specific muscle activity patterns.

In addition to examining absolute levels of muscle tension, relative patterns of muscle activity may contribute to CBP. These include asymmetries in muscle tension, or abnormal patterns of muscle activity during dynamic movement. Donaldson, Romney, Donaldson, and Skubick (1994) reported that CLBP patients who underwent single motor unit biofeedback training displayed immediate and sustained decreases in pain, as well as decreased EMG amplitude and asymmetries compared to a relaxation training group and controls. Wolf, Nacht, and Kelly (1982) suggested that neuromuscular retraining is an important aspect of treating CLBP. Based on data from normal subjects, they performed neuromuscular retraining on a back pain patient during trunk movements. The patient reported significantly less pain over time. Thus, biofeedback might be a beneficial adjunct in assisting patients with improving poor body posture, body mechanics, or muscle firing, and ultimately decrease their pain if these are contributing factors.

Relaxation is an important adjunct to biofeedback, as these techniques help generalize the skills learned during biofeedback and help to reduce the effects of stress. Although there is little information about specific relaxation techniques that might be particularly helpful for chronic pain, it is often helpful to teach patients techniques that are practical and can be used while the patient is active, such as deep breathing. Ohrbach and McCall (1996) suggested that myogenic pain may be maintained by changes in the muscle stretch receptors, whereby the contracted muscle state though painful actually feels more posturally "normal" to the patient. They suggested that contraction-relaxation techniques may be easier for patients with myogenic pain to tolerate, as stretching after the contraction phase is not accompanied by pain.

Cognitive-Behavioral Interventions

The earliest modern psychological interventions and theories of chronic pain management were based primarily on the work of Fordyce (1976), who proposed that suffering, the behavioral component of pain, can be modified by environmental contingencies. Pain treatment programs that followed an operant model were designed to extinguish pain behavior, and increase well behavior. Several authors suggested that these interventions are beneficial in treating CBP (Block, 1982; Keefe, Block, R. B. Williams, & Surwitt, 1981; Swanson, Maruta, & Swenson, 1979). A recent study by Roberts, Sternbach, and Polich (1993) found that even a brief, inexpensive outpatient behavioral rehabilitation program was effective in terms of reducing pain and increasing function.

In addition to assisting patients with developing more adaptive behavioral responses to pain, modern cognitive-behavioral therapies focus on helping patients reframe maladaptive thoughts about pain, and employ more adaptive cognitions when faced with pain. Several maladaptive pain beliefs have been identified in the literature including the belief (a) that pain is a signal of harm or damage to the body and therefore one should avoid activity or movement, (b) that pain is catastrophic, where patients respond to pain with thoughts that their pain is overwhelming, awful, and horrible, and (c) that there is no perceived control over pain, or that nothing one does will change their experience of pain. Turk (1990) suggested that because pain and fear of pain are aversive, many patients begin to avoid activities or situations that they expect will produce pain, even though this perception may not be accurate. Indeed, recent studies suggest that fear of movement/reinjury are significantly to disability and behavior during functional tasks (Jensen, Turner, & Romano, 1994; Jensen, Turner, Romano, & Lawler, 1994; Main & Watson, 1995; McCracken, Gross, Sorg, & Edmands, 1993; Vlaeyen, Kole-Snijders, Boeren, & van Eek, 1995; Vlaeyen, Kole-Snijders, Rotteveel, Ruesink, & Heuts, 1995). Catastrophizing has been shown to be related to increased disability, greater pain, and greater emotional distress (Flor & Turk, 1988; Geisser, Robinson, & Henson, 1994; Geisser, Robinson, Keefe, & Weiner, 1994; Keefe, Brown, Wallston, & Caldwell, 1989; Tuttle, Shutty, & DeGood, 1991). Increasing the patient's perceived control over their pain appears to be related to more favorable chronic pain adjustment and treatment outcome (Buckelew et al., 1994; Jacob, Kerns, Rosenberg, & Haythornthwaite, 1993; Jensen, Turner, Romano, & Lawler, 1994). Patients can be taught increased control over pain not only through the use of different cognitive-behavioral techniques (e.g., relaxation), but also by remembering to simultaneously use strategies taught by other disciplines, such as the use of icing or stretching encouraged by the physical therapist. Keefe et al. (1990) demonstrated that teaching adaptive pain-coping strategies to patients, such as ignoring pain sensations, using coping self-statements, and changing activity patterns decreased pain and disability. Holzman, Turk and Kerns (1986) reported that distraction may also be an effective coping strategy for patients who tend to focus a great deal on their pain and other bodily sensations.

Recent studies suggest that additional cognitive-behavioral interventions might be particularly useful for chronic pain patients whose pain etiology is related to injury or trauma. For example, many authors have reported a high incidence of posttraumatic stress disorder (PTSD) among patients with chronic pain, ranging from 9.5% (Muse, 1985) among patients seen at a multidisciplinary pain clinic, to as high as 50% (Hickling & Blanchard, 1992) and 75% (Hickling, Blanchard, Silverman, & Schwarz, 1992) for consecutive patients referred to a psychologist for treatment of headache and other pain resulting from a motor vehicle accident (MVA). Among patients with chronic pain, Geisser, Roth, Bachman, and Eckert (1996) found that patients with traumatic pain and high PTSD symptoms displayed the highest levels of disability and pain. Turk, Okifuji, Starz and Sinclair (1996) found that patients with traumatic onset of fibromyalgia demonstrated greater pain, disability, life interference, and affective distress compared to fibromyalgia patients whose pain onset was insidious. These studies suggest that specific interventions for psychological difficulties that may arise from trauma, such as exposure therapy for PTSD, may useful adjuncts to treating chronic pain patients whose pain onset is caused by trauma.

Another important psychological aspect of treating patients with accident-related pain may be the development of feelings of victimization (i.e., one wrongfully suffers because of someone else's mistake or carelessness) and entitlement (i.e., the belief that one is "owed" or should be compensated). DeGood and Kiernan (1996) found that chronic pain patients who blamed their injury on their employer or other source tended to have significantly higher affective distress compared to patients who indicated that no one was at fault for their pain. The patients who placed blame also tended to be more refractory to past treatments, were more likely to indicate that their pain would limit their activity, and had higher levels of anticipated pain. Patients who blamed their employer for their pain were also more likely to be unemployed at follow-up.

Work Hardening

Work-hardening programs generally attempt to assist clients with achieving a level of work productivity such that they would be acceptable in the competitive labor market (King, 1993). The procedures employed generally include gradually increasing engagement in functional activities, particularly activities that are vocationally related, feedback regarding ergonomic issues, encouraging the patient to employ various pain management strategies such as posture breaks, and assisting the patient with work adaptation including the use of adaptive devices. Some work-hardening programs are part of a larger, multidisciplinary pain program, whereas others may serve to begin the vocational rehabilitation of the patients treatment following initial pain management treatment. Few controlled outcome studies have examined work hardening among chronic pain patients, but these services, along with vocational counseling, are an important aspect of the rehabilitation of the CBP patient.

King (1993) examined data collected from 928 clients from 22 work-hardening programs in Wisconsin. Most clients were men, and the most frequent condition treated was lumbar spine injury (47%). Of patients with lumbar injury, 59% returned to their usual job, some with modifications, and 12% returned to an alternative job with the same employer. It is unclear, however, how many of these individuals had ongoing pain, for what duration, or of what intensity.

Multidisciplinary Treatment

It is estimated that there are over 1,000 multidisciplinary pain clinics and pain centers in the United States (Crue, 1985). Given the complexity and multidimensional nature of pain, multidisciplinary treatment is often recommended as the preferred treatment for a number of chronic pain conditions. Although the specific components of multidisciplinary treatment programs differ, they generally include (a) ongoing medical care or supervision, (b) exercise or specific physical therapy intervention, (c) psychosocial intervention, and (d) occupational therapy or other services related to daily functioning and/or vocational rehabilitation. Some programs also offer specialization in pharmacology, dietetics, nursing, and case management. Programs are housed in both inpatient and outpatient settings, although the general trend has been shifting toward providing services through less costly, outpatient settings.

A recent meta-analytic review of multidisciplinary pain treatment for CBP conducted by Flor, Fydrich, and Turk (1992) concluded that chronic pain patients treated in multidisciplinary programs were functioning better than 75% of control patients who either received no treatment or were

treated by conventional unimodal approaches. For example, multidisciplinary treatment was superior to conventional physical therapy alone. Furthermore, these effects appeared to persist over time, and the benefits of
multidisciplinary treatment seemed to extend beyond just pain and included increased return to work and decreased use of health care.

A specific type of multidisciplinary approach, labeled *functional restoration*, has been proposed to be highly effective in treating chronic pain.
Given the lack of knowledge regarding "treatable" organic pathology in
many chronic pain patients, functional restoration methods have been
proposed as an alternative treatment paradigm. Typically, the focus of the
treatment program is to promote function despite the fact that patients
experience ongoing pain and other difficulties. Hazard (1995) outlined
the critical elements of a functional restoration approach, including an
interdisciplinary staff, quantification of function to monitor patient status
and progress, physical training, and counseling. Two initial studies (Hazard
et al., 1989; T. G. Mayer, Gatchel, & H. Mayer, 1987) reported that over
80% of patients treated in a functional restoration program were able to
return to work following treatment, and a high percentage were still working at 1-year follow-up. These studies have been criticized, however, as one
of the comparison groups were patients who were not treated due to lack
of insurance funding, a group that may differ from the treatment group
in terms of other important characteristics (Teasell & Harth, 1996).

Feuerstein, Menz, Zastowny, and Barron (1994) presented a program
they termed *mutidisciplinary rehabilitation* (MDR), which is a combination
of medical management, physical conditioning, pain and stress management, vocational counseling/placement, and education regarding back
safety. The authors indicated that work reentry is the primary focus of the
program. Among people with CBP, the authors report that 71% of patients
who completed the program were working or in vocational rehabilitation
at 12-month-follow-up, compared to only 44% in corresponding comparison groups.

CONCLUSIONS

The physical causes of CBP are largely undetermined. Does this mean that
CBP is primarily psychological, or does it reflect our lack of knowledge or
recognition of certain pathophysiological causes of CBP? Although advances need to be made regarding the various physical and psychosocial
factors that influence CBP, some research suggests that musculoskeletal
causes of pain tend to go unnoticed or undetected. Specific treatments
for and education regarding the nature of musculoskeletal pain may be
useful interventions. Accepted reliable and valid criteria for these disorders

need to be developed, and potential interventions for these disorders, such as manual therapy, need to be empirically examined.

Numerous individual interventions appear to have some efficacy for reducing the patient's perception of pain, or decreasing physical contributions to pain. These include medications, TENS, neural blockade, exercise, biofeedback, and cognitive-behavior therapy. Typically, biofeedback is included as part of a cognitive-behavioral approach, and some suggest this intervention may change muscle activity patterns that contribute to pain. Tricylic antidepressant treatment may be particularly beneficial among patients with sleep disturbance. Special medication regimens need to be considered for patients that have significant depression. Studies conducted on neural blockade suggest that the efficacy is small and of short duration, however, injections may be beneficial in conjunction with other therapies as even brief relief may help patients make greater gains, for example, in their exercise program. Acupuncture has some demonstrated efficacy for CBP, however its use is somewhat controversial. Manual therapy for CBP appears to have some initial support, however its effectiveness in patients with disabling CBP has not been demonstrated. Exercise appears to have both treatment benefits as well as preventative benefits in terms of reduced risk of recurrence. The issue of compliance with exercise for pain treatment has not been adequately addressed, and empirical studies related to strategies for increasing compliance, such as simplifying prescribed regimens, would be beneficial. The impact of specific exercises and instruction on body mechanics and posture for musculoskeletal dysfunctions as an adjunct to manual therapy has not been examined empirically.

In practice, many of these individual therapies are used as part of multidisciplinary treatment. In general, multidisciplinary treatment appears to be superior to unimodal or no treatment, suggesting that multidimensional treatment should be the preferred method of treatment for CBP. Given that cost-effectiveness is becoming more of an issue in patient care, studies of multidisciplinary treatment might consider examining the optimal cost-effective parameters of multidisciplinary treatment, such as determining effective number of sessions or length of treatment, examining which components of treatment are particularly effective, or whether outpatient treatment is more cost-effective than inpatient treatment. In relation to this latter issue, Peters, Large, and Elkind (1992) found no differences in the outcomes of in- and outpatient chronic pain patients, whereas A. C. de C. Williams et al. (1996) found that inpatients made greater gains, and maintained them at 1-year follow-up. The authors were able to present the total cost of the programs but not necessarily demonstrate the cost-effectiveness of each individual type of treatment. It would be particularly useful to determine the utility of treatments tailored to empirically determined subgroups of pain patients, as some groups of patients may require more intensive multidisciplinary treatment, whereas some may respond well to less intensive and less costly interventions. For example, Turk, Rudy, Kubinski, Zaki, and Greco (1996) demonstrated that a treatment tailored for patients with temporomandibular disorder who had a dysfunctional profile type on the Multidimensional Pain Inventory produced the best outcomes.

Another controversial but important issue to address in relation to CBP treatment is the balance between functional activity and pain. For many patients, complete pain control is not achievable, thus they must work toward managing their pain and increasing their daily functioning despite the fact that they experience chronic pain. Treatments differ to a large degree in their emphasis on pacing or restricting activities to avoid pain versus performing prescribed activities despite increased pain. The progression of increased activity may be critical among patients with musculoskeletal pain as improving their strength and conditioning may ultimately decrease pain. However, overemphasis on activity pacing to provide pain relief in these patients may actually inhibit the patient's rehabilitation. In addition, patients who are fearful of certain activities because they overestimate the amount of pain they will experience may benefit from exposure to these activities, as performing them without experiencing unmanageable pain will likely decrease their fear of movement and increase their functioning. It would be useful to compare the long-term outcomes of different treatment paradigms that emphasize these different approaches to balancing the relationship of pain and functioning. We as pain practitioners do not want to contribute to the disability of patients with CBP, or to their suffering, yet little is known how to best balance progression of activity with managing pain.

REFERENCES

Abram, S. E., & O'Connor, T. C. (1996). Complications associated with epidural steroid injections. *Regional Anesthesia, 21,* 149–162.

Arena, J. G., Sherman, R. A., Bruno, G. M., & Young, T. R. (1989). Electromyographic recordings of 5 types of low back pain subjects and non-patient controls in different positions. *Pain, 37,* 57–65.

Aronoff, G. M. (1991). Chronic pain and the disability epidemic. *The Clinical Journal of Pain, 7,* 330–338.

Biering-Sorensen, F. (1984). Physical measurements as risk indicators for low-back trouble over a one-year period. *Spine, 9,* 106–119.

Block, A. R. (1982). Mutidisciplinary treatment of chronic low back pain: A review. *Rehabilitation Psychology, 27,* 51–63.

Bookhout, M. R. (1996). Exercise and somatic dysfunction. *Physical Medicine and Rehabilitation Clinics of North America, 7,* 845–862.

Buckelew, S. P., Parker, J. C., Keefe, F. J., Deuser, W. E., Crews, T. M., Conway, R., Kay, D. R., & Hewett, J. E. (1994). Self-efficacy and pain behavior among subjects with fibromyalgia. *Pain, 59,* 377–384.

Cady, L. D., Bischoff, D. P., O'Connell, E. R., Thomas, P. C., & Allan, J. H. (1979). Strength and fitness and subsequent back injuries in firefighters. *Journal of Occupational Medicine, 21*, 269–272.

Coste, J., Paolaggi, J. B., & Spira, A. (1992). Classification of nonspecific low back pain: I. Psychological involvement in low back pain. *Spine, 17*, 1028–1037.

Crue, B. L. (1985). Multi-disciplinary pain treatment programs: Current status. *The Clinical Journal of Pain, 1*, 31–38.

DeGood, D. E. (1993). What is the role of biofeedback in the treatment of chronic pain patients? *American Pain Society Bulletin, 3*(3), 1–5.

DeGood, D. E., & Kiernan, B. (1996). Perception of fault in patients with chronic pain. *Pain, 64*, 153–159.

Deyo, R. A. (1993). Practice variations, treatment fads, rising disability: Do we need a new clinical research paradigm? *Spine, 18*, 2153–2162.

Deyo, R. A. (1996). Drug therapy for back pain: Which drugs help which patients? *Spine, 21*, 2840–2850.

Dishman, R. K. (1982). Compliance/adherence in health-related exercise. *Health Psychology, 1*, 237–267.

Donaldson, S., Romney, D., Donaldson, M., & Skubick, D. (1994). Randomized study of the application of single motor unit biofeedback training to chronic low back pain. *Journal of Occupational Rehabilitation, 4*, 23–37.

Evans, D. P., Burke, M. S., Lloyd, K. N., Roberts, E. E., & Roberts, G. M. (1978). Lumbar spinal manipulation on trial: Part I. Clinical assessment. *Rheumatology and Rehabilitation, 17*, 46–53.

Fast, A. (1977). Low back disorders: Conservative management. *Archives of Physical Medicine and Rehabilitation, 69*, 880–891.

Feuerstein, M., Menz, L., Zastowny, T., & Barron, B. A. (1994). Chronic back pain and work disability: Vocational outcomes following multidisciplinary rehabiliation. *Journal of Occupational Rehabilitation, 4*, 229–251.

Flor, H., & Birbaumer, N. (1993). Comparison of the efficacy of electromyographic biofeedback, cognitive-behavior therapy, and conservative medical interventions on the treatment of chronic musculoskeletal pain. *Journal of Consulting and Clinical Psychology, 61*, 653–658.

Flor, H., Fydrich, T., & Turk, D. C. (1992). Efficacy of multidisciplinary pain treatment centers: a meta-analytic review. *Pain, 49*, 221–230.

Flor, H., Haag, G., & Turk, D. C. (1986). Long-term efficacy of EMG biofeedback for chronic rheumatic back pain. *Pain, 27*, 195–202.

Flor, H., Schugens, M. M., & Birbaumer, N. (1992). Discrimination of muscle tension in chronic pain patients and healthy controls. *Biofeedback and Self-Regulation, 17*, 165–177.

Flor, H., & Turk, D. C. (1988). Chronic back pain and rheumatoid arthritis: Predicting pain and disability from cognitive variables. *Journal of Behavioral Medicine, 11*, 251–265.

Fordyce, W. E. (1976). *Behavioral methods for chronic pain and illness.* St. Louis, MO: Mosby.

Fordyce, W. E. (1979). Environmental factors in the genesis of low back pain. In J. J. Bonica, J. C. Liebeskind, & D. G. Albe-Fessard (Eds.), *Advances in pain research and therapy: Vol. 3. Proceedings of the 2nd World Congress on Pain* (pp. 659–666). New York: Raven.

Fox, E. J., & Melzack, R. (1976). Transcutaneous electrical stimulation and acupuncture: Comparison of treatment for low-back pain. *Pain, 2*, 141–148.

France, R. D., & Krishnan, K. R. R. (1988). Pain in psychiatric disorders. In R. D. France & K. R. R. Krishnan (Eds.), *Chronic pain* (pp. 117–141). Washington, DC: American Psychiatric Press.

Fried, T., Johnson, R., & McCracken, W. (1984). Transcutaneous electrical nerve stimulation: Its role in the control of chronic pain. *Archives of Physical Medicine and Rehabilitation, 65*, 228–231.

Gamsa, A. (1990). Is emotional disturbance a precipitator or a consequence of chronic pain? *Pain, 42,* 183–195.

Geisser, M. E., Robinson, M. E., & Henson, C. D. (1994). The Coping Strategies Questionnaire and chronic pain adjustment: A conceptual and empirical reanalysis. *The Clinical Journal of Pain, 10,* 98–106.

Geisser, M. E., Robinson, M. E., Keefe, F. J., & Weiner, M. L. (1994). Catastrophizing, depression and the sensory, affective and evaluative aspects of chronic pain. *Pain, 59,* 79–84.

Geisser, M. E., Robinson, M. E., & Richardson, C. (1995). A time series analysis of the relationship between ambulatory EMG, pain, and stress in chronic low back pain. *Biofeedback and Self-Regulation, 20,* 339–355.

Geisser, M. E., & Roth, R. S. (1998). Knowledge of and agreement with chronic pain diagnosis: Relation to pain beliefs, pain severity, disability and psychological distress. *Journal of Occupational Rehabilitation, 8,* 73–88.

Geisser, M. E., Roth, R. S., Bachman, J. E., & Eckert, T. A. (1996). The relationship between symptoms of post-traumatic stress disorder and affective disturbance, pain and disability among patients with accident and non-accident related pain. *Pain, 66,* 207–214.

Gilliar, W. G., Kuchera, M. L., & Giulianetti, D. A. (1996). Neurologic basis of manual medicine. *Physical Medicine and Rehabilitation Clinics of North America, 7,* 693–714.

Greenman, P. E. (1989). *Principles of manual medicine.* Baltimore, MD: Williams & Wilkins.

Gregg, R. V. (1991). Should nerve blocks be used for chronic noncancer pain? *American Pain Society Bulletin, 1,* 1–4.

Hameroff, S. R., Cork, R. C., Scherer, K., Crago, B. R., Neuman, C., Womble, J. R., & Davis, T. P. (1982). Doxepin effects on chronic pain, depression and plasma opioids. *Journal of Clinical Psychiatry, 43,* 22–27.

Hameroff, S. R., Weiss, J. L., Lerman, J. C., Cork, R. C., Watts, K. S., Crago, B. R., Neuman, C., Womble, J. R., & Davis, T. P. (1984). Doxepin's effects on chronic pain and depression: A controlled study. *Journal of Clinical Psychiatry, 45,* 47–52.

Hansson, P., & Ekblom, A. (1983). Transcutaneous electrical nerve stimulation (TENS) as compared to placebo TENS for the relief of acute oro-facial pain. *Pain, 15,* 157–165.

Hazard, R. G. (1995). Spine update: functional restoration. *Spine, 20,* 2345–2348.

Hazard, R. G., Fenwick, J. W., Kalish, S. M., Redmond, J., Reeves, V., Reid, S., & Frymoyer, J. W. (1989). Functional restoration with behavioural support: A one year prospective study of patients with chronic low back pain. *Spine, 14,* 157–161.

Hazard, R. G., Haugh, L. D., Reid, S., Preble, J. B., & MacDonald, L. (1996). Early prediction of chronic disability after occupational low back injury. *Spine, 21,* 945–951.

Hazlett, R. L., & Haynes, S. N. (1992). Fibromyalgia: A time series analysis of the stressor-physical symptom association. *Journal of Behavioral Medicine, 15,* 541–557.

Hickling, E. J., & Blanchard, E. B. (1992). Post-traumatic stress disorder and motor vehicle accidents. *Journal of Anxiety Disorders, 6,* 285–291.

Hickling, E. J., Blanchard, E. B., Silverman, D. J., & Schwarz, S. P. (1992). Motor vehicle accidents, headaches, and post-traumatic stress disorder: Assessment findings in a consecutive series. *Headache, 32,* 147–151.

Hogan, Q. H., & Abram, S. E. (1997). Neural blockade for diagnosis and prognosis: A review. *Anesthesiology, 86,* 216–241.

Holzman, A. D., Turk, D. C., & Kerns, R. D. (1986). The cognitive-behavioal approach to the management of chronic pain. In A. D. Holzman & D. C. Turk (Eds.), *Pain management: A handbook of psychological treatment approaches* (pp. 31–50). New York: Pergamon.

Hughes, G. S., Lichstein, P. R., Whitlock, D., & Harker, C. (1984). Response of plasma beta-endorphins to transcutaneous electrical nerve stimulation in healthy subjects. *Physical Therapy, 64,* 1062–1066.

Indahl, A., Velund, L., & Reikeraas, O. (1995). Good prognosis for low back pain when left untampered: A randomized clinical trial. *Spine, 20,* 473–477.

Jacob, M. C., Kerns, R. D., Rosenberg, R., & Haythornthwaite, J. (1993). Chronic pain: Intrusion and accommodation. *Behaviour Research and Therapy, 31,* 519–527.

Jensen, M. P., Turner, J. A., & Romano, J. M. (1994). Correlates of improvement in multidisciplinary treatment of chronic pain. *Journal of Consulting and Clinical Psychology, 62,* 172–179.

Jensen, M. P., Turner, J. A., Romano, J. M., & Lawler, B. K. (1994). Relationship of pain specific beliefs to chronic pain adjustment. *Pain, 57,* 301–309.

Johnson, M. I., Ashton, C. H., Bousfield, D. R., & Thompson, J. W. (1989). Analgesic effects of different frequencies of transcutaneous electrical nerve stimulation on cold-induced pain in normal subjects. *Pain, 39,* 231–236.

Keefe, F. J., Block, A. R., Williams, R. B., Jr., & Surwit, R. S. (1981). Behavioral treatement of chronic low back pain: Clinical outcome and individual differences in pain relief. *Pain, 11,* 221–231.

Keefe, F. J., Brown, G. K., Wallston, K. A., & Caldwell, D. S. (1989). Coping with rheumatoid arthritis pain: Catastrophizing as a maladaptive strategy. *Pain, 37,* 51–56.

Keefe, F. J., Caldwell, D. S., Williams, D. A., Gil, K. M., Mitchell, D., Robertson, C., Martinez, S., Nunley, J., Beckham, J. C., Crisson, J. E., & Helms, M. (1990). Pain coping skills training in the management of osteoarthritic knee pain: A comparative study. *Behavior Therapy, 21,* 49–62.

Keefe, F. J., Schapira, B., Williams, R. B., Brown, C., & Surwit, R. S. (1981). EMG-assisted relaxation training in the management of chronic low back pain. *American Journal of Clinical Biofeedback, 4,* 93–103.

King, P. M. (1993). Outcome analysis of work-hardening programs. *The American Journal of Occupational Therapy, 47,* 595–603.

Koes, B. W., Scholten, R. J. P. M., Mens, J. M. A., & Bouter, L. M. (1996). Efficacy of epidural steroid injections for low-back pain and sciatica: A systematic review of the literature. *Pain, 63,* 279–288.

Kohler, T., & Haimerl, C. (1990). Daily stress as a trigger of migraine attacks: Results of thirteen single-subject studies. *Journal of Consulting and Clinical Psychology, 58,* 870–872.

Kremer, E. F., & Atkinson, J. H., Jr. (1983). Pain language as a measure of affect in chronic pain patients. In R. Melzack (Ed.), *Pain measurement and assessment* (pp. 119–127). New York: Raven.

Lacroix, J. M., Powell, J., Lloyd, G. J., Doxey, N. C. S., Mitson, G. L., & Aldam, C. F. (1990). Low-back pain: Factors of value in predicting outcome. *Spine, 15,* 495–499.

Lewit, K. (1979). The needle effect in the relief of myofascial pain. *Pain, 6,* 83–90.

Lewit, K. (1990). Management of muscular pain associated with articular dysfunction. In J. R. Fricton & E. A. Awad (Eds.), *Advances in pain research and therapy: Vol. 17. Myofascial pain and fibromyalgia* (pp. 315–317). New York: Raven.

Lewith, G., & Vincent, C. (1995). Evaluation of the clinical effects of acupuncture: A problem reassessed and a framework for future research. *Pain Forum, 4,* 26–39.

Linton, S. J., Hellsing, A.-L., & Bergstrom, G. (1996). Exercise for workers with musculoskeletal pain: Does enhancing compliance decrease pain? *Journal of Occupational Rehabilitation, 6,* 177–190.

Loeser, J. D., & Sullivan, M. (1995). Disability in the chronic low back pain patient may be iatrogenic. *Pain Forum, 4,* 114–121.

Lofland, K. R., Cassisi, J. E., & Blonsky, E. R. (1996, November). *Lumbar paraspinal EMG: Somatization as a potential unifying construct to this conflicting literature.* Paper presented at the meeting of the American Pain Society, Washington, DC.

Main, C. J., & Watson, P. J. (1995). Screening for patients at risk of developing chronic incapacity. *Journal of Occupational Rehabilitation, 5,* 207–217.

Martin, J. E., & Dubbert, P. M. (1985). Adherence to exercise. In R. L. Terjung (Ed.), *Exercise and sport sciences reviews* (Vol. 13, pp. 137–167). New York: Macmillan.

Max, M. B., Lynch, S. A., Muir, J., Shoaf, S. E., Smoller, B., & Dubner, R. (1992). Effects of desipramine, amitriptyline, and fluoxetine on pain in diabetic neuropathy. *New England Journal of Medicine, 326,* 1250–1256.

Mayer, T. G., Gatchel, R. J., & Mayer, H. (1987). A prospective two year study of functional restoration in industrial low back injury: An objective assessment procedure. *Journal of the American Medical Association, 258,* 1763–1767.

Mayer, T. G., Polatin, P., Smith, B., Smith, C., Gatchel, R., Herring, S. A., Hall., H., Donelson, R. G., Dickey, J., & English, W. (1995). Contemporary concepts in spine care: Spine rehabilitation. *Spine, 20,* 2060–2066.

McCracken, L. M., Gross, R. T., Sorg, P. J., & Edmands, T. A. (1993). Prediction of low back pain in patients with chronic low back pain: Effects of inaccurate prediction and pain-related anxiety. *Behaviour Research and Therapy, 31,* 647–652.

Mein, E. A. (1996). Low back pain and manual medicine: A look at the literature. *Physical Medicine and Rehabilitation Clinics of North America, 7,* 715–729.

Melzack, R. (1975). Prolonged relief of pain by brief, intense transcutaneous somatic stimulation. *Pain, 1,* 357–373.

Mense, S. (1993). Nociception from skeletal muscle in relation to clinical pain. *Pain, 54,* 241–289.

Meyler, W. J., de Jongste, M. J. L., & Rolf, C. A. M. (1994). Clinical evaluation of pain treatment with electrostimulation: A study on TENS in patients with different pain syndromes. *The Clinical Journal of Pain, 10,* 22–27.

Muse, M. (1985). Stress-related, posttraumatic chronic pain syndrome: Criteria for diagnosis, and preliminary report on prevalence. *Pain, 23,* 295–300.

Nachemson, A. L. (1981). Disc pressure measurements. *Spine, 6,* 93–97.

Nash, T. P., Williams, J. D., & Machin, D. (1990). TENS: Does the type of stimulus really matter. *The Pain Clinic, 3,* 161–168.

Nigl, A. J., & Fischer-Williams, M. (1980). Treatment of low back strian with electromyographic biofeedback and relaxation training. *Psychosomatics, 21,* 495–499.

Nouwen, A., & Solinger, J. W. (1979). The effectiveness of EMG biofeedback training in low back pain. *Biofeedback and Self-Regulation, 4,* 103–111.

O'Brien, W. J., Rutan, F. M., Sanborn, C., & Omer, G. E. (1984). Effect of transcutaneous electrical nerve stimulation on human blood beta-endorphin levels. *Physical Therapy, 64,* 1367–1374.

Ohrbach, R. O., & McCall, W. D., Jr. (1996). The stress-hyperactivity-pain theory of myogenic pain: Proposal for a revised theory. *Pain Forum, 5,* 51–66.

Ongley, M. J., Klein, R. G., Dorman, T. A., Eek, B. C., & Hubert, L. J. (1987). A new approach to the treatment of chronic low back pain. *Lancet, 2,* 143–146.

Peters, J., Large, R. G., & Elkind, G. (1992). Follow-up results from a randomised controlled trial evaluating in- and outpatient pain managment programs. *Pain, 50,* 41–50.

Roberts, A. H., Sternbach, R. A., & Polich, J. (1993). Behavioral management of chronic pain and excess disability: Long-term follow-up of an outpatient program. *The Clinical Journal of Pain, 9,* 41–48.

Rodriquez, A. A., Bilkey, W. J., & Agre, J. C. (1992). Therapeutic exercise in chronic neck and back pain. *Archives of Physical Medicine and Rehabilitation, 73,* 870–875.

Romano, J. M., & Turner, J. A. (1985). Chronic pain and depression: Does the evidence support a relationship? *Psychological Bulletin, 97,* 18–34.

Rosomoff, H. L., Fishbain, D. A., Goldberg, M., Santana, R., & Rosomoff, R. S. (1989). Physical findings in patients with chronic intractable benign pain of the neck and/or back. *Pain, 37,* 279–287.

Roth, R. S., Horowitz, K., & Bachman, J. E. (in press). Knowledge of diagnosis and satisfaction with medical care in chronic myofascial pain. *Archives of Physical Medicine and Rehabilitation.*

Rudy, T. E., & Greco, C. M. (1996). Stretching psychophysiological models of TMD: But do the muscles respond? *Pain Forum, 5,* 67–69.

Sanders, S. H. (1985). Cross-validation of the back pain classification scale with chronic, intractable pain patients. *Pain, 22,* 271–277.

Simons, D. G. (1987). Myofascial pain syndrome due to trigger points. *International Rehabilitation Medicine Association Monograph Series, 1,* 1–39.

Spengler, D. M., Bigos, S. J., Martin, N. A., Zeh, J., Fisher, L. & Nachemson, A. (1986). Back injuries in industry: A retrospective study: I. Overview and cost analysis. *Spine, 11,* 241–245.

Sullivan, M. J. L., Reesor, K., Mikail, S., & Fisher, R. (1992). The treatment of depression in chronic low back pain: Review and recommendations. *Pain, 50,* 5–13.

Swanson, D. W., Maruta, T., & Swenson, W. M. (1979). Results of behavior modification in the treatment of chronic pain. *Psychosomatic Medicine, 41,* 55–61.

Teasell, R. W., & Harth, M. (1996). Functional restoration: Returning patients with chronic low back pain to work—revolution or fad? *Spine, 21,* 844–847.

Thomas, M., & Lundeberg, T. (1996). Does acupuncture work? *Pain Clinical Updates, 4*(3), 1–4.

Timm, K. E. (1994). A randomized-control study of active and passive treatments for chronic low back pain following L5 laminectomy. *Journal of Orthopaedic and Sports Physical Therapy, 20,* 276–286.

Troup, J. D., Martin, J. W., & Lloyd, D. C. (1981). Back pain in industry: A prospective survey. *Spine, 6,* 61–69.

Tulgar, M., McGlone, F., Bowsher, D., & Miles, J. B. (1991a). Comparative effectiveness of different stimulation modes in relieving pain: Part I. A pilot study. *Pain, 47,* 151–155.

Tulgar, M., McGlone, F., Bowsher, D., & Miles, J. B. (1991b). Comparative effectiveness of different stimulation modes in relieving pain: Part II. A double-blind controlled long-term clinical trial. *Pain, 47,* 157–162.

Turk, D. C. (1990). Psychological assessment of patients with persistent pain: Part II. Alternative views. *Pain Management, 3,* 227–237.

Turk, D. C., Okifuji, A., Starz, T. W., & Sinclair, J. D. (1996). Effects of type of symptom onset on psychological distress and disability in fibromyalgia syndrome patients. *Pain, 68,* 423–430.

Turk, D. C., Rudy, T. E., Kubinski, J. A., Zaki, H. S., & Greco, C. M. (1996). Dysfunctional patients with temporomandibular disorders: Evaluating the efficacy of a tailored treatment protocol. *Journal of Consulting and Clinical Psychology, 64,* 139–146.

Turner, J. A. (1996). Educational and behavioral interventions for back pain in primary care. *Spine, 21,* 2851–2857.

Tuttle, D., Shutty, M., & DeGood, D. (1991). Empirical dimensions of coping in chronic pain patients: A factorial analysis. *Rehabilitation Psychology, 36,* 179–188.

Vlaeyen, J. W. S., Kole-Snijders, A. J. M., Boeren, R. G. B., & van Eek, H. (1995). Fear of movement/(re)injury in chronic low back pain and its relation to behavioral performance. *Pain, 62,* 363–372.

Vlaeyen, J. W. S., Kole-Snijders, A. J. M., Rotteveel, A. M., Ruesink, R., & Heuts, P. H. T. G. (1995). The role of fear of movement/(re)injury in pain disability. *Journal of Occupational Rehabilitation, 5,* 235–252.

Waagen, G. N., Haldeman, S., Cook, G., Lopez, D., & DeBoer, K. F. (1986). Short term trial of chiropractic adjustments for the relief of chronic low back pain. *Manual Medicine, 2,* 63–67.

Ward, N., Bokan, J. A., Phillips, M., Benedetti, C., Butler, S., & Spengler, D. (1984). Antidepressants in concomitant chronic back pain and depression: Doxepin and desipramine compared. *Journal of Clinical Psychiatry, 45,* 54–57.

Weintraub, M. I. (1988). Regional pain is usually hysterical. *Archives of Neurology, 45,* 914–915.

White, A. A., & Gordon, S. C. (1982). Synopsis: Workshop on idiopathic low back pain. *Spine*, 7, 141–149.

Williams, A. C. de C., Richardson, P. H., Nicholas, M. K., Pither, C. E., Harding, V. R., Ridout, K. L., Ralphs, J. A., Richardson, I. H., Justins, D. M., & Chamberlain, J. H. (1996). Inpatient vs. outpatient pain management: Results of a randomised controlled trial. *Pain, 66*, 13–22.

Wolf, S. L., Gersh, M. R., & Rao, V. R. (1981). Examination of electrode placements and stimulating parameters in treating chronic pain with conventional transcutaneous electrical nerve stimuation (TENS). *Pain, 11*, 37–47.

Wolf, S. L., Nacht, M., & Kelly, J. L. (1982). EMG feedback training during dynamic movement for low back pain patients. *Behavior Therapy, 13*, 395–406.

Chapter 10

Surgery for Chronic Spine Pain: Procedures for Patient Selection and Outcome Enhancement

Andrew R. Block
The WellBeing Group

Craig Callewart
Baylor University Medical Center

Pain arising from the spine is most often successfully treated using a nonoperative approach. Most individuals experiencing back pain can recover with 2 to 3 days of bed rest and anti-inflammatory medication (Deyo, Diehl, & Rosenthan, 1986). Even those patients who experience protracted pain rarely undergo invasive treatment. Although approximately 70% of individuals in the United States experience back pain at some point in their lives (Fordyce, Brockway, & Spengler, 1986), only about 1% of back pain sufferers have medical conditions requiring surgery (Spitzer, 1987). Yet the number of spine surgeries performed in the United States is still quite large. Approximately 280,000 surgeries for low back pain are performed yearly (Taylor, Deyo, Cherkin, & Kreuter, 1994). Thus, spine surgery is a not infrequent approach when nonoperative measures have failed to produce relief.

Unfortunately, the outcome of spine surgery is far from uniform. For example, Turner et al. (1992) reviewed 47 studies examining the outcome of lumbar spinal fusions. They found that, on average, 68% had satisfactory results, although satisfactory outcome ranged from 16% to 95%. The outcome for the somewhat simpler and less invasive procedure of laminectomy/discectomy is a little better. Hoffman, Wheeler, and Deyo (1993) reviewed the results of 81 published studies on discectomy and concluded that about 75% of patients receive short-term relief of sciatica (leg pain), with a 10% reoperation rate.

Despite such inconsistent results, spine surgery does offer the promise of pain relief and improved lifestyle for certain patients with unremitting pain. A study by Malter, Larson, Urban, and Deyo (1996) illustrates such benefits. Reexamining data on lumbar discectomy outcome originally obtained by Weber (1983), the authors found that quality of life for patients with herniated lumbar discs was significantly greater when they underwent discectomy than when they were given only medical treatment, with such differential improvement lasting for 5 years. An additional quantitative analysis in this study demonstrated that the cost-effectiveness for discectomy is quite high—in fact greater than that found for such procedures as coronary artery bypass grafting for single-vessel coronary artery disease, and medical therapy for moderate hypertension.

Spine surgery, although obviously not a panacea, can be very beneficial in many cases. The critical issue for the physician is to determine those patients most likely to be responsive to surgery. The relief of pain and improvements in function that can result from spine surgery do not rest simply upon correcting physical pathology. The patient's lifestyle, emotional state, and social environment also play large roles. If such psychosocial factors do not allow the patient to experience relief of pain, or if minimal incentives exist for improvement in function, then good surgical results are unlikely.

The present chapter provides an introduction to both the general conditions necessitating spine surgery, as well as an examination of psychological factors associated with poor surgical outcome. Further, we discuss some additional "medical" factors that may be overlooked by the physician but can be associated with poor outcome. A model is presented for predicting surgical outcome by combining these medical and psychological risk factors. Some implications and treatment plans based on this model are also presented. (For a more detailed treatment of many of the topics covered in this chapter see Block, 1996.)

DIAGNOSIS AND SURGICAL TREATMENT OF SPINAL DISORDERS

The current understanding of the physical basis of spinal pain ascribes its generation to both an anatomic anomaly and a corresponding biochemical inflammatory response. The role of the surgeon is to correct the anatomic defect, reduce the corresponding inflammatory response, and minimize the pain.

To appreciate the pathological anatomy, the cascade of degeneration model must be understood. The spine is composed of segments, each containing two adjoining vertebrae. The vertebrae are joined in front by a cartilaginous joint (the disc), and in back by two bony joints, the facets. Together they form a three-pronged connection. On the posterior side of the vertebra, spinous processes provide the location for muscular attachment. The muscles manipulate the vertebral bodies to twist, turn, and bend to provide spinal motion. Painful derangement of the spine usually starts with the front of the disc, and subsequently involves the facets. It is this progression of derangement, beginning in the discs and proceeding to the facet, that is known as the degenerative cascade.

Not all spinal pain fits this model, nor comes from degeneration. There are medical causes (spondyloarthropies), cancers, visceral (pancreatitis, prostatitis), fractures, and congenital conditions that can cause pain. Given its nature, pain usually does not afflict patients until the third decade of life, with the prevalence increasing in each decade.

With the cascade of degeneration model in mind, painful spinal conditions can be classified as derangements of one of the structures. Anteriorly, cartilaginous disc disorders begin as a prolapse or displacement of the internal shock absorbing gel-like substance comprising the disc nucleus. Known as herniation, the cartilaginous gel can directly compress nerves and cause painful back and lower extremity pain. Additionally, disc herniation will elicit an inflammatory response that leads to more pain. Removal of the displaced gel eliminates the neural compression and diminishes the inflammatory response. Occasionally, for reasons poorly understood, the inflammation may persist, and be a cause of chronic neck or back pain syndromes. The procedure to remove the displaced gel is known as a discectomy. Typically, only the 5%–10% displaced portion will be removed, the remaining stable portion left undisturbed. To a varying degree, the portion of the overlying lamina will be removed for exposure, resulting in a laminectomy/discectomy. The disc portion can also be removed from the front, resulting in an anterior discectomy. The laminectomy/discectomy represents the most common of surgical spinal treatments.

If the deterioration progresses to involve more than a focal herniation, then the disc space usually diminishes in height, collapsing to rest on the two posterior facets. In turn these facets are forced to carry a disproportionate load, and can become painful. They may enlarge in response to the increased mechanical stress, and occlude the neuroforamen. This is known as stenosis and it causes nerve root compression and pain. More broad than a herniation, its treatment requires more than a partial laminectomy. Typically, the whole lamina, part of the facet, and part of the disc are removed, in a procedure known as decompression. The goal is to free all compressed neural structures.

Finally, the degeneration may progress sufficiently that spinal alignment is lost. Loss of alignment in the forward or lateral planes is termed spondylolisthesis. If a rotary displacement also is included, it is known as scoliosis. As the vertebrae become maligned, nerves are compressed or stretched. Surgery is performed to prevent further malignment or slippage.

This is accomplished by surgically constructing a bridge between the vertebrae, in a procedure known as spinal fusion. Bone is harvested from the pelvis to use in the fusion. Alignment is achieved by the use of hooks, screws, and/or rods that are permanently implanted in to the spine. The fusion mass eventually grows over these implants. Occasionally, sufficient bone is removed during the decompression of nerves that alignment is at risk of being lost in the future. In this situation, a fusion may be done prophylactically. This loss of alignment is the final stage of the degeneration cascade and represents the most difficult challenge surgically.

The term *failed spine syndrome* is applied to the patient who continues to experience disabling pain symptoms, despite aggressive treatment. Various factors lead to the entity of the failed spine syndrome. Surgical complication such as infection, vascular event, or damage to the neural structures during decompression can cause this syndrome. Additionally, the inability of the spinal fusion to consolidate (much like concrete must cure) can cause pain. Inability to fully decompress the nerve is also a common cause of "failure." Many patients develop failed spine syndrome due to inadequate postoperative rehabilitation. However, for many patients the impact of psychosocial factors upon both pain and surgical recovery are the strongest cause for the failure of operative intervention.

PSYCHOLOGICAL FACTORS ASSOCIATED WITH POOR SURGICAL OUTCOME

Clearly, the most immediate goal of elective spine surgery is to correct the pathological condition that is the source of the pain. However, pain is a subjective experience, and correction of the objective pathology underlying it may fail to achieve relief. The experience of pain may linger even after successful surgery, due to many factors that lie far beyond the operating room, in the realm of the patient's psychological makeup and social situation. Consideration of such factors is critical to the patient selection process in elective spine surgery.

Personality and Emotional Factors

The most stable psychological aspects of each individual are subsumed under the term *personality*. According to the American Psychiatric Association (APA, 1994), personality is defined as, "deeply ingrained patterns of behaviors, which includes the way one relates to, perceives and thinks about, the environment and oneself" (p. 1). One of the most significant areas of psychological assessment has been the development of "objective" tests that can assess such personality patterns. The most widely used of these personality tests, and the most frequently in cases of chronic spine pain, is the Minnesota Multiphasic Personality Inventory (MMPI), which has also been the subject of numerous studies on screening for spine surgery.

Pain Sensitivity: MMPI Scales Hs (Hypochondriasis) and Hy (Hysteria). The Hs and Hy scales are the ones most commonly elevated in general chronic pain syndromes (Keller & Butcher, 1991) and in spine surgery candidates. Scales Hs and Hy assess several similar characteristics, including "somatic preoccupation"—a patient's tendency for excessive and multiple physical complaints (Graham, 1990). The major difference between the two scales is that Hy measures, in addition, a tendency to deny psychological and emotional problems, as well as to minimize discomfort experienced in social situations. There is a strong correlation (.53) between the two scales and they are often both elevated at about the same level, with no other scales showing particular elevation. Such a profile is often called a "Conversion V profile."

Every study examining the value of the MMPI in predicting spine surgery outcome has found at least one, if not both, of the scales Hs and Hy to strongly predict poor surgical outcome (see, e.g., Cashion & Lynch, 1979; Herron, Turner, Ersek, & Weiner, 1992; Long, 1981; Wiltse & Rochio, 1975). In some studies (e.g., Spengler, Oulette, Battie, & Zeh, 1990) the predictive value of these two scales far exceeds that of medical diagnostic tests, such as X rays, computerized tomography scans, or neurological signs. Such results parallel those in other chronic pain syndromes, finding that Hs and Hy elevations predict poor treatment outcome for syndromes as diverse as temporomandibular joint dysfunction (TMD; Milstein-Prentky & Olson, 1979; R. A. Schwartz, Greene, & Laskin, 1979), gastrointestinal disorder (Whitehead, 1993), and nonsurgical back pain (Kleinke & Spangler, 1988).

Clinical Depression: MMPI Scale D (Depression). Depression is a frequent concomitant of chronic pain. In some studies, up to 85% of chronic pain patients are found to meet the diagnostic criteria for clinical depression. Such depressive symptoms include: depressed mood, diminished interest in almost all activities, weight loss or gain, insomnia or hypersomnia, agitation or psychomotor retardation, fatigue or energy loss, feelings of worthlessness or guilt, impaired concentration, recurrent thoughts of death (adapted from APA, 1994). Individuals with depression have been found to be more likely to focus on negative rather than positive events (Seligman, 1975), and to have a low threshold for induced pain (Merskey, 1965). Further, they tend to underreport their ability to function (Kremer, Block, & Atkinson, 1983). Thus, it is not surprising to observe that depression is frequently associated with poor outcome of elective spine surgery (see Dvorak, Valach, Fuhrimann, & Heim, 1988; Herron et al., 1992; Sorenson & Mors, 1988),

In examining depression, it is critical to consider whether the symptoms are long standing (i.e., they predate the back injury) or of relatively recent onset. For some patients, depressive symptoms—such as decreased motivation and concentration, sleep disturbance, and weight change—may be a direct result of the experience of protracted pain or disability (Cavanaugh, Clark, & Gibbons, 1983). For another large group of patients, depression may be more of personality style or a chronic emotional condition like dysthymia (neurotic depression). Chronically depressed patients are those who may respond poorly to any surgical procedure aimed at pain relief.

Anger: MMPI Scale Pd (Psychopathic Deviate).   The Pd scale of the MMPI assesses a number of patient characteristics, the most salient of which are hostility, rebelliousness toward authority, and aggressiveness (Graham, 1990). Elevations on scale Pd have been found in at least five studies to be associated with poor surgical outcome (e.g., Dvorak et al., 1988; Herron et al., 1992; Long, 1981). This should not be surprising, because feelings of anger have been found, in a number of studies, to be both common among general chronic pain patients and associated with reduced treatment outcome (cf. Fernandez & Turk, 1995).

Anger may have a negative impact on reduction of pain for a number of reasons. First, anger has been shown to have an adverse effect on many health conditions, including cardiovascular disease (Williams & Williams, 1993), headaches, asthma, and many others. Such adverse effects may be mediated by changes in the immune system or excessive activation of sympathetic nervous system efferents (Williams & Williams, 1993). Anger also may lead to maladaptive lifestyle changes, such as poor health habits, lack of physical exercise, or excessive use of drugs or alcohol (Leiker & Hailey, 1988). Further, anger may be focused at specific individuals or institutions. DeGood and Kiernan (1996) have found chronic pain patients who are angry and blame the employer for his or her injury, report high levels of emotional distress, and have poorer response to treatment. For such patients, continued postsurgical pain reports may be tied more closely to such attributions than to any improvement in the pathophysiological basis of the pain.

Chronic Anxiety and Obsessions: MMPI Scale Pt (Psychasthenia).   Scale Pt elevations have been found in four studies to be associated with adverse outcomes of spine surgery (e.g., Doxey, Dzioba, & Mitson, 1988; Dvorak et al., 1988; Sorenson & Mors, 1988). This scale, which is considered a good index of psychological turmoil (Graham, 1990), was originally designed to identify patients with a tendency toward obsessions, compulsions, excessive doubts, and fears. These patients also tend to be stubborn, rigid, and self-critical (APA, 1994). Such traits may be expected to lead to poor surgical outcome, because recovery from spine injuries requires adapting to changes in lifestyle, physical activity, and self-image.

Cognitive Factors

In recent years a great deal of research in chronic pain has focused on the assessment of the patient's viewpoint on the pain experience: the ways the patient thinks about and copes with the pain. From a cognitive-behavioral perspective, such thoughts and coping strategies play large roles in determining the level of pain experienced by the patient, as well as adjustment to the pain and efforts to overcome it (Turk & Rudy, 1988). A number of studies, which provide support for the cognitive-behavioral perspective on pain, have found that such factors can be strongly associated both with the etiology and maintenance of chronic pain syndromes, as well as with the outcome of different types of treatment (for a review, cf. Jensen, Turner, Romano, & Karoly, 1991).

Coping Strategies. *Coping strategies* refer to specific thoughts and behaviors people use to manage their pain or their emotional reactions to pain (Brown & Nicassio, 1987). Of the many pain-coping questionnaires available, the largest body of research (and the only research directly applied to surgical screening) has used the Coping Strategies Questionnaire (CSQ; Rosenstiel & Keefe, 1983). The CSQ defines six types of cognitive coping strategies: diverting attention, reinterpreting pain sensations, coping self-statement, ignoring pain sensations, praying or hoping, and catastrophizing. Also defined are two behavioral coping strategies: increasing activity level and increasing pain behavior. Finally, the CSQ asks patients to rate the ability to control pain and the ability to reduce pain.

Gross (1986) gave the CSQ preoperatively to 50 patients about to undergo lumbar laminectomy. She examined the relationship of three CSQ combined scales to different aspects of surgical outcome, including pain intensity, sleep disturbance, and self-rated improvement. Although the findings are somewhat complicated to report, the general findings were that patients who responded well to surgery were those who felt they had some control over the pain and also felt they could rely on themselves to overcome the pain. Coping strategies identified on the CSQ have also been found in many studies to be associated with outcome of conservative pain treatment (cf. Turner & Clancy, 1986).

Feelings of self-reliance and self-control over pain have been examined using other questionnaires and have been found to be associated with good outcome of treatment for chronic pain. For example, Brown and Nicassio (1987) used the Vanderbilt Pain Management Inventory (VMPI) in patients with general pain syndromes. They found that active coping is associated with decreased pain, lower depression, and less functional impairment among these patients. Similarly, feelings of *self-efficacy* (the expectation that one has the ability to engage in specific pain-coping behaviors) have been examined in pain populations. Self-efficacy has been found to be associated with exercise performance during rehabilitation (Dolce, Crocker, Molettiere, & Doleys, 1986), and with the ability to perform activities of daily living (O'Leary, Shoor, Lorig, & Holman, 1988). Thus, it appears that recognition of the ability to cope with pain and to improve overall functioning carries great potential for motivating the patient, especially in the postoperative period, when rehabilitation efforts may be critical to success.

Behavioral Factors

Although chronic pain is inherently an unpleasant condition, many social, vocational, and economic reinforcers can prolong its occurrence. According to operant learning theory (Fordyce, 1976), pain behaviors increase in frequency to the extent that their emission is followed by rewarding consequences. In other words, pain behaviors, like any other response, occur more frequently when they are reinforced and decrease when they are ignored or actually punished. Such "rewards" for pain may be provided in many ways, some quite subtle. For example, patients may be involved in litigation concerning the accident that led to the pain, or may bring malpractice suits concerning treatments they have received. Similarly, patients injured on the job may receive worker's compensation wage replacement while undergoing treatment. To the extent that these incentives can be identified, the patient may be at risk for poor surgical outcome.

Spousal Reinforcement of Pain Behavior. Often it is the family that provides the greatest reinforcement for pain behavior. Such reinforcers might include actions such as: taking over the patient's jobs or responsibilities, giving the patient medication, and encouraging rest. In some cases, family members may be more likely to pay attention to the patient when the pain appears greatest, and to ignore the patient at other times, such as when the patient is engaging in alternative "well behaviors." Many studies have shown that spousal responses can play a large role in modulating patient pain behavior. Block, Kremer, and Gaylor (1980), for example, found that spouses who provide a relatively high level of reward for pain can become "discriminative cues" for pain behavior. Thus, the patient is more likely to display pain in the presence of such a spouse than in his or her absence.

This finding has been replicated and extended, with some modifications, in a number of other studies (Kerns et al., 1991; Lousberg, Schmidt, & Groenman, 1992; Romano et al., 1992, 1995).

Kerns, Turk, and Rudy (1985) have developed an excellent questionnaire, The West Haven–Yale Pain Management Inventory (WHYMPI), which assesses, among other things, spousal or partner reinforcement of pain behavior.

Litigation. Kennedy (1946), in an oft-cited quotation about patients involved in litigation, coined the term *compensation neurosis*—"a state of mind born out of fear, kept alive by avarice, stimulated by lawyers, and cured by verdict." Indeed, it appears that pending legal actions can influence spine surgery outcome. Junge, Dvorak, and Ahrens (1995) found that Swiss patients who were applying for disability pensions had poorer disc-ectomy outcome that did nonapplicants. Finneson and Cooper (1979) found that both "history of law suits for medicolegal problems" (p. 142) and "secondary gain" (p. 142) predicted negative results of disc surgery, a result corroborated by Manniche et al. (1994). Such results do not mean that litigation patients are making up their symptoms (i.e., malingering), because surgical candidates do have a pathophysiological basis for the pain. However, the results with litigating patients may imply that, most often, financial incentives increase sensitivity to pain, making patients "somatically hypervigilant" (Chapman, 1978, p. 177).

Worker's Compensation and Disability Payments. Patients injured while working often receive some form of wage replacement, or temporary disability payments, while undergoing treatment. Such payments often continue until the patient has been declared at maximum medical improvement by the treating physician. A number of studies have shown that patients receiving worker's compensation respond to surgery more poorly than do noncompensation patients (Davis, 1994; Greenough & Fraser, 1989; Haddad, 1987). Hudgins (1976), for example, examining patients 1 year postlaminectomy, found that those receiving worker's compensation were the least likely to be working and to report pain relief. As with patients involved in litigation, the reasons for such poor results may not be purely economic. Patients injured on the job may display many other problems associated with high pain levels and poor treatment outcome. Such frequently encountered problems may include job dissatisfaction (Bigos et al., 1991), heavy physical job demands (Davis, 1994; Junge et al., 1995), or having a high level of anger or blame toward the employer (DeGood & Kiernan, 1996). However, regardless of the cause, worker's compensation is so widely recognized as a risk factor that Frymoyer and Cats-Baril (1987) have proposed that "compensability" is one of the strongest predictors of excessive disability among back injury patients.

Environmental and Historical Factors

If the causes and types of treatment for spine pain are many, the backgrounds and histories of spine pain patients are even more diverse. Examination of many features in the patient's history can also improve the selection process for spine surgery patients.

Prior Psychological Problems. Patients with chronic back pain often have diagnosable psychological or psychiatric problems. Kinney, Gatchel, Polatin, Fogarty, and T. G. Mayer (1993), for example, assessed pain patients using a standardized interview procedure, and found that 61% fit the diagnostic criteria for a mental health disorder.

For many chronic pain patients, emotional and behavioral difficulties are a direct reaction to the injury (Gamsa, 1994), whereas for others major psychological problems predate the injury (see earlier discussion of depression; see also Polatin, Kinney, Gatchel, Lillo, & T. G. Mayer, 1993). There is evidence that patients with more long-standing psychological problems fare poorly in response to spine surgery. For example, in the Manniche et al. (1994) study, one component of the composite score predicting diminished surgical outcome was "poor psychological background." Thus, in screening spine surgery candidates, one must consider not only the existence of mental health problems, but also whether such problems are premorbid (i.e., predate the onset of the pain symptoms).

Marital Distress. It is a truism that chronic pain amplifies many preexisting problems experienced by the patient. In no aspect of life is this more recognizable than in the nature of patients' most intimate relationships. When pain occurs in the context of marital distress, communication difficulties, or sexual problems, the marriage may go downhill quickly. A number of studies have shown that marital problems and dissatisfaction are both common among chronic pain patients (Romano, Turner, & Clancy, 1989) and may negatively influence treatment outcome. Dissatisfied spouses have been found to have more negative outcome expectations for patients (Block, Boyer, & Silbert, 1985), and to attribute the patient's pain to psychological, rather than medical, problems (Block & Boyer, 1984). Sexual difficulties are also common (Maruta & Osborne, 1976). Thus, consideration of the quality of intimate relationships may provide valuable information in the screening process.

Abuse and Abandonment. Physical and sexual abuse are unfortunate tragic realities of modern life. Such problems are found quite frequently in the histories of chronic pain patients. Haber and Roos (1985) found that 53% of woman evaluated at a chronic pain clinic were physically or sexually abused and that for 90% of the women the abuse occurred during adulthood. Such rates, although distressingly high, are still somewhat lower than those found in other pain syndromes. For example, in chronic pelvic pain Walker et al. (1988) found that 64% of women had been sexual abuse victims, either as adults or children.

It appears that patients who have experienced physical, sexual, or emotional abuse are less likely to respond well to spine surgery. Schofferman, Anderson, Hinds, Smith, and White (1992) questioned spine surgery candidates about five categories of childhood psychological trauma: sexual abuse, physical abuse, parental substance abuse, abandonment, and emotional abuse. The authors found that the spine surgery failure rate was astoundingly high (85%) among patients reporting at least three of these types of abuse, compared to a very low failure rate (5%) among patients reporting no such trauma. It appears that both childhood abuse and trauma, as well as current physical and sexual abuse, bode poorly for the outcome of spine surgery.

Substance Overuse and Abuse. For many spine surgery candidates the only, even partially, effective means of pain control is through the use of narcotic medications. Unfortunately, as the pain is refractory and the physiologic basis of the pain is unresolved, some spine surgery candidates may become quite dependent on or even addicted to such medication. Prescription medication dependence can be determined if at least three of the following symptoms are present: (a) increasing medication tolerance, (b) withdrawal symptoms present, (c) medications taken in larger amounts and over longer periods than prescribed, (d) persistent, unsuccessful efforts to reduce medication, (e) spending a great deal of time and energy obtaining the medication (e.g., calling multiple doctors to obtain the medication), (f) important work and social activities reduced because of medication use, and (g) continued use of medicine even though the patient knows it is causing additional physical or mental problems (APA, 1994).

There has been a notable paucity of research on both the frequency of substance abuse and dependence and their effect on outcome in spine surgery candidates. The two studies addressing this topic both have found it to be associated with poor outcome. Spengler, Freeman, Westbrook, and Miller (1980) reviewed 30 of their spine surgery failures and found that 25 of these patients "were continually abusing medication and alcohol" (p. 359). Uomoto, Turner, and Herron (1988) also found alcohol abuse to be associated with poor surgical results. Both of these studies are quite limited, because neither specifically examined dependence on prescription medication. Further, in both of these studies it is unclear whether the substance abuse occurred before or after surgery, so that the abuse may have been a result of the failed surgery, rather than a cause of it. However, given these results, substance abuse or dependence (as defined by criteria from APA, 1994) should be considered risk factors for poor surgical outcome, especially when such behaviors predate the onset of pain.

MEDICAL RISK FACTORS

The surgeon considering invasive procedures for chronic back pain brings to bear his or her years of experience and is able to draw upon incredibly sophisticated technology to obtain a clear picture of the pathological basis of the patient's pain. However, there may still exist a number of quasi-medical risk factors that can predict poor surgical outcome. These are not risk factors that relate either to identification of the physical basis of the pain, or to diseases that make the candidate a poor surgical risk, but to less specific factors that lie on the interface of medicine and psychology. Some of these "medical" factors include the following:

Chronicity. The probability of good surgical outcome decreases with increasing duration of pain. For example, Junge et al. (1995) found that patients obtaining poor outcome of discectomy had longer duration of acute and chronic pain, as well as longer time out of work. Perhaps greater pain duration allows for the development of "deconditioning syndrome" (T. G. Mayer et al., 1987), a pain-induced downward spiral in physical activity. It may also be that the highly chronic patient experiences greater fear of activity or has fewer incentives for improvement. Whatever the case it appears that pain duration over 1 year in length is particularly problematic.

Number of Previous Surgeries. Numerous studies have shown that successful spine surgery is less likely if the patient has had a previous surgery for the same problem. Waddell (1987) found that the probability of good surgical outcome decreases with each successive surgery. Similar results have been obtained by many authors (Ciol, Deyo, Kreuter, & Bigos, 1994; Franklin, Haug, Heyer, McKeefrey, & Picciano, 1994; Pheasant, Gelbert, Goldfarb, & Herron, 1979; Turner et al., 1992). Thus, multiple prior surgeries must be considered a significant risk factor.

Surgical Destructiveness. All surgery involves some amount of tissue damage, in order to reach and then repair the physical basis of the pain. Procedures such as many types of spinal fusion, of necessity, involve more destructiveness than minimally invasive or microsurgical techniques, such as may be involved in discectomy. Further, procedures performed on more than one level, and those involving the use of hardware (such as plates, screws, cages, etc.) are more destructive than single-level, uninstrumented types. In general, results show that the more destructive the surgery the less likely is good surgical outcome (see Franklin et al., 1994; Turner et al., 1992).

Nonorganic Signs. Waddell, McCulloch, Kummel, and Venner (1980) developed a series of physical and verbal tests to determine "nonorganic" signs associated with back pain. Some of the nonorganic signs include "superficial pain" (pain in response to light pinch of the skin), pain with axial loading (i.e., pushing down on the top of the head), and nondermatomal distribution of pain. Dzioba and Doxey (1984) found that the presence of such nonorganic signs predicted poor surgical outcome (see also Sorenson, 1992). Such inconsistent, nonphysiologically based pain indicators are, therefore, considered a surgical risk factor.

Multiple Prior Medical Problems and Medical Utilization. Several studies suggest that, just like a history of psychological problems, a history of multiple medical problems (especially problems of a vague nature) can be associated with poor surgical outcome. For example, Ciol et al. (1994) found that Medicare patients with a higher number of previous nonspine hospitalizations were at greater risk of lumbar spine reoperations (see also Hoffman et al., 1993). Wiltse and Rochio (1975) found that high scores on the Cornell Medical Index, which measures bodily symptoms and illness, were associated with poor results from chemonucleolysis. Thus, patients who have received a great many treatments for non-spine-related complaints tend to be at greater risk to respond poorly to surgery for pain.

Smoking. Smokers have been found to be at risk for the development of disc herniation (An et al., 1994) and to have greatly diminished probability of good discectomy results (Manniche et al., 1994). Although the negative effects of smoking can be at least partially overcome through the use of a bone stimulator in spinal fusion, smoking more than one pack per day should still be considered a significant risk factor.

Obesity. Obesity, defined as greater than 50% above ideal body weight, is considered by many surgeons to be a risk factor for poor surgical results. There is, however, little direct evidence to support this contention in the case of spine surgery. Surgical failure is greater among patients with poorer general health status (Von Korff, Dworkin, & LeResche, 1990) and those with a low fitness level (Frymoyer & Cats-Baril, 1987). Both of these characteristics might apply to those who are highly overweight. However, in the absence of direct evidence, obesity must be considered only a moderate surgical risk factor.

DETERMINATION OF SURGICAL PROGNOSIS

Presurgical Psychological Screening (PPS) Scorecard

If spine surgery is to obtain good results, risk factors must be identified and minimized. The current review has shown that many of the risk factors for spine surgery are psychological or quasi-psychological in nature. PPS can identify such risk factors, through a careful clinical interview as well as standardized psychological testing. Further, the PPS can reveal even some "medical" risk factors that may not be considered by the physician but that can have a negative effect on surgical outcome. The determination of surgical prognosis follows from identifying, quantifying, and then combining these psychological and medical risk factors.

The identification and measurement of these risk factors are summarized using a "scorecard" approach. Figure 10.1 displays our PPS scorecard. (For other scorecards see Finneson & Cooper, 1979; Junge et al., 1995; Spengler et al., 1990). The top of the PPS scorecard contains some demographic information about the patient, as well as the patient's score on the Oswestry Disability Index (Fairbank, Couper, Davies, & O'Brien, 1980), which gives a general measure of function impairment in back pain patients. The bulk of the PPS scorecard catalogs risk factors in two domains: medical and psychological. The psychological factors are further divided into those identified through clinical interview and those identified through psychometric testing. Regardless of the type, individual risk factors are defined as either "moderate" risk or "high" risk. On the PPS scale each risk factor is assigned a certain number of points. All moderate-risk factors are assigned 1 point and all high-risk factors are assigned 2 points. Total medical risk and total psychological risk are determined by addition.

Within the psychological dimension, the interview and psychometric testing factors are handled somewhat differently. Interview risk points are determined by simple addition of all points in the interview column. For psychometric testing the patient can earn a maximum of 4 points on the MMPI and a maximum of 2 points on the CSQ. Without such restrictions the psychometric testing results could overwhelm results obtained in the interview portion of the PPS. Interview and testing points are added to determine total psychological risk.

PPS Model

Once the medical and psychological total points are determined, they must be combined in order to determine whether the patient has good, fair, or poor surgical risk. A heuristic model (Fig. 10.2) is used to guide decision making. In this model a high-risk threshold is established on each of the

Presurgical Psychological Screening (PPS) Scale

Name: _____   Oswestry _____   Date _____
Med DX: _____   Onset _____   ID _____
MD: _____   Surg. Type _____   Psych _____

Medical	Risk	Interview	Risk	Testing	Risk
Chronicity		**Litig./SSDI**		**MMPI (T > 70)**	
6-12 mos	med	pending	high	(max 4 pts.)	
> 12 mos	high	**Work Comp**			
Prev. Spine Surg.		receiving	high	Hs	high
One	med	**Job Disatis**		D (pre-inj.)	high
Two +	high	moderate	med	D (reactive)	med
Destructiveness		extreme	high	Hy	high
Min-Mod	med	**Heavy Job**		Pd	high
Highly	high	>50 lb lift	high	Pt	med
Salvage	high	**Sub. Abuse**			
Nonorganic		pre-injury	med	**CSQ**	
Present	high	current	high	(max 2 pts.)	
Nonspine Med		**Family Rein.**			
moderate	med	moderate	med	low self-rel	high
multiple	high	extreme	high	low cont.	high
Smoking		**Mar. Disatis.**			
< 1 pack/day	med	present	med		
> 1 pack/day	high	**Abuse**			
Obesity		pre-injury	med	**Test Total**	____
>50% over	med	current	high		
		Preinjury Psy		**Psych total**	
Med Total	____	outpatient	med	**(Int. + Test)**	____
Threshold	= 8 ± 2	inpatient	high	**Threshold =**	10 ± 3
Med Risk	= ____	**Inter. Total**	____	**Psych Risk**	= ____

PROGNOSIS	MED TREATMENT RECOMMENDATIONS
GOOD	Clear for surgery, no psych necessary
	Clear for surgery, postop psych
FAIR	Hold, pending psych intervention
	Do not operate, conservative care only
POOR	Do not operate, recommend discharge

© Andrew R. Block, Ph.D., 1996

FIG. 10.1. The PPS scorecard.

Psychological risk factors

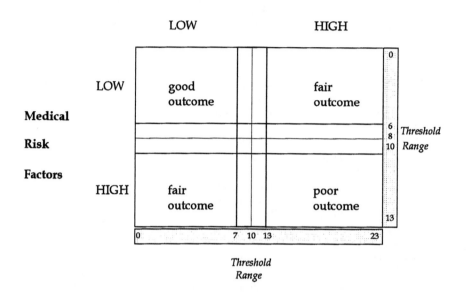

FIG. 10.2. Surgical prognosis determined by medical and psychological risk factors.

psychological and medical dimensions. Thus, a 2 × 2 decision matrix is formed. Patients who score above the high-risk threshold on both dimensions are considered to be at high risk, and those below threshold on both dimensions are considered to have a good prognosis. Patients who are high on one dimension and low on the other have a fair prognosis. The high-risk threshold is defined as 10 points on the psychological dimension and 8 points on the medical dimension.

Note also that a threshold range is defined on each dimension. When a patient's scores fall into the threshold range, the evaluator is free to place the patient either above or below threshold on that dimension. The determining factor in making this decision involves the evaluator's clinical judgment of nonquantified factors revealed in the PPS. Including such a threshold range allows decision making to be tied primarily to clearly identifiable risk factors, but does not overrely on such data. The evaluator's experience and expertise, thus, become critical parts of the PPS process. For the psychological dimension this range is 10 ± 3 points and for the medical dimension the range is 8 ± 2 points.

In using clinical judgment the evaluator may rely on many sources of information. Such information should be documented on PPS scorecard. Some suggestions for factors that may cause the patient to be placed on the high-risk side of the threshold are the following:

1. Noncompliance: The patient has a history of unwillingness to carry out treatment plans or missing appointments.
2. Staff splitting: The patient complains about other staff members, or relates unlikely information given by other physicians or staff. Also may "idealize" some health care providers.
3. Extortion: The patient makes threats if demands for treatment are not met, for example, threatening suicide if he or she does not receive surgery.

There are also factors that might cause the borderline patient to be placed on the low-risk side of the threshold, including:

1. Extenuating circumstances: Some high-risk factors may have plausible alternative explanations. For example, a patient may have a very extended pain as a result of the inaction of a thoughtless physician.
2. Overcoming past risk factors: The patient may have previously coped successfully with current risk factors. For example, the patient who has evidence of substance abuse or dependence may have overcome similar problems in the past.

Psychological Treatment Plans

In addition to determining a surgical prognosis, the evaluator should provide a plan of psychological treatment. The nature of this treatment plan will depend on the surgical prognosis determined through the PPS. For patients in the good category, psychological treatments should aim to augment or facilitate surgical outcome. For example, such patients may benefit from information about community resources, such as support groups, or referral to a state-funded rehabilitation agency. Also of value may be psychological treatments, including hypnosis or biofeedback for pain control, smoking cessation or weight reduction. For patients in the fair prognosis category, treatments can be designed to demonstrate and augment the patient's compliance with treatment recommendations in order to improve surgical outcome. Such treatments might involve: requiring reduction in narcotic medication to a predetermined level, cessation of smoking prior to surgery, required weight loss, or requirement to attend all scheduled appointments. The poor prognosis patient is one who will likely not benefit from surgery and may require an intense, coordinated treatment effort, such as a multidisciplinary pain treatment approach involving psychological, physical therapy, occupational therapy, and medical interventions. Such approaches have been found to be fairly effective even for quite difficult patients (Flor, Fydrich, & Turk, 1992). However, some patients (about 5% of the total patients evaluated) have such intense psychosocial difficulties that no treatment could be expected to be effective and discharge should be recommended.

Conclusion

The widespread use of spine surgery for relief of chronic back pain has recently come into question, due to reports of its limited effectiveness. However, a large body of research, discussed in this chapter, indicates that many patients who display poor spine surgery results have identifiable psychosocial risk factors. These studies suggest that the outcome of spine surgery can be dramatically improved through the judicious use of PPS techniques. PPS elucidates personality, emotional, social, and vocational issues that have been found to be associated with poor surgery results. PPS procedures screen out potential poor surgical responders, and can improve results in patients who undergo invasive treatments, through the development of adjunctive psychological treatment plans. Thus, PPS offers the promise of not only improving outcome for individual patients but also of allowing the effectiveness of operative spine procedures to be recognized and augmented.

REFERENCES

American Psychiatric Association. (1994). *Diagnostic and statistical manual of mental disorders* (4th ed.). Washington, DC: Author.
An, H. S., Silveri, C. P., Simpson, M., File, P., Simmons, C., Simeone, A., & Balderston, R. A. (1994). Comparison of smoking habits between patients and surgically confirmed herniated lumbar and cervical disc disease and controls. *Journal of Spinal Disorders, 7*(5), 369–373.
Bigos, S. J., Battie, M. C., Spengler, D. M., Fisher, L. D., Fordyce, W. E., Hansson, T., Nachemson, A. L., & Worthly, M. D. (1991). A prospective study of work perceptions and psychosocial factors affecting the report of back injury. *Spine, 16*, 1–6.
Block, A. R. (1996). *Presurgical psychological screening in chronic pain syndromes: A guide for the behavioral health practitioner.* Mahwah, NJ: Lawrence Erlbaum Associates.

Block, A. R., & Boyer, S. L. (1984). The spouse's adjustment to chronic pain: Cognitive and emotional factors. *Social Science and Medicine, 19,* 1313–1317.

Block, A. R., Boyer, S. L., & Silbert, R. V. (1985). Spouse's perception of the chronic pain patient: Estimates of exercise tolerance. In H. L. Fields, R. Dubner, & F. Cervero (Eds.), *Advances in pain research and therapy* (Vol. 9, pp. 897–904). New York: Raven.

Block, A. R., Kremer, E. F., & Gaylor, M. (1980). Behavioral treatment of chronic pain: The spouse as a discriminative cue for pain behavior. *Pain, 9,* 243–252.

Brown, G. K., & Nicassio, P. M. (1987). Development of a questionnaire for the assessment of active and passive coping strategies in chronic pain patients. *Pain, 31,* 53–64.

Cashion, E. L., & Lynch, W. J. (1979). Personality factors and results of lumbar disc surgery. *Neurosurgery, 4,* 141–145.

Cavanaugh, S., Clark, D. C., & Gibbons, R. D. (1983). Diagnosing depression in the hospitalized medically ill. *Psychosomatics, 24,* 809–815.

Chapman, R. C. (1978). Pain: The perception of noxious events. In R. A. Sternbach (Ed.), *The psychology of pain* (pp. 169–202). New York: Raven.

Ciol, M. A., Deyo, R. A., Kreuter, W., & Bigos, S. J. (1994). Characteristics in Medicare beneficiaries associated with reoperation after lumbar spine surgery. *Spine, 19*(12), 1329–1334.

Davis, R. A. (1994). A long-term outcome analysis of 984 surgically treated herniated lumbar discs. *Journal of Neurosurgery, 80,* 514–521.

DeGood, D. E., & Kiernan, B. (1996). Perception of fault in patient with chronic pain. *Pain, 64,* 153–159.

Deyo, R. A., Diehl, A., & Rosenthan, M. (1986). How many days of bedrest for acute low back pain? *New England Journal of Medicine, 315,* 1064–1070.

Dolce, J. J., Crocker, M. F., Moletteire, C., & Doleys, D. M. (1986). Exercise quotas, anticipatory concern and self-efficacy expectancies in chronic pain: A preliminary report. *Pain, 24,* 365–372.

Doxey, N. C., Dzioba, R. B., & Mitson, G. L. (1988). Predictors of outcome in back surgery candidates. *Journal of Clinical Psychology, 44,* 611–622.

Dvorak, J., Valach, L., Fuhrimann, P., & Heim, E. (1988). The outcome of surgery for lumbar disc herniation: II. A 4–17 years' follow-up with emphasis on psychosocial aspects. *Spine, 13*(12), 1423–1427.

Dzioba, R. B., & Doxey, N. C. (1984). A prospective investigation in the orthopedic and psychologic predictors of outcome of first lumbar surgery following industrial injury. *Spine, 9,* 614–623.

Fairbank, J. C. T., Couper, J., Davis, J., & O'Brien, J. P. (1980). The Oswestry low back pain disability questionnaire. *Physiotherapy, 66,* 271–273.

Fernandez, E., & Turk, D. C. (1995). The scope and significance of anger in the experience of chronic pain. *Pain, 61,* 165–175.

Finneson, B. E., & Cooper, V. R. (1979). A lumbar disc surgery predictive scorecard: A retrospective evaluation. *Spine, 4,* 141–144.

Flor, H., Fydrich, T., & Turk, D. C. (1992). Efficacy of multidisciplinary pain treatment centers: A meta-analytic review. *Pain, 49,* 221–230.

Fordyce, W. E. (1976). *Behavioral methods for chronic pain and illness.* St. Louis, MO: Mosby.

Fordyce, W. E., Brockway, J. A., & Spengler, D. (1986). Acute back pain: A control group comparison of behavioral versus traditional management models. *Journal of Behavioral Medicine, 4,* 127.

Franklin, G. M., Haug, J., Heyer, N. J., McKeefrey, S. P., & Picciano, J. F. (1994). Outcome of lumbar fusion in Washington State workers' compensation. *Spine, 19*(17), 1897–1904.

Frymoyer, J. W., & Cats-Baril, W. L. (1987). An overview of the incidences and cost of low back pain. *Orthopedic Clinics of America, 22,* 263–271.

Gamsa, A. (1994). The role of psychological factors in chronic pain: II. A critical appraisal. *Pain, 57*, 17–29.

Graham, J. R. (1990). *The MMPI-2: Assessing personality and psychopathology.* New York: Oxford University Press.

Greenough, C. G., & Fraser, R. D. (1989). The effects of compensation on recovery from low-back injury. *Spine, 14*(9), 947–955.

Gross, A. R. (1986). The effect of coping strategies on the relief of pain following surgical intervention for lower back pain. *Psychosomatic Medicine, 48*, 229–238.

Haber, J., & Roos, C. (1985). Effects of spouse abuse and/or sexual abuse in the development and maintenance of chronic pain in women. *Advances in Pain and Research Therapy, 9*, 889–895.

Haddad, G. H. (1987). Analysis of 2932 workers' compensation back injury cases: The impact of the cost to the system. *Spine, 12*(8), 765–771.

Herron, L., Turner, J. A., Ersek, M., & Weiner, P. (1992). Does the Millon Behavioral Health Inventory (MBHI) predict lumbar laminectomy outcome? A comparison with the Minnesota Multiphasic Personality Inventory (MMPI). *Journal of Spinal Disorders, 5*(2), 188–192.

Hoffman, R. M., Wheeler, K. J., & Deyo, R. A. (1993). Surgery for herniated lumbar discs: A literature synthesis. *Journal of General Internal Medicine, 8*, 487–496.

Hudgins, W. R. (1976). Laminectomy for treatment of lumbar disc disease. *Tex Med, 72*, 65–69.

Jensen, M. P., Turner, J. A., Romano, J. M., & Karoly, P. (1991). Coping with chronic pain: A critical review of the literature. *Pain, 47*, 249–283.

Junge, A., Dvorak, J., & Ahrens, S. (1995). Predictors of bad and good outcomes of lumbar disc surgery: A prospective clinical study with recommendations for screening to avoid bad outcomes. *Spine, 20*(4), 460–468.

Keller, L. S., & Butcher, J. N. (1991). *Assessment of chronic pain patients with the MMPI-2 [MMPI-2 Monographs]* (Vol. 2). Minneapolis: University of Minnesota Press.

Kennedy, F. (1946). The mind of the injured worker: Its affect on disability periods. *Compensation Medicine, 1*, 19–24.

Kerns, R. D., Southwick, S., Giller, E. L. Haythornthwaite, J. A., Jacob, M. C., & Rosenberg, R. (1991). The relationship between reports of pain-related social interactions and expression of pain and affective distress. *Behavior Therapy, 22*, 101–111.

Kerns, R. D., Turk, D. C., & Rudy, E. E. (1985). The West Haven–Yale Multidimensional Pain Inventory (WHYMPI). *Pain, 23*, 345–356.

Kinney, R. K., Gatchel, R. J., Polatin, P. B., Fogarty, W. T., & Mayer, T. G. (1993). Prevalence of psychopathology in acute and chronic low back pain patients. *Journal of Occupational Rehabilitation, 3*(2), 95–103.

Kleinke, C. L., & Spangler, A. D. (1988). Psychometric analysis of the audiovisual taxonomy for assessing pain behavior in chronic back pain patients. *Journal of Behavioral Medicine, 11*, 83–94.

Kremer, E. F., Block, A. R., & Atkinson, J. J. (1983). Assessment of pain behavior: Factors that distort self-report. In R. Melzack (Ed.), *Pain management and assessment* (pp. 165–171). New York: Raven.

Leiker, M., & Hailey, B. (1988). A link between hostility and disease: Poor health habits? *Behavioral Science, 14*, 129–133.

Long, C. (1981). The relationship between surgical outcome and MMPI profiles in chronic pain patients. *Journal of Clinical Psychology, 37*, 744–749.

Lousberg, R., Schmidt, A. J., & Groenman, N. H. (1992). The relationship between spouse solicitousness and pain behavior: Searching for more evidence. *Pain, 51*, 75–79.

Malter, A. D., Larson, E. B., Urban, N., & Deyo, R. A. (1996). Cost-effectiveness of lumbar discectomy for the treatment of herniated intervertebral disc. *Spine, 21*, 1048–1055.

Manniche, C., Asmussen, K. H., Vinterberg, H., Rose-Hansen, E. B. R., Kramhoft, J., & Jordan, A. (1994). Analysis of preoperative prognostic factors in first-time surgery for lumbar disc herniation, including Finneson's and modified Spengler's score systems. *Danish Medical Bulletin, 41,* 110–115.

Maruta, T., & Osborne, D. (1976). Sexual activity in chronic pain patients. *Psychosomatics, 19,* 531–537.

Mayer, T. G., Gatchel, R. J., Mayer, H., Kishino, N. D., Keeley, J., & Mooney, V. (1987). A prospective two-year study of functional restoration in industrial low back injury. *Journal of the American Medical Association, 258*(13), 1763–1768.

Merskey, H. (1965). The effect of chronic pain upon the response to noxious stimuli by psychiatric patients. *Journal of Psychosomatic Research, 9,* 291–298.

Millstein-Prentky, S., & Olson, R. (1979). Predictability of treatment outcome inpatients with myofascial pain-dysfunction (MPD) syndrome. *Journal of Dental Research, 58*(4), 1341–1346.

O'Leary, A., Shoor, S., Lorig, K., & Holman, H. R. (1988). A cognitive-behavioral treatment for rheumatoid arthritis. *Health Psychology, 7,* 527–544.

Pheasant, H. C., Gelbert, D., Goldfarb, J., & Herron, L. (1979). The MMPI as predictor of outcome in low-back surgery. *Spine, 4*(1), 78–84.

Polatin, P. B., Kinney, R. K., Gatchel, R. J., Lillo, E., & Mayer, T. G. (1993). Psychiatric illness and chronic low-back pain. The mind and the spine—Which goes first? *Spine, 18,* 66–71.

Romano, J. M., Turner, J. A., & Clancy, S. L. (1989). Sex differences in the relationship of pain patient dysfunction to spouse adjustment. *Pain, 39,* 289–296.

Romano, J. M., Turner, J. A., Friedman, L., Bulcroft, R. A., Jensen, M, P., Hops, H., & Wright, S. F. (1992). Sequential analysis of chronic pain behaviors and spouse responses. *Journal of Consulting and Clinical Psychology, 60,* 777–782.

Romano, J. M., Turner, J. A., Jensen, M. P., Friedman, L. S., Bulcroft, R. A., Hops, H., & Wright, S. F. (1995). Chronic pain patient-spouse behavioral interactions predict patient disability. *Pain, 63,* 353–360.

Rosensteil, A. K., & Keefe, F. J. (1983). The use of coping strategies in chronic low back pain patients: Relationship to patient characteristics and current adjustment. *Pain, 17,* 33–44.

Schofferman, J., Anderson, D., Hinds, R., Smith, G., & White, A. (1992). Childhood psychological trauma correlates with unsuccessful lumbar spine surgery. *Spine, 17*(Suppl. 6), S1381–S1384.

Schwartz, R. A., Greene, C. S., & Laskin, D. M. (1979). Personality characteristics of patients with myofascial pain-dysfunction (MPD) syndrome unresponsive to conventional therapy. *Journal of Dental Research, 58,* 1435–1439.

Seligman, M. E. P. (1975). *Helplessness: On depression, development, and death.* San Francisco: Freeman.

Sorenson, L. V. (1992). Preoperative psychological testing with the MMPI at first operation for prolapsed lumbar disc. *Danish Medical Bulletin, 39,* 186–190.

Sorenson, L. V., & Mors, O. (1988). Presentation of a new MMPI scale to predict outcome after first lumbar diskectomy. *Pain, 34,* 191–194.

Spengler, D. M., Freeman, C., Westbrook, R., & Miller, J. W. (1980). Low-back pain following multiple lumbar spine procedures: Failure of initial selection? *Spine, 5*(4), 356–360.

Spengler, D. M., Ouelette, E. A., Battie, M., & Zeh, J. (1990). Elective discectomy for herniation of a lumbar disc. *Journal of Bone and Joint Surgery [American], 12,* 230–237.

Spitzer, W. O. (1987). Scientific approach to the assessment and management of activity-related spinal disorders. *Spine, 12*(Suppl.), 1.

Taylor, V. M., Deyo, R. A., Cherkin, D. C., & Kreuter, W. (1994). Low back pain hospitalization: Recent United States trends and regional variations. *Spine, 19,* 1207–1212.

Turk, D. C., & Rudy, T. E. (1988). Toward an empirically driven taxonomy of chronic pain patients: Integration of psychological assessment data. *Journal of Consulting and Clinical Psychology, 56*(2), 233–238.

Turner, J. A., & Clancy, S. (1986). Strategies for coping with chronic low back pain: Relationship to pain and disability. *Pain, 24,* 355–364.

Turner, J. A., Ersek, M., Herron, L., Haselkorn, J., Kent, D., Ciol, M. A., & Deyo, R. (1992). Patient outcomes after lumbar spinal fusions. *Journal of the American Medical Association, 268*(7), 907–911.

Uomoto, J. M., Turner, J. A., & Herron, L. D. (1988). Use of the MMPI and MCMI in predicting outcome of lumbar laminectomy. *Journal of Clinical Psychology, 44,* 191–197.

Von Korff, M., Dworkin, S. F., & LeResche, L. (1990). Graded chronic pain status: An epidemiologic evaluation. *Pain, 40,* 279–291.

Waddell, G. (1987). A new clinical model for the treatment of low-back pain. *Spine, 12*(7), 632–644.

Waddell, G., McCulloch, J. A., Kummel, E., & Venner, R. M. (1980). Nonorganic physical signs in low-back pain. *Spine, 5*(2), 117–125.

Walker, E., Katon, W., Harrop-Griffiths, J., Holm, L., Russo, J., & Hickok, L. R. (1988). Relationship of chronic pelvic pain to psychiatric diagnoses and childhood sexual abuse. *American Journal of Psychiatry, 145,* 75–80.

Weber, H. (1983). Lumbar disc herniation: A controlled perspective study with ten years of observation. *Spine, 8,* 131–140.

Whitehead, W. E. (1993). Behavioral medicine approaches to gastrointestinal disorders. *Journal of Consulting and Clinical Psychology, 60*(4), 605–612.

Williams, R., & Williams, V. (1993). *Anger kills.* New York: Harper Perennial.

Wiltse, L. L., & Rochio, P. D. (1975). Preoperative psychological tests as predictors of success of chemonucleolysis in the treatment of low-back syndrome. *Journal of Bone and Joint Surgery [American], 75,* 478–483.

Chapter 11

Psychological Factors Influencing Treatment of Temporomandibular Disorders

D. L. Massoth
Department of Oral Medicine
University of Washington

Temporomandibular disorders (TMD) are a heterogeneous set of clinical conditions characterized by pain in the masticatory and related muscles of the head and neck, the temporomandibular joint and associated hard and soft tissues; limitations in jaw function such as the inability to open one's mouth wide; and/or clicking, popping, or grating sounds in the temporomandibular joint (American Dental Association, 1983). Headache, neck, and shoulder pain, as well as changes in how the teeth articulate, or fit together, also may be associated with TMD. Among individuals seeking treatment for TMD, pain is the most common symptom (Dworkin, Huggins, et al., 1990).

Although a heterogeneous group of disorders, TMD can be categorized into three main conditions. The most common form of TMD is myofascial pain, which may be accompanied by limitations in jaw opening. The second and third categories of TMD include internal derangements of the temporomandibular joint (TMJ) and degenerative joint diseases. Persons with TMD can have one or more of these conditions at the same time. The clinical course of TMD varies from a brief single occurrence that can resolve in weeks to months, to a chronic episodic or chronic persistent pain problem with duration from 6 months to 20 or more years. TMD-related pain, limitations in jaw function, and pain-related disability vary from mild to severe and do not consistently relate to duration of the TMD problem.

Historically, there have been a variety of factors implicated in the etiology and maintenance of TMD symptoms. These have included physical factors such as trauma, anatomic variation and malocclusion; behavioral factors such as parafunction (e.g., tooth clenching and grinding), gum chewing, and maladaptive posturing of the jaw, head, and neck; as well as an array of psychological variables that have been extensively reported in the literature (Clark, 1987; DeBoever & Carlsson, 1994; Glaros & Glass, 1993; Laskin, 1969; Moss, Garrett, & Chiodo, 1982; Pullinger & Monteiro, 1988). The psychological factors that have received the most attention include anxiety, depression, somatization, and substance abuse; psychosocial factors such as stress, coping, social support, pain-related dysfunction, abuse history, health care use, and secondary gain; and, a variety of cognitive factors such as perception and appraisal, explanatory models of illness, perceived control, and motivation (Dworkin, 1994; Dworkin, LeResche, et al., 1992; Grzesiak, 1991; LeResche & Massoth, 1995; Speculand & Goss, 1985; Turk & Rudy, 1988; Turner & Romano, 1990).

This chapter focuses on behavioral and psychological variables that can influence TMD treatment outcome. Following a general review of the literature, special attention is paid to three variables—chronic pain dysfunction, somatization, and explanatory models of illness—and their influence on TMD treatment expectations, treatment-seeking behavior, and TMD treatment.

TEMPOROMANDIBULAR DISORDERS: OVERVIEW

The prevalence of self-reported signs and symptoms of TMD is estimated between 5% and 15%, with a prevalence of around 12% for TMD-related pain. TMD is most prevalent in young adults age 20 to 40 years, and is overrepresented in women. In clinic populations, women may outnumber men 5:1; however, the ratio is closer to 2:1 in community samples. The natural history of TMD is not well defined, however, the lower prevalence of TMD signs and symptoms at older ages is supportive of a condition that is generally self-limiting in nature.

Contemporary perspectives derived from epidemiologic and clinical studies of TMD emphasize TMD as a chronic pain condition (Dworkin, Huggins, et al., 1990; Keefe & Dolan, 1986; McCreary, Clark, Merril, & Oakley, 1991; Rudy, Turk, Brena, & Brody, 1990; Turk & Rudy, 1988; Von Korff, Dworkin, et al., 1988). In fact, TMD shares many characteristics with other chronic pain conditions, most notably headache and back pain (Von Korff, Dworkin, et al., 1988). For example, like headache and back pain, TMD is characterized by variability in symptom presentation and associated treatments. Overall duration of the condition as well as pain episodes can be brief for some individuals and quite long for others, whereas the level of symptoms can vary greatly from mild to severely disabling. Like other

TABLE 11.1
TMD and Other Chronic Pain States

Pain Variables (Means)	Primary Care Patients		
	TMD	Headache	Back Pain
Pain Intensity	5.0	6.0	4.7
Disability Days	10.4	10.1	19.8
Days in Pain	91.7	55.5	78.5
Years Since Onset	6.0	17.5	12.3
Psychologic/Behavioral (% of Patients)			
Elevated Depression	25.6	28.4	22.0
Frequent Pain Visits	7.5	9.2	8.1
High Pain Impact	23.8	35.4	32.8

Note. TMD, headache, and back pain are comparable for important pain and psychologic/behavioral variables, including means on ratings of pain intensity, disability days, days in pain, and prevalence rates for depression (SCL 90–R subscales).

chronic pain conditions, TMD often presents as a chronic or recurrent condition, even though in many cases it appears to be physically nonprogressive. Similarly, the symptomatic report of TMD pain and the psychosocial impact to the individual are not consistently related to observable pathology. Much like headache and back pain, TMD can have significant impact on the individual with respect to disability days and days in pain (Table 11.1) (Von Korff, Ormel, Keefe, & Dworkin, 1992). In addition, TMD, headache, and back pain show comparable means on ratings of pain intensity and comparable prevalence rates for depression, measured from the Symptom Checklist–90–R (SCL 90–R) subscales (Derogatis, 1983; Von Korff et al., 1992).

MANAGEMENT OF TEMPOROMANDIBULAR DISORDERS

Generally accepted, scientifically based guidelines for the management of TMD are still unavailable. Therapeutic modalities for TMD range from very conservative to very invasive, and may include some combination of occlusal change therapies, physical therapy, pharmacological treatments, surgical therapies (both arthroscopic and open joint surgery), and a wide range of psychological and behavioral modalities (Clark, 1987; Glaros & Glass, 1993; Laskin & Greene, 1990; Rugh & Dahlstrom, 1995). High treatment success rates (60%–80%) have been reported for vastly differing treatments (Okeson & Hayes, 1986; Von Korff, Howard, et al., 1988); yet, there is a paucity of sound clinical research to both support these claims and guide therapeutic management of TMD patients.

Physically based dental therapies aimed at modifying the dental occlusion include direct modification of tooth structure (i.e., occlusal adjustment), use of intraoral repositioning appliances, orthodontic braces or placement of crowns to modify the occlusal scheme, and surgery to reposition the jaw bones. Advocates of these therapies argue that occlusal abnormalities (e.g., discrepancies in how the upper and lower teeth fit together) and/or functional abnormalities within the TM joint precipitate the development of TMD. However, the role of occlusion in the etiology and management of TMD remains controversial and the superiority of these irreversible therapies over reversible therapies has not been demonstrated in randomized, controlled, prospective trials (Clark et al., 1997; McNamara, 1997).

Physical therapy applications to TMD include massage; gentle stretching of the jaw and neck muscles, often following the application of a cold spray, heat packs, or ultrasound; diet modification and reduction in pathogenic oral behaviors (e.g., bruxism); as well as the use of non-repositioning stabilization splints (known as "night guards"). These conservative and reversible therapies are used relatively frequently in the treatment of TMD. However, even for these benign treatments, there remains a paucity of sound clinical data demonstrating their benefit in producing long-lasting reductions in TMD signs and symptoms (Feine et al., 1997)

A variety of medications are commonly used in the management of TMD and are similar to those used for other painful musculoskeletal conditions. Pharmacological therapy, which is typically used in combination with other TMD treatments, includes use of nonsteroidal anti-inflammatory drugs (NSAIDs), muscle relaxant medications, and/or low-dose antidepressants. There remains a paucity of well-controlled, randomized clinical trials to provide guidance for the most efficacious use of these medications, and the risk of side effects must always be weighed against the potential benefits of these agents (Dionne, 1997).

A variety of surgical interventions have been applied to the management of TMD, particularly when specific joint pathology is suspected. Surgical approaches include arthrocentesis, arthroscopy, arthrotomy/arthroplasty, condylotomy, orthognathic surgery, and total TMJ replacement. Although surgeons who perform these procedures claim high rates of success when these procedures are applied to select patients, randomized controlled clinical trials to support the efficacy of individual surgical procedures have not been performed (National Institutes of Health, 1997). It should also be noted that the use of certain alloplastic implants in TMD surgery has resulted in disastrous consequences for many patients; thus, the surgical management of TMJ pathology with implants should be pursued with great caution.

A variety of psychological and behavioral therapies, subsumed under the term *biobehavioral* therapies, are generally agreed to be useful and effective modalities in the management of chronic pain conditions, including TMD (Dworkin, 1997). Biobehavioral therapies for TMD include patient education about the condition; self-monitoring of TMD symptoms, parafunctional activity, jaw posture, and other pathogenic habits; self-care approaches such as correcting jaw posture, limiting parafunctional activity, diet modification, and daily jaw-stretching exercises; relaxation and stress reduction techniques; and strategies for modifying negative cognitions (i.e., pain-related perception and appraisal) that often contribute to pain-related disability. Biobehavioral therapies are advocated at most chronic pain centers around the world and are considered to be conservative and reversible. Conservative treatments do not invade the tissues of the face, jaw, or joint, and reversible treatments do not cause permanent changes in the structure or position of the jaw or teeth (Sheridan & Hall, 1996). These standard biobehavioral treatments seem to produce a positive response in approximately 75% of TMD patients (Clark, Lanham, & Flack, 1988).

BIOMEDICAL VERSUS BIOPSYCHOSOCIAL MODEL OF PAIN

Until recent years, physically based dental treatment such as occlusal adjustment, occlusal repositioning splints, orthodontics, and surgery were favored in the management of TMD. Behavioral treatments, when used, often followed unsuccessful trials of physically based modalities (McCreary, Clark, Oakley, & Flack, 1992). The exclusive use of physically based treatment modalities for chronic TMD was driven largely by a biomedical model of disease (Engel, 1977). The biomedical model assumes that an individual's complaints and ailments are likely to result from a specific disease state associated with specific physical pathology. The biomedical model has been criticized for its failure to account for psychological and psychosocial variables in health and disease, as well as their dynamic interactions with pathophysiologic factors. With its narrow focus on disease, the biomedical model is inadequate in accounting for discrepancies between the patient's complaints and the degree of "observable" pathology, a situation that is quite common in chronic pain conditions.

More recently, emphasis has been placed on evaluating and treating TMD from a biopsychosocial perspective that focuses on illness rather than disease, and emphasizes the complex interaction of biological, psychological, and social variables (Dworkin, 1991). Dworkin, Von Korff, and Le-Resche (1992) have presented a biopsychosocial or ecologic model for understanding chronic pain, including TMD, which emphasizes the fundamental role of noxious nociceptive signals that recruit the higher order central processes of perception, appraisal, emotional arousal and, eventually, pain behavior (Fig. 11.1). According to this model, the individual's

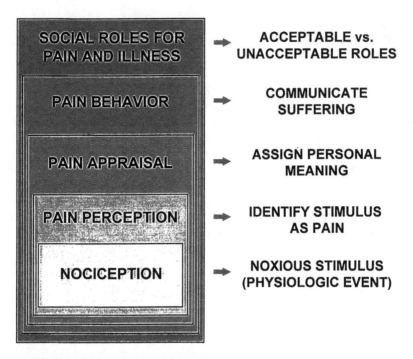

FIG. 11.1. The ecologic model for chronic pain. Adapted from Dworkin, Von Korff, and LeResche (1992).

perceptual processes identify the noxious stimulus as painful and allow for characterization of the pain, which may be dull or sharp, mild or severe, well localized or diffuse, brief or long lasting. The perception of pain leads to a cognitive-emotional appraisal process in which the individual assigns personal meaning to the pain (e.g., does the pain signal serious illness, is it ominous or nonthreatening, does it require medical treatment?). The appraisal process yields simultaneous emotional arousal that further reinforces the meaning ascribed to the painful event or condition. These processes of nociception, perception, and appraisal lead to observable pain behaviors that serve to communicate to others the suffering being experienced and the strategies (e.g., seeking home remedies and visiting doctors or other health care providers) used by the individual to cope with their pain. Finally, these chronic pain behaviors are also understood within the context of societally defined norms for the sick role. For example, the chronic pain patient may be relieved of responsibilities at home, work, or school and allowed to withdraw socially. Simultaneously, the socially defined sick role may promote increased reliance on health care delivery in the form of increased medical visits, diagnostic tests, hospitalization, surgery, and the use of medications.

PSYCHOLOGICAL VARIABLES INFLUENCING
TMD TREATMENT: REVIEW OF LITERATURE

The emergence of the biopsychosocial model for understanding TMD was both accompanied and facilitated by a number of early studies investigating the influence of psychological variables on a range of standard, conservative TMD treatments. Gessel and Alderman (1971) reported that TMD patients with poor response to tension-control relaxation training had multiple somatic complaints, high pain-related disability, and high depressive symptomatology. In a separate study, Gessel (1975) reported that patients who showed no improvement in TMD symptoms following biofeedback training and a course of tricyclic antidepressants suffered from severe depression and pain-related disability.

Other early studies also reported relationships between psychological factors noted before treatment and poor TMD treatment outcome. Speculand, Goss, Hughes, Spence, and Pilowsky (1983) reported an increase in abnormal illness behavior in TMD patients considered resistant to conservative TMD treatments. Studies by Millstein-Prentky and Olson (1979) and Schwartz, Greene, and Laskin (1979) demonstrated pretreatment elevations of several MMPI (Minnesota Multiphasic Personality Inventory) subscales in TMD treatment nonresponders compared with responders. Salter, Brooke, and Merskey (1986) reported poor treatment outcome in patients with the highest depression and somatization scores, but also noted the best treatment outcomes in patients with mild elevations in pretreatment depression and somatization scores. In addition, it was noted that patient's ratings of treatment outcome at 3-month follow-up were not related to the severity or duration of symptoms at initial presentation, and, interestingly, the outcomes of patients who received no treatment did not differ from those receiving treatment. These authors speculated that mild psychological distress may actually facilitate a successful treatment outcome.

In other early studies, Lipton and Marbach (1984) reported that myofascial pain (MPD) patients demonstrating poor treatment response tended to describe their pain using more emotional or expressive terms, whereas treatment responders had shorter pretreatment histories of pain and consulted fewer than three doctors. Finally, Gale and Funch (1984) reported that short- and long-term treatment response to behavioral therapies was best in TMD patients who were less depressed, more motivated to follow treatment recommendations, and more likely to endorse self-care activities than other patients.

Although these early studies were provocative, they suffered from a variety of methodological problems (McCreary et al., 1992). Most notably, the studies used different psychological distress measures that claim to assess variables such as depression, anxiety, and somatic preoccupation, often with little empirical validation of these measures. Many of these studies did not control for pretreatment levels of pain and used single and somewhat simplistic measures of treatment outcome. In addition, these studies suffered from a number of statistical problems, most notably the inappropriate use of multiple t tests contrasting good versus poor outcome groups on several variables, thereby increasing the likelihood of Type I errors (i.e., rejecting the null hypothesis when it is true).

Several more recent studies have focused on differential response to conservative TMD treatments based on psychosocial and behavioral characteristics. Tversky, Reade, Gerschman, Holwill, and Wright (1991) noted differential response to TMD treatments for depressed versus nondepressed TMD patients. A nondepressed group receiving occlusal splint therapy was compared to three depressed TMD treatment groups—one receiving occlusal splint therapy alone, one receiving a tricyclic antidepressant (doxepin) alone, and the third receiving occlusal splint and antidepressant therapy. Reduction in pain intensity was seen for all four groups but was greatest in the nondepressed and combined therapy depressed group. These authors noted that when depression is present, it must be managed concurrent with physical medicine strategies for adequate resolution of the TMD problem.

TEMPOROMANDIBULAR DISORDERS AND CHRONIC PAIN DYSFUNCTION

The importance of assessing and treating TMD within a biopsychosocial framework cannot be overemphasized. Research diagnostic criteria (RDC) are now established that specify a dual-axis approach for classifying TMD (Dworkin & LeResche, 1992). Axis I is devoted to clinical diagnosis using clinical parameters like vertical jaw opening, joint sounds, and muscle palpation tenderness, which reflect physical TMD status. Axis II, which emphasizes psychosocial classification, includes measures of chronic pain dysfunction, depression, and somatization.

The notion of chronic pain dysfunction has been introduced to account for the observation that in chronic pain conditions, the degree of pain-related disability is often not commensurate with the degree of observable pathology. Turk and Rudy (1988) have used the Multidimensional Pain Inventory (MPI) to distinguish among psychosocially "dysfunctional" chronic pain patients, "interpersonally distressed" pain patients, and their functional counterparts, termed "adaptive copers." The dysfunctional pain patients are distinguished by their high levels of pain severity and pain-related interference in daily activities; the interpersonally distressed patients share a common perception that significant others are not very supportive of their pain problem; and the adaptive copers are patients who report high levels of social support, relatively low levels of pain and pain-related disability, and high levels of activity. The authors have demonstrated that these groups differ on behavioral and psychosocial factors but did not differ on physical findings associated with TMD (e.g., dental examination findings, disc displacements, degenerative conditions of the TMJ). Rudy, Turk, Kubinski, and Zaki (1995) reported differential TMD treatment response to a combination of intraoral appliance, biofeedback, and stress management as a function of psychosocial subgroup. They reported that although the majority of patients demonstrated and maintained improvements in response to standard, conservative treatment, the dysfunctional patients displayed significantly greater improvements on measures of pain, catastrophizing, depression, and disability, when contrasted with the interpersonally distressed and adaptive coper patient subgroups. The authors noted that even with these gains, there was still room for improved treatment outcome, particularly among the dysfunctional subgroup. They suggested that adding components to treatments that specifically target problematic areas (e.g., targeting dysphoric mood for dysfunctional patients or targeting interpersonal problems for the interpersonally distressed subgroup) could lead to even greater improvements and maintenance of treatment gains.

Von Korff and colleagues (1992) have developed an alternate classification system for ratings of chronic pain dysfunction, measured using an easy-to-use 0–IV scale. The scale incorporates characteristic pain level, degree of interference due to pain, and number of days of activity lost due to pain. Patients receiving Grades I and II are termed "functional" and include individuals who report TMD pain of either low or high intensity that is not associated with significant disability. Patients receiving Grades III and IV are associated with increasing levels of pain-related disability, independent of pain level. The estimated prevalence of dysfunctional TMD patients (Grade III/IV) ranges from 19% in clinic cases referred to a large health maintenance organization (in the metropolitan Seattle area) for TMD treatment to 25%–30% in the more highly specialized and tertiary care TMD clinic at the University of Washington. Pain patients classified as dysfunctional are found to be more depressed, to report more nonspecific physical symptoms, and to use more medications and health care than functional pain patients.

Dworkin, Turner, and colleagues (1994) conducted a randomized clinical trial of a brief group cognitive-behavioral (CB) intervention for TMD that validates the use of the graded chronic pain scale. The brief CB intervention, which was administered after a comprehensive dental examination for TMD but prior to initiation of dental treatment, was designed to increase knowledge about the etiology and treatment of TMD, as well as provide skills in self-monitoring the condition and in use of behavioral strategies to manage chronic TMD pain. These authors reported a differential response to treatment for subjects by chronic pain grade that was independent of study group assignment. That is, pain patients who were classified as dysfunctional (Grade III/IV) were reported to be more resistant to usual TMD treatment both with and without a minimal CB intervention. Specifically, somatization scores for functional pain patients (Grade I/II), which were slightly elevated at baseline, were observed to return to the population mean at 12-month follow-up. By contrast, somatization scores at 12-month follow-up for the dysfunctional patients, although lower than baseline scores, still remained high (i.e., 75th percentile), even in the group receiving the CB intervention. The authors concluded that dysfunctional chronic pain patients might not respond readily to modest CB interventions that do not address the more complex aspects of their pain dysfunction, such as somatization.

TEMPOROMANDIBULAR DISORDERS AND SOMATIZATION

McCreary and colleagues (1992) compared TMD treatment outcome assessed in terms of pain levels, limitations in jaw function, and satisfaction with care among patients receiving an evaluation only or an evaluation followed by conservative physical medicine/dental procedures (occlusal appliance, physical therapy, and anti-inflammatory medications). They reported that high somatization (represented by a factor score combining scales #1, 2, 3 of MMPI Hs, D, Hy) was a consistent predictor of poor TMD outcome, especially with respect to posttreatment levels of pain in both the treated and evaluation only patients. This relationship held even after controlling for pretreatment pain levels.

Somatization, which has been described as a relatively common problem among large numbers of patients in primary medical care settings (Escobar, Burnam, Karno, Forsythe, & Golding, 1987; Katon et al., 1991; A. Kleinman, 1988; Simon, 1993), has also been heavily implicated in chronic pain, including TMD (Dworkin, Von Korff, et al., 1990; Dworkin, Wilson, et al., 1994; McCreary et al., 1992; Wilson, Dworkin, Whitney, & LeResche, 1994). Somatization is characterized as the predisposition to report numerous nonspecific physical symptoms (e.g., pounding heart, sweating, trembling) and pain complaints (e.g., headache, back pain, stomach upset); the tendency to seek medical treatment, often from multiple providers; and the presence of emotional or affective disturbance (Dworkin & Wilson, 1993; Katon et al., 1991). Nonspecific physical symptoms, one dimension of somatization, can be measured using age- and gender-adjusted scores for the 12 items that comprise the somatization subscale of the SCL 90–R (Dworkin, LeResche, et al., 1992).

Somatization may be most usefully understood as a dimension of personal functioning characterized by the tendency to report distress arising from physical symptoms that often are not consistent with measurable physiologic change. The predisposition to focus on physical signals as symptoms of a problem in the body can be mild for some individuals and quite intense for others, and can also fluctuate within an individual across situations and the life span. Important to note here, the somatizer's heavy focus on physical symptoms is accompanied by an insensitivity to associated psychological distress. In addition, the behavioral predisposition toward symptom reporting and treatment seeking can evolve into a subset of maladaptive illness behaviors, which include severe limitations in meeting social responsibilities and excessive use of health care in pursuit of a cure for a physical problem. Such behaviors have been characterized by Fordyce (1976) as chronic pain behaviors and by others as dysfunctional chronic pain (Von Korff, Ormel, Keefe, & Dworkin, 1992).

Dworkin, Wilson, and colleagues (1994) have proposed that somatization may be a risk factor for chronic pain. They have presented data demonstrating that TMD patients with the highest SCL 90–R somatization scores reported seeking TMD treatment from the greatest number of providers and reported receiving more and varied treatments for TMD. When patients continue to seek treatment for nonspecific physical symptoms, they are at increased risk for iatrogenic sequelae of multiple diagnostic and treatment procedures.

Using data from a different study, the same researchers grouped subjects according to low and high quartiles on SCL 90–R somatization subscales (Dworkin, 1995). At baseline examination, about 18% of patients in the lowest quartile for somatization reported seeking TMD treatment from five or more providers, whereas about 50% of patients in the top quartile reported seeking care from five or more providers (Fig. 11.2). A similar pattern was observed for level of pain dysfunction. A much higher percentage of patients who scored as "dysfunctional" reported seeing five or more health care providers compared to their "functional" counterparts (Fig. 11.3). Again, these findings are relevant to treatment outcome because seeking multiple treatments from multiple providers places these individuals at increased risk for iatrogenic effects of health care.

TEMPOROMANDIBULAR DISORDERS
AND EXPLANATORY MODELS OF ILLNESS

The major link that connects these theoretical and conceptual perspectives of chronic pain dysfunction and somatization with the clinical realities of working with chronic pain patients may reside in the nature of the patient's explanatory model for their pain and other physical symptoms. Explanatory models of illness were defined by A. Kleinman (1988) as the notions that patients, families and practitioners have about a specific illness episode.

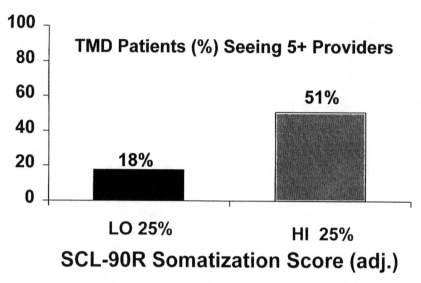

FIG. 11.2. Clinic cases (%) seeing five or more TMD providers by low and high quartiles for SCL 90–R somatization subscores.

Explanatory models represent an attempt by the individual to make sense of the illness experience—that is, how one perceives, experiences, and copes with illness. Each individual carries a set of illness beliefs about the etiology of their illness, time and mode of onset of symptoms, what maintains or aggravates their symptoms, expected course of their illness, and appropriate treatments. These beliefs and expectancies are shaped by past illness episodes as they are personally experienced or observed in others. Once an individual notices symptoms, a process of retrospectively linking symptoms with beliefs generated from personal or vicarious experience occurs (Chrisman, 1977). Whether the explanatory models that emerge are simple, obscure, complex, or precise, they serve to organize the patient's perceptions, motivations, and behavior with regard to what he or she will or will not do about their chronic pain. The processes that interact in chronic pain and illness are also influenced by ethnocultural variables governing perception, labeling, explanation, and valuation of the illness experience (Litman, 1974).

The explanatory beliefs model posits that in health care interactions, it is particularly important to identify and correct discrepancies between patient's and clinician's explanatory models in order to: enhance the patient–provider relationship; help organize strategies for clinical care and enhance patient compliance; enhance the patient's sense of control; and, decrease patient's use and/or misuse of health care services. The following is a brief example of an explanatory model from a patient suffering from TMD:

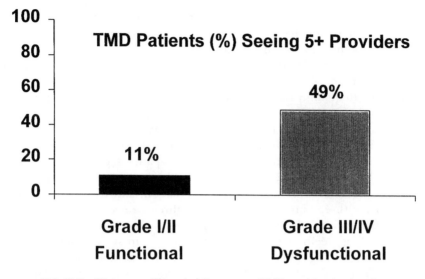

FIG. 11.3. Clinic cases (%) seeing five or more TMD providers by chronic pain grade. Grade I and II represent psychosocially functional pain patients and Grades III and IV represent psychosocially dysfunctional pain patients.

This is a condition that I've had most of my adult life. This past fall it got real bad but I don't know why. As an infant [I was told that] I chewed the wood on my crib and that might have affected my [jaw] joints. Now I avoid hard foods and wear a night guard. Now it's livable and the pain isn't that bad. It doesn't affect me emotionally at all. I moved from Alaska last fall but I don't think that is related to anything. When I get the money together, I want to get some jaw surgery and braces to improve my bite and hopefully help me get rid of this thing.

This brief explanatory model is rich with clinical information about how this TMD patient views her condition and about her expectations for treatment. In the patient's view, her current TMD condition is located in the TM joints, and may have been caused by her habit of chewing the wood on her crib during infancy. She does not seem to identify any current variables that may influence her condition and denies the possibility that a geographical relocation (with its inherent stresses) may have contributed to the exacerbation of her symptoms. Interestingly, although the patient maintains that her condition is livable, the pain is manageable, and there is little emotional impact from her symptoms, she desires a treatment plan that includes jaw surgery and braces, two lengthy treatments that are both irreversible and costly. It is also significant to note that this patient expects a cure for her condition. Thus, this patient may not be accepting of biobehavioral treatments for TMD, specifically those that are conservative and reversible, unless she receives significant education about biopsychosocial management of her chronic pain condition, and subsequently changes her explanatory model about her condition.

Although originally advanced as a qualitative approach to understanding illness from the patient's perspective, Massoth and colleagues (1992) have attempted to quantify patient explanatory models of TMD concerning the relative roles that physical factors, behaviors, and psychological factors play in patients' explanations for the cause, exacerbation, and perceived treatment efficacy of their TMD problem (Fig. 11.4). Explanatory model scores were derived from a measure designed to assess patients' global explanations of the relative roles played by physical factors, behavior, and/or stress in each of three TMD dimensions—cause, exacerbation, and treatment efficacy. Each of the three dimensions is assigned three scores depicting patients' global perceptions of the relative importance played by physical factors, behavior (e.g., teeth clenching and grinding), and stress along that one dimension, yielding a total of nine explanatory model scores, with ranges of 0%–100%. Together, the physical, behavior, and stress scores total 100% for each TMD dimension of cause, exacerbate, and treatment efficacy.

Composite measures were also developed to represent patients' global beliefs about factors that influence the *course* of TMD—that is, what makes their TMD worse, and concomitantly, what makes it better. Although an individual has little opportunity to change the initial causes of TMD, the course of TMD may be modified following the recognition of TMD-exacerbating agents and the initiation of effective strategies to ameliorate symptoms. The composite scores that integrate the TMD exacerbation and treatment efficacy dimensions are summed across physical, behavior, and stress domains yielding three composite scores, with potential ranging between 0 and 200%.

Massoth and colleagues (1994) reported a study of 71 patients undergoing treatment in a TMD specialty clinic known to advocate a biopsychosocial explanatory model of TMD and to emphasize use of conservative and reversible dental therapies. These authors reported on the relationships among various psychosocial variables and patients' global beliefs about the relative importance of physical factors, pathogenic behaviors (e.g., teeth clenching and grinding), and stress in the exacerbation and treatment of TMD symptoms. They found that SCL 90–R somatization scores (with pain items removed) and the endorsement of passive pain-coping strategies were positively correlated with global beliefs about the importance of physical factors in TMD and negatively correlated with global beliefs about the importance of pathogenic behaviors in TMD (Table 11.2). By comparison, self-report of pain and clinical TMD measures such as muscle palpation tenderness were not related to explanatory model scores; thus, it is unlikely that the patients with primarily physical explanations of their symptoms simply had more physically wrong with them. The observation that SCL 90–R

People who have TMD often say that it was **originally caused** by some combination of 1) physical factors, 2) harmful habits to the jaws/head/neck, and/or 3) stress and emotional upset. What combination would seem appropriate for your particular TMD problem?

Please distribute 100 percentage points between these three categories to describe how they may have **originally caused** your TMD problem?   For example, one could assign 34% to physical factors, 33% to harmful habits and 33% to stress to indicate that all three categories were equally important in originally causing his/her TMD. Any combination that adds up to 100% is fine.

What percentage of your TMD problem was **originally *caused* by:**

▲ Physical Factors (such as) ____ ____

▲ Harmful Habits to Jaws/Head/Neck ____ ____

▲ Stress or Emotional Upset ____ ____

_____

100%

What percentage of your TMD problem is ***aggravated*** by:

▲ Physical Factors (such as) ____ ____

▲ Harmful Habits to Jaws/Head/Neck ____ ____

▲ Stress or Emotional Upset ____ ____

_____

100%

What percentage of ***TMD treatments*** should be directed toward eliminating or lessening the impact of:

▲ Physical Factors ____ ____

▲ Harmful Habits to Jaws, Head or Neck ____ ____

▲ Stress or Emotional Upset ____ ____

_____

100%

FIG. 11.4. The Explanatory Models Questionnaire for TMD assesses patients' global perceptions of the relative importance of physical factors, behavior, and/or stress in each of three TMD dimensions—cause, exacerbation, and treatment efficacy. Composite explanatory model (EM) scores utilize only the exacerbation and treatment efficacy dimensions.

TABLE 11.2
TMD Explanatory Models, Clinical and Psychosocial Variables

	Physical (r)	Behavioral (r)	Stress (r)
Mean Average Pain (VAS: 0–10)	0.20	–0.08	–0.18
Muscle Palpation Score (0–20)	0.19	–0.16	–0.08
Somatization (SCL 90–R, adj)	0.25*	–0.23*	–0.09
Passive Coping	0.32**	–0.31**	0.10

Note. Although self-report of pain and muscle palpation tenderness were not related to explanatory model scores, SCL 90–R somatization scores and passive coping (VPMI) were positively related to patients' endorsements of a physical explanatory model and negatively related to patients' endorsements of a behavioral explanatory model.
*$p < .05$; **$p < .01$.

somatization scores were higher in patients reporting primarily physical explanations of TMD and lower in patients reporting behavioral explanations of TMD is potentially explained by the view that physical symptoms may be a somatic "idiom of expression" that focuses the report of personal and social distress on physical rather than psychological symptoms (Katon et al., 1991; A. Kleinman & J. Kleinman, 1985). Alternately, the tendency to explain TMD as a physically mediated disorder may be a characteristic explanatory style of the individual that reveals a predisposition to label bodily sensations as negative physical symptoms (Dworkin, Wilson, et al., 1994). These data also suggest that patients who endorse physical explanatory models may be less likely to embrace behavioral self-care practices and assume personal responsibility for effective coping with their symptoms.

Similarly, TMD patients classified as dysfunctional are also more likely to endorse a physical explanatory model (Fig. 11.5). When the association between explanatory model and graded chronic pain status was examined, it was observed that on average, functional patients gave behavioral factors more than twice the weight given by dysfunctional patients when explaining their TMD. Dysfunctional patients, conversely, gave twice as much weight to physical factors. That is, patients who report the most pain-related interference are more likely to implicate physical factors, and exclude behavioral and stress factors, as important in maintaining their TMD symptoms. Additionally, the more dysfunctional patients ascribe greater importance to physical TMD treatments.

SUMMARY AND TREATMENT IMPLICATIONS

Although there are a number of psychological variables associated with TMD treatment outcome, this chapter has focused on three distinct factors, that is, somatization, dysfunctional chronic pain, and explanatory models

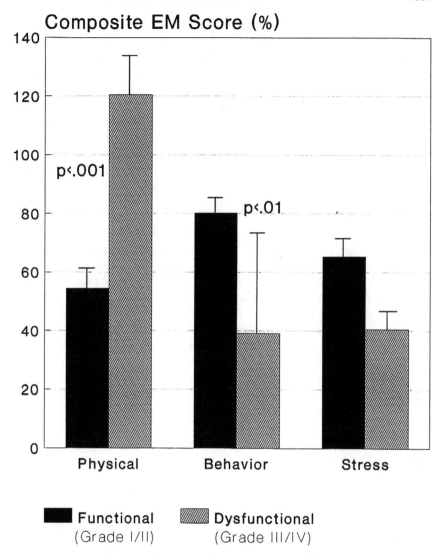

FIG. 11.5. Composite explanatory model (EM) scores for low (chronic pain Grades I/II) versus high (chronic pain Grades III/IV) pain-related disability.

of illness. It appears that highly somatizing and/or dysfunctional TMD patients, because they are guided by a biologic explanatory model for their condition, are at risk for poor treatment outcome; seek more treatment, often from multiple providers; and use more health care services. These patients often present for treatment seeking the "magic bullet" or "cure," typically some physical intervention, that will eliminate their pain problem. These data suggest that patients who endorse physical explanatory models may be less amenable to broad-based treatment approaches that include modifying behaviors that cause or exacerbate their pain condition.

Reports by Foreman, Harold, and Hay (1994) on treatment outcome among patients with chronic, protracted orofacial pain referred to inter-disciplinary pain management clinics are consistent with data presented in this chapter. These authors reported that patients who made good progress in treatment tended to be those motivated to take charge of, and responsibility for, their own rehabilitation. Those patients still seeking a cure, or who felt it was not up to them to take an active part in the management of their pain problem, tended to make poor or no progress.

Explanatory models of illness organize patient's perceptions, motivations, and behavior with respect to what they will or will not do about their chronic pain. Patients with a physical explanatory model tend to pursue physical treatment approaches that are often irreversible, more invasive, and have a higher risk for iatrogenic effects of health care, even though these treatment modalities show no better track record than conservative approaches that include modifying behaviors that cause or exacerbate the pain condition. A major therapeutic objective in management of chronic pain involves modifying the patient's presenting explanatory model away from its typically preeminent physical focus—a focus that also carries the expectations that factors in the environment, such as doctors, hold the cure to their condition. The patient is then directed toward acceptance of biobehavioral interventions, such as home-based physical exercises and relaxation techniques, that emphasize increased reliance on self-care and the assumption of greater self-responsibility for effective coping.

REFERENCES

American Dental Association. (1983). *The President's Conference on the Examination, Diagnosis and Management of Temporomandibular Disorders.* Chicago: American Dental Association.

Chrisman, N. (1977). The health seeking process: An approach to the natural history of illness. *Culture, Medicine and Psychiatry, 1,* 351–377.

Clark, G. T. (1987). Diagnosis and treatment of painful temporomandibular disorders. *Dental Clinics of North America, 31,* 645–674.

Clark, G. T., Lanham, F., & Flack, V. F. (1988). Treatment outcome results for consecutive TMJ clinic patients. *Journal of Craniomandibular Disorders: Facial & Oral Pain, 2,* 87–95.

Clark, G. T., Tsukiyama, Y., Baba, K., & Simmons, M. (1997). The validity and utility of disease detection methods and of occlusal therapy for temporomandibular disorders. *Oral Surgery, Oral Medicine, Oral Pathology, Oral Radiology and Endodontics, 83,* 101–106.

DeBoever, J. A., & Carlsson, G. E. (1994). Etiology and differential diagnosis. In G. A. Zarb, G. E. Carlsson, B. J. Sessle, & N. D. Mohl (Eds.), *Temporomandibular Joint and Masticatory Muscle Disorders* (pp. 171–187). Copenhagen: Munksgaard.

Derogatis, L. R. (1983). *SCL-90-R: Administration, Scoring and Procedures Manual—II for the Revised Version.* Towson, MD: Clinical Psychometric Research.

Dionne, R. A. (1997). Pharmacologic treatments for temporomandibular disorders. *Oral Surgery, Oral Medicine, Oral Pathology, Oral Radiology and Endodontics, 83*(1), 134–142.

Dworkin, S. F. (1997). Behavioral and educational modalities. *Oral Surgery, Oral Medicine, Oral Pathology, Oral Radiology and Endodontics, 83*(1), 128–133.

Dworkin, S. F. (1991). Illness behavior and dysfunction: Review of concepts and application to chronic pain. *Canadian Journal of Physiology and Pharmacology, 69,* 662–671.

Dworkin, S. F. (1994). Behavioral, emotional, and social aspects of orofacial pain. In C. S. Stohler & D. S. Carlson (Eds.), *Biological and Psychological Aspects of Orofacial Pain* (pp. 93–112). Ann Arbor: The University of Michigan.

Dworkin, S. F. (1995). Personal and societal impact of orofacial pain. In J. R. Fricton & R. B. Dubner (Eds.), *Orofacial Pain and Temporomandibular Disorders* (pp. 15–32). New York: Raven Press.

Dworkin, S. F., Huggins, K. H., LeResche, L., Von Korff, M., Howard, J., Truelove, E., & Sommers, E. (1990). Epidemiology of signs and symptoms in temporomandibular disorders: Clinical signs in cases and controls. *Journal of the American Dental Association, 120,* 273–281.

Dworkin, S. F., & LeResche, L. (1992). Research Diagnostic Criteria for Temporomandibular Disorders: Review, criteria, examinations and specifications, critique. *Journal of Craniomandibular Disorders: Facial & Oral Pain, 6*(4), 301–355.

Dworkin, S. F., Turner, J. A., Wilson, L., Massoth, D., Whitney, C., Huggins, K. H., Burgess, J., Sommers, E., & Truelove, E. (1994). Brief group cognitive-behavioral intervention for temporomandibular disorders. *Pain, 59,* 175–187.

Dworkin, S. F., Von Korff, M., & LeResche, L. (1992). Epidemiologic studies of chronic pain: A dynamic-ecologic perspective. *Annals of Behavioral Medicine, 14,* 3–11.

Dworkin, S. F., Von Korff, M. R., & LeResche, L. (1990). Multiple pains and psychiatric disturbance: An epidemiologic investigation. *Archives of General Psychiatry, 47,* 239–244.

Dworkin, S. F., & Wilson, L. (1993). Somatoform pain disorder and its treatment. In D. Dunner (Ed.), *Current Psychiatric Treatment* (pp. 321–328). Philadelphia: W. B. Saunders.

Dworkin, S. F., Wilson, L., & Massoth, D. L. (1994). Somatizing as a risk factor for chronic pain. In R. C. Grzesiak & D. S. Ciccone (Eds.), *Psychologic Vulnerability to Chronic Pain* (pp. 28–54). New York: Springer Publishing Company, Inc.

Engel, G. (1977). The need for a new medical model: A challenge for biomedicine. *Science, 196,* 129–136.

Escobar, J. I., Burnam, A., Karno, M., Forsythe, A., & Golding, J. M. (1987). Somatization in the community. *Archives of General Psychiatry, 44,* 713–718.

Feine, J. S., Widmer, C. G., & Lund, J. P. (1997). Physical therapy: A critique. *Oral Surgery, Oral Medicine, Oral Pathology, Oral Radiology and Endodontics, 83*(1), 123–127.

Fordyce, W. E. (1976). *Behavioral Methods in Chronic Pain and Illness.* St. Louis, MO: Mosby.

Foreman, P. A., Harold, P. L., & Hay, K. D. (1994). An evaluation of the diagnosis, treatment, and outcome of patients with chronic orofacial pain. *New Zealand Dental Journal, 90*(400), 44–48.

Gale, E. N., & Funch, D. P. (1984). Factors associated with successful outcome from behavioral therapy for chronic temporomandibular joint (TMJ) pain. *Journal of Psychosomatic Research, 28*(6), 441–448.

Gessel, A. H. (1975). Eletromyographic biofeedback and tricyclic antidepressants in myofascial pain-dysfunction syndrome: Psychological predictors of outcome. *Journal of the American Dental Association, 91,* 1048–1052.

Gessel, A. H., & Alderman, M. M. (1971). Management of myofascial pain dysfunction syndrome of the temporomandibular joint by tension control training. *Psychosomatics, 12*(5), 302–309.

Glaros, A. G., & Glass, E. G. (1993). Temporomandibular disorders. In R. J. Gatchel & E. B. Blanchard (Eds.), *Psychophysiological Disorders* (pp. 299–356). Washington, DC: American Psychological Association.

Grzesiak, R. C. (1991). Psychological aspects of chronic orofacial pain: Theory, assessment, and management. *Pain Digest*, *1*, 100–119.

Katon, W., Lin, E., Von Korff, M., Russo, J., Lipscomb, P., & Bush, T. (1991). Somatization: A spectrum of severity. *American Journal of Psychiatry*, *148*, 34–40.

Keefe, F. J., & Dolan, E. (1986). Pain behavior and pain coping strategies in low back pain and myofascial pain dysfunction syndrome patients. *Pain*, *24*, 49–56.

Kleinman, A. (1988). *The Illness Narratives: Suffering, Healing and the Human Condition*. New York: Basic Books, Inc.

Kleinman, A., & Kleinman, J. (1985). Somatization: Interconnections between Chinese culture, depressive meanings and the experience of pain. In A. Kleinman & B. Good (Eds.), *Culture and Depression*. Berkeley: University of California Press.

Laskin, D. M. (1969). Etiology of the pain-dysfunction syndrome. *Journal of the American Dental Association*, *79*, 147–153.

Laskin, D. M., & Greene, C. S. (1990). Technological methods in the diagnosis and treatment of temporomandibular disorders. *International Journal of Technology Assessment in Heath Care*, *6*, 558–568.

LeResche, L., & Massoth, D. L. (1995). Psychologic aspects of treating myofascial pain and dysfunction. *Oral and Maxillofacial Surgery Clinics of North America*, *7*(1), 113–127.

Lipton, J. A., & Marbach, J. J. (1984). Predictors of treatment outcome in patients with myofascial pain-dysfunction syndrome and organic temporomandibular joint disorders. *Journal of Prosthetic Dentistry*, *51*, 387–393.

Litman, T. J. (1974). The family as a basic unit in health and medical care. *Social Science and Medicine*, *8*, 495–519.

Massoth, D. L. (1992). *Explanatory models for illness: Applicability of the construct to the qualitative and quantitative description of Temporomandibular Disorders*. Unpublished doctoral dissertation, University of Washington, Seattle, WA.

Massoth, D. L., Dworkin, S. F., Whitney, C. W., Harrison, R. G., Wilson, L., & Turner, J. (1994). Patient explanatory models for temporomandibular disorders. In G. F. Gebhart, D. L. Hammond, & T. S. Jensen (Eds.), *Proceedings of the 7th World Congress on Pain* (pp. 187–200). Seattle: IASP Press.

McCreary, C. P., Clark, G. T., Merril, V., & Oakley, M. A. (1991). Psychological distress and diagnostic subgroups of temporomandibular patients. *Pain*, *44*, 29–34.

McCreary, C. P., Clark, G. T., Oakley, M. E., & Flack, V. (1992). Predicting response to treatment for temporomandibular disorders. *Journal of Craniomandibular Disorders: Facial & Oral Pain*, *6*(3), 161–169.

McNamara, J. A., Jr. (1997). Orthodontic treatment and temporomandibular disorders. *Oral Surgery, Oral Medicine, Oral Pathology, Oral Radiology and Endodontics*, *83*(1), 107–117.

Millstein-Prentky, S., & Olson, R. E. (1979). Predictability of treatment outcome in patients with myofacial pain-dysfunction (MPD) syndrome. *Journal of Dental Research*, *58*, 1341–1346.

Moss, R. A., Garrett, J., & Chiodo, J. F. (1982). Temporomandibular joint dysfunction and myofascial pain dysfunction syndromes: Parameters, etiology, and treatment. *Psychological Bulletin*, *92*, 331–346.

National Institutes of Health. (1997). National Institutes of Health Technology Assessment Conference Statement: Management of temporomandibular disorders, April 29–May 1, 1996. *Oral Surgery, Oral Medicine, Oral Pathology, Oral Radiology and Endodontics*, *83*(1), 177–183.

Okeson, J. P., & Hayes, D. K. (1986). Long-term results of treatment for temporomandibular disorders: An evaluation by patients. *Journal of the American Dental Association*, *112*, 473–478.

Pullinger, A. G., & Monteiro, A. A. (1988). History factors associated with symptoms of temporomandibular disorders. *Journal of Oral Rehabilitation*, *15*, 117–124.

Rudy, T. E., Turk, D. C., Brena, S. F., & Brody, M. C. (1990). Quantification of biomedical findings of chronic pain patients: Development of an index of pathology. *Pain*, *42*, 167–182.

Rudy, T. E., Turk, D. C., Kubinski, J. A., & Zaki, H. S. (1995). Differential treatment responses of TMD patients as a function of psychological characteristics. *Pain, 61*(1), 103–112.

Rugh, J. D., & Dahlstrom, L. (1995). Psychological management of the orofacial pain patient. In C. F. Stohler & D. S. Carlsson (Eds.), *Biological and psychological aspects of orofacial pain* (pp. 133–147). Ann Arbor: University of Michigan Press.

Salter, M. W., Brooke, R. I., & Merskey, H. (1986). Temporomandibular pain and dysfunction syndrome: The relationship of clinical and psychological data to outcome. *Journal of Behavioral Medicine, 9*(1), 97–109.

Schwartz, R. A., Greene, C. S., & Laskin, D. M. (1979). Personality characteristics of patients with myofacial pain dysfunction syndrome unresponsive to conventional therapy. *Journal of Dental Research, 58,* 1435–1439.

Sheridan, P., & Hall, B. (1996). NIH panel makes recommendations for temporomandibular disorders. *NIDR Research Digest, July,* 2–3.

Simon, G. E. (1993). Somatization and psychiatric disorders. In L. J. Kirmayer & J. M. Robbins (Eds.), *Progress in psychiatry: No. 31. Current concepts of somatization: Research and clinical perspectives* (pp. 37–61). Washington, DC: American Psychiatric Press, Inc.

Speculand, B., & Goss, A. N. (1985). Psychological factors in temporomandibular joint dysfunction pain. A review. *Int. J. Oral Surg., 14*(2), 131–137.

Speculand, B., Goss, A. N., Hughes, A., Spence, N. D., & Pilowsky, I. (1983). Temporomandibular joint dysfunction: Pain and illness behaviour. *Pain, 17,* 139–150.

Turk, D. C., & Rudy, T. E. (1988). Toward an empirically derived taxonomy of chronic pain patients: Integration of psychological assessment data. *Journal of Consulting and Clinical Psychology, 56*(2), 233–238.

Turner, J. A., & Romano, J. M. (1990). Psychological and psychosocial evaluation. In J. J. Bonica (Ed.), *The Management of Pain, Vol II* (pp. 595–609). Philidelphia: Lea and Febiger.

Tversky, J., Reade, P. C., Gerschman, J. A., Holwill, B. J., & Wright, J. (1991). Role of depressive illness in the outcome of treatment of temporomandibular joint pain-dysfunction syndrome. *Oral Surgery, Oral Medicine, Oral Pathology, Oral Radiology and Endodontics, 71,* 696–699.

Von Korff, M., Dworkin, S. F., LeResche, L., & Kruger, A. (1988). An epidemiologic comparison of pain complaints. *Pain, 32,* 173–183.

Von Korff, M., Ormel, J., Keefe, F. J., & Dworkin, S. F. (1992). Grading the severity of chronic pain. *Pain, 50,* 133–149.

Von Korff, M. R., Howard, J. A., Truelove, E. L., Sommers, E., Wagner, E. H., & Dworkin, S. F. (1988). Temporomandibular disorders: Variation in clinical practice. *Medical Care, 26(3),* 307–314.

Wilson, L., Dworkin, S. F., Whitney, C., & LeResche, L. (1994). Somatization and pain dispersion in chronic temporomandibular pain. *Pain, 57,* 55–61.

Chapter 12

Whiplash Injuries

Robert W. Teasell
University of Western Ontario

Allan P. Shapiro
London Health Sciences Centre,
London, Ontario, Canada

Whiplash injuries are a controversial clinical entity and in the developed industrialized world remain a significant public health problem with significant socioeconomic consequences. In 1990, the Societe d'Assurance Automobile du Quebec, a provincial government no-fault insurance carrier in Canada's second largest province, commissioned a group of clinicians, scientists, and epidemiologists to exhaustively review the scientific literature and make public policy recommendations regarding the prevention and treatment of whiplash and its associated disorders. The stated reasons for commissioning this study reflected a grievous concern with both the magnitude of the problem and the paucity of strategies to effectively address it:

> The frequency of the clinical entity labelled as whiplash is high; the residual disability of victims appears significant in magnitude, and the costs of care and indemnity are high and rising. There is considerable inconsistency about diagnostic criteria, indications for therapeutic intervention, rehabilitation and the appropriate role of clinicians at all phases of the syndrome. Little is known about primary prevention of the condition, and virtually nothing is known about tertiary prevention of serious disability. (Spitzer et al., 1995, p. 10S)

DEFINITION AND SCOPE OF THE PROBLEM

The Quebec Task Force (QTF; Spitzer et al., 1995) adopted the following definition of whiplash: "Whiplash is an acceleration-deceleration mechanism of energy transfer to the neck. It may result from rear-end or side-impact motor vehicle collisions, but can also occur during diving or other mishaps. The impact may result in bony or soft tissue injuries (whiplash injuries), which in turn may lead to a variety of clinical manifestations (Whiplash-Associated Disorders)" (Spitzer et al., 1995, p. 22S). In 1971, the National Safety Council estimated that there were approximately 4 million rear-end collisions in the United States resulting in as many as 1 million reported injuries per year (Croft, 1988; National Safety Council, 1971). In that same year the Insurance Institute for Highway Safety reported a 24% incidence of these injuries following rear-end collisions. Similarly, Macnab (1964, 1969, 1971, 1982) estimated that neck injuries occurred in one fifth of all accidents involving rear-end collisions. Schutt and Dohan (1968) calculated the number of neck injuries sustained in automobile accidents to be 14.5 per thousand industrial employees. The cost of whiplash injuries is high. In British Columbia and Saskatchewan, two Canadian provinces with single-payer motor vehicle insurance programs, 68% and 85% respectively, of all claims paid out, were for whiplash injuries (Giroux, 1991; Sobeco, Ernst, & Young, 1989; Spitzer et al., 1995). The QTF (Spitzer et al., 1995) estimated that the annual incidence of compensated whiplash in the province of Quebec in 1987 was 70 per 100,000 inhabitants.

BIOMECHANICS AND PATHOPHYSIOLOGY
OF WHIPLASH INJURIES

Typically, the injured individual is the occupant of a stationary vehicle that is struck from behind (Bogduk, 1986; Commack, 1957; Deans, 1986; Frankel, 1976; Hohl, 1974; LaRocca, 1978; Macnab, 1964, 1969, 1971, 1973, 1982) although injury frequently occurs following side-on and head-on collisions (Deans, 1986). Injury results when neck musculature is unable to compensate for the rapidity of head and torso movement resulting from the acceleration forces generated at the time of impact (Hohl, 1989). When the physiological limits of cervical structures are exceeded, anatomical disruption of the "soft tissues" of the neck (including muscles, ligaments, and joint capsules) results.

Although the mechanism of injury is relatively well understood and generally agreed upon, the actual *pathological lesions* accounting for chronically symptomatic whiplash injuries are by no means certain. Possible pathological lesions following whiplash injuries are listed in Table 12.1. The anterior and posterior longitudinal spinal ligaments can theoretically undergo stretching and possible tearing (Bogduk, 1986; Clemens & Burrow, 1972; Macnab, 1964, 1969, 1971, 1973, 1982) although the recent introduction of MRI (magnetic resonance imaging) scanning has failed to reveal major injuries to these structures. Injuries occurring to the muscles of the

TABLE 12.1
Possible Pathological Lesions in Whiplash Injuries

- Muscle strain
- Zygapophyseal joint sprain or fracture
- Anterior and/or posterior longitudinal ligament strain or tear
- Intervertebral ligament sprain or tear
- Intervertebral disk herniation
- Retropharyngeal hematoma
- Sympathetic trunk injury
- Vertebral artery ischemia
- Concussion or mild traumatic brain injury
- Thoracic outlet syndrome
- Temporomandibular joint dysfunction

neck including stretching, tearing, and hemorrhaging of the longus colli, longus capitis, scalenes, and sternocleidomastoid, muscles that have long been thought to be the primary reason for pain (Lieberman, 1986). A critical element of the debate regarding persistent pain revolves around the normal anticipated time for musculoligamentous healing to occur. The QTF (Spitzer et al., 1995) noted:

> Apart from anatomic studies, much of the scientific understanding of soft tissue injury and healing is derived from animal models, and there is little information on the normal recuperation period. In the animal model of soft tissue healing, there is a brief period (less than 72 hours) of acute inflammation and reaction, followed by a period of repair and regeneration (approximately 72 hours to up to 6 weeks), and finally by a period of re-modeling and rematuration that can last up to 1 year. (p. 22S)

This limited animal data and the fact that most whiplash injuries resolve quickly has led to a commonly held belief that physiologically all whiplash injuries should heal.

This assumption that all whiplash injuries should heal has been seriously challenged with evidence that supporting structures around facet joints may also be sprained or the facet joint can suffer cartilaginous damage or fracture (Barnsley, Lord, Wallis, & Bogduk, 1995; Lord, Barnsley, & Bogduk, 1993; Lord, Barnsley, Wallis, & Bogduk, 1996). These researchers demonstrated in a carefully controlled trial of diagnostic local anaesthetic blocks that chronic whiplash pain can be relieved. In these blinded studies, 50 and 68 consecutively referred patients with chronic neck pain after whiplash injury were studied by means of controlled diagnostic blocks of cervical zygapophyseal joints (Barnsley et al., 1995; Lord, Barnsley, Wallis, & Bogduk, 1996). Each joint was separately injected with a short-acting (lignocaine) and a long-acting (bupivicaine) local anaesthetic. In the latter study (Lord,

Barnsley, Wallis, & Bogduk, 1996) normal saline blocks were also used. Well over half the patients obtained pain relief with injection concordant with the expected duration of the anaesthetic, thereby dealing with the placebo effect. Postmortem studies of motor vehicle accident victims have confirmed that zygapophyseal joint injuries are very common. Such injuries include capsular tears, intraarticular hemorrhages, and small fractures (Lord et al., 1993). In a recent randomized controlled trial, the same investigators clearly demonstrated statistically and clinically significant relief for cervical zygapophyseal joint pain for periods in excess of 6 months with radiofrequency neurotomy of the dorsal cervical rami (Lord, Barnsley, Wallis, McDonald, & Bogduk, 1996). It is notable that this treatment study was a randomized, double-blind trial incorporating a sham surgical control procedure in patients with a median pain duration of 34 months.

THE CLINICAL PICTURE OF WHIPLASH INJURIES

The Clinical Syndrome

The clinical syndrome of whiplash is dominated by head, neck, and upper thoracic pain and often is associated with a variety of poorly explained symptoms such as dizziness, tinnitus, and blurred vision. The symptom complex is remarkably consistent from patient to patient and is frequently complicated by psychological sequelae such as anger, anxiety, depression, and concerns over litigation or compensation. In their cohort study, the QTF (Spitzer et al., 1995) found the highest incidence of whiplash claims among the 20–24 year age group. The potential array of physical and psychosocial complaints is listed in Table 12.2.

TABLE 12.2
Potential Physical and Psychosocial Complaints
Associated With Whiplash Injuries

- Neck and shoulder pain
- Headache
- Arm pain/parasthesias/weakness
- Dizziness
- Tinnitus
- Low back pain
- Temporomandibular joint pain
- Depression
- Anxiety
- Anger and frustration
- Loss of job and income
- Marital and family disruption
- Drug dependency

Women appear to experience whiplash injuries more often than do men (Balla, 1980; Spitzer et al., 1995). Women generally have slimmer, less muscular necks which, theoretically, are less able to resist damaging acceleration forces generated at the time of impact. Other possible reasons for the gender difference are that women may be more likely to seek medical attention, be sent to medical specialists for complaints of pain, respond to their injuries in a way that aggravates their condition, or be subjected to more external stressors making it more difficult for them to cope. At present, the exact reason for this gender difference with respect to those presenting with whiplash symptoms remains undetermined.

A delay in onset of symptoms of several hours following impact is characteristic of whiplash injuries (Deans, McGailliard, Kerr, & Rutherford, 1987; Dunsker, 1982; Evans, 1992). Most patients feel little or no pain for the first few minutes following injury after which symptoms gradually intensify over the next few days. In the first few hours, findings on examination are generally minimal (Hohl, 1975). After several hours, limitation of neck motion, tightness, muscle spasm, and/or swelling and tenderness of both anterior and posterior cervical structures become apparent (Hohl, 1975; Wickstrom & LaRocca, 1975). This delay is likely due to the time required for traumatic edema and hemorrhage to occur in injured soft tissues (Jeffreys, 1980; Lieberman, 1986).

Neck Pain. Patients with whiplash injuries invariably complain of an achy discomfort in the posterior cervical region radiating out over the trapezius muscle and shoulders, down to the interscapular region, up to the occiput, and/or down the arms. This deep aching discomfort is often associated with burning and stiffness with the latter typically being most apparent in the morning. Tenderness is often present over the posterior spinous prominence of the sixth cervical vertebra and the posterior paracervical musculature. Initially, there is marked restricted range of motion of the cervical spine, which may be associated with palpable muscle spasm.

Headaches. Headache is a common symptom following whiplash injury. Within 24 hours of the accident, many patients complain of diffuse neck and head pain. The headache may be limited to the occipital area or may spread to the vertex, temporal-frontal, and retro-orbital areas (Speed, 1987). The pain may be a dull pressure or a squeezing sensation and include pounding and throbbing (migrainous) components (Balla & Moraitis, 1970; Speed, 1987). Muscle contraction and vascular headaches often are present simultaneously (posttraumatic mixed headache). Patients may experience concomitant nausea, vomiting, and photophobia. The frequency of these various forms of headache in whiplash is not known. However, the incidence of unspecified headache in a retrospective analysis of 320 cases referred for medical-legal assessment was 55% (Wiley, Lloyd, Evans, Stewart, & Sanchez, 1986). In our experience, vascular-like headaches are common following whiplash injuries and often occur in individuals with no previous history of migraines.

Visual Disturbances, Dizziness, and Tinnitus. Whiplash patients may complain of intermittent blurring of vision (Horwich & Kasner, 1962; LaRocca, 1978; Macnab, 1971, 1982). Blurring of vision by itself is not believed to have diagnostic significance unless associated with damage to the cervical sympathetic trunk, which is regarded as rare. Complaints of dizziness or vertigo-like symptoms are common following whiplash injuries (Oosterveld, Kortschot, Kingma et al., 1991). Several theories have been postulated to explain these features, including vertebral artery insufficiency, inner-ear damage, injury to the cervical sympathetic chain, and an impaired neck-righting reflex (Bogduk, 1986; Toglia, 1976). The "reflex," or "neuromuscular," theory proposes that interference with normal signals coming from the upper cervical joints, muscles, or nerves to the inner ear produces a feeling of ataxia (DeJong, DeJong, Cohen, & Jongkees, 1977; Macnab, 1971). The entire concept of chronic vertigo arising from the cervical region has been questioned because of the relatively small cervical afferent input to the vestibular nuclei and the capacity of the system for making adjustments (Balch, 1984; Evans, 1992).

Tinnitus or difficulties with auditory acuity are frequently reported in association with whiplash injuries (Chrisman & Gervais, 1962; Lieberman, 1986; Macnab, 1971). Tinnitus may theoretically be due to vertebral artery insufficiency, injury to the cervical sympathetic chain, or inner-ear damage (Bogduk, 1986; Medical News, 1965). Tinnitus alone does not appear to have prognostic significance (Macnab, 1971), although anecdotally we have noted it to be common with more severe injuries. Additional auditory complaints include decreased hearing and loudness recruitment (Gibson, 1974; Lieberman, 1986). Electronystagmographic abnormalities have been reported in a number of whiplash victims in uncontrolled studies (Compere, 1968; Pang, 1971).

Arm Pain and Thoracic Outlet Syndrome. Arm pain and paresthesiae frequently are reported following whiplash injury. Historically, these symptoms were attributed to cervical disk herniation and nerve root compression following whiplash trauma (Gay & Abbott, 1953). However, modern imaging techniques have shown that disk herniations occurring in association with whiplash injuries are distinctly uncommon. Even when present, their significance is uncertain given the significant number of asymptomatic individuals who exhibit disk herniations or foraminal stenosis on MRI (Boden et al., 1990). Arm symptoms also have been attributed to *thoracic outlet syndrome* (TOS) secondary to intermittent or transient compression of the brachial plexus (Capistrant, 1977). However, objective evidence for TOS as a pathophysiological entity is lacking, causing some authors to dispute its existence (Nelson, 1990; Wilbourn, 1990). Attributing symptoms to TOS may lead to surgery to decompress the brachial plexus, which is of dubious efficacy (Cherington, Happer, Marchanic, & Parry, 1986).

A frequent extracervical complaint of whiplash victims is numbness or a "pins and needles" sensation down the arm, most commonly noted along the ulnar aspect of the forearm and hand. Macnab (1971) speculated that these symptoms may be the result of a form of TOS with spasm of the scalene muscles compressing the trunks of the brachial plexus. No data supporting this hypothesis have emerged. Trauma to the zygapophyseal or facet joint, which may have been fractured or had its capsule injured at the time of the accident, has also been suggested as a cause (Bogduk, 1986). This hypothesis proposes that in the acute stage, edema of this joint, or surrounding hemorrhage, may compromise the adjacent nerve roots posteriorly. In the chronic stage, nerve root fibrosis may ensue from pericapsular exudates. Objective evidence for this proposed pathophysiology is also lacking.

Low Back Pain. During motor vehicle accidents (MVAs), the lumbar and thoracolumbar spine may be suddenly forced into extension or flexed forward as the torso moves in an arc over a fixed pelvis. In selected groups of whiplash patients, the incidence of low back pain ranges from 25% to 60% (Braaf & Rosner, 1955; Hildingsson & Toolanen, 1990; Hohl, 1974; Wiley et al., 1986). Factors that have been reported to increase the risk of low back pain include side-on collisions, a soft seat back, and a lap belt with no shoulder strap (Croft, 1988; McKenzie & Williams, 1971). Low back pain usually resolves before the neck symptoms, but in some cases may persist indefinitely and in some patients may become the prominent complaint. A particularly confusing group of patients are those with onset of low back pain some time after the initial development of neck pain following MVA.

Psychosocial Problems and Pain Attributed to a Psychological Etiology

Psychosocial problems frequently develop as a reaction to chronic pain and disability. Depression, anxiety, anger, frustration, preoccupation with somatic complaints, marital stress, financial pressures, and difficulty maintaining employment are common.

Unfortunately, the psychosocial sequelae of chronic pain often are misinterpreted as the cause of pain. This belief has enjoyed significant, albeit declining, popularity and has resulted in patients with chronic pain and disability secondary to whiplash injuries being labeled as hysterical, somatizers, hypochondriacs, and malingerers. Attribution of whiplash symptoms to a psychological etiology persists for many reasons including: a lack of appreciation for psychological sequelae of chronic pain; a high selection bias with the most psychologically distressed overrepresented in tertiary specialty clinics; outmoded, dualistic conceptualizations of pain as either physical or psychological; failure to adopt a biopsychosocial perspective; and frequent involvement with adversarial legal or insurance systems, which tends to encourage more extreme viewpoints among health care professionals. Misdiagnosis of whiplash and other chronic pain conditions as hysterical is discussed in more detail elsewhere (Shapiro & Teasell, 1997). It is of note that the only study to prospectively follow a representative sample of whiplash patients from injury onset did not find that personality (neuroticism) or premorbid psychiatric history predicted nonresolution of symptoms (Radanov, DeStefano, Schnidrig, & Ballinari, 1991; Radanov, Sturzenegger, DeStefano, & Schnidrig, 1994). Although we regard whiplash as a physiologically based pain problem, it is inappropriate to disregard the potential impact of psychosocial factors. The constellation and interplay of pathophysiological mechanisms, emotional concomitants, premorbid personality, and sociodemographic factors and their impact on pain and disability are indeed complex and await further elucidation.

Although the role of emotional distress in exacerbating musculoskeletal pain is controversial, evidence suggests that stress-induced elevations in muscle tension over an extended period of time lead to increased pain in patients with facial, back, and head pain (Borgeat, Hade, Elie, & Larouche, 1984; Christensen, 1986a, 1986b). This tension may increase pain through reflex muscle spasm, ischemia, and/or the release of pain-eliciting neurotransmitters (Turk & Flor, 1984). As well, because the perception of pain represents an interaction of sensory, affective, and cognitive processes (Melzack & Wall, 1983), depression and/or anxiety may heighten the affective component of pain perception. Anecdotally, we often see perfectionistic patients who become increasingly depressed and irritable because they cannot maintain their premorbid standards. Continuous attempts to "push through" the pain in association with anxiety and depression often result in significant emotional and physical deterioration. This, in turn, may lead to interpersonal and occupational difficulties, which heighten anxiety. Financial and job security stressors further compound the problem.

NATURAL HISTORY OF WHIPLASH INJURIES

It is difficult to be definitive regarding the natural history of whiplash as there continues to be a paucity of longitudinal studies in anything but selected populations, for example, individuals who attend a specialist's office or who seek attention in a local emergency room. Only two studies, the QTF study (Spitzer et al., 1995) and the Lithuanian study (Schrader, Obelieniene, Bovin, et al., 1996), have attempted to study a cohort of patients *with minimal or no selection bias*. Both studies were *retrospective* in nature and suffered from serious methodological flaws. However, because they are being widely cited as evidence that chronic whiplash syndrome is a questionable entity, they warrant closer scrutiny.

The QTF cohort study (Spitzer et al., 1995) retrospectively determined that 87% and 97% of insurance claimants recover at 6 and 12 months, respectively; however, the criterion for recovery was that the claimant was no longer receiving insurance payments. Using this outcome criterion, it is unclear how many subjects actually recovered versus those who remained both symptomatic and disabled but had their benefits discontinued for lack of a demonstrable organic basis (as is the case for all soft tissue pain) for their symptoms. Although it is impossible to say, it is instructive to consider a recent study (Corey, Koepflen, Etlin, & Day, 1996) that followed a group of patients who at 3 to 6 months postinjury were not working and collecting Worker's Compensation Board benefits. At 18 months postinjury, the majority (80%) of these patients were deemed "recovered" (Mitchell & Carmen, 1994) because they were no longer receiving wage replacement benefits. Corey and his colleagues found that in contrast to the 80% recovery rate calculated on the basis of being off benefits, telephone follow-up at 18 months revealed that only 50% reported that they were either working (24%) or "looking for work" (26%). Although the direct extrapolation of these findings to the QTF whiplash cohort is not possible, it is clear that the criterion of discontinuance of insurance benefits significantly overestimates actual "recovery" in soft tissue injuries.

Schrader and his colleagues (1996) used police accident records from a city in Lithuania to identify 202 individuals whose cars were rear-ended in automobile collisions 1 to 3 years earlier. They compared these subjects to a nonaccident control group selected randomly from the population register and found no statistically significant differences between groups in the incidence of neck/back pain, headache, or memory/concentration difficulties. They concluded that "the late whiplash syndrome has little validity" (p. 1210) and argued that reports of chronic whiplash in other countries are likely due to the existence of a medical-legal context that compensates whiplash injury—in Lithuania few drivers are covered by auto insurance. However, closer analysis reveals significant methodological shortcomings that render the authors' conclusions regarding whiplash dubious, at best.

The gender ratio in the Lithuanian accident group was four men to one woman, whereas most studies on chronic whiplash report a higher ratio of women to men, ostensibly because women have smaller neck musculature, which renders them less able to resist the damaging acceleration forces generated at the time of impact (Teasell & Shapiro, 1993). A review of the scientific literature on gender variation and pain concluded that women are more likely than men to experience a variety of recurrent pains and report more severe levels of pain, more frequent pains, and pain of longer duration (Unreh, 1996). Likewise, relative to men, women report higher rates of disability for cervical pain (Hasvold & Johnson, 1993) and headache (H. Taylor & Curran, 1985). Accordingly, the gender bias in the Lithuanian study likely resulted in a significantly lower incidence of chronic pain and disability.

Only 31 of the 202 accident subjects in the Lithuanian study actually reported any acute injury and of these, only 9 reported that their pain lasted a week or more. A prospective study of acute whiplash injury from Switzerland (Radanov et al., 1994) of subjects who had pain at initial intake, which was, on average, on 1 week postinjury, found that 24% continued to report symptoms at 2-year follow-up. Based on this research we would expect that of the nine Lithuanian accident victims whose pain lasted more than a week, 24% or two subjects would continue to report symptoms long term. Indeed, the Lithuanian study reported that three more subjects in the accident group reported chronic neck pain relative to the nonaccident group, a difference that, given the small sample, could not have reached (and did not reach) statistical significance.

The Radanov et al. (1994) study is widely regarded as the best study of whiplash. They looked at whiplash patients who were solicited from family doctors and were insured under a typical no-fault insurance plan with no compensation for "noneconomic" loss, that is, pain and suffering. One hundred and sixty-four consecutive patients were referred of whom 27 did not meet study criteria and 20 dropped out at 6 months. One hundred and seventeen subjects (74 women, 43 men) completed the study at 1 year. Within 10 days of injury, patients underwent a thorough physical and psychosocial assessment. Recovery at 3-, 6-, and 12-month follow-up was 56%, 69%, and 76%, respectively. No difference between symptomatic and asymptomatic patients on baseline personality inventories was noted. The authors concluded that psychological and cognitive problems were the result of somatic symptoms. Persistence of symptoms at 1 year was predicted by physical aspects of the injury including initial intensity of neck pain and headache, rotated or inclined head position at impact, unpreparedness at the time of impact, and the car being stationary when hit.

Prospective studies without selection bias utilizing objective measures of recovery are lacking. The Radanov et al. (1994) trial comes the closest to avoiding the selection bias that besets most prospective studies. There are other studies looking at selected populations, either attending an emergency room or a specialty clinic, that have demonstrated failure to recover in 62%

TABLE 12.3
Cohort Studies on Whiplash Patients:
Percentage of Acute Patients Who "Recover"

Time Since MVA	QTF[a]	Radanov[b]
3 months	70%	56%
6 months	87%	69%
1 year	97%	76%

[a]Retrospective, all claims in jurisdiction and recovery defined as claim no longer compensated.

[b]Prospective, representative cases from family doctors and recovery defined as asymptomatic.

(Gargan & Bannister, 1994) and 58% (Hildingsson & Toolanen, 1990) of whiplash patients, respectively. However, as is evident from Table 12.3, the majority of individuals who recover do so within the first 3–6 months.

MANAGEMENT OF WHIPLASH INJURIES

Radiological Investigations

Radiological studies of the cervical spine taken at the time of the accident are generally unremarkable or reveal evidence of preexisting degenerative changes. The most commonly reported abnormal X-ray finding is straightening of the normal cervical lordotic curve (Hohl, 1974). However, Hohl (1989) noted that straightening of the cervical spine was not necessarily indicative of a pathological condition (Borden, Rachtman, & Gershom-Cohen, 1960; Hohl, 1974; Rachtman, Borden, & Gershom-Cohen, 1961) and can be regarded as a normal variant. Rarely, X rays may reveal evidence of bony injury such as posterior joint crush fractures or minimal subluxation (Macnab, 1971). Radiological investigations are of limited value in diagnosis and prognosis and their main use is in ruling out surgically correctable anatomical injuries. Computerized tomography (CT) scanning and MRI imaging should be reserved for cases where cervical disk protrusion or spinal cord injury are suspected. Radionucleotide bone scanning is warranted only when there is significant clinical suspicion of an undiagnosed fracture (Hohl, 1989).

Quebec Task Force Review of Interventions and Treatment Guidelines

The QTF (Spitzer et al., 1995) reviewed the research literature on treatment interventions for whiplash patients. For almost every treatment, the QTF found either no studies or a lack of independent studies; that is, the specific intervention was included only as a part of a multi-intervention treatment or in conditions other than whiplash. Only facet joint injections, pulsed electromagnetic treatment, and magnetic necklace were *not* found to be of benefit in acceptable clinical trials and even these conclusions were based on only one study for each treatment. Table 12.4, based on the QTF review, lists conclusions for each treatment; the most common

TABLE 12.4
Specific Interventions for Whiplash-Associated Disorder (WAD)

Immobilization	
Soft Collars	Only studied in control groups. May delay recovery by promoting inactivity (3).
Rest	No studies. Prolonged rest likely detrimental to recovery.
Cervical pillows	No studies.
Activation	
Manipulation	No acceptable studies establishing short-term or long-term effectiveness.
Mobilization	No studies. Likely beneficial over short-term. Long-term benefit not established.
Exercise	Not independently studied. As part of a "multimodal intervention" may be beneficial.
Traction	Not independently studied. No benefit demonstrated.
Postural Advice	Not independently studied.
Spray and Stretch	No studies.
Passive Modalities and Electrotherapies	
TENS	No studies.
Pulsed Electromagnetic Rx	No benefit (1).
Electrical Stimulation	No studies.
Ultrasound	No studies.
Laser, Heat, Ice, Massage	No studies.
Surgery	No studies.
Injections	
Nerve Block	No studies.
Epidural Injections	No studies.
Facet Joint Injection	No benefit (1).
Subcutaneous Sterile Water Injections	Some benefit compared to normal saline in unblinded study.
Pharmacological Interventions	No studies.
Psychological Treatments	No studies.
Other Interventions	
Prescribed Function	Improved outcome in one study.
Acupuncture	No studies.
Magnetic Necklace	No benefit (1).

Note. From Spitzer et al. (1995). Copyright 1995 by Societe d'Assurance Automobile du Quebec. Adapted by permission.

conclusion was "no studies." Therefore, based on the QTF review one cannot definitively conclude whether these interventions are effective *or* ineffective, just that they have not been studied in isolation. However, for many of these treatments, multimodal interventions did not suggest they would be effective.

Although the QTF concluded that their "systematic review of the original research literature yielded little scientifically rigorous information" they nonetheless developed consensus guidelines "based on the best evidence available, or where evidence was lacking, on the combined experience and judgement emerging from extended in-depth discussions of the Task Force Members" (Spitzer et al., 1995, p. 34S). One weakness of these treatment guidelines is that, although they give the impression of being built upon a foundation of scientific data, they are, in fact, based on admittedly little scientific evidence. As well, the guidelines address interventions only in the first 12 weeks and therefore are particularly suspect if applied to chronic whiplash patients.

As is apparent from Table 12.4, a wide variety of interventions are available to treat patients with whiplash injuries with reports of efficacy largely anecdotal. No treatment consistently "cures" the pain of acute or chronic whiplash injuries. Treatment programs should attempt to balance *pain control* with *increased function*, although in recent years there has been a trend toward focusing primarily on the latter. The concept that some injuries resulting in pain may be inaccessible to physical and pharmacological treatments is a difficult one for many patients (and some clinicians) to grasp and accept. Because there is a lack of good clinical trials, the discussion that follows is based largely on our own anecdotal experience.

Treatments Generally Agreed to Be of Benefit

Education of the patient (and family) is a critical element of any treatment program. Patients must clearly understand the goals of treatment, that is, return of function, control of pain, and the likely prognosis. Education helps patients plan realistically for their future, provides them with a sense of control, and increases their confidence in treating clinicians. Patients must understand that "hurt is not equal to harm." Many patients excessively limit their activities and movement of their neck in a logical attempt to avoid pain and by inference tissue damage. This may result in general deconditioning and constriction of neck muscles. Alternatively, a subset of patients repeatedly push themselves to extremely high levels of pain necessitating several days of relative inactivity until pain returns to manageable levels. Exhorting these patients to "push through the pain" only reinforces an already maladaptive and ineffective strategy. It is often difficult to identify this latter group, as they tend to emphasize their frustrations with their periods of inactivity and underreport the extent of their activity on "good" days because it is still significantly below their premorbid levels of activities and standards.

McKinney, Dornon, and Ryan (1989), in a study of acute whiplash injuries, found that advice to mobilize, exercise, limit activity to pain tolerance, and avoid dependence on collars and analgesics was as effective as a physiotherapy-directed program. Information and advice regarding activities that aggravate pain (heavy lifting or maintaining prolonged postures) help prevent significant exacerbations of pain. For chronic whiplash patients, an emphasis on proper pacing of activities is helpful, often critical, to pain management.

Exercise-Oriented Physical Therapy. In acute whiplash injuries early mobilization of the neck that is gentle and graduated is thought to promote maximal healing of damaged soft tissues. Patients are then enrolled in a program of stretching and aerobic exercise. Stretching of muscles and ligaments to their normal length has long been thought to maximize functioning. Strengthening exercises are controversial and often aggravate pain, particularly if introduced too early or too aggressively. Isometric strengthening exercises may be tolerated better. Theoretically, strong neck musculature is desirable to provide an active physiological splint, which can potentially reduce pain. Formal exercise programs should be time limited with a shift over time to a home exercise program. Exercise-oriented treatments were divided by the QTF (Spitzer et al., 1995) into mobilization and exercise. Regarding mobilization they noted, "The cumulative evidence suggests that mobilization techniques can be used as an adjunct to strategies that promote activation. In combination with activating interventions, they appear to be beneficial in the short term but the long term benefit has not been established" (p. 29S). Regarding exercise they noted, "The cumulative evidence suggests that active exercise as part of a multimodal intervention may be beneficial in the short and long term. This suggestion should be confirmed in future studies" (p. 29S).

Two studies are of note. McKinney et al. (1989) reported that acute whiplash patients receiving 2 weeks of physiotherapy that combined McKenzie and Maitland mobilization techniques demonstrated greater improvement/recovery 1 week after a treatment than patients prescribed rest and soft collars. However, there was no difference between the two groups at 2-year follow-up. Moreover, a third group simply given advice on early activation and a home program of exercises did better than either group. Mealey, Brennan, and Fenelon (1986) reported that patients receiving Maitland mobilization techniques had more short-term relief of pain and range of motion than did patients prescribed rest and a soft cervical collar. These studies suggest that one must promote activity and on balance, physiotherapy exercises are likely helpful in the short term.

Treatments That Serve Primarily to Decrease Pain

These treatments are the most commonly used treatments in the management of whiplash injuries. They often provide subsets of patients with consistent reduction of pain. Unfortunately, it is impossible to predict in advance whether a particular treatment will relieve pain for a given patient. As well, the benefits of these treatments are invariably short-lived. It is of note that some of these treatments are more readily funded (e.g., medications) than others. Passive treatments such as physical modalities, massage, manipulation, and even medications, if not performed within the framework of an active rehabilitation program, may potentially result in greater dependency on the part of the patient and discourage them from taking active responsibility for their own rehabilitation.

Cervical Collar. Initial use of a cervical collar in acute whiplash injuries still enjoys popularity although its use appears to be declining. Research has failed to demonstrate its efficacy. A controlled study demonstrated that patients mobilized early without a collar experienced a greater reduction of pain and improved cervical range of motion relative to rest and use of a collar (Mealey et al., 1986). Similar findings were reported by McKinney (McKinney, 1989; McKinney et al., 1989). However, another prospective study failed to demonstrate differences between early active treatment with traction and physiotherapy compared with rest in a collar and unsupervised mobilization (Pennie & Agambar, 1991). A soft cervical collar does not truly immobilize the neck (Colachis, Strohm, & Ganter, 1973; Fisher, Bowar, Awad, & Gullickson, 1977; Johnson, Simmons, Ramsby, & Southwick, 1977). If a cervical collar is prescribed, continuous use for more than 2 weeks should be discouraged (Teasell & Shapiro, 1993). According to Lieberman (1986), *prolonged collar use* leads to a variety of complications, including disuse atrophy of the neck muscles, soft tissue contractures, shortening of muscles, thickening of subcapsular tissues, increased dependency, and enhancement of feelings of disability.

Physical Modalities. Ice packs may be helpful in the early acute phase of whiplash (3 to 10 days after the accident) to limit muscle swelling. After the acute phase, local hot packs, ultrasound, and interferential current or transcutaneous electrical nerve stimulation (TENS) may serve to reduce pain temporarily. Recent research on TENS in low back pain showed it to be no better than placebo (Deyo, Walsh, Martin, Schoenfeld, & Ramamurthy, 1990). In patients who benefit initially from TENS, the positive effect decreases over time. Moist heat tends to be more effective than dry heat. Many patients find it useful to apply ice for 3 to 5 minutes before stretching the involved regional muscles. There is some limited evidence that pulsed electromagnetic treatment may be useful in the early stages of whiplash (Foley-Nolan et al., 1992). The use of physical modalities serves primarily as an adjunct to therapeutic exercise and should not take the place of an active exercise program (Teasell & Shapiro, 1993).

Medications. Drugs have a limited role in the management of whiplash injuries despite their widespread use. They have significant potential for misuse and adverse side effects. Medications are frequently overused in chronic whiplash injuries because the treating physician is uncertain how else to ease the pain and emotional distress of the suffering patient. *Analgesic medications* have their greatest application in the acute stage. Nonsteroidal anti-inflammatory drugs (NSAIDs) are more likely of benefit due to their analgesic properties than their anti-inflammatory properties. Long-term usage carries with it a substantial risk of stomach ulceration. Muscle relaxants appear to work primarily through their anxiolytic effect but have not been adequately studied (Spitzer et al., 1995). Narcotic analgesics must be carefully monitored and their use limited because of the risk of tolerance and addiction; the issue of narcotic use in chronic pain is not fully resolved (Brena & Sanders, 1991). Long-term narcotic use has traditionally been discouraged (Lieberman, 1986), and in our opinion, patients are generally better served by avoiding them. A recent (Moulin et al., 1996) randomized, controlled trial found that morphine reduced pain in chronic pain sufferers, many of whom had suffered whiplash injuries. However, there was no corresponding improvement in function.

Tricyclic antidepressants (TCAs), administered either in small doses before bedtime or in full antidepressant doses are sometimes helpful in chronic pain patients, especially those with a nonrestorative sleep pattern (Butler, 1984; Ward, 1986). TCAs have been shown to have an analgesic effect in animal studies (Spiegel, Kalb, & Pasternak, 1983). TCAs' mechanism of action is not clear but may be related to the ability of TCAs to block the reuptake of serotonin, thereby enhancing endogenous pathways of pain control, improving nonrestorative sleep patterns, and/or treating co-occurring depression. The major side effects of TCAs are dry mouth, morning drowsiness, and weight gain, which many patients find intolerable.

Manipulation. There is no definitive research on the efficacy of cervical manipulation in whiplash patients (Spitzer et al., 1995). Anecdotal experience and one published study (Cassidy, Lopes, & Yong-Hing, 1992) suggest it offers short-term relief of symptoms in chronic whiplash patients. Physicians are concerned most about the high-velocity/low-amplitude thrust maneuver and the rare but serious complication of vertebral artery dissection (Teasell & Marchuk, 1994).

Cervical Traction. Although this treatment has been advocated for cervical whiplash injuries (Jackson, 1978; Macnab, 1971), there is no evidence it is of benefit in whiplash injuries. The only controlled trial failed to demonstrate any effect (Zylbergold & Piper, 1985). In our experience, mechanical cervical traction often aggravates symptoms. In the initial stage, traction is contraindicated because the distractive forces may increase pain and further damage healing tissue (Weinberger, 1976).

Massage. Massage therapy is a time-honored treatment for musculoskeletal problems, in particular myofascial pain and muscle tension. There is no evidence that it produces long-lasting benefits and controlled trials are lacking. Massage can play a role in keeping the patient functional by providing temporary relief of pain. Anecdotally, benefits have been observed in some whiplash patients who are in situations in which muscle tension and pain gradually build up (e.g., an office worker or a student studying for an exam). Massage therapy must be gentle because aggressive or deep friction massage is often poorly tolerated, resulting in increased pain.

Trigger Point Injections. Tender points within cervical and upper thoracic muscles can produce an abrupt onset of pain from the point of palpation with distal referral of pain in a characteristic pattern (Travell & Simons, 1983). Injections of local anaesthetics and corticosteroids is a popular, albeit unproven, treatment. It is not clear that anaesthetics are essential to the therapeutic effect, because injections of sterile water, normal saline, or dry needling into trigger points may also produce a therapeutic response. Recent reports found that subcutaneous injections of sterile water were more effective than injections of normal saline in patients with chronic neck and shoulder pain from whiplash injury (Byrn, Borenstein, & Linder, 1991; Byrn, Olsson, Falkheden, et al., 1993).

Treatments That Improve Coping Skills and Increase Function

The QTF (Spitzer et al., 1995) found no quality research regarding psychosocial interventions in the treatment of whiplash injuries. These treatments are usually employed to help patients cope better or move on with their lives in the face of chronic pain. They do not necessarily reduce pain per se although, in some cases, they can significantly decrease emotional distress and improve whiplash patients' overall level of coping. These interventions are often provided within functional restoration programs (FRPs) or multidisciplinary pain programs. FRPs have become very popular because of the limitations of current treatment programs and the frequently observed discordance between pain, impairment, and disability (Gatchel, 1994). FRPs combine aggressive exercise regimens, discourage pain behaviors, and attempt to address psychosocial issues. FRPs have arisen as a natural evolution of behavioral theories of pain (Fordyce, 1976; Fordyce, Roberts, & Sternbach, 1985). Most FRPs provide a multidisciplinary approach designed to improve factors contributing to disability apart from the pain itself. FRPs have been described as a tertiary, medically directed, interdisciplinary amalgam of a sports medicine approach to restoring physical capacity and a cognitive crisis intervention technique for disability management (Gatchel, Mayer, Hazard, Rainville, & Mooney, 1992). Unfortunately, there is a paucity of properly controlled evidence that FRPs actually work for chronic low back pain (Teasell & Harth, 1995) and there are no published studies specific to whiplash. FRPs offer a promising approach but must be considered unproven in the absence of adequate controlled trials with whiplash patients.

Treatments of Dubious Value

There are no controlled studies on the use of *occipital nerve blocks* in treating whiplash injuries. *Cervical facet joint corticosteroid blocks* have been subjected to a randomized, controlled, double-blind study, which failed to demonstrate effectiveness in whiplash patients with pain of greater than 3 months' duration (Barnsley, Lord, Wallis, & Bogduk, 1994). In this study, the level of facet joint pathology was identified using cervical facet joint diagnostic blocks. Hamer and colleagues (Hamer et al., 1992) utilized *diskectomy/fusion* in 0.5% of cases and found significant relief of pain in only 10% of those operated on. This lack of efficacy is consistent with our experience. The QTF (Spitzer et al., 1995) found no acceptable studies on surgical interventions in whiplash injuries. *Cervical epidural injections* have been reported to be beneficial in uncontrolled trials. Theoretically, they should not be helpful because the damaged tissue are presumably outside the epidural space. The *magnetic necklace* was mentioned by the QTF (Spitzer et al., 1995) because of its widespread use among laypeople. A controlled trial using active and sham treatment in chronic neck pain patients failed to demonstrate any benefit (Hong et al., 1982).

Treatments That Show Some Promise

Percutaneous Facet Joint Denervation. These procedures have been reported to offer benefit to a subset of patients in uncontrolled studies. Hildebrant and Argyrakis (1986) reported on 35 patients presenting with headache, neck, shoulder, and arm pain who underwent apophyseal joint or dorsal rami diagnostic blocks. The involved joints were then partially denervated using radiofrequency electrocoagulation. Thirteen of 35 patients reported significant relief, 10 some improvement, and 12 no benefit. Verkest and Stolker (1991) performed facet joint denervation procedures on 53 patients with cervical facet joint pain. They reported that over 80% received long-lasting improvement in this uncontrolled study. As described previously, a recent randomized, double-blind trial demonstrated the efficacy of this treatment in patients determined to have pain of cervical facet joint origin (Lord, Barnsley, Wallis, McDonald, & Bogduk, 1996).

SUMMARY

Patients with chronic whiplash injuries are difficult to treat. It is important to recognize that the natural history of acute whiplash is such that many patients will improve or recover relatively quickly. Supportive education and a progressive program of exercises, involving stretching of the involved region as well as an aerobic exercise program, are regarded as the mainstays of medical management. Other physical treatments (physical modalities, manipulation, TENS) and pharmacological treatments provide short-term pain reduction at best and should not be used in isolation. Injections and surgical interventions are rarely useful in uncomplicated whiplash. The one exception is percutaneous facet joint denervation, which appears effective for patients with demonstrable (via diagnostic blocks) facet joint involvement. Psychosocial interventions including vocational counseling are becoming more popular as we recognize the importance of treating the person with a whiplash injury and not just the injury itself. However, psychosocial interventions remain unproven. Similarly functional restoration programs are a potentially useful but unproven treatment approach. The challenge of treatment is to integrate the art and science of medicine to efficiently and effectively increase function and reduce pain and suffering.

REFERENCES

Balch, R. W. (1984). *Dizziness, hearing loss and tinnitus, the essentials of neurology.* Philadelphia: Davis.

Balla, J. I. (1980). The late whiplash syndrome. *Austrailia and New Zealand Journal of Surgery, 50,* 610–614.

Balla, J. I., & Moraitis, S. (1970). Knights in armour. A follow-up study of injuries after legal settlement. *Medical Journal of Australia, 2,* 355–361.

Barnsley, L., Lord, S. M., Wallis, B. J., & Bogduk, N. (1994). Lack of effect of intra-articular corticosteroids for chronic cervical zygapophyseal joint pain. *New England Journal of Medicine, 330,* 1047–1050.

Barnsley, L., Lord, S. M., Wallis, B. J., & Bogduk, N. (1995). The prevalence of chronic cervical zygapophysial joint pain after whiplash. *Spine, 20,* 20–25.

Boden, S. D., McCowin, P. R., Davis, D. O., Dina, T. S., Mark, A. S., & Wiesel, S. (1990). Abnormal magnetic-resonance scans of the cervical spine in asymptomatic subjects. *Journal of Bone and Joint Surgery [American]*, 72, 1178–1184.

Bogduk, N. (1986). The anatomy and pathophysiology of whiplash. *Clinical Biomechanics, 1,* 92–101.

Borden, A. G. B., Rachtman, A. M., & Gershom-Cohen, J. (1960). The normal cervical lordosis. *Radiology, 74,* 806.

Borgeat, F., Hade, B., Elie, R., & Larouche, I. M. (1984). Effects of voluntary muscle tension increases in tension headaches. *Headache, 24,* 199–202.

Braaf, M. M., & Rosner, S. (1955). Symptomatology and treatment of injuries of the neck. *New York Journal of Medicine, 55,* 237.

Brena, S. F., & Sanders, S. H. (1991). Opioids in nonmalignant pain: Questions in search of answers. *Clinical Journal of Pain, 7,* 342–345.

Butler, S. (1984). Present status of tricyclic antidepressants in chronic pain therapy. In C. Benedette et al. (Eds.), *Advances in pain research and therapy* (Vol. 7, pp. 173–197). New York: Raven.

Byrn, C., Borenstein, P., & Linder, L. E. (1991). Treatment of neck and shoulder pain in whiplash syndrome patients with intracutaneous sterile water injections. *Acta Anesthesiology Scandinavica, 35,* 52–53.

Byrn, C., Olsson, I., Falkheden, L., Lindh, M., Hösterey, U., Fogelberg, M., et al. (1993). Subcutaneous sterile water injection for chronic neck and shoulder pain following whiplash injuries. *Lancet, 341,* 449–452.

Capistrant, T. D. (1977). Thoracic outlet syndrome in whiplash injury. *Annals Surgery, 185,* 175–178.

Cassidy, J. D., Lopes, A. A., & Yong-Hing, K. (1992). The immediate effect of manipulation versus mobilization on pain and range of motion in the cervical spine: A randomized control trial. *Journal Manipulative Physiological Therapy, 15,* 570–575.

Cherington, M., Happer, I., Marchanic, B., & Parry, L. (1986). Surgery for thoracic outlet syndrome may be hazardous to your health. *Muscle & Nerve, 9,* 632–634.

Chrisman, O. D., & Gervais, R. F. (1962). Otologic manifestations of the cervical syndrome. *Clinical Orthopedics, 24,* 34–39.

Christensen, L. V. (1986a). Physiology and pathophysiology of skeletal muscle contractions: Part 1. Dynamic activity. *Journal of Oral Rehabilitation, 13,* 451–461.

Christensen, L. V. (1986b). Physiology and pathophysiology of skeletal muscle contractors: Part 2. Static activity. *Journal of Oral Rehabilitation, 13,* 463–477.

Clemens, H. J., & Burrow, K. (1972). Experimental investigation on injury mechanisms of cervical spine at frontal and rear-front vehicle impacts. In *Proceedings of the Sixteenth Stapp Car Crash Conference* (pp. 76–104).

Colachis, S. C., Strohm, B. R., & Ganter, E. L. (1973). Cervical spine motion in normal women: Radiographic study of effect of cervical collar. *Archives of Physical Medicine and Rehabilitation, 54,* 161–169.

Commack, K. V. (1957). Whiplash injuries to the neck. *American Journal of Surgery, 93,* 663–666.

Compere, W. E. (1968). Electronystagmographic finding in patients with "whiplash" injuries. *Laryngoscope, 78,* 1226–1232.

Corey, D. T., Koepfler, L. E., Etlin, D., & Day, I. H. (1996). A limited functional restoration program for injured workers: A randomized trial. *Journal of Occupational Rehabilitation, 6,* 239–249.

Croft, A. C. (1988). Biomechanics. In S. M. Foreman & A. C. Croft (Eds.), *Whiplash injuries. The cervical acceleration deceleration syndrome* (p. 1072). Baltimore: Williams & Wilkins.

Deans, G. T. (1986). Incidence and duration of neck pain among patients injured in car accidents. *British Medical Journal, 292,* 94–95.

Deans, G. T., McGailliard, J. N., Kerr, M., & Rutherford, W. H. (1987). Neck pain—A major cause of disability following car accidents. *Injury, 18,* 10–12.

DeJong, P. T. V. M., DeJong, J. M. B. V., Cohen, B., & Jongkees, L. B. W. (1977). Ataxia and nystagmus induced by injection of local anaesthetics in the neck. *Annals Neurology, 1,* 240–246.

Deyo R. A., Walsh, N. E., Martin, D. C., Schoenfeld, L. S., & Ramamurthy, S. (1990). A controlled trial of transcutaneous electrical nerve stimulation (TENS) and exercise for chronic low back pain. *New England Journal of Medicine, 322,* 1627–1634.

Dunsker, S. B. (1982). Hyperextension and hyperflexion injuries of the cervical spine. In J. R. Youmans (Ed.), *Neurological surgery* (2nd ed., pp. 2332–2343). Philadelphia: Saunders.

Evans, R. W. (1992). Some observations on whiplash injuries. *Neurologic Clinics, 10*(4), 975–995.

Fisher, S. V., Bowar, J. F., Awad, E. A., & Gullickson, G. (1977). Cervical orthoses effect on cervical spine motion: Roentgenographic and gonometric method of study. *Archives of Physical Medicine and Rehabilitation, 58,* 109–115.

Foley-Nolan, D., Moore, K., Codd, M., Barry, C., O'Connor, P., & Coughlan, R. J. (1992). Low energy high frequency pulsed electromagnetic therapy for acute whiplash injuries. A double blind randomized controlled study. *Scandinavian Journal of Rehabilitation Medicine, 24,* 51–59.

Fordyce, W. E. (1976). *Behavioural methods for chronic pain and illness.* St. Louis, MO: Mosby.

Fordyce, W. E., Roberts, A. H., & Sternbach, R. A. (1985). The behavioural management of chronic pain: A response to critics. *Pain, 22,* 113–125.

Frankel, V. H. (1976). Pathomechanics of whiplash injuries to the neck. In T. P. Morley (Ed.), *Current controversies in neurosurgery* (pp. 39–50). Philadelphia: Saunders.

Gargan, M. F., & Bannister, G. C. (1994). The rate of recovery following whiplash injury. *European Spine Journal, 3,* 162–164.

Gatchel, R. J. (1994). Occupational low back pain disability: Why function needs to "drive" the rehabilitation process. *American Pain Society Journal, 3*(2), 107–110.

Gatchel, R. J., Mayer, T. G., Hazard, R. G., Rainville, J., & Mooney, V. (1992). Functional restoration: Pitfalls in evaluating efficacy [Editorial]. *Spine, 17*(8), 988–995.

Gay, J. R., & Abbott, K. H. (1953). Common whiplash injuries of the neck. *Journal of the American Medical Association, 152,* 1698–1704.

Gibson, J. W. (1974). Cervical syndromes: Use of comfortable cervical collar as an adjunct in their management. *Southern Medical Journal, 67,* 205–208.

Giroux, M. (1991, September). Les blessmes a la colonne cervicale; importance du probleme. *Le Medicin du Quebec,* pp. 22–26.

Hamer, A. J., Prasad, R., Gargan, M. F., et al. (1992, November). *Whiplash injury and cervical disc surgery.* Paper presented at the meeting of the British Cervical Spine Society Meeting, Bowness-on-Windermere, England.

Hasvold, T., & Johnsen, R. (1993). Headache and neck as shoulder pain-frequent and disabling complaints in the general population. *Scandinavian Journal of Primary Health Care, 11,* 219–224.

Hildebrant, J., & Argyrakis, A. (1986). Percutaneous nerve block of the cervical facets—A relatively new method in the treatment of chronic headache and neck pain. *Manual Medicine, 2,* 48–52.

Hildingsson, C., & Toolanen, G. (1990). Outcome after soft tissue injury of the cervical spine. *Acta Orthopedics Scandinavica, 61,* 357–359.

Hohl, M. (1974). Soft tissue injuries of the neck in automobile accidents: Factors influencing prognosis. *Journal of Bone and Joint Surgery, 56A,* 1675–1682.

Hohl, M. (1975). Soft tissue injuries of the neck. *Clinical Orthopedics, 109,* 42–49.

Hohl, M. (1989). Soft tissue neck injuries: In The Cervical Spine Research Society Editorial Committee (Eds.), *The cervical spine* (2nd ed., pp. 436–441). Philadelphia: Lippincott.

Hong, C. Z., Lin, J. C., Bender, L. F., Schaeffer, J. N., Meltzer, R. J., & Causin, P. (1982). Magnetic necklace: Its therapeutic effectiveness on neck and shoulder pain. *Archives Physical Medicine and Rehabilitation, 63,* 462–466.

Horwich, H., & Kasner, D. (1962). The effect of whiplash injuries on ocular functions. *Southern Medical Journal, 55,* 69–71.

Jackson, R. (1978). *The cervical syndrome* (4th ed.). Springfield, IL: Thomas.

Jeffreys, E. (1980). *Disorders of the cervical spine.* London: Butterworth.

Johnson, R. M., Hart, D. L., Simmons, E. F., Ramsby, G. R., & Southwick, W. O. (1977). Cervical orthoses—A study comparing their effectiveness in restricting cervical motion in normal subjects. *Journal of Bone and Joint Surgery [American], 59,* 332–339.

LaRocca, H. (1978). Acceleration injuries of the neck. *Clinical Neurosurgery, 25,* 205–217.

Lieberman, J. S. (1986). Cervical soft tissue injuries and cervical disc disease. In *Principles of physical medicine and rehabilitation in the musculoskeletal diseases* (pp. 263–286). New York: Grune & Stratton.

Lord, S., Barnsley, L., & Bogduk, N. (1993). Cervical zygapophyseal joint pain in whiplash. *Spine: State of the Art Reviews, 7*(3), 355–372.

Lord, S. M., Barnsley, L., Wallis, B. J., & Bogduk, N. (1996). Chronic cervical zygapophysial joint pain after whiplash: A placebo-controlled prevalence study. *Spine, 21*(5), 1737–1745.

Lord, S. M., Barnsley, L., Wallis, B. J., McDonald, G. J., & Bogduk, N. (1996). Percutaneous radio-frequency neurotomy for chronic cervical zygapophyseal joint pain. *New England Journal of Medicine, 335,* 1721–1726.

Macnab, I. (1964). Acceleration injuries of the cervical spine. *Journal of Bone and Joint Surgery [American], 46,* 1797–1799.

Macnab, I. (1969). Acceleration extension injuries of the cervical spine. In *AAOS Symposium of the Spine* (pp. 10–17). St. Louis, MO: Mosby.

Macnab, I. (1971). The "whiplash syndrome." *Orthopedic Clinics of North America, 2,* 389–403.

Macnab, I. (1973). The whiplash syndrome. *Clinical Neurosurgery, 20,* 232–241.

Macnab, I. (1982). Acceleration extension injuries of the cervical spine. In R. H. Rothman & F. A. Simeone (Eds.), *The Spine* (2nd ed., pp. 647–660). Philadelphia: Saunders.

McKenzie, J. A., & Williams, J. F. (1971). The dynamic behavior of the head and cervical spine during "whiplash." *Journal of Biomechanics, 4,* 474–490.

McKinney, L. A. (1989). Early mobilization and outcome in acute sprains of the neck. *British Medical Journal, 299,* 1006–1008.

McKinney, L. A., Dornon, J. O., & Ryan, M. (1989). The role of physiotherapy in the management of acute neck sprains following road-traffic events. *Archives of Emergency Medicine, 6,* 27–33.

Mealey, K., Brennan, H., & Fenelon, G. C. C. (1986). Early mobilization of acute whiplash injuries. *British Medical Journal, 292,* 656–657.

Medical News. (1965). Animals riding in carts show effects of "whiplash" injury. *Journal of the American Medical Association, 194,* 40–41.

Melzack, R., & Wall, P. D. (1983). *The challenge of pain.* New York: Basic Books.

Mitchell, R. I., & Carmen, G. (1994). The functional restoration approach to the treatment of chronic pain in patients with soft tissue and back injuries. *Spine, 19,* 633–642.

Moulin, D. E., Iezzi, A., Amireh, R., Sharpe, W. K. J., Boyd, D., & Merskey, H. (1996). Randomized trial of oral morphine for chronic non-cancer pain. *Lancet, 347,* 143–147.

National Safety Council. (1971). *Accident facts.* Chicago: Author.

Nelson, D. A. (1990). Thoracic outlet syndrome and dysfunction of the temporomandibular joint: Proved pathology or pseudosyndromes? *Perspectives of Biological Medicine, 33,* 567–576.

Oosterveld, W. J., Kortschot, H. W., Kingma, G. G., de Jong, H. A. A., & Saatchi, M. R. (1991). Electronystagmographic findings following cervical whiplash injuries. *Acta Otolaryngology [Stockholm], 111,* 201–205.

Pang, L. Q. (1971). The otological aspects of whiplash injuries. *Laryngoscope, 81,* 1381–1387.

Pennie, B., & Agambar, L. (1991). Patterns of injury and recovery in whiplash. *Injury, 22,* 57–99.

Rachtman, A. A., Borden, A. G. B., & Gershom-Cohen, J. (1961). The lordotic curve of the cervical spine. *Clinical Orthopedics, 20*, 208.

Radanov, B. P., DeStefano, G., Schnidrig, A., & Ballinari, P. (1991). Role of psychosocial stress in recovery from common whiplash. *Lancet, 388*, 712–715.

Radanov, B. P., Sturzenegger, M., DeStefano, G., & Schnidrig, A. (1994). Relationship between early somatic, radiological, cognitive and psychosocial findings and outcome during a one-year follow-up in 117 patients suffering from common whiplash. *British Journal of Rheumatology, 33*, 442–448.

Schrader, H., Obelieniene, D., Bovim, G., Surkiene, D., Mickeviciene, D., Miseviciene, I., & Sand, T. (1996). Natural evolution of the late whiplash syndrome outside the medical legal context. *Lancet, 347*, 1207–1211.

Schutt, C. H., & Dohan, F. C. S. (1968). Neck injuries to women in auto accidents: A metropolitan plague. *Journal of the American Medical Association, 206*, 2689–2692.

Shapiro, A. P., & Teasell, R. W. (1997). Misdiagnosis of chronic pain as hysterical. *NeuroRehabilitation, 8*, 201–222.

Sobeco, Ernst, & Young (1989). *Saskatchewan government insurance automobile injury study* (Report to the Saskatchewan Government Insurance Office). Cited in Spitzer et al. (1995).

Speed, W. G. (1987). Psychiatric aspects of post-traumatic headaches. In C. S. Adler et al. (Eds.), *Psychiatric aspects of headache* (pp. 210–216). Baltimore: Williams & Wilkins.

Spiegel, K., Kalb, R., & Pasternak, G. W. (1983). Analgesic activity of tricyclic antidepressants. *Annals of Neurology, 13*, 462–465.

Spitzer, W. O., Skovron, M. L., Salmi, L. R., Cassidy, J. D., Durancean, J., Suissa, S., & Zeiss, E. (1995). Quebec Task Force on Whiplash-Associated Disorders. *Spine, 20*(85), 1S–73S.

Taylor, H., & Curran, N. M. (1985). *The Nuprin Pain Report.* New York: Louis Harris.

Teasell, R. W., & Harth, M. (1996). Functional restoration in returning patients with chronic low back pain to work: Revolution or fad? *Spine, 21*(7), 844–847.

Teasell, R. W., & Marchuk, Y. (1994). Vertebro-basilar artery stroke as a complication of cervical manipulation. *Critical Reviews in Physical Rehabilitation Medicine, 6*(1), 121–129.

Teasell, R. W., & Shapiro, A. P. (1993). Flexion-extension injuries and chronic pain. In H. Merskey & H. Vaeroy (Eds.), *Pain research and clinical management: Progress on fibromyalgia and myofascial pain* (Vol. 6, pp. 253–266). Amsterdam: Elsevier.

Toglia, J. V. (1976). Acute flexion-extension injury of the neck: Electronystagmographic study of 309 patients. *Neurology, 26*, 808–814.

Travell, J., & Simons, D. G. (1983). *Myofascial pain and dysfunction: The trigger point manual.* Baltimore: Williams & Wilkins.

Turk, D. C., & Flor, H. (1984). Etiological theories and treatments for chronic pain: II. Psychosocial factors and interventions. *Pain, 19*, 209–233.

Unreh, A. M. (1996). Gender variations in clinical pain experience. *Pain, 65*, 123–167.

Verkest, A. C. M., & Stolker, R. J. (1991). The treatment of cervical pain syndromes with radiofrequency procedures. *Pain Clinic, 4*(2), 103–112.

Ward, N. G. (1986). Tricyclic antidepressants for chronic low back pain. *Spine, 11*, 661–665.

Weinberger, L. M. (1976). Trauma or treatment? The role of intermittent traction in the treatment of cervical soft tissue injuries. *Journal of Trauma, 15*, 377–382.

Wickstrom, J. K., & LaRocca, H. (1975). Management of patients with cervical spine and head injuries from acceleration forces. *Current Practices in Orthopedic Surgery, 6*, 83.

Wilbourn, A. J. (1990). The thoracic outlet syndrome is overdiagnosed. *Archives of Neurology, 47*, 328–330.

Wiley, A. M., Lloyd, J., Evans, J. G., Stewart, B. M., & Sanchez, J. (1986). Musculoskeletal sequelae of whiplash injuries. *Advocates Quarterly, 7*, 65–73.

Zylbergold, R. S., & Piper, M. C. (1985). Cervical spine disorders. A comparison of three types of traction. *Spine, 10*, 867–871.

Chapter 13

Pain in Patients
With Rheumatic Disease

Laurence A. Bradley
University of Alabama at Birmingham

Patients with rheumatic disease view pain as one of the most important and challenging consequences of their illnesses (Bradley, 1996). It has been found, for example, that pain is more important than physical or psychological disability in explaining medication usage among patients with rheumatoid arthritis (RA) (Kazis, Meenan, & Anderson, 1983). Pain is also a significant predictor of patient and physician assessments of the patients' general health status as well as their future levels of pain and disability (Kazis et al., 1983). However, perceptions of pain intensity and displays of pain behavior are not highly associated with measures of rheumatic disease activity such as joint counts (Bradley, 1994a, 1994b). Indeed, it is quite common to observe patients in rheumatology clinic with few inflamed joints who display multiple pain behaviors (e.g., stiffness, guarded movement, grimacing) as well as patients with numerous inflamed joints who behave in a relatively stoic manner. Moreover, despite the advances that have been made in the medical management of the rheumatic diseases, patients rarely experience complete pain relief in response to their medication and physical treatment regimens (Bradley, 1996).

Psychological and social variables affect patients' pain experiences (Bradley, 1994b). Thus, optimal management of patients' pain problems can be achieved only if treatment providers recognize these psychosocial factors and can use the behavioral interventions that have been shown to influence these factors and reduce pain in patients with rheumatic disease. The primary purposes of this chapter are to (a) review the relationships that have been established between psychosocial factors and pain associated with three common rheumatic diseases: RA, osteoarthritis (OA), and fibromyalgia (FM); and (b) examine the behavioral methods that have been shown to help patients with these disorders to manage their pain. However, prior to examining these issues, the chapter presents information regarding the prevalence, pathogenesis, and medical treatment of these three diseases. The interested reader may wish to consult *Arthritis and Allied Conditions* (Koopman, 1997) for additional information regarding rheumatic disease.

THREE COMMON RHEUMATIC DISEASES

Rheumatoid Arthritis

Rheumatoid arthritis is a systemic disease that is found in 0.5% to 1% of the population across many cultures (Pincus, 1996). It is characterized by an acute inflammatory response, with symmetric polyarticular joint pain and swelling, morning stiffness, and fatigue. For most persons, RA is a progressive illness in which the inflammatory activity produces irreversible joint damage. However, the course of the disease, the amount of joint damage, as well as the severity of pain, are quite variable among individuals with RA. There is no cure for RA, although some individuals experience spontaneous remissions of their disease. Current medical therapies for patients with RA include nonsteroidal anti-inflammatory drugs (e.g., naproxen), corticosteroids (e.g., prednisone), and "disease-modifying" antirheumatic drugs or DMARDS (e.g., methotrexate). Physical therapy in conjunction with joint protection strategies is also an important part of treatment. For some individuals, joint replacement surgery may greatly reduce pain and increase functional ability.

Osteoarthritis

Osteoarthritis is the most common of the joint diseases (Stein, Griffin, & Brandt, 1996). The prevalence of OA depends on age. That is, radiographic evidence of OA is found in less than 1% of individuals in their 20s but is present in more than 50% of persons in their 70s and 80s. Nevertheless, fewer than one half of persons in their 70s with radiographic evidence of OA experience pain or functional disability (Bagge, Bjelle, Eden, & Svanborg, 1991). Predictors of the development of OA include female gender, obesity, physical trauma, and genetic factors. Moreover, numerous factors may contribute to the pathogenesis of OA such as abnormal biomechanical properties of joint structures, excessive biomechanical loading on joints, inflammation, cytokine release, and high release of matrix-degrading enzymes in the articular cartilage and subsequent morphologic changes in joint tissue (Stein et al., 1996).

As is the case with RA, there is no cure for OA. Medical approaches to the management of OA are designed to reduce pain and increase function. These approaches include weight loss interventions, exercise, joint protection devices (e.g., knee brace), local pain relief interventions (e.g., application of heat or cold), drug therapy (e.g., acetaminophen), and, for some individuals, surgery (e.g., joint replacement).

Fibromyalgia

Fibromyalgia is a syndrome characterized by widespread pain and exquisite tenderness at specific anatomic sites known as tender points (Bradley & Alarcón, 1997). Other symptoms include fatigue, disturbed sleep, and irritable bowel. The prevalence of FM is 2% in population studies across cultures; however, approximately 90% of persons with FM are women. The etiopathogenesis of FM is unknown but several biological abnormalities have been identified in patients with this syndrome. These include alpha EEG (electroencephelography) intrusion during non-REM (rapid eye movement) sleep, abnormal function of the hypothalamic-pituitary-adrenal (HPA) axis, and inhibited functional activity of two brain structures, the thalamus and caudate nucleus, during resting conditions. Only recently, however, have investigators attempted to develop models of the pathogenesis of FM that incorporate all of these biological abnormalities (Bradley & Alarcón, 1997; Weigent, Bradley, Blalock, & Alarcón, in press).

There is no cure for FM. However, randomized, controlled trials have shown that several interventions are superior to placebo in reducing pain. These include cardiovascular training exercise and pharmacologic therapies such as amitriptyline and cyclobenzaprine (Bradley & Alarcón, 1997).

PSYCHOSOCIAL FACTORS AND PAIN IN THE RHEUMATIC DISEASES

Depression and Anxiety

Depression and anxiety are negative psychological states that are frequently found in patients with rheumatic disease. For example, the frequency with which depression and anxiety disorders are diagnosed among RA patients ranges from 14% to 42% (Ahles, Khan, Yunus et al., 1991; Blalock, DeVellis, Brown et al., 1989; Frank, Beck, Parker et al., 1988). Similarly, the frequency of lifetime diagnoses of major depression and anxiety disorders in patients with FM ranges from 26% to 71% (Aaron et al., 1996; J. I. Hudson, Goldenberg, Pope, Keck, & Schlesinger, 1992; J. I. Hudson, M. S. Hudson,

Pliner, Goldenberg, & Pope, 1985). Clinically significant levels of depression are found in 14% to 23% of patients with OA (Dexter & Brandt, 1994); little is known, however, regarding the frequency of anxiety disorders in these patients. Although there are large differences in the frequency of depression and anxiety among patients with rheumatic disease, all of the frequency rates just noted are substantially greater than the population base rates for these psychological disorders (Frank & Hagglund, 1996).

Depression and anxiety are associated with several other health status variables in patients with rheumatic disease. For example, patients with RA who experience depression report significantly higher levels of pain, greater number of painful joints, and poorer functional ability, and they spend significantly more days in bed than patients who are not depressed (Katz & Yelin, 1993). Depression also is associated with higher levels of pain and functional disability in patients with OA and FM (Bradley & Alarcón, 1997; Summers, Haley, Reveille, & Alarcón, 1988). Moreover, psychological distress is associated with high levels of medical service use among patients with RA. For example, it was found that over a 5-year period, RA patients with elevated scores on a geriatric depression scale reported a significantly greater number of physician visits and hospitalizations related to their disease than patients whose depression scores were within normal limits (Katz & Yelin, 1993).

Some effort has been devoted to identifying the predictors of depression and anxiety in patients with RA. There is evidence that measures of disease activity, such as the number of tender or painful joints, are associated with anxiety and depression (Parker, Smarr, Anderson et al., 1992; Parker, Smarr, Walker et al., 1991). However, pain severity, age, neuroticism, lack of satisfaction with current lifestyle, and degree of functional impairment are better predictors of psychological distress than are joint counts and other measures of disease activity (Affleck, Tennen, Urrows et al., 1992; Frank et al., 1988; Hawley & Wolfe, 1988). It has been suggested that disease activity might be a more powerful predictor of depression or anxiety if patients were studied intensively over short time periods. This hypothesis was tested in a study that required RA patients to make multiple ratings of mood status on a daily basis over 75 consecutive days (Affleck, Tennen et al., 1992). Consistent with the findings noted earlier, disease activity did not predict daily mood. Instead, the most powerful predictors of daily mood states were age, neuroticism, and chronic pain.

Several studies of patients with FM also have delineated the importance of depression and anxiety in health status. For example, a cross-sectional investigation revealed that the frequency of lifetime psychiatric diagnoses assessed by the Diagnostic Interview Schedule (Robins, Helzer, Croughan, & Ratcliff, 1981) reliably differentiated three groups of individuals from one another. These groups were: (a) patients with FM recruited from a university-based rheumatology clinic, (b) community residents with FM who had not sought treatment for their pain during a 10-year period prior to their participation in the study (i.e., nonpatients), and (c) healthy community residents without FM (Aaron et al., 1996). The mean number of lifetime psychiatric diagnoses among the FM patients was nearly three times greater than those of both the nonpatients and the controls. Moreover, major depression and anxiety disorders were found most frequently among the FM patients (Table 13.1). Psychiatric morbidity did not distinguish the nonpatients from the healthy controls. These results suggested, then, that lifetime history of psychiatric disorders is an important determinant of health care–seeking behavior among persons with FM.

This conclusion received additional support in a 2½-year longitudinal study of the nonpatients. That is, it was found that only 25% of the nonpatients obtained medical treatment for their pain during the 2½-year follow-up study (Aaron, Bradley, Alexander et al., 1997). Several measures of work stress, psychiatric illness, and prescription medication usage assessed at baseline were associated with receiving medical care during follow-up. However, the best predictor of seeking medical treatment was the number of lifetime psychiatric diagnoses assessed at the beginning of the investigation. Indeed, the mean number of lifetime psychiatric diagnoses among the nonpatients who obtained medical care during the follow-up was commensurate with that of the FM patients assessed in the initial cross-sectional study.

Psychosocial factors also are associated with frequency of health care–seeking behavior among established patients with FM. For example, rheu-

TABLE 13.1
Percentage of Fibromyalgia (FM) Patients, FM Nonpatients,
and Healthy Controls With Lifetime Psychiatric Diagnoses

Diagnosis	FM Patients (N = 64)	FM Nonpatients (N = 28)	Healthy Controls (N = 23)	P[a]
Anxiety Disorders	60	36	26	0.008
Simple Phobia	38	18	4	0.001
Panic Disorder with Agoraphobia	11	0	0	0.050
Mood Disorders	52	18	22	0.002
Major Depressive Episode	39	11	9	0.001
Major Depression-Recurrent Episode	25	7	4	0.014
Dysthymic Disorder	22	7	0	0.004
Bipolar Disorder	13	4	0	0.043
Body Image Disorders	34	14	4	0.002
Somatization Disorder	23	10	0	0.004

[a]Probability of meeting criteria for at least one diagnosis in this category: $p < 0.01$, FM patients versus controls; $p > 0.05$, FM nonpatients versus controls.

matology clinic patients with FM who report that psychological trauma preceded or coincided with the onset of their pain more frequently obtain medical consultations and report significantly higher levels of functional disability than do FM patients without trauma (Aaron, Bradley, Alarcón, Triana-Alexander et al., 1997). One form of psychological trauma that has received particular attention from investigators is sexual and/or physical abuse. It has been found that between 53% and 67% of rheumatology clinic patients with FM report one or more incidents of sexual or physical abuse during childhood or adulthood (R. W. Alexander, Bradley, Alarcón et al., in press). Patients with histories of abuse, relative to nonabused patients, report significantly higher levels of pain and functional disability as well as significantly greater frequencies of physician visits for medical problems other than FM. The abused patients also report using a significantly greater number of medications for pain than do nonabused patients. These findings suggest that early identification and effective treatment of psychiatric disorders and other sources of psychological distress might reduce FM patients' health care costs as well as improve their overall health status.

Stress

Rheumatologic disorders produce numerous stressors, in addition to psychological distress, that may influence pain. These stressors include activity limitations and functional impairments in the home and workplace as well as financial hardships produced by loss of income and high health care costs (Clarke et al., 1993; Felts & Yelin, 1989; Liang, Larson, Thompson et al., 1984; Pincus, Mitchell, & Burkhauser, 1989; Yelin, 1992). Another important source of stress is change in patients' social relationships and in their appearance. It has been found, for example, that between 43% and 52% of patients with RA report dysfunction in the areas of social interaction, communication with others, and emotional behavior (Deyo, Inui, Leininger et al., 1982). In addition, two independent studies have reported that about 60% of patients with RA experience at least one major psychosocial change related to family functioning such as increased arguments with spouses, changes in the health of family members, and sexual dysfunction (Liang, Rogers, Larson et al., 1984; Yelin, Feshbach, Meenan et al., 1979).

Most of the research concerning stress and pain has been performed with patients with RA. It has been found that these patients frequently report that stress tends to precede flare-ups in disease activity (Affleck, Tennen, Pfeiffer et al., 1987). Indeed, there is evidence that the hypothalamus and other neural structures involved in stress responses are also involved in the inflammatory process in RA (Chikanza, Petrou, Kingsley et al., 1992). Abnormal function of the HPA axis also may be involved in abnormal pain perception among patients with FM through its effects on production of nerve growth factor and on the function of brain limbic system structures involved in pain processing (Crofford et al., 1994; Weigent et al., in press). Finally, there is some evidence that daily stressors and mood are both involved in immune system responses and pain among patients with RA. That is, it has been shown that daily stresses are associated with mood disturbances which, in turn, are related to decreases in soluble interleukin-2 receptor levels and increases in joint pain (Harrington, Affleck, Urrows et al., 1993).

Sleep Disturbance

High frequencies of sleep disturbances have been documented in patients with a variety of rheumatologic disorders including RA and OA (Wegener, 1996). However, sleep disturbance is most consistently found among patients with FM. These patients frequently show a specific anomaly characterized by intrusion of alpha waves during non-REM delta (i.e., slow wave) sleep (Moldofsky, 1986). This "alpha-delta" sleep anomaly, which is associated with local tenderness, pain, and stiffness in patients with FM, may be induced by emotionally arousing environmental events. It also has been demonstrated in healthy persons that noise-induced disruption of non-REM delta sleep directly leads to the appearance of the alpha-delta sleep anomaly as well as to onset of musculoskeletal pain and negative mood changes (Moldofsky & Scarisbrick, 1976). A return to undisturbed sleep in these healthy persons is followed by normalized sleep physiology and alleviation of symptoms. However, patients with FM who display the alpha-delta sleep anomaly do not report greater symptom severity than those without the anomaly. Moreover, the anomaly does not respond to a nightly regimen of low-dosage amitriptyline (Carette, Oakson, Guimont, & Steriade, 1995). Thus, disturbed sleep plays a role in symptom production and amplification in FM but the precise physiologic mechanism underlying the relationship has not yet been identified.

Beliefs and Coping Strategies

There is consistent evidence that patients' beliefs about their abilities to control or influence their symptoms are associated with pain. Two beliefs that have been studied extensively in patients with rheumatic diseases are *learned helplessness* and *self-efficacy*. These beliefs also may influence patients' abilities to effectively use various *coping strategies* to reduce or adapt to their pain and other symptoms.

Learned Helplessness. This is a phenomenon characterized by emotional, motivational, and cognitive deficits in adaptive coping with stressful situations. The deficits are produced by the belief that no viable solutions are available to eliminate or reduce the source of stress (Garber & Seligman, 1980). It has been hypothesized that learned helplessness may underlie a portion of the psychological distress and pain experienced by patients with RA and other rheumatologic disorders (Bradley, 1985). That is, many patients may develop the belief that their diseases are beyond their effective control because they tend to be characterized by causes that are not well understood, chronic and unpredictable courses, and variable responses to medical treatments. These patients tend to perceive that, regardless of their actions, they will not be able to substantially reduce the pain or other symptoms associated with their conditions. This perception of uncontrollability may cause patients to experience depression and anxiety (i.e., emotional deficits) that, in turn, may lead to increased pain and reduced attempts to either engage in activities of daily living (i.e., motivational deficits), or to develop new means of adapting to their pain, disabilities, and distress (i.e., cognitive deficits). These deficits may be particularly profound and resistant to change among patients who view the consequences of their conditions as relatively stable over time and global in nature (i.e., adversely affecting numerous vocational, recreational, social, and marital or sexual activities).

The importance of helplessness beliefs in adaptation to rheumatic disease has been demonstrated in many studies (Bradley, 1996). For example, high levels of helplessness are associated with high levels of pain, depression, and functional disability among patients with RA both at baseline and over follow-up periods of up to 3 years (Lorish, Abraham, Austin, Bradley, & Alarcón, 1991; Smith, Peck, & Ward, 1990). These studies initially led many health professionals to believe that the perception of control over pain and other symptoms (low helplessness) is desirable for patients with rheumatologic illnesses. Subsequently, however, it was found that RA patients who believe they can control their symptoms tend to suffer psychological distress in response to flares in disease activity and pain unless they are able to cognitively restructure their pain experiences (Tennen, Affleck, Urrows et al., 1992). An example of cognitive restructuring would be the adoption of the belief that one's pain has allowed one to better appreciate the preciousness of life. Thus, psychologists and other health professionals currently tend to focus on enhancing both perceptions of control and coping with flare-induced losses of control among their patients with rheumatic disease (Keefe & Van Horn, 1993).

Self-Efficacy. This construct is closely related to belief in one's level of symptom control or helplessness. However, in contrast to perceptions of loss of control over symptoms, self-efficacy (SE) represents a belief that one can perform specific behaviors to achieve specific health-related goals. Thus, whereas loss of control as manifested in learned helplessness tends to represent a relatively consistent belief regarding a wide array of symptoms, an individual may vary with respect to SE beliefs concerning different behaviors. An individual with RA, for example, may have high SE for pacing her daily activities to reduce pain and fatigue, but she also may have low SE for performing water-based exercise to improve physical function (Lorig, Chastain, Ung et al., 1989).

The importance of SE is that it tends to predict pain and other dimensions of health status if individuals believe that the relevant behaviors will lead to improved health status (Bradley, 1994b). Indeed, it has been reported that high SE for pain is correlated with low frequencies of observable displays of pain behavior among patients with RA and FM even after controlling for demographic factors and disease activity (Buckelew et al., 1994; Buescher et al., 1991). Given these findings, current behavioral interventions for patients with rheumatic disease are designed to foster patients' development of high levels of SE for pain control through rehearsal of adaptive behaviors in the home, social, and work environments. Many of these adaptive behaviors may be considered as coping strategies.

Coping Strategies. *Coping* is defined as behaviors that are performed to manage environmental and internal demands (i.e., stressors and conflicts among them) that tax or exceed a person's resources (Bradley, 1994a, 1994b). The coping process consists of several stages. These are (a) appraisal of the threat associated with a particular stressor, (b) performing the adaptive behaviors or coping strategies that may control the effects of the stressor, and (c) evaluating the outcomes produced by these behaviors and, if necessary, performing alternative coping responses. It should be noted that coping strategies may be categorized as either direct action or palliative strategies (Burish & Bradley, 1983). Direct action strategies consist of behaviors that contribute to the removal of the stressor whereas palliative strategies are responses that diminish the negative impact of the stressor. For example, a patient with RA who experiences a flare in disease activity may seek treatment from her physician (direct action) and use relaxation or other cognitive distracters (palliative) to better control the impact of pain associated with the flare.

Numerous studies have been performed on the coping responses of patients with rheumatic disease. Three instruments have been used to evaluate coping among patients with these illnesses. The instruments are the Ways of Coping scale (Lazarus & Folkman, 1984), Coping Strategies Questionnaire or CSQ (Rosenstiel & Keefe, 1983), and the Vanderbilt Pain Management Inventory (Brown & Nicassio, 1987). Despite the variability in these instruments, there has been remarkable consistency in the findings reported across investigations and across disorders. For example, it has been shown repeatedly that passive coping strategies, such as catastrophizing (e.g., believing that if medication is not effective, no other coping strategy will effectively control pain and other symptoms) and escapist fantasies (e.g., hoping that pain will get better someday) are correlated with high levels of pain (Brown & Nicassio, 1987; Martin et al., 1996) and psychological distress (Keefe, Brown, Wallston et al., 1989; Martin et al., 1996) in patients with RA, OA, and FM. In addition, it recently has been found that catastrophizing among FM patients moderates the relationships between morning levels of pain intensity and evening levels of pain intensity, functional impairment, and fatigue severity (Aaron, Bradley, Alarcón, Alberts et al., 1997). That is, FM patients who produce relatively high scores on the CSQ measure of catastrophizing report stronger relationships between morning pain intensity and evening levels of pain, impairment, and fatigue than do patients who produce relatively low catastrophizing scores. However, catastrophizing does not moderate the relationships between morning pain levels and evening levels of depression, anxiety, and hassles. In contrast to the findings reported previously, psychological adjustment and relatively low levels of pain tend to be associated with strategies such as attempts to derive personal meaning from the illness experience, seeking information about arthritis, focusing on positive thoughts during pain episodes, and infrequent use of catastrophizing (e.g., Affleck, Urrows, Tennen et al., 1992).

BEHAVIORAL INTERVENTIONS FOR PAIN MANAGEMENT

Given the relationships that have been documented between pain and patients' beliefs and coping strategies, several behavioral interventions have been developed to alter patients' perceptions of control, SE beliefs, as well as their coping strategies and thereby improve pain and other health status variables. All of these interventions tend to share similar treatment components. These include education, training in relaxation and other coping skills, rehearsal of these newly learned skills in patients' home and work environments, and relapse prevention.

Education

The primary purposes of the educational component are to present a credible rationale for the treatment intervention, to elicit the active collaboration of patients and spouses or other caregivers with the therapist, and to help patients and spouses begin to alter negative perceptions regarding their abilities to manage the pain and other consequences of their disease. During this phase of treatment, it is especially important to encourage the patients and spouses to adopt the belief that they can learn the skills necessary to cope better with the patients' pain and other illness-related problems. This frequently may be facilitated through (a) discussions of the relationships among perceived uncontrollability of rheumatic disease symptoms, negative behavior (e.g., low adherence with medication regimes), and poor health status, and (b) demonstrations of the power of behavioral interventions such as relaxation to enhance control of these symptoms. In a behavioral intervention study performed with RA patients, the educational component comprised the first two treatment sessions. The therapists initiated the education component by discussing with the patients and their spouses the learned helplessness construct and the relationships between perceptions of helplessness and pain, depression, and functional disability (Bradley et al., 1987). Once the patients and spouses acknowledged the importance of those relationships in their experiences, the therapists described the major components of the behavioral intervention to them, and explained how the components of the intervention were designed to help the patients maintain better control of their pain, psychological reactions, and health-related behaviors. This was followed by a brief demonstration with the patients of the power of relaxation and deep breathing to temporarily reduce perceptions of stress and pain.

Coping Skills Training: Cognitive and Behavioral Rehearsal

The purpose of the coping skills–training component is to help patients and spouses engage actively in the process of learning new behaviors and cognitions that will help them better manage pain and other problems related to rheumatic disease. The purpose of the rehearsal component is to help patients and spouses practice and consolidate new pain management behaviors and cognitions, and to apply these effectively in their home and work environments.

The Bradley et al. (1987) intervention study featured 11 sessions of training in and rehearsal of three major coping skills. These skills were (a) progressive muscle relaxation training with relaxation imagery and deep breathing, (b) thermal biofeedback aimed at increasing skin temperature at joints affected by RA, and (c) behavioral goal setting by patients and spouses with reinforcements provided by the spouses and other family members following patients' displays of adaptive coping. For example, patients and spouses who reported fatigue as a problem frequently identified spending more time together in leisure activities as a behavioral goal. Therefore, these couples usually agreed to develop written daily time schedules for patients' activity and rest periods, in an attempt to reduce patients' fatigue behaviors and to create more opportunities for shared leisure activities. The rewards for following these time schedules often included verbal self-reinforcement, as well as allowing the patients to choose the leisure activities they desired.

Relapse Prevention

The purpose of this component is to help patients retain their newly learned coping skills and to avoid increases in pain or other unpleasant symptoms following treatment. Keefe and Van Horn (1993) have suggested that relapses among patients with rheumatic disease tend to occur when patients' symptoms begin to increase in intensity and their perceptions of symptoms control are diminished. Indeed, these circumstances can be expected to occur relatively often given the unpredictable courses of most of the rheumatic diseases. At these times, patients are likely to experience psychological distress, reduce their efforts to cope with their symptoms, and thus experience a relapse in pain, emotional distress, and functional ability. Relapse prevention training, then, is designed to help patients respond effectively to potential relapse situations. Specifically, training includes (a) identification of high-risk situations that are likely to tax patients' coping resources, (b) identification of the early signs of relapse, such as increases in pain or depression, (c) rehearsal of cognitive and behavioral skills for coping with these early relapse signs, and (d) provision of self-rewards for effective performance of coping responses to potential relapse.

The Bradley et al. (1987) intervention study devoted the final two sessions of the treatment protocol to relapse prevention. During these sessions, patients and their spouses discussed their beliefs and feelings regarding new problems they might encounter after the termination of the treatment intervention. These problems often were associated with possible increases in disease activity or disability with advancing age. Therefore, the therapists asked the patients and spouses to describe possible goals, behavioral strategies, and rewards for coping with their anticipated problems. The therapists also frequently encouraged them to use their newly learned skills to cope with problems unrelated to RA that they might confront in the future. It should be noted that 1-year follow-up analyses suggested that this relapse prevention component was effective in producing a sustained reduction in health care services usage but failed to maintain improvement in pain behavior (Young, Bradley, & Turner, 1995). Findings such as these have led Keefe and Van Horn (1993) to suggest that relapse prevention training should be introduced early in treatment and repeated throughout the protocol.

Outcomes Produced by Behavioral Interventions

Rheumatoid Arthritis. Bradley and colleagues (1987) produced one of the earliest studies of the effects of behavioral interventions on the pain behavior of patients with RA. The components of this intervention, which were described in preceding section, primarily emphasized training in progressive muscle relaxation, thermal biofeedback, and behavioral goal setting. It was found that, relative to a credible attention-placebo (i.e., social support group meetings) and no adjunct treatment conditions, the intervention produced significant reductions in patients' displays of pain behavior (e.g., guarded movement during walking) and number of painful or tender joints. Indeed, the joint count reduction produced by this relaxation-based therapy has been replicated by several other investigators (e.g., O'Leary, Shoor, Lorig et al., 1988). Moreover, during a 1-year follow-up period, patients who received the intervention reported significantly lower usage of outpatient health care services and incurred lower medical service costs than did patients in the other two study conditions (Young et al., 1995). The former patient group also reported significantly lower levels of pain intensity and depression than patients who received no adjunct treatment. However, posttreatment reductions in pain behavior and joint counts produced by the behavioral intervention were not maintained at 1-year follow-up.

Unpublished post hoc analyses of the data from this study suggested that treatment gains on all variables, including pain behavior and joint counts, were best maintained at follow-up by patients who reported good adherence with at least two of the major treatment components (i.e., relaxation, biofeedback, behavioral goal setting). Similar observations by other investigators have led to increased interest in improving relapse prevention among large numbers of patients who participate in behavioral treatment protocols. Indeed, a recent study of a stress management intervention that incorporated the relapse prevention procedures advocated by Keefe and Van Horn (1993) showed that, relative to attention-placebo and no adjunct treatment conditions, stress management produced significant improvements in RA patients' pain ratings, reports of helplessness, and coping strategy usage that persisted for 15 months following treatment (Parker, Smarr, Buckelew et al., 1995).

Osteoarthritis. Two investigations have examined the effects of a coping skills–training intervention on patients with OA of the knee (Keefe et al., 1990a, 1990b). This training program, relative to arthritis education and no adjunct treatment, produced significant reductions in patients' ratings of pain and psychological disability that generally were maintained at 6-month follow-up. The coping skills intervention also produced significant improvements in patients' reports of physical disability from posttreatment to follow-up.

The Arthritis Self-Management Program (ASMP) is a standardized intervention that is designed to enhance patients' perceptions of SE for pain, disability, and other arthritis symptoms. It has been evaluated primarily with large groups of patients with OA and RA. The most recent study of the effectiveness of the ASMP with these patients showed that it produced significant increases in SE for pain and other symptoms as well as significant reductions in pain ratings and arthritis-related physician visits that persisted up to 4 years after treatment (Lorig, Mazonson, & Holman, 1993).

Provision of behavioral counseling by telephone represents a new, inexpensive method for improving patients' health status. The first of these interventions, developed for patients with OA, reviewed educational information, medications, and clinical problems identified by the patients. Moreover, it taught them strategies for increasing their involvement in their encounters with their physicians (Weinberger et al., 1993). The intervention produced significant reductions in patients' reports of pain and functional ability and did not substantially increase their health care costs.

Recently, telephone-based counseling interventions have been tested with patients with RA and systemic lupus erythematosus (Maisiak, Austin, West, & Heck, 1996). However, the results produced by these interventions have not been uniformly positive. It remains to be determined, then, whether the promising initial results of telephone-based counseling can be consistently reproduced in OA patients as well as in patients with other rheumatic diseases.

Fibromyalgia. Bradley (1989) first suggested that behavioral interventions might prove to be beneficial for patients with FM. Since then, several investigators have produced studies of the outcomes produced by behavioral interventions with FM patients. Most of these investigators have reported that behavioral interventions produce significant reductions in patients' ratings of pain, other clinical symptoms, and functional disability as well as in pain behavior and pain thresholds at the tender points (Bennett et al., 1996; Bennett et al., 1991; Goldenberg, Kaplan, Nadeau et al., 1994; Nielson, Walker, & McCain, 1992; White & Nielson, 1995). However, none of these investigators employed attention-placebo comparison groups to control for the nonspecific effects of prolonged or frequent contact with concerned health professionals. Thus, it is not possible to attribute the treatment gains to the interventions, although it is promising that two studies found that patient improvements in observed pain behavior, reports of functional ability, and the tender point count were maintained for periods ranging from 6 to 30 months after treatment termination (Bennett et al., 1996; White & Nielson, 1995).

Three groups of investigators have performed controlled studies of behavioral treatments for patients with FM. Each group examined the effects of cognitive-behavioral interventions, which included electromyographic (EMG) biofeedback and/or relaxation training as well as training in coping strategies (Buckelew et al., in press; Nicassio, Rodojevic, Weisman et al., 1997; Vlaeyen et al., 1996). Vlaeyen and colleagues and Nicassio et al.

reported that patients who received behavioral intervention did not show greater improvements on any measure of pain or health status than patients who received education-based, attention-placebo intervention. It should be noted, however, that Vlaeyen et al. reported there was poor compliance among the behavioral condition patients with home practice of the pain control and coping skills; this intervention, then, may have failed to produce change because many patients did not attempt to fully learn these skills or to incorporate their use in their home and work environments. In contrast, the results reported by Nicassio et al. are perplexing as patients in both the behavioral and attention-placebo conditions showed improvement on several outcome measures. Therefore, it appears that the negative findings produced by this study may have been due to the unanticipated development of a powerful attention-placebo intervention.

Unlike the preceding investigators, Buckelew and colleagues (in press) compared the effects of brief (six sessions) behavioral intervention, exercise training, and a combination of the two treatments with an education-based, attention-placebo condition. At 2-year follow-up, all of the active treatments had produced significant improvements in a tender point index relative to the attention-placebo condition. Only exercise training and the combination of exercise and behavior therapy produced significant improvements in physical activity relative to attention-placebo. There were no other group differences on any measure of pain or health status. However, the investigators suggested that the effects of the behavioral and exercise interventions may have been enhanced if the treatments had not been limited to only six training sessions.

In summary, well-controlled studies of the effects of behavioral interventions for patients with FM have produced modest effects that generally are inferior to those produced by similar interventions for patients with RA and OA. It should be emphasized, however, that the potential power of behavioral intervention has not been adequately assessed with FM patients due to difficulties with patient compliance, inclusion of powerful attention-placebo interventions, and the use of training periods that were much shorter than those used for patients with RA (6 vs. 15) (Bradley et al., 1987; Buckelew et al., in press). These methodological problems must be resolved before the value of behavioral interventions for patients with FM may be accurately assessed.

Future Directions

Investigators recently have become interested in documenting abnormal functional brain activity, as measured by regional cerebral blood flow, in patients with chronic pain using neuroimaging methods such as positron emission tomography (PET) and single photon emission computed tomography (SPECT) (Mountz, Bradley, & Alarcón, in press). Several investigations have found evidence of decreased functional activity in the thalamus among patients with advanced cancer pain (Di Piero, Jones, Iannoti et al., 1991) and neuropathic pain (e.g., Iadarola, Max, Berman et al., 1995). One study has documented low levels of functional activity in both the thalamus and caudate nucleus among patients with FM (Mountz et al., 1995) (Table 13.2). This finding recently was replicated by a group of investigators in Australia (Kwiatek, Barnden, Rowe, & Pile, 1997). Mountz and colleagues have speculated that diminished functional activity in these brain structures may reflect impaired capacity to inhibit transmission of sensory information from ascending spinal afferents to the cortex or other brain structures. Therefore, some investigators have begun to examine whether pharamacologic and surgical interventions produce changes in functional brain activity that may mediate changes in pain perception (e.g., Di Piero et al., 1991). Similar studies currently are being performed with FM patients at the University of Alabama at Birmingham (Mountz et al., in press). It is anticipated that neuroimaging of functional brain activity will lead to new insights regarding altered pain perception among patients with RA and OA as well as those with FM. Moreover, neuroimaging may help us better understand the changes in brain function produced by interventions such as relaxation training and psychoactive medications that might mediate changes in patients' reports of pain.

TABLE 13.2

Mean (± SEM) Measures of Functional Brain Activity Assessed by Regional Cerebral Blood Flow (rCBF) in the Thalamus and Caudate Nucleus of Patients With Fibromyalgia (FM) and Healthy Controls

Location of rCBF Measurement	FM Patients	Controls	p
Right Thalamus	0.84 ± 0.04	1.05 ± 0.03	0.003
Left Thalamus	0.87 ± 0.05	1.04 ± 0.03	0.010
Right Caudate	0.77 ± 0.03	0.88 ± 0.02	0.020
Left Caudate	0.77 ± 0.04	0.90 ± 0.02	0.010

Note. From Mountz et al. (1995). A detailed description of the semiquantitative methods used to measure functional brain activity is provided in the article just cited. Briefly, rCBF is obtained by high-resolution SPECT imaging in the Picker prism (Triple-head) Anger Gamma Camera after injection of 30 mCi of Technetium-99m HMPAO tracer. A precise coregistration method allows translation of regions of interest from both the thalamus and caudate anatomic structure identified by an MRI scan to the correct thalamus and caudate region on the SPECT scan of rCBF. The numerical values shown in Table 13.2 represent the average counts per pixel in the caudate or thalamic regions of interest normalized to the average counts per pixel in a midcerebellar slice. Using the coregistration method, all of these regions can be accurately and consistently defined in the patients and in controls such that comparable and nonsubjective, semiquantitative measures of rCBF are used in the analysis.

Conclusions

This review has shown there are strong relationships between psychosocial factors and pain perceptions as well as pain behaviors in patients with rheumatic disease. Factors that tend to increase pain include the presence of depression and anxiety, stress, sleep disturbances, and maladaptive pain beliefs or coping strategies such as perceived helplessness or catastrophizing. In contrast, relatively adaptive pain beliefs, such as perceived SE, tend to be associated with lower levels of pain. These findings have led investigators to devote considerable effort to studying the effects of behavioral interventions on pain and other symptoms among patients with RA, OA, and FM.

These studies have produced consistent evidence that behavioral interventions produce significant reductions in ratings of pain and psychological distress among patients with RA and OA. The small number of well-controlled intervention studies performed with FM patients generally have not produced positive results. However, resolution of methodological problems in this area of the behavioral intervention literature may produce improved outcomes for FM patients.

It is anticipated that four issues will receive greater attention from investigators during the next 5 years. First, greater emphasis will be devoted to the prevention of relapse among patients following behavioral treatment. Second, increased attention will be focused on documenting treatment-related reductions in health care usage and other costs of chronic pain in addition to changes in patients' reports of symptoms. Third, special attention will be devoted to the development and evaluation of "minimal" interventions, such as telephone-based counseling therapies, that may contribute to health care cost savings. Finally, it is expected that investigators will devote particular attention to treatment-related alterations in brain function that may mediate changes in patients' perceptions of pain. The latter development will certainly strengthen the development of biopsychosocial models of and interventions for chronic pain in patients with rheumatic disease.

ACKNOWLEDGMENTS

The research in this chapter was supported by National Institute of Arthritis, Musculoskeletal and Skin Diseases Grants 1RO1-AR-43136-04 and PO-AR-20164, National Center for Research Resources Grant 5-MO1-00032, and grants from the American Fibromyalgia Syndrome Association.

REFERENCES

Aaron, L. A., Bradley, L. A., Alarcón, G. S., Alberts, K. R., Martin, M. Y., & Sotolongo, A. (1997). Catastrophizing is a specific moderator of daily pain and health status in patients with fibromyalgia (FMS). *Arthritis and Rheumatism, 40,* S129.

Aaron, L. A., Bradley, L. A., Alarcón, G. S., Alexander, R. W., Alexander, M. T., Martin, M. Y., & Alberts, K. R. (1996). Psychiatric diagnoses are related to health care seeking behavior rather than illness in fibromyalgia. *Arthritis and Rheumatism, 39,* 436–445.

Aaron, L. A., Bradley, L. A., Alarcón, G. S., Triana-Alexander, M., Alexander, R. W., Martin, M. Y., & Alberts, K. R. (1997). Perceived physical and emotional trauma as precipitating events in fibromyalgia: Associations with health care seeking and disability status but not pain severity. *Arthritis and Rheumatism, 40,* 453–460.

Aaron, L. A., Bradley, L. A., Alexander, M. T., Alexander, R. W., Alberts, K. R., Martin, M. Y., & Alarcón, G. S. (1997). Work stress, psychiatric history, and medication usage predict initial use of medical treatment for fibromyalgia symptoms: A prospective analysis. In T. S. Jensen, J. A. Turner, & Z. Weisenfeld-Hallin (Eds.), *Proceedings of the 8th World Congress on Pain: Progress in pain research and management* (Vol. 5, pp. 683–691). Seattle: IASP Press.

Affleck, G., Tennen, H., Pfeiffer, C., & Fifield, J. (1987). Appraisals of control and predictability in adapting to a chronic disease. *Journal of Personality and Social Psychology, 53,* 273–279.

Affleck, G., Tennen, H., Urrows, S. et al. (1992). Neuroticism and the pain-mood relation in rheumatoid arthritis: Insights from a prospective daily study. *Journal of Consulting Clinical Psychology, 60,* 119–126.

Affleck, G., Urrows, S., Tennen, H., & Higgins, P. (1992). Daily coping with pain from rheumatoid arthritis: Patterns and correlates. *Pain, 51,* 221–230.

Ahles, T. A., Khan, S., Yunus, M. B., Spiegel, D. A., & Masi, A. T. (1991). Psychiatric status of patients with primary fibromyalgia, patients with rheumatoid arthritis, and subjects without pain: A blind comparison of *DSM–III* diagnoses. *American Journal of Psychiatry, 148,* 1721–1726.

Alexander, R. W., Bradley, L. A., Alarcón, G. S., Triana-Alexander, M., Aaron, L. A., Alberts, K. R., Martin, M. Y., & Stewart, K. E. (1998). Sexual and physical abuse is associated with outpatient health care utilization and pain medication usage in women with fibromyalgia. *Arthritis Care and Research, 11,* 102–115.

Bagge, E., Bjelle, A., Eden, S., & Svanborg, A. (1991). Osteoarthritis in the elderly: Clinical and radiographic findings in 79–85 year olds. *Annals of the Rheumatic Diseases, 50,* 535–539.

Bennett, R. M., Burckhardt, C. S., Clark, S. R., O'Reilly, C. A., Wiens, A., & Campbell, S. M. (1996). Group treatment of fibromyalgia: A 6 month outpatient program. *Journal of Rheumatology, 23,* 521–528.

Bennett, R. M., Campbell, S., Burckhardt, C., Clark, S., O'Reilly, C., & Weins, A. (1991). Balanced approach provides small but significant gains: A multidiscplinary approach to fibromyalgia management. *Journal of Musculoskeletal Medicine, 8,* 21–32.

Blalock, S. J., DeVellis, R. F., Brown, G. K., & Wallston, K. A. (1989). Validity of the Center for Epidemiologic Studies—Depression scale in arthritis populations. *Arthritis and Rheumatism, 32,* 991–997.

Bradley, L. A. (1985). Psychological aspects of arthritis. *Bulletin on the Rheumatic Diseases, 35,* 1–12.

Bradley, L. A. (1989). Cognitive-behavioral therapy for primary fibromyaglia. *Journal of Rheumatology, 16*(Suppl.), 131–136.

Bradley, L. A. (1994a). Behavioral interventions for managing chronic pain. *Bulletin on the Rheumatic Diseases, 43,* 2–5.

Bradley, L. A. (1994b). Psychological dimensions of rheumatoid arthritis. In F. Wolfe & T. Pincus (Eds.), *Rheumatoid arthritis: Critical issues in etiology, assessment, prognosis, and therapy* (pp. 273–295). New York: Marcel Dekker.

Bradley, L. A. (1996). Pain. In S. T. Wegener, B. L. Belza, & E. P. Gall (Eds.), *Clinical care in the rheumatic diseases* (pp. 111–115). Atlanta: American College of Rheumatology.

Bradley, L. A., & Alarcón, G. S. (1997). Fibromyalgia. In W. J. Koopman (Ed.), *Arthritis and allied conditions* (13th ed., pp. 1619–1640). New York: Lippincott.

Bradley, L. A., Young, L. D., Anderson, K. O., Turner, R. A., Agudelo, C. A., McDaniel, L. K., Pisko, E. J., Semble, E. L., & Morgan, T. M. (1987). Effects of psychological therapy on pain behavior of rheumatoid arthritis patients: Treatment outcome and six-month follow-up. *Arthritis and Rheumatism, 30,* 1105–1114.

Brown, G. K., & Nicassio, P. M. (1987). Development of a questionnaire for the assessment of active and passive coping strategies in chronic pain patients. *Pain, 31,* 53–64.

Buckelew, S. P., Conway, R., Parker, J., Deuser, W. E., Read, J., Jennings, J., Witty, T. E. Hewett, J. E., Minor, M., Johnson, J. C., Van Mole, L., McIntosh, M. J., Nigh, M., & Kay, D. R. (1998). Biofeedback/relaxation training and exercise interventions for fibromyalgia: A prospective trial. *Arthritis Care and Research, 11,* 196–209.

Buckelew, S. P., Parker, J. C., Keefe, F. J., Deuser, W. E., Crews, T. M., Conway, R., Kay, D. R., & Hewett, J. E. (1994). Self-efficacy and pain behavior among subjects with fibromyalgia. *Pain, 59,* 377–384.

Buescher, K. L., Johnston, J. A., Parker, J. C., Smarr, K. L., Buckelew, S. P., Anderson, S. K., & Walker, S. E. (1991). Relationship of self-efficacy to pain behavior. *Journal of Rheumatology, 18,* 968–972.

Burish, T. G., & Bradley, L. A. (1983). Coping with chronic disease: Definitions and issues. In T. G. Burish & L. A. Bradley (Eds.), *Coping with chronic disease: Research and applications* (pp. 3–12). New York: Academic Press.

Carette, S., Oakson, G., Guimont, C., & Steriade, M. (1995). Sleep electroencephalography and the clinical response to amitriptyline in patients with fibromyalgia. *Arthritis and Rheumatism, 38,* 1211–1217.

Chikanza, I. C., Petrou, P., Kingsley, G. et al. (1992). Defective hypothalamic response to immune and inflammatory stimuli in patients with rheumatoid arthritis. *Arthritis and Rheumatism, 35,* 1281–1288.

Clarke, A. E., Esdaile, J. M., Bloch, D. A., Lacaille, D., Danoff, D. S., & Fries, J. F. (1993). A Canadian study of the total medical costs for patients with systemic lupus erythematosus and the predictors of costs. *Arthritis and Rheumatism, 36,* 1548–1559.

Crofford, L. F., Pillemer, S. R., Kalogeras, K. T., Cash, J. M., Michelson, D., Kling, M. A., Sternberg, E. M., Gold, P. W., Chrousos, G. P., & Wilder, R. L. (1994). Hypothalamic-pituitary-adrenal axis perturbations in patients with fibromyalgia. *Arthritis and Rheumatism, 37,* 1583–1592.

Dexter, P., & Brandt, K. (1994). Distribution and predictors of depressive symptoms in osteoarthritis. *Journal of Rheumatology, 21,* 279–286.

Deyo, R. A., Inui, T. S., Leininger, J., & Overman, S. (1982). Physical and psychosocial function in rheumatoid arthritis: Clinical use of a self-administered health status instrument. *Archives of Internal Medicine, 142,* 879–882.

Di Piero, V., Jones, A. K. P., Iannotti, F. et al. (1991). Chronic pain: A PET study of the central effects of percutaneous high cervical cordotomy. *Pain, 46,* 9–12.

Felts, W., & Yelin, E. H. (1989). The economic impact of the rheumatic diseases in the United States. *Journal of Rheumatology, 16,* 867–884.

Frank, R. G., Beck, N. C., Parker, J. C., Kashami, J. H., Elliott, T. R., Haw, A. E., Smith, E., Alwood, C., Brownlee-Duffeck, M., & Kay, D. R. (1988). Depression in rheumatoid arthritis. *Journal of Rheumatology, 15,* 920–929.

Frank, R. G., & Hagglund, K. J. (1996). Mood disorders. In S. T. Wegener, B. L. Belza, & E. P. Gall (Eds.), *Clinical care in the rheumatic diseases* (pp. 125–130). Atlanta: American College of Rheumatology.

Garber, J., & Seligman, M. E. P. (Eds.). (1980). *Human helplessness: Theory and applications.* New York: Academic Press.

Goldenberg, D. L., Kaplan, K. H., Nadeau, M. G., Brodeur, C., Smith, S., & Schmid, C. H. (1994). A controlled study of a stress-reduction, cognitive-behavioral treatment program in fibromyalgia. *Journal of Musculoskeletal Pain, 2,* 53–66.

Harringon, L., Affleck, G., Urrows, S., Tennen, H., Higgins, P., Zautra, A., & Hoffman, S. (1993). Temporal covariation of soluble interleukin-2 receptor levels, daily stress, and disease activity in rheumatoid arthritis. *Arthritis and Rheumatism, 36,* 199–203.

Hawley, D. J., & Wolfe, J. (1988). Anxiety and depression in patients with rheumatoid arthritis: A prospective study of 400 patients. *Journal of Rheumatology, 15,* 932–941.

Hudson, J. I., Goldenberg, D. L., Pope, H. G., Keck, P. E., & Schlesinger, L. (1992). Comorbidity of fibromyalgia with medical and psychiatric disorders. *American Journal of Medicine, 92,* 363–367.

Hudson, J. I., Hudson, M. S., Pliner, L. F., Goldenberg, D. L., & Pope, H. G. (1985). Fibromyalgia and major affective disorder: A controlled phenomenology and family history study. *American Journal of Psychiatry, 142,* 441–446.

Iadarola, M. J., Max, M. G., Berman, K. F., Byas-Smith, M. G., Coghill, R. C., Gracely, R. H., & Bennett, G. J. (1995). Unilateral decrease in thalamic activity observed with positron emission tomography in patients with chronic neuropathic pain. *Pain, 63,* 55–64.

Katz, P. P., & Yelin, E. H. (1993). Prevalence and correlates of depressive symptoms among persons with rheumatoid arthritis. *Journal of Rheumatology, 20,* 790–796.

Kazis, L. E., Meenan, R. F., & Anderson, J. J. (1983). Pain in the rheumatic diseases: Investigation of a key health status component. *Arthritis and Rheumatism, 26,* 1017–1022.

Keefe, F. J., Brown, G. K., Wallston, K. A., & Caldwell, D. S. (1989). Coping with rheumatoid arthritis pain: Catastrophizing as a maladaptive strategy. *Pain, 37,* 51–56.

Keefe, F. J., Caldwell, D. S., Williams, D. A., Gil, K. M., Mitchell, D., Robertson, C., Martinez, S., Nunley, J., Beckham, J. C., Crisson, J. E., & Helms, M. (1990a). Pain coping skills training in the management of osteoarthritic knee pain: A comparative study. *Behavior Therapy, 21,* 49–62.

Keefe, F. J., Caldwell, D. S., Williams, D. A., Gil, K. M., Mitchell, D., Robertson, C., Martinez, S., Nunley, J., Beckham, J. C., Crisson, J. E., & Helms, M. (1990b). Pain coping skills training in the management of osteoarthritic knee pain: II. Follow-up results. *Behavior Therapy, 21,* 435–447.

Keefe, F. J., & Van Horn, Y. (1993). Cognitive-behavioral treatment of rheumatoid arthritis pain: Maintaining treatment gains. *Arthritis Care and Research, 6,* 213–222.

Koopman, W. J. (Ed.). (1997). *Arthritis and allied conditions* (13th ed.). New York: Lippincott.

Kwiatek, R., Barnden, K., Rowe, C., & Pile, K. (1997). Pontine tegmental regional cerebral blood flow (rCBF) is reduced in fibromyalgia. *Arthritis and Rheumatism, 40,* S43.

Lazarus, R. S., & Folkman, S. (1984). *Stress, appraisal, and coping.* New York: Springer.

Liang, M. H., Larson, M., Thompson, M. et al. (1984). Costs and outcomes in rheumatoid arthritis and osteoarthritis. *Arthritis and Rheumatism, 27,* 522–529.

Liang, M. H., Rogers, M., Larson, M. et al. (1984). The psychosocial impact of systemic lupus erythematosus and rheumatoid arthritis. *Arthritis and Rheumatism, 27,* 13–19.

Lorig, K., Chastain, R. L., Ung, E., Shoor, S., & Holman, H. R. (1989). Development and evaluation of a scale to measure perceived self-efficacy in people with arthritis. *Arthritis and Rheumatism, 32,* 37–44.

Lorig, K. R., Mazonson, P. D., & Holman, H. R. (1993). Evidence suggesting that health education for self-management in patients with chronic arthritis has sustained health benefits while reducing health care costs. *Arthritis and Rheumatism, 36,* 439–446.

Lorish, C. D., Abraham, N., Austin, J., Bradley, L. A., & Alarcón, G. S. (1991). Disease and psychosocial factors related to physical functioning in rheumatoid arthritis patients. *Journal of Rheumatology, 18,* 1150–1157.

Maisiak, R., Austin, J. S., West, S. G., & Heck, L. (1996). The effect of person-centered counseling on the psychological status of persons with systemic lupus erythematosus or rheumatoid arthritis: A randomized controlled trial. *Arthritis Care and Research, 9,* 60–66.

Martin, M. Y., Bradley, L. A., Alexander, R. W., Alarcón, G. S., Triana-Alexander, M., Aaron, L. A., & Alberts, K. R. (1996). Coping strategies predict disability in fibromyalgia. *Pain, 68,* 45–53.

Moldofsky, H. (1986). Sleep and musculoskeletal pain. *American Journal of Medicine, 81*(Suppl. 3A), 85–89.

Moldofsky, H., & Scarisbrick, P. (1976). Induction of neurasthenic musculoskeletal pain syndrome by selective sleep stage deprivation. *Psychosomatic Medicine, 38,* 35–44.

Mountz, J. M., Bradley, L. A., & Alarcón, G. S. (in press). Abnormal functional activity of the central nervous system in fibromyalgia syndrome. *American Journal of Medical Sciences.*

Mountz, J. M., Bradley, L. A., Modell, J. J., Alexander, R. W., Triana-Alexander, M., Martin, M. Y., & Alberts, K. R. (1995). Fibromyalgia in women: Alterations of regional cerebral blood flow in the thalamus and caudate nucleus are associated with low pain threshold levels. *Arthritis and Rheumatism, 38,* 926–938.

Nicassio, P. M., Padojevic, V., Weisman, M. H., Schuman, C., Kim, J., Schoenfeld-Smith, T., & Kral, T. (1997). A comparison of behavioral and educational interventions with fibromyalgia. *Journal of Rheumatology, 24,* 2000–2007.

Nielson, W., Walker, G., & McCain, G. A. (1992). Cognitive-behavioral treatment of fibromyalgia syndrome: Preliminary findings. *Journal of Rheumatology, 19,* 98–103.

O'Leary, A., Shoor, S., Lorig, K., & Holman, H. R. (1988). A cognitive-behavioral treatment for rheumatoid arthritis. *Health Psychology, 7,* 527–544.

Parker, J., Smarr, K., Anderson, S., Hewett, J., Walker, S., Bridges, A., & Caldwell, W. (1992). Relationship of changes in helplessness and depression to disease activity in rheumatoid arthritis. *Journal of Rheumatology, 19,* 1901–1905.

Parker, J. C., Smarr, K. L., Buckelew, S. P., Sturky-Ropp, R. C., Hewett, J. E., Johnson, J. C., Wright, G. E., Irvin, W. S., & Walker, S. E. (1995). Effects of stress management on clinical outcomes in rheumatoid arthritis. *Arthritis and Rheumatism, 38,* 1807–1818.

Parker, J. C., Smarr, K. L., Walker, S. E. et al. (1991). Biopsychosocial parameters of disease activity in rheumatoid arthritis: A prospective study of 400 patients. *Arthritis Care Res, 4,* 73–80.

Pincus, T. (1996). Rheumatoid arthritis. In S. T. Wegener, B. L. Belza, & E. P. Gall (Eds.), *Clinical care in the rheumatic diseases* (pp. 147–155). Atlanta: American College of Rheumatology.

Pincus, T., Mitchell, J., & Burkhauser, R. V. (1989). Substantial work disability and earnings losses in individuals less than age 65 with osteoarthritis: Comparisons with rheumatoid arthritis. *Journal of Clinical Epidemiology, 42,* 449–457.

Robins, L. N., Helzer, J. E., Croughan, J., & Ratcliff, K. S. (1981). National Institute of Mental Health Diagnostic Interview Schedule. *Archives of General Psychiatry, 38,* 381–389.

Rosenstiel, A. K., & Keefe, F. J. (1983). The use of coping strategies in chronic low back pain patients: Relationship to patient characteristics and current adjustment. *Pain, 17,* 33–44.

Smith, T. W., Peck, J. R., & Ward, J. R. (1990). Helplessness and depression in rheumatoid arthritis. *Health Psychology, 9,* 377–389.

Stein, C. M., Griffin, M. R., & Brandt, K. D. (1996). Osteoarthritis. In S. T. Wegener, B. L. Belza, & E. P. Gall (Eds.), *Clinical care in the rheumatic diseases* (pp. 177–182). Atlanta: American College of Rheumatology.

Summers, M. N., Haley, W. E., Reveille, J. D., & Alarcón, G. S. (1988). Radiographic assessment and psychologic variables as predictors of pain and functional impairment in osteoarthritis of the knee or hip. *Arthritis and Rheumatism, 31,* 204–209.

Tennen, H., Affleck, G., Urrows, S., Higgins, P., & Mendola, R. (1992). Perceiving control, construing benefits, and daily processes in rheumatoid arthritis. *Canadian Journal of Behav Sci, 24,* 186–203.

Vlaeyen, J. W. S., Teeken-Gruben, N. J. G., Goosens, M. E. J. B., Rutten-van Molken, M. P. M. H., Pelt, R. A. G. B., van Eek, H., & Heuts, P. H. T. G. (1991). Cognitive-educational treatment of fibromyalgia: A randomized clinical trial: I. Clinical effects. *Journal of Rheumatology, 23,* 1237–1245.

Wegener, S. T. (1996). Sleep disturbance. In S. T. Wegener, B. L. Belza, & E. P. Gall (Eds.), *Clinical care in the rheumatic diseases* (pp. 121–124). Atlanta: American College of Rheumatology.

Weigent, D. A., Bradley, L. A., Blalock, J. E., & Alarcón, G. S. (in press). Current concepts in the pathophysiology of abnormal pain perception in fibromyalgia. *American Journal of Medical Sciences.*

Weinberger, M., Tierney, W. M., Cowper, P. A., Katz, B. P., & Booher, P. A. (1993). Cost-effectiveness of increased telephone contacts for patients with osteoarthritis: A randomized controlled trial. *Arthritis and Rheumatism, 36,* 243–246.

White, K. P., & Nielson, W. R. (1995). Cognitive behavioral treatment of fibromyalgia syndrome: A follow-up assessment. *Journal of Rheumatology, 22,* 717–721.

Yelin, E. (1992). Arthritis: The cumulative impact of a common chronic condition. *Arthritis and Rheumatism, 35,* 489–497.

Yelin, E., Feshbach, D. M., Meenan, R. F., & Epstein, W. (1979). Social problems, services, and policy for persons with chronic disease: The case of rheumatoid arthritis. *Soc Sci Med, 13,* 13–20.

Young, L. D., Bradley, L. A., & Turner, R. A. (1995). Decreases in health care resource utilization in patients with rheumatoid arthritis following a cognitive-behavioral intervention. *Biofeedback and Self-Regulation, 20,* 259–268.

Neurological Conditions

Chapter 14

Headache

Edwin F. Kremer
James Hudson
Thomas Schreiffer
Headache Rehabilitation Program
Mary Free Bed Hospital and Rehabilitation Center

Headaches comprise the second most prevalent chronic, nonmalignant pain problem in the general population (Sternbach, 1986). The majority of headache patients perform some type of self-care that may include avoidance of stress, missed time from work, curtailment of activities of daily living, or use of nonprescription medications. As Rasmussen and Olesen (1996) have noted, there are now several studies documenting that only a minority of headache sufferers ever seek medical treatment. Even so, headache complaint still comprises over 18 million office visits per year for diagnosis and treatment (Stewart & Lipton, 1993).

Migraines, tension-type, and mixed headache comprise the vast majority of headache sufferers (Rasmussen & Olesen, 1992). This chapter focuses on these three headache patient populations as they are the most likely to comprise clinical case load. The less common headaches, such as cluster headache, temporal arteritis, and so on, are addressed in several comprehensive headache texts (e.g., Dalessio & Silberstein, 1993; Diamond & Dalessio, 1992; Olesen, Tfelt-Hansen, & Welch, 1993).

The focus of the present chapter is on the multidisciplinary behavioral care of the headache patient. Despite a rich literature attesting to the efficacy of pharmacologic (Holroyd, Penzien, & Cordingley, 1991) as well as behavioral (Blanchard, 1992) treatment of headache, many patients continue to suffer with their head pain. This would suggest that headache is multidetermined. Successful headache resolution then would seem to require comprehensive treatment. Moreover, as at least some headache variables are interactive, multidisciplinary treatment would necessarily be delivered in a coordinated or programmatic manner. Multidisciplinary treatment of pain is by no means a novel concept. Fordyce (1976) proposed programmatic behavioral treatment for chronic musculoskeletal pain, and that approach has developed over the past two decades to essentially constitute the standard of care. Also, multidisciplinary programmatic care has been available for headache for at least as many years (Freitag, 1992), but these programs, although offering behavioral interventions, have tended to heavily emphasize pharmacologic therapies.

The specific design of this chapter is to briefly review conventional headache treatment in terms of pharmacologic and behavioral interventions, to discuss their relative efficacy, and finally, to describe behavioral programmatic care, its efficacy, and long-term results.

PHARMACOLOGIC MANAGEMENT OF HEADACHE

Headache treatment typically begins with medication. Although some physicians offer at least brief counseling regarding diet and lifestyle changes, most rely on medication as their initial and primary approach to the headache patient (Becker et al., 1988; Von Korff, Galer, & Stang, 1995). No definite rules govern whom and how to treat. This decision is based largely on the physician's bias and the patient's wishes. Some patients do not require or desire treatment with medication. Some merely seek reassurance that their headaches are not indicative of a serious underlying problem such as brain tumor or aneurysm. Others begin headache treatment by making appropriate diet and lifestyle changes. A smaller number prefer nonpharmacologic treatment such as biofeedback, relaxation training, or physical therapy. Most headache patients, however, leave the office with a prescription or recommendation for some sort of medication.

These medicines fall into three broad groups—preventative, abortive, and symptomatic. Preventative medication, taken on a daily basis, reduces headache frequency and intensity by blocking physiologic events that putatively lead to headache. Abortive therapy, taken as needed only when acute headaches occur, decreases headache severity by blocking or even reversing the neurogenic and vascular mechanisms that may lead to headache. Symptomatic therapy, taken as needed during acute or chronic headaches, seeks to dull headache pain with analgesics until the headache resolves in its own time. Many drugs fall neatly into one of these three categories. Others employ more than one mechanism of action. The distinction between abortive and symptomatic treatment strategies is often blurred. Drugs from more than one of these categories may be used in the same patient. For example, a preventative medication may be prescribed for a patient and, in addition, an abortive agent given for those headaches that still occur despite headache prophylaxis.

Symptomatic Treatment

Whether prescribed by a physician or obtained over the counter, symptomatic medications represent the most common approach to migraine treatment. The potency of these analgesics varies from mild (aspirin, acetaminophen) to marked (hydrocodone, meperidine). These diverse agents are united by their ability to relieve headache intensity without necessarily addressing the underlying mechanisms causing the headache. Symptomatic medications may be used alone or in combination with other symptomatic, abortive, or prophylactic agents. Although a detailed description of all symptomatic therapies is not practical, a few representative agents are discussed further.

Acetominophen may be effective in mild headaches, particularly if taken early. Low cost, ready availability, and relative safety are its greatest advantages. Acetaminophen is limited by its lack of effect for more severe headaches as well as the risk for hepatotoxicity at higher doses.

Nonsteroidal anti-inflammatory drugs (NSAIDS) enjoy a reputation for being more effective than acetaminophen (Continuum, 1995). This increased efficacy is due not only to their analgesic properties but also to their ability to inhibit prostaglandin synthesis, platelet aggregation, and subsequent serotonin release (Diamond & Freitag, 1989). No one NSAID preparation has demonstrated clear superiority for headache treatment, and there is wide individual variation in response to NSAIDS (Elkind, 1996). Ibuprofen's low cost and over-the-counter availability make it a popular choice. Naproxen and Indocin have traditionally been two of the most commonly studied drugs for migraine treatment. NSAID use may be limited by its gastrointestinal toxicity.

When used properly, oral narcotic analgesics such as propoxyphene, codeine, and butalbital are highly effective for the treatment of acute headaches. Although nausea, drowsiness, and cognitive dysfunction are the most common side effects, of great concern for the physician is their addictive potential. This risk is minimized by allowing their use no more than 2 to 3 days a week. More frequent use not only increases the risk of addiction and tolerance but also may lead to rebound headaches (Kudrow, 1982). Similar precautions are required with using intranasal opiods such as butorphanol nasal spray.

Abortive Treatment

Although symptomatic medications may be useful for headaches no matter what their etiology, the use of abortive medication is limited to migrainous-type headaches. Abortive therapy may be used alone or in combination with symptomatic or preventative treatments. For most agents, abortive therapy is most effective when instituted at the onset of headache. This creates two problems. The first is that patients must carry their medicine with them at all times or risk initiating abortive treatment too late for any relief. This is not as great a problem for oral medications as it is for injectables and suppositories requiring refrigeration or other special handling. Second, when faced with a small headache, the eventual severity of which cannot be predicted, patients are faced with a difficult choice. Delaying treatment until the headache is severe may render the abortive medication ineffective. Consequently, some opt to treat even mild headaches early to prevent the chance that they will get severe. As a result, some headaches are treated abortively even though, left alone, they might never have gotten severe enough to require treatment. This indiscriminate use of abortive medications often leads to rebound headaches (Saper, 1987).

An exhaustive listing of all abortive headache medicines is beyond the scope of this chapter, but a few representative medicines are discussed. Ergotamine preparations have historically been among the most commonly used abortive agents. Although ergotamines are best known for their vasoconstrictor effect, their ability to abort migraine may arise more from their action as a 5-hydroxytryptamine$_1$ (5-HT$_1$) receptor agonist. Ergotamines offer many advantages over other abortive agents. They are generally effective if taken at the onset of headache. Several different routes of administration are available, including oral tablets, sublingual tablets, and suppositories. Their cost may be considerably less than that of some newer medications, an advantage under managed care.

Ergotamines are limited primarily by their inability to provide relief of headaches that have been present several hours. Many patients also require concurrent antiemetics, given the propensity of ergotamines to cause nausea. Ergotamines are contraindicated in patients with coronary or peripheral arterial disease, uncontrolled hypertension, and in pregnancy. They should not be administered within 24 hours of sumatriptan. Overuse of ergotamines may lead to tolerance and rebound headaches. To avoid this, ergotamine use should be restricted to no more than 2 days in a week.

In addition to the role in symptomatic treatment of headaches, NSAIDS display efficacy in the abortive treatment of migraine. NSAIDS offer several advantages over ergotamines. They typically do not cause nausea and may be used in some patients (those at risk for vascular disease) where ergotamines are contraindicated. NSAIDS are also less likely to cause rebound headaches than ergotamines. Because of their analgesic effect, NSAIDS may provide some relief even when administered hours after headache onset. NSAID use is limited primarily by gastrointestinal side effects, most notably gastritis and ulcers. Intranasal lidocaine 4% has enjoyed recent publicity for its role in migraine treatment (Maizels, Scott, Cohen, & Chen, 1996). Advantages of intranasal lidocaine include its rapid onset of action, absence of clinically important adverse effects, and low cost. Disadvantages include a response rate of only 55% and a significant relapse rate of 42%.

No discussion of abortive medication would be complete without mention of sumatriptan. Available in both injectable and oral tablet form, sumatriptan is one of the most effective medications for the treatment of acute migraine headaches. This effectiveness relates to sumatriptan's action as a selective 5-HT$_1$ receptor agonist. Not only does sumatriptan provide significant improvement of headaches in 70% of patients with migraine, it also helps relieve migraine-induced nausea and photophobia. Unlike other abortive agents, sumatriptan may be effective even when administered later in the course of the headache.

Given orally, sumatriptan's most common side effect is tingling. Injectable sumatriptan may cause transient tightness in the neck, jaw, and chest. Neither preparation should be used in patients with complicated migraine. Likewise, sumatriptan is contraindicated during pregnancy and in those with uncontrolled hypertension or who are at risk for ischemic heart disease. Rebound headaches can be avoided by limiting its use to no more than 2 days in a week. Sumatriptan's expense limits its use in the underinsured and in some managed care settings.

Preventative Therapy

Preventative therapy may benefit those whose headaches are too frequent or severe to be controlled with abortive or symptomatic medicines. A frequently quoted guideline is that those with two or more headaches a month should be considered for prophylactic treatment. However, oftentimes patients with more frequent headaches decline preventative treatment whereas some with less frequent, but more intense, headaches welcome it. Prophylactic therapy requires a committed patient because compliance is far more important in preventative strategies than in abortive or symptomatic.

A myriad of medication choices faces the patient who requests preventative treatment. As with abortive and symptomatic therapy, a medication's perceived effectiveness and side effects are of paramount importance in the physician's recommendation and the patient's acceptance. A third factor influencing physician prescribing practice is the opportunity to treat comorbid conditions. In the migraineur with hypertension, for example, beta-blockers or calcium channel blockers offer the opportunity to treat both conditions with one drug. Tricyclic antidepressants are useful for treatment of migraine coexisting with insomnia or depression. Valproate is an ideal drug for patients where seizures and migraine are comorbid.

As with symptomatic and abortive treatment, no single preventative agent works for everyone. Sometimes effective prophylaxis is obtained only after the third or fourth medication is tried, testing the perseverance of both physician and patient. A minimum of 4 to 6 weeks' treatment is required before a medicine should be considered ineffective. Sometimes a combination of drugs that work by different mechanisms, for example, a beta-blocker and tricyclic antidepressant, may work better together than either drug individually.

Beta-blockers are the most commonly prescribed class of drug for migraine prophylaxis, producing a 50% reduction in headache frequency in 60% to 80% of migraine patients (Andersson & Vinge, 1990; Continuum, 1995). Proposed mechanisms of action include inhibition of arterial dilation and decrease in platelet aggregation and adhesion (Diamond, 1991). Although controlled studies have demonstrated that propranolol, metoprolol, timolol, nadolol, and atenolol are all effective in migraine prophylaxis, only propranolol and timolol are FDA approved for this indication. The relative efficacy of these various beta-blockers for migraine prophylaxis is not established (Continuum, 1995). Common side effects of beta-blockers include fatigue, lightheadedness, sleep disturbance, and cognitive dysfunction. Their use is contraindicated in patients with asthma and Raynaud's disease, and they should be used with caution in patients with congestive heart failure, bradycardia, brittle diabetes, and depression. If migraine prophylaxis fails with an adequate dose of one beta-blocker, switching to a different beta-blocker is usually ineffective (Elkind, 1996).

Tricyclic antidepressants (TCAs) are widely used for the treatment of migraine, tension-type headaches, and mixed headache syndromes. Their efficacy is similar to that of beta-blockers (Ziegler et al., 1987). The precise mechanism of their antimigraine effect is uncertain, but believed to be relatively independent of their antidepressant effect (Martscci, Monna, & Agnoli, 1985). Amitriptyline, nortriptyline, and doxepin are among the most commonly used TCAs for migraine prophylaxis. TCA use is often limited by side effects including sedation, dry mouth, orthostatic hypotension, and weight gain. Starting with a low dose and gradually increasing the level helps minimize these side effects. TCAs should be used with caution in patients with underlying cardiovascular disease, glaucoma, and obstructive urinary tract disease.

Serotonin selective reuptake inhibitors (SSRIs) deserve mention as an alternative to TCAs when migraine prophylaxis with an antidepressant is desired. Although not as extensively studied as TCAs and lacking FDA approval for this indication, their use is endorsed by most headache specialists (Continuum, 1995). SSRIs are particularly useful in patients who cannot tolerate TCAs or have found TCA prophylaxis ineffective.

Calcium channel blockers make up the third major class of migraine prophylactic medications. As with beta-blockers, several mechanisms of actions are proposed, including inhibition of vasoconstriction in the migraine prodrome by blocking calcium entry into vascular smooth muscle, inhibition of platelet aggregation, and inhibition of platelet serotonin release (Solomon, 1990). Despite their widespread use for migraine prophylaxis, none of the calcium channel blockers are FDA approved for this indication. Although nomodapine, nifedipine, and diltiazem have all proven useful for migraine prophylaxis, verapamil appears to be most effective (Solomon, 1990). The relative efficacy of calcium channel blockers compared to beta-blockers has not been established (Elkind, 1996). Calcium channel blockers are generally well tolerated, the most common side effects being constipation and edema. They are particularly useful in patients where beta-blockers are contraindicated or have produced intolerable side effects. Other migraine prophylactic agents, which are mentioned in name only, include divalproex, methycergide, cyproheptadine, and NSAIDs.

Though in some senses more convenient than behavioral interventions (e.g., taking medication does not require instrumentation nor practice), some patients elect to forego pharmacologic interventions and focus on behavioral strategies for headache management. This can occur in situations where (a) pregnancy prevents the use of medications, (b) coexisting medical conditions render at least some medications imprudent (e.g., use of Amitriptyline in elderly patients with a cardiovascular problem), (c) numerous medication trials have been attempted and the patient remains symptomatic, or (d) the patient simply prefers not to unnecessarily ingest a pharmacologic agent when an alternative strategy is available.

BEHAVIORAL MANAGEMENT OF HEADACHE

Behavioral interventions for treatment of headache include biofeedback, various forms of relaxation training, cognitive-behavioral therapy, and combinations thereof. The literature has been fairly consistent in demonstrating the efficacy of these various interventions relative to various control groups (see reviews by Arena & Blanchard, 1996; Blanchard & Andrasik, 1985; Roberts, 1993). Representative literature for each of these interventions is reviewed next.

Tension-Type Headache

The efficacy of electromyographic (EMG) biofeedback training in treatment of tension-type headache has been well established. Early work by Budzynski and Stoyva (Stoyva, 1976) was followed by extensive work by Blanchard and colleagues at the State University of New York at Albany (for a summary of this work, see Blanchard & Andrasik, 1985, or Blanchard, 1992). In a meta-analytic study of frontal EMG biofeedback, Blanchard, Andrasik, Ahles, Teders, and O'Keefe (1980) found an average percent improvement of 60.9% in the 12 studies included. Though not appreciably better than relaxation training (average improvement 59.2%) or frontal EMG plus relaxation training (average improvement 58.8%), all three behavioral interventions were substantially more beneficial than physiological placebo (average improvement 35.3%) and medication placebo (average improvement 34.8%). More recent work (Reich, 1989) found similar comparability in the efficacy of EMG biofeedback and relaxation training for tension-type headache. In reality, proposed treatment protocols typically include instruction in some form of relaxation followed by EMG biofeedback to enhance skills (e.g., Nash & Holroyd, 1992; Schwartz, 1995).

Mechanism of Change. Though early conceptual models focused on muscle tension reduction as the mechanism of action for headache reduction (see Blanchard & Andrasik, 1985), there are a number of observations that demonstrate that this surely cannot be the mechanism of change. First, Andrasik and Holroyd (1980) compared headache reduction among groups of tension headache subjects under four conditions. One group was instructed to reduce frontal EMG activity and received accurate feedback. A second group received feedback of a lowering EMG level for holding tension levels constant. A third group received feedback of a lowering EMG level but for increasing tension levels. The fourth group was a waiting list control group that simply monitored headache. All three treatment groups achieved the EMG activity trained, that is, decrease, constant, and increase, respectively. At the same time, all three groups showed significant decreases in headache activity relative to the control group but did not differ from each other. Obviously then, decreasing muscle tension cannot underlie headache relief. As is noted later, however, this is not to say that increased levels of muscle tension do not play some role in the genesis of tension-type headache.

Though some researchers have failed to find a relationship between EMG levels and subjective pain ratings (Martin & Matthews, 1978; A. L. Peterson, Talcott, Kelleher, & Haddock, 1995; Schoenen, Gerard, DePasqua, & Juprelle, 1991), other researchers have been more successful. Pritchard (1989) compared EMG measures from frontal, occipital, and neck muscles of migrainous and tension-type headache sufferers with no headache controls. Readings were taken during baseline, a stress task, and a headache. Results revealed that both headache groups had substantially greater EMG activity in neck muscle relative to controls during all phases of the study. Further, measures obtained from occipital muscles during the headache phase showed higher EMG activity in tension headache and lower EMG activity in migrainous headache. Pritchard (1995) found the same effect of tonic tension in neck muscles in comparing children who "complained of severe headache" to a headache-free group. Similarly, Bansevicius and

Sjaastad (1996), in studying patients with cervicogenic headache and recording EMG activity from frontal, temporal, splenius, and trapezius muscles, found elevated EMG readings in trapezius on the symptomatic side both at baseline and under a stress condition. EMG levels for frontal readings were greater on the symptomatic side at baseline but not during the stress condition.

In a novel experiment assessing the role of muscle tension, Jensen and Olesen (1996) had tension headache patients and matched controls engage in 30 minutes of sustained teeth clenching. Within 24 hours of the clenching, 69% of the patients developed a headache relative to 17% of the controls. Further, muscle tenderness increased in those patients who subsequently developed headache but not in patients who did not.

All things considered then, it would appear that muscle tension increases either at baseline and/or in response to cognitive (Pritchard, 1989) or mechanical stressors (Jensen & Olesen, 1996) might play some role in the genesis of tension-type headache. At the same time, the Andrasik and Holroyd (1980) study makes it clear that headache relief vis-à-vis EMG biofeedback is more complex than simple reduction of muscle tension. Subsequent work by Holroyd and coworkers (1984) suggests an underlying mechanism. In that work, four groups of patients were provided biofeedback training. One group was given feedback to assist in lowering frontal EMG. A second group was given feedback that would lead the patient to believe the task was to lower EMG, but in fact, they were increasing muscle tension. Within each of these conditions, half of the patients were given feedback that they were successful whereas the other half was given feedback that they were not being successful. Again, EMG frontal readings indicated successful training (i.e., decreases in the first overall group and increases in the second overall group), but headache reduction was associated with perception of success rather than acquired skills in tension reduction/tension induction. Specifically, patients who increased tension but felt successfully in control, experienced greater headache reduction than those who actually reduced tension but because of bogus feedback did not feel the same level of self-regulation. This would suggest, as Blanchard and Andrasik (1985) have already noted, that concepts such as self-efficacy and self-control play the more fundamental role in headache management.

Originally formalized by Julian Rotter (1966) as locus of control, the concept was elaborated by Bandura (1977) as self-efficacy and more recently substantially expanded in the work of Martin E. P. Seligman on learned helplessness (Seligman, 1975), learned optimism (Seligman, 1991), and explanatory style (C. Peterson, Maier, & Seligman, 1993). Work reported by Kremer and Kremer (1995) using the Survey of Pain Attitudes with both tension-type and migrainous headache patients found significant change in the control dimension (a measure of self-efficacy or self-control) following successful treatment in a multidisciplinary behavioral program. Also, Hudzinski and Levenson (1985) found that tension-type headache patients with an internal locus of control (reflecting an attitude of self-efficacy) attained significantly greater headache relief using EMG biofeedback than did patients with an external locus.

Migrainous Headache

Sargent, Green, and Walters (1973) first demonstrated reduction of migrainous headache with hand warming using a combination of autogenic phrases and temperature biofeedback. As Blanchard and Andrasik (1985) have already noted, proposed mechanisms of migrainous headache suggest that thermal feedback allows the patient to gain control of vasodynamics and hence migrainous headache. Holroyd et al. (1988) noted that, at the time of their publication, there had been more than 80 studies examining the efficacy of behavioral interventions for vascular headache. The majority of studies focused on relaxation training and/or thermal biofeedback and consistently demonstrated significant reductions in headache activity.

Blanchard et al. (1991) provided an example of a standard thermal biofeedback protocol. They trained pure migrainous and mixed headache patients in 12 sessions of temperature biofeedback. Subjects were provided a 10-minute adaptation period, followed by 4 minutes of hand warming without feedback, then 16 minutes of warming with feedback, and finally, 4 minutes of warming without feedback. During the initial session, subjects were assisted by autogenic phrases. Results indicated a significant reduction in headache index with a significantly greater percentage of migrainous headache patients (64.3%) improving relative to the mixed headache group (27.8%). Other work found greater mean effect when relaxation training was used rather than autogenic phrases (Blanchard et al., 1990). Further, Holroyd et al. (1988) found significant reduction in migrainous headache with as few as three clinical sessions of relaxation training and thermal biofeedback.

RELATIVE EFFICACY OF PHARMACOLOGIC
AND BEHAVIORAL INTERVENTIONS

Holroyd and co-workers have published work that directly compared pharmacologic and behavioral treatment of both vascular and tension-type headache. In the first study, Holroyd et al. (1988) compared vascular headache patients treated with a behavioral intervention modeled after the protocol developed by Blanchard and Andrasik (1985) to patients treated with either cafergot or ergostat. The behavioral intervention was brief and largely home based. There were a total of three clinic visits with 1 month intervening between each. In the first two visits, patients were instructed in relaxation training and thermal biofeedback with manuals and audiotapes provided for home practice. In addition, there was brief telephone contact for problem solving at the end of the second and sixth weeks. The pharmacologic group had the same number of clinic visits and phone consultations, but the contacts were used to prescribe and monitor medication as well as to problem-solve compliance issues.

Analysis of headache index measures indicated that overall improvement was comparable with mean posttreatment headache index at 4.59 for the behavioral group and 4.81 for the pharmacologic group. The rate of improvement, however, was more rapid in the pharmacologic group, which showed 30% reduction in headache activity in the first month relative to only 2% decrease in the behavioral group. Using the standard of 50% reduction in headache activity as successful treatment (Blanchard & Schwarz, 1988), 53% of the behavioral group eventually achieved this standard relative to 61% of the pharmacologic group. Further, the groups differed significantly in analgesic use with the pharmacologic group showing no change over treatment as compared to a statistically significant reduction by the behavioral group. This obviously has important implications for long-term cost of headache treatment as well as potential for treatment complications such as rebound headache.

Holroyd, Nash, Pingel, Cordingley, and Jerome (1991) compared cognitive-behavioral therapy to amitriptyline in effectiveness in treating chronic tension headaches. The cognitive-behavioral therapy was brief, consisting only of three 1-hour sessions and two 15-minute telephone contacts. The first session dealt with overall treatment strategy and relaxation training. This session was augmented by manuals and audiotapes to be used for home practice. The second session addressed headache-related stress and essentially consisted of problem-solving psychotherapy. For appropriate patients, this session was augmented by homework material on cognitive restructuring or problem-solving skills. The final session was devoted to review and reinforcement of the strategies the patient found more useful. The amitriptyline group met with the neurologist on three occasions. During the first visit, 50 mg of amitriptyline was prescribed, and medication use and side effects were explained. At the second session, if indicated, the dosage was increased to 75 mg. At the third encounter, the maximum dosage was selected.

Analysis of the results indicated that cognitive-behavioral therapy yielded a 56% reduction in headache index as compared to 27% reduction for the group treated with amitriptyline. Further, the cognitive-behavioral group had a threefold increase in headache-free days as compared to a twofold increase for the amitriptyline group. The headache index effect was statistically significant between the two treatment groups, whereas headache-free days improvement was not reliably different. On balance then, one would have to consider the behavioral intervention the treatment of choice.

Finally, Holroyd and Penzien (1990) used meta-analysis to compare the relative efficacy of behavioral interventions to propranolol in treatment of recurrent migraine headache. In the literature reviewed, 73 studies provided usable date with 60 treatment groups and 37 control groups. Behavioral treatment was defined as relaxation training of some form (e.g., progressive muscular relaxation, autogenic training, etc.) and thermal biofeedback. The meta-analysis indicated that average group percent improvement for both groups was 55.1% as compared to 12.2% for placebo and 1.1% for untreated patients.

These three studies then indicate that behavioral interventions are at least as efficacious as some conventional pharmacologic interventions for both migrainous and tension-type headache. This result is particularly impressive when one considers the brevity of the behavioral interventions. To put this in some perspective, in their review of literature involving relaxation training/thermal biofeedback in the treatment of migrainous headache, Holroyd and Penzien (1990) reported training sessions to range from 2 to 24 sessions with 57% of the studies reporting 8 to 12 sessions. As Holroyd et al. (1988) found a significant correlation between finger temperature increases in posttreatment psychophysiologic assessment and reduction in headache index, one could speculate that more extensive behavioral treatment might produce greater benefit relative to pharmacologic interventions. Indeed, Hudzinski and Levenson (1985) found that among their patients, those attending four or more sessions attained significantly greater relief than those attending fewer sessions.

MULTIDISCIPLINARY HEADACHE TREATMENT

Scharff and Marcus (1994) have cogently iterated the logic for multidisciplinary headache treatment. This logic notes that many patients respond equally well to pharmacologic or behavioral treatment. Moreover, they noted the contribution of physical therapy interventions in headache treatment (e.g., Hammill, Cook, & Rosecrance, 1996). Despite these various individual approaches, there continues to be a group of treatment-resistant patients. Interdisciplinary treatment approaches have been shown to be efficacious for other types of pain problems (Flor, Fydrich, & Turk, 1992). It would make sense then to treat these difficult patients by combining treatment options in a group format.

A MODEL MULTIDISCIPLINARY TREATMENT PROGRAM

At the Mary Free Bed Hospital and Rehabilitation Center, a multidisciplinary team has offered chronic pain rehabilitation treatment since 1975. In 1992, a separate multidisciplinary program was offered for treatment of chronic, intractable headache patients. This program combined the expertise of the Committee for Accreditation of Rehabilitation Facilities (CARF) accredited chronic pain treatment team with a team of board-certified neurologists to evaluate and treat headache patients in the milieu of a sophisticated regional rehabilitation center.

Evaluation Process

After referral by the treating physician, previous records, including original imaging studies, are obtained for review. The patient begins a headache diary and completes medical history and headache history questionnaires.

In the evaluation clinic, the patient is evaluated sequentially by a board-certified neurologist, a behavioral medicine psychologist, and a family physician who is a fellow of the American Board of Pain Medicine. Prior to the clinic, the patient completed psychological testing.

The breadth and depth of the multidisciplinary evaluation usually identifies areas of concern that have not been previously elucidated. In the neurological exam, particular care is given to identifying the uncommon headaches that are secondary to a primary neurologic disease or represent an atypical headache syndrome.

The general medical exam screens for unidentified medical conditions that need further treatment or that may limit the patient's ability to participate in a rehabilitation program. Conditions such as hypertension, diabetes mellitus, coronary artery disease, and arthritis are as common in headache patients as they are in the rest of the population and are just as frequently undiagnosed or inadequately controlled. Specific conditions such as chronic sinus disease, cervical spine disease, temporal arteritis, temporal mandibular joint dysfunction, and Acquired Immune Deficiency must be carefully ruled out.

The psychological evaluation seeks to identify underlying psychological problems such as depression, anxiety, personality disorders, or other psychiatric diseases. The interview also explores the patient's attitude and understanding of their headaches. Attention is paid to identifying specific stressors and separating pre- and postmorbid contributors to the patient's pain state.

The evaluation team conferences immediately following the clinic. This open interaction is important in arriving at a common diagnosis and an appropriate treatment plan. Patients who are not considered good candidates include those with long-standing significant psychiatric illness, headaches secondary to as yet untreated primary medical problems, primary substance abuse problems not originating from headache treatment, headaches likely to resolve with single specialty treatment, and cluster headache.

If traditional medical management has not been adequately pursued previously, such a course is suggested when headaches are intermittent, not disabling, and when no significant mood or thought disorder is identified. A multidisciplinary behavioral program is recommended when traditional medical management has been unsuccessful or poorly tolerated, or if significant problems with medication dependency or abuse, rebound headaches, or depression or anxiety are identified.

When a multidisciplinary approach is recommended, an individualized program is designed. A typical program will include 12 weeks of treatment. The first week is intensive, involving a physical therapy evaluation and daily education sessions, physical therapy sessions to initiate a conditioning program, instruction in body mechanics and proper posture, as well as flare-up management and pacing. During the first week, the patient is also introduced to relaxation training and biofeedback. This intensive week of therapy also immerses patients in a therapeutic environment and takes them out of their usual daily setting for significant parts of their day. All of this reinforces the belief that real change can and will take place during the course of their treatment. For the remainder of their programs, the patients are seen between 3 and 4 hours per week divided up on 1 or 2 days as their schedule dictates.

Initial medical treatment focuses on controlling analgesic and abortive medication use. Medications that have been used on a daily basis via a PRN (*pro re nata*, or as needed) schedule are placed on a timed basis at dosages that are equivalent to pretreatment levels. This eliminates the contingency between headache and medication (Fordyce, 1976). Prophylactic medications that have not been effective are gradually eliminated. If the patient has significant problems with sleep disturbance and/or depression, a starting dose of a tricyclic antidepressant is often introduced.

When prophylactic medications have not been used previously, these may also be initiated, but the importance of medications in chronic headache management is downplayed and poly-pharmacy is assiduously avoided. Physician lectures on commonly used headache medications and headache syndromes are used to increase patient understanding of their disease and its treatment.

Psychological treatment starts with individual sessions focused on personal, family, and workplace stressors with an emphasis on problem solving and stress management. Group lectures on stress management, relaxation, meditation and self-hypnosis, biofeedback, pain and mood changes, pain and relationships, and self-efficacy and self-control are scheduled over the course of the program. The focus of psychological care is on behavioral change, cognitive restructuring, and education. Couples sessions are scheduled when deemed necessary by the treating therapist.

Biofeedback training is extensively used. Patients are initiated using either progressive muscular relaxation, meditative breathing, or autogenic techniques. Feedback modality is a function of diagnosis and often is used more as an educational tool than instrumentation to facilitate skill acquisition. By the same token, the psychology assistant might work in collaboration with the physical therapist in using EMG biofeedback for postural retraining where postural derangement contributes to the headache. Portable units allow the patient to integrate these skills into their daily lives.

Our dedicated physical therapist performs an initial evaluation of posture, aerobic conditioning, and spinal and joint range of motion. Careful evaluation of temporomandibular joint function and muscular evaluation of the head, neck, and thorax is completed in the first week. The importance and benefits of aerobic exercise are reviewed in physical therapy sessions and reinforced in psychology lectures and during biofeedback training.

Articulation of treatment components and treatment intensity is guided by a number of considerations. First, as noted earlier, the development of a sense of self-efficacy or self-control by the patient is fundamental to successful resolution of headache. Second, Dolce, Crocker, Moleteteire, and Doleys (1986) have shown that a sense of self-efficacy develops only after demonstrable behavioral gains or acquisition of skills has occurred. Third, as noted earlier, Blanchard and Andrasik (1985) found only a 2% decrease in headache over the first month of behavioral treatment. It would follow then the treatment intensity would be greater in the early stages of the program as the patient struggles with skill acquisition. As skill is acquired and a sense of self-efficacy develops, treatment intensity is decreased and components such as medication withdrawal are introduced.

Team conferences are held every other Friday to review progress and refine each patient's treatment plan. These conferences include most members of the treatment team but do not include the patient. When patients are having difficulty, the team will develop a specific plan to deal with the problem. This may have to do with challenging the patient on excessive pain talk or behavior. It may involve increasing the focus on individual or couples counseling while decreasing physical therapy, or it may involve a decision to discharge the patient early for lack of progress. When an early discharge is recommended, the patient is almost always in agreement that the approach was not working.

At discharge, patients most frequently cite the biofeedback and physical therapy components as the most beneficial parts of the program. Patients who are openly hostile to the idea of managing their headaches without narcotic analgesics are also frequently very positive about the improvements they notice in overall functioning when they are discharged off all medication or on only a low-dose antidepressant.

A discharge conference is held at the conclusion of treatment, and the patient is officially returned to the care of their primary-care or referring physician. A single follow-up appointment is scheduled 4–6 weeks after discharge to evaluate progress and reinforce the patient's self-management techniques. We encourage patients and their physicians to contact us if successfully treated patients experience a flare-up of their symptoms after discharge. Short refresher programs of 3–6 weeks' duration can then be specifically tailored to each patient's need and have been successful in helping patients regain control of headache flare-ups.

OUTCOME OF MULTIDISCIPLINARY BEHAVIORAL TREATMENT.

Scharff and Marcus (1994) reported the results of behavioral treatment in a program conducted in 3-hour group sessions over a 5-week period. Various components of education and intervention were delivered by a neurologist, a physical therapist, an occupational therapist, and a psychologist. Follow-up data over an average of 7.4 months posttreatment revealed that 71.4% of the patients continued with a 50% or greater reduction in headache. Moreover, this improvement occurred in the context of a 70.9% reduction in medication index.

In the same programmatic setting, Scharff, Marcus, and Turk (1996) treated pregnant headache patients and found a significant (greater than 50%) improvement for 80% of the patients. These patients were then followed over the 12 months postpartum. Even at 1-year postpartum, patients as a group maintained a 63.6% improvement.

Kremer and Kremer (1995) presented the results of evaluation and treatment of 99 consecutive referrals to the previously described multidisciplinary headache treatment program. Of the 99 patients evaluated, 65 were recommended for treatment with 31 having completed treatment at the time of the study and 5 were discharged early for noncompliance. The insurance carriers for 15 of the recommended patients would not authorize treatment following the evaluation.

Admission to discharge comparisons for pain, depression, anxiety, and belief system all revealed significant improvement over the course of treatment. The McGill Pain Questionnaire sensory dimension score on admission was 0.59 as compared to 0.30 on discharge. Similarly, the affective dimension score was 0.42 on admission and 0.17 at discharge. The Zung Depression Scale and Zung Anxiety Scale indicated mild levels of depression and anxiety on admission, but both measures were within normal

TABLE 14.1
Percentage of Patients Using Various Classes
of Medications on Admission and at Discharge

Medication	Admission % Patients	Discharge % Patients
NSAIDs	8	6
Narcotics	50	0
Anxiolytics	11	9
Ergotamines	14	6
B-Blockers	8	0
CA Channel	8	0
Anticonvulsants	11	12
Antidepressants	64	68

limits at discharge. Finally, analysis of the Survey of Pain Attitudes found significantly greater feelings of control and significant decreases in feelings of disability. Consistent with this, there were also significant decreases in the medication and medical cure scales, indicating that the patients were less focused on medication as a means of managing their headaches. These, of course, are precisely the cognitive changes that many workers feel are fundamental to successful headache management.

Table 14.1 presents the percentage of patients using various classes of headache medications at admission and on discharge. Note that half of the patients were using narcotic analgesics on a regular basis as compared to none at discharge. Overall, the only class of medications maintained by any significant number of patients was the antidepressants. Thus, medications known to result in rebound headache (Rapoport, 1988) were eliminated whereas the class of medication designed to reduce depression and stabilize sleep pattern was introduced or maintained.

All things considered, the multidisciplinary treatment proved an efficacious intervention for vascular, tension-type, and mixed headache. It is important to note that these benefits were derived after long histories of headache suffering and relative failure of many conventional medical and nonmedical interventions. Many of these patients had previously undergone aggressive poly-pharmacy interventions and derived greater benefit from a less pharmacologically focused multidisciplinary treatment. Obviously, with the pain studies available, much more research is needed before the full promise of multidisciplinary behavioral treatment can be appreciated.

REFERENCES

Andersson, K. E., & Vinge, E. (1990). B-Adrenoceptor blockers and calcium-antagonists in the prophylaxis and treatment of migraine. *Drugs, 39*, 355–373.

Andrasik, F., & Holroyd, K. (1980). A test of specific and non-specific effects in the biofeedback treatment of tension headache. *Journal of Consulting Clinical Psychology, 48*, 575–586.

Arena, J. G., & Blanchard, E. B. (1996). Biofeedback and relaxation therapy for chronic pain disorders. In R. J. Gatchel & D. C. Turk (Eds.), *Psychological approaches to pain management: A practitioner's handbook* (pp. 179–230). New York: Guilford.

Bandura, A. (1977). Self-efficacy: Toward a unifying theory of behavioral change. *Psychological Review, 84,* 191–215.

Bansevicius, D., & Sjaastad, O. (1996). Cervicogenic headache: The influence of mental load on pain level and EMG of shoulder-neck and facial muscles. *Headache, 36,* 372–378.

Becker, L., Iverson, D. C., Reed, F. M., Calonge, N., Miller, R. S., & Freeman, W. L. (1988). Patients with new headache in primary care: A report from ASPN. *Journal of Family Practice, 27,* 41–47.

Blanchard, E. B. (1992). Psychological treatment of benign headache disorders. *Journal of Consulting Clinical Psychology, 60,* 537–551.

Blanchard, E. B., & Andrasik, F. (1985). *Management of chronic headache: A psychological approach.* Elmsford, NY: Pergamon.

Blanchard, E. B., Andrasik, F., Ahles, T. M., Teders, S. J., & O'Keefe, D. (1980). Migraine and tension headache: A meta-analytic review. *Behavior Therapy, 11,* 613–631.

Blanchard, E. B., Appelbaum, K. A., Radnitz, C. L., Michulta, D. M., Morrell, B., Kirsch, C., Hillhouse, J., Evans, D. D., Guarnieri, P., Altanasio, V., Andrasik, F., Jaccard, J., & Dentinger, M. P. (1990). A placebo-controlled evaluation of abbreviated progressive muscle relaxation and relaxation combined with cognitive therapy in the treatment of tension headache. *Journal of Consulting Clinical Psychology, 58,* 210–215.

Blanchard, E. B., Nicholson, N. L., Radnitz, C. L., Steffek, B. D., Appelbaum, K. A., & Dentinger, M. P. (1991). The role of home practice in thermal biofeedback. *Journal of Consulting Clinical Psychology, 59,* 507–512.

Blanchard, E. B., & Schwarz, S. P. (1988). Clinically significant changes in behavioral medicine. *Behavioral Assessment, 10,* 171–188.

Continuum. (1995). *A program of the American Academy of Neurology, 1,* 36.

Dalessio, D. J., & Silberstein, S. D. (Eds.). (1993). *Wolff's headache and other head pain* (6th ed.). New York: Oxford University Press.

Diamond, S. (1991). Migraine headaches. *Medical Clinics of North America, 75,* 545–578.

Diamond, S., & Dalessio, D. J. (Eds.). (1992). *The practicing physician's approach to headache* (5th ed.). Baltimore: Williams & Wilkins.

Diamond, S., & Freitag, F. (1989). Do non-steroidal anti-inflammatory agents have a role in the treatment of migraine headaches? *Drugs, 37,* 755–760.

Dolce, J. J., Crocker, M. F., Moleteteire, C., & Doleys, D. M. (1986). Exercise quotas, anticipatory concern and self-efficacy expectancies in chronic pain: A preliminary report. *Pain, 24,* 365–375.

Elkind, A. H. (Ed.). (1996). *Therapeutic guide for the treatment of headache.* Austin, TX: Silent Partners.

Flor, H., Fydrich, T., & Turk, D. C. (1992). Efficacy of multidisciplinary pain treatment centers: A meta-analytic review. *Pain, 49,* 221–230.

Fordyce, W. E. (1976). *Behavioral methods for chronic pain and illness.* St. Louis, MO: Mosby.

Freitag, F. G. (1992). Headache clinics and inpatient units for treatment of headache. In S. Diamond & D. J. Dalessio (Eds.), *The practicing physician's approach to headache* (5th ed., pp. 270–280). Baltimore: Williams & Wilkins.

Hammill, J. M., Cook, T. M., & Rosecrance, J. C. (1996). Effectiveness of a physical therapy regimen in the treatment of tension-type headache. *Headache, 36,* 149–153.

Holroyd, K. A., Holm, J. E., Hursey, K. G., Penzien, D. B., Cordingley, G. E., Theofanous, A. G., Richardson, S. C., & Tobin, D. L. (1988). Recurrent vascular headache: Home-based behavioral treatment *versus* abortive pharmacological treatment. *Journal of Consulting Clinical Psychology, 56,* 218–223.

Holroyd, K. A., Nash, J. M., Pingel, J. D., Cordingley, G. E., & Jerome, A. (1991). A comparison of pharmacological (amitriptyline HCL) and non-pharmacological (cognitive-behavioral) therapies for chronic tension headaches. *Journal of Consulting Clinical Psychology, 59*, 387–393.

Holroyd, K. A., & Penzien, D. B. (1990). Pharmacological versus non-pharmacological prophylaxis of recurrent migraine headache: A meta-analytic review of clinical trials. *Pain, 42*, 1–13.

Holroyd, K. A., Penzien, D. B., & Cordingley, M. D. (1991). Propranolol in the management of recurrent migraine: A meta-analytic review. *Headache, 31*, 333–340.

Holroyd, K. A., Penzien, D. B., Hursey, K. G., Tobin, L. R., Holm, J. E., Marcille, P. J., Hall, J. R., & Chila, A. G. (1984). Change mechanisms in EMG biofeedback training: Cognitive changes underlying improvements in tension headache. *Journal of Consulting Clinical Psychology, 52*, 1039–1053.

Hudzinski, L. G., & Levenson, H. (1985). Biofeedback behavioral treatment of headache with locus of control pain analysis: A 20-month retrospective study. *Headache, 25*, 380–386.

Jensen, R., & Olesen, J. (1996). Initiating mechanisms of experimentally induced tension-type headache. *Cephalgia, 16*, 175–182.

Kremer, E. F., & Kremer, A. M. (1995, November). *Psychological factors influencing medical treatment outcome: Headache.* Paper presented at the Annual Scientific Meeting of the American Pain Society, Los Angeles.

Kudrow, L. (1982). Paradoxical effects of frequent analgesic use. *Advances in Neurology, 33*, 335–341.

Maizels, M., Scott, B., Cohen, W., & Chen, W. (1996). Intranasal lidocaine for treatment of migraine: A randomized double-blind, controlled trial. *Journal of the American Medical Association, 276*, 319–321.

Martin, P. R., & Matthews, A. M. (1978). Tension headaches: Psychophysiological investigation and treatment. *Journal of Psychosomatic Research, 22*, 389–399.

Martscci, N., Monna, V., & Agnoli, A. (1985). Antidepressant drugs and migraine. *Cephalgia, 5*(Suppl. 2), 225–228.

Nash, J. M., & Holroyd, K. A. (1992). Home-based behavioral treatment for recurrent headache: A cost-effective alternative. *American Pain Society Bulletin, 2*, 1–6.

Olesen, J., Tfelt-Hansen, P., & Welch, K. M. A. (1993). *The headaches.* New York: Raven.

Peterson, A. L., Talcott, W., Kelleher, W. J., & Haddock, K. (1995). Site specificity of pain and tension in tension-type headaches. *Headache, 35*, 89–92.

Peterson, C., Maier, S. F., & Seligman, M. E. P. (1993). *Learned helplessness: A theory for the age of personal control.* New York: Oxford University Press.

Pritchard, D. W. (1989). EMG cranial muscle levels in headache sufferers before and during headache. *Headache, 29*, 103–108.

Pritchard, D. (1995). EMG levels in children who suffer from severe headache. *Headache, 35*, 554–556.

Rapoport, A. M. (1988). Analgesic rebound headache. *Headache, 28*, 662–665.

Rasmussen, B. K., & Olesen, J. (1992). Symptomatic and non-symptomatic headaches in a general population. *Neurology, 42*, 1225–1231.

Rasmussen, B. K., & Olesen, J. (1996, March/April). Epidemiology of headache. *IASP Newsletter*, pp. 3–6.

Reich, B. A. (1989). Non-invasive treatment of vascular and muscle contraction headache: A comparative longitudinal study. *Headache, 29*, 34–41.

Roberts, A. (1993). Behavioral management of headache. In D. J. Dalessio & S. D. Silberstein (Eds.), *Wolff's headache and other head pain* (6th ed., pp. 483–501). New York: Oxford University Press.

Rotter, J. B. (1966). Generalized expectancies for internal *versus* external control of reinforcement. *Psychological Monograph, 80*, 1–28.

Saper, J. R. (1987). Ergotamine dependency: A review. *Headache, 27,* 435–438.

Sargent, J. D., Green, E. E., & Walters, E. D. (1973). Preliminary report on the use of autogenic training in the treatment of migraine and tension headaches. *Psychosomatic Medicine, 35,* 129–135.

Scharff, L., & Marcus, D. A. (1994). Interdisciplinary outpatient group treatment of intractable headache. *Headache, 34,* 73–78.

Scharff, L., Marcus, D. A., & Turk, D. C. (1996). Maintenance of effects in the non-medical treatment of headaches during pregnancy. *Headache, 36,* 285–290.

Schoenen, J., Gerard, P., DePasqua, V., & Juprelle, M. (1991). EMG activity in pericranial muscles during postural variation and mental activity in healthy volunteers and patients with chronic tension-type headache. *Headache, 31,* 321–324.

Schwartz, M. S. (1995). Headache: Selected issues and considerations in evaluation and treatment: Part B. Treatment. In M. S. Schwartz (Ed.), *Biofeedback: A practitioner's guide* (2nd ed., pp. 354–407). New York: Guilford.

Seligman, M. E. P. (1975). *Helplessness: On depression, development, and death.* San Francisco: Freeman.

Seligman, M. E. P. (1991). *Learned optimism.* New York: Knopf.

Solomon, G. D. (1990). The action and uses of calcium channel blockers in migraine and cluster headache. *Headache Quarterly, 1,* 152–159.

Sternbach, R. A. (1986). Survey of pain in the United States: The Nuprin pain report. *Clinical Journal of Pain, 2,* 49–53.

Stewart, W. F., & Lipton, R. B. (1993). Societal impact of headache. In J. Olesen, P. Tfelt-Hansen, & K. M. A. Welch (Eds.), *The headaches* (pp. 29–34). New York: Raven.

Stoyva, J. (1976). Self-regulation and the stress-related disorders: A perspective on biofeedback. In D. I. Mostofsky (Ed.), *Behavior control and modification of psychological activity* (pp. 366–398). Englewood Cliffs, NJ: Prentice-Hall.

Von Korff, M., Galer, B. S., & Stang, P. (1995). Chronic use of symptomatic headache medications. *Pain, 62,* 179–186.

Ziegler, D. K., Huruitz, A., Hassanein, R. S., Kodanaz, H. A., Prekorn, S. H., & Mason, J. (1987). Migraine prophylaxis: A comparison of propranolol and amitriptyline. *Archives of Neurology, 44,* 486–489.

Chapter 15

Chronic Posttraumatic Headache

Paul N. Duckro
John T. Chibnall
Saint Louis University

Mild closed head trauma, including acceleration/deceleration injury to the head and neck without direct head strike, is associated with short-term or no loss of consciousness; short-term or no amnesia; and near-normal eye, motor, and verbal responses posttrauma without subsequent deterioration (Packard & Ham, 1994a). Headache is the most common and intractable complication of mild closed head trauma. Although estimates are variable across studies, the best evidence suggests that 50% to 90% of mild head trauma victims will experience acute headache, 30% to 50% will have headache up to 2 months posttrauma, 20% to 25% will have headache up to 6 months posttrauma, and as many as 10% to 15% will continue to experience significant posttraumatic symptoms, including headache, for 1 year or longer (cf. Alexander, 1995; Alves, Colohan, O'Leary, Rimel, & Jane, 1986; Appenzeller, 1987; Bailey & Gudeman, 1989; Brown, Fann, & Grant, 1994; Jensen & Nielsen, 1990; Moore, 1996; Packard, 1993). With millions of head injuries in the United States each year (Brown et al., 1994), these percentages represent substantial human and economic costs.

The present chapter is focused on the minority of persons for whom headache becomes chronic (i.e., lasts longer than 6 months) following minor head trauma. Chronic headache does not typically present as a solitary symptom following trauma. Although headache is the most common complication of minor head injury, it is usually one aspect of a syndrome that may include physical (e.g., fatigue, dizziness, tinnitus), psychosocial (e.g., mood swings, depression, irritability, anxiety, anger), and/or cognitive (e.g., memory impairment, distractibility, poor comprehension) symptoms (Alves et al., 1986; Bailey & Gudeman, 1989; Binder, 1986; J. Goldstein, 1991; Speed, 1989). This cluster of symptoms has been designated posttraumatic syndrome or postconcussion syndrome. Because the chronic posttraumatic headache (CPTH) patient will often present with this constellation and because the nonheadache symptoms can greatly complicate the assessment and treatment of CPTH, any discussion of CPTH must consider headache within the context of the syndrome (Packard, 1996).

Posttraumatic headache is a complex phenomenon that is poorly understood with regard to its etiology, prognosis, and treatment (R. W. Evans, 1994). Historically, it has also carried with it significant stigma centered around the issues of psychogenesis and malingering for financial profit (Miller, 1968). Thus, a comprehensive and rational approach to its assessment and treatment is imperative for clinical success. A comprehensive approach must include attention to the presenting characteristics of CPTH, the many factors that affect onset and persistence, comorbid psychological and cognitive symptoms, and the value of multimodal assessment and treatment approaches. These features form the outline for the present chapter.

CLINICAL PRESENTATION OF CHRONIC POSTTRAUMATIC HEADACHE

"Posttraumatic headache" is a descriptive term; it does not identify a specific type of headache. On the contrary, the literature suggests that any of the major benign headache disorders may occur following head trauma, although not with equal incidence (Appenzeller, 1987; Duckro et al., 1992; Haas, 1996; Packard, 1993; Saper, 1983; Speed, 1989).

Tension-Type Headache. Chronic tension-type headache appears to be the most common form of posttraumatic headache and may account for as much as three fourths of CPTH (Diamond & Freitag, 1992; Duckro et al., 1992; Haas, 1996; Mandel, 1989). Clinically, it appears indistinguishable from chronic tension-type headache not associated with trauma (Haas, 1996).

Migraine. Variations of migraine appear to be the second most prevalent type of CPTH, accounting for perhaps 10% to 20% of cases (Duckro et al., 1992; Haas, 1996). As with tension-type headache, its clinical presentation appears identical to that of migraine not associated with trauma.

Chronic Daily Headache. No single accepted term exists to describe this clinical presentation. Other names that have been used include *transformational migraine* and *mixed headache.* Chronic daily headache typically presents as daily headache of dull to moderate intensity consistent with chronic tension-type headache, but with periodic exacerbations with symptoms suggestive of migraine headache (Duckro & Chibnall, 1995; Duckro et al., 1992; Packard, 1993). Because chronic daily headache is not an IHS headache diagnosis (Headache Classification Committee of the International Headache Society, 1988), it is difficult to estimate the prevalence of this syndrome from the literature on mild head trauma patients. However, a number of studies have identified it in CPTH samples (Appenzeller, 1987; Duckro & Chibnall, 1995; Duckro et al., 1992; Speed, 1989) and in at least one sample it was more prevalent than migraine alone (21% vs. 14%, respectively) (Duckro et al., 1992).

Cluster Headache. There is considerable debate regarding the validity of cluster headache following mild trauma. Although several studies have identified cases of posttraumatic cluster headache (Duckro et al., 1992; Gfeller, Chibnall, & Duckro, 1994; Mandel, 1989; Mathew & Rueveni, 1988; Reik, 1987) and the IHS classification lists cluster headache as a type of headache associated with head trauma (Headache Classification Committee, 1988), Packard and Ham (1996) have recently presented findings from a large sample of consecutive CPTH patients in which no cases of cluster headache were identified. The authors suggested that differences in sample characteristics (e.g., severity of head injury) or the application of diagnostic criteria (e.g., headaches may be "clusterlike" but not meet strict IHS criteria for cluster headache) may account for the discrepancy.

Local Head Pain. Finally, there are instances of local head pain that do not meet criteria for any of the major headache categories. These pain syndromes appear to be associated with musculoskeletal dysfunction of the neck (e.g., cervicogenic headache) or jaw (e.g., temporomandibular dysfunction [TMD]). Cervicogenic headache is characterized by localized pain, thought to originate from the neck, but presenting in some area of the head. Pain may be exacerbated by movement of the neck. It may be transient or enduring. Several studies have documented this headache in patients who have experienced acceleration/deceleration injuries and its prevalence in samples of CPTH patients has ranged from 7% to 20% (e.g., Duckro, Chibnall, & Greenberg, 1995; Duckro et al., 1992; Mandel, 1989; Treleaven, Jull, & Atkinson, 1994).

Local head pain associated with TMD is a controversial diagnosis independent of issues of trauma. Nevertheless, several studies have identified cases of posttraumatic facial pain associated with symptoms of TMD (Braun, DiGiovanna, Schiffman, Bonnema, & Fricton, 1992; Duckro, Chibnall, Greenberg, & Schultz, 1997; Romanelli, Mock, & Tenenbaum, 1992; Weinberg & LaPointe, 1987). In his review of trauma-related headaches, Packard

(1993) identified "headache secondary to temporomandibular joint syndrome" as a "less common" form of posttraumatic headache. In some cases, TMD may serve as a trigger of one of the common headache types, most notably posttraumatic tension-type headache (Headache Classification Committee of the IHS, 1988).

ETIOLOGY OF POSTTRAUMATIC HEADACHE

There is considerable controversy and uncertainty regarding the etiology of posttraumatic headache and, more generally, posttraumatic syndrome. There are at least five competing models, each briefly reviewed next.

Psychogenic Model. In this model, CPTH is the result of preexisting psychopathology interacting with the experience of trauma, a negative psychological reaction to trauma, or both. There are no significant biological constructs in this model; "posttraumatic syndrome" becomes "posttraumatic neurosis" (Lidvall, Linderoth, & Norlin, 1974). This position is supported in part by the well-validated finding of an inverse relationship between severity of head injury and the incidence and chronicity of posttraumatic symptoms (R. W. Evans, 1992; Yamaguchi, 1992). Other reports support the role of preexisting or trauma-induced psychopathology in the maintenance of CPTH (cf. Haas, 1993; Lishman, 1988; Moore, 1996; Packard, 1993, 1994; Pearce, 1995). In related work, depression and anxiety have consistently emerged as salient correlates of pain (Arena, Blanchard, & Andrasik, 1984; M. K. Chung & Kraybill, 1990; Ham, Andrasik, Packard, & Bundrick, 1994; Spierings & van Hoof, 1996), and suppressed anger appears to augment depression and disability associated with chronic headache (Duckro, Chibnall, & Tomazic, 1995; Hatch et al., 1991; Tschannen, Duckro, Margolis, & Tomazic, 1992). However, these data allow no definitive statement regarding the role of psychological variables as causal agents of the pain syndrome.

Historically, the psychogenic model of CPTH has implicitly or explicitly proposed a relationship between posttraumatic symptoms and the prospect of financial compensation (Miller, 1968). Contrary to the common wisdom (R. W. Evans, R. I. Evans, & Sharp, 1994; Packard & Ham, 1994a), litigation status has not been found to be a reliable predictor of the incidence or persistence of posttraumatic syndrome or CPTH (Gfeller et al., 1994; Karzmark, Hall, & Englander, 1995; McKinlay, Brooks, & Bond, 1983; Mendelson, 1995; Packard, 1992).

Physical Pathology Model. In this model, CPTH and posttraumatic syndrome are primarily the result of neuronal, cervical spine, or soft tissue pathology. Several hypotheses based on some form of neuronal derangement have emerged, including diffuse axonal damage (Goodman, 1994; Levi, Guilburd, Lemberger, Soustiel, & Feinsod, 1990; Mittl et al., 1994), irregular cerebral circulation (Elson & Ward, 1994), and altered neurotransmitter function (Hayes & Dixon, 1994). Other research has focused on cervical spine pathology and soft tissue damage in the neck as contributors to posttraumatic headache, vertigo, and local pain (Nagasawa, Sakakibara, & Takahashi, 1993). The weakness of this hypothesis is that it fails to account for (a) the greater incidence and intractability of posttraumatic symptoms in mild head trauma relative to severe head injury, and (b) the greater intractability of symptoms in mild head trauma patients without objective physical signs relative to those with positive signs (R. W. Evans, 1992; Norris & Watt, 1983). In addition, the prevalence of chronic headache following trauma varies with the sample. If posttraumatic symptoms were primarily attributable to neuronal pathologies, one would not expect to see much lower prevalences of posttraumatic headache in certain populations in which there are actually higher rates of mild head trauma (e.g., athletes) (Cook, 1969).

Identity Model. A few observers dismiss entirely the idea that there is any separate biologic etiology for posttraumatic headaches (Haas, 1996). They base their argument on the lack of distinctive features of posttraumatic headaches relative to benign headache syndromes. As noted, nearly the whole range of common benign headache classifications have been observed following trauma. Advocates of this model maintain that the underlying causes or mechanisms of posttraumatic and naturally occurring headaches are the same, even if they are poorly understood or unknown at the present time. Unfortunately, these observers fail to adequately account for the fact that the headaches themselves typically present as part of a broader posttraumatic syndrome.

Organic Genesis/Psychogenic Persistence Model. Lishman (1988) was the first to form this hypothesis into a model of postconcussion syndrome. Lishman proposed that posttraumatic headache has a biological basis in the acute phase but is chronically maintained by "neurotic" developments secondary to trauma. Others have suggested that certain types of persons are dispositionally predisposed to experience these neurotic developments posttrauma and, consequently, the perpetuation of symptoms (Haas, 1993; Lishman, 1988; Moore, 1996; Pearce, 1995). This position has received some empirical and clinical support and fits well with the evolution toward psychobiological models of chronic headache syndromes (Long & Novack, 1986). However, the rather strict "organic versus psychogenic" conceptualization is a limiting factor.

Integrative Model. Recently, Jacobson (1995) has expanded on Lish-man's (1988) model and proposed a multifactorial model that integrates biological mechanisms with psychological, psychosocial, and cognitive-be-havioral processes to explain the onset and intractability of posttraumatic symptoms. For example, Jacobson argued that cognitive-behavioral factors like coping style may significantly influence the course of posttraumatic syndrome. In this model, failure to assess and monitor all four influences on patient presentation and symptom course will lead to less effective or inappropriate treatment choices.

If a consensus position from the available literature can be formulated, it is that both physical and psychosocial issues are important in CPTH and the posttraumatic syndrome (Moore, 1996). What remains to be explored through further research are the specific interrelationships among the myriad variables represented in the categories of "physical" and "psychoso-cial" factors. A recent synthesis statement by Von Korff and Simon (1996) regarding the relationship between pain and depression may have general application for the biopsychosocial approach to CPTH. The authors ar-ticulated three mechanisms that may explain the relationship between pain and depression (or other psychological distress): (a) susceptibility to both depression and pain, (b) maladaptive behavioral and cognitive coping that develops over time in response to acute pain, and (c) the natural psy-chosocial distress that follows significant and prolonged pain. Clearly, Von Korff and Simon view pain and psychological distress, in part, as reciprocal phenomena; their relationship may be set into motion by a third variable (or constellation of variables) called susceptibility. Versions of this model have also been proposed by Gualtieri (1995) and Moore (1996).

COGNITIVE DYSFUNCTION IN CHRONIC POSTTRAUMATIC HEADACHE

Although the psychological correlates of CPTH are generally not in dispute, the proposed link between chronic cognitive deficits and mild head trauma is quite controversial. Several studies have identified cognitive deficits or relatively (compared with nonpatient samples) lower levels of cognitive performance in CPTH patients (e.g., Barth, Macciocchi, & Giordani, 1983; Cremona-Meteyard & Geffen, 1994; F. C. Goldstein et al., 1994; Packard, Weaver, & Ham, 1993; Shum, McFarland, & Bain, 1994; Shum, McFarland, Bain, & Humphreys, 1990). Other reports have demonstrated that greater cognitive deficit is associated with more severe posttraumatic symptoms generally (e.g., Gfeller et al., 1994). Research of this type, however, has been criticized for one or more of the following reasons: (a) reliance on subjective self-reports of cognitive problems, (b) failure to use adequate control groups, and (c) failure to follow patients longitudinally (Bohnen & Jolles, 1992). An alternative study design has allowed the comparison of neuropsychological deficit over time in mild head trauma patients who do and do not develop posttraumatic symptoms, including headache (e.g., Bohnen, Jolles, & Twijnstra, 1992; Bohnen, Jolles, Twijnstra, Mellink, & Wijnen, 1995).

The picture that emerges from the current literature is not clear. We know that patients themselves report cognitive dysfunction. However, when assessed with objective neuropsychological instruments, those deficits that can be identified (in particular, deficits in attentional processes) appear to be subtle and transient (Bohnen & Jolles, 1992; Levin et al., 1987; M. A. Levitt, Sutton, Goldman, Mikhail, & Christopher, 1994; Moore, 1996). Even so, neuropsychological testing cannot determine whether demonstrated deficits are due to psychological variables (e.g., depression, anxiety) or medication side effects, or might have existed prior to the trauma (Moore, 1996; Newcombe, Rabbitt, & Briggs, 1994). Where attempts are made to control for such factors, the association between the trauma and neuropsychological performance has not been corroborated (e.g., Fisher & Williams, 1994; Levin et al., 1987; Tsushima & Tsushima, 1993). Gronwall (1989) has suggested that posttrauma patients who continue to report cognitive deficits beyond the "normal" recovery period are more likely to be older, to have had a previous head injury, to have high-achieving/highly demanding lifestyles, and/or to have high levels of psychosocial stress. Fisher and Williams have warned clinicians that evidence of cognitive deficit after mild head trauma must be interpreted in the light of premorbid factors, comorbid factors, and base rates of dysfunction.

ASSESSMENT OF CHRONIC POSTTRAUMATIC HEADACHE

Given the large number of potentially relevant etiologic factors, effective clinical assessment of CPTH patients must be comprehensive and multimodal. The literature suggests at least three critical components of a thorough assessment, corresponding to the three major symptom categories of CPTH patients: physical, emotional, and cognitive (Gronwall, 1989).

Medical/Dental. The medical evaluation should include a careful history and physical, including a neurological examination, followed by imaging or radiographic studies if there is any suggestion of undiagnosed neurological injury (often, however, CPTH patients will already have had imaging or X-ray studies—usually negative—by the time they present to a headache clinic or headache specialist) (Packard, 1993). Unfortunately, there is as yet no scientifically documented connection between identified abnormalities and posttraumatic symptoms in mild head trauma patients. Some authors have advocated multiple imaging studies to increase sensitivity (Landy, Donovan, & Laster, 1996; Stein, Spettell, Young, & Ross, 1993). However, current technology is not sufficient to evaluate all suggested etiologies. For example, diffuse axonal injury, a condition that has been detected on autopsy in severe, fatal closed head injuries, would not be revealed on an MRI (magnetic resonance imaging). For the present, the relevance of imaging studies in CPTH is primarily as a means of ruling out less subtle neurological injury (e.g., hemorrhages, hematomas); more sophisticated imaging techniques may soon change this (Packard & Ham, 1994b; Young & Silberstein, 1994).

The medical evaluation must also generate detailed information concerning the patient's medication use (types and quantities), because it is not uncommon for CPTH patients to consume large quantities of over-the-counter analgesics, which may exacerbate headache. Moore (1996) has noted that neurophysiologic procedures like EEG or evoked potentials appear to have minimal value in the diagnostic workup of CPTH patients due to the wide intrasubject variability and low specificity of these procedures.

Recent work by Duckro and colleagues (Duckro, Chibnall, & Greenberg, 1995; Duckro et al., 1997; Duckro et al., 1992) and others (cf. Balla & Karnaghan, 1987; Bennett, 1988; Bring & Westman, 1991; Jensen, Justesen, Neilsen, & Brixen, 1990; Jensen, Nielsen, & Vosmar, 1990) has supported the importance of cervical and facial muscle irritation in some cases of CPTH. Patients should be routinely evaluated for masticatory and cervical muscle sensitivity. This can be screened with a relatively simple protocol including manual palpation of muscles and joints, range of motion of the neck and jaw, and self-report of pain with palpation or movement. The examination can be standardized with simple tools for the quantification of palpation pressure and the range of movement achieved (cf. Chibnall, Duckro, & Baumer, 1994; S. C. Chung, Um, & Kim, 1992; Hogeweg, Langereis, Bernards, Faber, & Helders, 1992; Kosek, Ekholm, & Nordemar, 1993). The TMJ Scale™ (Pain Resource Center, Durham, NC) is a well-researched self-report instrument for screening TMD (S. R. Levitt, Lundeen, & McKinney, 1987). Positive findings on any of these screening protocols suggest referral for further evaluation by a physical therapist and/or dentist experienced in working with CPTH.

Psychological Factors. No workup of the CPTH patient is complete without a thorough evaluation of premorbid and comorbid affective, social, cognitive, and behavioral factors. We suggest that the integrative model of CPTH is the more effective and most consistent with current evidence. In that model, psychological factors may be premorbid, predisposing factors, comorbid aggravating factors, or sequelae of pain that exacerbate the condition or associated disability. A wide range of potentially important factors must be considered in each case, though all are not operative in any given patient. The more common affective factors include depression, anxiety, anger, and the indirect expression of emotion in somatic symptoms. Affect, as a reflection of the subjective effect of trauma, should not be underestimated. King (1996) found that measures of anxiety, depression, and "impact of event" were the best predictors of persistent posttraumatic symptoms following mild head trauma. Increased disability (e.g., social, occupational, familial, and sexual role dysfunction) is likely to be associated with clinically significant emotional factors (Duckro, Chibnall, & Tomazic, 1995).

The traumatic onset of CPTH may heighten the emotional distress. In a subset of CPTH patients, the level of anxiety meets diagnostic criteria for posttraumatic stress disorder (PTSD) (Blanchard et al., 1996; Blanchard, Hickling, Taylor, Loos, & Gerardi, 1994; Chibnall & Duckro, 1994). Several studies have documented decreases in pain intensity following the treatment of PTSD in chronic posttraumatic pain patients. The important point is that attention must be paid to psychopathology in CPTH patients of all types. Failure to address emotional distress may reduce the effectiveness of other treatments or complicate the treatment process.

Social factors are legion, but the more common include legal-financial disputes, loss of occupation, family and marital strain, and loss of social network. Cognitive-behavioral influences include coping style and its "fit" with acute or chronic pain, understanding of the posttraumatic syndrome, attribution of blame for the trauma, relationship with the treatment team, pain behavior, and expectations of control over symptoms (Andrasik & Wincze, 1994; Couch, 1995; Fenton, McClelland, Montgomery, MacFlynn, & Rutherford, 1993). The most efficient method for screening psychological variables remains the clinical interview, conducted by a clinician experienced in the behavioral management of headache, and supplemented by paper-and-pencil screening instruments. (For further discussion of the clinical interview in the psychological assessment of headache patients, see Duckro & Tschannen, in press.)

Neuropsychological. Most cognitive symptoms are expected to be resolved within 3 months of mild head trauma. Patients who complain of cognitive deficits beyond that time should be evaluated by a neuropsychologist. Diagnostic accuracy requires attention to a host of premorbid and comorbid cognitive, psychological (e.g., depression, anxiety), medical (e.g., medication, pain), and psychosocial factors, as well as careful attention to base rates of impairment and the sensitivity/specificity of tests in a mild head trauma population (Fisher & Williams, 1994).

TREATMENT OF CHRONIC POSTTRAUMATIC HEADACHE

Treatment must also be multimodal and multidisciplinary. In addition to the specific elements of the treatment plan, the nonspecific factors are critically important in forming an effective therapeutic alliance with the CPTH patient (Andrasik, 1990; Packard & Ham, 1994a; Parker, 1995). Moore (1996) and Gronwall (1989) have used the term *reassurance* to represent one facet of this attitude. *Empathy* is certainly another. By the time CPTH patients present to a headache clinic, they may well have had to work their way through frustrating encounters with disbelieving and/or bewildered health care professionals, supervisors, insurers, or family (Barnat, 1986; Chibnall, Duckro, & Richardson, 1995). Finally, the importance of education lies not only in its content but in the nonspecific benefits of bringing some (even tentative) order to a confusing situation. Explanations for the headache can be offered honestly as hypotheses, to be supported or rejected based on empirical experience in evaluation and treatment.

There is consistent clinical evidence that a multimodal approach is effective in the alleviation of chronic pain syndromes generally (NIH Technology Assessment Panel, 1996). In this report, published in the *Journal of the American Medical Association*, the panel noted a consistent positive effect of multimodal programs on several categories of pain, including headache, facial pain, neck pain, and low back pain (see Duckro, Richardson, Marshall, Marshall, & Cassabaum, 1995, for a clinical, patient-oriented discussion of multimodal treatment). Medina (1992) has conducted one of the only clinical evaluations of multimodal treatment specifically for CPTH, demonstrating in that study the effectiveness of an individualized, multimodal outpatient program. Twenty patients received individualized therapy that included, as a minimum, medication, biofeedback, and educational sessions. In addition, patients received, where applicable, exercise therapy, TENS (transcutaneous electrical nerve stimulation), neuromuscular education, and stress management therapy. After an average of 9 weeks of treatment, 70% of the patients experienced marked improvement in their headache symptoms (20% improved moderately). These percentages are comparable to those reported by clinicians treating patients with chronic, refractory headache syndromes in specialty clinics. Thus, there is empirical support for the integration of therapies in a multimodal, often multidisciplinary response to refractory pain, the components of which are detailed later.

Medication. Although attempts to treat CPTH with medication alone often have proven frustrating, medication remains an important component of the multimodal treatment plan. Antidepressant medications (in particular, doxepin, phenelizine, amitriptyline, nortriptyline, maprotiline) alone or in combination with propanolol have proven successful in reducing the emotional distress of CPTH patients as well as the severity and frequency of certain types of headache (Tyler, McNeely, & Dick, 1980; Weiss, Stern, & Goldberg, 1991). At least one study (Saran, 1988), however, failed to find significant value in tricyclic antidepressants (TCAs) and phenelzine for depression and headache following mild head injury. Packard (1994) has suggested that the selective serotonin-reuptake inhibitors (e.g., fluoxetine) may be more useful for CPTH, given their equivalent efficacy with fewer of the side effects common to TCAs, but this observation requires more extensive empirical confirmation. Other medications that have demonstrated efficacy for symptom management include systematic use of nonsteroidal anti-inflammatory drugs (e.g., aspirin, naproxen) on a timed schedule and abortive medications to limit the duration of severe headache episodes (e.g., sumatriptan, ergotamines) (Gawel, Rothbart, & Jacobs, 1993; McBeath & Nanda, 1994).

Physical Therapy. The use of physical therapy and exercise has proven effective in the treatment of headache (e.g., Jay, Brunson, & Branson, 1989), including CPTH, in which triggering factors include muscle tension or soft tissue injury (Balla & Karnaghan, 1987; Bennett, 1988; Bring & Westman, 1991; Jensen, Justesen et al., 1990; Jensen, Nielsen et al., 1990). The most effective type of physical therapy appears to be an active, exercise-based intervention as opposed to passive, palliative techniques. An integration of active techniques such as stretching, strengthening, and conditioning is typically used in addition to more passive measures like heat, massage, or ultrasound.

There is also some evidence for the effectiveness of manipulation or manual therapy as a component of the physical therapy intervention. Manipulation comprises any number of planned, managed movements of the musculoskeletal system with the goal of enhancing motion or alignment. Recent studies and commentary support the value of manipulation in the treatment of headaches with cervical involvement (often a factor in CPTH) (cf. Cassidy, Lopes, & Yong-Hing, 1992; Di Fabio, 1992; Nilsson, 1995; Twomey, 1992; Vernon, 1989; Whittingham, Ellis, & Molyneux, 1994).

Psychological Treatments. Relaxation, hypnosis, biofeedback, and cognitive-behavioral therapy have all proven effective in reducing chronic pain and its related symptoms (NIH Technology Assessment Panel, 1996). Relaxation therapies seek to induce generalized relaxation resulting in decreased metabolic activity and muscle tension. There are many types of relaxation therapy including diaphragmatic breathing, meditation, imagery, yoga, autogenic phrases, and progressive muscle relaxation. In the clinical setting, biofeedback is used much more often to facilitate relaxation training than as an alternative way to induce relaxation. Biofeedback devices are used to provide information regarding physiologic activity relevant to relaxation such as muscle tension, central neural activity, skin moisture, and skin temperature. Hypnotic approaches use relaxation, imagery, and distraction to focus attention on a specific therapeutic goal introduced through suggestion. According to the NIH Technology Assessment Panel (1996), relaxation and hypnosis are the most universally efficacious interventions across the range of chronic pain syndromes. With respect to CPTH in particular, Ham and Packard (1996) have recently demonstrated the effectiveness of biofeedback-assisted relaxation therapy.

Cognitive-behavioral therapy is the most common type of psychotherapy used for the management of chronic pain syndromes. Such therapy emphasizes education, cognitive and behavioral restructuring, management of dysfunctional emotions, skills acquisition, and the application and maintenance of those skills outside the clinical setting (Parker, 1995). Education was an important component of successful CPTH treatment in Medina's (1992) program evaluation.

Dental. CPTH may be associated with TMD (cf. Braun et al., 1992; Duckro et al., 1992; Duckro et al., 1997; Romanelli et al., 1992; Weinberg & LaPointe, 1987). When TMD is indicated on the basis of a screening assessment, referral to a dentist experienced in the systematic clinical assessment and treatment of TMD should be considered. Conservative use of oral appliances has been shown to decrease symptoms of TMD and associated pain/headache (Ahlin, 1991; Forssell, Kirveskari, & Kangasniemi, 1986; Johansson, Wenneberg, Wagersten, & Haraldson, 1991; Kemper & Okeson, 1983; Magnusson & Carlsson, 1983; Schokker, Hansson, & Ansink, 1990).

RESEARCH ISSUES

Despite the widespread use of multimodal, multidisciplinary treatment programs for CPTH, there is relatively little research documenting its effectiveness as practiced in the clinical setting. The Medina (1992) study, previously cited, is the notable exception. The bulk of the available research has been in the form of efficacy studies. Such studies stress the internal validity of the research design, the careful operationalization and administration of treatments, strict inclusion/exclusion criteria for samples, and the isolation of specific effects associated with narrowly defined causes. Although efficacy studies make an important contribution to the understanding of mechanisms, the relative strength of specific components of multimodal plans, and the relative strength of specific versus nonspecific factors, they necessarily sacrifice external validity. In the clinical setting, treatments are often delivered as a package, patients are heterogenous, and clinicians rather than researchers administer the treatments.

In the view of an increasing number of clinicians and researchers alike, there is a clear need for more effectiveness studies that would evaluate program outcomes in a naturalistic setting, without unrealistic constraints on therapists, patients, and treatment. There also remains a high level of confusion regarding the interplay of biological, social, and psychological factors in the development of CPTH and syndrome. Prospective studies are clearly needed to unravel these relationships.

REFERENCES

Ahlin, J. H. (1991). Clinical application of remoldable appliances for craniomandibular disorder. *Cranio Clinics International, 1*, 65–79.

Alexander, M. P. (1995). Mild traumatic brain injury: Pathophysiology, natural history, and clinical management. *Neurology, 45*, 1253–1260.

Alves, W. M., Colohan, A. R., O'Leary, T. J., Rimel, R. W., & Jane, J. A. (1986). Understanding post-traumatic symptoms after minor head injury. *Journal of Head Trauma and Rehabilitation, 1*, 1–12.

Andrasik, F. (1990). Psychologic and behavioral aspects of chronic headache. *Neurologic Clinics, 8*, 961–976.

Andrasik, F., & Wincze, J. P. (1994). Emotional and psychosocial aspects of mild head injury. *Seminars in Neurology, 14*, 60–66.

Appenzeller, O. (1987). Post-traumatic headaches. In D. J. Dalessio (Ed.), *Wolff's headache and other head pain* (5th ed., pp. 289–303). New York: Oxford University Press.

Arena, J. G., Blanchard, E. B., & Andrasik, F. (1984). The role of affect in the etiology of chronic headache. *Journal of Psychosomatic Research, 28*, 29–86.

Bailey, B. N., & Gudeman, S. K. (1989). Minor head injury. In D. P. Becker & S. K. Gudeman (Eds.), *Textbook of head injury* (pp. 308–318). Philadelphia: Saunders.

Balla, J., & Karnaghan, J. (1987). Whiplash headache. *Clinical and Experimental Neurology, 23*, 179–182.

Barnat, M. R. (1986). Post-traumatic headache patients: II. Special problems, perceptions, and service needs. *Headache, 26*, 332–338.

Barth, J. T., Macciocchi, S. N., & Giordani, B. (1983). Neuropsychological sequelae of minor head injury. *Neurosurgery, 13*, 529–533.

Bennett, T. (1988). Post-traumatic headaches: Subtypes and behavioral treatments. *Cognitive Rehabilitation, 6*, 34–39.

Binder, L. M. (1986). Persisting symptoms after mild head injury. *Journal of Clinical and Experimental Neuropsychology, 8*, 323–346.

Blanchard, E. B., Hickling, E. J., Taylor, A. E., Loos, W. R., Forneris, C. A., & Jaccard, J. (1996). *Behavioral Research and Therapy, 34*, 1–10.

Blanchard, E. B., Hickling, E. J., Taylor, A. E., Loos, W. R., Gerardi, R. J. (1994). Psychological morbidity associated with motor vehicle accidents. *Behavioral Research and Therapy, 32*, 283–290.

Bohnen, N., & Jolles, J. (1992). Neurobehavioral aspects of postconcussive symptoms after mild head injury. *Journal of Nervous and Mental Disease, 180*, 683–692.

Bohnen, N., Jolles, J., & Twijnstra, A. (1992). Neuropsychological deficits in patients with persistent symptoms six months after mild head injury. *Neurosurgery, 30,* 692–695.

Bohnen, N. I., Jolles, J., Twijnstra, A., Mellink, R., & Wijnen, G. (1995). Late neurobehavioural symptoms after mild head injury. *Brain Injury, 9,* 27–33.

Braun, B. L., DiGiovanna, A., Schiffman, E., Bonnema, J., & Fricton, J. (1992). A cross-sectional study of temporomandibular joint dysfunction in post-cervical trauma patients. *Journal of Craniomandibular Disorders, Facial and Oral Pain, 6,* 24–31.

Bring, G., & Westman, G. (1991). Chronic posttraumatic syndrome after whiplash injury. *Scandinavian Journal of Primary Health Care, 9,* 135–141.

Brown, S. J., Fann, J. R., & Grant, I. (1994). Postconcussional disorder: Time to acknowledge a common source of neurobehavioral morbidity. *Journal of Neuropsychiatry and Clinical Neuroscience, 6,* 15–22.

Cassidy, J. D., Lopes, A. A., & Yong-Hing, K. (1992). The immediate effect of manipulation versus mobilization on pain range of motion in the cervical spine: A randomized controlled trial. *Journal of Manipulative and Physiological Therapeutics, 15,* 570–575.

Chibnall, J. T., & Duckro, P. N. (1994). Post-traumatic stress disorder in chronic post-traumatic headache patients. *Headache, 34,* 357–361.

Chibnall, J. T., Duckro, P. N., & Baumer, K. (1994). The influence of body size on linear measurements used to reflect cervical range of motion. *Physical Therapy, 74,* 1134–1137.

Chibnall, J. T., Duckro, P. N., & Richardson, W. R. (1995). Physician frustration with chronic pain patients can and should be avoided. *Headache Quarterly, 6,* 123–125.

Chung, M. K., & Kraybill, D. E. (1990). Headache: A marker of depression. *Journal of Family Practice, 31,* 360–364.

Chung, S. C., Um, B. Y., & Kim, H. S. (1992). Evaluation of pressure pain threshold in head and neck muscles by electronic algometer: Intrarater and interrater reliability. *Cranio, 10,* 28–34.

Cook, J. B. (1969). The effects of minor head injuries sustained in sport and the postconcussional syndrome. In A. E. Walker, W. F. Caveness, & M. Critchley (Eds.), *The late effects of head injury* (pp. 408–413). Springfield, IL: Thomas.

Couch, J. R. (1995). Post-concussion (post-trauma) syndrome. *Journal of Neurologic Rehabilitation, 9,* 83–89.

Cremona-Meteyard, S. L., & Geffen, G. M. (1994). Persistent visuospatial attention deficits following mild head injury in Australian Rules Football players. *Neuropsychology, 32,* 649–662.

Diamond, S., & Freitag, F. G. (1992). Headache following cervical trauma. In C. D. Tollison & J. R. Satterthwaite (Eds.), *Painful cervical trauma* (pp. 381–394). Baltimore: Williams & Wilkins.

Di Fabio, R. P. (1992). Efficacy of manual therapy. *Physical Therapy, 72,* 853–864.

Duckro, P. N., & Chibnall, J. T. (1995). Chronic daily headache as a sequela of minor head and/or neck trauma: A multiple case study. *Headache Quarterly, 6,* 297–302.

Duckro, P. N., Chibnall, J. T., & Greenberg, M. S. (1995). Myofascial involvement in chronic post-traumatic headache. *Headache Quarterly, 6,* 34–38.

Duckro, P. N., Chibnall, J. T., Greenberg, M. S., & Schultz, K. S. (1997). Prevalence of temporomandibular dysfunction in chronic post-traumatic headache patients. *Headache Quarterly, 8,* 228–233.

Duckro, P. N., Chibnall, J. T., & Tomazic, T. J. (1995). Anger, depression, and disability: A path analysis of relationships in a sample of chronic posttraumatic headache patients. *Headache, 35,* 7–9.

Duckro, P. N., Greenberg, M., Schultz, K. T., Burton, S. M., Tait, R. C., Deshields, T. L., & Richardson, W. D. (1992). Clinical features of chronic post-traumatic headache. *Headache Quarterly, 3,* 295–308.

Duckro, P. N., Richardson, W. D., Marshall, J. E., Marshall, G., & Cassabaum, S. (1995). *Taking control of your headaches.* New York: Guilford.

Duckro, P. N., & Tschannen, T. (in press). Psychological assessment of the headache patient. In M. L. Diamond & G. D. Solomon (Eds.), *Diamond's and Dalessio's The practicing physician's approach to headache* (6th ed.). New York: Saunders.

Elson, L. M., & Ward, C. C. (1994). Mechanics and pathophysiology of mild head injury. *Seminars in Neurology, 14,* 8–18.

Evans, R. W. (1992). The postconcussion syndrome and the sequelae of mild head injury. *Seminars in Neurology, 14,* 8–18.

Evans, R. W. (1994). The postconcussion syndrome: 130 years of controversy. *Seminars in Neurology, 14,* 32–39.

Evans, R. W., Evans, R. I., & Sharp, M. J. (1994). The physician survey on the post-concussion and whiplash syndromes. *Headache, 34,* 268–274.

Fenton, G., McClelland, R., Montgomery, A., MacFlynn, G., & Rutherford, W. (1993). *British Journal of Psychiatry, 162,* 493–497.

Fisher, A. D., & Williams, A. D. (1994). Neuropsychologic investigations of mild head injury: Ensuring diagnostic accuracy in the assessment process. *Seminars in Neurology, 14,* 53–59.

Forssell, H., Kirveskari, P., & Kangasniemi, P. (1986). Effect of occlusal adjustment on mandibular dysfunction. A double-blind study. *Acta Odontologica Scandinavica, 44,* 63–69.

Gawel, M. J., Rothbart, P., & Jacobs, H. (1993). Subcutaneous sumatriptan in the treatment of acute episodes of posttraumatic headache. *Headache, 33,* 96–97.

Gfeller, J. D., Chibnall, J. T., & Duckro, P. N. (1994). Postconcussion symptoms and cognitive functioning in posttraumatic headache patients. *Headache, 34,* 503–507.

Goldstein, F. C., Levin, H. S., Presley, R. M., Searcy, J., Colohan, A. R. T., Eisenberg, H. M., Jann, B., & Bertolino-Kusnerik, L. (1994). Neurobehavioral consequences of closed head injury in older adults. *Journal of Neurology, Neurosurgery, and Psychiatry, 57,* 961–966.

Goldstein, J. (1991). Posttraumatic headache and the postconcussion syndrome. *Medical Clinics of North America, 75,* 641–651.

Goodman, J. C. (1994). Pathologic changes in mild head injury. *Seminars in Neurology, 14,* 19–24.

Gronwall, D. (1989). Cumulative and persisting effects of concussion on attention and cognition. In H. S. Levin, I. M. Eisenberg, & A. I. Benton (Eds.), *Mild head injury* (pp. 153–162). New York: Oxford University Press.

Gualtieri, C. T. (1995). The problem of mild brain injury. *Neuropsychiatry, Neuropsychology, and Behavioral Neurology, 8,* 127–136.

Haas, D. C. (1993). Chronic post-traumatic headache. In J. Olesen, P. Tfelt-Hansen, & K. M. A. Welch (Eds.), *The headaches* (pp. 629–637). New York: Raven.

Haas, D. C. (1996). Chronic post-traumatic headaches classified and compared with natural headaches. *Cephalalgia, 16,* 486–493.

Ham, L. P., Andrasik, F., Packard, R. C., & Bundrick, C. M. (1994). Psychopathology in individuals with post-traumatic headaches and other pain types. *Cephalalgia, 14,* 118–126.

Ham, L. P., & Packard, R. C. (1996). A retrospective, follow-up study of biofeedback-assisted relaxation therapy in patients with posttraumatic headache. *Biofeedback and Self Regulation, 21,* 93–104.

Hatch, J. P., Schoenfeld, L. S., Boutros, N. N., Seleshi, E., Moore, P. J., & Cyr-Provost, M. (1991). Anger and hostility in tension-type headache. *Headache, 32,* 302–304.

Hayes, R., & Dixon, C. E. (1994). Neurochemical changes in mild head injury. *Seminars in Neurology, 14,* 25–31.

Headache Classification Committee of the International Headache Society. (1988). Classification and diagnostic criteria for headache disorders, cranial neuralgias and facial pain. *Cephalalgia, 8*(Suppl. 7), 1–96.

Hogeweg, J. A., Langereis, M. J., Bernards, A. T., Faber, J. A., & Helders, P. J. (1992). Algometry. Measuring pain threshold, method and characteristics in healthy subjects. *Scandinavian Journal of Rehabilitation Medicine, 24,* 99–103.

Jacobson, R. R. (1995). The post-concussional syndrome: Physiogenesis, psychogenesis and malingering. An integrative model. *Journal of Psychosomatic Research, 39,* 675–693.

Jay, G. W., Brunson, J., & Branson, S. J. (1989). The effectiveness of physical therapy in the treatment of chronic daily headaches. *Headache, 29,* 156–162.

Jensen, O. K., Justesen, T., Neilsen, F. F., & Brixen, K. (1990). Functional radiographic examination of the cervical spine in patients with post-traumatic headache. *Cephalalgia, 10,* 295–303.

Jensen, O. K., & Nielsen, F. F. (1990). The influence of sex and pre-traumatic headache on the incidence and severity of headache after head injury. *Cephalalgia, 10,* 285–293.

Jensen, O. K., Nielsen, F. F., & Vosmar, L. (1990). An open study comparing manual therapy with the use of cold packs in the treatment of post-traumatic headache. *Cephalalgia, 10,* 241–250.

Johansson, A., Wenneberg, B., Wagersten, C., & Haraldson, T. (1991). Acupuncture in treatment of facial muscular pain. *Acta Odontologica Scandinavica, 49,* 153–158.

Karzmark, P., Hall, K., & Englander, J. (1995). Late-onset post-concussion symptoms after mild brain injury: The role of premorbid, injury-related, environmental, and personality factors. *Brain Injury, 9,* 21–26.

Kemper, J. T. Jr., & Okeson, J. P. (1983). Craniomandibular disorders and headaches. *Journal of Prosthetic Dentistry, 49,* 702–705.

King, N. S. (1996). Emotional, neuropsychological, and organic factors: Their use in the prediction of persisting postconcussion symptoms after moderate and mild head injuries. *Journal of Neurology, Neurosurgery, and Psychiatry, 61,* 75–81.

Kosek, E., Ekholm, J., & Nordemar, R. (1993). A comparison of pressure pain thresholds in different tissues and body regions. Long-term reliability of pressure algometry in healthy volunteers. *Scandinavian Journal of Rehabilitation Medicine, 25,* 117–124.

Landy, S. H., Donovan, T. B., & Laster, R. E. (1996). Repeat CT or MRI in posttraumatic headache. *Headache, 36,* 44–47.

Levi, L., Guilburd, J. N., Lemberger, A., Soustiel, J. F., & Feinsod, M. (1990). Diffuse axonal injury: Analysis of 100 patients with radiological signs. *Neurosurgery, 27,* 429–432.

Levin, H. S., Mattis, S., Ruff, R. M., Eisenberg, H. M., Marshall, L. F., Tabaddor, K., High, W. M. Jr., & Frankowski, R. F. (1987). Neurobehavioral outcome following minor head injury: A three-center study. *Journal of Neurosurgery, 66,* 234–243.

Levitt, M. A., Sutton, M., Goldman, J., Mikhail, M., & Christopher, T. (1994). Cognitive dysfunction in patients suffering minor head trauma. *American Journal of Emergency Medicine, 12,* 172–175.

Levitt, S. R., Lundeen, T. F., & McKinney, M. W. (1987). *The TMJ Scale manual.* Durham, NC: Pain Resource Center.

Lidvall, H. F., Linderoth, B., & Norlin, B. (1974). Causes of the post-concussional syndrome. *Acta Neurologica Scandinavica, 50*(Suppl. 56), 7–144.

Lishman, W. A. (1988). Physiogenesis and psychogenesis in the "post-concussional syndrome." *British Journal of Psychiatry, 153,* 460–469.

Long, C. J., & Novack, T. A. (1986). Postconcussion symptoms after head trauma: Interpretation and treatment. *Southern Medical Journal, 79,* 728–732.

Magnusson, T., & Carlsson, G. E. (1983). A 2½-year follow-up of changes in headache and mandibular dysfunction after stomatognathic treatment. *Journal of Prosthetic Dentistry, 49,* 398–402.

Mandel, S. (1989). Minor head injury may not be "minor." *Postgraduate Medicine, 85,* 213–225.

Mathew, N. T., & Rueveni, U. (1988). Cluster-like headache following head trauma. *Headache, 28,* 297.

McBeath, J. G., & Nanda, A. (1994). Use dihydroergotamine in patients with postconcussion syndrome. *Headache, 34,* 148–151.

McKinlay, W., Brooks, D., & Bond, M. (1983). Post-concussional symptoms, financial compensation and outcome of severe blunt head injury. *Journal of Neurology, Neurosurgery, and Psychiatry, 46,* 1084–1091.

Medina, J. L. (1992). Efficacy of an individualized outpatient program in the treatment of chronic post-traumatic headache. *Headache, 32,* 180–183.

Mendelson, G. (1995). "Compensation neurosis" revisited: Outcome studies of the effects of litigation. *Journal of Psychosomatic Research, 39,* 695–706.

Miller, H. (1968). Posttraumatic headache. In P. J. Vinken & G. W. Bruyn (Eds.), *Handbook of clinical neurology: Vol. 5. Headaches and clinical neuralgias* (pp. 178–184). New York: Wiley.

Mittl, R. L., Grossman, R. I., Hiehle, J. F., Hurst, R. W., Kauder, D. R., Gennarelli, T. A., & Alburger, G. W. (1994). Prevalence of MR evidence of diffuse axonal injury in patients with mild head injury and normal head CT findings. *American Journal of Neuroradiology, 15,* 1583–1589.

Moore, K. L. (1996). Trauma and headaches. *Headache Quarterly, 7,* 21–29.

Nagasawa, A., Sakakibara, T., & Takahashi, A. (1993). Roentgenographic findings of the cervical spine in tension-type headache. *Headache, 33,* 90–95.

Newcombe, F., Rabbitt, P., & Briggs, M. (1994). Minor head injury: Pathophysiological or iatrogenic sequelae? *Journal of Neurology, Neurosurgery, and Psychiatry, 57,* 709–716.

NIH Technology Assessment Panel on Integration of Behavioral and Relaxation Approaches Into the Treatment of Chronic Pain and Insomnia. (1996). Integration of behavioral and relaxation approaches into the treatment of chronic pain and insomnia. *Journal of the American Medical Association, 276,* 313–318.

Nilsson, N. (1995). A randomized controlled trial of the effect of spinal manipulation in the treatment of cervicogenic headache. *Journal of Manipulative and Physiological Therapeutics, 18,* 435–440.

Norris, S. H., & Watt, I. (1983). The prognosis of neck injuries resulting from rear-end vehicle collisions. *Journal of Bone and Joint Surgery [British], 65,* 608–611.

Packard, R. C. (1992). Posttraumatic headache: Permanency and relationship to legal settlement. *Headache, 32,* 496–500.

Packard, R. C. (1993). Mild head injury. *Headache Quarterly, 4,* 42–52.

Packard, R. C. (1994). Posttraumatic headache. *Seminars in Neurology, 14,* 40–45.

Packard, R. C. (1996). Post-traumatic headache: More than a headache. *Headache Quarterly, 7,* 115–116.

Packard, R. C., & Ham, L. P. (1994a). Posttraumatic headache. *Journal of Neuropsychiatry and Clinical Neuroscience, 6,* 229–236.

Packard, R. C., & Ham, L. P. (1994b). Promising techniques in the assessment of mild head injury. *Seminars in Neurology, 14,* 74–83.

Packard, R. C., & Ham, L. P. (1996). Incidence of cluster-like post-traumatic headache: An inconsistency. *Headache Quarterly, 7,* 139–141.

Packard, R. C., Weaver, R., & Ham, L. P. (1993). Cognitive symptoms in patients with post-traumatic headache. *Headache, 33,* 365–368.

Parker, R. S. (1995). The distracting effect of pain, headaches, and hyper-arousal upon employment after "minor head injury." *Journal of Cognitive Rehabilitation, 13,* 14–23.

Pearce, J. M. S. (1995). Post-traumatic syndrome and whiplash injuries. In C. Kennard (Ed.), *Recent advances in clinical neurology* (Vol. 8, pp. 133–150). New York: Churchill-Livingstone.

Reik, L. (1987). Cluster headache after head injury. *Headache, 27,* 509–510.

Romanelli, G. G., Mock, D., & Tenenbaum, H. C. (1992). Characteristics and response to treatment of posttraumatic temporomandibular disorders: A retrospective study. *Clinical Journal of Pain, 8,* 6–17.

Saper, J. R. (1983). *Headache disorders: Current concepts and treatment strategies.* Boston: John Wright.

Saran, A. (1988). Antidepressants not effective in headache associated with minor closed head injury. *International Journal of Psychiatry and Medicine, 18,* 75–83.

Schokker, R. P., Hansson, T. L., & Ansink, B. J. (1990). The result of treatment of the masticatory system of chronic headache patients. *Journal of Craniomandibular Disorders, 4,* 126–130.

Shum, D. H., McFarland, K., Bain, J. D. (1994). Effects of closed-head injury on attentional processes: Generality of Sternberg's additive factor method. *Journal of Clinical and Experimental Neuropsychology, 16,* 547–555.

Shum, D. H., McFarland, K., Bain, J. D., & Humphreys, M. S. (1990). Effects of closed-head injury on attentional processes: An information-processing stage analysis. *Journal of Clinical and Experimental Neuropsychology, 12,* 247–264.

Speed, M. (1989). Closed head injury sequelae: Changing concepts. *Headache, 29,* 643–647.

Spierings, E. L. H., & van Hoof, M. J. (1996). Anxiety and depression in chronic headache sufferers. *Headache Quarterly, 7,* 235–238.

Stein, S. C., Spettell, C., Young, G., & Ross, S. E. (1993). Delayed and progressive brain injury in closed-head trauma: Radiological demonstration. *Neurosurgery, 32,* 25–31.

Treleaven, J., Jull, G., & Atkinson, L. (1994). Cervical musculoskeletal dysfunction in post-concussional headache. *Cephalalgia, 14,* 273–279.

Tschannen, T. A., Duckro, P. N., Margolis, R. B., & Tomazic, T. J. (1992). The relationship of anger, depression, and perceived disability among headache patients. *Headache, 32,* 501–503.

Tsushima, W. T., & Tsushima, V. G. (1993). Relation between headaches and neuropsychological functioning among head injury patients. *Headache, 33,* 139–142.

Twomey, L. T. (1992). A rationale for the treatment of back pain and joint pain by manual therapy. *Physical Therapy, 72,* 885–892.

Tyler, G., McNeely, H., & Dick, M. (1980). Treatment of post-traumatic headache with amitriptyline. *Headache, 20,* 213–216.

Vernon, H. T. (1989). Spinal manipulation and headache of cervical origin. *Journal of Manipulative and Physiological Therapeutics, 12,* 455–468.

Von Korff, M., & Simon, G. (1996). The relationship between pain and depression. *British Journal of Psychiatry, 30*(Suppl.), 101–108.

Weinberg, S., & LaPointe, H. (1987). Cervical extension-flexion injury (whiplash) and internal derangement of the temporomandibular joint. *Journal of Oral and Maxillofacial Surgery, 45,* 653–656.

Weiss, H. D., Stern, J., & Goldberg, J. (1991). Post-traumatic migraine: Chronic migraine precipitated by minor head or neck trauma. *Headache, 31,* 451–456.

Whittingham, W., Ellis, W. B., & Molyneux, T. P. (1994). The effect of manipulation (toggle recoil technique) for headaches with upper cervical joint dysfunction: A pilot study. *Journal of Manipulative and Physiological Therapeutics, 17,* 369–375.

Yamaguchi, M. (1992). Incidence of headache and severity of head injury. *Headache, 32,* 427–431.

Young, W. B., & Silberstein, S. D. (1994). Imaging and electrophysiologic testing in mild head injury. *Seminars in Neurology, 14,* 46–52.

Chapter 16

Complex Regional Pain Syndromes: An Interdisciplinary Perspective

Herbert G. Steger
Department of Anesthesiology
University of Kentucky College of Medicine

Stephen Bruehl
R. Norman Harden
Department of Physical Medicine and Rehabilitation
Northwestern University Medical School

Complex regional pain syndrome (CRPS) is characterized by constant, severe, deep, diffuse, burning pain; abnormal pain response; autonomic dysfunction; and difficulty in motor functioning. It typically affects the extremities, but less frequently also affects other areas of the body, including head and breast. CRPS usually develops following surgery, trauma (such as a sprain, fracture, or crush injury), or injury to a peripheral nerve, although it may develop without an initiating event. The condition also has been reported in association with other medical conditions, including myocardial infarction, cerebral vascular accident, traumatic brain injury, neoplastic tumor, cervical and lumbar radiculopathy, and spinal cord injury. Although long thought to affect only adults, CRPS has been found to affect children and adolescents (Wilder, Berde, Wolohan, Vieyra, & Masek, 1992). The condition develops at variable rates, can spread to other parts of the body, often responds poorly to treatment, and can progress to become a disabling chronic pain syndrome.

CRPS has posed a diagnostic and treatment challenge since its initial description during the American Civil War (Mitchell, Morehouse, & Keen, 1864). Psychological factors have been presumed to play an integral role in the etiology, maintenance, and outcome of the condition throughout its long history. Recent developments have led to improved understanding of the pathophysiology, diagnosis, treatment, and role of psychological and behavioral factors in CRPS. This chapter reviews these developments and discusses the current interdisciplinary approach to treatment, with an emphasis on the role of behavioral medicine in understanding and treating the disorder.

Historically, CRPS has been known by a variety of names (Kozin, 1992). The most commonly used terms have been *reflex sympathetic dystrophy* (RSD) and *causalgia*, although terms such as *Sudeck's atrophy, shoulder-hand syndrome,* and *algoneurodystrophy* are also used. Because of difficulties associated with lack of standardized diagnostic criteria and nomenclature, the International Association for the Study of Pain (IASP) created consensus nomenclature and a set of diagnostic criteria to supersede those previously used (Merskey & Bogduk, 1994; Stanton-Hicks et al., 1995). Table 16.1 presents IASP diagnostic criteria for CRPS. Two distinct subtypes of CRPS were identified, Types I and II. CRPS-Type I (previously labeled RSD) refers to the syndrome occurring without nerve injury, whereas CRPS-Type II (previously known as causalgia) refers to syndromes that develop following injury to a peripheral nerve. Differences between these two syndromes are presented in Table 16.2. We focus on CRPS-Type I because it has an established interdisciplinary treatment protocol and because there is little clinical or research literature on Type II from a behavioral medicine perspective.

There are two approaches to characterizing CRPS-Type I (hereafter referred to as CRPS); one describes distinct stages and the other identifies relative grades of severity. CRPS has been described as passing through three overlapping phases or stages as shown in Table 16.3. The appropriateness of staging CRPS has been questioned because (a) it is impossible to tell whether patients will pass from the first to subsequent stages without

TABLE 16.1
Signs and Symptoms of CRPS

Primary Features

Diffuse burning or deep aching pain, usually in an extremity.
Presence of initiating noxious event or immobilization.
Persistent pain, allodynia, or hyperalgesia out of proportion to inciting event.
Symptoms of autonomic dysfunction in area of pain, including swelling, blood flow abnormalities, increased or decreased sweating.
No other disorder can account for the symptoms.

Associated Signs and Symptoms

Skin, hair, and nail growth changes.
Diminished joint range of motion.
Loss of bone density (osteoporosis).
Impaired motor function (weakness, tremor).
Contractures.
Thermal sensitivity.

TABLE 16.2
Differences Between CRPS Types I and II

	CRPS I	*CRPS II*
Etiology	Any type of lesion except to peripheral nerve	Partial nerve lesion
Localization	Distal part of extremity	Any peripheral body site
Spreading of symptoms	Always present	Rare
Spontaneous pain	Common	Always present
	Mostly deep and superficial	Predominantly superficial
	Orthostatic component (pain decreases when limb elevated and increases when lowered)	No orthostatic component
Mechanical allodynia (painful response to nonpainful stimulus)	Present in most patients Tends to spread	Present in area served by nerve
Autonomic symptoms (blood flow abnormalities, disturbed sweating, swelling)	Distally generalized with tendency to spread	Related to nerve lesion
Motor symptoms (weakness, tremor, dystonia)	Distally generalized	Related to nerve lesion
Sensory symptoms (spontaneous pain, allodynia, hyperalgesia, hyperpathia)	Distally generalized with spreading tendency	Related to nerve lesion

Note. From Baron, Blumberg, & Jänig (1996). Copyright 1996 by IASP Press. Adapted by permission.

TABLE 16.3
Stages of CRPS Type I

CRPS Stage	*Time Frame*	*Characteristics*
Stage I: Acute	0 to 3 months	Localized symptoms of pain, swelling, joint stiffness, altered hair & nail growth; skin warm & dry; diminished sympathetic activity.
Stage II: Dystrophic	3 to 6 months	Pain more diffuse & severe, edema more widespread, skin cold & sweaty, diminished hair & nail growth, sympathetic overactivity.
Stage III: Atrophic	6+ months	Pain intractable & may spread to entire limb & beyond, skin smooth & glossy, muscles atrophied, joints fused, tendons contracted, bones demineralized. Characterized by functional disability & chronicity.

treatment, (b) patients do not always pass through each stage in sequence, and (c) none of the symptoms are specific to the first two stages (Baron, Blumberg, & Jänig, 1996; Blumberg & Jänig, 1994). Instead of staging, these authors suggested grading the severity of sensory, autonomic, motor, and growth symptoms. Table 16.4 presents severity ratings used with CRPS. Although rating according to severity or to presumed stages is a common clinical practice, there is little research to support either as meaningful categories in terms of reliability and validity or clinical utility in guiding treatment interventions. Indeed, it appears that treatment typically has progressed through the complete range of available options irrespective of the supposed stage or severity of the condition.

Early intervention is critical in treatment of CRPS because response to treatment decreases rapidly as time passes. Wang, Johnson, and Ilstrup (1985), for example, reported that the rate of improvement following sympathetic blocks decreased steadily with increasing time since onset. Eighty-seven percent of their patients were improved after 1 year when sympathetic blocks were administered within 1 month of onset, whereas only 50% improved if blocks were delayed until 6 to 12 months after onset.

Good results are reported for various medical and surgical interventions, with improvement ranging up to 95% for sympathetic blocks (Carron & Weller, 1974), 82% for epidural blocks with physical therapy (Ladd, De-Haven, Thanik, Patt, & Feuerstein, 1989), 91% for spinal cord stimulation (Robaina, Domingues, Diaz, Rodriguez, & de Vera, 1989), 70% with intravenous regional blocks (Eulry et al., 1991), 82% with high doses of oral corticosteroids (Kozin, Ryan, Carrera, & Soin, 1981), 80% with physical therapy alone (Pak, Martin, Magness, & Kavanaugh, 1970), and 80% with surgical sympathectomy (Kleinert et al., 1973).

Our clinical experience, lack of good long-term outcome data, and reports of others in the literature suggest that claims of high success rates in treating CRPS are extremely optimistic. McLeskey, Balestrieri, and Weeks (1993) noted, "despite the many techniques available to treat patients with

TABLE 16.4
Classification of CRPS by Symptom Severity

Classification	Characteristics
Severe	Pain is severe, burning, knifelike or lancinating, unrelieved by rest, and subject to exacerbation by slightest emotional or physical stimulation; associated with significant autonomic, motor, and sensory disturbances.
Moderate	Pain is dull, throbbing, aching, burning, and diffuse; moderate or mild autonomic, motor, and sensory disturbances.
Mild	Most common form, the border between normal response to trauma and the more severe forms. Often not diagnosed because of mildness of pain and associated symptoms.

sympathetic dystrophies, most clinicians and authors remain frustrated with the results of therapy" (p. 231). Subbarao and Stillwell (1981) reported that nearly 60% of 125 cases reviewed continued to have persistent symptoms despite adequate treatment. Kozin (1992) reviewed seven studies of over 500 patients treated with sympathetic blocks and found that the majority had only transient or no pain relief from this type of treatment. Inhofe and Garcia-Moral (1994) studied treated patients an average of 5 years after diagnosis. Fifty-six percent of their subjects experienced a worsening of symptoms and 78% reported activities of daily living were negatively affected. Greipp and Thomas (1986) also reported that survey data from Reflex Sympathetic Dystrophy Syndrome Association members indicated 96% continued to suffer from pain despite a variety of treatments, after an average of 4.2 years since onset. Thus, it appears that long-term outcome may be considerably less positive than suggested by shorter term results reported in some treatment studies.

DIAGNOSIS OF COMPLEX REGIONAL PAIN SYNDROME

Diagnosis of CRPS is based primarily on clinical examination because there are no objective physical findings or laboratory results that are pathognomonic (Kozin, 1992). Although thermography often is used to identify areas of temperature asymmetry associated with autonomic dysfunction (Cooke et al., 1989), validity studies indicate that its sensitivity and specificity are not sufficient for definitive diagnosis (Bruehl, Lubenow, Nath, & Ivankovich, 1996). A radiologic study, the three-phase bone scan, reliably identifies early changes in bone metabolism that later develop into osteoporosis (Kozin, 1992). The role of the sympathetic nervous system in CRPS pain is frequently evaluated by use of local anesthetics that temporarily block sympathetic ganglia, or by infusion of systemic blockade that cause temporary pain reduction by blocking sympathetic receptors (Baron et al., 1996). However, this diagnostic block approach may be problematic because current CRPS criteria include patients whose pain may not be sympathetically mediated.

PATHOPHYSIOLOGY OF COMPLEX REGIONAL PAIN SYNDROME

The pathophysiology of CRPS remains enigmatic (Harden, 1994). Although multiple hypotheses have been proposed as to how CRPS develops and is maintained, none have received sufficient empirical support. Most hypotheses include the presence of a peripheral nociceptive generator, such as minor nerve damage. Because most etiologies include damage to deep tissues of a limb, this nociception is most often presumed to be carried on traditional peripheral nociceptive pathways (i.e., small and unmyelinated C-fibers and A-delta fibers). Chronic maintenance of a nociceptive generator may be an intrinsic feature of the disease (Gracely, Lynch, & Bennett, 1992). It has been hypothesized, with some research support, that the presumed nociceptive generator alters signal processing in the spinal cord, and a pathological feedback loop is set up that ultimately involves the sympathetic efferents (Roberts, 1986). This altered central processing (probably through dorsal horn to interomediolateral horn connections) clearly affects the sympathetic efferents, but probably also creates pathologic processes that maintain amplified and abnormal spinal transmission of the pain (Gracely et al., 1992).

Increased sympathetic efferent outflow may act in the periphery to maintain and amplify activity in the nociceptive generator (e.g., area of nerve injury). The impact of central feedback from midbrain, limbic system, thalamus, and cortex may serve to amplify and sustain positive feedback and feed-forward loops that reverberate throughout the peripheral and central nervous systems. The coexistence of psychological states such as anxiety and depression may perpetuate the syndrome at brainstem levels (such as locus coeruleous and bulbar raphae) through their effects on the sympathetic nervous system (Bruehl & Carlson, 1992). Data from one of our pain centers suggest that patients with CRPS have higher levels of systemic catecholamines, which could be the result of preexisting or coexisting depression and anxiety disorders (Harden, Rudin, & Parikh, 1995). Whether these biochemical markers of anxiety and depression exist prior to the development of CRPS remains uncertain.

ROLE OF PSYCHOLOGICAL FACTORS IN COMPLEX REGIONAL PAIN SYNDROME

Covington (1996) has suggested five ways that psychological factors could be active in this condition: (a) Psychological factors can be seen as expected reactions to chronic pain and disability, (b) personality traits or psychiatric illness can cause a predisposition for the condition, (c) CRPS can represent a conversion or psychogenic phenomenon, (d) behavior can modify the condition's course and symptoms, and (e) psychological issues that are important in other chronic pain conditions also may be involved with CRPS. We consider what is known regarding the role of these factors.

The psychogenic approach focuses on the role of psychological trauma in the etiology of CRPS. Repressed emotions about the trauma can be expressed physically in the form of somatic symptoms and pain. This view of CRPS pain became widely accepted by both mental health professionals and physicians for several reasons. First, there was no accepted pathophysiological mechanisms or theory to explain the unusual nature of the symptoms, for example, pain in a "glove" or "stocking" pattern unrelated to dermatomal or peripheral nerve distributions. There also was often no known injury sufficient to explain symptom severity. A frequent temporal relationship between symptom onset and significant psychological events can lead to an attribution of causation to these psychological factors. When pain is unresponsive to what is considered to be appropriate treatment, it is often labeled as psychogenic (Dworkin & Burgess, 1987). Because there are no specific tests or objective evaluation procedures that definitively indicate the presence of CRPS, physicians often were left with no other explanation than a psychological one.

Although the psychogenic view continues to be espoused (Ochoa & Verdugo, 1995; Weiss, 1994), it has no empirical support and also has significant logical and conceptual problems. This approach confuses the absence of evidence with evidence of absence; that is, failure to find a known pathological condition was taken as proof that there was no physiological basis for the disorder. It also makes the mistake of using an absence of identifiable physical pathology as positive evidence for a psychological causation.

Another model for understanding the relationship between psychological and physiological factors in CRPS is the psychophysiological model (Bruehl & Carlson, 1992; Ecker, 1989). The key element in this model is the relationship between psychological arousal and sympathetic nervous system activity. Autonomic dysfunction, particularly sympathetic arousal, appears to be responsible for key symptoms of CRPS, for example, hyperalgesia, allodynia, and temperature dysregulation. Psychological factors such as anxiety and depression are associated with neurohumoral changes and with sympathetic nervous system arousal (Abelson et al., 1991; Gold, Goodwin, & Chrousos, 1988). Additional psychosocial stresses associated with the condition, its treatment, and its impact on the person's life keep the patient in a chronic state of sympathetic arousal. To the extent that sympathetic arousal causes or exacerbates CRPS symptoms, psychological factors may play an etiological, maintenance, or exacerbating role in the condition.

There is much speculation about possible predisposing personality variables in CRPS (Bruehl & Carlson, 1992; Horowitz, 1984; Weiss, 1994). Patients have been labeled variously as insecure, fearful, unstable, and chronic complainers (Lankford & Thompson, 1977); as having inadequate personalities and neurotic tendencies (McLeskey et al., 1993); as having personality traits such as anxiety, hyperirritability, and intolerance for cold and pain (Lankford, 1983); and even as exceptionally energetic and hysterical (Zachariae, 1964). There is, however, little empirical evidence to support the notion that there is a predisposing CRPS personality type.

It has been suggested that patients who develop CRPS have a constitutional psychophysiologic predisposition or susceptibility related to a chronic state of the nervous system, a "diathesis" (Sternbach, 1966) that includes a highly active or reactive sympathetic nervous system (Lankford, 1983; Lankford & Thompson, 1977). This predisposition is considered to be associated with psychological factors including underlying anger, passive-aggressiveness, extreme dependency, insecurity, instability, proneness to psychosomatic symptoms, and repression (Weiss, 1994). Although a psychophysiological diathesis is a very attractive concept, no empirical data support such a predisposition, so its presence and influence, as with personality variables, remain speculative.

Situational factors also have been proposed to be critical in onset and exacerbation of CRPS symptoms. Some support for an association between situational stress and CRPS onset can be found in a study by Geertzen, de Bruijn, de Bruijn-Kofman, and Arendzen (1994), who found that 80% of CRPS patients reported a stressful life event prior to the onset of the condition, whereas only 20% of controls reported such an event. All individuals experiencing significant stress of any origin will experience sympathetic arousal that can impact the severity of CRPS symptoms. Psychiatric disorders also may impact CRPS by similar mechanisms (Bruehl & Carlson, 1992).

Van Houdenhove and colleagues (1992) have presented a biopsychosocial hypothesis relating situational psychophysiological stress to the onset and maintenance of CRPS. This model proposes that a significant and fundamental loss is associated with the initiating physical trauma. The individual responds to this loss with a characteristic helplessness, resulting in sympathetic overactivity that contributes to the precipitation, reinforcement, and maintenance of CRPS symptoms. A vicious cycle results in which helplessness leads to passive coping, reinforcement of exaggerated pain behavior and prolonged disability, and further sympathetic reactivity. Although empirical support for this theory is lacking, it does present the potential for integrating psychophysiological, behavioral, and psychological factors.

Another alternative to the psychogenic model involves operant learning. According to some physiological models of CRPS, many of the symptoms result from chronic disuse of the affected extremity (Hooshmand, 1993). Negative reinforcement can be a useful concept in understanding disuse phenomena in CRPS. From this perspective, the patient does not use the extremity in order to avoid the aversive consequence of increased pain that has been associated with its use in the past. Avoidance of pain reinforces disuse with resulting loss of range of motion and strength, increase in edema and bone mineral loss, and difficulty in proprioception and body awareness (Galer, Butler, & Jensen, 1995). Operant learning can also affect the behavior of CRPS patients in a manner similar to that of patients with other chronic pain conditions, for example, by increasing pain, disability, or sick role behaviors through the effects of environmental consequences (Fordyce, 1976).

Dysfunctional cognitive responses to chronic pain (i.e., negative distortions such as catastrophizing and overgeneralizing) can contribute to stress and emotional distress. When such thought patterns result in elevated stress and depression, pain experience is exacerbated, contributing to further disuse, disability, and disruptions in life and functioning. These negative effects on quality of life can lead to additional distress and continued dysfunctional thinking, thus resulting in a vicious cycle of distress, pain, and dysfunction.

Research Evidence for Role of Psychological Factors in Complex Regional Pain Syndrome

Although theory supports a role for psychological factors in CRPS, extensive reviews of the pain literature find no prospective studies to support their etiological role (Bruehl & Carlson, 1992; Haddox, 1990; Lynch, 1992). Empirical studies have investigated possible psychological differences between CRPS patients and other patients with chronic pain. The results of these studies have been mixed, depending in part on how the disorder is defined and on the patients to whom CRPS patients are compared. DeGood, Cundiff, Adams, and Shutty (1993) failed to find evidence of psychological differences on standardized psychological tests between patients with CRPS and those with headache or low back pain. Haddox, Abram, and Hopwood (1988) found no differences between those with CRPS and a group with radicular back pain. However, Bruehl and colleagues (Bruehl, Husfeldt, Lubenow, Nath, & Ivankovich, 1996) found that CRPS patients with sympathetically maintained pain were more anxious than low back pain patients when age and duration of pain were controlled. Although this finding is consistent with a differential impact of psychological factors in CRPS, Bruehl et al. found that patients with extremity pain resulting from CRPS were not different on measures of psychological distress than control patients who had nonsympathetic limb pain. However, many of these control patients would meet current diagnostic criteria for nonsympathetically maintained CRPS (Bruehl, 1997).

Patients with CRPS do not appear to comprise a distinct population or subset of chronic pain patients. Many of the emotional and personality factors cited as causal in CRPS are understood equally well as the result of ongoing severe pain and disability. In fact, it has been noted that these psychological problems cleared when pain was relieved (Ecker, 1989; Schwartzman & McLellan, 1987). It appears reasonable to conclude that CRPS patients are psychologically similar to other patients with chronic pain, especially those with extremity pain, with psychological characteristics determined more by the chronicity of the pain than by any distinctive characteristic common to them.

TREATMENT APPROACHES TO COMPLEX REGIONAL PAIN SYNDROME

In previous treatment approaches to CRPS, the focus often has been on modification of the disease process, with psychological, emotional, and behavioral factors seen as epiphenomena or complicating reactions to the disease and treatment. In the rehabilitation treatment paradigm presented here (Harden, Stanton-Hicks, & Covington, 1996), the condition and its treatment are approached from a biopsychosocial perspective in which psychological-behavioral, physical, and physiological interventions are primary and integrated.

Rehabilitation

Figure 16.1 presents an outline of an algorithm utilized in the rehabilitation-based approach to CRPS. Reactivation and functional normalization are guiding principles of therapy in CRPS (Charlton, 1990; Harden et al.,

Reactivation
Contrast Baths
Desensitization
⇓
Flexibility
Edema Control
Isometric Strengthening
Peripheral Electrostimulation
Diagnosis & Treatment of Secondary Myofascial Pain
⇓
ROM (gentle!)
Stress Loading
Isotonic Strengthening
General Aerobic Conditioning
Postural Normalization & Balanced Use
⇓
Ergonomics
Movement Therapies
Normalization of Use
Vocational/Functional Rehabilitation

FIG. 16.1. Rehabilitation algorithm for CRPS. If the patient cannot perform any step due to pain, then consider block and/or medication change. If there are frequent inconsistencies, inordinate pain behavior, or poor compliance, increase psychological intervention.

1996; Wilson, 1990). Adherence to objective and measurable rehabilitation goals is essential. The algorithm for functional improvement by rehabilitation ideally is followed to completion in a stepwise, time-contingent way. Other treatment modalities (e.g., behavioral medicine interventions and sympathetic blocks) are delivered only as needed to achieve this functional improvement. Although the differing presentation of CRPS across patients requires flexibility in applying treatment protocols to the individual, some general principles apply to all. One essential component is an interdisciplinary, coordinated team approach where there is communication between patient and treatment team, with the patient involved in all therapeutic decisions. Emphasis is placed on self-management, low-technology interventions, and active patient participation. A high level of patient motivation and compliance is absolutely essential to success. Frequent physical and occupational therapy, often daily or hourly, is often necessary.

With early intervention, each step in the algorithm is completed ideally in 2 to 3 weeks. This pace is adjusted individually according to the patient's particular pathophysiology and clinical response. More chronic or complicated cases may need longer at each step, but if progress is not seen after 3 weeks, aggressive medical and behavioral medicine interventions should be initiated. If a time frame longer than 3 weeks is adopted because of severity of disease, or entrenchment of pain behaviors and/or psychological pathology, definitive time lines should still be established.

The first step in treatment primarily involves development of a therapeutic alliance and rapport. A focus on the principles of motivation, mobilization, and desensitization is absolutely essential. Movement phobia is gently overcome, and the patient actually begins to move and allow the limb to be touched.

In the second step the patient begins to overcome barriers to movement (e.g., edema) and works on increasing flexibility. Isometric strengthening and electrostimulation should be explored (Richlin et al., 1978). Identification and treatment of secondary myofascial pain syndromes in supporting joints should begin. Such myofascial pain problems may develop in part because of fear of pain and operantly reinforced disuse, which can lead to deconditioning.

In the third step, isotonic strengthening can be started and stress loading begun (e.g., walking, carrying weights; Carlson & Watson, 1988). General aerobic conditioning should be encouraged to facilitate general reactivation. Range of motion work (ROM) must be gentle and primarily patient directed (i.e., "active" rather than "passive" ROM). Aggressive passive ROM done with the patient in an insensate condition (e.g., after a somatic block) must be avoided. Consistency and gentle, steady increase in ROM should be the goal. Postural normalization, balanced use of the limbs, and stabilization exercises also may be helpful.

In the final stage the goal is complete functional recovery, emphasizing normalization of use of the affected limb. Specific interventions to overcome residual disability are appropriate, such as ergonomic assessment and intervention. Vocational rehabilitation with work hardening, functional capacity evaluation, and written work restrictions and modifications are appropriate for adult patients who were working. Return to school or to other productive life activities should be goals when competitive employment is not possible. Therapeutic recreation can be an invaluable aid in improving the patient's quality of life.

If the patient's subjective pain experience causes significant limitations in treatment progress, more aggressive treatment of any inferred nociceptive generator is called for. Medications, behavioral medicine interventions, sympathetic blocks, and specific physical modalities (e.g., electrostimulation) may be utilized, alone or in combination, to facilitate progression through the algorithm.

The presence of severe cutaneous allodynia may call for specific interventions. In addition to sympathetic blockade, a course of desensitization is recommended. This should involve cutaneous desensitization using progressively coarse textures for massage as well as proprioceptive challenge up to and including scrubbing during a weight-bearing activity. If dependent edema is a significant problem, it should be treated by elevation, active ROM, lymphedema massage, and antiedema garments or pumps.

Contractures may require very slow progression through the algorithm. Although it is often necessary to provide analgesia for initial stretching maneuvers, it is important for the patient be able to provide feedback in order to avoid injury. Frequent gentle work done by the patient is essential. Dynamic splinting and serial casting that progressively increase joint ROM also may be helpful on a limited basis. Casting or splinting that results in immobility of the limb is counterproductive in the long run and should be considered only for use at night. It is critical to progress slowly and within patient defined limits with these techniques. Use of adequate and liberal analgesia in these steps may be important for assuring continuing progress.

Active loading (weight-bearing exercises) and distraction (progressive weights added distally to the extremity) of the extremity have become key concepts during all stages of the algorithm. If weight bearing is particularly difficult for the patient, loading may be conducted from any position or therapy may be initiated in water and gradually progressed to upright and dry land exercises. Normalization of gait during ambulation, with or without assistive devices, should be encouraged to tolerance. Progressively heavier weights are attached to the extremity during upright functional activities. Treatment activities increasingly utilize the extremity in activities that approximate normal functioning in home, avocational, and vocational settings.

Medical Interventions

Regional Anesthetic Techniques. If the patient has difficulty at any step in the algorithm, regional anesthetic, pharmacologic, and behavioral medicine interventions should be considered to initiate or continue steady progress. Regional anesthetic techniques should be considered only to allow patients to become comfortable enough to participate in rehabilitation activities (Harden, 1994; Wilson, 1990). Paravertebral sympathetic blocks (e.g., stellate and lumbar) are frequently used with sympathetically maintained pain to relieve pain and also may improve associated symptomatology such as poor blood flow and motor abnormalities (Bonica, 1990). Paravertebral sympathetic blocks also can be useful diagnostic purposes.

If sympathetic blockade is helpful, it is often reserved as a powerful tool for promoting progression through stages of the algorithm. A planned series of blocks can be incorporated as part of the therapeutic regime. Alternatively, a prolonged block can be utilized in which a catheter is implanted in the epidural space or paravertebral plexus, allowing for constant infusion. Because this technique is associated with a significant increase in risk (infection) and expense (it usually involves hospitalization), it should be considered only in carefully selected patients.

Other ways to block sympathetic outflow include the intravenous (IV) regional techniques (e.g., Bier blocks) and epidural injections (Hannington-Kiff, 1990). Epidurals have the advantage of being easier to perform and less painful for the patient. They also hold a relative advantage of blocking nociceptive input into the spinal cord, but the disadvantage in some cases of causing a temporary decrease in motor strength, thereby hindering physical therapies. Bier blocks,[1] although very invasive and often quite painful, offer the advantage of causing prolonged sympathetic blockade. The increase in expense of these procedures and their morbidity need to be carefully considered before they are utilized.

Neuromodulation. Spinal cord stimulation (SCS) and peripheral nerve stimulation (PNS) represent invasive and expensive techniques that as yet are unproven in the treatment of CRPS. Although SCS has been in use since 1967, there are no well-designed studies of its efficacy in any specifically defined condition at this point. PNS is even less well studied (Hassenbach, Stanton-Hicks, Schoppa, Walsh, & Covington, 1996). Although some small studies have shown good results, they need to be interpreted with caution because they are not experimentally well controlled. Neuromodulation procedures continue to be unproven in their potential for helping patients achieve goals of functional restoration. Pain control by

---

[1]An extended infusion of local anesthetic into an extremity after it has been made ischemic, with the ischemia maintained by a tourniquet.

these invasive techniques is also questionable, so they only should be considered as experimental and as "last resort" interventions in efforts at facilitating functioning and rehabilitation.

Pharmacotherapies. Double-blind, randomized controlled studies of drug therapies for CRPS are rare. Information presented here is anecdotal or is drawn from empirically validated treatment of other painful conditions such as neuropathies (Harden, 1994; Wilson, 1990). Pharmacotherapy of any chronic painful condition falls into two types: prophylactic therapies (aimed at suppressing general pain levels) and abortive therapies (used for breakthrough pain). Table 16.5 presents an overview of medications currently used in the treatment of CRPS.

Behavioral Medicine Interventions

Behavioral medicine services for CRPS patients include: (a) psychological and behavioral evaluation, (b) preventive interventions for at-risk patients, (c) interventions to support participation in treatment, and (d) psychological treatment directed at reducing sympathetic arousal, managing psychological consequences of CRPS, improving the patient's self-management of pain and related symptoms, preventing psychological and behavioral complications, and assisting the patient in adjusting to the emotional demands of chronic pain and disability. Although physical and occupational therapy form the core of treatment for CRPS, behavioral medicine interventions are not merely ancillary; rather they can facilitate response to treatment and prevent complications that can lead to treatment failure and to chronicity.

There are no large-scale or controlled studies to guide us in designing behavioral medicine intervention strategies for CRPS. What are available, however, are case studies, small-scale uncontrolled clinical reports, theory-based interventions, and an extensive literature on approaches used with other forms of chronic pain. All of these are relied upon in the following discussion of psychological management of CRPS within a rehabilitation-based treatment algorithm.

Evaluation

Patients should be evaluated as early as possible to identify potential problem areas and to introduce the patient to the role of behavioral medicine in CRPS treatment. Patients with chronic pain often fear that others believe their pain is "all in their heads." This concern can be heightened by early experiences in the course of the illness by clinicians inexperienced with CRPS who doubt the veracity of the patient's pain because of the high level of emotional distress, unusual symptom pattern, apparent symptom magnification, and relatively minor nature of the inciting trauma in

TABLE 16.5
Medications Used With CRPS

Class	Examples	Effects	Comments
Prophylactic Agents:			
Tricyclic Antidepressants	amitriptyline, nortriptyline	antidepressant, sedative, analgesic, normalize sleep	TCAs appear to be more effective as adjuvant analgesics than are newer serotonin specific reuptake inhibitors.
Anticonvulsants	GABApentin, valproic acid, phenytoin, lamotrigine	analgesic	Believed to be effective primarily in neuropathic pain conditions.
Alpha Blockers	prazosine, phenoxybenzamine, clonidine	reduce sympathetic-mediated symptoms	No good clinical trials; have significant side effects.
Topical Agents	capsaicin, eutectic mixture of local analgesics	analgesic	Anecdotal support, but few well-designed studies.
Opioids	Oxycontin, MS-Contin, Duragesic	analgesic	Long-term effectiveness unproven. Tolerance, cognitive impairment, and dependency are concerns.
Abortive Agents:			
Nonsteroidal Anti-Inflammatory Drugs	Ketoprofen, Naproxen, Ibuprofen	anti-inflammatory, weaker analgesic	Ketoprofen may be best for CRPS. Potential long-term side effects (e.g., GI, ulcers, kidney damage)
Corticosteroids	methylprednisolone	anti-inflammatory	May be useful as rescue agents and for breaking up patterns of extreme pain. Substantial long-term side effects.
Opioids	codeine, morphine, hydrocodone, oxycodone	analgesic	May be more appropriate abortively than prophylactically. Same concerns as above.
Spinal Agents:			
Opioids	Epidural or intrathecal morphine	analgesic	Tolerance is an issue, problems with infection, catheter migration, and malfunction of drug delivery pumps.

comparison to the patient's pain complaint. If psychological evaluation and treatment are initiated only after problems have developed, the patient's fears can be reinforced and needed interventions become more difficult. Table 16.6 presents some of the areas explored as in psychological evaluation or CRPS patients.

Psychological assessment instruments commonly used in evaluation of chronic pain patients may also be of use for patients with CRPS. The MMPI (Minnesota Multiphasic Personality Inventory) historically has been the primary psychological assessment tool used with chronic pain. It has been noted that patients with chronic pain often display similar MMPI profiles (Bradley & Van der Heide, 1984). Studies using the MMPI with CRPS patients indicate that, as a group, they produce similar profiles to those found with patients suffering from other forms of chronic pain (Haddox et al., 1988). Turk (1996) has noted that patients with chronic pain will come to share common behavioral, psychological, and social characteristics because of common experiences despite differing pathophysiology.

Work using other instruments such as the SCL–90 also indicates that CRPS patients are similar psychologically to other patients with chronic pain, including those with headache and low back pain (DeGood et al., 1993). However, Bruehl et al. (1996), using a short form of the SCL–90, found that CRPS patients with sympathetically maintained pain reported higher levels of phobic anxiety and somatization than were reported by low back pain patients. These authors found the magnitude of the relationship between anxiety and pain to be stronger in CRPS patients than in other pain patients. Based on this finding and the relationship between anxiety and sympathetic arousal, questionnaires assessing anxiety should be included among assessment instruments used with CRPS patients.

TABLE 16.6
Areas Addressed in Psychological Evaluation

1. Personality and situational factors that increase risk for increased sympathetic arousal.
2. Emotional reactions to pain and disability, including depression, anxiety, anger, somatization.
3. Emotional and psychological factors associated with initiating trauma.
4. Coping efforts and resources.
5. Premorbid psychiatric difficulties.
6. Treatment-related issues including previous and current conflicts with health care providers.
7. Cognitive factors that interfere with treatment or contribute to increased pain and disability.
8. Extent of learned disability related to fear of pain.
9. Problematic behavioral factors including environmental reinforcers for pain, sick role, or disability behaviors.
10. Family support for well-behaviors or reinforcement of disability.
11. Disincentives for improvement or increased function.

Assessment of depressive symptoms is also important because there is approximately a 30% incidence of major depression among chronic pain patients (Barkin et al., 1996). Although the Beck Depression Inventory (Beck & Steer, 1987) is widely used with chronic pain, other instruments such as Center for Epidemiological Studies Depression Scale (Radloff, 1977) and the Multiscore Depression Inventory (Berndt, 1986), which are not as influenced by physical symptoms, may be more appropriate with this population.

Areas of CRPS patients' lives that may be negatively affected by pain can be assessed by the Multidimensional Pain Inventory (MPI; Kerns, Turk, & Rudy, 1985). The MPI assesses a number of pain-relevant areas, including pain level, perceived control over pain, degree that pain interferes in life, level of affective distress, perceived level of support from significant others, and functional activity levels. The Coping Strategies Questionnaire (CSQ; Rosenstiel & Keefe, 1983) is useful in assessing positive and negative ways in which patients attempt to cope with pain. Given findings that negative cognitive coping predicts dysfunction in pain patients (Rosenstiel & Keefe, 1983) and the importance of coping skills in managing chronic pain, the CSQ is a valuable instrument in evaluation and treatment planning for patients with CRPS.

Psychological Interventions

As with other types of chronic pain conditions, behavioral medicine treatment of patients with CRPS must be in a closely coordinated interdisciplinary environment. For many CRPS patients, especially those who have begun treatment early in the course the condition, psychological and behavioral interventions primarily support participation in core rehabilitation treatment and in medical interventions. However, patients with complicating psychological and behavioral issues, as well as those whose pain and disability do not respond favorably to treatment efforts, will require more extended and intensive treatment.

Supporting Interdisciplinary Treatment and Managing Painful Treatment Procedures. Patients with CRPS often struggle with the painful demands of physical and occupational therapy treatment and the additional acute pain and distress associated with invasive medical procedures. Cooperation and compliance with these treatments can be problematic because short-term consequences (e.g., temporarily increased pain) are often more salient for the patient than promises of long-term benefits. Patients who have learned to avoid activity to prevent added pain often find it difficult to comply with requirements for exercise of the involved extremity. Patients may become so apprehensive about these procedures, often after stressful initial experiences, that they decline further treatment, even though some benefit might have been evident from earlier treatments. These patients can benefit from self-directed acute pain or anxiety-coping strategies including cognitive-behavioral coping skills, self-hypnosis, and relaxation skills that have proven useful in managing acute pain from injuries, surgery, and painful medical interventions (Bruehl, Carlson, & McCubbin, 1993; Kendall, 1983). Behavioral strategies (Fordyce, 1976), including use of goal setting, baselines, quotas, activity graphing, and planned reinforcing consequences, can be helpful in assisting the patient's compliance with home exercise and activity programs. Compliance also can be enhanced through education directed at correcting cognitive distortions about treatment outcomes (e.g., overly optimistic or pessimistic), at increasing knowledge of the CRPS disease process, and at enhancing understanding and acceptance of the importance of early aggressive treatment in prevention of chronicity.

Psychotherapeutic Treatment. Psychotherapy is mentioned frequently as an important component of treatment for CRPS (Bonica, 1990; Raj & Kelly, 1994; Shelton & Lewis, 1990; Sullivan, 1991). Although cognitive-behavior therapy is the primary approach cited in the literature on CRPS and other types of chronic pain (e.g., Van Houdenhove et al., 1992; Wilder et al., 1992), psychodynamic psychotherapy also has been reported in treatment of patients with chronic pain (Grzesiak, 1996; Pilowsky & Bassett, 1982). A primary focus of psychotherapy with this population is reduction of sympathetic arousal resulting from emotional distress associated with pain and disability (Ecker, 1989; Van Houdenhove et al., 1992; Weiss, 1994). Another major goal is to assist the patient in dealing effectively with the chronic pain and life impact so that a positive adjustment is achieved despite the presence of continuing pain (Steger, Fox, & Feinberg, 1980; Turk, 1979). Reactive depression and anxiety are common issues that must be addressed in treatment because they can interfere with participation in treatment, cause interpersonal and social withdrawal, disrupt sleep, enhance suffering from pain, and increase the experience of pain through sympathetic effects on nociception.

Cognitive-behavior therapy for patients with chronic pain (Turk, Meichenbaum, & Genest, 1983) enters patients into an active role in treatment by helping them to develop expectations that the pain and associated problems can be managed, and then by helping them gain the knowledge and skills needed to manage these issues effectively. Development of an enhanced sense of control is an important predictor of treatment outcome for chronic pain (Keefe et al., 1991) and should be a focus of treatment. Many of the techniques used in this form of treatment are discussed in other sections of this chapter, for example, training in coping skills, behavioral and social skills, flare-up management, and self-hypnosis and relaxation. These skills are rehearsed to increase the patient's confidence in implementing them in the real world. Wilder et al. (1992) found that children with CRPS whose cognitive-behavioral coping techniques were useful in managing pain at follow-up had better outcomes in terms of pain ratings, functional status, and presence of autonomic signs.

Cognitive-behavior therapy also focuses on the way negative beliefs, expectations, and distortions, and maladaptive behavior patterns impact distress and dysfunction. Patients learn to assess and modify negative or inaccurate thoughts that affect pain through their impact on the sympathetic nervous system and through the depression and distress that accompanies expectations of helplessness and hopelessness. They explore how maladaptive behavior patterns can result in excess disability and needless pain, suffering, and emotional distress. Patients engage in problem solving to identify, practice, and implement alternative adaptive behavior patterns that recognize both the reality of pain-related limitations and the need for increased and better modulated activity levels.

Biofeedback. Thermal biofeedback training directed at learned voluntary control over sympathetic functioning can help patients gain control over their pain (Alioto, 1981; Grunert, Devine, Sanger, Matloub, & Green, 1990). In addition to reducing sympathetic arousal and increasing peripheral blood flow, this skill can give patients an increased sense of self-control and participation in treatment. Surface electromyograhic (sEMG) training can be used to identify chronic muscle tension that often develops in the patient's involved extremity and associated musculature as a result of continued guarding or bracing. Additional pain that patients experience from chronic muscle tension may be interpreted incorrectly as spreading of the CRPS, leading to catastrophizing and increased distress. Secondary muscular pain can be controlled through increased tension awareness and control gained from sEMG biofeedback. sEMG biofeedback may also be helpful in reducing the neglectlike syndrome found with some CRPS patients (Galer et al., 1995) by increasing awareness and normal use of the involved extremity.

Relaxation Training and Hypnosis. Relaxation training provides the patient with a self-directed way of reducing sympathetic arousal (Davison, 1966) and is also useful in conjunction with other coping skills in managing episodes of increased pain. Because patients with CRPS often find it painful to tense muscles of the involved extremity, progressive muscle relaxation techniques (Jacobson, 1962) generally should be avoided in favor of more cognitive techniques, such as autogenic (Schultz & Luthe, 1969) or guided imagery (Rossman & Bresler, 1990) approaches. Initial relaxation training is best practiced during periods of lower pain, for example, following nerve blocks or medication intake, rather than during intense pain episodes, to provide the opportunity for successful experiences before attempts are made under more stressful circumstances.

Hypnotic pain control techniques, which are well described in the literature on hypnosis (Hammond, 1990; Sacerdote, 1982), can be adapted readily for use with CRPS patients. Gainer (1992, 1993) has reported on several cases of refractory CRPS where pain relief was achieved using hypnosis. Self-hypnosis can provide the patient with an additional tool for controlling sympathetic arousal, and for managing pain experiences during daily activities, during flare-ups, and treatment procedures.

Social Skill Training. Chronic pain patients often have difficulties in communicating with health care providers as well as with family and friends. Verbal and nonverbal pain behavior can become an alternative to direct communication. Communication between patient and health care providers can become problematic because of passivity inherent in the social sick role, because of patients' concerns about being labeled as uncooperative, and because of stresses in the doctor–patient relationship that arise when pain does not improve despite the best efforts of physician and patient. If patients believe those involved in their care are neither taking them seriously nor addressing their problems adequately, increased pain behavior can communicate dissatisfaction. Training in communication skills, including assertiveness and active listening, offers patients more effective means of interacting with others and can help in developing more mature relationships with health care providers.

Problems with anger arise from a variety of sources, including reactions to pain-related losses, reactions to health care providers who fail to provide expected pain relief, helplessness the patient experiences in controlling pain, feelings toward those held responsible for the pain, reactions to perceived obstruction by insurers or employers, or feelings about others because of their continued good health. Anger, especially chronic and unexpressed, can increase sympathetic arousal and subsequent pain experience, and also can impact communication and adjustment to the chronic pain. The intensity of anger and the way in which it is expressed can also influence the intensity of pain, pain behavior, and the degree pain interferes with activity (Kerns, Rosenberg, & Jacob, 1994). Anger management training (Novaco, 1978) can be an important component of psychological treatment of CRPS.

Flare-Up Prevention and Management. CRPS is prone to intermittent flare-up of symptoms. Flare-ups can become crises if the patient does not expect, understand, or have skills in managing them. Symptom flare-ups can result in increased emotional distress, fears the condition has worsened permanently, despair that everything that has been done and everything the patient has learned are useless, abandonment of self-management efforts, and deterioration of the patient's overall condition. Training in flare-up prevention and management follows the general relapse prevention approach described by Marlatt and Gordon (1985). Training begins during the patient's active treatment program. Typical flare-up management plans include: (a) identifying factors that can increase symptoms, (b) learning early signs of symptom flare-up, (c) developing a personal symptom management plan including crisis management strategies, (d) preventing negative emotional and cognitive reactions to the flare-up, and (e) using the experience to help contain future flare-ups. Patients identify and use personal and health care resources to contain the flare-up and maintain a sense of personal control. Personal resources can include increased use of strategies to reduce emotional arousal and to cope with pain, using cognitive coping skills, or contacting support group members. Patients are encouraged to develop understandings with health care providers about the nature of the provider's availability and involvement during flare-ups.

Treatment of Sleep Complaints. Sleep problems are common for many patients with chronic pain, with long sleep-onset and maintenance insomnia (Atkinson, Ancoli-Israel, Slater, Garfin, & Gillin, 1988). These sleep problems may arise from the direct effects of pain and from maladaptive behaviors such as loss of a regular diurnal cycle, daytime napping, use of bed for non-sleep-related activities, chronic use of narcotic and hypnotic medications, excessive use of stimulants, and chronic physical and emotional tension. CRPS patients especially may be prone to insomnia, because individuals who are more sympathetically reactive and cope poorly tend to have difficulty with insomnia (Waters, Adams, Binks, & Varnado, 1993). With chronic sleep loss come complaints of fatigue, increased irritability, and difficulty in coping with pain and stress. Patients with sleep problems may benefit from behavioral interventions to improve sleep hygiene, including restricting use of stimulants such as caffeine and nicotine, establishing regular times for going to bed and arising, implementing environmental stimulus control, restricting the bed to sleep-related activities, using relaxation techniques and other soothing activities prior to bedtime, and avoiding hypnotic sleep medications (Morin, Kowatch, & Wade, 1989).

Group Therapy. Several components of behavioral medicine treatment can be provided more efficiently in group than in individual treatment format. Groups are especially suited for instruction about CRPS, and for training in communication skills, relaxation techniques, activity pacing, and coping skills. Open-ended groups allow patients further along in treatment to serve as role models in demonstrating the value of cognitive-behavioral coping strategies. The support and shared experience of other group members can be helpful in reducing emotional isolation and the feeling of not being understood that often characterizes relationships with family, friends, coworkers, and many health care providers.

Community Support Groups. Because many with CRPS must live with pain for years after completion of active treatment, patients often benefit from involvement with community support groups. Although the value of participation in these groups has not been demonstrated empirically, in our experience they can be useful unless unguided and focused on expression of complaints of suffering and disability. Potential benefits of support groups include social and emotional support, reduction of social isolation, and reinforcement of self-management concepts and skills learned during treatment. The RSDS Association (P.O. Box 821, Haddonfield, NJ 08033) provides information and support nationwide to people with CRPS. The American Chronic Pain Association (P.O. Box 850, Rocklin, CA 95677) and The National Chronic Pain Outreach Association (7979 Old Georgetown Road, Suite 100, Bethesda, MD 20814-2429), which are oriented toward persons with chronic pain rather than with specific chronic pain syndromes, have local support groups in communities throughout the country.

CONCLUSIONS

CPRS continues to present a significant challenge to both patients and health care teams. The recent introduction of standard diagnostic criteria and an interdisciplinary treatment approach provides an opportunity for improved understanding and treatment of the condition. Psychological factors are involved in determining pain severity and adjustment to pain, can affect outcome of medical and rehabilitation treatment, and may prove to be etiologic factors in CRPS following injury. Treatment of CRPS requires an interdisciplinary approach that integrates physical and occupational therapy, medical, and behavioral medicine interventions. Medical and behavioral medicine treatments are provided in support of the patient's orderly progress in rehabilitation efforts. Behavioral medicine services play an important role in interdisciplinary treatment for patients with CRPS; however, much research remains to be done in (a) demonstrating efficacy of behavioral medicine interventions, (b) understanding the optimal integration of behavioral interventions with medical and rehabilitation treatment, (c) understanding how psychological factors affect the onset and course of CRPS, and (d) determining what psychological factors are related to outcome and maintenance of treatment gains.

REFERENCES

Abelson, J. L., Glitz, D., Cameron, O. G., Lee, M. A., Bronzo, M., & Curtis, G. C. (1991). Blunted growth hormone response to clonidine in patients with generalized anxiety disorder. *Archives of General Psychiatry, 48,* 157–162.

Alioto, J. T. (1981). Behavioral treatment of reflex sympathetic dystrophy. *Psychosomatics, 22,* 539–540.

Atkinson, J. H., Ancoli-Israel, S., Slater, M. A., Garfin, S. R., & Gillin, J. H. (1988). Subjective sleep disturbance in chronic back pain. *Clinical Journal of Pain, 4,* 225–232.

Barkin, R. L., Lubenow, T. R., Bruehl, S., Husfeldt, B., Ivankovich, O., & Barkin, S. J. (1996). Management of chronic pain. Part II. *Disease-a-Month, 42,* 469–507.

Baron, R., Blumberg, H., & Jänig, W. (1996). Clinical characteristics of patients with complex regional pain syndrome in Germany with special emphasis on vasomotor function. In W. Jänig & M. Stanton-Hicks (Eds.), *Reflex sympathetic dystrophy: A reappraisal* (pp. 25–48). Seattle: IASP Press.

Beck, A., & Steer, R. (1987). *The Beck Depression Inventory manual.* New York: Harcourt Brace.

Berndt, D. J. (1986). *Multiscore Depression Inventory (MDI) manual.* Los Angeles: Western Psychological Services.

Blumberg, H., & Jänig, W. (1994). Clinical manifestations of reflex sympathetic dystrophy and sympathetically maintained pain. In P. D. Wall & R. Melzack (Eds.), *Textbook of pain* (pp. 685–698). New York: Churchill Livingstone.

Bonica, J. J. (1990). Causalgia and other reflex sympathetic dystrophies. In J. J. Bonica (Ed.), *The management of pain* (2nd ed., pp. 220–243). Philadelphia: Lea & Febiger.

Bradley, L. A., & Van der Heide, L. H. (1984). Pain-related correlates of MMPI profile subgroups among back pain patients. *Health Psychology, 3,* 157–174.

Bruehl, S. (1997). Reply to B. S. Galer. *Pain, 71,* 210.

Bruehl, S., & Carlson, C. R. (1992). Predisposing psychological factors in the development of reflex sympathetic dystrophy: A review of the empirical evidence. *The Clinical Journal of Pain, 8,* 287–299.

Bruehl, S., Carlson, C. R., & McCubbin, J. A. (1993). Two brief interventions for acute pain. *Pain, 54,* 29–36.

Bruehl, S., Husfeldt, B., Lubenow, T. R., Nath, H., & Ivankovich, A. D. (1996). Psychological differences between reflex sympathetic dystrophy and non-RSD chronic pain patients. *Pain, 67,* 107–114.

Bruehl, S., Lubenow, T. R., Nath, H., & Ivankovich, O. (1996). Validation of thermography in the diagnosis of reflex sympathetic dystrophy. *The Clinical Journal of Pain, 12,* 316–325.

Carlson, L. K., & Watson, H. K. (1988). Treatment of reflex sympathetic dystrophy using the stress-loading program. *Journal of Hand Therapy, 1,* 149–154.

Carron, H., & Weller, R. M. (1974). Treatment of post-traumatic sympathetic dystrophy. *Advances in Neurology, 4,* 485–490.

Charlton, J. E. (1990). Reflex sympathetic dystrophy: Non-invasive methods of treatment. In M. Stanton-Hicks, W. Jänig, & R. A. Boas (Eds.), *Reflex sympathetic dystrophy* (pp. 153–164). Boston: Kluwer Academic.

Cooke, E. D., Glick, E. N., Bowcock, S. A., Smith, R. E., Ward, C., Almond, N. E., & Beachum, J. A. (1989). Reflex sympathetic dystrophy (algoneurodystrophy): Temperature studies in the upper limb. *British Journal of Rheumatology, 28,* 399–403.

Covington, E. C. (1996). Psychological issues in reflex sympathetic dystrophy. In W. Jänig & M. Stanton-Hicks (Eds.), *Reflex sympathetic dystrophy: A reappraisal* (pp. 191–215). Seattle: IASP Press.

Davison, G. C. (1966). Anxiety under total curarization: Implications for the role of muscular relaxation in the desensitization of neurotic fears. *Journal of Nervous and Mental Disease, 143,* 443–448.

DeGood, D. E., Cundiff, G. W., Adams, L. E., & Shutty, J. S. (1993). A psychosocial and behavioral comparison of reflex sympathetic dystrophy, low back pain, and headache patients. *Pain, 54,* 317–322.

Dworkin, S. F., & Burgess, J. A. (1987). Orofacial pain of psychogenic origin: Current concepts and classification. *Journal of the American Dental Association, 115,* 565–571.

Ecker, A. (1989). Norepinephrine in reflex sympathetic dystrophy: An hypothesis. *The Clinical Journal of Pain, 5,* 313–315.

Eulry, F., Lechevalier, B., Pats, B., Alliaume, C., Crozes, P., Vasseut, P., Coutant, G., Felten, D., & Pattin, S. (1991). Regional intravenous guanethidine blocks in algodystrophy. *Clinical Rheumatology, 10,* 377–383.

Fordyce, W. E. (1976). *Behavioral methods for chronic pain and illness.* St. Louis, MO: Mosby.

Gainer, M. J. (1992). Hypnotherapy for reflex sympathetic dystrophy. *American Journal of Clinical Hypnosis, 34,* 227–232.

Gainer, M. J. (1993). Somatization of dissociated traumatic memories in a case of reflex sympathetic dystrophy. *American Journal of Clinical Hypnosis, 36,* 124–131.

Galer, B. S., Butler, S., & Jensen, M. P. (1995). Case reports and hypothesis: A neglect-like syndrome may be responsible for the motor disturbance in reflex sympathetic dystrophy (complex regional pain syndrome-I). *Journal of Pain and Symptom Management, 10,* 385–391.

Geertzen, J. H., de Bruijn, H., de Bruijn-Kofman, A. T., & Arendzen, J. H. (1994). Reflex sympathetic dystrophy: Early treatment and psychological aspects. *Archives of Physical Medicine and Rehabilitation, 75,* 442–446.

Gold, P. W., Goodwin, F. K., & Chrousos, G. P. (1988). Clinical and biochemical manifestations of depression: Relation to the neurobiology of stress. *New England Journal of Medicine, 319,* 413–420.

Gracely, R. H., Lynch, S. A., & Bennett, G. J. (1992). Painful neuropathy: Altered central processing maintained dynamically by peripheral input. *Pain, 51,* 175–194.

Greipp, M. E., & Thomas, A. F. (1986). Reflex sympathetic dystrophy syndrome: Pain that doesn't stop. *Journal of Neuroscience Nursing, 18,* 23–25.

Grunert, B. K., Devine, C. A., Sanger, J. R., Matloub, H. S., & Green, D. (1990). Thermal self-regulation for pain control in reflex sympathetic dystrophy syndrome. *The Journal of Hand Surgery, 15A,* 615–618.

Grzesiak, R. C. (1996). Psychodynamic psychotherapy with chronic pain patients. In R. J. Gatchel & D. C. Turk (Eds.), *Psychological approaches to pain: A practitioner's handbook* (pp. 148–178). New York: Guilford.

Haddox, J. D. (1990). Psychological aspects of reflex sympathetic dystrophy. In M. Stanton-Hicks (Ed.), *Pain and the sympathetic nervous system* (pp. 207–224). Norwell, MA: Kluwer Academic.

Haddox, J. D., Abram, S. E., & Hopwood, M. H. (1988). Comparison of psychometric data in RSD and radiculopathy. *Regional Anesthesia, 13,* 27.

Hammond, C. D. (Ed.). (1990). *Handbook of hypnotic suggestions and metaphors.* New York: Norton.

Hannington-Kiff, J. G. (1990). Intravenous regional sympathetic blocks. In M. Stanton-Hicks, W. Jänig, & R. A. Boas (Eds.), *Reflex sympathetic dystrophy* (pp. 113–124). Boston: Kluwer Academic.

Harden, R. N. (1994). Reflex sympathetic dystrophy and other sympathetically maintained pains. In J. M. Conroy (Ed.), *Anesthesia for orthopedic surgery* (pp. 367–372). New York: Raven.

Harden, R. N., Rudin, N. J., & Parikh, D. (1995, November). *Elevated systemic catecholamines in complex regional pain syndrome.* Poster presented at the meeting of the American Pain Society, Los Angeles.

Harden, R. N., Stanton-Hicks, M., & Covington, E. (1996, November). *A rehabilitation based algorithm for the treatment of CRPS: Consensus of the Malibu closed workshop.* Symposium conducted at the meeting of the American Pain Society, Washington, DC.

Hassenbach, S. J., Stanton-Hicks, M., Schoppa, D., Walsh, J. G., & Covington, E. C. (1996). Long-term results of peripheral nerve stimulation for reflex sympathetic dystrophy. *Journal of Neurosurgery, 84,* 415–123.

Hooshmand, H. (1993). *Chronic pain: Reflex sympathetic dystrophy prevention and management.* Boca Raton, FL: CRC Press.

Horowitz, L. H. (1984). Iatrogenic causalgia: Classification, clinical findings, and legal ramifications. *Archives of Neurology, 41,* 821–824.

Inhofe, P. D., & Garcia-Moral, C. A. (1994). Reflex sympathetic dystrophy: A review of the literature and a long-term outcome study. *Orthopedic Review, 23,* 655–661.

Jacobson, E. (1962). *You must relax* (4th ed.). New York: McGraw-Hill.

Keefe, F. J., Caldwell, D. S., Martinez, S., Nunley, J., Beckham, J., & Williams, D. A. (1991). Analyzing pain in rheumatoid arthritis patients. Pain coping strategies in patients who have had knee replacement surgery. *Pain, 46,* 153–160.

Kendall, P. C. (1983). Stressful medical procedures: Cognitive-behavioral strategies for stress management and prevention. In D. Meichenbaum & M. E. Jaremko (Eds.), *Stress reduction and prevention* (pp. 159–190). New York: Plenum.

Kerns, R. D., Rosenberg, R., & Jacob, M. C. (1994). Anger expression and chronic pain. *Journal of Behavioral Medicine, 17,* 57–67.

Kerns, R. D., Turk, D. C., & Rudy, T. E. (1985). The West Haven–Yale Multidimensional Pain Inventory (WHYMPI). *Pain, 23,* 345–356.

Kleinert, H. E., Cole, N. M., Wayne, L., Harvey, R., Kutz, J. E., & Atasoy, E. (1973). Post traumatic sympathetic dystrophy. *Orthopedic Clinics of North America, 4,* 917–927.

Kozin, F. (1992). Reflex sympathetic dystrophy syndrome: A review. *Clinical and Experimental Rheumatology, 10,* 401–409.

Kozin, F., Ryan, L. M., Carrera, G. F., & Soin, J. S. (1981). Reflex sympathetic dystrophy syndrome. III: Scintigraphic studies, further evidence for the therapeutic efficacy of systemic corticosteroids, and proposed diagnostic criteria. *American Journal of Medicine, 70,* 23–30.

Ladd, A. L., DeHaven, K. E., Thanik, J., Patt, R. B., & Feuerstein, M. (1989). Reflex sympathetic imbalance: Response to epidural blockade. *American Journal of Sports Medicine, 17,* 660–667.

Lankford, L. L. (1983). Reflex sympathetic dystrophy. In C. M. Everts (Ed.), *Surgery of the musculoskeletal system* (pp. 145–174). New York: Churchill Livingstone.

Lankford, L. L., & Thompson, J. E. (1977). Reflex sympathetic dystrophy, upper and lower extremity: Diagnosis and management. *Instructional Course Lectures, 26,* 163–178.

Lynch, M. E. (1992). Psychological aspects of reflex sympathetic dystrophy: A review of the adult and paediatric literature. *Pain, 49,* 337–347.

Marlatt, G. A., & Gordon, J. R. (1985). *Relapse prevention.* New York: Guilford.

McLeskey, C. H., Balestrieri, F. J., & Weeks, D. B. (1993). Sympathetic dystrophies. In C. A. Warfield (Ed.), *Principles and practice of pain management* (pp. 219–234). New York: McGraw-Hill.

Merskey, H., & Bogduk, N. (Eds.). (1994). *Classification of chronic pain: Descriptions of chronic pain syndromes and definition of pain terms* (2nd ed.). Seattle: IASP Press.

Mitchell, S. W., Morehouse, G. R., & Keen, W. W. (1864). *Gunshot wounds and other injuries of nerves.* Philadelphia: Lippincott.

Morin, C. M., Kowatch, R. A., & Wade, J. B. (1989). Behavioral management of sleep disturbances secondary to chronic pain. *Journal of Behavior Therapy and Experimental Psychiatry, 20,* 295–302.

Novaco, R. W. (1978). Anger and coping with stress: Cognitive behavioral interventions. In J. P. Foreyt & D. P. Rathjen (Eds.), *Cognitive behavior therapy: Research and applications* (pp. 135–173). New York: Plenum.

Ochoa, J. L., & Verdugo, R. J. (1995). Reflex sympathetic dystrophy: A common clinical avenue for somatoform expression. *Neurology Clinics, 13,* 351–363.

Pak, T. J., Martin, G. M., Magness, J. L., & Kavanaugh, G. J. (1970). Reflex sympathetic dystrophy: Review of 140 cases. *Minnesota Medicine, 53,* 507–512.

Pilowsky, I., & Bassett, D. (1982). Individual dynamic psychotherapy for chronic pain. In R. Roy & E. Tunks (Eds.), *Chronic pain: Psychosocial factors in rehabilitation* (pp. 107–125). Baltimore: Williams & Wilkins.

Radloff, L. (1977). The CES-D scale: A self-report depression scale for research in the general population. *Applied Psychological Measurement, 1,* 385–401.

Raj, P. P., & Kelly, J. F. (1994, Winter). Multidisciplinary management of reflex sympathetic dystrophy. *PSNS SIG: A Publication on Pain and Sympathetic Nervous System,* pp. 4–6.

Richlin, D. N., Carron, H., Rowlingson, J. C., Sussman, M. D., Brugher, W. H., & Goldner, R. D. (1978). Reflex sympathetic dystrophy: Successful treatment by transcutaneous nerve stimulation. *Journal of Pediatrics, 93,* 84–86.

Robaina, F. J., Domingues, M., Diaz, M., Rodriguez, J. L., & de Vera, J. A. (1989). Spinal cord stimulation for relief of chronic pain in vasospastic disorders of the upper limbs. *Neurosurgery, 24,* 63–67.

Roberts, W. J. (1986). A hypothesis on the physiological basis for causalgia and related pains. *Pain, 24,* 297–311.

Rosenstiel, A. K., & Keefe, F. J. (1983). The use of coping strategies in chronic low back pain patients: Relationship to patient characteristics and current adjustment. *Pain, 17,* 33–44.

Rossman, M. L., & Bresler, D. E. (1990). *Guided imagery: An intensive training program for clinicians* (3rd ed.). Mill Valley, CA: Academy for Guided Imagery.

Sacerdote, P. (1982). Techniques of hypnotic intervention with pain patients. In J. Barber & C. Adrian (Eds.), *Psychological approaches to the management of pain* (pp. 60–83). New York: Bruner/Mazel.

Schultz, J. H., & Luthe, W. (1969). *Autogenic therapy: Vol. 1. Autogenic methods.* New York: Grune & Stratton.

Schwartzman, R. J., & McLellan, T. L. (1987). Reflex sympathetic dystrophy: A review. *Archives of Neurology, 44,* 555–561.

Shelton, R. M., & Lewis, C. W. (1990). Reflex sympathetic dystrophy: A review. *Journal of the American Academy of Dermatology, 22,* 513–520.

Stanton-Hicks, M., Jänig, W., Hassenbusch, S., Haddox, J. D., Boas, R., & Wilson, P. (1995). Reflex sympathetic dystrophy: Changing concepts and taxonomy. *Pain, 63,* 127–133.

Steger, H. G., Fox, C. D., & Feinberg, S. D. (1980). Behavioral assessment and management of chronic pain. In D. S. Bishop (Ed.), *Behavior and the disabled: Assessment and management* (pp. 302–336). Baltimore: Williams & Wilkins.

Sternbach, R. A. (1966). *Principles of psychophysiology.* New York: Academic Press.

Subbarao, J., & Stillwell, G. K. (1981). Reflex sympathetic dystrophy syndrome of the upper extremity: An analysis of total outcome of management of 125 cases. *Archives of Physical Medicine and Rehabilitation, 62,* 549–554.

Sullivan, M. (1991). Integrated treatment of a woman with chronic hand pain. *Hospital and Community Psychiatry, 42,* 474–475.

Turk, D. C. (1979). Factors influencing the adaptive process with chronic illness. In I. G. Sarason & C. D. Spielberger (Eds.), *Stress and anxiety* (Vol. 6, pp. 291–308). Washington, DC: Hemisphere.

Turk, D. C. (1996). Biopsychosocial perspective on chronic pain. In R. J. Gatchel & D. C. Turk (Eds.), *Psychological approaches to pain management: A practitioner's handbook* (pp. 3–32). New York: Guilford.

Turk, D. C., Meichenbaum, D., & Genest, M. (1983). *Pain and behavioral medicine: A cognitive-behavioral perspective.* New York: Guilford.

Van Houdenhove, B., Vasquez, G., Onghena, P., Stans, L., Vandeput, C., Vermaut, G., Vervaeke, G., Igodt, P., & Vertommen, H. (1992). Etiopathogenesis of reflex sympathetic dystrophy: A review and biopsychosocial hypothesis. *The Clinical Journal of Pain, 8,* 300–306.

Waters, W. F., Adams, S., Binks, P., & Varnado, P. (1993). Attention, stress, and negative emotion in persistent sleep-onset and sleep-maintenance insomnia. *Sleep, 16,* 128–136.

Wang, J. K., Johnson, K. A., & Ilstrup, D. M. (1985). Sympathetic blocks for reflex sympathetic dystrophy. *Pain, 23,* 13–17.

Weiss, W. U. (1994). Psychophysiologic aspects of reflex sympathetic dystrophy. *American Journal of Pain Management, 4,* 67–72.

Wilder, R. T., Berde, C. B., Wolohan, M., Vieyra, M. A., & Masek, B. J. (1992). Reflex sympathetic dystrophy in children: Clinical characteristics and follow-up of seventy patients. *Journal of Bone and Joint Surgery (Am), 74,* 910–919.

Wilson, P. R. (1990). Sympathetically maintained pain, principles of diagnosis and therapy. In M. Stanton-Hicks, W. Jänig, & R. A. Boas (Eds.), *Reflex sympathetic dystrophy* (pp. 25–28). Boston: Kluwer Academic.

Zachariae, L. (1964). Incidence and course of posttraumatic dystrophy following operation for Dupuytren's contracture. *Acta Chirurgica Scandavica, 336*(Suppl.), 7–51.

Chapter 17

Pain in Multiple Sclerosis and the Muscular Dystrophies

Frederick M. Perkins
Richard T. Moxley, III
Anthony S. Papciak
University of Rochester,
School of Medicine and Dentistry

Individuals with any disease may experience pain from the usual nociceptive stimuli, but some disorders predispose patients to particular pain problems. In this chapter we review the causes for the pains that occur commonly in patients with multiple sclerosis and the muscular dystrophies. In the closing portion of the chapter we discuss the medical and psychological management of these typical pain problems.

MULTIPLE SCLEROSIS

Multiple sclerosis (MS), a demyelinating disease of the central nervous system (CNS), is "the great crippler of young adults," having its onset between the second to fifth decades. MS varies in its geographic distribution, being rare in tropical and subtropical zones and having a disease rate that increases with increasing latitude in both the Northern Hemisphere and the Southern Hemisphere (Hogancamp, Rodriguez, & Weinshenker, 1997). The occurrence of MS varies considerably among ethnic groups. There is a low incidence in Native Americans, Asians, and Africans, and a high incidence in Whites (Hogancamp et al., 1997; Poser, 1994), especially those having certain HLA (human leukocyte antigen) genotypes (Ebers & Sadovnick, 1994). For example, there are no reported cases of MS in full-blooded American Indians in British Columbia, Canada, whereas there is an incidence of 2/1000 in certain populations in Scotland (Sadovnick & Ebers, 1993).

Clinical symptoms in MS are variable and usually cumulate over time. The specific symptoms depend on the sites of demyelination within the CNS (Hunter, Weinshenker, Carter, & Noseworthy, 1997). For example, unpleasant tingling paresthesiae and Lhermitte's sign usually result from lesions in the dorsal column. Radicular pain comes from damage in the dorsal horn, whereas trigeminal neuralgia develops with lesions in the trigeminal entry zone in the brainstem. Tonic spasms can occur with demyelination in the brain stem or spinal cord, and spasticity may develop following lesions affecting either the corticospinal, corticobulbar, or bulbospinal tracts (Hunter et al., 1997; Thompson, 1996).

Acute pain is usually not the primary presenting symptom (Ramirez-Lassepas, Tulloch, Quinones, & Snyder, 1992). The majority of the pain problems in MS develop later in the disease and are chronic. Eventually, pain becomes an important management concern in most patients with its prevalence as a significant complaint being approximately 55% (Archibald et al., 1994; Moulin, Foley, & Ebers, 1988).

Certain pain problems are frequent in MS (Table 17.1). Dysesthetic pains are the most common, and they usually develop slowly. Muscle pains are also common (Archibald et al., 1994; Clifford & Trotter, 1984; Moulin et al., 1988), typified by (a) pain in the legs and back due to spasms directly provoked by spasticity, and (b) pain in the back and paraspinal muscles due to abnormal stresses related to weakness from CNS demyelination independent of any spasticity. These two types of muscular pain often coexist and interact in the same patient. Controlling these muscular pains usually requires treatment of both spasticity and pain.

Moulin and colleagues (1988), in their study of 182 MS patients, have reported that dysesthetic leg pain, chronic back pain, and recurrent leg spasms that cause pain, were the three most common pain problems. They found that patients with chronic dysesthetic leg pain had less disability than patients with either chronic back pain or recurrent spasms with pain in their leg muscles. Another study by Clifford and Trotter (1984) involving a chart review of 317 MS patients reported similar results. They found that burning extremity pain was the most frequent pain complaint.

Acute pain problems in MS are less common than the chronic pain complaints noted previously. However, acute or subacute pain sometimes becomes a dominant complaint. For example, Lhermitte's sign and trigeminal neuralgia are two important acute pain complaints that may require long-term treatment. Lhermitte's sign occurs commonly in MS, and in some patients occasionally these sensations are quite painful (Moulin et al., 1988). Trigeminal neuralgia is more frequent in MS than in the general population. Jensen and coworkers (Jensen, Rasmussen, & Reske-Nielsen, 1982) found that 2.4% of 900 patients with trigeminal neuralgia had MS. This frequency of trigeminal neuralgia in MS ranges from 20 to 50 times

TABLE 17.1
Pains Associated With Multiple Sclerosis

Pain Syndrome	Classification	Pain Character
Trigeminal neuralgia	Acute, neuropathic	Sharp, shooting facial pain that is triggered.
Tonic seizures	Acute, neuropathic & muscular	Burning, electric, or tingling pain associated with muscle spasms. They can be triggered by light touch. Attacks appear to be brief, 1 minute, and recurring.
Lhermitte's sign	Acute, neuropathic	Electrical sensation passing down the back to the legs with neck flexion.
Optic neuritis	Subacute, neuropathic	Aching periorbital pain, made worse by eye movement.
Pressure neuropathies	Subacute, neuropathic	Most commonly ulnar or peroneal nerves in wheelchair-bound patients.
Dysesthetic extremity	Chronic, neuropathic	Probably the most common pain syndrome in MS, usually burning pain with hyperpathia. Sensory loss is not always noted.
Leg spasms	Chronic, muscular	Muscle spasms associated with demyelination.
Shoulder	Chronic, muscular	Noted in Charcot's description, probably related to scapula levator weakness and overuse of accessory muscles of the shoulder girdle.
Low back	Chronic, muscular & skeletal	Spasms of the back muscles result in pain and possibly deterioration of disk and facet joints. Also secondary muscular pain in the pelvic girdle associated with poor posture.

greater than in the general population of Denmark. Jensen and coworkers also noted that MS patients with trigeminal neuralgia tended to be younger and more likely to have bilateral neuralgia. It is prudent to consider the presence of MS in any patient referred to a pain clinic with trigeminal neuralgia, but especially a younger patient 20–40 years of age.

The common pain complaints occurring in MS, listed in Table 17.1, do not occur with an increased frequency in any particular form of MS. Archibald and colleagues (1994) have found no significant difference in the prevalence of pain among the four subgroups of MS patients (relapsing-remitting, relapsing-progressive, chronic progressive, or benign). These investigators have observed only a weak correlation between either the duration of MS or its severity, and the number of hours per week of pain; and, they have found no significant correlation between the severity of the pain, and either the duration of MS or its severity. Of those MS patients complaining of pain, 60% used NSAIDs (nonsteroidal anti-inflammatory drugs) or acetaminophen, 42% took neuropathic pain medications, and 4% received treatment with opioids. Of those patients reporting pain in the preceding month, 36% had not taken any analgesics.

Patient Management

In general, the pain that occurs in MS patients will respond to conservative medical management. With close coordination of care between the patient and his or her care providers, which usually include family members, the primary-care physician, neurologist, nursing staff, physical therapist, occupational therapist, and psychologist/psychiatrist, treatment of common pain problems rarely will require long-term care in a pain treatment center. Controlled studies of pain management in MS are lacking. As a general rule, if a patient with MS has worsening symptoms, an infection needs to be ruled out. Also, most patients will benefit from a daily stretching regimen as the disease progresses and spasticity worsens.

Patients presenting with optic neuritis are usually managed by neurologists or opthalmologists with steroids (Beck et al., 1993). Acute optic neuritis may be a presenting symptom of MS, and appropriate treatment is important (Beck et al., 1993).

Standard treatment of trigeminal neuralgia is with carbamazepine, and if necessary the addition of phenytoin or baclofen (Dalessio, 1991). Some patients may not tolerate these medications or have less than satisfactory pain control. Percutaneous trigeminal neurolysis with glycerol or radiofrequency lesioning has been fairly successful (Broggi & Franzini, 1982; Linderoth & Hakanson, 1989) with 80% to 90% short-term efficacy and 60% to 80% long-term efficacy.

The pain from tonic seizures can also be controlled with carbamazepine (Clifford & Trotter, 1984; Shibasaki & Kuroiwa, 1974).

Muscle spasms are common and need to be managed by the patient's primary physician because excessive loss of muscle tone may compromise the patient's functional status. In our experience, control of these spasms with muscle relaxants such as baclofen (Roussan, Terrence, & Fromm, 1985) or tinanidine (Wallace, 1994) will usually control the associated pain.

Pains that are secondary to positioning may be attended to by careful attention to position and support of the patient. A soft collar for Lhermitte's sign, padding for pressure sores, and encouragement to practice good posture are all appropriate measures. The use of tricyclic antidepressants is usually advocated for the management of chronic dysesthetic pain as well as generalized muscular pains (Clifford & Trotter, 1984; Moulin et al., 1988). Success rates are relatively low (30% to 50%), and whether this is different from a placebo response has not been determined. The use of NSAIDs, opioids, and cannabis all have advocates, but in our experience they have a long-term efficacy of less than 30% for this symptom.

Despite the well-documented prevalence of pain, there have been no controlled group psychological interventions to manage pain in this population. There has been one published case report on the effects of hypnosis on pain and neuromuscular function (Dane, 1996).

There is a significant body of literature on cognitive and emotional disturbances in multiple sclerosis (Beatty, 1993), which is not reviewed here. The majority of the psychological research has focused on coping with the illness and the impact it has on the intra- and interpersonal environments of the patient (Murray, 1995; VanderPlate, 1984). Depression associated with MS has received the most attention in the literature (Schiffer, 1987, 1990) with exacerbations or progression of the disease postulated to be a significant precipitant (Dalos, Rabins, Brooks, & O'Donnell, 1983). However, these reports did not identify pain as a specific variable contributing to the exacerbation or progression of the illness in their sample. Jonsson, Korfitzen, Heltberg, Ravnborg, and Byskov-Ottosen (1993) had MS patients rate the symptoms and signs of the illness that they considered the most disabling. These included fatigue, getting readily tired, gait disturbances, dependence on others, and worry about deterioration, but did not include pain.

Archibald et al. (1994) examined pain prevalence, severity, and impact of pain on social role in a sample of MS patients. The prevalence of pain in their sample was 53%, which included headache related to MS. They found that pain was equally distributed across gender and disease subtype: relapsing-remitting, relapsing-progressive, chronic progressive, and benign. Of the subjects who reported pain, 57% indicated that their ability to perform as a worker was reduced by 50% or more due to their pain. Number of hours in pain per week was correlated with disease duration and neurologic symptom severity. However, neurologic symptom severity was not correlated significantly with pain severity, number of pain sites, or pain-related distress.

Pain has been identified as a risk factor for suicide in medical patients. E. N. Stenager, E. Stenager, and Jensen (1994) found that patients who suffered from a somatic disease differed from other attempters in terms of depression score, age, pain, and presence of psychosis. Of the suicide attempters they interviewed who had somatic disease, 22% reported having neurological diseases. In another study, E. N. Stenager, Koch-Henriksen, and E. Stenager (1996) investigated risk factors for suicide in MS specifically. Although they were unable to distinctly characterize female patients successfully committing suicide, they were able to come up with a profile for men. They found that the male patient successful at suicide was 40–49 years of age, died by the use of a violent method 68% of the time, had previous expression of suicidal thoughts in half the cases, had depression as the most frequent condition in half the cases, and was suffering from a recent neurological deterioration in half the cases. The role that pain played in the perceived exacerbation of symptoms was not specified.

Psychological pain management intervention in MS patients has not been investigated in a controlled group study. Mandel and Keller (1986) reported the results of a group stress management intervention comprised of patients with chronic pain, chronic obstructive pulmonary disease, and MS. The MS patients comprised 23% of the sample. Pain was not the target of intervention, which included instruction in relaxation techniques, cognitive reappraisal, thought stopping, cognitive restructuring, assertiveness training, and skill consolidation. Although it was found overall that learning the techniques reduced the levels of perceived stress, it appears that the investigators did not control for the type of MS and whether their patients were in remission during the eight-session intervention.

Jonsson, Dock, and Ravnborg (1996) studied the effects of neuropsychotherapy and its effects on quality-of-life variables in a multidisciplinary rehabilitation program for MS. A variable measured on the quality-of-life scale was pain (Laman & Lankhorst, 1994). Neuropsychotherapy focused on remediation of cognitive deficits and instruction in coping skills to minimize the effects of their illness (Jonsson et al., 1993). Pre- and posttest data revealed no change in reported levels of pain. Depression as measured by the Beck Depression Inventory was reduced posttreatment and the authors associated improvement in mood with improvement in physical endurance and ability to work.

Dane (1996) reported a detailed case study using hypnosis to manage pain and assist in neuromuscular rehabilitation with multiple sclerosis. The author indicated that pretreatment psychotherapy was used to reduce the patient's denial of illness and make her more amenable to the hypnosis intervention. Dane found that the sustained use of self-hypnosis was helpful in the short term in reducing the patient's pain. However, given the progressive nature of the disease in this patient, only minimal benefits of the treatment persisted 1 year later. It appears that during treatment with hypnosis, the subject improved her neuromuscular functioning in the absence of changes in medical treatment or medication. The author suggested that utilization of hypnosis, perhaps in combination with cognitive-behavioral interventions for pain (Kirsch, Montgomery, & Sapirstein, 1995), may prove to be beneficial.

Based on a careful review of the literature, there is little published about psychological pain management in MS patients. Given the uncertain course of the disease and the associated cognitive and emotional disturbances, it makes a challenging group of patients to investigate. Future research directions in working with MS patients who report pain include utilizing a standardized pain assessment battery with a constructed validity scale, which could help ensure that the more severely cognitively impaired patients understood the meaning of the question and the correct way to rate their response (Jonsson et al., 1996). Also, it would be potentially beneficial to administer an index of coping strategies for pain (Smith, Wallston, Dwyer, & Dowdy, 1997) that identifies a preferred style of pain coping by the patient. Such information could be a useful means of identifying which patients may be at risk for developing mood disturbance should they experience an exacerbation in their illness and pain.

THE MUSCULAR DYSTROPHIES

The *muscular dystrophies* are a group of inherited myopathies characterized by progressive weakness. Pain is usually not a severe problem in the different forms of muscular dystrophy, and for this reason these patients are not seen frequently at most pain clinics. However, a word of caution is necessary. Patients with certain forms of muscular dystrophy may go unidentified within the general population and may come undiagnosed to pain clinics for management of relatively common complaints, such as persistent or recurrent chronic low back or shoulder pain. This type of patient may pose a diagnostic challenge to the clinicians providing pain management. Because the different forms of muscular dystrophy are uncommon, clinicians may overlook the diagnosis in their initial evaluation of a patient with acute or chronic pain. They may assume that when patients with a muscular dystrophy come for treatment, they will come with an established diagnosis. For example, it is unlikely that a boy with acute low back pain related to weakness and muscle strain from Duchenne dystrophy will present to a pain clinic without a prior diagnosis. This is similar to the situation with MS, in which most patients come to the pain clinic with an established diagnosis. This is not always the case.

The two most common forms of adult muscular dystrophy, myotonic dystrophy (Griggs, Mendell, & Miller, 1995a; Harper, 1989; Moxley, 1992, 1997) and facioscapulohumeral dystrophy (Griggs, Mendell, & Miller, 1995b; Lunt & Harper, 1991; Padberg et al., 1995; Tawil & Griggs, 1996), are highly variable in their clinical manifestations. This variability occurs in age of onset, in side-to-side differences of wasting/weakness, in degree of symptoms both within and between kindreds, and in the severity of the different manifestations. The same is true for the less common, recently delineated disorder, proximal myotonic (Meola, Sansone, Radice, Skradski, & Ptacek, 1996; Ricker et al., 1994, 1995; Thornton, Griggs, & Moxley, 1994). We have seen patients with myotonic muscular dystrophy and proximal myotonic myopathy present for evaluation and treatment, and neither the patient nor the referring physician is aware of the underlying diagnosis. We suspect that we have probably treated patients with fascioscapulo-humeral dystrophy and may not have identified the disorder. Those of us involved primarily in pain management need to consider the possibility of a mild form of adult muscular dystrophy in our initial evaluation of patients, especially those with back and shoulder pain, and we need to include clinical testing that screens for characteristic features of the common forms of adult muscular dystrophy (Griggs et al., 1995b; Harper, 1989; Meola et al., 1996; Moxley, 1992, 1997; Padberg et al., 1995; Ricker et al., 1994, 1995; Tawil & Griggs, 1996; Thornton et al., 1994).

Tips for the Initial Clinical Evaluation. As indicated in Table 17.2, myotonic dystrophy, fascioscapulohumeral dystrophy, and proximal myotonic myopathy may present with muscle or muscular/tendon-associated pain in the shoulders or thighs, and occasionally with recurrent knee pain due

TABLE 17.2
The Muscular Dystrophies

Syndrome	Affected Areas	Pain Character
Myotonic	Low back pain; shoulder-rotator cuff; subscapular muscle pain; temporal mandibular joint pain; knee pain due to hyperextension and abnormal mobility.	Pain with arising from sitting; point tenderness and with motion; with prolonged or wide jaw opening; pain with arising from sitting, descending stairs, or prolonged standing.
Facioscapulohumeral	Upper back, shoulder, posterior neck pains; low back strain; knee pain with effusion and increased mobility; calf muscle.	Scapular instability with muscular aches and spasms; pain on arising from sitting; pain with weight bearing and activity; due to overuse to compensate for hip girdle and dorsiflexion weakness.
PROMM	Upper arms, shoulders, chest, and thighs.	Burning, tearing, and aching in various combinations. Pain fluctuates.
Duchenne	Flexion contractures of the feet and gastrocnemius; occasional low back pain.	Muscular cramps secondary to overuse usually at rest at bedtime; muscle strain to compensate for proximal hip girdle weakness.
Becker	Muscle cramps	With activity; also symptoms similar to Duchenne.
Emery–Dreifuss	Neck-spine contracture; elbow contracture.	Aching and sharp muscle strains; joint stress.

to joint instability caused by muscle weakness. Chronic or acute low back pain is also a common pain problem in these adult muscular dystrophies. The initial assessment of patients referred to a pain treatment specialist with muscle pain or knee pain, especially patients without clear evidence of radicular or peripheral nerve damage, should include (a) testing for grip and percussion myotonia, (b) functional testing, such as the ability to walk on heels and tiptoe, and (c) specific testing of the strength of the facial muscles, neck flexors, scapular fixators, long finger flexors, and foot dorsiflexors. Patients with myotonic dystrophy and proximal myotonic myopathy often have grip and/or percussion myotonia. Myotonic dystrophy and proximal myotonic myopathy cause weakness of neck flexors, whereas facioscapulohumeral dystrophy leads to weakness of neck extensors, sparing to a large degree the neck flexors. Patients with myotonic dystrophy and fascioscapulohumeral dystrophy usually have a limitation in their ability to bury their eyelashes during forceful closure of the eyes. Both of these disorders also have weakness of foot dorsiflexion and scapular fixation, although weakness of scapular fixation is usually much more pronounced in fascioscapulohumeral dystrophy. Patients with myotonic dystrophy often have a prominent weakness of the long flexors of the fingers. In contrast, patients with proximal myotonic myopathy have weakness of hip flexors without weakness of foot dorsiflexors or of the long flexors of the fingers. Table 17.2 lists the more common forms of the muscular dystrophies and summarizes the commonly associated pain syndromes.

Myotonic muscular dystrophy is a multisystem autosomal dominant disorder, and is the most common of the muscular dystrophies with a prevalence of 1/8000 (Harper, 1989; Moxley, 1992). Onset occurs throughout life, being at birth in the severe congenital form, occurring between the second and third decades of life in the moderate-classical form, and presenting later in life with the mild form, often with only restricted manifestations, such as cataracts, heart block, or very mild distal weakness in the hands and legs. The gene defect in myotonic dystrophy is an unstable trinucleotide repeat expansion, [CTG]n, on chromosome 19 (Brook et al., 1992; Fu et al., 1992; Mahadevan et al., 1992; Redman, Fenwick, Fu, Pizzuti, & Caskey, 1993; Shelbourne et al., 1993), and a standard leucocyte DNA test is available to identify affected individuals (Redman et al., 1993; Shelbourne et al., 1993). Unlike most myopathies, myotonic dystrophy affects the distal (rather than proximal) muscles of the arms and legs along with facial and bulbar muscles. Life span is shortened for most patients due to complications, such as respiratory insufficiency, aspiration/atelectatic pneumonitis, heart block, and other cardiac arrhythmias.

Certain pain problems are common in myotonic dystrophy, the most prominent being low back pain (Harper, 1989). Because of weakness in the ankle-stabilizing muscles, patients develop a compensatory backward tilt of their pelvis. There is an associated flattening of the normal lumbar lordosis. The combination of abnormal pelvic-spinal alignment, underlying muscle stiffness/myotonia, and weakness of distal muscles of the legs, places myotonic dystrophy patients at constant risk for low back strain. As the disease progresses, weakness and wasting of the knee extensors develop, and is accompanied by further worsening of weakness and wasting of the ankle stablizers. This pattern of progressive weakness causes more strain on the paraspinous muscles and increases the strain on the relatively spared proximal thigh and hip girdle muscles. As time passes patients have more back, pelvic girdle, and medial thigh muscle strains and pain.

Other common pain problems in myotonic dystrophy involve strain or tears of the rotator cuff, strain and overuse of the scapular stabilizing muscles, traumatic arthritis in the knees secondary to abnormally increased mobility, especially in hyperextension, and pain in the temporomandibular joint and masseter muscles. The jaw pain, which fortunately is a less common complaint, results from the selective pattern of facial muscle weakness. Not only is there weakness of facial movement, including limited ability to bury the eyelashes during forceful eye closure, but there is also weakness of the muscles of mastication, swallowing, and neck flexion. The weakness of the masseter and temporalis muscles produces the open-mouth appearance so typical in moderate to severe cases of myotonic dystrophy. Weakness of these muscles predisposes to dislocation and strain on the temporomandibular joint, and there is an associated abnormal stretch of the muscles of mastication. This stretch in turn stimulates myotonic muscle spasms in the muscles closing the mouth. Patients can have their mouths stuck in the closed position for many hours and can sometimes have moderately severe pain during these spasms. In some circumstances the inability to open the mouth can pose a medical emergency. If the patient requires oral medications or has chronic nasal obstruction and relies on mouth breathing, urgent treatment of this problem is necessary. As a rule, however, most of the pain complaints in myotonic dystrophy can be safely managed in an outpatient in a nonemergency setting.

Facioscapulohumeral muscular dystrophy is the second most common form of adult muscular dystrophy with a prevalence of 1 in 20,000 (Tawil & Griggs, 1996). Weakness usually appears between the second and fifth decades of life. The weakness and wasting progress very slowly, are restricted to relatively few muscles, and seldom shorten life expectancy (Griggs et al., 1995b; Padberg et al., 1995; Tawil & Griggs, 1996). The vast majority of patients who have undergone DNA analysis have shown linkage to a locus on chromosome 4 and have had a deletion in the subtelomeric region (Tawil & Griggs, 1996). However, the exact gene lesion remains unknown, and at present there is no standard genetic test to identify affected individuals.

In the years immediately after the onset of facioscapulohumeral dystrophy, weakness is restricted mainly to the scapular fixators, producing the hallmark symptom of scapular winging. Less marked weakness appears in the face and neck extensor muscles (as opposed to weak flexors in myotonic dystrophy, proximal myotonic myopathy, and Duchenne dystrophy). One clinical feature requires special emphasis. There is an extraordinary variability in the severity of the disease as measured by the age of onset, side-to-side symmetry, rate of progression, and distribution of affected muscles (Tawil & Griggs, 1996). Interestingly, this variability can exist both within and between kindreds (Tawil & Griggs, 1996).

Marked, selective weakness of scapular fixation prevents patients from elevating their outstretched arms fully above their head, despite having good power in their deltoid muscles. This scapular fixator weakness combined with weakness of the lower trapezius causes patients to have characteristic bulges in the upper trapezius muscles and lateral regions of the neck during lifting of their outstretched arms. In the later stages of the disease, weakness and wasting develop in the elbow flexors and extensors, the anterior abdominal muscles, the knee extensors, and the dorsiflexors of the feet. Often the lower abdominal muscles are selectively weaker than the upper abdominal muscles, leading to the interesting clinical finding of an elevation of the umbilicus during forceful flexion of the neck. This finding is relatively specific to facioscapulohumeral muscular dystrophy and is not commonly observed in other myopathic disorders.

Acute and chronic low back pain are the most common pain complaints. Back pain occurs in large part because patients inadvertently use poor body mechanics when lifting or arising from a squat. The older, more affected patients with significant weakness of foot dorsiflexors and knee extensors have more back complaints. Pain and spasm in the upper trapezius, rotator cuff, and deltoid muscles are frequent. Pain develops in these relatively strong muscles as they attempt to compensate for the weakness of the scapula fixator muscles, which usually are quite weak in facioscapulohumeral dystrophy, even in the early stages.

Other pain complaints in facioscapulohumeral dystrophy include knee pain with effusion due to traumatic arthritis, and occasional calf muscle pain and spasm. The knee symptoms worsen as joint mobility becomes abnormally increased. Increasing weakness of the knee extensors leads to the abnormal mobility in the knee and increasing weakness of the foot dorsiflexors places more stress on the knee joint and the plantar flexors of the feet. Greater reliance on plantar flexors to correct for the mild foot drop and to help stabilize the knee in extension occurs and also predisposes the calf muscles to overuse, pain, and spasm. This calf pain is like the painful cramps that develop with overuse in athletes or patients with mild L5-S1 radiculopathy, and management of this particular pain is for the most part similar.

Proximal myotonic myopathy (PROMM) is a recently delineated, autosomal dominant muscular dystrophy that typically presents in midadult life (Meola et al., 1996; Ricker et al., 1994, 1995; Thornton et al., 1994). The gene defect is unknown. The core features of PROMM are (a) proximal weakness, usually in the hip flexors with difficulty arising from a squat or climbing stairs (Ricker et al., 1994, 1995; Thornton et al., 1994), (b) myotonia, typically in the grip or thigh muscles, which fluctuates so that at times there may be no clinical signs of myotonia (Von Roenn, Cleeland, Gonin, Hatfield, & Pandya, 1993), and (c) cataracts, which are irridescent, posterior capsular, lens opacities indistinguishable from the cataracts in myotonic dystrophy (Ricker et al., 1994, 1995; Thornton et al., 1994). Many affected individuals have minimal weakness and their myotonia and cataracts go unnoticed. Patients commonly attribute their stiffness, pain, and difficulty climbing steps to "arthritis." Tendon reflexes, sensation, cerebellar function, and cranial nerve function are normal, except for weakness of neck flexors. The diagnosis has to be suspected or it will be overlooked. The onset of myotonia in the grip and thighs occurs in the second through fifth decades. Weakness usually develops later. Cataracts begin early in life but usually do not require removal until patients are over 50 years of age. Occasionally patients with PROMM complain about a peculiar muscle pain (tearing, burning) that is most pronounced at rest and can worsen with pressure on the symptomatic muscle groups (Ricker et al., 1995). This pain is most prominent in the upper arms, shoulders, chest, and thighs. It is not typically related to exercise or the degree of myotonia. It fluctuates over hours to days to weeks, and can resolve without specific therapy for months at a time. Some patients never have this pain. Its cause is unknown, but its source seems to be within skeletal muscle.

Duchenne dystrophy is an X-linked recessive disease and is the most common form of muscular dystrophy in childhood (Dubowotz, 1995; Engel, Yamamoto, & Fischbeck, 1994; Roberts, 1995; Samaha & Quinlan, 1996a, 1996b). Onset of symptoms occurs early in childhood. Weakness of neck flexors and anterior abdominal muscles is apparent during the first year of life. Patients have a delay in walking, and never achieve the ability to run normally. They are unable to "keep up" with their peers at play. Clumsiness, toe walking, and a greater number of falls than normal occur between 4 and 8 years of age, along with more difficulty in arising quickly from the floor and climbing stairs. The early weakness of hip extensors, hip abductors, and knee extensors leads to increased lumbar lordosis and an increased reliance on the calf muscles to ambulate. Because the gastrocnemius muscle acts to both plantar flex the foot and stabilize the knee in extension, it becomes hypertrophied. The calf muscles bear an increasing work load as the disease worsens, which accounts for the frequent occurrence of calf muscle cramps and pain, especially at bedtime following a day of vigorous exertion. As proximal hip girdle weakness becomes more pronounced, the lordosis becomes more marked, placing an increased load on the paraspinous muscles. This predisposes to episodes of recurrent acute low back pain, and rarely to chronic persistent low back pain.

Weakness of scapular fixators, arm adductors, and elbow flexors/extensors progresses in parallel with weakness of hip extensors/abductors and knee extensors. However, shoulder and upper back pain rarely occur. Pain from transient distraction of the humerus in the shoulder joint can occur when someone moves or lifts the patient by improperly pulling on the arms rather than using the "hug technique" for lifting. Older and/or heavier patients require a Hoyer lift to be moved safely to avoid risking joint or muscle strain in the patient and in the person performing the lifting. Dropping a patient during lifting or falls in which the patient lands abruptly on his buttocks can lead to compression fractures in the lower thoracic and lumbar vertebrae and can provide a nidus for chronic low back pain. Osteopenia is often marked in Duchenne dystrophy, and compression fractures and fractures of long bones occur more readily than in normal children undergoing the identical trauma.

Duchenne dystrophy results from a lack of the large, sarcolemmal membrane associated protein, dystrophin, and is due to a mutation in the dystrophin gene located in the Xp21 region of the X-chromosome (Dubowotz, 1995; Engel et al., 1994; Roberts, 1995). Up to one third of patients represent spontaneous mutations, but prenatal and perinatal genetic counseling is available for carriers who have the typical deletion/duplication mutations that occur in about 60% to 70% of patients and carriers (Dubowotz, 1995; Engel et al., 1994; Roberts, 1995). Duchenne dystrophy causes a shortened life span with patients often succumbing in their teens or 20s. Most patients die from respiratory failure and a small number from congestive heart failure. Recently, the symptoms and life span have benefited from long-term treatment with prednisone (Fenichel et al., 1991; Griggs et al., 1991, 1993; Higuchi et al., 1993; Mendell et al., 1989; Sansome, Royston, & Dubowitz, 1993), and the combination of improved supportive care plus prednisone has prolonged the period of ambulation and standing and delayed the development of respiratory failure (Fenichel et al., 1991; Griggs et al., 1993).

Becker type muscular dystrophy, like Duchenne dystrophy, is an X-linked recessive disease resulting from a mutation in the dystrophin gene on the X-chromosome with a frequency one tenth that of Duchenne dystrophy (Dubowotz, 1995; Engel et al., 1994; Roberts, 1995; Samaha & Quinlan, 1996a, 1996b). Unlike Duchenne dystrophy, the clinical course is more slowly progressive (Dubowotz, 1995; Engel et al., 1994; Roberts, 1995) and on muscle biopsy there is usually preservation of a small amount of dystrophin (Dubowotz, 1995; Engel et al., 1994; Roberts, 1995; Samaha & Quinlan, 1996b). The preservation of dystrophin and milder clinical course appears to be due to the fact that the gene defect represents an inframe deletion in Becker dystrophy, whereas Duchenne dystrophy has out-of-frame deletions (Dubowotz, 1995; Engel et al., 1994; Roberts, 1995; Samaha & Quinlan, 1996a, 1996b). Onset typically occurs in late childhood or the teens, although later onset can occur (Dubowotz, 1995; Engel et al., 1994; Roberts, 1995; Samaha & Quinlan, 1996a, 1996b). The pattern of weakness eventually mimics that of Duchenne dystrophy, but in the early years manifests primarily in the legs. Patients are able to run and perform vigorous exercise in childhood, and occasionally pain develops with exercise as one of the earliest complaints (Samaha & Quinlan, 1996a, 1996b). Pain can develop in the calves and low back as the disease worsens, due to overuse, and the mechanism for the muscle overload is identical to that described previously for Duchenne dystrophy. The clinical course is slowly progressive weakness with patients maintaining their ability to ambulate into the late teens or 20s. Upper-body strength remains relatively well preserved until the 20s and 30s. Respiratory insufficiency eventually becomes a life-threatening complication and there is not uncommonly coexisting congestive heart failure (Dubowotz, 1995; Engel et al., 1994; Roberts, 1995). DNA testing is available to screen at-risk carriers for prenatal and perinatal counseling (Dubowotz, 1995; Engel et al., 1994; Roberts, 1995).

Emery-Dreifuss dystrophy is an X-linked recessive muscular dystrophy caused by mutations in the region of Xq28, which encodes a serine rich protease of unknown function (Bione et al., 1994, 1995; Dubowotz, 1995; Klauck, Wilgenbus, Yates, Muller, & Poustka, 1995; Nagano et al., 1996). On antibody staining the protease, emerin, appears in the nuclear membrane of nuclei from skeletal, cardiac, and smooth muscles in normal controls and in various neuromuscular disease controls, but not in the nuclear membranes of these same tissues from patients with Emery-Dreifuss muscular dystrophy (Nagano et al., 1996). Emery-Dreifuss dystrophy usually presents in adolescence or adult life with mild stiffness and contractures of limb joints as initial complaints. Occasionally there is associated chronic muscle and joint pain. Flexion contractures at the elbows, Achilles shortening, and inability to touch the chin to the sternum or to bend forward to touch the toes are all complications that slowly develop (Bione et al., 1994, 1995; Dubowotz, 1995; Grimm & Janka, 1994; Klauck et al., 1995; Nagano et al., 1996). Rigidity of the spine, especially in the cervical region, predisposes patients to paraspinous muscle strain and pain. Weakness is often mild, although striking wasting can occur in the upper arms with sparing of the deltoid and forearm muscles as the disease becomes fully manifest. Calf muscles are sometimes wasted. Mildly affected patients presenting to a pain clinic may be difficult to recognize without performing a careful evaluation to check for contractures. Unlike Duchenne dystrophy and Becker dystrophy in which there is a marked elevation of creatine kinase level in the blood, Emery-Dreifuss dystrophy shows a mild two- to four-fold elevation. Muscle biopsy reveals normal dystrophin content and a pattern of changes typical for muscular dystrophy (Dubowotz, 1995; Grimm & Janka, 1994).

Serious complications occur in Emery-Dreifuss dystrophy. Arrhythmias, including atrial paralysis and complete heart block, occur typically, and subsequently, a generalized cardiomyopathy develops (Bione et al., 1994, 1995; Grimm & Janka, 1994; Klauck et al., 1995; Nagano et al., 1996). Syncope is often the heralding sign of the cardiac disease. Occasionally nocturnal hypoventilation occurs, as in rigid spine syndrome, and can exacerbate the cardiac arrhythmias. A cardiac pacemaker is often required and is life saving. Physical therapy is helpful to lessen the rate of progression and severity of contractures. Genetic counseling is especially important for all at risk of carrying the mutation. Special emphasis is necessary to perform serial ECG (electrocardiogram) examinations on known and suspected carriers, in view of their increased risk of developing cardiac arrhythmias (Bione et al., 1994, 1995; Dubowotz, 1995; Grimm & Janka, 1994; Klauck et al., 1995; Nagano et al., 1996).

Patient Management

In general, the pain that occurs in muscular dystrophy patients will respond to conservative medical management. Pain is not a common feature of muscular dystrophies other than mild muscle aching (Gardner-Medwin, 1995). With close coordination of care between the patient and care providers, which usually includes family members, the primary-care physician, neurologist, nursing staff, physical therapist, occupational therapist, and psychologist/psychiatrist, treatment of pain problems rarely will require long-term care in a pain treatment center.

Medical pain management in the muscular dystrophies is highly symptomatic. That is, most of the pains are from overuse and are expected to respond to NSAIDs and stretching. In addition, patients need to learn how to both pace their activities and maintain activity to maintain muscle mass as long as possible.

Myotonic Dystrophy. Low back pain and shoulder pain due to muscle overuse are the most common pain problems and usually respond to NSAIDs and stretching. Occasionally, recurrent pain and intense spasm require acute and/or long-term treatment of the underlying myotonia. Mexiletine, tocainide, and phenytoin are all effective in the control of myotonia (Ceccarelli, Rossi, Siciliano, Calevro, & Tarantino, 1992; Kwiecinski, Ryniewicz, & Ostrzycki, 1992), but mexiletine is our preference. Treatment of the myotonia is best coordinated with the patient's neurologist. Occasionally, the treatment of acute muscle pain/spasm/myotonia may benefit from the addition cyclobenzaprine treatment for a few days.

Low back pain becomes more frequent as the weakness of ankle stabilizers and knee extensors increase. This pattern of weakness leads to increased stress on the extensor muscles of the spine during attempts to arise from a chair or the floor. Shoulder pain develops due to muscle overuse in the upper trapezius and in the rotator cuff muscles and relates to degree of weakness and fatigue of the scapular fixators. Tear of the rotator cuff occurs with an increased frequency and pain management needs to consider this possibility along with overuse. Referral to an orthopedist may be necessary. Physical therapy evaluation to advise patients in proper body mechanics to avoid placing undue stress on the paraspinous muscles and on the scapular fixators is very helpful for both acute and long-term management.

Hypermobility of the knee occurs as weakness of the knee extensors worsens. Patients develop a "back-knee" posture during walking, which predisposes them to develop knee effusions and pain in the joint. NSAIDs, rest, and lightweight, long leg bracing is often useful in decreasing the pain and permitting a longer period of ambulation and weight bearing before the patient becomes fully wheelchair dependent. Sometimes thigh adductor muscle pain accompanies the knee effusion/pain. This due to increased reliance on the adductors to assist in arising from sitting and this adductor pain usually responds to rest and NSAIDs. Physical therapy consultation is useful in developing strategies to lessen the stress, for example, elevated seats, powered riser chair, and so forth.

Occasionally, severe muscle spasm and pain develops in the jaw and relates to the tendency for dislocation of the mandible in myotonic dystrophy patients with advanced weakness of the masseter and temporalis muscles, for example, in the cases of congenital myotonic dystrophy who have reached their teens and 20s. Hot packs and NSAIDs are often helpful. Chronic treatment with mexiletine may become necessary to reduce the myotonia and lessen the likelihood of stretch induced myotonic spasm. This treatment needs to be coordinated with the neurologist.

A few general guidelines about pain management in myotonic dystrophy need to be remembered. Myotonic dystrophy causes altered gastrointestinal motility (Moxley, 1992). NSAIDs, especially those that have a high potential to stimulate gastroesophageal reflux, may be poorly tolerated. Myotonic dystrophy patients have an abnormal sensitivity to opiates and barbiturates and can develop apnea or depressed respiration following their administration (Moxley, 1992). Delayed onset of respiratory depression has occurred in patients following general anesthesia, even several hours after extubation (Moxley, 1992). Patients also have an abnormal sensitivity to depolarizing muscle relaxants, and they should be avoided (Moxley, 1992). Any operative procedure to alleviate pain that requires sedation, whether as an adjunct to local anesthesia or as premedication for general anesthesia, is best discussed with the patient's neurologist and primary-care physician before proceeding with the procedure.

Facioscapulohumeral Dystrophy. Low back pain and knee pain are common in facioscapulohumeral dystrophy and usually respond to the approach just outlined for myotonic dystrophy. Shoulder pain due to overuse is also common, because patients early in their course develop prominent winging of their scapulae. Physical therapy consultation to advise patients in proper body mechanics is particularly important and is necessary to prevent recurrent bouts of back and shoulder muscle pain from strain and overuse. Surgery to stabilize the scapula is not commonly used and should be reserved for a selected number of patients (Tawil & Griggs, 1996). These patients tolerate sedative medications and general anesthesia without complication.

Proximal Myotonic Myopathy. There are no published trials of treatment to evaluate different medications for the peculiar tearing, burning pain described previously that afflicts patients with PROMM. Anecdotal treatment with carbamazepine, phenytoin, and mexiletine has not controlled the pain although the myotonia has lessened with mexiletine. NSAIDs have helped. The muscle pain in PROMM may be a candidate for treatment with tricyclic antidepressants.

Duchenne Dystrophy, Becker Dystrophy, Emery–Dreifuss Dystrophy. Pain management in these forms of muscular dystrophy focuses on treatment of low back strain and calf muscle cramping. The approach is similar to that described earlier for myotonic dystrophy. Physical therapy and nighttime calf muscle stretching serve to lessen the progression or development of contractures, and decrease the likelihood of nighttime muscle cramps. Usually the combination of NSAIDs, stretching, and low dose of a tricyclic antidepressant is effective in controlling the muscle pain. Infrequently, compression fracture with persistent pain occurs in Duchenne dystrophy and requires the use of lightweight corset support to accompany these medications. Becker dystrophy patients sometime have exercise-provoked muscle pain, particularly in their legs. One report indicates that corticosteroid therapy was effective (Nagano et al., 1996). However, other than the established use of prednisone as a treatment for preserving muscle strength in Duchenne dystrophy (Fenichel et al., 1991; Griggs et al., 1991, 1993; Higuchi et al., 1993; Mendell et al., 1989; Sansome et al., 1993), there is no specific role for corticosteroids in the control of pain in these muscular dystrophies.

Psychological Management of Pain in the Muscular Dystrophies

No psychological intervention strategies targeted at pain in this population have been reported. Depending on the type of dystrophy, psychological interventions have usually consisted of assessment of cognitive abilities, supportive group therapy for family members and patients, genetic counseling, grief counseling, improving coping skills, facilitating adherence to medical regimens, and providing support for caregivers of this challenging population of patients (Charash, Kutschner, Lovelace, & Hale, 1983).

CONCLUSIONS

The treatment of pain in either multiple sclerosis or a muscular dystrophy needs to be integrated into the overall management of the patient. The etiology of the pain will need to be determined, and then appropriate treatment started. Management is highly symptomatic, and is dependent on both the overall condition of the patient and the etiology of the pain.

REFERENCES

Archibald, C. J., McGrath, P. J., Ritvo, P. G., Fisk, J. D., Bhan, V., Maxner, C. E., & Murray, T. J. (1994). Pain prevalence, severity and impact in a clinic sample of multiple sclerosis patients. *Pain, 58,* 89–93.

Beatty, W. W. (1993). Cognitive and emotional disturbances in multiple sclerosis. *Neurologic Clinics, 11,* 189–204.

Beck, R. W., Cleary, P. A., Trobe, J. D., Kaufman, D. I., Kupersmith, M. J., Paty, D. W., & Brown, C. H. (1993). The effect of corticosteroids for acute optic neuritis on the subsequent development of multiple sclerosis. The Optic Neuritis Study Group. *New England Journal of Medicine, 329,* 1764–1769.

Bione, S., Maestrini, E., Rivella, S., Mancini, M., Regis, S., Romeo, G., & Toniolo, D. (1994). Identification of a novel X-linked gene responsible for Emery–Dreifuss muscular dystrophy. *Nature Genetics, 8,* 323–327.

Bione, S., Small, K., Aksmanovic, V. M., D'Urso, M., Ciccodicola, A., Merlini, L., Morandi, L., Kress, W., Yates, J. R., Warren, S. T., & Toniolo, D. (1995). Identification of new mutations in the Emery-Dreifuss muscular dystrophy gene and evidence for genetic heterogeneity of the disease. *Human Molecular Genetics, 4,* 1859–1863.

Broggi, G., & Franzini, A. (1982). Radiofrequency trigeminal rhizotomy in treatment of symptomatic non-neoplastic facial pain. *Journal of Neurosurgery, 57,* 483–486.

Brook, J. D., McCurrach, M. E., Harley, H. G., Buckler, A. J., Church, D., Aburatani, H., Hunter, K., Stanton, V. P., Thirion, J. P., Hudson, T., Sohn, R., Zemelman, B., Snell, R. G., Rundle, S. A., Crow, S., Davies, J., Shelbourne, P., Buxton, J., Jones, C., Juvonen,

V., Johnson, K., Harper, P. S., Shaw, D. J., & Housman, D. E. (1992). Molecular basis of myotonic dystrophy: expansion of a trinucleotide (CTG) repeat at the 3′ end of a transcript encoding a protein kinase family member. *Cell, 68,* 799–808.

Ceccarelli, M., Rossi, B., Siciliano, G., Calevro, L., & Tarantino, E. (1992). Clinical and electrophysiological reports in a case of early onset myotonia congenita (Thomsen's disease) successfully treated with mexiletine. *Acta Paediatrica, 81,* 453–455.

Charash, L. I., Kutschner, A. H., Lovelace, R. E., & Hale, M. S. (1983). *Psychosocial aspects of muscular dystrophy and allied diseases.* Springfield, IL: Thomas.

Clifford, D. B., & Trotter, J. L. (1984). Pain in multiple sclerosis. *Archives of Neurology, 41,* 1270–1272.

Dalessio, D. J. (1991). Diagnosis and treatment of cranial neuralgias. *Medical Clinics of North America, 75,* 605–615.

Dalos, N. P., Rabins, P. V., Brooks, B. R., & O'Donnell, P. (1983). Disease activity and emotional state in multiple sclerosis. *Annals of Neurology, 13,* 573–577.

Dane, J. R. (1996). Hypnosis for pain and neuromuscular rehabilitation with multiple sclerosis: Case summary, literature review, and analysis of outcomes. *International Journal of Clinical & Experimental Hypnosis, 44,* 208–231.

Dubowotz, V. (1995). Muscular dystrophies. In V. Dubowitz (Ed.), *Muscular disorders in childhood* (2nd ed., pp. 34–133). Philadelphia: Saunders.

Ebers, G. C., & Sadovnick, A. D. (1994). The role of genetic factors in multiple sclerosis susceptibility. *Journal of Neuroimmunology, 54,* 1–17.

Engel, A., Yamamoto, M., & Fischbeck, K. H. (1994). Dystrophinopathies. In A. G. Engel & C. Franzini-Armstrong (Eds.), *Myology* (2nd ed., pp. 1133–1187). New York: McGraw-Hill.

Fenichel, G. M., Florence, J. M., Pestronk, A., Mendell, J. R., Moxley, R. T., Griggs, R. C., Brooke, M. H., Miller, J. P., Robison, J., King, W., Signore, L., Pandya, S., Schierbecker, J., & Wilson, B. (1991). Long-term benefit from prednisone therapy in Duchenne muscular dystrophy. *Neurology, 41,* 1874–1877.

Fu, Y. H., Pizzuti, A., Fenwick, R. G., Jr., King, J., Rajnarayan, S., Dunne, P. W., Dubel, J., Nasser, G. A., Ashizawa, T., de Jong, P., Wieringa, B., Korneluk, R., Perryman, M. B., Epstein, H. F., & Caskey, C. T. (1992). An unstable triplet repeat in a gene related to myotonic muscular dystrophy. *Science, 255,* 1256–1258.

Gardner-Medwin, D. (1995). New questions about the muscular dystrophies. *Annals of the Rheumatic Diseases, 54,* 536–538.

Griggs, R. C., Mendell, J. R., & Miller, R. G. (1995a). Facioscapulohumeral muscular dystrophy. In R. C. Griggs, J. R. Mendell, & R. G. Miller (Eds.), *Evaluation and treatment of myopathies* (pp. 122–126). Philadelphia: Davis.

Griggs, R. C., Mendell, J. R., & Miller, R. G. (1995b). Myotonic muscular dystrophy. In R. C. Griggs, J. R. Mendell, & R. G. Miller (Eds.), *Evaluation and treatments of myopathies* (pp. 114–121). Philadelphia: Davis.

Griggs, R. C., Moxley, R. T., Mendell, J. R., Fenichel, G. M., Brooke, M. H., Pestronk, A., & Miller, J. P. (1991). Prednisone in Duchenne dystrophy. A randomized, controlled trial defining the time course and dose response. Clinical Investigation of Duchenne Dystrophy Group. *Archives of Neurology, 48,* 383–388.

Griggs, R. C., Moxley, R. T., Mendell, J. R., Fenichel, G. M., Brooke, M. H., Pestronk, A., Miller, J. P., Cwik, V. A., Pandya, S., Robison, J., King, W., Signore, L., Schierbecker, J., Florence, J., Matheson-Burden, N., & Wilson, B. (1993). Duchenne dystrophy: Random-ized, controlled trial of prednisone (18 months) and azathioprine (12 months). *Neurology, 43,* 520–527.

Grimm, T., & Janka, M. (1994). Emery–Dreifuss muscular dystrophy. In A. G. Engel & C. Franzini-Armstrong (Eds.), *Myology* (2nd ed., pp. 1188–1191). New York: McGraw-Hill.

Harper, P. S. (1989). *Myotonic dystrophy* (2nd ed.). London: Saunders.

Higuchi, I., Nakamura, K., Nakagawa, M., Nakamura, N., Usuki, F., Inose, M., & Osame, M. (1993). Steroid-responsive myalgia in a patient with Becker muscular dystrophy. *Journal of the Neurological Sciences, 115,* 219–222.

Hogancamp, W. E., Rodriguez, M., & Weinshenker, B. G. (1997). The epidemiology of multiple sclerosis. *Mayo Clinic Proceedings, 72,* 871–878.

Hunter, S. F., Weinshenker, B. G., Carter, J. L., & Noseworthy, J. H. (1997). Rational clinical immunotherapy for multiple sclerosis. *Mayo Clinic Proceedings, 72,* 765–780.

Jensen, T. S., Rasmussen, P., & Reske-Nielsen, E. (1982). Association of trigeminal neuralgia with multiple sclerosis: Clinical and pathological features. *Acta Neurologica Scandinavica, 65,* 182–189.

Jonsson, A., Dock, J., & Ravnborg, M. H. (1996). Quality of life as a measure of rehabilitation outcome in patients with multiple sclerosis. *Acta Neurologica Scandinavica, 93,* 229–235.

Jonsson, A., Korfitzen, E. M., Heltberg, A., Ravnborg, M. H., & Byskov-Ottosen, E. (1993). Effects of neuropsychological treatment in patients with multiple sclerosis. *Acta Neurologica Scandinavica, 88,* 394–400.

Kirsch, I., Montgomery, G., & Sapirstein, G. (1995). Hypnosis as an adjunct to cognitive-behavioral psychotherapy: A meta-analysis. *Journal of Consulting & Clinical Psychology, 63,* 214–220.

Klauck, S. M., Wilgenbus, P., Yates, J. R., Muller, C. R., & Poustka, A. (1995). Identification of novel mutations in three families with Emery–Dreifuss muscular dystrophy. *Human Molecular Genetics, 4,* 1853–1857.

Kwiecinski, H., Ryniewicz, B., & Ostrzycki, A. (1992). Treatment of myotonia with antiarrhythmic drugs. *Acta Neurologica Scandinavica, 86,* 371–375.

Laman, H., & Lankhorst, G. J. (1994). Subjective weighting of disability: An approach to quality of life assessment in rehabilitation. *Disability & Rehabilitation, 16,* 198–204.

Linderoth, B., & Hakanson, S. (1989). Paroxysmal facial pain in disseminated sclerosis treated by retrogasserian glycerol injection. *Acta Neurologica Scandinavica, 80,* 341–346.

Lunt, P. W., & Harper, P. S. (1991). Genetic counselling in facioscapulohumeral muscular dystrophy. *Journal of Medical Genetics, 28,* 655–664.

Mahadevan, M., Tsilfidis, C., Sabourin, L., Shutler, G., Amemiya, C., Jansen, G., Neville, C., Narang, M., Barcelo, J., O'Hoy, K., Leblond, S., Earle-MacDonald, J., De Jong, P. J., Wieringa, B., & Korneluk, R. G. (1992). Myotonic dystrophy mutation: an unstable CTG repeat in the 3′ untranslated region of the gene. *Science, 255,* 1253–1255.

Mandel, A. R., & Keller, S. M. (1986). Stress management in rehabilitation. *Archives of Physical Medicine & Rehabilitation, 67,* 375–379.

Mendell, J. R., Moxley, R. T., Griggs, R. C., Brooke, M. H., Fenichel, G. M., Miller, J. P., King, W., Signore, L., Pandya, S., Florence, J., Schierbecker, J., Robison, J., Kaiser, K., Mandel, S., Arfken, C., & Gilder, B. (1989). Randomized, double-blind six-month trial of prednisone in Duchenne's muscular dystrophy. *New England Journal of Medicine, 320,* 1592–1597.

Meola, G., Sansone, V., Radice, S., Skradski, S., & Ptacek, L. (1996). A family with an unusual myotonic and myopathic phenotype and no CTG expansion (proximal myotonic myopathy syndrome): A challenge for future molecular studies. *Neuromuscular Disorders, 6,* 143–150.

Moulin, D. E., Foley, K. M., & Ebers, G. C. (1988). Pain syndromes in multiple sclerosis. *Neurology, 38,* 1830–1834.

Moxley, R. T. (1992). Myotonic muscular dystrophy. In L. P. Rowland (Ed.), *Handbook of clinical neurology* (Vol. 18, pp. 209–259). Amsterdam: Elsevier Scientific.

Moxley, R. T. (1997). Carrell–Krusen Symposium Invited Lecture—1997. Myotonic disorders in childhood: Diagnosis and treatment. *Journal of Child Neurology, 12,* 116–129.

Murray, T. J. (1995). The psychosocial aspects of multiple sclerosis. *Neurologic Clinics, 13,* 197–223.

Nagano, A., Koga, R., Ogawa, M., Kurano, Y., Kawada, J., Okada, R., Hayashi, Y. K., Tsukahara, T., & Arahata, K. (1996). Emerin deficiency at the nuclear membrane in patients with Emery–Dreifuss muscular dystrophy. *Nature Genetics, 12,* 254–259.

Padberg, G. W., Frants, R. R., Brouwer, O. F., Wijmenga, C., Bakker, E., & Sandkuijl, L. A. (1995). Facioscapulohumeral muscular dystrophy in the Dutch population. *Muscle & Nerve, 2*, S81–S84.

Poser, C. M. (1994). The epidemiology of multiple sclerosis: A general overview. *Annals of Neurology, 36*(Suppl. 2), S180–S193.

Ramirez-Lassepas, M., Tulloch, J. W., Quinones, M. R., & Snyder, B. D. (1992). Acute radicular pain as a presenting symptom in multiple sclerosis. *Archives of Neurology, 49*, 255–258.

Redman, J. B., Fenwick, R. G., Jr., Fu, Y. H., Pizzuti, A., & Caskey, C. T. (1993). Relationship between parental trinucleotide GCT repeat length and severity of myotonic dystrophy in offspring. *Journal of the American Medical Association, 269*, 1960–1965.

Ricker, K., Koch, M. C., Lehmann-Horn, F., Pongratz, D., Otto, M., Heine, R., & Moxley, R. T. (1994). Proximal myotonic myopathy: A new dominant disorder with myotonia, muscle weakness, and cataracts. *Neurology, 44*, 1448–1452.

Ricker, K., Koch, M. C., Lehmann-Horn, F., Pongratz, D., Speich, N., Reiners, K., Schneider, C., & Moxley, R. T. (1995). Proximal myotonic myopathy. Clinical features of a multisystem disorder similar to myotonic dystrophy. *Archives of Neurology, 52*, 25–31.

Roberts, R. G. (1995). Dystrophin, its gene, and the dystrophinopathies. *Advances in Genetics, 33*, 177–231.

Roussan, M., Terrence, C., & Fromm, G. (1985). Baclofen versus diazepam for the treatment of spasticity and long-term follow-up of baclofen therapy. *Pharmatherapeutica, 4*, 278–284.

Sadovnick, A. D., & Ebers, G. C. (1993). Epidemiology of multiple sclerosis: A critical overview. *Canadian Journal of Neurological Sciences, 20*, 17–29.

Samaha, F. J., & Quinlan, J. G. (1996a). Dystrophinopathies: Clarification and complication. *Journal of Child Neurology, 11*, 13–20.

Samaha, F. J., & Quinlan, J. G. (1996b). Myalgia and cramps: Dystrophinopathy with wide-ranging laboratory findings. *Journal of Child Neurology, 11*, 21–24.

Sansome, A., Royston, P., & Dubowitz, V. (1993). Steroids in Duchenne muscular dystrophy; pilot study of a new low-dosage schedule. *Neuromuscular Disorders, 3*, 567–569.

Schiffer, R. B. (1987). The spectrum of depression in multiple sclerosis. An approach for clinical management. *Archives of Neurology, 44*, 596–599.

Schiffer, R. B. (1990). Disturbances of affect. In S. M. Rao (Ed.), *Neurobehavioral aspects of multiple sclerosis* (pp. 186–195). New York: Oxford University Press.

Shelbourne, P., Davies, J., Buxton, J., Anvret, M., Blennow, E., Bonduelle, M., Schmedding, E., Glass, I., Lindenbaum, R., Lane, R., Williamson, R., & Johnson, K. (1993). Direct diagnosis of myotonic dystrophy with a disease-specific DNA marker. *New England Journal of Medicine, 328*, 471–475.

Shibasaki, H., & Kuroiwa, Y. (1974). Painful tonic seizure in multiple sclerosis. *Archives of Neurology, 30*, 47–51.

Smith, C. A., Wallston, K. A., Dwyer, K. A., & Dowdy, S. W. (1997). Beyond good and bad coping: A multidemensional examination of coping with pain in persons with rheumatoid arthritis. *Annals of Behavioral Medicine, 19*, 11–21.

Stenager, E. N., Koch-Henriksen, N., & Stenager, E. (1996). Risk factors for suicide in multiple sclerosis. *Psychotherapy & Psychosomatics, 65*, 86–90.

Stenager, E. N., Stenager, E., & Jensen, K. (1994). Attempted suicide, depression and physical diseases: A 1-year follow-up study. *Psychotherapy & Psychosomatics, 61*, 65–73.

Tawil, R., & Griggs, R. C. (1996). Facioscapulohumeral muscular dystrophy. In R. N. Rosenberg, S. B. Pruisiner, S. DiMauro, & R. L. Barchi (Eds.), *Molecular and genetic basis of neurological disease* (pp. 931–937). Newton, MA: Butterworth Heinemann.

Thompson, A. J. (1996). Multiple sclerosis: Symptomatic treatment. *Journal of Neurology, 243*, 559–565.

Thornton, C. A., Griggs, R. C., & Moxley, R. T. (1994). Myotonic dystrophy with no trinucleotide repeat expansion. *Annals of Neurology, 35*, 269–272.

VanderPlate, C. (1984). Psychological aspects of multiple sclerosis and its treatment: Toward a biopsychosocial perspective. *Health Psychology, 3,* 253–272.

Von Roenn, J. H., Cleeland, C. S., Gonin, R., Hatfield, A. K., & Pandya, K. J. (1993). Physician attitudes and practice in cancer pain management. *Annals of Internal Medicine, 119,* 121–126.

Wallace, J. D. (1994). Summary of combined clinical analysis of controlled clinical trials with tizanidine. *Neurology, 44,* S60–S69.

Chapter 18

A Belt of Roses From Hell: Pain in Herpes Zoster and Postherpetic Neuralgia

Robert H. Dworkin
University of Rochester School of Medicine and Dentistry, Rochester, New York

Robert W. Johnson
Bristol Royal Infirmary, Bristol, England

> *The Norwegians have an admirable name for zoster (which like shingles means belt)—"a belt of roses from Hell"—while the Danes call it "hell-fire."*
> —Anonymous (1979, p. 5)

The varicella-zoster virus establishes latency in sensory ganglia following a primary varicella infection (chicken pox) that typically occurs in children. Herpes zoster (shingles) is the recrudescence of the virus and its spread from a sensory ganglion to the corresponding dermatome and neural tissue of the same segment (Hope-Simpson, 1954, 1965; Straus et al., 1984; Weller, Witton, & Bell, 1958). The onset of herpes zoster is marked by the appearance of a characteristic rash, with thoracic dermatomes being the most commonly affected sites (Glynn et al., 1990; Hope-Simpson, 1965; Portenoy, Duma, & Foley, 1986). The rash usually heals within 2 to 4 weeks, leaving pain as the most distressing symptom of herpes zoster. The nature and duration of this pain varies greatly among patients, and in a percentage of cases pain in the affected dermatome persists after the acute infection and healing of the rash. Pain that persists beyond a defined interval is termed postherpetic neuralgia (PHN). This pain syndrome is often refractory to treatment and can last for years, causing substantial physical and social disability and psychological distress.

In this chapter, we review the results of research on the natural history, pathogenesis, and treatment of pain in herpes zoster and PHN. Because several excellent literature reviews of these topics have appeared (Kost &

Straus, 1996; Loeser, 1990; Portenoy et al., 1986; Rowbotham, 1994b; C. P. N. Watson, 1993a; P. N. Watson & Evans, 1986), we emphasize recent studies and attempt to update and extend our own prior reviews of some of this material (Dworkin, 1997a; Dworkin & Banks, in press; Dworkin, Carrington et al., 1997; Dworkin & Portenoy, 1996; Johnson, 1995, 1996a, 1996b, 1997a, 1997b). We first discuss the natural history of herpes zoster pain, then review risk factors for PHN and selected hypotheses regarding its pathogenesis, and conclude with an evaluation of the treatments that are presently available for patients suffering from this chronic pain syndrome.

NATURAL HISTORY

In approximately 75% of patients, a prodrome of dermatomal pain begins several days before the appearance of the herpes zoster rash (Beutner, Friedman, Forszpaniak, Andersen, & Wood, 1995; Cobo et al., 1986; Dworkin, Boon, Griffin, & Phung, in press; Rogers & Tindall, 1971). A few patients have longer prodromes, and a series of patients with prodromal pain preceding the rash by 7 to more than 100 days has been reported (Gilden et al., 1991). Almost all herpes zoster patients experience pain during their acute infection, and patients who have not had a painful prodrome typically begin to experience pain at rash onset or shortly afterwards. Dermatomal pain without a rash, referred to as zoster sine herpete, has also been described (Gilden, Dueland, Devlin, Mahalingam, & Cohrs, 1992; Gilden, Wright, Schneck, Gwaltney, & Mahalingam, 1994; Lewis, 1958).

For the majority of patients, herpes zoster is a short-lived disorder that has no lasting adverse impact. A percentage of herpes zoster patients, however, suffer from the prolonged pain of PHN. A variety of definitions of PHN have been proposed. Some authors have defined it as any pain persisting after the herpes zoster rash has healed (Bamford & Boundy, 1968; Burgoon, Burgoon, & Baldridge, 1957). Others have defined it as pain persisting beyond a specified interval following rash onset—for example, 4 weeks (Rogers & Tindall, 1971), 6 weeks (Brown, 1976), 3 months (Max et al., 1988), or 6 months (Harding, Lipton, & Wells, 1987) after rash onset. Yet another approach is to consider PHN as pain persisting beyond a specified interval following rash healing—for example, 1 month (Rowbotham, Davies, & Fields, 1995) or 3 months (Baron & Saguer, 1993) after rash healing.

Because the number of patients with pain declines with time, estimates of the proportion of patients with acute herpes zoster who develop PHN range from 9% to 34% and vary depending on the definition of PHN used

(Dworkin & Portenoy, 1996). Perhaps the most useful data for estimating the risk of PHN are provided by the results of a meta-analysis of the results of 14 placebo-controlled trials of acyclovir (Crooks, Jones, & Fiddian, 1991). Of the herpes zoster patients studied in the placebo groups in these trials, 22% had pain that persisted at least 3 months, a duration of pain that is consistent with definitions of PHN that consider it a chronic pain syndrome. However, three antiviral medications—acyclovir, famciclovir, and valacyclovir—are now used in acute herpes zoster, and there is evidence that they reduce the duration of pain and the risk of PHN (Beutner et al., 1995; Dworkin et al., in press; Jackson, Gibbons, Meyer, & Inouye, 1997; Tyring et al., 1995; Wood, Kay, Dworkin, Soong, & Whitley, 1996). It is therefore possible that at the present time fewer than 22% of acute herpes zoster patients still have pain 3 months or more after rash onset. The magnitude of this reduction in the risk of PHN is difficult to estimate; it will depend on several factors, including the percentage of acute herpes zoster patients in a sample prescribed adequate antiviral treatment, patient compliance in completing an adequate course of treatment, and, if antiviral medications differ in efficacy, the proportions of patients administered different medications.

Until recently, it was believed that there were no pain-free intervals in patients with PHN. However, there is now evidence that pain in PHN can be discontinuous, with pain-free intervals of varying durations (Huff et al., 1993; McKendrick, Care, Ogan, & Wood, 1994; C. P. N. Watson, Watt, Chipman, Birkett, & Evans, 1991). In a study of 156 patients with PHN, "25% of patients with a poor outcome said that they could recall a time after the rash when they had little or no pain for a period of weeks to as much as 12 months" (C. P. N. Watson, Watt et al., 1991, p. 198). A long-term follow-up study of patients originally enrolled in an acyclovir trial conducted in the United Kingdom found that 16 of 132 patients who had reported no pain at the end of the trial 9 years earlier reported pain within the preceding year (McKendrick et al., 1994). Moreover, in an acyclovir trial conducted in the United States, 4 of 187 patients (2 acyclovir and 2 placebo subjects) first reported pain at 1 month after enrollment and continued to report pain until the final follow-up assessment 7 months later (Huff et al., 1993). The data from these four patients suggest that PHN can develop even in herpes zoster patients who have not had acute pain.

The quality of pain in acute zoster and PHN has been examined in two studies using the McGill Pain Questionnaire (Bhala, Ramamoorthy, Bowsher, & Yelnoorker, 1988; Bowsher, 1993; see also Dubuisson & Melzack, 1976). One third or more of acute herpes zoster patients endorsed the sensory adjectives *sharp, tender, stabbing, shooting, throbbing, itching,* and/or *hot* to describe their pain; one third or more of patients with PHN endorsed the sensory adjectives *tender, burning, throbbing, stabbing, shooting,* and/or *sharp.* Sharp, stabbing pain was found to be more common in patients with acute herpes zoster than in patients with PHN, whereas burning pain was found to be more common in PHN patients and was much less likely to be reported by acute zoster patients. The investigators noted that the word *tender* was chosen by both groups of patients to describe allodynia (i.e., pain in response to a stimulus that does not normally provoke pain). These adjectives therefore reflect the three different types of pain that have been distinguished in research on PHN—a steady throbbing or burning pain, an intermittent sharp or shooting pain, and allodynia (Rowbotham & Fields, 1989; C. P. N. Watson, Chipman, Reed, Evans, & Birkett, 1992). The results of a recent study, however, suggest that throbbing and burning pain should be examined separately. In a sample of patients with PHN, those who had received acyclovir during their acute herpes zoster infection were found to be much less likely to report burning pain than those who had not received acyclovir; reports of throbbing pain in these two groups did not differ (Bowsher, 1992, 1993). It will therefore be important to distinguish steady burning pain from steady throbbing pain in future research.

Quality of life is adversely affected by acute herpes zoster, especially in patients with severe acute pain (Mauskopf, Austin, Dix, & Berzon, 1994), but apparently returns to normal levels in most patients after recovery from the acute infection (Lydick, Epstein, Himmelberger, & White, 1995). In patients with PHN, however, "alterations in mood, personality, activity levels, and social interactions are common" (Satterthwaite, 1989, p. 467). As is true of other chronic pain syndromes, PHN patients can develop depression as well as physical, occupational, and social disability as a consequence of their unremitting pain (Portenoy et al., 1986; Schmader, 1995). In one recent study, it was reported that 59% of a sample of PHN patients attending a pain clinic in Liverpool had taken time off from their usual activities and that these patients had been prevented from pursuing these activities for up to 16 years, with the average being 1.4 years (Davies, Cossins, Bowsher, & Drummond, 1994). In another study of the psychosocial impact of PHN, patients who had PHN for longer than 6 months were found to have greater disability and psychological distress than patients who had PHN for fewer than 6 months (Graff-Radford, Kames, & Naliboff, 1986). The results of this study suggest that increases in psychosocial distress may occur as a result of the chronic pain of PHN (although it is also possible that prolonged pain is a consequence of greater distress).

Not surprisingly, there is also evidence of substantial utilization of health care resources by patients with PHN. For example, it has been reported that PHN patients in a pain clinic sample had visited their general physicians an average of 19 times (range: 0 to 69 visits) and had required visits by home health aides an average of 16 times (range: 0 to 507 visits; Davies et al., 1994).

Approaches to Examining Prolonged Herpes Zoster Pain

Because of the existence of different definitions of PHN, the use of a diagnosis of PHN in research on herpes zoster pain has recently become controversial. It has been suggested that pain in herpes zoster be considered "as a continuum, rather than distinguishing acute pain from an arbitrary definition of postherpetic neuralgia" (Huff et al., 1993, p. 93). Several recent studies have used this approach to examine the efficacy of antiviral medications and other treatments in reducing the duration of herpes zoster pain (Beutner et al., 1995; Crooks et al., 1991; Degreef, 1994; Huff et al., 1993; Whitley et al., 1996; Wood et al., 1994, 1996). In these trials, the primary endpoint used in evaluating efficacy was the time from enrollment to complete cessation of all zoster–associated pain; no distinction is made between acute pain and PHN when herpes zoster pain is examined in this manner (Wood, 1995).

Considering herpes zoster pain as a continuum can provide a worthwhile overview of factors associated with pain duration, not only in studies of treatment efficacy but also in research on risk factors for prolonged pain. One important advantage of examining herpes zoster pain as a continuum is that no assumption is required regarding the point at which PHN begins. However, to the extent that acute herpes zoster pain and PHN differ clinically and have different pathophysiologies, examining pain only as a continuum would be misleading and could impede progress in understanding herpes zoster.

The results of research on natural history, risk factors, pathophysiology, and impact on quality of life suggest that PHN is a discrete disorder that differs from acute herpes zoster pain in important respects (Dworkin, 1997a; Dworkin, Carrington et al., 1997). The results of these studies provide considerable support for the validity of examining acute pain and PHN separately and suggest that analyses of zoster pain as a simple continuum of pain duration may fail to reveal those aspects of PHN that are not shared with acute herpes zoster pain. Nevertheless, these two different approaches are not mutually exclusive; data on pain collected on multiple occasions beginning during the acute infection and continuing for several months thereafter can be examined by using a continuum of pain duration as well as by analyzing the prevalence and duration of PHN. Accordingly, in the following discussions of risk factors, pathogenesis, and treatment, findings based on a diagnosis of PHN, however defined, are considered together with findings based on analyses in which herpes zoster pain is considered as a continuum of overall pain duration.

PATHOGENESIS

Risk Factors for PHN

The identification of risk factors for PHN has the potential to contribute to a greater understanding of its pathogenesis (Dworkin, 1997b; Dworkin & Banks, in press; Johnson, 1995). Knowledge of these risk factors could also be used to guide research on the development of interventions to prevent PHN. In addition, the identification of acute zoster patients with an increased risk of developing PHN would make it possible to deliver interventions to those patients most in need of preventive efforts.

Until recently, the only factor that had been consistently associated with an increased risk of PHN was older age (e.g., Burgoon et al., 1957; De Moragas & Kierland, 1957; Hope-Simpson, 1975; Raggozzino, Melton, Kurland, Chu, & Perry, 1982; Rogers & Tindall, 1971). PHN is infrequent in patients under the age of 40, but as many as 65% of patients over 60 and 75% of those over 70 have pain at 1 month following healing; the proportion of patients with pain at 1 year approaches 50% in those over 70 (De Moragas & Kierland, 1957).

An increasing number of studies are now being conducted in which other risk factors for PHN are examined. Because we have recently reviewed this literature in detail (Dworkin & Banks, in press; Dworkin & Portenoy, 1996), we provide only a summary of these studies in this chapter. In addition to age, five risk factors for PHN have been identified by independent groups of investigators—greater pain severity, rash severity, and sensory dysfunction in the affected dermatome during acute herpes zoster, as well as the presence of a prodrome and the absence of antiviral therapy.

Of these five risk factors, the most well established is greater acute pain severity. The results of a considerable number of studies have demonstrated that patients with more severe pain during acute herpes zoster are at greater risk for prolonged herpes zoster pain (assessed as a continuum) and PHN. A variety of research designs, pain measures, and approaches to examining persisting pain were used in these studies. Despite various methodological shortcomings, including small sample sizes and the use of retrospective methods, when considered together these studies clearly indicate that greater acute pain severity is as robust a risk factor for PHN as older age. The focus of future research should therefore be to determine the actual mechanism by which greater acute pain produces chronic pain (Dworkin, 1997b).

Four additional risk factors—more pronounced humoral and cell-mediated immune responses, fever, generalized impairment of large fiber afferents, and psychosocial distress—have been identified either in a single study or by a single group of investigators and therefore await replication by others. With respect to gender and dermatome the literature is inconsistent, with some studies finding that women and patients with trigeminal zoster are at increased risk for the development of PHN and other studies finding no evidence in support of these relationships (Dworkin & Banks, in press).

Rowbotham and Fields (1989) noted several years ago that the prospective study of patients with acute herpes zoster "is necessary to learn more about the development of the clinical syndrome of PHN including the characteristics of the pain. . . . Comparison of patients who do not progress to post-herpetic neuralgia with those who do is important in determining causality" (pp. 142–143). Such studies have considerable potential to elucidate the pathogenesis of PHN. Most of the studies summarized in this section, however, were not specifically designed to examine risk factors— few examined more than one or two risk factors and none investigated interactions between risk factors (e.g., does the relationship between greater acute pain severity and increased risk of PHN vary as a function of age?). It is only when such multivariate analyses are conducted that it will become possible to specify the combinations of risk factors that identify which acute herpes zoster patients have the greatest risk of developing PHN (Dworkin & Banks, in press).

Why Is Older Age a Risk Factor for PHN?

Perhaps the most interesting unanswered question about risk factors for PHN is also the one with the longest history—that is, why is older age a risk factor for PHN (Wall, 1993)? It has been hypothesized that age is associated with the development of PHN because older patients have more severe acute herpes zoster infections (Higa, Dan, Manabe, & Noda, 1988; Higa et al., 1997). The results of several studies, however, are not entirely consistent with this hypothesis. Although significant associations between older age and greater rash duration have been reported (Harding et al., 1987; Wildenhoff et al., 1981; Wildenhoff, Ipsen, Esmann, Ingemann-Jensen, & Poulsen, 1979), older age is inconsistently associated with greater lesion severity (Higa et al., 1988, 1997) and is not associated with greater acute pain severity (Bamford & Boundy, 1968; Dworkin, Cooper, Walther, & Sweeney, 1997; Harding et al., 1987). Moreover, the results of several recent studies suggest that age and acute pain severity make independent contributions to predicting which herpes zoster patients develop PHN (Beutner et al., 1995; Dworkin et al., in press; Dworkin, Cooper et al., 1997; Wood et al., 1996). To the extent that acute pain severity reflects a more severe acute infection, these findings suggest that the increased risk of PHN in the elderly is not fully accounted for by more severe acute infections, and that this increased risk reflects an additional pathophysiologic process. Indeed, Hope-Simpson (1967) recognized that although severe acute infections are frequently associated with PHN, even mild cases of zoster are sometimes followed by PHN.

One process that might contribute to an increased risk of PHN in the elderly is nervous system senescence. As noted by Baron, Haendler, and Schulte (1997), "subclinical impairment of peripheral neuronal function, in particular degeneration of myelinated afferent fibers, is a well-known physiological aspect of aging" (p. 237). Their recent report that generalized impairment of A-beta fiber function (i.e., large fiber polyneuropathy) in acute herpes zoster patients predicts the development of PHN is consistent with the hypothesis that nervous system senescence contributes to the greater risk of PHN in the elderly and merits continued investigation.

A second process that might explain the increased risk of PHN in the elderly involves immunopathogenesis. It is well established that aging is accompanied by a substantial deterioration in the functioning of the immune system and an increased incidence of autoimmune disorders. With aging, there is an increased production of autoantibodies, including antineuronal antibodies. Inflammatory and immune mechanisms have been implicated in the pathophysiology of Alzheimer's Disease (Aisen & Davis, 1994), and antineuronal antibodies have been examined in a number of other neuropsychiatric disorders (Nandy & Nandy, 1986). With respect to PHN, it has been hypothesized that autoimmune phenomena and age-associated disturbances in cytokine production, possibly involving cytokine neurotoxicity, may result in nerve damage and contribute to the development of prolonged pain in patients with herpes zoster (Dworkin & Porteny, 1996; Weksler, 1994).

To our knowledge, there have not been any studies in which the contribution of immunopathogenesis to the development of PHN has been examined. However, the hypothesis that age-associated immunopathological processes play a role in PHN is consistent not only with the greater risk of PHN in the elderly but also with several other recent findings. One is the existence of the pain-free intervals, discussed earlier, that have been reported in patients with herpes zoster and PHN. Because many autoimmune disorders have a chronic course with intermittent exacerbations, the results of these studies are consistent with the hypothesis that immunopathological processes play a role in the development of PHN.

The evidence of inflammatory changes found in postmortem studies of patients with PHN (Head & Campbell, 1900; Smith, 1978; C. P. N. Watson, Deck, Morshead, Van der Kooy, & Evans, 1991) is also consistent with this hypothesis. In the most detailed of these studies, C. P. N. Watson and colleagues reported the presence of a marked inflammatory process in a patient who had PHN for 2 years and suggested that such processes may play an ongoing role in the pathogenesis of either chronic or recurrent pain in PHN patients.

Equivalent risks of PHN in immunocompromised and immunocompetent patients have appeared to suggest that the greater severity of acute herpes zoster infections in immunocompromised patients is not accompanied by an increased risk of PHN (Balfour, 1988; Gershon, 1993; Rusthoven et al., 1988; Wood, 1991). This *absence* of an increased risk of PHN in immunocompromised patients—who suffer from immune deficiency but not necessarily from the immunopathological changes that occur with aging—suggests that the severity of the acute infection does not fully account for PHN and would be consistent with a role for immunopathogenesis in the development of prolonged pain (Dworkin & Portenoy, 1996). However, the results of a recent study indicated that patients with HIV infection, connective tissue diseases, and organ transplants had a higher risk of developing PHN (Choo et al., 1997); additional studies of immunocompromised and immunocompetent herpes zoster patients matched for age are therefore needed.

Recent Approaches to the Pathophysiology of PHN

Thirty years ago, Hope-Simpson (1967) proposed that patients with more severe acute herpes zoster infections are more likely to develop PHN. Most of the risk factors for PHN that have now been identified can be considered aspects of a more severe acute infection. More severe acute herpes zoster infections are presumably accompanied by greater neural damage, and it has been hypothesized that this neural damage contributes prominently to the development of PHN in patients with herpes zoster (Bennett, 1994a; Dworkin & Portenoy, 1996).

But the nature of this damage and the specific mechanisms by which it causes the persisting pain of PHN remain unclear. Although it is beyond the scope of this chapter to comprehensively review the diverse hypotheses and relevant data regarding the pathophysiology of PHN, fortunately this literature has been discussed in a number of recent publications (Baron & Saguer, 1993, 1995; Bennett, 1994a, 1994b; Bowsher, 1993; Choi & Rowbotham, 1997; Fields, 1997; Fields & Rowbotham, 1994; Fromm, 1993; Johnson, 1996b; Nurmikko, 1994, 1995; Rowbotham, 1994b; Rowbotham & Fields, 1989, 1996; Wall, 1993; C. P. N. Watson & Deck, 1993). What limited knowledge we have of the pathophysiology of PHN derives from studies of neuropathology, sensory dysfunction, and pharmacologic response. At the present time, there is considerable agreement that different pathophysiologic processes probably contribute to prolonged pain in herpes zoster, and that the qualitatively different types of pain that characterize PHN probably have different underlying mechanisms. This suggests that there may be pathophysiologically distinct subgroups of patients with PHN or that more than one mechanism may be involved in individual patients or both (different mechanisms may even produce the same type of pain; Bennett, 1994b). Beyond this consensus, the literature on the pathophysiology of PHN can be characterized as one in which there are many hypotheses but relatively little data. In the following selective review, we discuss several of the more prominent current approaches to research on the pathophysiology of PHN.

C. P. N. Watson and colleagues (C. P. N. Watson & Deck, 1993; C. P. N. Watson, Deck et al., 1991; C. P. N. Watson, Morshead, Van der Kooy, Deck, & Evans, 1988) have conducted an elegant series of postmortem studies of patients with PHN at the time of death and of patients with a history of zoster whose pain did not persist beyond rash healing. Atrophy of the dorsal horn and pathological changes in the sensory ganglion were found on the affected side (and not on the unaffected side) in patients with PHN, but not in patients with zoster whose pain did not persist. These pathological features were therefore characteristic of only those patients with PHN. Other findings—for example, marked loss of myelin in the peripheral nerve and sensory root—were found in those who did not develop PHN as well as in those who did. Although these results are based on a small number of patients, they constitute important preliminary evidence that different pathophysiologic mechanisms account for the acute pain of herpes zoster and the chronic pain of PHN (Bennett, 1994a). An apparent imbalance of small and large fiber types in peripheral nerves was also found in these postmortem studies, but various explanations of these findings are possible (C. P. N. Watson & Deck, 1993).

Rowbotham and Fields (1989, 1996; see also Fields, 1997; Rowbotham, 1994b) have conducted an important series of studies on sensory dysfunction and pharmacologic response that address the pathophysiology of PHN. In their first study, PHN patients with prominent allodynia were found to have less sensory loss than PHN patients with continuous pain. In addition, the patients with prominent allodynia reported pain relief following local anesthetic infiltration with lidocaine, whereas patients with primarily constant pain did not respond to lidocaine (Rowbotham & Fields, 1989). As discussed in more detail later, there is also increasing evidence that PHN patients with allodynia benefit from the topical application of analgesic agents (e.g., Rowbotham, Davies, Verkempinck, & Galer, 1996).

In a recent study, Rowbotham and Fields (1996) found that greater pain intensity and allodynia in PHN patients were associated with relatively normal sensory function as assessed by thermal thresholds. They concluded that at least two different mechanisms may contribute to PHN. They propose that allodynia in PHN is due to abnormal activity in *preserved* primary afferent nociceptors that have been damaged by the varicella-zoster virus but remain in continuity with their peripheral and central targets (Fields, 1997; Rowbotham & Fields, 1996). Activity in these relatively intact nociceptors may initiate and then maintain a state of central sensitization in which input from large-fiber afferents that respond to nonpainful mechanical stimuli becomes painful (i.e., allodynia). It is also possible that sensitized primary afferent nociceptors contribute to allodynia, but following differential neural blockade in PHN patients, pain, allodynia, and tactile sensation (mediated by A-fibers) reappear when thermal sensation (mediated by C-fibers) is still absent (Nurmikko, Wells, & Bowsher, 1991); this suggests that nociceptor sensitization does not contribute significantly to allodynia in PHN (Bowsher, 1993; Nurmikko, 1994).

As opposed to patients with prominent allodynia, PHN patients with continuous pain have their greatest sensory loss in the areas where they have the most pain (Rowbotham & Fields, 1996). This suggests that continuous pain in PHN is caused by a different mechanism, possibly involving the central structural and functional changes that accompany deafferentiation. These changes may include a structural reorganization of the spinal cord that involves abnormal synaptic connections of neurons that no longer have their normal input, as well as functional abnormalities resulting from deafferentiation, such as hyperexcitability of dorsal horn neurons (Fields, 1997; Fields & Rowbotham, 1994).

A number of investigators have emphasized such central processes in interpreting data on sensory dysfunction and its relationship to pain in patients with PHN (e.g., Bowsher, 1993; Nurmikko, 1994). Baron and Saguer (1993, 1995) examined primary afferent nociceptor function in 10 patients with PHN by measuring axon reflex vasodilatation after iontophoresed histamine. Responses were significantly reduced in the areas where patients reported allodynia. In addition, pain intensity was significantly correlated with the degree of primary afferent nociceptor dysfunction as assessed by vasodilatation and flare measures (these correlations included three additional subjects with a history of herpes zoster but no PHN). Baron and Saguer (1995) concluded that their results suggest allodynia is not maintained by ongoing input from sensitized nociceptors, and that in accounting for pain in PHN "an anatomic synaptic reorganization depending on *afferent C-fiber degeneration* seems to be more likely" (p. S64; italics in original). Although these results are provocative, it has been noted that because histamine activates only a subset of primary afferent nociceptors these conclusions should be considered tentative (Rowbotham & Fields, 1996). Importantly, the nature of any central structural reorganization in PHN remains obscure and must be addressed in future research.

It is likely that both peripheral and central mechanisms contribute to pain in PHN patients. This could account not only for the different types of pain that patients report but also for the incomplete response of many patients to topical treatments and other therapies. An apt summary of our current understanding of the pathophysiology of PHN has been provided by Rowbotham (1994b), who noted that "What is perhaps unique to PHN compared with other pain syndromes is that all hypotheses could be correct and no two are mutually exclusive" (p. 248).

A Diathesis-Stress Model of PHN

Research on chronic pain is usually based on an assumption that both biological and psychosocial processes contribute, but explicit hypotheses regarding the manner in which these processes interact to bring about the development of chronic pain have rarely been specified. Recently, a diathesis-stress model of PHN was proposed that is consistent with the literature reviewed in this section (Dworkin & Banks, in press; Dworkin & Portenoy, 1996). In this model, neural impairment—whether peripheral or central or both—is considered the diathesis for PHN. The extent of this impairment is largely a consequence of the severity of the acute herpes zoster infection, but preexisting neural impairment may also be a component of the diathesis (Baron et al., 1997; Oaklander et al., in press). Various psychosocial factors constitute the stress (broadly defined) that is hypothesized to interact with this diathesis in accounting for prolonged herpes zoster pain and the development of PHN. It was hypothesized that the risk of PHN increases as both the severity of the neural impairment and the severity of the psychosocial stress increase, and that stress may have a greater effect on the risk of PHN when the diathesis is more severe (see Fig. 18.1). Of course, it is possible that other forms of interaction could

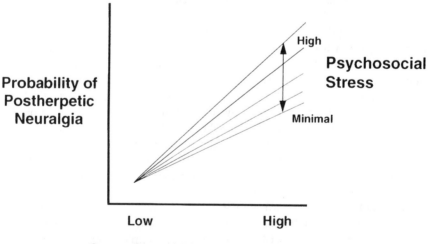

FIG. 18.1. A diathesis-stress model of postherpetic neuralgia.

characterize a relationship between neural impairment, psychosocial stress, and PHN; for example, stress could have a greater effect on the risk of PHN when the diathesis is moderate in severity than when it is mild or severe. Compared to the biopsychosocial approach—the prevailing orientation in research and theory on chronic pain—the most important advantage of diathesis-stress models is their greater emphasis on the identification of *specific* interactions among etiologic processes, as well as their "in-depth probing of associations between the components of the model, often multidirectional and transpiring over time" (Monroe & Simons, 1991, p. 422).

TREATMENT

> If a great many remedies are suggested for a disease, it means that the disease is incurable.
>
> —Chekhov (1904/1964, p. 333)

Chekhov's astute observation might well have applied to the management of PHN. Lack of evidence of efficacy is not evidence of inefficacy, and physicians may be excused for using unproven therapies for PHN as so few randomized, controlled trials have been undertaken. PHN is notoriously difficult to treat and patients (and their relatives and physicians) become desperate.

However, there is little excuse for first-line use of therapies that have been shown not to work in any but a very few patients. Similarly, it seems inappropriate to embark on treatments that have little chance of success and have a poor risk/benefit ratio. Whatever drug, invasive, or stimulation therapies may be offered, humane explanation of the pain associated with herpes zoster and ongoing psychological care are essential accompaniments.

Assessment

The key to good management is first to understand the problem. A comprehensive history and physical examination will ascertain the extent of the problem in terms of duration, quality and quantity of pain, and effects on quality of life for patients and their caregivers. Compliance with past and current therapy and adverse effects of such therapy are also important to note.

Recording and quantifying these observations allows monitoring of response to treatment or spontaneous resolution. A data collection form specific for herpes zoster pain and appropriate for elderly patients has been developed (Johnson, Shukla, & Fletcher, 1995). This form, which can be used in the routine assessment of patients with acute herpes zoster and PHN, is presented in Fig. 18.2. Standard illness behavior, anxiety, depression, and quality-of-life questionnaires provide additional valuable information and may also be used with these patients.

The management of pain associated with herpes zoster falls into early and late phases. All too often, patients are referred to pain management centers 2 or 3 years (and many failed therapies) into established PHN. At this stage, it is rare to cure the condition but common to improve quality of life. There is growing experience with energetic management of early PHN (from, say, 6 to 8 weeks following acute herpes zoster) and experienced clinicians are producing data in support of such referral and care (Bowsher, 1997).

Physical Treatments

Pain, sensory changes, abnormal sensations (such as formication), and allodynia are common in patients with PHN. Reduced stimulation to the affected area may be valuable in reducing symptoms, and natural fiber clothing may be preferable to artificial fibers. A protective layer between the skin and provoking stimuli may be helpful; cling film (e.g., Saran Wrap), cut to size and shape, or a layer of "plastic skin" may be applied intermittently. Transcutaneous electrical nerve stimulation (TENS) is occasionally helpful in established PHN (Nathan & Wall, 1974), but one

Please ✔ appropriate boxes

	Yes*	No
1. Have you had any shingles pain and/or burning in the last week?	☐	☐

*If yes, please record the frequency of EACH type of pain and/or burning that you felt on the day that they were worst during the last week:

	Never (✔)	Occasionally (✔)	Quite often (✔)	Very often/ All of time (✔)
BURNING e.g. hot, scalding	☐	☐	☐	☐
DULL e.g. heavy, aching, pulling	☐	☐	☐	☐
SHARP e.g. flashing, shooting, stabbing	☐	☐	☐	☐

	Yes*	No
2. Have you had any abnormal sensations or discomfort related to your shingles (e.g. itching, tingling, sensitivity to touch, loss of feeling) in the last week?	☐	☐

	Occasionally (✔)	Quite often (✔)	Very often/ All of time (✔)
*If yes, please record the frequency of abnormal sensations or discomfort that you felt on the day that they were worst during the last week:	☐	☐	☐

	Yes*	No
3. Is any of your pain, burning, abnormal sensations or discomfort set off by being touched?	☐	☐

4. Please record the number of days in the last week on which you have had pain, burning, abnormal sensations or discomfort:...................... days

FIG. 18.2. Data form for pain assessment in acute herpes zoster and PHN. From Johnson, Shukla, and Fletcher (1995).

study reported no benefit in a series of 17 patients (Gerson, R. B. Jones, & Luscombe, 1977). Ultrasound has a poor record in a few small series of PHN patients (R. J. Jones & Silman, 1987; Payne, 1984) but may be helpful for acute herpes zoster pain. Acupuncture seems to provide little benefit in PHN (Lewith, Field, & Machin, 1983), although early treatment may be more effective (Dung, 1987). Cold pack application often provides short-term relief and is always worth trying—a small pack of frozen peas is ideal, and some patients may even request advice on the brand that should be used!

Pharmacological Approaches

Many classes of medication are used for the management of PHN. Few have been evaluated in randomized, double-blind, placebo-controlled trials. No doubt many drugs have helped some patients; probably few have helped many. Most have adverse effects.

Topical Agents. Various local anesthetic preparations may be applied to allodynic skin, including lidocaine and EMLA (eutectic mixture of local anesthetics—prilocaine and lidocaine). They may be adsorbed onto various dressing materials, applied under occlusive dressings, or administered by iontophoresis. Several publications suggest that these treatments may have value, but this conclusion has been based on case reports or uncontrolled series (Collins, 1991; Stow, Glynn, & Minor, 1989; Wheeler, 1991). Rowbotham and colleagues, however, recently presented the results of double-blind vehicle-controlled studies in which topical 5% lidocaine in either gel or patch form relieved pain in PHN patients with allodynia (Rowbotham et al., 1995, 1996).

Nonsteroidal anti-inflammatory drug (NSAID) creams have been investigated in several studies and may help some patients, although the evidence is inconclusive (Alexander, 1985; Coniam & Hunton, 1988; McQuay, Carroll, Moxon, Glynn, & Moore, 1990). Limited studies of aspirin suspended in chloroform, ether, or acetone have been reported (De Beneditis, Besana, & Lorenzetti, 1992; Haines, 1989; King, 1988, 1993). There is doubt regarding the extent of clinical benefit of this treatment, and concern regarding the safety and stability of the mixtures has been expressed. It is but one of many therapies that helps some patients.

Capsaicin—an extract of capsicum frutescans (hot peppers) prepared as a cream—has received considerable attention as a treatment for PHN. Capsaicin is relatively expensive and may need long-term use to establish whether or not it offers benefit in an individual patient. Up to 3 weeks of four times daily use may be required to achieve an effect and application must be continued to maintain the effect. Some patients reject it soon after beginning treatment because of intense burning after application; this burning sensation, however, may lessen with time. Capsaicin may induce selective C-fiber substance P depletion. As discussed earlier, it has been hypothesized that allodynia in PHN may arise from large-fiber mechanoreceptors behaving as nociceptors. However, unless activity from C-fiber nociceptors also contributes to pain in PHN, the peripheral depletion of substance P would not be expected to provide relief (Rowbotham & Fields, 1996). An alternative mechanism might involve an effect from central migration of capsaicin. Controlled studies are difficult because of the problem of blinding and placebo control. C. P. N. Watson et al. (1993) studied 143 patients with PHN of more than 6 months' duration for 6 weeks in a double-blind vehicle-controlled study. Analysis of the whole group, and of a subset of 93 patients with PHN of more than 12 months' duration, showed significant benefit for capsaicin in both groups, an effect that was enhanced or maintained by ongoing open-label use in 86% of patients. The beneficial effect of capsaicin may derive from pharmacologic mechanisms or a response to counterirritation or both.

Oral Medications: Antidepressants.   Tricyclic antidepressant medications are widely prescribed for chronic pain and their analgesic effects have been found to be independent of their effects on mood. Although noradrenaline reuptake blocking effects seem most important, amitriptyline, with mixed noradrenergic and serotonergic effects, has been most frequently used and has been found to provide a significant beneficial effect in chronic pain patients (Bryson & Wilde, 1996; McQuay et al., 1996). Max (1994, 1995) reviewed five controlled trials of antidepressant drugs in PHN. In these studies, reduced severity of pain in PHN was found in patients treated with amitriptyline or desipramine, as compared to placebo in three trials (Kishore-Kumar et al., 1990; Max et al., 1988; C. P. N. Watson et al., 1982) and to maprotiline (C. P. N. Watson, 1992) and zimelidine (C. P. N. Watson & Evans, 1985) in two others. Beneficial therapeutic response was defined somewhat differently in these studies, but generally included relief that was moderate or greater at the end of treatment.

Because the side effects of tricyclic antidepressants limit their use in many patients by preventing dose escalation to therapeutic levels, selective serotonin reuptake inhibitors (SSRIs) have been examined in recent studies. Although paroxetine was found to have a beneficial effect in patients with pain from diabetic neuropathy (Sindrup, Gram, Brøsen, Eshøj, & Mogensen, 1990), fluoxetine was found to be no more effective than placebo in these patients (Max et al., 1992). Surprisingly, with the exception of one trial in which zimelidine was examined and found to have no beneficial effect (C. P. N. Watson & Evans, 1985), controlled trials of SSRIs in patients with PHN have not been reported. The newer antidepressant venlafaxine inhibits both noradrenaline and serotonin reuptake but lacks significant muscarinic side effects. Anecdotal reports suggest that venlafaxine may have an analgesic effect in patients with neuropathic pain; although it has been shown to reduce thermal hyperalgesia in rats with experimentally produced neuropathic pain (Lang, Hord, & Denson, 1996), no controlled clinical trials of this antidepressant have been reported.

It remains uncertain whether a dose-response relationship exists for treatment with antidepressants in chronic pain patients or whether there is a therapeutic window below and above which pain control is suboptimal (Max et al., 1988; McQuay, Carroll, & Glynn, 1993; Sindrup, Gram, Skjold, Frøland, & Beck-Nielsen, 1990; Zitman, Linssen, Edelbroek, & Stijnen, 1990). At the present time, therefore, titration to a clinically beneficial effect or to side effects requiring discontinuation of treatment is the best treatment strategy. Significant numbers of patients achieve worthwhile relief if drug compliance is good. In addition to side effects, inadequate explanation of the rationale for the use of antidepressant medications in chronic pain and of the length of time before onset of beneficial effects frequently lead to poor compliance. Starting dose and rate of dose escalation are often inappropriate. The elderly and frail may be commenced on amitriptyline 10mg increasing every 7 days by 10mg, and the younger and more robust may be started on 25mg increasing every 7 days by 25mg (Max, 1994; C. P. N. Watson, 1993b). The more common side effects of tricyclics—drowsiness, dry mouth, increased appetite, constipation, blurring of vision, and, rarely, urinary retention—and the means of minimizing them should be fully explained to all patients. Nortriptyline and desipramine cause fewer side effects than amitriptyline and may be preferable in many circumstances. Attention to diet, artificial saliva spray or lozenges (chewing gum is also useful), gradual dose escalation, and once-daily dosing 1 hour before bedtime (except for desipramine, which causes insomnia in some patients) are usually effective in reducing dry mouth, constipation, and sedation. If drowsiness is excessive, desipramine given in the morning may be effective. If one drug fails, another may work.

Anticonvulsants. Carbamazepine, phenytoin, and sodium valproate have traditionally been used for the management of neuropathic pain and may be beneficial in trigeminal neuralgia and diabetic neuropathy. Evidence for benefit in PHN is lacking and their side effects, particularly in the elderly, are unpleasant. A recent review of published studies of these drugs in pain patients provides no support for their use in PHN (McQuay, Carroll, Jadad, Wiffen, & Moore, 1995), and C. P. N. Watson (1993b) concluded that the benefit of treatment with anticonvulsants has often been unimpressive (Killian & Fromm, 1968) or difficult to interpret because of concomitant use of antidepressants (Gerson et al., 1977; Hatangdi, Boas, & Richards, 1976;

Raftery, 1979). Newer anticonvulsants such as gabapentin and lamotrigine may stabilize neuronal membrane sodium channels. These agents might be expected to have greater benefit in the treatment of PHN and other neuropathic pain syndromes than earlier anticonvulsants. Anecdotal reports, the results of retrospective studies (e.g., Rosenberg, Harrell, Ristic, Werner, & de Rosayro, 1997), and the preliminary report of the results of a placebo-controlled trial of gabapentin treatment in patients with diabetic neuropathy pain (Backonja et al., 1997) have been promising. Anticonvulsant drugs have a variety of side effects and their use should be monitored carefully; gabapentin, however, has fewer side effects than the older anticonvulsants. Prophylactic treatment in patients with acute herpes zoster to prevent PHN (perhaps by preventing central sensitization) might yield a greater benefit than use in patients whose PHN is already well established.

Analgesics. Oral NSAIDs seem to be of little benefit in acute herpes zoster pain or in PHN. Acetaminophen combined with weak opioids is often prescribed for acute herpes zoster pain. Patients who escalate their dose to achieve adequate pain relief risk acetaminophen toxicity so pure opioids are often indicated. Strong opioids are often avoided for fear of addiction and because traditionally it has been considered that narcotic analgesics have no value in patients with neuropathic pain. However, like all such generalizations, this is not true. Some patients derive significant benefit from these medications, but this should be assessed under controlled conditions with skilled observation of response and frequent review.

Intravenous infusion of morphine has been shown to reduce pain and allodynia in a placebo-controlled trial in PHN patients (Rowbotham, 1994a; Rowbotham, Reisner-Keller, & Fields, 1991). Pappagallo and Campbell (1994) conducted an open-label trial of long-acting opioids in 20 patients with PHN, 17 of whom had responded poorly to treatment with one or more tricyclic antidepressants. Most patients received oral controlled-release morphine; two received controlled-release oxycodone. At 6-month follow up, five patients reported excellent relief, nine reported good relief, and two reported slight to moderate relief. There was no significant impairment of cognitive function, and side effects—for example, drowsiness, nausea, and constipation—were not problematic. C. P. N. Watson and Babul (1997) have recently presented a preliminary report of the results of a placebo-controlled crossover trial of controlled-release oxycodone in patients with PHN. In this important study, oxycodone treatment was associated with significantly greater pain relief, decreased disability, and greater patient preference compared with placebo.

Ketamine and NMDA Receptor Antagonists. The N-methyl-D-aspartate (NMDA) receptor is involved in peripheral and central components of pain and its control. Little is known of peripheral effects in clinical pain but centrally acting drugs, such as ketamine and dextromethorphan, are available, albeit with unwanted side effects. These include ataxia, somnolence, dysphoria, short-term memory loss, and other psychological symptoms which limit use. An indirect effect on the receptor may be achieved by agents acting at the glycine site. In central sensitization states, it is possible that potentiation of opiates may provide a useful benefit of NMDA receptor function.

NMDA receptors are involved in the development and maintenance of changes in neuronal excitability that might be relevant to central sensitization, allodynia, and the persistence of pain after zoster-mediated neural damage. Ketamine is known to produce analgesia at least partially as a result of blocking these receptors. Recent studies have shown that ketamine reduces or abolishes some components of PHN in some patients (Backonja, Arndt, Gombar, Check, & Zimmermann, 1994; Bushnell, Vijay, Thwaites, Tidy, & Hester, 1996; Eide, Jørum, Stubhaug, Bremnes, & Breivik, 1994; Hoffmann, Coppejans, Vercauteren, & Adriaesen, 1994), but with adverse side effects and possibly other complications of ongoing use (Kato, Homma, & Ichiyanagi, 1995). The experimental NMDA receptor antagonist 3-(2-carboxypiperazin-4-yl)propyl-1-phosphonic acid (CPP) appears to have similar effects to ketamine (Kristensen, Svensson, & Gordh, 1992). Dextromethorphan (usually used as a cough suppressant) has NMDA receptor antagonist activity and appears to also have an analgesic effect, but there is presently limited evidence of its efficacy and the optimal dosage and long-term adverse effects are largely unknown. Dextromethorphan in doses usually reported (approximately 20mg three times daily) has not produced lasting analgesia in significant numbers of patients and may be rejected because of side effects (McQuay et al., 1994).

Other Drugs. There exists a long list of drugs supported by publications varying from single-case reports to uncontrolled studies. Although many provide relief in a few patients with PHN, the natural history of pain in herpes zoster, placebo effects, and regression to the mean must be considered in any evaluation of their effectiveness (Whitney & Von Korff, 1992). A very partial list of drugs used in the treatment of herpes zoster pain includes amantadine (Galbraith, 1973; Parkes, 1975), adenosine (Sherlock & Corey, 1985; Sklar, Blue, Alexander, & Bodian, 1985), various phenothiazines, baclofen, iontophoresis with vincristine (Csillik, Knyihar-Csillik, & Szucs, 1982), and calcium channel blockers (Ikebe et al., 1995). Rarely, analgesic effects of systemic lidocaine may be reproduced by oral mexiletine or flecainide. These drugs are often rejected by patients because of side effects.

Nerve Blocks. Interpleural nerve blocks have been used for both acute herpes zoster pain (Reiestad, Kvalheim, & McIlvaine, 1989) and PHN (Reiestad et al., 1990; Thwaites & Powell, 1995). Lidocaine administered intravenously has been shown to produce pain relief equivalent to that of morphine and superior to infusion of placebo, although the site of action is uncertain (Rowbotham et al., 1991). Subcutaneous injections of local anesthetics may produce a temporary reduction of allodynia and hyperpathia (a painful syndrome characterized by an abnormally painful reaction to a stimulus, especially a repetitive stimulus, as well as an increased threshold) and it is possible that this effect is prolonged by the addition of depot steroid. "Pain holidays" may be cautiously offered for major events, such as weddings, to those patients in whom a few days of symptom relief follows such injection. Peripheral blocks may reduce allodynia and hyperpathia but whether the temporary effects of a local anesthetic block can be prolonged by neurolysis—be it chemical, heat, or cold induced—remains uncertain. Abolition of sensory input by nerve destruction may, at times, lead to increased pain resulting from deafferentation. Sympathetic nerve blocks are often effective in relieving acute pain in herpes zoster, and they may possibly have a role in the prevention of PHN. However, these blocks rarely, if ever, provide lasting relief in patients with established PHN.

Drug-Licensing Considerations. The intractability of PHN leads pain specialists to try non-approved drugs or novel routes of administration. These actions should only be taken by experienced pain specialists, with careful monitoring of benefits and adverse effects and preferably as part of clinical research. Before such treatment is begun, the results of an objective prognostic test should ideally have shown a favorable outcome; such tests, however, are rarely available for the treatments considered for patients with PHN. Of course, patients should receive a thorough explanation of their treatment and provide informed consent. In addition, the rationale of the treatment plan and its implications should be explained to the patient's primary-care physician.

Psychosocial Interventions

Elderly patients are often lonely and major life stressors such as bereavement or loss of independence are common. They may have preexisting anxiety or depression or may develop such changes secondary to a severe acute herpes zoster infection and the development of prolonged pain. As in every other chronic pain syndrome, such factors should be carefully evaluated in patients with PHN. Patients should always be questioned about symptoms of depression, and appropriate treatments and referrals made. Providing the patient with an understanding of the disease as well as recommending an appropriate level of social activity are frequently helpful. As with all chronic pain syndromes, an individual management strategy should be developed for each patient. Thomsen's (1994) book makes helpful reading for thoughtful patients with PHN.

Cognitive-behavioral therapy—including such specific interventions as relaxation training, biofeedback, and hypnosis—has a well-established role in the treatment of patients with chronic pain (Gatchel & Turk, 1996; Turk, Meichenbaum, & Genest, 1983). Although no studies have been reported that have specifically examined this form of treatment in patients with PHN, there is no reason to doubt that cognitive-behavioral therapy provides as significant a benefit in PHN as it does in all of the other chronic pain syndromes in which it has been studied.

Neuroinvasive Measures

Noordenbos (1959) noted the intractability of PHN and illustrated this with a case reported by Sugar and Bucy (1951). In this patient, who suffered from PHN in the eye, cheek, and nose, the following methods were used in sequence, with appropriate lapses of time to evaluate the results: injection of alcohol into the infra-orbital nerve, roentgen radiation of the Gasserian ganglion, partial division of the sensory component of the trigeminal nerve, total resection of the sensory root of the trigeminal nerve, cocainization of the sphenopalatine ganglion, procaine block of the stellate ganglion, excision of the contralateral sensory cortex for the face, excision of the ipsilateral sensory cortex for the face, a series of electroconvulsive treatments, and bilateral prefrontal lobotomy. After this course of treatment the patient still suffered from pain although it was not as troublesome as it had been. This case report should be read and reread before considering any neuroinvasive treatment for PHN. Study of the reports of neurodestructive techniques does not provide encouragement to those considering such treatments. Pain is currently a justifiably feared complication of shingles and may be truly intractable for some patients.

An Illustrative Treatment Plan

Various algorithms have been presented for the treatment of acute herpes zoster and PHN (see Kost & Straus, 1996, for one recent example). An illustrative treatment plan for a 70-year-old patient with pain at 6 months or more after acute herpes zoster would include: thorough explanation of the disease and the reasons for ongoing pain; encouragement and advice on quality of life matters, including early return to premorbid activity levels; advice on clothing, cold packs, massage, and the use of cling film; prescription of a tricyclic antidepressant (with clear explanation of rationale and common side effects and their avoidance) in the manner suggested earlier; gradual titration of the antidepressant to a dose that provides pain relief or produces unacceptable side effects; and frequent review at clinic or by telephone with reassurance and support and counseling when needed. If allodynia is significant, EMLA or amethocaine cream under an occlusive dressing should be tried; other appropriate topical local anesthetic applications are likely to appear soon.

If less than adequate relief occurs within 3 weeks, the following may be considered: capsaicin cream four times daily for a minimum of 3 weeks, TENS, and continued increase in tricyclic antidepressant or change to a different antidepressant if further increases are limited by side effects. After a further 3 weeks, the following should be considered: intravenous lidocaine or ketamine prognostic tests with use of mexiletine or oral dextromethorphan respectively if positive; carefully monitored use of a long-acting opiate such as oxycodone; gabapentin with cautious dose escalation and hematological monitoring; appropriate injections of local anesthetic or local anesthetic and depot steroid mixtures; topical application three times daily of aspirin in ether, chloroform, or acetone; and referral to a psychologist or psychiatrist for cognitive-behavioral therapy.

What May Be Offered Patients With Inadequate Treatment Response?

Pain management centers specialize in the treatment of patients who suffer from chronic pain syndromes such as chronic back pain. These centers typically offer patients a multidisciplinary treatment program aimed at improving function (i.e., reducing disability), decreasing psychological distress, and increasing quality of life. The treatment plan usually includes medical management and some form of cognitive-behavioral therapy, and may also involve consideration for indwelling pumps and augmentive and ablative neurosurgical procedures. The reduction of pain intensity is not considered the primary goal in the majority of pain management centers. However, the reduction of pain intensity may occur in these settings, either as a result of the medical treatments provided or because cognitive-behavioral therapy has reduced suffering and psychological distress and increased the patient's ability to cope effectively with prolonged pain. These programs are appropriate for PHN patients but must take account of the fact that most patients with this chronic pain syndrome are elderly and return to work is not a relevant goal. In our view, a contingency to improve quality of life is mandatory for those patients in whom inadequate pain relief is common.

FUTURE DIRECTIONS

The number of patients suffering from PHN may increase substantially in the future for several reasons (Weller, 1992). First, the results of a recent epidemiological study suggested that the incidence of herpes zoster has increased in recent decades, although the explanation for this was unclear (Donohue, Choo, Manson, & Platt, 1995). In addition, the incidence of herpes zoster is expected to increase in coming decades, not only as the number of older individuals in the population increases but also as a result of the increasing prevalence of immunosuppression associated with various diseases and medical treatments. Finally, because PHN is more likely to develop in older individuals, it can be expected to become more prevalent as the population ages (Johnson, 1997a). Unfortunately, although numerous approaches are available for the treatment of PHN, some patients fail to respond and many derive only partial benefit and then continue to suffer from pain for months or even years. Because patients with PHN also suffer from physical and occupational disability, psychological distress, and increased health care utilization, a substantial increase in the prevalence of PHN would have major public health implications.

An important goal for future research, therefore, is the development of more effective treatments for PHN. C. P. N. Watson and Chipman (1993) have provided an excellent discussion of methodological issues in research on the treatment of PHN, and have noted that a better understanding of its pathogenesis may be of value in developing improved treatments. However, even though better treatment is a very important goal, it has become clear that the prevention of PHN is a more effective strategy than management of the established condition (Dworkin, 1997b; Johnson, 1995; Kost & Straus, 1996). As discussed previously, those patients most likely to develop PHN should be identified at the time of diagnosis of acute herpes zoster. At present, antiviral drugs combined with analgesic medications to control pain (and possibly a tricyclic antidepressant; Bowsher, 1997) provide the greatest likelihood of reducing the risk of PHN. Use of corticosteroids in combination with antiviral therapy during the acute disease has been recommended in the treatment of patients with a high risk of developing PHN (Kost & Straus, 1996). Although steroids appear not to reduce the overall duration of herpes zoster pain, they may hasten return to premorbid quality of life (Whitley et al., 1996; Wood et al., 1994); in one recent study, however, a greater number of adverse events was reported in herpes zoster patients treated with steroids (Wood et al., 1994).

Further reductions in the prevalence and severity of PHN may soon occur. Administration of the varicella vaccine to older adults who have not had herpes zoster results in increases in VZV-specific cell-mediated immunity to levels comparable to those found in individuals with a history of zoster (Hayward, Levin, Wolf, Angelova, & Gilden, 1991). Herpes zoster might therefore be attenuated by routine administration of the varicella vaccine to older adults (Levin et al., 1992; Levin, Murray, Zerbe, White, & Hayward, 1994; Oxman, 1995). If such immunization has a beneficial impact on herpes zoster, then appreciable reductions in the incidence and severity of PHN would be likely (Kost & Straus, 1997).

To evaluate the impact on herpes zoster and PHN of administering the varicella vaccine to older adults, placebo-controlled trials have been designed and subject enrollment is anticipated to begin in the near future. These large prospective studies of herpes zoster have important implications. They will provide rich sets of data on the epidemiology, natural history, and immunologic aspects of herpes zoster and PHN, and this information may lead to substantial increases in our understanding of the pathogenesis of PHN. But if the results of these trials demonstrate that the varicella vaccine markedly attenuates herpes zoster and immunization of older adults becomes widespread, PHN may become so rare that it ceases to be a feared complication of herpes zoster.

ACKNOWLEDGMENTS

Preparation of this chapter was supported by a research grant from the National Institute of Neurological Disorders and Stroke (NS-30714) to the first author. The authors would like to express their appreciation to Anne Louise Oaklander, M.D., Ph.D., for her thoughtful comments on an earlier version of this chapter, and to the VZV Research Foundation for its ongoing support of research, scientific conferences, and collegial gatherings relevant to the diseases caused by the varicella-zoster virus.

REFERENCES

Aisen, P. S., & Davis, K. L. (1994). Inflammatory mechanisms in Alzheimer's disease: Implications for therapy. *American Journal of Psychiatry, 151,* 1105–1113.

Alexander, J. I. (1985). Postherpetic neuralgia. *Anaesthesia, 40,* 1133–1134.

Anonymous. (1979). Shingles: A belt of roses from hell. *British Medical Journal, 1,* 5.

Backonja, M., Arndt, G., Gombar, K. A., Check, B., & Zimmermann, M. (1994). Response of chronic neuropathic pain syndromes to ketamine: A preliminary study. *Pain, 56,* 51–57.

Backonja, M., Hes, M. S., LaMoreaux, L. K., Garofalo, E. A., Koto, E. M., & the US Gabapentin Study Group. (1997, October). *Gabapentin (GBP; Neurontin®) reduces pain in diabetics with painful peripheral neuropathy: Results of a double-blind, placebo-controlled clinical trial (945-210).* Paper presented at the meeting of the American Pain Society, New Orleans.

Balfour, H. H., Jr. (1988). Varicella zoster virus infections in immunocompromised hosts: A review of the natural history and management. *American Journal of Medicine, 85*(Suppl. 2A), 68–73.

Bamford, J. A. C., & Boundy, C. A. P. (1968). The natural history of herpes zoster (shingles). *Medical Journal of Australia, No. 13,* 524–528.

Baron, R., Haendler, G., & Schulte, H. (1997). Afferent large fiber polyneuropathy predicts the development of postherpetic neuralgia. *Pain, 73,* 231–238.

Baron, R., & Saguer, M. (1993). Postherpetic neuralgia: Are C-nociceptors involved in signalling and maintenance of tactile allodynia? *Brain, 116,* 1477–1496.

Baron, R., & Saguer, M. (1995). Mechanical allodynia in postherpetic neuralgia: Evidence for central mechanisms depending on nociceptive C-fiber degeneration. *Neurology, 45*(Suppl. 8), S63–S65.

Bennett, G. J. (1994a). Hypotheses on the pathogenesis of herpes zoster-associated pain. *Annals of Neurology, 35*(Suppl.), S38–S41.

Bennett, G. J. (1994b). Neuropathic pain. In P. D. Wall & R. Melzack (Eds.), *Textbook of pain* (3rd ed., pp. 201–224). Edinburgh: Churchill Livingstone.

Beutner, K. R., Friedman, D. J., Forszpaniak, C., Andersen, P. L., & Wood, M. J. (1995). Valaciclovir compared with acyclovir for improved therapy for herpes zoster in immunocompetent adults. *Antimicrobial Agents and Chemotherapy, 39,* 1546–1553.

Bhala, B. B., Ramamoorthy, C., Bowsher, D., & Yelnoorker, K. N. (1988). Shingles and postherpetic neuralgia. *Clinical Journal of Pain, 4,* 169–174.

Bowsher, D. (1992). Acute herpes zoster and postherpetic neuralgia: Effects of acyclovir and outcome of treatment with amitriptyline. *British Journal of General Practice, 42,* 244–246.

Bowsher, D. (1993). Sensory change in postherpetic neuralgia. In C. P. N. Watson (Ed.), *Herpes zoster and postherpetic neuralgia* (pp. 97–107). Amsterdam: Elsevier.

Bowsher, D. (1997). The effects of pre-emptive treatment of postherpetic neuralgia with amitriptyline: A randomized, double-blind, placebo-controlled trial. *Journal of Pain and Symptom Management, 13,* 327–331.

Brown, G. R. (1976). Herpes zoster: Correlation of age, sex, distribution, neuralgia, and associated disorders. *Southern Medical Journal, 69,* 576–578.

Bryson, H. M., & Wilde, M. I. (1996). Amitriptyline. A review of its pharmacological properties and therapeutic use in chronic pain states. *Drugs & Aging, 8,* 459–76.

Burgoon, C. F., Burgoon, J. S., & Baldridge, G. D. (1957). The natural history of herpes zoster. *Journal of the American Medical Association, 164,* 265–269.

Bushnell, T., Vijay, V., Thwaites, R., Tidy, L., & Hester, J. (1996). Ketamine is an analgesic in refractory postherpetic neuralgia. *Journal of the Pain Society, 12,* 37.

Chekhov, A. (1964). The cherry orchard. In A. Chekhov, *The major plays* (A. Dunnigan, Trans.) (pp. 313–380). New York: Penguin. (Original work published 1904)

Choi, B., & Rowbotham, M. C. (1997). Effect of adrenergic receptor activation on post-herpetic neuralgia pain and sensory disturbances. *Pain, 69,* 55–63.

Choo, P. W., Galil, K., Donahue, J. G., Walker, A. M., Spiegelman, D., & Platt, R. (1997). Risk factors for postherpetic neuralgia. *Archives of Internal Medicine, 157,* 1217–1224.

Cobo, L. M., Foulks, G. N., Liesegang, T., Lass, J., Sutphin, J. E., Wilhelmus, K., Jones, D. B., Chapman, S., Segreti, A. C., & King, D. H. (1986). Oral acyclovir in the treatment of acute herpes zoster ophthalmicus. *Ophthalmology, 93,* 763–770.

Collins, P. D. (1991). EMLA Cream and herpetic neuralgia. *Medical Journal of Australia, 155,* 206–207.

Coniam, S. W., & Hunton, J. (1988). A study of benzydamine cream in post-herpetic neuralgia. *Research and Clinical Forums, 10,* 65–67.

Crooks, R. J., Jones, D. A., & Fiddian, A. P. (1991). Zoster-associated chronic pain: An overview of clinical trials with acyclovir. *Scandinavian Journal of Infectious Diseases, Suppl. 78,* 62–68.

Csillik, B., Knyihar-Csillik, E., & Szucs, A. (1982). Treatment of chronic pain syndromes with iontophoresis of vinca alkaloids to the skin of patients. *Neuroscience, 31,* 87–90.

Davies, L., Cossins, L., Bowsher, D., & Drummond, M. (1994). The cost of treatment for post-herpetic neuralgia in the UK. *PharmacoEconomics, 6,* 142–148.

De Benedittis, G., Besana, F., & Lorenzetti, A. (1992). A new topical treatment for acute herpetic neuralgia and postherpetic neuralgia: The aspirin/dietyl ether mixture: An open-label study plus a double-blind, controlled clinical trial. *Pain, 48,* 383–390.

Degreef, H. (1994). Famciclovir, a new oral antiherpes drug: Results of the first controlled clinical study demonstrating its efficacy and safety in the treatment of uncomplicated herpes zoster in immunocompetent patients. *International Journal of Antimicrobial Agents, 4*, 241–246.

De Moragas, J. M., & Kierland, R. R. (1957). The outcome of patients with herpes zoster. *AMA Archives of Dermatology, 75*, 193–196.

Donohue, J. G., Choo, P. W., Manson, J. E., & Platt, R. (1995). The incidence of herpes zoster. *Archives of Internal Medicine, 155*, 1605–1609.

Dubuisson, D., & Melzack, R. (1976). Classification of clinical pain descriptions by multiple group discriminant analysis. *Experimental Neurology, 51*, 480–487.

Dung, H. C. (1987). Acupuncture for the treatment of post-herpetic neuralgia. *American Journal of Acupuncture, 15*, 5–14.

Dworkin, R. H. (1997a). Pain and its assessment in herpes zoster. *Antiviral Chemistry & Chemotherapy, 8*(Supp. 1), 31–36.

Dworkin, R. H. (1997b). Which individuals with acute pain are most likely to develop a chronic pain syndrome? *Pain Forum, 6*, 127–136.

Dworkin, R. H., & Banks, S. M. (in press). A vulnerability-diathesis-stress model of the pathogenesis of chronic pain: Herpes zoster and the development of postherpetic neuralgia. In R. J. Gatchel & D. C. Turk (Eds.), *Psychosocial factors in pain: Evolution and revolutions.* New York: Guilford.

Dworkin, R. H., Boon, R. J., Griffin, D. R. G., & Phung, D. (in press). Postherpetic neuralgia: Impact of famciclovir, age, rash severity, and acute pain in herpes zoster patients. *Journal of Infectious Diseases.*

Dworkin, R. H., Carrington, D., Cunningham, A., Kost, R., Levin, M., McKendrick, M., Oxman, M., Rentier, B., Schmader, K. E., Tappeiner, G., Wassilew, S. W., & Whitley, R. J. (1997). Assessment of pain in herpes zoster: Lessons learned from antiviral trials. *Antiviral Research, 33*, 73–85.

Dworkin, R. H., Cooper, E. M., Walther, R. R., & Sweeney, E. W. (1997, March). *Risk factors for postherpetic neuralgia: A prospective study of acute herpes zoster patients.* Paper presented at the Third International Conference on the Varicella-Zoster Virus, Palm Beach, FL.

Dworkin, R. H., & Portenoy, R. K. (1996). Pain and its persistence in herpes zoster. *Pain, 67*, 241–251.

Eide, P. K., Jørum, E., Stubhaug, A., Bremnes, J., & Breivik, H. (1994). Relief of post-herpetic neuralgia with the N-methyl-D-aspartic acid receptor antagonist ketamine: A double-blind, cross-over comparison with morphine and placebo. *Pain, 58*, 347–354.

Fields, H. L. (1997, December). *Mechanisms and treatment of post-herpetic neuralgia.* Paper presented at the meeting on Current Concepts in Acute, Chronic, and Cancer Pain Management, New York.

Fields, H. L., & Rowbotham, M. C. (1994). Multiple mechanisms of neuropathic pain: A clinical perspective. In G. F. Gebhart, D. L. Hammond, & T. S. Jensen (Eds.), *Proceedings of the 7th World Congress on Pain* (pp. 437–454). Seattle: IASP Press.

Fromm, G. H. (1993). Facial pain with herpes zoster and postherpetic neuralgia and a comparison with trigeminal neuralgia. In C. P. N. Watson (Ed.), *Herpes zoster and postherpetic neuralgia* (pp. 109–122). Amsterdam: Elsevier.

Galbraith, A. W. (1973). Treatment of acute herpes zoster with amantadine hydrochloride (Symmetrel). *British Medical Journal, 4*, 693–695.

Gatchel, R. J., & Turk, D. C. (Eds.). (1996). *Psychological approaches to pain management: A practitioner's handbook.* New York: Guilford.

Gershon, A. A. (1993). Zoster in immunosuppressed patients. In C. P. N. Watson (Ed.), *Herpes zoster and postherpetic neuralgia* (pp. 73–86). Amsterdam: Elsevier.

Gerson, G. R., Jones, R. B., & Luscombe, D. K. (1977). Studies of the concomitant use of carbamazepine and clomipramine for the relief of postherpetic neuralgia. *Postgraduate Medical Journal, 54*(Supp. 4), 104–109.

Gilden, D. H., Dueland, A. N., Cohrs, R., Martin, J. R., Kleinschmidt-DeMasters, B. K., & Mahalingam, R. (1991). Preherpetic neuralgia. *Neurology, 41,* 1215–1218.

Gilden, D. H., Dueland, A. N., Devlin, M. E., Mahalingam, R., & Cohrs, R. (1992). Varicella-zoster virus reactivation without rash. *Journal of Infectious Diseases, 166*(Suppl. 1), S30–S34.

Gilden, D. H., Wright, R. R., Schneck, S. A., Gwaltney, J. M., & Mahalingam, R. (1994). Zoster sine herpete, a clinical variant. *Annals of Neurology, 35,* 530–533.

Glynn, C., Crockford, G., Gavaghan, D., Cardno, P., Price, D., & Miller, J. (1990). Epidemiology of shingles. *Journal of the Royal Society of Medicine, 83,* 617–619.

Graff-Radford, S. B., Kames, L. D., & Naliboff, B. D. (1986). Measures of psychological adjustment and perception of pain in postherpetic neuralgia and trigeminal neuralgia. *Clinical Journal of Pain, 2,* 55–58.

Haines, D. R. (1989). Topical aspirin in chloroform for post-herpetic neuralgia. *Journal of the Intractable Pain Society, 7,* 15–16.

Harding, S. P., Lipton, J. R., & Wells, J. C. D. (1987). Natural history of herpes zoster ophthalmicus: Predictors of postherpetic neuralgia and ocular involvement. *British Journal of Opthalmology, 71,* 353–358.

Hatangdi, V. S., Boas, R. A., & Richards, E. G. (1976). Postherpetic neuralgia: Management with antiepileptic and tricyclic drugs. In J. J. Bonica & D. Albe-Fessard (Eds.), *Advances in pain research and therapy* (Vol. 1, pp. 583–587). New York: Raven.

Hayward, A., Levin, M., Wolf, W., Angelova, G., & Gilden, D. (1991). Varicella-zoster virus-specific immunity after herpes zoster. *Journal of Infectious Diseases, 163,* 873–875.

Head, H., & Campbell, A. W. (1900). The pathology of herpes zoster and its bearing on sensory localization. *Brain, 23,* 353–523.

Higa, K., Dan, K., Manabe, H., & Noda, B. (1988). Factors influencing the duration of treatment of acute herpetic pain with sympathetic nerve block: Importance of severity of herpes zoster assessed by the maximum antibody titers to varicella-zoster virus in otherwise healthy patients. *Pain, 32,* 147–157.

Higa, K., Mori, M., Hirata, K., Hori, K., Manabe, H., & Dan, K. (1997). Severity of skin lesions of herpes zoster at the worst phase rather than age and involved region most influences the duration of acute herpetic pain. *Pain, 69,* 245–253.

Hoffmann, V. H. Coppejans, H., Vercauteren, M., & Adriaensen, H. F. (1994). Successful treatment of postherpetic neuralgia with oral ketamine. *Clinical Journal of Pain, 10,* 240–242.

Hope-Simpson, R. E. (1954). Studies on shingles: Is the virus ordinary chicken pox virus? *Lancet, ii,* 1299–1302.

Hope-Simpson, R. E. (1965). The nature of herpes zoster: A long-term study and a new hypothesis. *Proceedings of the Royal Society of Medicine, 58,* 9–20.

Hope-Simpson, R. E. (1967). Herpes zoster in the elderly. *Geriatrics, 22,* 151–159.

Hope-Simpson, R. E. (1975). Postherpetic neuralgia. *Journal of the Royal College of General Practitioners, 25,* 571–575.

Huff, J. C., Drucker, J. L., Clemmer, A., Laskin, O. L., Connor, J. D., Bryson, Y. J., & Balfour, H. H., Jr. (1993). Effect of oral acyclovir on pain resolution in herpes zoster: A reanalysis. *Journal of Medical Virology, Supp. 1,* 93–96.

Ikebe, H., Miyagawa, A., Mizutani, A., Miyamoto, M., Taniguchi, K., & Honda, N. (1995). The effect of iontophoresis with several Ca channel blockers for PHN patients. *Masui, 44,* 428–33.

Jackson, J. L., Gibbons, R., Meyer, G., & Inouye, L. (1997). The effect of treating herpes zoster with oral acyclovir in preventing postherpetic neuralgia: A meta-analysis. *Archives of Internal Medicine, 157,* 909–912.

Johnson, R. W. (1995). The future of predictors, prevention, and therapy in postherpetic neuralgia. *Neurology, 45*(Suppl. 8), S70–S72.

Johnson, R. W. (1996a). Aspects of postherpetic neuralgia: Can we zap Z-ap? *Pain Reviews, 3*, 117–135.

Johnson, R. W. (1996b). Pathophysiology of pain with reference to herpes zoster. *Reviews in Medical Virology, 6*, 17–23.

Johnson, R. W. (1997a). Current and future management of herpes zoster. *Antiviral Chemistry & Chemotherapy, 8*(Suppl. 1), 11–20.

Johnson, R. W. (1997b). Herpes zoster and postherpetic neuralgia: Optimal treatment. *Drugs & Aging, 10*, 80–94.

Johnson, R. W., Shukla, S., & Fletcher, P. (1995). *Qualitative aspects of zoster-associated pain: Evaluation of a new approach.* Paper presented at the meeting of the European Federation of IASP Chapters, Verona, Italy.

Jones, R. J., & Silman, G. M. (1987). Trials of ultrasonic therapy for acute herpes zoster. *Practitioner, 231*, 1336–1340.

Kato, Y., Homma, I., & Ichiyanagi, K. (1995). Postherpetic neuralgia. *Pain, 11*, 336–337.

Killian, J. M., & Fromm, G. H. (1968). Carbamazepine in the treatment of neuralgia. *Archives of Neurology, 19*, 129–136.

King, R. B. (1988). Concerning the management of pain associated with herpes zoster and of postherpetic neuralgia. *Pain, 33*, 73–78.

King, R. B. (1993). Topical aspirin in chloroform and the relief of pain due to herpes zoster and postherpetic neuralgia. *Archives of Neurology, 88*, 556–561.

Kishore-Kumar, R., Max, M. B., Schafer, S. C., Gaughan, A. M., Smoller, B., Gracely, R. H., & Dubner, R. (1990). Desipramine relieves postherpetic neuralgia. *Clinical Pharmacology and Therapeutics, 47*, 305–312.

Kost, R. G., & Straus, S. E. (1996). Postherpetic neuralgia: Pathogenesis, treatment, and prevention. *New England Journal of Medicine, 335*, 32–42.

Kost, R. G., & Straus, S. E. (1997). Postherpetic neuralgia: Predicting and preventing risk. *Archives of Internal Medicine, 157*, 1166–1167.

Kristensen, J. D., Svensson, B., & Gordh, T. (1992). The NMDA-receptor antagonist CPP abolishes neurogenic "wind-up pain" after intrathecal administration in humans. *Pain, 51*, 249–253.

Lang, E., Hord, A. H., & Denson, D. (1996). Venlafaxine hydrochloride (Effexor) relieves thermal hyperalgesia in rats with an experimental mononeuropathy. *Pain, 68*, 151–155.

Levin, M. J., Murray, M., Rotbart, H. A., Zerbe G. O., White, C. J., & Hayward, A. R. (1992). Immune response of elderly individuals to a live attenuated varicella vaccine. *Journal of Infectious Diseases, 166*, 253–259.

Levin, M. J., Murray, M., Zerbe, G. O., White, C. J., & Hayward, A. R. (1994). Immune responses of elderly persons 4 years after receiving a live attenuated varicella vaccine. *Journal of Infectious Diseases, 170*, 522–526.

Lewis, G. W. (1958). Zoster sine herpete. *British Medical Journal, 2*, 418–421.

Lewith, G. T., Field, F., & Machin, D. (1983). Acupuncture versus placebo in postherpetic pain. *Pain, 17*, 361–368.

Loeser, J. D. (1990). Herpes zoster and postherpetic neuralgia. In J. J. Bonica (Ed.), *The management of pain* (2nd ed., pp. 257–263). Philadelphia: Lea & Febiger.

Lydick, E., Epstein, R. S., Himmelberger, D., & White, C. J. (1995). Herpes zoster and quality of life: A self-limited disease with severe impact. *Neurology, 45*(Suppl. 8), S52–S53.

Mauskopf, J., Austin, R., Dix, L., & Berzon, R. (1994). The Nottingham Health Profile as a measure of quality of life in zoster patients: Convergent and discriminant validity. *Quality of Life Research, 3*, 431–435.

Max, M. B. (1994). Treatment of post-herpetic neuralgia: Antidepressants. *Annals of Neurology, 35*(Suppl.), S50–S53.

Max, M. B. (1995). Thirteen consecutive well-designed randomized trials show that antidepressants reduce pain in diabetic neuropathy and postherpetic neuralgia. *Pain Forum, 4,* 248–253.

Max, M. B., Lynch, S. A., Muir, J., Shoaf, S. E., Smoller, B., & Dubner, R. (1992). Effects of desipramine, amitriptyline, and fluoxetine on pain in diabetic neuropathy. *New England Journal of Medicine, 326,* 1250–1256.

Max, M. B., Schafer, S. C., Culnane, M., Smoller, B., Dubner, R., & Gracely, R. H. (1988). Amitriptyline, but not lorazepam, relieves postherpetic neuralgia. *Neurology, 38,* 1427–1432.

McKendrick, M. W., Care, C. D., Ogan, P., & Wood, M. J. (1994, July). *A retrospective study of the epidemiology of zoster with particular reference to factors pertinent to the development of chronic pain.* Paper presented at the Second International Conference on the Varicella-Zoster Virus, Paris.

McQuay, H. J., Carroll, D., & Glynn, C. J. (1993). Dose-response for analgesic effect of amitriptyline in chronic pain. *Anaesthesia, 48,* 281–285.

McQuay, H. J., Carroll, D., Jadad, A. R., Glynn, C. J., Jack, T., Moore, R. A., & Wiffen, P. J. (1994). Dextromethorphan for the treatment of neuropathic pain: A double-blind, randomised controlled crossover trial with integral *n*-of-1 design. *Pain, 59,* 127–133.

McQuay, H. J., Carroll, D., Jadad, A. R., Wiffen, P., & Moore, A. (1995). Anticonvulsant drugs for management of pain: A systematic review. *British Medical Journal, 311,* 1047–1052.

McQuay, H. J., Carroll, D., Moxon, A., Glynn, C. J., & Moore, R. A. (1990). Benzydamine cream for the treatment of post-herpetic neuralgia: Minimum duration of treatment periods in a cross-over trial. *Pain, 40,* 131–135.

McQuay, H. J., Tramèr, M., Nye, B. A., Carroll, D., Wiffen, P. J., & Moore, R. A. (1996). A systematic review of antidepressants in neuropathic pain. *Pain, 68,* 217–227.

Monroe, S. M., & Simons, A. D. (1991). Diathesis-stress theories in the context of life stress research: Implications for the depressive disorders. *Psychological Bulletin, 110,* 406–425.

Nandy, K., & Nandy, L. K. (1986). Immunological and autoimmune phenomena in senile brain disease. In A. B. Scheibel, A. F. Wechsler, & M. A. B. Brazier (Eds.), *The biological substrates of Alzheimer's disease* (pp. 167–176). New York: Academic Press.

Nathan, P. W., & Wall, P. D. (1974). Treatment of postherpetic neuralgia by prolonged electrical stimulation. *British Medical Journal, 3,* 645–647.

Noordenbos, W. (1959). *Pain.* Amsterdam: Elsevier.

Nurmikko, T. (1994). Sensory dysfunction in postherpetic neuralgia. In J. Boivie, P. Hansson, & U. Lindblom (Eds.), *Touch, temperature, and pain in health and disease: Mechanisms and assessments* (pp. 133–141). Seattle: IASP Press.

Nurmikko, T. (1995). Clinical features and pathophysiological mechanisms of postherpetic neuralgia. *Neurology, 45*(Suppl. 8), S54–S55.

Nurmikko, T., Wells, C., & Bowsher, D. (1991). Pain and allodynia in postherpetic neuralgia: Role of somatic and sympathetic nervous systems. *Acta Neurologica Scandinavica, 84,* 146–152.

Oaklander, A. L., Romans, K., Horasek, S., Stocks, A., Hauer, P., & Meyer, R. A. (in press). Unilateral postherpetic neuralgia is associated with bilateral sensory neuron damage. *Annals of Neurology.*

Oxman, M. (1995). Immunization to reduce the frequency and severity of herpes zoster and its complications. *Neurology, 45*(Supp. 8), S41–S46.

Pappagallo, M., & Campbell, J. N. (1994). Chronic opioid therapy as alternative treatment for post-herpetic neuralgia. *Annals of Neurology, 35*(Suppl.), S54–S56.

Parkes, D. (1975). Amantadine. *Advances in Drug Research, 8,* 11–81.

Payne, C. (1984). Ultrasound for post-herpetic neuralgia. *Physiotherapy, 70,* 96–97.

Portenoy, R. K., Duma, C., & Foley, K. M. (1986). Acute herpetic and postherpetic neuralgia: Clinical review and current management. *Annals of Neurology, 20,* 651–664.

Raftery, H. (1979). The management of postherpetic pain using sodium valproate and amitriptyline. *Irish Medical Journal, 72,* 399–401.

Raggozzino, M. W., Melton, L. J., III, Kurland, L. T., Chu, C. P., & Perry, H. O. (1982). Population-based study of herpes zoster and its sequelae. *Medicine, 61,* 310–316.

Reiestad, F., Kvalheim, L., & McIlvaine, W. B. (1989). Pleural analgesia for the treatment of acute severe thoracic herpes zoster. *Regional Anesthesia, 14,* 244–246.

Reiestad, F., McIlvaine, W. B., Barnes, M., Kvalheim, L., Haraldstad, M. D., & Pettersen, B. (1990). Interpleural analgesia in the treatment of severe thoracic postherpetic neuralgia. *Regional Anesthesia, 15,* 113–117.

Rogers, R. S., III, & Tindall, J. P. (1971). Geriatric herpes zoster. *Journal of the American Geriatric Society, 19,* 495–504.

Rosenberg, J. M., Harrell, C., Ristic, H., Werner, R. A., & de Rosayro, A. M. (1997). The effect of gabapentin on neuropathic pain. *Clinical Journal of Pain, 13,* 251–255.

Rowbotham, M. C. (1994a). Managing post-herpetic neuralgia with opioids and local anesthetics. *Annals of Neurology, 35*(Suppl.), S46–S49.

Rowbotham, M. C. (1994b). Postherpetic neuralgia. *Seminars in Neurology, 14,* 247–254.

Rowbotham, M. C., Davies, P. S., & Fields, H. L. (1995). Topical lidocaine gel relieves post-herpetic neuralgia. *Annals of Neurology, 37,* 246–253.

Rowbotham, M. C., Davies, P. S., Verkempinck, C., & Galer, B. S. (1996). Lidicaine patch: Double-blind controlled study of a new treatment method for post-herpetic neuralgia. *Pain, 65,* 39–44.

Rowbotham, M. C., & Fields, H. L. (1989). Post-herpetic neuralgia: The relation of pain complaint, sensory disturbance, and skin temperature. *Pain, 39,* 129–144.

Rowbotham, M. C., & Fields, H. L. (1996). The relationship of pain, allodynia and thermal sensation in post-herpetic neuralgia. *Brain, 119,* 347–354.

Rowbotham, M. C., Reisner-Keller, L., & Fields, H. L. (1991). Both intravenous lidocaine and morphine reduce the pain of postherpetic neuralgia. *Neurology, 41,* 1024–1028.

Rusthoven, J. J., Ahlgren, P., Elhakim, T., Pinfold, P., Reid, J., Stewart, L., & Feld, R. (1988). Varicella-zoster infection in adult cancer patients: A population study. *Archives of Internal Medicine, 148,* 1561–1566.

Satterthwaite, J. R. (1989). Postherpetic neuralgia. In C. D. Tollison (Ed.), *Handbook of chronic pain management* (pp. 460–474). Baltimore: Williams & Wilkins.

Schmader, K. (1995). Management of herpes zoster in elderly patients. *Infectious Diseases in Clinical Practice, 4,* 293–299.

Sherlock, C. H., & Corey, L. (1985). Adenosine monophosphate for the treatment of varicella zoster infections: A large dose of caution. *Journal of the American Medical Association, 253,* 1444–1445.

Sindrup, S. H., Gram, L. F., Brøsen, K., Eshøj, O., & Mogensen, E. F. (1990). The selective serotonin reuptake inhibitor paroxetine is effective in the treatment of diabetic neuropathy symptoms. *Pain, 42,* 135–144.

Sindrup, S. H., Gram, L. F., Skjold, T., Frøland, A., & Beck-Nielsen, H. (1990). Concentration-response relationship in imipramine treatment of diabetic neuropathy symptoms. *Clinical Pharmacology and Therapeutics, 47,* 509–515.

Sklar, S. H., Blue, W. T., Alexander, E. J., & Bodian, C. A. (1985). Herpes zoster: The treatment and prevention of neuralgia with adenosine monophosphate. *Journal of the American Medical Association, 253,* 1427–1445.

Smith, F. P. (1978). Pathological studies of spinal nerve ganglia in relation to intractable intercostal pain. *Surgical Neurology, 19,* 50–53.

Stow, P. J., Glynn, C. J., & Minor, B. (1989). EMLA cream in the treatment of postherpetic neuralgia: Efficacy and pharmacokinetic profile. *Pain, 39,* 301–305.

Straus, S. E., Reinhold, W., Smith, H. A., Ruyechan, W. T., Henderson, D. K., Blaese, R. M., & Hay, J. (1984). Endonuclease analysis of viral DNA from varicella and subsequent zoster infections in the same patient. *New England Journal of Medicine, 311,* 1362–1364.

Sugar, O., & Bucy, P. C. (1951). Post-herpetic trigeminal neuralgia. *Archives of Neurology and Psychiatry, 65,* 131.

Thomsen, T. C. (1994). *Shingles and PHN.* New York: Cross River Press.

Thwaites, B. K., & Powell, D. R. (1995). Interpleural block for acute combined cervical and thoracic herpes zoster. *Regional Anesthesia, 20,* 255–256.

Turk, D. C., Meichenbaum, D., & Genest, M. (1983). *Pain and behavioral medicine: A cognitive-behavioral perspective.* New York: Guilford.

Tyring, S., Barbarash, R. A., Nahlik, J. E., Cunningham, A., Marley, J., Heng, M., Jones, T., Rea, T., Boon, R., Saltzman, R., & the Collaborative Famciclovir Herpes Zoster Study Group. (1995). Famciclovir for the treatment of acute herpes zoster: Effects on acute disease and postherpetic neuralgia: A randomized, double-blind, placebo-controlled trial. *Annals of Internal Medicine, 123,* 89–96.

Wall, P. D. (1993). An essay on the mechanisms which may contribute to the state of postherpetic neuralgia. In C. P. N. Watson (Ed.), *Herpes zoster and postherpetic neuralgia* (pp. 123–138). Amsterdam: Elsevier.

Watson, C. P. N. (Ed.). (1993a). *Herpes zoster and postherpetic neuralgia.* Amsterdam: Elsevier.

Watson, C. P. N. (1993b). The medical treatment of postherpetic neuralgia: Antidepressants, other therapies, and practical guidelines for management. In C. P. N. Watson (Ed.), *Herpes zoster and postherpetic neuralgia* (pp. 205–219). Amsterdam: Elsevier.

Watson, C. P. N., & Babul, N. (1997, March). *Placebo-controlled evaluation of the efficacy and safety of controlled release oxycodone in postherpetic neuralgia.* Paper presented at the Third International Conference on the Varicella-Zoster Virus, Palm Beach Gardens, FL.

Watson, C. P. N., & Chipman, M. (1993). Suggestions for research and unanswered questions regarding postherpetic neuralgia. In C. P. N. Watson (Ed.), *Herpes zoster and postherpetic neuralgia* (pp. 239–253). Amsterdam: Elsevier.

Watson, C. P. N., Chipman, M., Reed, K., Evans, R. J., & Birkett, N. (1992). Amitriptyline versus maprotiline in postherpetic neuralgia: A randomized, double-blind, crossover trial. *Pain, 48,* 29–36.

Watson, C. P. N., & Deck, J. H. (1993). The neuropathology of herpes zoster with particular reference to postherpetic neuralgia and its pathogenesis. In C. P. N. Watson (Ed.), *Herpes zoster and postherpetic neuralgia* (pp. 139–157). Amsterdam: Elsevier.

Watson, C. P. N., Deck, J. H., Morshead, C., Van der Kooy, D., & Evans, R. J. (1991). Post-herpetic neuralgia: Further post-mortem studies of cases with and without pain. *Pain, 44,* 105–117.

Watson, C. P. N., & Evans, R. J. (1985). A comparative trial of amitriptyline and zimelidine in post-herpetic neuralgia. *Pain, 23,* 387–394.

Watson, C. P. N, & Evans, R. J., Reed, K., Merskey, H., Goldsmith, L., & Warsh, J. (1982). Amitriptyline versus placebo in postherpetic neuralgia. *Neurology, 32,* 671–673.

Watson, C. P. N., Morshead, C., Van der Kooy, D., Deck, J., & Evans, R. J. (1988). Post-herpetic neuralgia: Post-mortem analysis of a case. *Pain, 34,* 129–138.

Watson, C. P. N., Tyler, K. L., Bickers, D. R., Millikin, L. E., Smith, S., & Coleman, E. (1993). A randomized vehicle-controlled trial of topical capsaicin in the treatment of postherpetic neuralgia. *Clinical Therapeutics, 15,* 510–526.

Watson, C. P. N., Watt, V. R., Chipman, M., Birkett, N., & Evans, R. J. (1991). The prognosis of postherpetic neuralgia. *Pain, 46,* 195–199.

Watson, P. N., & Evans, R. J. (1986). Postherpetic neuralgia: A review. *Archives of Neurology, 43,* 836–840.

Weksler, M. E. (1994). Immune senescence. *Annals of Neurology, 35*(Suppl.), S35–S37.

Weller, T. H. (1992). Varicella and herpes zoster: A perspective and overview. *Journal of Infectious Diseases, 166*(Suppl. 1), S1–S6.

Weller, T. H., Witton, H. M., & Bell, E. J. (1958). The etiologic agents of varicella and herpes zoster: Isolation, propagation, and cultural characteristics in vitro. *Journal of Experimental Medicine, 108,* 843–868.

Wheeler, J. G. (1991). EMLA cream and herpetic neuralgia. *Medical Journal of Australia, 154,* 781.

Whitley, R. J., Weiss, H., Gnann, J. W., Jr., Tyring, S., Mertz, G. J., Pappas, P. G., Schleupner, C. J., Hayden, F., Wolf, J., Soong, S-J., & the National Institute of Allergy and Infectious Diseases Collaborative Antiviral Study Group. (1996). Acyclovir with and without prednisone for the treatment of herpes zoster: A randomized, placebo-controlled trial. *Annals of Internal Medicine, 125,* 376–383.

Whitney, C. W., & Von Korff, M. (1992). Regression to the mean in treated versus untreated chronic pain. *Pain, 50,* 281–285.

Wildenhoff, K. E., Esmann, V., Ipsen, J., Harving, H., Peterslund, N. A., & Schonheyder, H. (1981). Treatment of trigeminal and thoracic zoster with idoxuridine. *Scandinavian Journal of Infectious Diseases, 13,* 257–262.

Wildenhoff, K. E., Ipsen, J., Esmann, V., Ingemann-Jensen, J., & Poulsen, J. H. (1979). Treatment of herpes zoster with idoxuridine ointment, including a multivariate analysis of symptoms and signs. *Scandinavian Journal of Infectious Diseases, 11,* 1–9.

Wood, M. J. (1991). Herpes zoster and pain. *Scandinavian Journal of Infectious Diseases, Suppl. 78,* 53–61.

Wood, M. J. (1995). For debate: How should zoster trials be conducted? *Journal of Antimicrobial Chemotherapy, 36,* 1089–1101.

Wood, M. J., Johnson, R. W., McKendrick, M. W., Taylor, J., Mandal, B. K., & Crooks, J. (1994). A randomized trial of acyclovir for 7 days or 21 days with and without prednisolone for treatment of acute herpes zoster. *New England Journal of Medicine, 330,* 896–900.

Wood, M. J., Kay, R., Dworkin, R. H., Soong, S-J., & Whitley, R. J. (1996). Oral acyclovir therapy accelerates pain resolution in patients with herpes zoster: A meta-analysis of placebo-controlled trials. *Clinical Infectious Diseases, 22,* 341–347.

Zitman, F. G., Linssen, A. C. G., Edelbroek, P. M., & Stijnen, T. (1990). Low dose amitriptyline in chronic pain: The gain is modest. *Pain, 42,* 35–42.

Chapter 19

Phantom Limb Pain

Joel Katz
The Toronto Hospital and Acute Pain Research Unit,
Mount Sinai Hospital, and University of Toronto

Many patients awake from the anesthetic after an amputation believing that the operation has not been performed. Their continued sense of the lost limb is so real that not until they lift the bed sheets to see it do they realize it has been cut off. This startling realization has little effect on the reality of the limb they experience, and in some cases may even intensify the sensations that define it. Mitchell (1871) coined the term *phantom limb* to describe the persisting sensory awareness of a limb after amputation.

A distinction is usually made between the painful and nonpainful phantom limb (Melzack & Wall, 1988). The most salient property of the nonpainful phantom is its tingling, "pins and needles" or *paresthestic* quality, but sensations of temperature, posture, length, volume, and movement are also very common (T. S. Jensen & Rasmussen, 1994). Recent studies estimate the incidence of the nonpainful phantom at approximately 80% to 100% (T. S. Jensen & Rasmussen, 1994). For many amputees, however, a distressing problem is phantom limb pain (R. A. Sherman, 1989). Many patients report a painful intensification of the paresthesias (i.e., dysesthesias) that define the nonpainful phantom limb. Some sufferers describe bouts of paroxysmal shooting pain that travel up and down the limb. Others report the phantom to be in a cramped or otherwise unnatural posture that gives rise to excruciating pain. Many amputees describe the pain in the phantom limb as indistinguishable from the pain they experienced in the limb prior to amputation. In still others, the phantom may be immobile or paralyzed so that attempts to move it generate pain. Finally, the phantom is often the seat of an intense burning pain as if the hand or foot were being held too close to an open flame. Frequently, amputees suffer from several types of pain (T. S. Jensen & Rasmussen, 1994). A recent survey based on several thousand amputees reveals that more than 70% continue to experience phantom limb pain of considerable intensity more than 25 years after amputation (R. A. Sherman, C. J. Sherman, & Parker, 1984). Equally striking is the low success rate of treatments for phantom limb pain: In the long term only 7% of patients are helped by the more than 50 types of therapy used to treat phantom limb pain (R. A. Sherman, 1989). This intractability reflects our ignorance about the mechanisms that contribute to phantom limb pain.

This chapter evaluates the joint influence of peripheral neurophysiological factors and higher order cognitive and affective processes in triggering or modulating a variety of phantom limb experiences, including pain. The first section outlines one way in which the sympathetic nervous system may influence phantom limb pain. A model involving a sympathetic-efferent somatic-afferent cycle is presented to explain fluctuations in the intensity of sensations referred to the phantom limb. In the second section, the model is extended to explain the puzzling finding that only *after* amputation are thoughts and feelings capable of evoking referred sensations to the (phantom) limb. Whereas phantom pains and other sensations frequently are triggered by thoughts and feelings, there is no evidence that the painful or painless phantom limb is a symptom of a psychological disorder. The available literature on coping with phantom limb pain is then reviewed. In the third section, the concept of a pain "memory" is introduced and described with examples. The data show that pain experienced prior to amputation may persist in the form of a memory referred to the phantom limb causing continued suffering and distress. It is argued that two independent and potentially dissociable memory components underlie the unified experience of a pain memory. This conceptualization is evaluated in the context of the surgical arena, raising the possibility that under certain conditions postamputation pain may, in part, reflect the persistent central neural memory trace left by the surgical procedure. Preemptive analgesia and other preventive approaches to the management of phantom limb pain are briefly reviewed. In the final section, the immobile or paralyzed phantom is presented along with recent evidence that a simple, nonpharmacological intervention may prove helpful in restoring a sense of movement to the phantom limb. Treatment implications and options are presented at the end of each section.

SYMPATHETIC NERVOUS SYSTEM CONTRIBUTIONS TO PHANTOM LIMB EXPERIENCE

Phantom Limb Pain

A controversy has arisen over the origin of the phantom limb. In an attempt to find a single explanatory mechanism, theories have focused on only one aspect of phantom limb experience and have ignored or discounted others (Melzack & Wall, 1988). The cause has been sought in the activity of primary afferent fibers, spinal cord cells, and supra-spinal sensory nuclei (T. S. Jensen & Rasmussen, 1994; Melzack & Wall, 1988). A review of these mechanisms is beyond the scope of this chapter. The interested reader is referred to several recent publications for more detail (Devor, 1994; T. S. Jensen & Rasmussen, 1994; R. A. Sherman, Devor, Jones, Katz, & Marbach, 1997). Another class of theory has attempted to account for the phantom solely on the basis of psychological and emotional processes (Szasz, 1975). It is becoming increasingly clear, however, that the phantom limb cannot be explained by a unitary mechanism—whether peripheral, central, or psychological (Melzack, 1989). This conceptualization proposes that the simultaneous outputs of neural networks in widespread regions of the brain combine to produce the various qualities of human experience—including phantom limb experience.

Sherman and Arena (1992) have also argued that phantom limb pain is not a unitary syndrome, but a symptom class, with each class subserved by different etiologic mechanisms. For example, one class of phantom limb pain, which is characterized by a cramping quality, is associated with electromyographic (EMG) spike activity in muscles of the stump whereas burning phantom limb pain shows no such association (R. A. Sherman & Arena, 1992). Katz and Melzack (1990) have identified a class of phantom limb pain that resembles in quality and location a pain experienced in the limb before amputation. Although the precise physiological mechanisms that underlie these somatosensory pain memories are unknown, the presence of preamputation pain clearly is a necessary condition for these phantom pains to develop. Another class of phantom limb pain may come about through involvement of the sympathetic nervous system. The interested reader is referred to a more detailed review of the role of the sympathetic nervous system in phantom limb pain (Katz, 1996).

Evidence That the Sympathetic Nervous System Is Involved in Phantom Limb Pain

Evidence of sympathetic involvement among amputees with phantom limb pain comes from studies that pharmacologically block (Livingston, 1938, 1943) or surgically interrupt (Bailey & Moersch, 1941; Kallio, 1950) the sympathetic supply to the involved limb producing at least temporary alleviation of pain. Long-term relief of phantom limb pain has been reported with propranolol, a beta-adrenergic blocking agent, although these reports are uncontrolled and unblinded (Ahmad, 1984; Marsland, Weekes, Atkinson, & Leong, 1982; Oille, 1970). An open trial of propranolol in six (nonamputee) patients with pain from peripheral nerve injuries showed very little benefit (Scadding, Wall, Wynn Parry, & Brooks, 1982). Electrical or mechanical stimulation of the lumbar sympathetic chain produces intense pain referred to the phantom limb (Echlin, 1949; Noordenbos, 1959), whereas sensations are referred to the abdomen or flank in pain patients without amputation (Noordenbos, 1959).

Regional sympathetic hyperactivity has also been hypothesized to contribute to the development of phantom limb pain through excessive vasoconstriction and sweating at the stump and surrounding regions (Livingston, 1943). The condition may spread centrally from the stump to involve the phantom limb. Hyperalgesia (heightened pain) and allodynia (pain arising from gentle touch) may be referred to the phantom limb upon stimulation of the stump whether or not the stump is painful or shows signs of trophic or vascular changes (Doupe, Cullen, & Chance, 1944; Livingston, 1938). The characteristic qualities of superficial burning pain and deep aching pain may provide additional evidence of sympathetic nervous system involvement (Doupe et al., 1944). However, just as some sympathetically maintained pains occur in the absence of regional sympathetic abnormalities (Campbell, Meyer, Davis, & Raja, 1992), not all patients with phantom limb pain due to sympathetic nervous system involvement would be expected to show signs of abnormal sympathetic nervous system activity at the stump (e.g., trophic changes, abnormal sympathetic reflexes and sweating, alterations in stump blood flow). This possibility suggests that the abnormality associated with sympathetically maintained pains of this type does not reside in the sympathetic nervous system but in the afferent supply of the involved extremity (Schott, 1993; Treede, Davis, Campbell, & Raja, 1992). The absence of signs of sympathetic nervous system abnormality points to the importance of diagnostic sympathetic blocks, the phentolamine test, or regional infusions of guanethidine to ascertain the presence of sympathetically maintained pain.

Even when sympathetic nervous system abnormalities are present, their relationship to pain in the stump and pain in the phantom is not always clear-cut (Sunderland, 1968). For example, Livingston (1938) reported cases of amputees with phantom limb pain who also showed abnormalities in sweating and large temperature differences between the stump and contralateral intact limb but who did not complain of stump pain. Local anesthetic infiltration into the sympathetic ganglia was followed by relief of phantom limb pain, a sense of warmth and relaxation in the phantom, and a reversal of the vasomotor, sudomotor, and trophic changes at the stump—all of which often extended well beyond the duration of action of the local anesthetic. Despite the correlation between the restoration of normal sympathetic functioning and the relief of phantom limb pain, it remains unclear whether the sympathetic abnormalities were responsible for the pain or whether both were caused by a common third factor (e.g., reduced sympathetic transmitter release).

Nyström and Hagbarth (1981) carried out microneurographic recordings of activity from skin and muscle nerve fascicles in two amputees with phantom limb pain. One patient had sustained a below-knee amputation and suffered from intense cramping pain referred to the phantom foot. Recordings from muscle nerve fascicles in the peroneal nerve showed that although bursts of activity in sympathetic fibers were accentuated by the Valsalva maneuver, the phantom pain remained unchanged, suggesting that the pain was not dependent on sympathetic activity. The second patient had undergone amputation of his left hand at the wrist secondary to extensive lacerations following an agricultural accident. Microneurographic recordings were taken from a skin nerve fascicle in the left median nerve at the wrist. In both patients, tapping the neuroma at the stump evoked marked neural activity, afterdischarge, and an intensification of the phantom limb pain. Interestingly, although local anesthetic infiltration into the tissue of the stump surrounding the neuroma abolished (or reduced) the tap-induced increase in neural activity and phantom limb pain, in neither patient was the spontaneous or background neural activity and phantom limb pain changed. In the light of recent work by Devor and colleagues (Devor, 1994; Devor, Jänig, & Michaelis, 1994), the ongoing neural activity that persisted after lidocaine infiltration may well have originated in the dorsal root ganglion and propagated antidromically to reach the recording electrode in the stump (Devor, 1994).

Further evidence of a possible connection between the sympathetic nervous system and pain after amputation comes from a single-blind study (Chabal, Jacobson, Russell, & Burchiel, 1992) of nine amputees with stump pain ($n = 5$) and concomitant phantom limb pain ($n = 3$) who received successive perineuromal injections of normal saline (0.5 ml), epinephrine (5 µg in 0.5 ml normal saline), and lidocaine (1 ml 1%). Within 1–2 seconds of injection of epinephrine all patients reported an increase in the intensity of local stump pain, although only one of the three patients noted an increase in phantom limb pain.

The quality of the pain following injection of epinephrine was described as "poorly localized shooting or electric shocklike" whereas the area of discomfort increased from baseline. Four patients remarked that the limb was "on fire." Lidocaine injection significantly decreased but did not abolish the pain. Five patients who also received a control injection of subcutaneous epinephrine (5 μg in 0.5 ml normal saline) in a region distant from the neuroma reported a localized, minor stinging of approximately 1–2 seconds in duration that was described as distinctly different from the pain experienced in response to perineuromal injection of epinephrine.

Sympathetic Nervous System Activity at the Stump Correlates With Phantom Limb Pain

Despite frequent assertions that the sympathetic nervous system is involved in the production and maintenance of phantom limb pain, surprisingly few studies have actually examined peripheral sympathetic nervous system activity at the stump and contralateral limb. Sliosberg (1948) studied 141 amputees and found that the stump was cooler than the intact limb in 94 patients, but he did not relate the temperature difference to the presence or absence of phantom limb pain. Kristen, Lukeschitsch, Plattner, Sigmund, and Resch (1984) reported that a "patchy asymmetrical temperature" distribution of stump thermograms was significantly more frequent among stump pain sufferers than in patients who were free from stump pain, but thermograms were no different for patients with or without phantom limb pain.

In contrast, R. A. Sherman and colleagues (R. A. Sherman, 1984; R. A. Sherman & Bruno, 1987) observed a negative correlation between temperature at the stump and the presence of burning, tingling, or throbbing phantom limb and stump pain, indicating that reduced blood flow to the stump is associated with increased levels of pain. Repeated measurements of the same patients on different occasions revealed that lower temperatures at the stump relative to the contralateral limb were associated with greater intensities of phantom limb and stump pain, suggesting that the reduced blood flow was in some way causally tied to the pain. However, in the majority of cases, the relationship between phantom pain and limb temperature was confounded by coexisting stump pain, so that it is not possible to unambiguously attribute the presence of phantom limb pain to altered blood flow at the stump.

Katz (1992) followed up this line of inquiry and compared skin conductance and surface skin temperature of the stump and contralateral limb in amputees reporting phantom limb pain (Group PLP), nonpainful phantom limb sensations (Group PLS), or no phantom limb at all (Group No PL). The results showed that although mean skin temperature was lower at the stump than the contralateral limb in all groups, the difference was significant for Groups PLP and PLS, but not Group No PL. Stump-intact limb temperature differences in excess of −1°C were associated with the presence of a phantom limb in the absence of concomitant stump pain.

These results suggest that the presence of a phantom limb, whether painful or painless, is related to the sympathetic-efferent outflow of cutaneous vasoconstrictor fibers in the stump and stump neuromas. The related finding that stump skin conductance responses over time correlated significantly with the intensity of phantom limb paresthesias, but not other qualities of sensation, supports the hypothesis (outlined later) of a sympathetic-efferent somatic-afferent mechanism involving both sudomotor and vasoconstrictor fibers. The most parsimonious explanation of these findings is that the paresthetic or dysesthetic component of the phantom limb may be triggered by sympathetic-efferent activity.

Psychophysical Correlates of Phantom Limb Paresthesias

Although a normal phantom occurs whenever nerve impulses from the periphery are blocked or otherwise removed (Wall, 1981), it is also true that direct stimulation of the amputation stump frequently exaggerates the tingling or paresthetic quality of sensation typical of the painless phantom limb (Carlen, Wall, Nadvorna, & Steinbach, 1978). Careful questioning of amputees reveals that the nonpainful phantom limb is not perceived as a static phenomenon. The paresthetic quality of sensation, which defines the phantom limb percept, is in a constant state of flux, with changes occurring in intensity, body part, or both. For example, Katz et al. (1989) reported on a subject whose phantom sensations consisted of a "numbness" that defined a region including the lateral three toes. Within this circumscribed area, he experienced rapid "waves of numbness" that increased and decreased the intensity of the involved phantom parts.

One mechanism that has been proposed to account for the paresthetic component of the phantom limb is a cycle of sympathetic-efferent somatic-afferent activity (Katz, 1992; Katz, France, & Melzack, 1989). As shown in Fig. 19.1, stump skin conductance levels correlate significantly over time with the intensity of phantom limb paresthesias. It is hypothesized that changes in the intensity of phantom limb paresthesias reflect the joint activity of cholinergic (sudomotor) and noradrenergic (vasomotor) postganglionic sympathetic fibers on primary afferents located in the stump and stump neuromas (Fig. 19.2). Release of acetylcholine and norepinephrine from postganglionic sympathetic fibers produces transient vasoconstriction and heightened skin conductance responses. As well, neurotransmitter release onto apposing peripheral fibers trapped in stump neuromas increases primary afferent discharge. This information is transmitted rostrally where it gives rise to referred phantom sensations upon

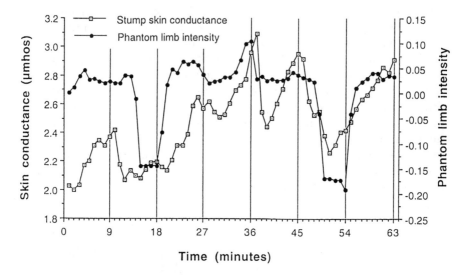

FIG. 19.1.   A minute-by-minute plot of the relationship between stump skin conductance and the intensity of nonpainful phantom limb paresthesias for a subject with an amputation above the knee. Skin conductance was continuously measured at the stump over a 63-minute period while the subject monitored the intensity of the phantom limb by turning a dial. Phantom limb intensity ratings have been transformed so that a value of 0.0 represents the intensity at the start of the session and deviations from zero correspond to increases and decreases in phantom limb intensity. Each data point represents a mean of 30 values consecutively sampled at 2-second intervals. Note that changes in the intensity of paresthesias (described by the subject as increases and decreases in "numb" sensations referred to the phantom toes) occur in concert with changes in stump skin conductance. From Katz, France, and Melzack, 1989. Copyright 1989 by Elsevier Press. Adapted with permission.

reaching central structures subserving the amputated parts of the limb. The moment-to-moment fluctuations in the intensity of phantom limb paresthesias reported by many amputees may, in part, reflect a cycle of sympathetic-efferent somatic-afferent activity. Increases in the intensity of phantom limb paresthesias would follow bursts of sympathetic activity and decreases would correspond to periods of relative sympathetic inactivity (Katz, 1992; Katz et al., 1989). If central sensitization has also developed either through prior injury, trauma during amputation, or peripheral inflammation, or, if the sympathetic-sensory coupling involves nociceptors (Roberts, 1986) the sensation may be one of dysesthesia. Direct support for this hypothesis would require that changes in the intensity of phantom limb paresthesias (or dysesthesias) be correlated with microneurographic recordings from postganglionic sympathetic and primary afferent fibers in

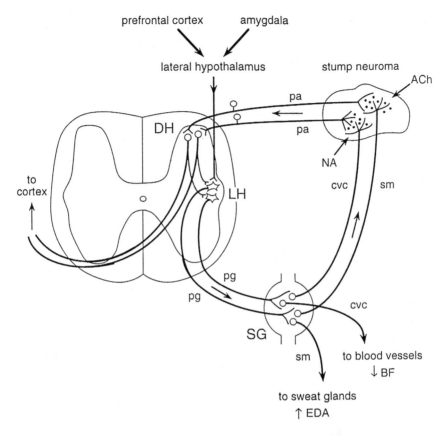

FIG. 19.2. Schematic diagram illustrating a mechanism of sympathetically generated phantom limb paresthesias. Spontaneous activity or excitatory inputs descending from cortex (e.g., due to the perception of a salient event, loud noise, thought, feeling, etc.) increase the discharge rate of preganglionic (pg) sympathetic neurons with cell bodies in the lateral horn (LH) of the spinal cord and terminals in the sympathetic ganglion (SG). These neurons excite postganglionic noradrenergic (NA) cutaneous vasoconstrictor (cvc) and cholinergic (ACh) sudomotor (sm) fibers that impinge on effector organs (vascular smooth muscle and sweat glands) in the stump and on sprouts from large-diameter primary afferent (pa) fibers that have been trapped in a neuroma. The release of ACh and NA on effector organs results in increased electrodermal activity (EDA) and decreased blood flow (BF) to the stump. Release of these chemicals in the neuroma activates primary afferents that project to spinal cord dorsal horn (DH) cells subserving the amputated parts of the limb. These neurons, in turn, feed back to the preganglionic sympathetic neurons and project rostrally where the impulses contribute to the perception of phantom limb paresthesias. If DH cells have been sensitized due to injury, or nociceptive primary afferents are activated, then the perception may be dysesthetic.

amputation stump neuromas. In the following section, this mechanism is elaborated to explain how psychological and emotional processes might alter phantom limb sensations through their actions on the sympathetic nervous system.

Treatment and Treatment Implications

The majority of studies of phantom limb pain lack the rigorous control conditions and adequate sample sizes to conclude with certainty that specific treatments are more effective than no treatment or placebo treatment. There is evidence of an adrenergic sympathetic-sensory coupling mechanism underlying stump pain and possibly phantom limb pain as well (Chabal et al., 1992). The results of early studies showing that local anesthetic infiltration into the sympathetic chain (Livingston, 1938, 1943) and sympathectomy (Bailey & Moersch, 1941; Kallio, 1950) at least temporarily relieve phantom limb pain also suggest that sympathetic ganglion blocks or surgical sympathectomies are effective because they block the release of norepinephrine from the peripheral sympathetic terminals.

It should be noted, however, that pain relief in response to a local anesthetic sympathetic block may be due to factors other than sympathetic blockade. Diffusion of the agent to the dorsal roots resulting in small-fiber block or a systemic action of the local anesthetic are limitations of diagnostic sympathetic blocks that reduce the specificity of the test (Raja, 1993). The lack of permanency of sympathectomy for phantom limb pain (Bailey & Moersch, 1941; Kallio, 1950) may be due to a variety of factors including inadequacy of diagnosis, extent of sympathectomy, surgical skill, and confusion about anatomy (Campbell, Raja, Selig, Belzberg, & Meyer, 1994). The finding that beta-adrenergic receptor blockade does not seem to be effective in relieving phantom limb pain (Scadding et al., 1982) is consistent with the negative results of propranolol for treatment of sympathetically maintained pain in nonamputees (Campbell, Raja, & Meyer, 1993).

Phantom limb pain and stump pain respond well to epidural or spinal administration of local anesthetics or opioids (Jacobson & Chabal, 1989; Jacobson, Chabal, & Brody, 1989; Jacobson, Chabal, Brody, Mariano, & Chaney, 1990). Although the relevant assessments to determine the presence of sympathetically maintained pain were not established in these studies, the possibility remains that the continuous sympathetic blockade achieved by epidural infusions of local anesthetic agents may prove effective in the management of patients with sympathetically maintained pain (Campbell et al., 1994). To date, neither the phentolamine test (Raja, Treede, Davis, & Campbell, 1991), nor regional infusions of guanethidine have been tried for phantom limb pain. Raja (1993) has published guidelines for evaluating patients suspected of having sympathetically maintained pain.

PSYCHOLOGICAL AND EMOTIONAL
CONTRIBUTIONS TO PHANTOM LIMB EXPERIENCE

It is not surprising that amputees suffering with phantom limb pain exhibit higher than normal levels of psychological and emotional distress. Depression (Caplan & Hackett, 1963; Lindesay, 1985; R. A. Sherman, C. J. Sherman, & Bruno, 1987; Shukla, Sahu, Tripathi, & Gupta, 1982), anxiety (Parkes, 1973; Shukla et al., 1982), and other forms of psychopathology are common (Morgenstern, 1970; Parkes, 1973; Shukla et al., 1982; Steigerwald, Brass, & Krainick, 1981). Moreover, amputees with severe phantom limb pain score higher on psychological inventories measuring depression (Lindesay, 1985) and neuroticism (Morgenstern, 1970) than do amputees who have little or no pain. However, amputees with phantom limb pain report higher levels of overall disability than do patients with musculoskeletal pain (Marshall, Helmes, & Deathe, 1992).

The co-occurrence of phantom limb pain and psychological disturbance has led to three conclusions: (a) Pain is a symptom of a psychological disorder (Parkes, 1973; Szasz, 1975), (b) psychological disturbance is a consequence of pain (R. A. Sherman & Bruno, 1987), or (c) the two are causally unrelated (Caplan & Hackett, 1963). At present, the consensus is that there is no difference in the prevalence rates of pain of psychological origin among amputees and the general population. There is no evidence to suggest that surgical amputation predisposes an individual to develop pain of psychological origin, nor that patients who undergo amputation are at greater risk for developing such pain. However, a prospective study has yet to be conducted in which preoperative measures of psychological and emotional functioning are obtained sufficiently prior to amputation so as to avoid the confounding effects of preamputation pain and hospitalization.

Psychodynamic Explanations

Psychodynamic explanations of phantom limb phenomena have been advanced as evidence of the amputee's difficulty in adapting to the mutilated state (Frazier & Kolb, 1970; Parkes, 1973; Parkes & Napier, 1975; Szasz, 1975). Denial (of the loss or the associated affect) and repression are the most common defense mechanisms proposed to explain the presence of a painless phantom (Szasz, 1975), painful phantom (Parkes, 1973; Parkes & Napier, 1975; Stengel, 1965; Szasz, 1975), and various alterations in the form of the phantom limb (Abramson & Feibel, 1981; Weiss, 1958).

Though often elegantly formulated, psychodynamic explanations are not consistent with the accumulation of physiological and psychological data. For example, many amputees become profoundly depressed after surgery, yet phantom pain and other sensations persist. The co-occurrence of depression and pain is inconsistent with the role of denial because the intense negative affect implies awareness, if not acceptance, of the loss (Caplan & Hackett, 1963). In fact, for many amputees, the affect associated with the loss is so overwhelming that it cannot be contained and seems to "spill over" into the phantom thereby increasing the intensity of paresthesias (Simmel, 1959).

There are other inconsistencies between psychodynamic theory and empirical evidence. Apparently healthy individuals who, by all objective measures, have adjusted to the amputation continue to report the presence of a phantom years after amputation (Simmel, 1959). Phantoms that occur after injury to the central nervous system (CNS) (e.g., when sensory and motor nerve roots are torn from the spinal cord or the spinal cord is transected) are similar to amputation phantoms in quality of sensation even though the real limb(s) is still present but totally anesthetic and paralyzed. One would not expect denial of the loss of function to produce a phantom defined by paresthesias (Weinstein, 1962). Phantoms do not develop if the process of sensory loss is gradual, as in leprosy (Price, 1976), yet there should be as great a need for denial in these cases. Finally, procedures that temporarily block the supply of afferent impulses from reaching the CNS (e.g., anesthetic nerve blocks, blood pressure cuff occlusion) reliably result in the perception of a phantom limb that persists until the flow of afferent input has been restored (Melzack & Bromage, 1973; Wall, 1981). Under these circumstances, it is difficult to see the need of a phantom limb to fulfill the putative ego-protective function of defending the individual from a loss.

Although denial is more commonly associated with diseases that have no visual evidence of infirmity (Caplan & Hackett, 1963), the foregoing does not imply that denial of the loss, affect, illness, or future implications plays no part in the overall adaptation to amputation (Rosen, 1950). Patients may demonstrate their denial of the importance of these realities in a variety of ways (Bradway, Malone, Racy, Leal, & Poole, 1984; Turgay & Sonuvar, 1983), but these do not include having a phantom. For the vast majority of amputees, the presence of a phantom limb—painful or painless—is not a symptom of a psychological disorder.

Characterological Disturbances

In addition to the role of specific defense mechanisms in the genesis of phantom limb pain, it is postulated that phantom limb pain may be psychologically determined by characterological disturbances such as "compulsive self-reliance" and "rigidity" (Parkes, 1973). With the exception of a recent review (R. A. Sherman et al., 1987), the idea that patients with persisting phantom limb pain are rigid and exhibit compulsively self-reliant personality characteristics has been uncritically accepted by researchers and clinicians working in the field of phantom limb pain (Dawson & Arnold, 1981; Dernham, 1986; Lundberg & Guggenheim, 1986; Shukla et al., 1982) despite the absence of empirical evidence to support this view.

The association between the presence of pain and psychological distress (e.g., depression and anxiety) or particular personality traits or styles (e.g., rigidity and compulsive self-reliance) may be influenced by biased sampling procedures so that the characteristics of a select group of patients (e.g., those referred to a pain center) come to define the population at large (Merskey, 1989; R. A. Sherman et al., 1987). Sherman et al. suggested that the low success rate of most treatments for phantom limb pain serves as a deterrent to all but the most persistent or self-reliant individuals. Long after less assertive patients have given up actively seeking help, these sufferers of phantom limb pain continue to search for relief despite repeated failures. According to Sherman et al., this self-selection bias explains the tendency for individuals with "compulsively self-reliant" personality characteristics *and* phantom limb pain to dominate the clinical picture of the typical patient with phantom limb pain.

Recent studies indicate that among an unselected sample of amputees, those with phantom limb pain, painless phantom limb sensations, or no phantom limb at all cannot be distinguished by their scores on personality, depression, or anxiety inventories (Katz & Melzack, 1990, 1991). Moreover, there are no significant intergroup differences in scores on a questionnaire designed to measure psychological "rigidity" as defined by a tendency to persist in behaviors that were effective at one time, or in a particular situation, but no longer are adequate to accomplish current goals (Katz & Melzack, 1990).

Coping With Phantom Limb Pain

Coping with chronic pain may be defined as the thoughts and actions people engage in in their efforts to manage pain on a daily basis (Katz, Ritvo, Irvine, & Jackson, 1996). These diverse efforts include interventions as global as cognitive-behavior therapy and other self-management programs developed to help patients cope with a multitude of problems associated with pain to specific strategies designed to manage the sensory intensity of a discrete episode of pain. In addition to the burden of pain, patients must contend with many secondary lifestyle changes that inevitably arise when pain becomes chronic. Among these downstream effects are loss of employment and income, mood disturbances such as depression and anxiety, changes in the marital relationship and family dynamics, and a reduction in social and leisure activities (Hitchcock, Ferrell, & McCaffery, 1994).

The literature on phantom limb pain spans more than 100 years, yet we know very little about the coping efforts and outcomes of amputees with phantom limb pain. To date, only a single study has evaluated use of coping strategies in patients with phantom limb pain (Hill, 1993). The Coping Strategies Questionnaire (CSQ; Rosenstiel & Keefe, 1983) was administered to 60 male, upper- or lower-extremity amputees. A principal components analysis yielded three factors (cognitive control, helplessness, and pain denial) accounting for 68% of the variance. The helplessness factor, made up of three subscales (increasing activity level, praying or hoping, and catastrophizing) of the CSQ accounted for approximately 20% of the variance in pain report and psychological distress.

These results are consistent with what is known about pain coping in other chronic pain populations, namely, patients who catastrophize fare worse than those who do not (M. P. Jensen, Turner, Romano, & Karoly, 1991). Factor analytic or principal component techniques often yield a factor that invariably includes the negative-thinking characteristic of catastrophizing (e.g., helplessness, pain control and rational thinking, self-control and rational thinking). In general, these factors tend to be strongly correlated with depression, measures of physical impairment, and poor psychosocial adjustment.

For example, a reduction in catastrophizing was associated with less pain and improved psychosocial functioning following either cognitive-behavioral or operant behavioral therapy for low back pain (Turner & Clancy, 1986). In another study (Flor, Behle, & Birbaumer, 1993), the degree of catastrophizing was reduced significantly from pre- to posttreatment among patients who improved but not among patients who did not. In contrast, improvement was not accompanied by a strengthening of adaptive self-statements and beliefs. The association between lower pain and a reduction in the use of catastrophizing but not a strengthening of adaptive self-statements and beliefs suggests that maladaptive cognitions may have a stronger influence on negative outcomes than the utilization of adaptive coping strategies. In other words, it may be more important *not to catastrophize* than to engage in positive self-statements. This is a challenging area for future research and treatment development given the tendency for certain qualities of phantom limb pain to occur episodically and unpredictably (Hill, 1993). These parameters are likely to contribute to a sense of helplessness and lack of personal control.

Primary pain prevention and early detection of individuals at risk for developing chronic pain is of paramount importance. Keefe, Salley, and Lefebvre (1992) advocate use of longitudinal designs in which subjects are identified and assessed in terms of coping strategies prior to the development of chronic pain. Following these individuals over time would clarify the relationship between pain coping strategies and the development of persistent pain. Future research might best accomplish this objective by targeting patient populations, such as amputees, at relatively high risk for developing long-term pain problems.

Psychological and Emotional Processes Influence Phantom Limb Experience

As reviewed previously, the idea that emotional and psychological processes can cause pain traditionally has been tied to the notion of psychopathology. However, it is becoming increasingly clear that under certain circumstances pain may be triggered by these processes in psychologically healthy individuals as well. Although instances of psychologically or emotionally triggered pain and psychopathology may be present in the same amputee, their co-occurrence should not be taken as *prima facie* evidence of a causal link.

It is commonly accepted that anxiety or stress influences pain perception and subsequent behavior (Merskey, 1989). The aggravation or alleviation of pain referred to phantom body parts also may be mediated in part by psychological processes that alter anxiety levels (Kolb, 1954). Phantom breast pain after mastectomy is provoked by emotional distress in 6% of women 3 weeks after surgery and in 29% 1 year later (Krøner, Krebs, Skov, & Jørgensen, 1989). Fifty percent of lower-extremity amputees report that attacks of phantom limb pain are triggered by emotional distress (T. S. Jensen, Krebs, Nielsen, & Rasmussen, 1985) as long as 7 years after amputation (Krebs, T. S. Jensen, Krøner, Nielsen, & Jørgensen, 1985). A combination of progressive relaxation training and EMG biofeedback of stump and forehead muscles produces significant reductions of phantom limb pain and anxiety (R. A. Sherman, 1976) that are sustained for up to 3 years (R. A. Sherman, Gall, & Gormly, 1979). Finally, stress levels and pain intensity ratings sampled over a 180-day observation period correlate significantly for most amputees (Arena, R. H. Sherman, & Bruno, 1990).

There are also examples of psychological or emotional processes precipitating transient but profound alterations in the quality and intensity of phantom limb sensations. These processes include hypnosis (Schilder, 1950), concentration (Morgenstern, 1964; Riddoch, 1941), distraction (Parkes, 1973), relaxation (R. A. Sherman, 1976; R. A. Sherman et al., 1979), fright (Henderson & Smyth, 1948), forceful reminders of the events that led to amputation (Simmel, 1956), the sight of other amputees (Simmel, 1956), and witnessing cruel and violent acts (Pilowsky & Kaufman, 1965; Stengel, 1965). One amputee, interviewed by the present writer, described his reaction to an accident involving his wife by reporting ". . . goose bumps and cold shivering down the phantom [leg]. It went through me. Everything emotional will get you that." Another amputee stated, "It's like everything I feel goes there—the good and the bad."

A Centrally Triggered Sympathetic-Efferent
Somatic-Afferent Mechanism

The material presented earlier indicates that cognitive and affective processes reliably trigger transient pains or sensations referred to the phantom limb. The model schematically represented in Fig. 19.2 outlines a mechanism through which cognitive and affective processes associated with higher cortical and limbic centers may alter phantom limb sensations. The reciprocal connections between cortical, limbic, and lateral hypothalamic structures are well documented (Brodal, 1981; Smith & DeVito, 1984). The lateral hypothalamus is involved in the control and integration of neural activity associated with affectively charged behavior (Brodal, 1981; Melzack & Casey, 1968; Smith & DeVito, 1984) and has direct projections to the lateral horn of the spinal cord. The intensity of phantom limb paresthesias and dysesthesias may thus be modulated by higher brain centers involved in cognitive and affective processes via a multisynaptic network of descending inputs that impinges on preganglionic sympathetic neurons producing diffuse peripheral autonomic discharge and activation of primary afferent fibers located in stump neuromas.

Occasionally, the effects of intense affect (e.g., fright, horror) are experienced diffusely over the entire body as *cutis anserina* associated with pilomotor contraction (i.e., "goose bumps"). Among amputees, however, a more frequent occurrence is that the perception of less salient events and emotions precipitate these sensations throughout only the phantom limb. The tendency for affectively charged and psychologically meaningful experiences to be referred to the phantom limb, but not to other parts of the body, is consistent with two lines of evidence suggesting that the threshold for impulse generation is lower both in regenerating primary afferents in the stump and in deafferented central cells subserving the phantom limb than it is in the intact nervous system.

First, regenerating sprouts, which are trapped in a neuroma, are exceedingly sensitive to the postganglionic sympathetic neurotransmitters noradrenaline (Wall & Gutnick, 1974) and acetylcholine (Diamond, 1959), and they discharge rapidly when these substances are present. In contrast, intact peripheral fibers do not show this chemosensitivity, and thus have a higher threshold compared with regenerating sprouts. Second, the loss of afferent nerve impulses (deafferentation) resulting from amputation produces a disinhibition of cells in the dorsal horn and more rostral sensory structures giving rise to the perception of a phantom limb (Melzack & Loeser, 1978; Wall, 1981). This consequence of deafferentation implies that the threshold for detecting sympathetically triggered afferent impulses arising from stump neuromas should be lower than at other, intact body sites because stump impulses would be subject to less inhibition upon reaching the spinal cord. This fits well with the observation that the threshold for detecting sensations in the phantom limb during stimulation of the stump is lower than at the site of stimulation itself (Carlen et al., 1978).

Another possibility is that amputation leads to increased expression of alpha-1 adrenergic receptors located on mechanoreceptors or nociceptors (Campbell et al., 1992) in stump neuromas. This hypothesis would explain the perception of phantom limb paresthesias or dyesthesias in the absence of regional sympathetic hyperactivity. Taken together, these observations may explain the puzzling finding that only after amputation does the (phantom) limb become the site of affectively or cognitively triggered sensations.

The suggestion that the perception of phantom limb sensations may reflect the activity of postganglionic sympathetic fibers on stump primary afferents is obviously not meant to imply that paresthesias arise only from a peripheral source. Blocking the afferent supply to a body region is sufficient to produce the experience of a painless phantom defined by paresthesias (Melzack & Bromage, 1973; Wall, 1981) and electrical stimulation of the medial lemniscal pathway gives rise to the sensation of paresthesias referred to the territory subserved by the cells being stimulated (Tasker, Organ, & Hawrylyshyn, 1982). Moreover, it is likely that through repeated activation, neural circuitry is strengthened among brain regions subserving cognitive, affective, and sensory processes so that phantom limb sensations and pain may be triggered by thoughts and feelings in the absence of primary afferent feedback from peripheral structures (LeDoux, 1989; Leventhal, 1982).

Implications for Treatment of Phantom Limb Pain

Given that cognitive and affective processes may trigger or exacerbate phantom limb pain, it is of the utmost importance that patients be prepared prior to amputation for the presence of a phantom limb. Patient education programs and treatment of stress prior to and after amputation have become standard practice (Butler, Turkal, & Seidl, 1992; McGrath & Hillier, 1992; R. A. Sherman, 1989). Patients who are ill prepared psychologically for amputation suffer needlessly with phantom limb pain and concern about their sanity (Solomon & Schmidt, 1978).

It is noteworthy that mental stress and anxiety not only provoke transient increases in the intensity of phantom limb sensations and pain (Arena et al., 1990; R. A. Sherman, 1976; R. A. Sherman et al., 1979), but they also induce reflex-bursting activity in cutaneous sudomotor and vasomotor sympathetic fibers (Delius, Hagbarth, Hongell, & Wallin, 1972; Hagbarth, Hallin, Hongell, Torebjörk, & Wallin, 1972). Moreover, distraction or attention diversion (and intense concentration) that reduces phantom limb pain (Morgenstern, 1964; Parkes, 1973) also diminishes peripheral sympathetic nervous system activity (Hagbarth et al., 1972). These findings provide support for the model shown in Fig. 19.2 and suggest that relaxation training and other cognitive strategies directed at anxiety reduction and increasing self-control may be effective in reducing phantom limb pain in certain amputees. To date controlled studies of this nature have not been carried out.

PAIN MEMORIES IN PHANTOM LIMBS

A striking property of phantom limb pain is the presence of a pain that existed in a limb prior to its amputation (Melzack, 1971). This class of phantom limb pain is characterized by the persistence or recurrence of a previous pain, has the same qualities of sensation, and is experienced in the same region of the limb as the preamputation pain (Katz & Melzack, 1990). Case studies of amputees have revealed pain "memories" of painful diabetic foot ulcers, bedsores, gangrene, corns, blisters, ingrown toenails, cuts and deep tissue injuries, and damage to joints and bony structures. As well, the phantom limb may assume the same painful posture as that of the real limb prior to amputation, especially if the arm or leg had been immobilized for a prolonged period.

The proportion of amputees who report similar pain before and after amputation may be as high as 79% (Katz & Melzack, 1990). Pain memories in phantom limbs appear to be less common when there has been a discontinuity, or a pain-free interval, between the experience of pain and amputation. This is consistent with the observation that relief of phantom limb pain by continuous epidural blockade for 3 days before amputation decreases the incidence of phantom limb pain 6 months later (Bach, Noreng, & Tjéllden, 1988). Furthermore, compared with pain that is temporally noncontiguous with amputation, pain experienced at or near the time of amputation has a higher probability of persisting into the phantom limb (T. S. Jensen et al., 1985; Katz & Melzack, 1990).

Pain also persists in patients with deafferentation that does not involve amputation. In these conditions, the involved body part is still present but it is devoid of sensibility due to an interruption in the supply of sensory (afferent) information (i.e., deafferentation). Brachial plexus avulsions, in which the sensory nerve roots supplying the arm and hand are torn from the spinal cord, often produce pain that is felt in the deafferented and anesthetic region (T. S. Jensen & Rasmussen, 1994; Reisner, 1981). Similarly, patients with spinal cord injuries (Berger & Gerstenbrand, 1981; Conomy, 1973) may complain of pain referred to body parts below the level of the transection. For example, Nathan (1962) described a patient who continued to feel the pain of an ingrown toenail after a complete spinal cord break. As well, patients undergoing spinal anesthesia (Van Bogaert, 1934; Wallgren, 1954) and those with injuries of the brachial plexus or spinal cord sometimes report that a limb is in the same uncomfortable, often painful, posture it was in prior to the injury of block. These postural phantom sensations do not usually persist beyond several days and in most cases are at least temporarily reversed by competing visual inputs that reveal a dissociation between the real and felt limb(s).

Painful and nonpainful sensations also persist or recur after surgical removal or deafferentation of body structures other than the limbs, such as breasts (Krøner et al., 1989), teeth (Marbach, 1978; Sicuteri, Nicolodi, Fusco, & Orlando, 1991), and internal and special sense organs. Ulcer pain has been reported to persist after subtotal gastrectomy with removal of the ulcer (Gloyne, 1954). Patients have reported labor pain and menstrual cramps after total hysterectomy (Dorpat, 1971), rectal pain (Boas, Schug, & Acland, 1993) and hemorrhoids (Oveson, Krøner, Ørnsholt, & Bach, 1991) after removal of the rectum and anus, the burning pain of cystitis after complete removal of the bladder (Brena & Sammons, 1979), and the pain of a severely ulcerated cornea after enucleation of an eye (Minski, 1943).

Taken together, these case reports and studies of amputees reveal that pain memories are not merely images or cognitive recollections; they are direct experiences of pain that resemble an earlier pain in location and quality. They are perceptually complex experiences that may even involve information from multiple sensory modalities including visual, olfactory, tactile, and motor components that had accompanied the original experience. The precise details of the experiences of pain involve localization, discrimination, affect, and evaluation—that is, all the dimensions of perceptual experience—and these properties are a function of integrated brain activity. It is likely that the outputs of sensitized spinal cells activate the neural structures in the brain that subserve memories of earlier events.

Separate Somatosensory and Cognitive Memory Components Underlie Pain Memories

A closer examination of the phenomenon suggests that the experience of a pain memory reflects the joint activity of two separate memory subsystems with properties and functions specialized for processing somatosensory and cognitive (declarative) information respectively. The somatosensory memory component consists of the same, or very similar, neural circuitry that was activated by the peripheral input prior to amputation. It is a higher order functional unit that codes the temporal and spatial patterning of nerve impulses specifying the body part, quality of sensation, and intensity of the somatosensory experience.

The cognitive memory component contains declarative information related to when and in what context the preamputation pain occurred as well as *meta*-information *about* the body part, quality of sensation, and intensity of the preamputation experience. The declarative information contained in the cognitive component provides the unique, personal meaning associated with the somatosensory component and provides a basis for the identifying label and response (e.g., "my pain," a corn, diabetic ulcer, etc.). The determination that a current sensory impression has occurred before involves a process of recognition: One must know, or have access to knowledge about, what one has (and therefore has not) previously experienced in order to state whether two experiences separated in time are the same or different.

Evidence of a Double Dissociation Between Somatosensory and Cognitive Components

There is evidence that it is possible to demonstrate a double dissociation of these two memory components. Evidence of the cognitive component in the absence of the somatosensory component is common and occurs whenever amputees recall details about a preamputation pain (e.g., its duration, quality of sensation, location, intensity) without also reexperiencing the somatosensory qualities of that pain (Katz & Melzack, 1990). Dissociation of the opposite kind is not as common and is more difficult to demonstrate, because without the knowledge (i.e., contents of the cognitive memory component) of what one has felt in the past, the reactivation of the somatosensory qualities of a past pain would be perceived as novel and therefore would not be recognized as having occurred before. Moreover, it is rare to find a situation in which (a) an amputee demonstrates amnesia or forgetting (of the contents of the cognitive memory component) and (b) an independent source had verified the nature of the pain at the time of injury before amputation.

Nevertheless, there are several lines of evidence supporting dissociation of this kind, both animal (Katz, Vaccarino, Coderre, & Melzack, 1991) and human (Lacroix, Melzack, Smith, & Mitchell, 1992). Lacroix et al. reported the case of a 16-year-old girl who was born with a congenital deformity of the right foot, which was amputated when she was just 6 years old. At the time of the interview, 10 years after amputation, the patient reported a flat phantom foot that was stuck in a forward position. This description corresponded to information subsequently obtained from her medical records verifying a right flatfoot that was locked in an equinovalgus position and incapable of movement. Interestingly, the patient was not aware that her foot had been deformed as a child, for she mistakenly described her foot as she "remembered" it prior to amputation as being normal and freely mobile. This case report demonstrates the remarkable capacity of the CNS to retain, for years after amputation, a complete representation of the cut-off part, including its somatosensory qualities, proprioceptive sensibility, and associated motor program. Moreover, the case demonstrates that the neural circuitry underlying the somatosensory component is capable of being activated and of influencing conscious awareness independent of the cognitive component.

Although separate representations of the somatosensory and cognitive components are formed during repeated occurrences of the preamputation pain, such frequent and temporally contiguous activity would result in a tendency for these representations to occur more often together than alone once the limb has been removed. There is evidence that the two memory systems may be reciprocally connected so that activation of either memory component can lead to activation of the other. The presence of the somatosensory component is sufficient to activate the contents of the cognitive component as implied by the process of recognition involved when a patient identifies the somatosensory qualities of the experience as having occurred before. The possibility also exists that the link is bidirectional. One subject in the study by Katz and Melzack (1990) reported that he could reproduce at will the sensation of the "hole" from a gangrenous ulcer he had on the medial aspect of his foot prior to amputation, but if he did not concentrate on it, the somatosensory component remained out of his awareness. It is important to note, however, that activation of the representation underlying the cognitive component is not to be equated with the conscious awareness of thoughts about the past pain, but when such thoughts occur, excitation of the corresponding neural assemblies must have been involved.

Implications of Separate Memory Components

There are important implications associated with the suggestion that separate somatosensory and cognitive memory systems underlie pain that persists after amputation. For one, conscious awareness of the contents of the cognitive memory component is not necessary for the *reactivation* of the somatosensory component (although it may facilitate the process when present). Second, it is clear that the conscious experience of pain is not a necessary condition for the *formation* of the somatosensory memory component. That is, the formation of the somatosensory component can occur even when there is no conscious awareness of pain at the time of injury or trauma (Katz et al., 1991, 1992, 1994) or when the cognitive component is not accessible through introspection (Lacroix et al., 1992).

These findings raise the possibility that just as brief, intense pain experienced in a limb shortly before its amputation persists as phantom limb pain memory (Katz & Melzack, 1990), the effects of the primary afferent "injury discharge" on spinal cord dorsal horn neurons produced by surgical incision (and subsequent cutting of muscle, nerve, and bone) may also produce lasting changes that later contribute to postoperative pain. This implies that both somatosensory and cognitive systems must be blocked in order to interfere with the formation of a pain memory arising from the surgical procedure (Fig. 19.3).

Patients who have sustained traumatic amputation either by accident, combat-related injury, or emergency surgical procedures carried out without anesthetics or analgesics (e.g., in war-ravaged parts of the world) are at highest risk for developing postamputation problems (Fig. 19.3a). Traumatic amputation would be expected to result in the formation of both the somatosensory and cognitive memory components. The expected outcome would include heightened stump pain (stump hyperalgesia), heightened phantom limb pain intensity, recognition of the somatosensory qualities of the pain, and a posttraumatic stress disorder arising from the traumatic events.

Amputation performed under general anesthesia alone (Fig. 19.3b) would interfere with the formation of the *cognitive* but not the *somatosensory* memory component. However, unlike a pain memory that resembles a long-standing preamputation lesion, the somatosensory qualities of postsurgical pain would not be recognized by a patient whose surgery was performed under a general anesthetic, because the patient would not have had any conscious experience of pain at the time of incision and amputation. Upon awakening from the general anesthetic, the patient's complaints of pain would reflect the persistent central neural memory trace left by the surgical procedure in addition to input from transected fibers in the amputation stump (Wall, 1989). This is hypothesized to result in enhanced postoperative phantom limb pain and heightened pain at the site of the incision (incisional hyperalgesia).

Administration of spinal local anesthesia alone (Fig. 19.3c) would block the formation of the *somatosensory* but not the *cognitive* memory component. The preincisional spinal blockade would prevent the injury barrage from reaching the CNS, resulting in less intense postoperative phantom limb pain and incisional pain. However, in the absence of a general anesthetic, awareness during amputation can produce vivid declarative memories of operating room events that develop into a posttraumatic stress disorder.

Combined use of spinal anesthesia and general anesthesia (Fig. 19.3d) would be expected to interfere with both *somatosensory* and *cognitive* memory systems by blocking the transmission of nociceptive impulses (arising from the cutting of tissue, nerve, and bone) at the level of the spinal cord, and by ensuring that the patient is unconscious during the surgical procedure. This model has yet to be tested in patients undergoing amputation.

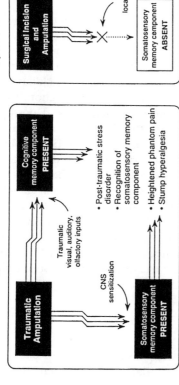

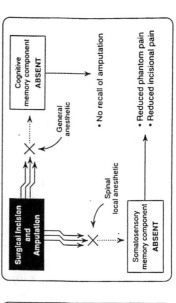

FIG. 19.3. Predicted postoperative pain status and psychological status following traumatic amputation or surgical amputation performed under general anesthesia, spinal local anesthesia, or combined spinal local anesthesia plus general anesthesia (see text for details).

Preemptive Analgesia and Other Preventive Approaches
to Phantom Limb Pain

Preemptive and other preventive approaches have considerable potential
for reducing the incidence and intensity of long-term phantom limb pain,
but well-designed clinical trials are required to establish this with certainty.
Short-term preemptive analgesic effects following major surgery have been
reported for lateral thoracotomy (Katz et al., 1992), lower abdominal surgery
(Katz et al., 1994), and abdominal hysterectomy (Katz, Clairoux et al., 1996;
Richmond, Bromley, & Woolf, 1993), but the majority of these surgical
procedures are not usually associated with long-term pain problems. On the
other hand, long-term reductions in phantom limb pain have been reported
when regional analgesia was used to block noxious inputs before, during,
and/or after limb amputation (Bach et al., 1988; Jahangiri, Bradley,
Jayatunga, & Dark, 1994; Schug, Burrell, Payne, & Tester, 1995), but
methodological problems limit valid interpretation.

The prospective intervention studies (Bach et al., 1988; Jahangiri et al.,
1994; Schug et al., 1995) provide some of the strongest evidence supporting
a link between acute injury and the development of long-term phantom
limb. Epidural anesthesia started before and continuing for the duration
of surgery (Bach et al., 1988) or for several days after amputation (Jahangiri
et al., 1994; Schug et al., 1995) appears to confer the most protection from
long-term pain. By contrast, blockade of late intraoperative and postoperative noxious inputs does not seem to alter the developmental course
of persistent pain (Elizaga, Smith, Sharar, Edwards, & Hansen, 1994; Fisher
& Meller, 1991), probably because the blockade is administered after central sensitization has been established. As noted earlier, a number of methodological problems limit the validity of these studies (e.g., small sample
sizes, nonrandom assignment of patients to treatment, nonblinded treatment and pain assessment, insufficient details about pain assessment).
Discovering the relative contributions to long-term pain of factors such as
preexisting pain, noxious perioperative events, and postoperative pain will
enable us to design multiagent, preemptive treatments aimed specifically
at minimizing the detrimental effects of these factors.

PHANTOM PARALYSIS

Phantom limb movements are reported by approximately 36% of patients
8 days after amputation and by 24% 2 years later (T. S. Jensen, Krebs,
Nielsen, & Rasmussen, 1984). In contrast, we do not know the percentage
of amputees who report that their phantom is "frozen" in a fixed posture,
incapable of voluntary movement. For some amputees, the problem of
"phantom paralysis" is associated with pain (Ramachandran, 1994). For
example, a common report is that the amputee's fingernails are felt to be

digging into the palm of the phantom hand (Mitchell, 1872; Ramachandran, 1994; Ramachandran & Rogers-Ramachandran, 1996). In some cases this may be related to the position of the limb before amputation (i.e., a postural pain memory) (Browder & Gallagher, 1948; Frederiks, 1963; T. S. Jensen & Rasmussen, 1994; Katz & Melzack, 1990; Mitchell, 1872; Riddoch, 1941). In others, the inability to move the phantom limb may develop progressively after amputation (Ramachandran, 1994; Ramachandran & Rogers-Ramachandran, 1996). Until recently, there has been nothing in the way of treatment for this painful problem.

A clever solution has been devised that promises to restore, at least temporarily, a sense of voluntary movement to the paralyzed phantom limb (Ramachandran, 1994; Ramachandran & Rogers-Ramachandran, 1996). The solution is based on the assumption that the brain has "learned" that the phantom is paralyzed. The learning occurs either as a function of past experience with a paralyzed limb before amputation or subsequent to amputation due to the absence of visual feedback from the limb following attempts to move the phantom. The experiments involve a "virtual reality box" that makes use of mirrors to trick the brain into thinking that the phantom is moving. The amputee looks into a mirror at the reflection of his or her contralateral intact hand while it is positioned to coincide spatially with the felt position of the phantom hand. The amputee is then instructed to carry out the same movement with both hands while looking at the phantom (i.e., the reflection of the intact hand). In the majority of cases, the sight of the hand moving determines the ultimate perception, and the amputee feels as if the once paralyzed hand is now moving freely. These findings support the idea that vision dominates over other sensory modalities in determining the phantom limb percept (Katz, 1993). When there is a discrepancy or contradiction between incoming information from different modalities, or when a state of uncertainty exists based on somatosensory input alone, additional information is sought via the visual sense, which usually determines the perceptual experience.

The initial experiments carried out by Ramachandran and colleagues (Ramachandran, 1994; Ramachandran & Rogers-Ramachandran, 1996) suggest that in most cases the initiation of movement in the phantom is also associated with pain relief. From a clinical standpoint, controlled studies are needed to assess the duration of the analgesic effect, the percentage of patients in whom it is effective and the possibility that a permanent effect can be achieved with repeated use of the mirrors.

CONCLUSIONS

The material presented in this chapter indicates that the phantom limb is not perceived as a static entity but as a frequently changing perceptual experience. Phantom limb phenomena range from simple, diffuse sensations of tingling to perceptually complex experiences of pains and lesions that originally were felt in the limb prior to amputation. Although phantom pains and other sensations frequently are triggered by the perception of salient events, thoughts, and feelings, there is no evidence that the painful or painless phantom limb is a symptom of a psychological disorder. The sympathetic nervous system may provide an important link between higher brain centers involved in cognitive and affective processes and phantom limb sensations through its peripheral actions on primary afferents located in stump neuromas. Pharmacological and nonpharmacological treatments geared toward reducing sympathetic outflow may prove effective in managing phantom limb pain for some amputees. Other qualities of phantom limb pain may be generated by different mechanisms. Thorough evaluation of patients is essential to isolate relevant mechanisms. Treatment options may include temperature biofeedback for burning phantom limb pain and muscle tension biofeedback for cramping phantom limb pain. Preamputation pain should be reduced as soon as possible to avoid the development of a pain memory. Preoperative and intraoperative spinal or epidural analgesia is expected to block the injury discharge associated with noxious surgical events and lead to a reduced incidence and intensity of phantom limb pain. Immobilized or paralyzed phantoms may acquire the capacity to move following restoration of visual information of the limb created by use of mirrors.

ACKNOWLEDGMENTS

Preparation of this chapter was supported by a Medical Research Council of Canada (MRC) Scholar Award and MRC Grant #MT-12052.

REFERENCES

Abramson, A. S., & Feibel, A. F. (1981). The phantom phenomenon: Its use and disuse. *Bulletin of the New York Academy of Medicine, 57*, 99–112.

Ahmad, S. (1984). Phantom limb pain. *Southern Medical Journal, 77*, 804.

Arena, J. G., Sherman, R. H., & Bruno, G. M. (1990). The relationship between situational stress and phantom limb pain: Cross-lagged correlational data from six month pain logs. *Journal of Psychosomatic Research, 34*, 71–77.

Bach, S., Noreng, M. F., & Tjéllden, N. U. (1988). Phantom limb pain in amputees during the first 12 months following limb amputation, after preoperative lumbar epidural blockade. *Pain, 33*, 297–301.

Bailey, A. A., & Moersch, F. P. (1941). Phantom limb. *Canadian Medical Association Journal, 45*, 37–42.

Berger, M., & Gerstenbrand, F. (1981). Phantom illusions in spinal cord lesions. In J. Siegfried & M. Zimmermann (Eds.), *Phantom and stump pain* (pp. 66–73). New York: Springer-Verlag.

Boas, R. A., Schug, S. A., & Acland, R. H. (1993). Perineal pain after rectal amputation: A 5-year follow-up. *Pain, 52,* 67–70.

Bradway, J. K., Malone, J. M., Racy, J., Leal, J. M., & Poole, J. (1984). Psychological adaptation to amputation: An overview. *Orthotics and Prosthetics, 38,* 46–50.

Brena, S. F., & Sammons, E. E. (1979). Phantom urinary bladder pain—Case report. *Pain, 7,* 197–201.

Brodal, A. (1981). *Neurological anatomy in relation to clinical medicine* (3rd ed.). New York: Oxford University Press.

Browder, J. G., & Gallagher, J. P. (1948). Dorsal cordotomy for painful phantom limbs. *Annals of Surgery, 128,* 128.

Butler, D. J., Turkal, N. W., & Seidl, J. J. (1992). Amputation: Preoperative psychological preparation. *Journal of the American Board of Family Practice, 5,* 69–73.

Campbell, J. N., Meyer, R. A., Davis, K. D., & Raja, S. N. (1992). Sympathetically maintained pain: A unifying hypothesis. In W. D. Willis (Ed.), *Hyperalgesia and allodynia* (pp. 141–149). New York: Raven.

Campbell, J. N., Raja, S. N., & Meyer, R. A. (1993). Pain and the sympathetic nervous system: Connecting the loop. In L. Vecchiet, D. Albe-Fessard, U. Lindblom, & M. A. Giamberadino (Eds.), *New trends in referred pain and hyperalgesia* (pp. 99–107). Amsterdam: Elsevier.

Campbell, J. N., Raja, S. N., Selig, D. K., Belzberg, A. J., & Meyer, R. A. (1994). Diagnosis and management of sympathetically maintained pain. In H. L. Fields & J. C. Liebeskind (Eds.), *Pharmacological approaches to the treatment of chronic pain: New concepts and critical issues* (pp. 85–97). Seattle: IASP Press.

Caplan, L. M., & Hackett, T. P. (1963). Emotional effects of lower-limb amputation in the aged. *New England Journal of Medicine, 269,* 1166–1171.

Carlen, P. L., Wall, P. D., Nadvorna, H., & Steinbach, T. (1978). Phantom limbs and related phenomena in recent traumatic amputations. *Neurology, 28,* 211–217.

Chabal, C., Jacobson, L., Russell, L. C., & Burchiel, K. J. (1992). Pain response to perineuromal injection of normal saline, epinephrine, and lidocaine in humans. *Pain, 49,* 9–12.

Conomy, J. P. (1973). Disorders of body image after spinal cord injury. *Neurology, 23,* 842–850.

Dawson, L., & Arnold, P. (1981). Persistent phantom limb pain. *Perceptual and Motor Skills, 53,* 135–138.

Delius, W., Hagbarth, K. E., Hongell, A., & Wallin, B. G. (1972). Manoeuvres affecting sympathetic outflow in human skin nerves. *Acta Physiologica Scandinavica, 84,* 177–186.

Dernham, P. (1986). Phantom limb pain. *Geriatric Nursing (New York), 7,* 34–37.

Devor, M. (1994). The pathophysiology of damaged peripheral nerves. In P. D. Wall & R. Melzack (Eds.), *Textbook of pain* (3rd ed., pp. 79–100). Edinburgh: Churchill Livingstone.

Devor, M., Jänig, W., & Michaelis, M. (1994). Modulation of activity in dorsal root ganglion neurons by sympathetic activation in nerve-injured rats. *Journal of Neurophysiology, 71,* 38–47.

Diamond, J. (1959). The effect of injecting acetylcholine into normal and regenerating nerves. *Journal of Physiology (London), 145,* 611–629.

Dorpat, T. L. (1971). Phantom sensations of internal organs. *Comprehensive Psychiatry, 12,* 27–35.

Doupe, J., Cullen, C. H., & Chance, G. Q. (1944). Post-traumatic pain and the causalgic syndrome. *Journal of Neurology, Neurosurgery and Psychiatry, 7,* 33–48.

Echlin, F. (1949). Pain responses on stimulation of the lumbar sympathetic chain under local anesthesia. *Journal of Neurosurgery, 6,* 530–533.

Elizaga, A. M., Smith, D. G., Sharar, S. R., Edwards, T., & Hansen, S. T. (1994). Continuous regional analgesia by intraneural block: Effect on postoperative opioid requirements and phantom limb pain following amputation. *Journal of Rehabilitation Research and Development, 31,* 179–187.

Fisher, A., & Meller, Y. (1991). Continuous postoperative regional analgesia by nerve sheath block for amputation surgery—A pilot study. *Anesthesia and Analgesia, 72,* 300–303.

Flor, H., Behle, D. J., & Birbaumer, N. (1993). Assessment of pain-related cognitions in chronic pain patients. *Behaviour Research and Therapy, 31*, 63–73.

Frazier, S. H., & Kolb, L. C. (1970). Psychiatric aspects of pain and the phantom limb. *Orthopedic Clinics of North America, 1*, 481–495.

Frederiks, J. A. M. (1963). Occurrence of phantom limb phenomena following amputation of body parts and following lesions of the central and peripheral nervous system. *Psychiatrica, Neurologica, Neurochirurgia, 66*, 73–97.

Gloyne, H. F. (1954). Psychosomatic aspects of pain. *Psychoanalytic Review, 41*, 135–139.

Hagbarth, K. E., Hallin, R. G., Hongell, A., Torebjörk, H. E., & Wallin, B. G. (1972). General characteristics of sympathetic activity in human skin nerves. *Acta Physiologica Scandinavica, 84*, 164–176.

Henderson, W. R., & Smyth, G. E. (1948). Phantom limbs. *Journal of Neurology, Neurosurgery and Psychiatry, 2*, 88–112.

Hill, A. (1993). The use of pain coping strategies by patients with phantom limb pain. *Pain, 55*, 347–353.

Hitchcock, L. S., Ferrell, B. R., & McCaffery, M. (1994). The experience of chronic nonmalignant pain. *Journal of Pain and Symptom Management, 9*, 312–318.

Jacobson, L., & Chabal, C. (1989). Prolonged relief of acute postamputation phantom limb pain with intrathecal fentanyl and epidural morphine. *Anesthesiology, 71*, 984–985.

Jacobson, L., Chabal, C., & Brody, M. C. (1989). Relief of persistent postamputation stump and phantom limb pain with intrathecal fentanyl. *Pain, 37*, 317–322.

Jacobson, L., Chabal, C., Brody, M. C., Mariano, A. J., & Chaney, E. F. (1990). A comparison of the effects of intrathecal fentanyl and lidocaine on established postamputation stump pain. *Pain, 40*, 137–141.

Jahangiri, M., Bradley, J. W. P., Jayatunga, A. P., & Dark, C. H. (1994). Prevention of phantom limb pain after major lower limb amputation by epidural infusion of diamorphine, clonidine and bupivacaine. *Annals of the Royal College of Surgeons of England, 76*, 324–326.

Jensen, M. P., Turner, J. A., Romano, J. M., & Karoly, P. (1991). Coping with chronic pain: A critical review of the literature. *Pain, 47*, 249–283.

Jensen, T. S., Krebs, B., Nielsen, J., & Rasmussen, P. (1984). Non-painful phantom limb phenomena in amputees: Incidence, clinical characteristics and temporal course. *Acta Neurologica Scandinavica, 70*, 407–414.

Jensen, T. S., Krebs, B., Nielsen, J., & Rasmussen, P. (1985). Immediate and long-term phantom pain in amputees: Incidence, clinical characteristics and relationship to pre-amputation pain. *Pain, 21*, 268–278.

Jensen, T. S., & Rasmussen, P. (1994). Phantom pain and other phenomena after amputation. In P. D. Wall & R. Melzack (Eds.), *Textbook of pain* (3rd ed., pp. 651–665). Edinburgh: Churchill Livingstone.

Kallio, K. E. (1950). Permanency of results obtained by sympathetic surgery in the treatment of phantom pain. *Acta Orthopaedica Scandinavica, 19*, 391–397.

Katz, J. (1992). Psychophysical correlates of phantom limb experience. *Journal of Neurology, Neurosurgery and Psychiatry, 55*, 811–821.

Katz, J. (1993). The reality of phantom limbs. *Motivation and Emotion, 17*, 147–179.

Katz, J. (1996). The role of the sympathetic nervous system in phantom limb pain. *Physical Medicine and Rehabilitation: State of the Art Reviews, 10*, 153–175.

Katz, J., Clairoux, M., Kavanagh, B. P., Roger, S., Nierenberg, H., Redahan, C., & Sandler, A. N. (1994). Pre-emptive lumbar epidural anaesthesia reduces postoperative pain and patient-controlled morphine consumption after lower abdominal surgery. *Pain, 59*, 395–403.

Katz, J., Clairoux, M., Redahan, C., Kavanagh, B. P., Carroll, S., Nierenberg, H., Jackson, M., Beattie, J., Taddio, A., & Sandler, A. N. (1996). High dose alfentanil pre-empts pain after abdominal hysterectomy. *Pain, 68*, 109–118.

Katz, J., France, C., & Melzack, R. (1989). An association between phantom limb sensations and stump skin conductance during transcutaneous electrical nerve stimulation (TENS) applied to the contralateral leg: A case study. *Pain, 36,* 367–377.

Katz, J., Kavanagh, B. P., Sandler, A. N., Nierenberg, H., Boylan, J. F., Friedlander, M., & Shaw, B. F. (1992). Preemptive analgesia: Clinical evidence of neuroplasticity contributing to post-operative pain. *Anesthesiology, 77,* 439–446.

Katz, J., & Melzack, R. (1990). Pain "memories" in phantom limbs: Review and clinical observations. *Pain, 43,* 319–336.

Katz, J., & Melzack, R. (1991). Auricular TENS reduces phantom limb pain. *Journal of Pain and Symptom Management, 6,* 73–83.

Katz, J., Ritvo, P., Irvine, M. J., & Jackson, M. (1996). Coping with chronic pain. In M. Zeidner & N. S. Endler (Eds.), *Handbook of coping: Theory, research, applications* (pp. 252–278). New York: Wiley.

Katz, J., Vaccarino, A. L., Coderre, T. J., & Melzack, R. (1991). Injury prior to neurectomy alters the pattern of autotomy in rats. *Anesthesiology, 75,* 876–883.

Keefe, F. J., Salley, A. N. J., & Lefebvre, J. C. (1992). Coping with pain: Conceptual concerns and future directions. *Pain, 51,* 131–134.

Kolb, L. C. (1954). *The painful phantom: Psychology, physiology and treatment.* Springfield, IL: Thomas.

Krebs, B., Jensen, T. S., Krøner, K., Nielsen, J., & Jørgensen, H. S. (1985). Phantom limb phenomena in amputees 7 years after limb amputation. In H. L. Fields, R. Dubner, & F. Cervero (Eds.), *Advances in pain research and therapy* (Vol. 9, pp. 425–429). New York: Raven.

Kristen, H., Lukeschitsch, G., Plattner, F., Sigmund, R., & Resch, P. (1984). Thermography as a means for quantitative assessment of stump and phantom pains. *Prosthetics and Orthotics International, 8,* 76–81.

Krøner, K., Krebs, B., Skov, J., & Jørgensen, H. S. (1989). Immediate and long-term phantom breast syndrome after mastectomy: Incidence, clinical characteristics and relationship to pre-mastectomy breast pain. *Pain, 36,* 327–334.

Lacroix, R., Melzack, R., Smith, D., & Mitchell, N. (1992). Multiple phantom limbs in a child. *Cortex, 28,* 503–507.

LeDoux, J. E. (1989). Cognitive-emotional interactions in the brain. *Cognition and Emotion, 3,* 267–289.

Leventhal, H. (1982). The integration of emotion and cognition: A view from the perceptual-motor theory of emotion. In M. Clark & S. Fiske (Eds.), *Affect and cognition: The 17th annual Carnegie Symposium on cognition* (pp. 121–156). Hillsdale, NJ: Lawrence Erlbaum Associates.

Lindesay, J. (1985). Multiple pain complaints in amputees. *Journal of the Royal Society of Medicine, 78,* 452–455.

Livingston, W. K. (1938). Fantom limb pain. A report of ten cases in which it was treated by injections of procaine hydrochloride near the thoracic sympathetic ganglions. *Archives of Surgery, 37,* 353–370.

Livingston, W. K. (1943). *Pain mechanisms.* New York: Macmillan.

Lundberg, S. G., & Guggenheim, F. G. (1986). Sequelae of limb amputation. *Advances in Psychosomatic Medicine, 15,* 199–210.

Marbach, J. J. (1978). Phantom tooth pain. *Journal of Endodontics, 4,* 362–372.

Marshall, M., Helmes, E., & Deathe, B. (1992). A comparison of psychosocial functioning and personality in amputee and chronic pain populations. *The Clinical Journal of Pain, 8,* 351–357.

Marsland, A. R., Weekes, J. W. N., Atkinson, R., & Leong, M. G. (1982). Phantom limb pain: A case for beta blockers? *Pain, 12,* 295–297.

McGrath, P. A., & Hillier, L. M. (1992). Phantom limb sensations in adolescents: A case study to illustrate the utility of sensation and pain logs in pediatric clinical practice. *Journal of Pain and Symptom Management, 7,* 46–53.

Melzack, R. (1971). Phantom limb pain: Implications for treatment of pathologic pain. *Anesthesiology, 35,* 409–419.

Melzack, R. (1989). Phantom limbs, the self, and the brain (The D. O. Hebb memorial lecture). *Canadian Psychology, 30,* 1–16.

Melzack, R., & Bromage, P. R. (1973). Experimental phantom limbs. *Experimental Neurology, 39,* 261–269.

Melzack, R., & Casey, K. L. (1968). Sensory, motivational, and central control determinants of pain. In D. Kenshalo (Ed.), *The skin senses* (pp. 423–439). Springfield, IL: Thomas.

Melzack, R., & Loeser, J. D. (1978). Phantom body pain in paraplegics: Evidence for a central "pattern generating mechanism" for pain. *Pain, 4,* 195–210.

Melzack, R., & Wall, P. D. (1988). *The challenge of pain* (2nd ed.). New York: Basic Books.

Merskey, H. (1989). Psychiatry and chronic pain. *Canadian Journal of Psychiatry, 34,* 329–336.

Minski, L. (1943). Psychological reactions to injury. In W. B. Doherty & D. D. Runes (Eds.), *Rehabilitation of the war injured* (pp. 115–122). New York: Philosophical Library.

Mitchell, S. W. (1871). Phantom limbs. *Lippincott's Magazine of Popular Literature and Science, 8,* 563–569.

Mitchell, S. W. (1872). *Injuries of nerves and their consequences.* Philadelphia: Lippincott.

Morgenstern, F. S. (1964). The effects of sensory input and concentration on post-amputation phantom limb pain. *Journal of Neurology, Neurosurgery and Psychiatry, 27,* 58–65.

Morgenstern, F. S. (1970). Chronic pain: A study of some general features which play a role in maintaining a state of chronic pain after amputation. In O. W. Hill (Ed.), *Modern trends in psychosomatic medicine* (Vol. 2, pp. 225–245). London: Butterworth.

Nathan, P. W. (1962). Pain traces left in the central nervous system. In C. A. Keele & R. Smith (Eds.), *The assessment of pain in man and animals* (pp. 129–134). Edinburgh: Livingstone.

Noordenbos, W. (1959). *Pain.* Amsterdam: Elsevier.

Nyström, B., & Hagbarth, K. E. (1981). Microelectrode recordings from transected nerves in amputees with phantom limb pain. *Neuroscience Letters, 27,* 211–216.

Oille, W. A. (1970). Beta adrenergic blockade and the phantom limb. *Annals of Internal Medicine, 73,* 1044–1045.

Oveson, P., Krøner, K., Ørnsholt, J., & Bach, K. (1991). Phantom-related phenomena after rectal amputation: Prevalence and clinical characteristics. *Pain, 44,* 289–291.

Parkes, C. M. (1973). Factors determining the persistence of phantom pain in the amputee. *Journal of Psychosomatic Research, 17,* 97–108.

Parkes, C. M., & Napier, M. M. (1975). Psychiatric sequelae of amputation [Special publication]. *British Journal of Psychiatry, 9,* 440–446.

Pilowsky, I., & Kaufman, A. (1965). An experimental study of atypical phantom pain. *British Journal of Psychiatry, 111,* 1185–1187.

Price, D. B. (1976). Phantom limb phenomenon in patients with leprosy. *Journal of Nervous and Mental Disease, 163,* 108–116.

Raja, S. N. (1993). Diagnosis of sympathetically maintained pain: The past, present, and future. *European Journal of Pain, 14,* 45–48.

Raja, S. N., Treede, R. D., Davis, K. D., & Campbell, J. N. (1991). Systemic alpha-adrenergic blockade with phentolamine: A diagnostic test for sympathetically maintained pain. *Anesthesiology, 74,* 691–698.

Ramachandran, V. S. (1994). Phantom limbs, neglect syndromes, repressed memories, and Freudian psychology. *International Review of Neurobiology, 37,* 291–333.

Ramachandran, V. S., & Rogers-Ramachandran, D. (1996). Synaesthesia in phantom limbs induced with mirrors. *Proceedings of the Royal Society of London B, 263,* 377–386.

Reisner, H. (1981). Phantom sensations (phantom arm) in plexus paralysis. In J. Siegfried & M. Zimmermann (Eds.), *Phantom and stump pain* (pp. 62–65). New York: Springer-Verlag.

Richmond, C. E., Bromley, L. M., & Woolf, C. J. (1993). Preoperative morphine pre-empts postoperative pain. *The Lancet, 342,* 73–75.

Riddoch, G. (1941). Phantom limbs and body shape. *Brain, 64,* 197–222.

Roberts, W. J. (1986). A hypothesis on the physiological basis for causalgia and related pains. *Pain, 24,* 297–311.

Rosen, V. H. (1950). The role of denial in acute postoperative affective reactions following removal of body parts. *Psychosomatic Medicine, 12,* 356–361.

Rosenstiel, A. K., & Keefe, F. J. (1983). The use of coping strategies in low-back pain patients: Relationship to patient characteristics and current adjustment. *Pain, 17,* 33–40.

Scadding, J. W., Wall, P. D., Wynn Parry, C. B., & Brooks, D. M. (1982). Clinical trial of propranolol in post-traumatic neuralgia. *Pain, 14,* 283–292.

Schilder, P. (1950). *The image and appearance of the human body: Studies in the constructive energies of the psyche.* New York: International Universities Press.

Schott, G. D. (1993). Pain and the sympathetic nervous system. In R. Bannister & C. J. Mathias (Eds.), *Autonomic failure. A textbook of clinical disorders of the autonomic nervous system* (pp. 904–917). Oxford, England: Oxford University Press.

Schug, S. A., Burrell, R., Payne, J., & Tester, P. (1995). Pre-emptive epidural analgesia may prevent phantom limb pain. *Regional Anesthesia, 20,* 256.

Sherman, R. A. (1976). Case reports of treatment of phantom limb pain with a combination of electromyographic biofeedback and verbal relaxation techniques. *Biofeedback and Self Regulation, 1,* 353.

Sherman, R. A. (1984). Direct evidence of a link between burning phantom pain and stump blood circulation: A case report. *Orthopedics, 7,* 1319–1320.

Sherman, R. A. (1989). Stump and phantom limb pain. *Neurologic Clinics, 7,* 249–264.

Sherman, R. A., & Arena, J. G. (1992). Phantom limb pain: Mechanisms, incidence, and treatment. *Critical Reviews in Physical and Rehabilitation Medicine, 4,* 1–26.

Sherman, R. A., & Bruno, G. M. (1987). Concurrent variation of burning phantom limb and stump pain with near surface blood flow in the stump. *Orthopedics, 10,* 1395–1402.

Sherman, R. A., Devor, M., Jones, D. E. C., Katz, J., & Marbach, J. J. (1997). *Phantom pain.* New York: Plenum.

Sherman, R. A., Gall, N., & Gormly, J. (1979). Treatment of phantom limb pain with muscular relaxation training to disrupt the pain-anxiety-tension cycle. *Pain, 6,* 47–55.

Sherman, R. A., Sherman, C. J., & Bruno, G. M. (1987). Psychological factors influencing chronic phantom limb pain: An analysis of the literature. *Pain, 28,* 285–295.

Sherman, R. A., Sherman, C. J., & Parker, L. (1984). Chronic phantom and stump pain among American veterans: Results of a study. *Pain, 18,* 83–95.

Shukla, G. D., Sahu, S. C., Tripathi, R. P., & Gupta, D. K. (1982). A psychiatric study of amputees. *British Journal of Psychiatry, 141,* 50–53.

Sicuteri, F., Nicolodi, M., Fusco, B. M., & Orlando, S. (1991). Idiopathic headache as a possible risk factor for phantom tooth pain. *Headache, 31,* 577–581.

Simmel, M. L. (1956). On phantom limbs. *Archives of Neurology and Psychiatry, 75,* 637–647.

Simmel, M. L. (1959). Phantoms, phantom pain and "denial." *American Journal of Psychotherapy, 13,* 603–613.

Sliosberg, A. (1948). *Les algies des amputés* [The pains of amputees]. Paris: Masson.

Smith, O. A., & DeVito, J. L. (1984). Central neural integration for the control of autonomic responses associated with emotion. *Annual Review of Neuroscience, 7,* 43–65.

Solomon, G. F., & Schmidt, K. M. (1978). A burning issue: Phantom limb pain and psychological preparation of the patient for amputation. *Archives of Surgery, 113,* 185–186.

Steigerwald, F., Brass, J., & Krainick, J. U. (1981). The analysis of personality factors in the prediction of phantom limb pain. In J. Siegfried & M. Zimmermann (Eds.), *Phantom and stump pain* (pp. 84–88). New York: Springer-Verlag.

Stengel, E. (1965). Pain and the psychiatrist. *British Journal of Psychiatry, 111,* 795–802.

Sunderland, S. (1968). *Nerve and nerve injuries.* Edinburgh: Livingstone.

Szasz, T. S. (1975). *Pain and pleasure* (2nd ed.). New York: Basic Books.

Tasker, R. R., Organ, L. W., & Hawrylyshyn, P. A. (1982). *The thalamus and midbrain of man.* Springfield, IL: Thomas.

Treede, R. D., Davis, K. D., Campbell, J. N., & Raja, S. N. (1992). The plasticity of cutaneous hyperalgesia during sympathetic ganglion blockade in patients with neuropathic pain. *Brain, 115,* 607–621.

Turgay, A., & Sonuvar, B. (1983). Emotional aspects of arm or leg amputation in children. *Canadian Journal of Psychiatry, 28,* 294–297.

Turner, J. A., & Clancy, S. (1986). Strategies for coping with chronic low back pain: Relationship to pain and disability. *Pain, 24,* 355–364.

Van Bogaert, L. (1934). Sur la pathologie de l'image de soi (Études anatomo-cliniques) [On the pathology of self-image (Anatomical-Clinical Studies)]. *Annales Médico Psychologiques (Paris), 14,* 519–555, 714–759.

Wall, P. D. (1981). On the origin of pain associated with amputation. In J. Siegfried & M. Zimmermann (Eds.), *Phantom and stump pain* (pp. 2–14). New York: Springer-Verlag.

Wall, P. D. (1989). To what would Gaston Labat be attending today? *Regional Anesthesia, 14,* 261–264.

Wall, P. D., & Gutnick, M. (1974). Properties of afferent nerve impulses originating from a neuroma. *Nature, 248,* 740–743.

Wallgren, G. R. (1954). Phantom experience at spinal anaesthesia. *Annales Chirurgicae et Gynaecologicae Fenniae, 43*(Suppl.), 486–500.

Weinstein, S. (1962). *Phantoms in paraplegia.* Paper presented at the Proceedings of Eleventh Annual Clinical Spinal Cord Injury Conference.

Weiss, S. A. (1958). The body image as related to phantom sensations: A hypothetical conceptualization of seemingly isolated findings. *Annals of the New York Academy of Science, 74,* 25–29.

Chapter 20

Trigeminal Neuralgia

Eli Eliav
Department of Oral Medicine, Oral Diagnosis
and Oral Radiology, and Department of Anatomy,
Hadassah School of Dental Medicine, The Hebrew University, Jerusalem

Richard H. Gracely
Pain and Neurosensory Mechanisms Branch
NIDR, National Institutes of Health

Trigeminal neuralgia (TN) is a distinct syndrome characterized by paroxysms of brief stabbing pain in the face, often near the mouth. The single episodes or clusters of episodes may be followed by long pain-free intervals. The pain is described as mild to extremely intense with an incisive, stabbing or jabbing quality (Fields, 1996; Stookey & Ransohoff, 1959). The pain is often accompanied by a characteristic unilateral, intense grimacelike motor response.

HISTORICAL BACKGROUND

Descriptions of TN can be traced to the first century A.D., in which Aretaeus described the combination of intense episodic pain and facial spasm of what he termed *heterocrania* (Stookey & Ransohoff, 1959). These same features were reported by the philosopher and physician John Locke following treatment of the wife of the English Ambassador during a visit to Paris in 1677. His careful description is a classic that clearly withstands the test of time (Stookey & Ransohoff, 1959). However, it was not until 1756 that the French physician Nicolaus André recognized the unique nature of the entity and proposed the term *tic douloureux* that captured both the pain and convulsive features of the paroxysmal attack. Independently, John Fothergill in 1773 described a series of 14 cases characterized by the dual features of pain and muscular contraction, with pain the primary component (Fothergill, 1773; Stookey & Ransohoff, 1959). Like Locke's, his description ". . . is as valid today as at the time it was written," (Stookey & Ransohoff, 1959, p. 24). In contrast to André's classification as a variant of convulsive disorder, Fothergill recognized TN as pain syndrome unique to the face. The anatomic locus in the trigeminal system is based in part on the seminal work of Charles Bell (1829), who divided the sensory and motor functions of the face between the trigeminal and facial nerve. The fact that attacks can be triggered by trigeminal stimulation resulted in the present nomenclature of trigeminal neuralgia.

FEATURES OF TRIGEMINAL NEURALGIA

TN is a unilateral disease of the mid- to late-aged that afflicts both genders. Incidence is 0.004% (Yoshimasu, Kurland, & Elveback, 1972). It is reported that a small (3%) subset of patients may experience shifts from one side to the other over long time periods, with no reports of bilateral symptoms. It occurs most frequently in patients aged 50 to 70, although the tails of the age distribution stretch from childhood years to 90 (Stookey & Ransohoff, 1959). Previous theories of predominance in women and on the right side have been discounted, and associations with multiple sclerosis have not advanced to evidence for causality (Loeser, 1994).

Sensory Features of the Attack

The main sensory feature is an abrupt, jolting, sharp, radiating pain that lasts usually from a few seconds to less than a minute. The pain can occur in all three divisions of the trigeminal nerve, and in all combinations of divisions. It most commonly occurs in the mandibular division and least commonly in the ophthalmic division; the maxillary and mandibular are the most common combination. Extratrigeminal involvement of the glossopharyngeal nerve and nervus intermedius are less frequently observed (Harris, 1940; Loeser, 1994; Stookey & Ransohoff, 1959; Wilkins, 1979). Attacks in the distribution of the glossopharyngeal nerve have been associated with syncope (Riley et al., 1942; Roulhac & Levy, 1950; Svien, Hill, & Daly, 1957).

Motoric Features of the Attack

The paroxysmal pain is usually accompanied by immediate movements in the head and face that are convulsive in nature. These convulsive-like movements earned both the appellation of "tic" and the hypothesis of a central epileptiform mechanism. The nature of these features varies among patients but the common appearance was captured by Pujol in 1787:

When we observe a patient who actually feels a pretty sharp attack of tic douloureux in the cheek we see him knit his brows, both eyelids are strongly compressed, and the commissure of the lips is drawn towards the ear as in sardonic laughter. The lower jaw remains immobile, and held in the same situation in which it was at the time of the attack: respiration is slow, as if suspended; and often the patient dares not make the least cry or utter a single exclamation. He seems to dread the slightest motion of the body; his forced attitude and almost ecstatic state much better express the violence of his pain than any verbal description. (Stookey & Ransohoff, 1959, p. 27)

The Triggering Stimulus

The nature of the triggering stimulus has been well characterized (Stookey & Ransohoff, 1959). Non-noxious touch, brushing, or stroking are sufficient to evoke an attack. Movement-related stimulation from eating, talking, and facial expressions can be sufficient, and may be the culprit when a trigger cannot be found. These stimuli are usually near the mouth or nose, and can include skin, lips, teeth, and mucosa. They are infrequently found outside of the trigeminal distribution. In heavily documented cases, stimulation of a single hair was sufficient to evoke an attack (Dubner, Sharav, Gracely, & Price, 1987; Kugleberg & Lindblom, 1959). The accumulated evidence indicates that the adequate stimulus activates the large-diameter, fast-conducting $A\beta$ low-threshold mechanoreceptor ($A\beta$-LTM) primary afferents that mediate fine touch. Administration of painful stimuli that preferentially activates the thinly myelinated $A\delta$ and unmyelinated C-fiber nociceptor afferents do not evoke the attack.

The trigger site is usually discrete, consisting of a small area of skin, small portion of the lip, a tooth, or facial hair. There are usually several sites that evoke the same attack. The location of these areas is always ipsilateral to the side of the attack, but otherwise is independent of the painful area, and both the number and location of sites can vary within a patient between weekly examinations. Table 20.1 shows the variation found in 11 examinations of a single patient.

Behavioral Antecedents

Patients report that both the frequency and severity of the attacks are increased by emotional or physical stress (Loeser, 1994).

Behavioral Consequences

Onset of attacks is unpredictable and can increase in frequency. The syndrome interferes with all aspects of life. Many behaviors that directly involve the affected region are avoided or modified. Patients may avoid brushing

TABLE 20.1
Trigger Zone Locations During Multiple Visits of a Single Patient

Session	R Upper Lip	R Lower Incisor	R Upper Molar Area	R Eyebrow	R Lower Lip
1	yes	yes			
2	yes				
3	yes	yes	yes		
4	yes	yes			
5	yes	yes			
6					
7		yes			
8		yes		yes	
9			yes		
10				yes	
11					yes

Note. From Dubner, Sharav, Gracely, and Price (1987).

or flossing teeth, or combing their hair. Men may avoid shaving whereas women may avoid makeup. Hair must be washed with care. Common outdoor activities such as riding a bicycle may become impossible, and driving a car with the window rolled down may evoke an attack. TN usually does not interfere with sleep (Maxwell, 1990).

Natural History

The attacks can occur individually or in clusters and can be separated from symptom-free intervals lasting from months to years. The attacks may increase in frequency with time. The trigger zone may move, resulting in adjustments in guarding behaviors. Alternatively, spontaneous remission is possible, which is good for the patient but increases the difficulty of evaluating therapeutic treatments.

Diagnosis

The unique nature of TN allows diagnosis solely on the basis of history and physical examination. Imaging is not required unless a surgical intervention is planned. However, Loeser (1994) pointed out that the syndrome is often accompanied by a background burning pain, due to deafferentation, that may be much more difficult to treat. In addition, TN may be confused with the rarer paroxysmal hemicrania, which presents with the TN feature of unilateral paroxysmal attacks of sharp, excruciating pain, often triggered by a mechanical stimulus. The pain of hemicrania is located in a broad area that includes the periorbital, periauricular, and temporal areas. This wide distribution is both responsible for the name and a distinguishing feature differentiating hemicrania from TN. In addition, the 13- to 29-minute attacks are longer than the 1- to 2-minute attacks of TN, and are accompanied by ipsilateral lacrimation, nasal congestion, and rhinnorrhea (Antonaci & Sjaastad, 1989; Sjaastad & Dale, 1974). Nocturnal attacks, common in paroxysmal hemicrania, are rare in TN. Lacrimation is not usually associated with TN, and the presence of lacrimation has been used to support other diagnoses. However a recent report cites a number of cases of TN accompanied by lacrimation (Benoliel & Sharav, 1998).

ETIOLOGY

There is increasing evidence that Dandy's (1934) proposal of vascular compression of a trigeminal root is likely the cause of many of the cases of TN. Pain in the second or third trigeminal division is associated with compression of the rostral and anterior portion of the nerve by the superior cerebellar artery; pain in the first division results usually from compression of the caudal and posterior portion of the nerve by the anterior inferior cerebellar artery (Dandy, 1934; Jannetta, 1967; Rhoton, 1990). Vascular compression is found in 90% to 95% of patients treated by surgical decompression. Surgery most often abolishes further attacks, and reverses both preoperative sensory deficits and suppressed trigeminally mediated evoked cortical potentials. This specificity is supported by an imaging study that revealed vascular compression in 51/55 of imaged affected areas and in only 4/45 contralateral evaluations (Meaney et al., 1995). These findings have also been confirmed in autopsy studies (Hamlyn & King, 1992). However, the caveats associated with inferring living anatomical relationships qualify this result as supportive but not conclusive (Loeser, 1994). In addition, the anatomical specificity in living tissue is not perfect. Five percent to 10% of surgery patients have no visible nerve lesion (Loeser, 1994). These cases may represent other pathologies that can affect the nerve, such as the theory that cavities in bone secondary to dentition loss may harbor chronic infections (Ratner, Person, Kleinman, Shklar, & Socransky, 1979; Roberts, Person, Candran, & Hori, 1984; Shaber & Kroll, 1980). This proposed mechanism of infection also lacks specificity; cavities can be observed in patients that do not have pain, and many TN patients do not have cavities. Finally, in terms of the nerve compression hypothesis, the frequency of asymptomatic patients with vascular compression is not known. Thus, although accumulated evidence is consistent with the hypothesis that vascular compression is responsible for most cases of TN, vascular compression does not result in TN in all cases. Factors other than visible nerve compression may exert similar effects and cause a small percentage of TN cases.

TREATMENT

A variety of effective treatments are available, including drug therapy, peripheral nerve block, several peripheral nerve destructive procedures, and craniotomy with vascular decompression. Evaluation of efficacy is complicated by the intermittent nature of the disease and by a fluctuating natural course that could result in exacerbation or spontaneous remission. A patient with uncomplicated TN can expect significant to complete relief. Medications trials will be effective in the majority of patients. Patients contemplating surgery must choose between relatively safe peripheral destructive procedures that can eliminate symptoms for a long period with minimal but unavoidable sensory loss, or a craniotomy that can essentially cure the disease with a minimal but increased morbidity.

Pharmacological Treatments

Carbamazepine. Carbamazepine is clearly the first choice. Efficacy is reported to be from 70% to 90% (Blom, 1962; Green & Selman, 1991; Loeser, 1994). Careful blood monitoring is required to guard against decline in platelets or white or red blood cells. This is usually achieved by monthly sampling the first year and at periods of 3 months thereafter. Carbamazepine is a gastric irritant and should be taken with food. A typical dosage regime begins with 100 mg twice daily, working up to 200 mg three times, and then four times, a day. Peak daily total can be 1,800 mg. Carbamazepine reaches peak concentration in 2 to 6 hours and is distributed in all body tissues by 24 hours. Recommended therapeutic serum level is 4 to 12 mcg/ml when used alone, and less when used in combination. However, correlation with serum levels is poor. Subjective side effects are dose dependent and include nausea, dizziness, slurred speech, ataxia, and somnolence (Green & Selman, 1991; Loeser, 1994). If treatment is otherwise successful, dosage should be reduced by 200 mg after 1 medication-free day. Carbamazepine stabilizes membranes by blocking sodium channels. Its efficacy in TN is due to inhibition of synaptic transmission within the spinal trigeminal nucleus (Green & Selman, 1991).

Phenytoin, Diphehylhydantoin. Phenytoin is the second choice for a pharmacological treatment. Two to three of four patients report initial relief whereas one of four report relief at 1 year (Blom, 1962; Braham & Saia, 1960). Five percent to 10% of patients experience side effects that can include ataxia, dizziness, slurred speech, somnolence, dermatitis, gingival hyperplasia, and hirustism. The therapeutic dose range is narrow. Patients are started on 100 mg three times a day, serum levels are checked at 3 weeks, and dosage is adjusted to reach levels of 10–20 mcg/ml (Green &

Selman, 1991). Side effects are treated by a 1-day drug holiday and dose reduction to 100 mg/day.

Clonazepam. Clonazepam is a benzodiazepine that was used originally as an anticonvulsant. The long-term efficacy for the treatment of TN is less than that of carbamazepine, with fewer side effects and reduced hepatoxicity (Green & Selman, 1991). Excellent results are obtained in about one half of the patients treated (Chandra, 1975; Court & Kase, 1976; Smirne & Scarlato, 1977). The side effects appear to be less bothersome; Swerdlow (1980) noted that 51% of carbamazepine users change medications because of unacceptable side effects, whereas only 17% of clonazepam users switch drugs. Side effects include sedation, which improves with tolerance, incoordination, ataxia, hyperactivity, and weight gain (Green & Selman, 1991). Clonazepam has a high lipid solubility and thus a fast distribution and long half-life (18–50 hours). Thus care must be taken in increasing doses. The initial dose is 0.5 to 1.0 mg/day in divided doses, which can be increased every 3 to 7 days by the same amount. Maximum dose is approximately 20 mg per day.

Valproic Acid. Valproic acid is an anticonvulsant used primarily for the treatment of epilepsy. It increases GABA (gamma-aminobutyric acid) activity by blocking degradation and facilitating synthesis (Engel, 1989). Forty-five percent of patients intolerant to the preceding drugs experienced relief for 1 to 2 years in a report of 20 patients (Peiris, Perera, Devendra, & Lionel, 1980). Initial dosage is 250 mg once or twice a day, which can be increased 75–150 mg at weekly intervals to 1,000–3,000 mg per day in divided doses. It is rapidly distributed (1–4 hours) with a 9- to 18-hour half-life. Primary side effects are gastrointestinal, including nausea, vomiting and anorexia, and hepatotoxicity, especially in children. Other side effects are transient hair loss, and pancreatitis, ataxia, weight gain, and tremor with long administration. Valproic acid may decrease plasma levels of phenytoin, and is actually recommended as a monotherapy due to other multiple drug reactions.

Baclofen. Baclofen is a GABA derivative used for spasticity in multiple sclerosis. Fromm and colleagues (Fromm, Shibuya, Nakata, & Terrence, 1990; Fromm, Terrence, & Marron, 1984) were instrumental in applying baclofen to the treatment of TN, and reported that 74% of TN patients who did not respond to, or discontinued, carbamazepine reported satisfactory relief when baclofen was used alone or in combination with carbamazepine. Baclofen can be used in combination with phenytoin if carbamazepine is poorly tolerated. Half-life is short (3–4 hours) and elimination is via the kidney. Initial dose is 5 mg two or three times per day with a maximum dose of 80 mg. Side effects are somnolence, dizziness, ataxia, and mental confusion. Abrupt discontinued use may result in hallucination, anxiety, and tachycardia. Patients must be withdrawn slowly.

Pimozide (Diphenylbutylpiperidine). Pimozide is a neuroleptic used primarily for management of Tourette's syndrome. It is the only neuroleptic drug effective for treatment of TN. Initial dose is 0.5 to 1.0 mg; peak effect occurs in 4 to 12 hours. Pimozide is metabolized in the liver; the long half-life (111 ± 57 hours) requires gradual dose elevation (Green & Selman, 1991; Lechin, van der Dijs, Lechin, Amat, & Leechin, 1989). Doses may be increased 0.5 to 1.0 mg every 4 to 7 days; less than 10 mg/day is sufficient. Side effects include overactivity or sedation, insomnia and restlessness, fatigue, increased gastrointestinal motility, nocturnal myoclonus, miosis, bradycardia, and hypersalivation. The mechanism is thought to be mostly dopaminergic with a serotonergic component.

Gabapentin. Gabapentin is a lipid soluble analog of GABA that penetrates the blood-brain barrier. A preliminary, small study suggests relief of TN when administered alone or in combination with other anticonvulsants (Ranieri, Longmire, Attia-Yon, McDonald, & Leak, 1996). Absorption is limited by an amino acid carrier mechanism, and thus not affected by increases in the sufficient dose. Suggested dose is 900–1,800 mg divided among three daily doses. Surprisingly, the drug is not GABA mimetic; there is no effect on sodium channels or major neurotransmitter systems. The side-effect profile (sedation and ataxia) is less severe than with other antiepileptic drugs used for treatment of TN.

Other Pharmacological Agents. Other agents that have been used for the treatment of TN include mephenesin and chloromephenesin (Loeser, 1994). Lidocaine-like drugs have also been used recently, and like gabapentin, their clinical potential will be established after adequate clinical trials.

Local Anesthetic Blocks. Local blockade of the trigger or painful area provides relief; some patients may obtain long-term relief after one or more of such blocks. Local blocks also allow patients to experience the anesthesia that would follow an ablative procedure.

Surgical/Ablative Methods

The patient and clinician must choose between two types of procedures: discrete lesioning of a peripheral nerve, or decompression of a nerve root. The ablative procedures result in long-term, but not permanent, relief at low cost. Side effects are minimal and there is some degree of sensory loss.

Decompression is more costly and is associated with greater morbidity and with rare mortality. Relief is highly likely and permanent. Loeser (1994) noted that all other treatments are palliative, whereas decompression can cure the disease. However, there is general agreement that, for most patients, surgery should be considered after medication trials.

Gangliolysis. Radiofrequency thermal gangliolysis has largely replaced ablative procedures such as peripheral neurectomy and rhizotomy. It is now the most commonly reported neurosurgical procedure (Sweet, 1986). Gangliolysis allows very good control of the sensory loss in the painful region. The original theoretical action that this method would preferentially lesion small fibers has been confirmed by clinical practice. One half of the treated patients report relief after 5 years and at least three fourths after 1 year. Side effects occur in less than 1% of patients, and are related to the amount of sensory deficit. These include the known effects of ablative procedures: anesthesia dolorosa, painful parathesia, and neuroparalytic keratitis. Gangliolysis of the ophthalmic division should be considered and performed with caution because there is a risk of corneal anesthesia as well as neuroparalytic keratitis. One advantage of the method is that surgeons can conservatively ablate only the minimally effective amount. The procedure can be repeated as needed with no loss of efficacy or change in complications.

Recent variants of this method include injection of glycerol (Håkanson, 1981; Rappaport, 1986; Saini, 1987; Young, 1988) or expansion of a balloon catheter introduced through a large-gauge needle (Belber & Rak, 1987; Connelly, 1982; Mullan & Lichtor, 1983; Sheldon, Pudenz, Freshwater, & Crue, 1955). The glycerol method may be useful in reducing the side effect of corneal anesthesia in treatment of ophthalmic division TN. Further evaluation of these variants is warranted.

Suboccipital Craniotomy With Microvascular Decompression (MVD). Based on Dandy's (1934) proposal of vascular compression, Taarnhøj (1952) introduced the logical restorative procedure of decompressing the affected root that has been popularized by Jannetta (1976). The procedure involves a retromastoid craniectomy or craniotomy under general anesthesia and examination of the trigeminal nerve for evidence of vascular compression near the point of reentry into the brainstem. Arteries and some veins that are found to compress the nerve are repositioned and an amount of muscle or synthetic material such as Ivalon or Dacron is inserted between the vessel and the nerve root. Veins may also be divided and sacrificed without untoward effects. Vascular compression is not found in 5% to 10% of the cases; the surgeon has the option of performing a partial rhizotomy in such instances (Loeser, 1994). The degree of rhizotomy must balance increased efficacy of major transection with increased side effects of sensory loss and increased probability of anesthesia dolorosa or dysethesia that are very difficult to treat.

The success of MVD has been evaluated in detail. A recent report from the Jannetta group describes the favorable long-term outcome in 1,185 patients treated over a 20-year period (Barker, Jannetta, Bissonette, Larkins, & Jho, 1966). Seventy percent of patients with one or two operations were free of pain after 10 years, with an annual recurrence rate of less than 1% at that time. An additional 4% of patients report periods of pain that are treated without resort to long-term medication. Four factors were found to predict long-term relief: immediate postoperative relief, male gender, an absence of a venous compression, and preoperative syndrome duration of less than 8 years. Outcome was not influenced by bilateral symptoms or presence of spasm. It is important to note that a history of previous ablative procedures did not reduce the relief from tic pain, but did increase the probabilities of aching and burning pain.

The authors reported that complications of MVD have been reduced by continued experience and introduction of intraoperative monitoring of evoked brainstem responses in 1980. Prior to that time, two patients, ages 69 and 79, died due to postoperative stroke or infarction, whereas no patient death has been reported since. Fifteen patients have experienced ipsilateral hearing loss; however the rate of hearing loss decreased from 3% to 1% after 1980.

The experience of this group includes other complications (infarction, edema or hemorrhage of ipsilateral hemisphere, supratentorial hematoma) that were treated successfully surgically. Eleven patients experienced numbness in the face, although no patient developed anesthesia dolorosa. Burning and aching pain were reported by 96 patients with a previous history of gangliolysis, but in only a small percentage of patients with previous ablative surgery.

This report likely represents a "best case" result because the authors have developed this method and are very experienced in the procedure. The general consensus is that the method is attended by a 1% mortality rate and a +1% rate of serious morbidity. The results of other groups and of other procedures have been reviewed by Sweet (1990), who provided both evidence against the MVD hypothesis and a note of caution for those contemplating surgical procedures.

Other Ablative Procedures. Although peripheral nerve avulsions have been replaced by gangliolysis and MVD, there is still a role for these procedures in the management of TN. Candidates include patients in which pharmacological approaches are or have become ineffective, gangliolysis has failed or pain has returned, and the patient declines MVD.

Another group includes those in which pharmacological therapy and both gangliolysis and MVD have been ineffective. A third group includes those in which exploration (or reexploration in the previous group) reveals no structural lesion. Loeser (1994) recommended a posterior fossa rhizotomy in these conditions but cautioned that 1- to 2-year relief is accompanied by profound sensory loss. Repeat avulsions are less successful.

If all else has failed, that patient may elect more invasive procedures that result in significant permanent loss of small-fiber sensation (pain and temperature) in the affected side of the face. Touch sensation is spared. Preliminary studies indicate a successful outcome for both descending trigeminal tractotomy and trigeminal nucleotomy (Loeser, 1994).

MECHANISMS

The features of an evoked abnormality such as TN can be subdivided into etiology, characteristics of activation, consequences of activation, and most important, the underlying mechanisms that link these components. The etiology was mentioned early in this chapter in conjunction with MVD. At least seven sites of structural lesions have been proposed. In addition to the compression of posterior root or peripheral branches of the trigeminal nerve, these include lesions of the Gasserion ganglion, trigeminal nerve nuclei, dental structures, vascular supply, or the skin. Present schools of thought favor vascular compression, although a theory based on infection in the mandible at the site of dentition loss has not been dismissed (Ratner et al., 1979).

As we noted previously, there is increasing evidence for the vascular compression hypothesis, although these findings are not completely specific. Vascular compression may not result in TN, and TN may occur in the absence of vascular compression. TN likely results from one of several antecedents that share the same general neural consequence. The notable success of just surgical exploration or minor mechanical stimulation suggests that the causative factor(s) may be minor misadjustments that are not specific to any gross structural lesion (Adams, 1989; Gybels & Sweet, 1989; Sweet, 1990).

CHARACTERISTICS OF ACTIVATION

The clinical findings presented earlier indicate that a paroxysm is initiated by gentle mechanical stimulation usually within or near the mouth. The characteristics of this activation have been described in countless clinical studies and in at least two complementary studies that experimentally triggered the paroxysm in participating patient volunteers. In the "group" study, Kugleberg and Lindblom (1959) examined activation in a group of 50 patients. In the "longitudinal" study, Dubner et al. (1987) examined the variability of the trigger locations in 11 examinations of a single patient during an 8-month period.

In the group study, the investigators used manual stimulation and controllable vibration to map the trigger zone in a series of 30 patients. The majority of these zones were small and well defined, with areas in some not larger than 1 or 2 mm^2. The severity of the attack was not related to the size of the zone.

The trigger location was not stable in the longitudinal study. Table 20.1 shows that the adequate trigger moved between examinations and the trigger sites included the lips and both intra- and extraoral sites. Two trigger sites were often found, and these could be from different trigeminal divisions. Both studies report evaluations during which movement of a single hair was sufficient to evoke a complete attack.

The trigger zones were activated by light tactile stimuli, and depended on the speed of activation. For example, rapid displacement of a few hairs or sudden application or release of pressure could evoke an attack, whereas slow movement or pulling of a hair or firm pressure failed to produce an attack. Painful and thermal stimuli were not effective. The results of both studies agree with the accumulated clinical evidence that light tactile stimuli exclusively activates the paroxysm. Apparent spontaneous attacks may be related to activation of sensitive tactile triggers by chewing, swallowing, or speaking.

These studies reached different conclusions about which primary afferents were activated by triggering stimuli. The original group study could not activate the paroxysm by weak or even painful electrical stimuli in two patients. Because these stimuli preferentially activate the large-diameter Aβ fibers, they concluded that the adequate stimuli was mediated by unmyelinated or thinly myelinated primary afferents sensitive to light touch. In contrast, the more recent longitudinal study provided several lines of evidence that suggest that the adequate trigger is the activation of the rapidly conducting, large-diameter Aβ low-threshold mechanoreceptors (Aβ-LTMs) that mediate fine touch: (a) Innocuous stimuli (touching, brushing, stroking) evoked both stimulation-related and paroxysmal pain whereas (b) activation of Aδ and C-fibers by warming, cooling, noxious heat, and electrical stimulation of the tooth pulp never produced the painful paroxysm or the throbbing stimulation-related pain; (c) the paroxysmal and stimulation-related pain could be evoked by movement of an eyebrow guard hair, which is known to be activated by Aβ-LTMs (Burgess & Perl, 1973), and (d) the evoked pains were produced after a local anesthetic began to wane and the patient reported lingering numbness. Because Aβ fibers recover first from such a block, this result suggests that the pain was evoked during the stage when some Aβ fibers had recovered but other Aβ fibers and the smaller diameter Aδ and C fibers were still blocked.

In the longitudinal study, the trigger produced two types of pain: a stimulation-related throbbing pain that lasted only 1 to 2 sec, and the episodic, severe paroxysmal pain that lasted 15 to 30 seconds, accompanied by facial flushing and muscle twitching. Interestingly, the spatial characteristics of these two evoked pains were completely different. The stimulation-related pain was perceived at the site of stimulation and could radiate beyond this site. The paroxysmal pain was always perceived in the right maxillary infraorbital region. In the group study, stimulation also could produce stimulation-related jabs of pain, a sustained pain that did not outlast a continued stimulus, or the full paroxysmal pain.

In both the longitudinal and group studies, stimulation of the trigger zone could be performed at rates, intensities, or areas that were insufficient to evoke the paroxysm. Increasing the area, rate, or intensity of stimulation could increase the magnitude of the stimulation-related pain, cause it to radiate, or produce an attack. For example, in the longitudinal study, in a session in which a trigger was located in an incisor tooth, this tooth was stimulated at different frequencies and forces by means of calibrated nylon monofilaments. Stimulation with 2 grams evoked the stimulation-related pain. At stimulation intervals less than 20 seconds, the magnitude of the evoked pain increased with successive stimuli, with the greatest increase at the 5-second interval. An increase in stimulation force to 29 grams resulted in increased stimulation-related pain, and stimulation at 2-second intervals resulted in a further increase and radiation of the pain beyond the stimulation site. However, none of these stimuli evoked the paroxysm, which was eventually evoked by a single application of 282 grams of force.

Temporal effects of stimulation were also investigated in a session with an eyebrow hair trigger. Flicking the hair at a 2-second rate resulted in increased stimulation-related pain and radiation of the pain beyond the eyebrow site. In this case, this temporal summation was sufficient to evoke the full paroxysm, which occurred after 26 stimulations.

These studies indicate that stimulus intensity, extent, and frequency can increase the stimulus effect. In the group study, Kugleberg and Lindblom (1959) determined the decay of this effect and found that the increased excitability quickly decreases in an exponential-like fashion, reaching near-baseline levels within 30 seconds.

CONSEQUENCES OF ACTIVATION

The clinical literature and the aforementioned investigations reveal two consequences of activation. The first is a stimulation-related pain that is modulated in magnitude and extent by characteristics of the stimulation.

The second is the classic paroxysmal attack, which appears to be evoked if a combination of stimulus features exceeds some stimulation threshold. This attack is accompanied by characteristic motor responses. In addition, it is followed by a refractory period lasting from 20 seconds to minutes during which further stimulation does not evoke either the stimulation-related or paroxysmal pain.

In the group study, Kugleberg and Lindblom (1959) found that the duration of the refactory period was directly related to the duration and intensity of the preceding attack. In addition, stimulation during the relative part of the refractory period diminished the intensity and duration of the next attack. This interdependence of refactory period and attack allowed the investigators to greatly modulate the attack by selective stimulation. In patients with only slight paroxysmal pain, the refractory period was increased by provoking a series of attacks in quick succession. It was also possible to maintain an attack continuously without any absolute refractory period. In this case the paroxysmal pain decreased in intensity throughout the attack and was replaced by a sensation of glowing warmth after 19 minutes.

A third consequence of activation might be revealed in sensory changes in the absence of a provoked attack. Sensory function generally is assumed to be normal in TN patients. However, studies employing quantitative sensory testing have found reduced sensitivity to touch, warm, and cold (Bowsher, Haggett, Miles, & Eldridge, 1996; Lewey & Grant, 1938; Miles, Eldridge, Haggett, & Bowsher, 1996; Nurmikko, 1991) and altered evoked cortical potentials to electrical infraorbital nerve stimulation (Bennett & Jannetta, 1983; Leandri, Miles, Eldridge, & Haggett, 1996) that normalized after MVD (Leandri et al., 1996; Miles et al., 1996).

This normalization of sensory function suggests that altered sensory function could serve as a marker for the underlying mechanisms. The issue is whether this underlying pathology is due to vascular compression, or is successively treated by some unknown and likely trivial consequence of surgical exploration.

Normalization of sensory deficits and other features of activation aid the development of models that attempt to account for the underlying mechanisms of TN. The system dynamics revealed by these investigations guide the choice of model and mechanism, and ultimately can be used to test the goodness of fit of proposed mechanisms.

Underlying Mechanism

The mechanisms linking nerve compression or other lesions to Aβ-triggered paroxysmal pain are not known. The obvious relation of TN to epileptic seizures and the disparity between trigger and paroxysmal zones has formed the basis of theories specifying a central origin, whereas the focus on events such as peripheral nerve compression and relief from surgical manipulation of nerve roots has led to theories of a peripheral etiology. The emerging consensus among several theories is that the mechanism combines both peripheral and more central features. The syndrome is initiated and maintained peripherally, but this peripheral etiology results in downstream consequences that result in the observed symptoms.

The location of the peripheral pathology has been assigned to various locations, but as E. J. Gardner (1962) noted, the success of surgical manipulation of the trigeminal nerve via either the middle or posterior fossa implicates the structure common to both, the trigeminal nerve root. Two types of nerve root mechanisms have been proposed. First, vascular compression or other peripheral events can produce partial deafferentation of primary afferent neurons. Partial deafferentation, consistent with observed sensory deficits, leads to central reorganization that can result in expansion of low-threshold receptive fields and alteration in center-surround inhibition mechanisms (Dubner et al., 1987; Hu et al., 1986; Hu & Sessle, 1989). This mechanism can explain stimulation-related pain produced by activation of Aβ fibers, and the radiation of this pain beyond the stimulation site (Dubner et al., 1987). Central reorganization following partial deafferentation may also explain both the disparity between the location of the trigger site and the location of the paroxysmal pain. Evolving reorganization results in a series of new receptive fields that are removed from the original; stimulation of these fields evokes pain in the original, now distant, location (Dubner et al., 1987).

Second, the central changes in TN may also reflect persistent peripheral input rather than the absence of inputs. Focal demyelination from mechanical compression or demyelinating plaques associated with multiple sclerosis can result in the formation of microneuromas at the site of the demyelination. Ephaptic activity from these microneuromas provide a source of persistent input that sensitizes central neurons. Demyelination may also increase primary afferent excitability, resulting also in enhanced central sensitivity to other peripheral inputs. This increase in excitability may be sufficient to account for Aβ-evoked pain, temporal summation, and radiation or stimulation-related pain beyond the stimulation site. However, the mechanisms of persistent input might be expected to result in both spontaneous pain and secondary hyperalgesia. In addition, all of these mechanisms cannot account for the features of painful paroxysm and subsequent refractory period. The similarities of TN to epileptic seizures provides an attractive explanation for an underlying mechanism, although the connection of epileptic foci to a peripheral etiology is not obvious.

The overwhelming evidence indicates that peripheral pathology interacts with neurons from other locations and modalities. The observed effects of the central consequences of demyelination and deafferentation have led to the formation of the proposed brainstem mechanisms described earlier. However, the afferent fibers have an opportunity to interact before this stage. They may communicate at the site of putative compression, forming "an artificial synapse" with neighboring neurons (W. J. Gardner & Pinto, 1953). They may also interact in a similar fashion with a greater number of neurons as they converge downstream in the Gasserion ganglion. A recent proposal suggests that all of the features of TN can be explained by trigeminal root pathologies and altered processing in the ganglion (Rappaport & Devor, 1994). In this proposal, increased sensitivity in ganglionic neurons would set the stage for a paroxysmal event. A triggering stimulus would set off this chain of events by the known mechanism of ganglionic crossed after discharge, in which populations of neighboring neurons, including nociceptors, are excited. This excitation would both spread and enter a positive feedback mode, explaining the intensity, spread, and duration of a paroxysmal attack. The indiscriminate activation of a population of neurons results in the unnatural "electric shock" nature of the paroxysmal sensation. A number of "self-quenching" mechanisms would temporarily stop rhythmic firing due to depletion of stores of a necessary substance or accumulated activation of an inhibitory mechanism.

This proposed ganglionic mechanism can account for many, but not all, of the features of TN. For example, it does not explain how the paroxysm in one trigeminal division can be triggered from another division. Of course, the proposed mechanisms need not operate in isolation; TN may represent a unique disease that is only expressed when a group of interacting factors are present.

In conclusion, TN is a specific disease that can be managed very effectively by pharmacological and minimally invasive techniques, and likely cured by more invasive procedures. For the patient, the prognosis is very good with current state-of-the-art techniques. For the scientist, TN provides an intriguing puzzle. Future advances may both help complete this puzzle and increase further the efficacy and safety of pharmacological and surgical treatments.

REFERENCES

Antonaci, F., & Sjaastad, O. (1989). Chronic paroxysmal hemicrania (CPH): A review of the clinical manifestations. *Headache, 29,* 648–656.

Adams, C. B. T. (1989). Microvascular compression: An alternative review and hypothesis. *Journal of Neurosurgery, 57,* 1–12.

Barrett, A. P., & Schifter, M. (1993). Trigeminal neuralgia. *Australian Dental Journal, 38,* 198–203.

Barker, F. G. II, Jannetta, P. J., Bissonette, D. J., Larkins, M. V., & Jho, H. D. (1996). The long-term outcome of microvascular decompression for trigeminal neuralgia. *New England Journal of Medicine, 334,* 1077–1082.

Belber, C. J., & Rak, R. A. (1987). Balloon compression rhizolysis in the surgical management of trigeminal neuralgia. *Neurosurgery, 20,* 908–913.

Bell, C. (1829). On the nerves of the face, being a second paper on that subject. *Philosophical Transactions of the Royal Society of London, 1,* 317–330.

Bennett, M. H., & Jannetta, P. J. (1983). Evoked potentials in trigeminal neuralgia. *Neurosurgery, 13,* 242–247.

Benoliel, R., & Sharav, Y. (1998). Trigeminal neuralgia with lacrimation or SUNCT syndrome? *Cephalgia, 18,* 85–89.

Blom, S. (1962). Trigeminal neuralgia: Its treatment with a new anticonvulsant drug. *Lancet, 1,* 839–840.

Bowsher, D., Haggett, C., Miles, J., & Eldridge, P. (1996). Sensory change in unoperated idiopathic trigeminal neuralgia. *Abstracts—Eighth World Congress on Pain, 152.*

Braham, J., & Saia, A. (1960). Phentoin in the treatment of trigeminal and other neuralgias. *Lancet, 2,* 892–893.

Burgess, P. R., & Perl, E. R. (1973). Cutaneous mechanoreceptors and nociceptors. In A. Iggo (Ed.), *Handbook of sensory physiology, somatosensory system* (Vol. 2, pp. 29–78). Heidelberg, Germany: Springer.

Chandra, B. (1975). The use of clonazepam in the treatment of trigeminal neuralgia. *Modern Medicine of Asia, 11,* 8–9.

Connelly, T. J. (1982). Balloon compression and trigeminal neuralgia. *Medical Journal of Australia, 2,* 119.

Court, J. E., & Kase, C. S. (1976). Treatment of tic douloureux with a new anticonvulsant (clonazepam). *Journal of Neurology, Neurosurgery, and Psychiatry, 39,* 297–299.

Dandy, W. E. (1934). Concerning the cause of trigeminal neuralgia. *American Journal of Surgery, 24,* 447–455.

Dubner, R., Sharav, Y., Gracely, R. H., & Price, D. C. (1987). Idiopathic trigeminal neuralgia: Sensory features and pain mechanisms. *Pain, 31,* 23–33.

Engel, J. (1989). *Seizures and epilepsy.* Philadelphia: Davis.

Fields, H. L. (1996). Treatment of trigeminal neuralgia. *New England Journal of Medicine, 334,* 1125–1126.

Fothergill, S. (1773). Of a painful affection of the face. *Medical Observations and Inquiries by a Society of Physicians, London, 5,* 129–142.

Fromm, G. H., Shibuya, T., Nakata, M., & Terrence, C. F. (1990). Effects of d-baclofen and l-baclofen on the trigeminal nucleus. *Neuropharmacology, 29,* 249–254.

Fromm, G. H., Terrence, C. F., & Maron, J. C. (1984). Baclofen in the treatment of trigeminal neuralgia: Double-blind study and long term follow-up. *Annals of Neurology, 15,* 240–244.

Gardner, E. J. (1962). Concerning the mechanism of trigeminal neuralgia and hemifacial spasm. *Journal of Neurosurgery, 19,* 947–957.

Gardner, W. J., & Pinto, J. P. (1953). The Taarnhoj operation: Relief of trigeminal neuralgia without numbness. *Cleveland Clinical Quarterly, 20,* 364–367.

Green, M. W., & Selman, J. E. (1991). The medical management of trigeminal neuralgia. *Headache, 31,* 588–592.

Gybels, J., & Sweet, W. H. (1989). *Neurosurgical treatment of persistent pain.* Basel, Switzerland: Karger.

Håkanson, S. (1981). Trigeminal neuralgia treated by the injection of glycerol into the trigeminal cistern. *Neurosurgery, 9,* 638–646.

Hamlyn, P. J., & King, T. T. (1992). Neurovascular compression in trigeminal neuralgia: A clinical and anatomical study. *Journal of Neurosurgery, 26,* 159–162.

Harris, W. (1940). Analysis of 1433 cases of paroxysmal trigeminal neuralgia (trigeminal-tic) and the end results of Gasserion alcohol injection. *Brain, 63,* 209–224.

Hu, J. W., Dostrovsky, J. O., Lenz, Y. E., Ball, G. J., & Sessle, B. J. (1986). Tooth pulp deafferentation is associated with functional alterations in the properties of neurons in the trigeminal spinal tract nucleus. *Journal of Neurophysiology, 56,* 1650–1668.

Hu, J. W., & Sessle, B. J. (1989). Effects of tooth pulp deafferentation on nociceptive and nonnociceptive neurons of the feline trigeminal subnucleus caudalis (medullary dorsal horn). *Journal of Neurophysiology, 61,* 1197–1206.

Jannetta, P. J. (1967). Arterial compression of the trigeminal nerve at the pons in patients with trigeminal neuralgia. *Journal of Neurosurgery, 26,* 159–162.

Jannetta, P. J. (1976). Microsurgical approach to the trigeminal nerve for tic douloureux. *Progress in Neurological Surgery, 7,* 180–200.

Kugleberg, E., & Lindblom, U. (1959). The mechanisms of the pain in trigeminal neuralgia. *Journal of Neurology, Neurosurgery, and Psychiatry, 22,* 36–43.

Leandri, M., Miles, J., Eldridge, P., & Haggett, C. (1996). Evoked potentials in proximal trigeminal root before and during microvascular decompression for trigeminal neuralgia. *Abstracts—Eighth World Congress on Pain, 152.*

Lechin, F., van der Dijs, B., Lechin, M., Amat, J., & Leechin, A. (1989). Pimmozide therapy for trigeminal neuralgia. *Archives of Neurology, 46,* 960–963.

Lewey, F. H., & Grant, F. C. (1938). Physiopathologic and pathoanatomic aspects of major trigeminal neuralgia. *Archives of Neurological Psychiatry, 40,* 1126–1134.

Loeser, J. D. (1994). Tic douloureux and atypical facial pain. In P. D. Wall & R. Melzack (Eds.), *Textbook of pain* (pp. 699–710). Edinburgh: Churchill Livingstone.

Maxwell, R. E. (1990). Clinical diagnosis of trigeminal neuralgia and differential diagnosis of facial pain. In R. L. Rovit, R. Muralli, & P. J. Jannetta (Eds.), *Trigeminal neuralgia* (pp. 53–77). Baltimore: Williams & Wilkins.

Meaney, J. F., Eldridge, P. R., Dunn, L. T., Nixon, T. E., Whitehouse, G. H., & Miles, J. B. (1995). Demonstration of neurovascular compression in trigeminal neuralgia with magnetic resonance imaging: Comparison with surgical findings in 52 consecutive operative cases. *Journal of Neurosurgery, 83,* 799–805.

Miles, J., Eldridge, P., Haggett, C., & Bowsher, D. (1996). Clinical and sensory effects of microvascular decompression on idiopathic trigeminal neuralgia. *Abstracts—Eighth World Congress on Pain, 152.*

Mullan, S. M., & Lichtor, T. (1983). Percutaneous microcompression of the trigeminal ganglion for trigeminal neuralgia. *Journal of Neurosurgery, 59,* 1007–1012.

Nurmikko, T. J. (1991). *Archives of Neurology, 48,* 523–527.

Peiris, J. B., Perera, G. L. S., Devendra, S. V., & Lionel, N. D. W. (1980). Sodium valproate in trigeminal neuralgia. *Medical Journal of Australia, 2,* 278.

Ranieri, T. A., Longmire, D. R., Attia-Yon, E., McDonald, R. T., & Leak, W. D. (1996). Symptom reduction in trigeminal neuralgia and atypical facial pain during treatment with gabapentin. *Abstracts—Eighth World Congress on Pain, 155.*

Rappaport, Z. H. (1986). Percutaneous retrogasserian glycerol injection for trigeminal neuralgia: One year follow-up. *Pain Clinic, 1,* 57–61.

Rappaport, Z. H., & Devor, M. (1994). Trigeminal neuralgia: The role of self-sustaining discharge in the trigeminal ganglion. *Pain, 56,* 127–138.

Ratner, E. J., Person, P., Kleinman, D. J., Shklar, G., & Socransky, S. W. (1979). Jawbone cavities and trigeminal and atypical facial neuralgias. *Oral Surgery, 48,* 3–20.

Rhoton, A. L. (1990). Microsurgical anatomy of decompression operations on the trigeminal nerve. In R. L. Rovit, A. Murali, & P. J. Jannetta (Eds.), *Trigeminal neuralgia* (pp. 165–200). Baltimore: Williams & Wilkins.

Riley, H. A., German, W. J., Wortis, H., Herbert, C., Zahn, D., & Eichna, L. (1942). Glossopharyngeal neuralgia initiating or associated with cardiac arrest. *Transactions of the American Neurological Association, 89,* 1742–1744.

Roberts, A. M., Person, P., Chandran, N. B., & Hori, J. M. (1984). Further observations on dental parameters of trigeminal and atypical facial neuralgias. *Oral Surgery, 58*, 121–129.

Roulhac, G. E., & Levy, I. (1950). Glossopharyngeal neuralgia associated with cardiac arrest and convulsions. *AMA Archives of Neurology and Psychiatry, 63*, 133–139.

Saini, S. S. (1987). Retrogasserian anhydrous glycerol injection therapy in trigeminal neuralgia: Observations in 552 patients. *Journal of Neurology, Neurosurgery, and Psychiatry, 50*, 1536–1538.

Shaber, E. P., & Kroll, A. J. (1980). Trigeminal neuralgia—A new treatment concept. *Oral Surgery, 49*, 286–293.

Sheldon, C. H., Pudenz, R. H., Freshwater, B., & Crue, B. L. (1955). Compression rather than decompression for trigeminal neuralgia. *Journal of Neurosurgery, 12*, 123–126.

Sjaastad, O., & Dale, I. (1974). Evidence for a new (?) treatable headache entity. *Headache, 14*, 105–108.

Smirne, S., & Scarlato, G. (1977). Clonazepam in cranial neuralgias. *Medical Journal of Australia, 1*, 93–94.

Stookey, B., & Ransohoff, J. (1959). *Trigeminal neuralgia: Its history and treatment*. Springfield, IL: Thomas.

Svien, H. J., Hill, N. C., & Daly, D. D. (1957). Partial glossopharyngeal neuralgia associated with syncope. *Journal of Neurosurgery, 14*, 452–457.

Sweet, W. H. (1986). The treatment of trigeminal neuralgia (tic douloureux). *New England Journal of Medicine, 315*, 174–177.

Sweet, W. H. (1990). Complications of treating trigeminal neuralgia; an analysis of the literature and response to a questionnaire. In R. L. Rovit, A. Murali, & P. J. Jannetta (Eds.), *Trigeminal neuralgia* (pp. 251–279). Baltimore: Williams & Wilkins.

Swerdlow, M. (1980). The treatment of "shooting" pain. *Postgraduate Medical Journal, 56*, 159–161.

Taarnhøj, P. (1952). Decompression of the trigeminal root and the posterior part of the ganglion as treatment in trigeminal neuralgia: Preliminary communication. *Journal of Neurosurgery, 9*, 288–290.

Wilkins, R. H. (1979). Tic douloureux. *Contemporary Neurosurgery, 1*, 1–6.

Yoshimasu, F., Kurland, L. T., & Elveback, L. R. (1972). Tic douloureux in Rochester, Minnesota, 1945–1969. *Neurology, 22*, 952.

Young, R. F. (1988). Glycerol rhizolysis for treatment of trigeminal neuralgia. *Journal of Neurosurgery, 69*, 39–45.

Pelvic and Abdominal Syndromes

Chapter 21

Chronic Pelvic Pain

Robert C. Reiter

The University of Iowa College of Medicine

Prevalence and Significance

Chronic pelvic pain (CPP) may be defined as noncyclic abdominal and pelvic pain of at least 6 months' duration. This syndrome, and the many adverse psychosocial outcomes with which it is associated, represent a primary health concern of women. Inappropriate health care utilization, high rates of undiagnosed psychological morbidity, and protracted disability have been documented in several studies (Walker, Katon, & Jemelka, 1991; Walling, O'Hara, et al., 1994).

The significance of CPP is readily appreciated. In one nonclinical sample of 651 women, the current prevalence rate of CPP was 12%, and the lifetime occurrence rate was 33% (Walker et al., 1991). This syndrome has been estimated to account for approximately 15% of outpatient gynecological consultations and is responsible for one third of laparoscopies performed in the United States (Reiter & Gambone, 1991).

In addition, CPP is listed as the indication for 12% to 16% of hysterectomies performed in the United States, accounting for approximately 80,000 procedures annually (Dicker et al., 1982; Gambone, Lench, Slesinski, Reiter, & Moore, 1989). Despite its high use, there are no controlled trials evaluating the long-term effectiveness of hysterectomy for chronic pain. However, approximately 25% of women referred for evaluation of CPP have previously undergone hysterectomy without resolution of symptoms (Slocumb, 1990).

The management of CPP has been the subject of considerable controversy, with forceful advocates of interventions ranging from psychotherapy to aggressive surgery. These widely divergent differences in management have tended to reflect underlining differences in training and understanding of the pathogenesis and maintenance of chronic pain, as well as significant professional uncertainty (Steege, Stout, & Somkuti, 1991).

CONCEPTUAL MODELS OF CHRONIC PAIN

Medical Model

The medical model of pain postulates that pain perception is the direct result of tissue trauma and that the severity of pain is proportional to the severity of the traumatic insult (Melzack, 1986). This model tends to emphasize technologically intensive and diagnostic and therapeutic procedures in the search for a single biological cause and specific quick cure. In this framework, pain unassociated with identifiable tissue injury is commonly regarded as spurious or psychogenic.

Despite anecdotal reports attempting to ascribe symptoms to specific gynecological causes, the etiology and maintenance of CPP defies any simple taxonomy. Prior to the 1950s, CPP was commonly attributed to a variety of incidental or even spurious conditions such as pelvic congestion syndrome, uterine retroflexion, uterine descensus, and broad ligament defects, many of which occur with similar frequency in asymptomatic women (Stenchever, 1990). With the widespread use of laparoscopic procedures, CPP has more recently been attributed to laparoscopic findings, such as endometriosis and pelvic adhesions. Controlled trials, however, have documented that the prevalence of many of these conditions is also similar in women with CPP and in pain-free controls (such as a women undergoing tubal sterilization), suggesting that they are incidentally— rather than causally—associated with symptoms (Rapkin, 1986; Walker et al., 1988). Several recent studies have implicated gastroenterological disorders, such as symptomatic dysmotility and irritable bowel syndrome, in many women with CPP (Reiter & Milburn, 1992; Walker et al., 1991).

Biopsychosocial Model

The medical model of pain has proven overly simplistic for understanding and managing most chronic pain syndromes, including chronic pelvic pain. Multiple psychosocial factors have been documented in hundreds of well-controlled trials to be equal or better predictors of chronic pain severity, associated disability, and treatment outcomes than degree of tissue injury

(Turk, Meichenbaum, & Genest, 1983). Among these are affective state (depression), attention to pain, general health status, attributions (beliefs) about pain, anxiety, social support, educational attainment, socioeconomic status, employment status and disability compensation, and familial models (family members) with chronic pain (Fordyce, 1976; Melzack, 1986; Turk et al., 1983).

We have investigated multiple clinical and nonclinical factors associated with CPP, including abuse history, spouse responses to pain, unemployment disability compensation, marital adjustment, and chronic pain experience among first-degree female relatives. These variables are found to be strongly predictive of several adverse health-related sequelae associated with chronic pain, including depression, pain severity, and sexual dysfunction (see Table 21.1). Furthermore, our data suggest that these variables are more accurate predictors of outcome than "classic" medical variables, such as laparoscopic findings.

Collectively, these data lend support to the *biopsychosocial model* of chronic pain (see Table 21.2). In this model, the occurrence and maintenance of adverse clinical and social outcomes is seen as the result of the complex interaction between chronic nociceptive stimuli and multiple psychological and social determinants. This model would predict that chronic symptoms (such as those associated with functional bowel disorders) that may be relatively prevalent in the general population would not lead to major adverse outcomes ("harm") in the absence of specific predisposing psychosocial conditions.

This model would also predict that eradication of a chronic symptom without alteration of the predisposing psychosocial state in a chronic pain patient would lead to temporary improvement in symptoms following by recurrent disabling symptoms, perhaps involving an alternate site or symptom (such as headache or chronic fatigue). These predications are con-

TABLE 21.1
Predictors of Pain Severity, Sexual Function,
and Depression in Women With CPP

	Dependent (Outcome) Variable		
Independent Variables	Pain Severity	Sexual Function	Depression
Spouse responses	$p < 0.05$	$p < 0.05$	$p < 0.05$
Marital adjustment	NS	$p < 0.05$	$p < 0.05$
Physical abuse	NS	NS	$p < 0.05$
Relative with CPP	NS	NS	$p < 0.05$
Depression	$p < 0.05$	$p < 0.05$	—
Laparoscopic findings	NS	NS	NS
Pain severity	—	NS	NS

TABLE 21.2
Biopsychosocial Model of Chronic Pelvic Pain

Precipitating Somatic Symptoms	+	Predisposing Psychosocial Variables	=	Adverse Outcomes
• Irritable bowel		• Familial pain models		• Pain severity
• Trigger points		• Marital adjustment		• Disability/impaired health status
• Cycle pain		• Spouse responses		• Inappropriate health care utilization
• Detrusor instability		• Abuse history		• Substance abuse
		• Mood/anxiety		• Depression
		• Somatization		

sistent with reported observations of a variety of chronic pain populations, including CPP. For this reason, appropriate expectations of outcome of treatment for chronic pain must be regarded as long-term resolution of all chronic disabling symptomatology and normalization of health-related quality of life, rather than short-term resolution of an isolated symptom.

The biopsychosocial model serves as the basis for multidisciplinary pain management in which treatment is provided by an interdisciplinary team and is directed not only toward identifiable medical diagnoses and symptoms, but simultaneously toward psychological and social outcomes, including depression, substance abuse, marital and sexual dysfunction, and current distress relating to previous or current abuse. Failure to recognize and treat these factors will undermine efforts to improve pain and restore normal function.

MULTIDISCIPLINARY MANAGEMENT OF CHRONIC PELVIC PAIN

This section summarizes the approach used in the Chronic Pelvic Pain Clinic at the University of Iowa. Although our experience represents only one model of multidisciplinary pain management, it incorporates many of the elements present in similar programs.

Assessment

Medical Evaluation

The goals of medical evaluation of CPP are to rule out potentially life-threatening pathology, such as cancer or major depression with suicidal ideation, and to identify treatable sources of pain.

Laparoscopy. Following the widespread reemergence of laparoscopy in the 1960s, CPP was attributed to a variety of laparoscopic findings, such as peritoneal defects, serousal pigmentation, adhesions, or dilated veins (Kresch, Seifer, & Sachs, 1984). Clinicians have commonly concluded that somatic diagnoses have been excluded if laparoscopy is negative. There are few objective data, however, to support these assumptions, and a growing body of investigation to suggest that they may be invalid.

Several studies, for example, have documented that the prevalence of findings such as mild endometriosis and adhesions is similar in patients with CPP and pain-free controls undergoing laparoscopy for infertility or tubal sterilization (Rapkin, 1986; Walker et al., 1991). Other investigators have reported high prevalences of nongynecological diagnoses, such as irritable bowel syndrome and abdominal "trigger points," in many women with laparoscopically negative abdominal and pelvic pain (Hogston, 1987; Reiter & Gambone, 1991; Slocumb, 1986; Walker et al., 1991). Of particular relevance is a recent prospective randomized trial that concluded that laparoscopy did not improve long-term outcome in women with CPP (Peters, VanDorst, & Jellis, 1991). Therefore, though advanced intrapelvic pathology, such as severe endometriosis or dense pelvic adhesions involving bowel, may be causally associated with CPP, we consider mild endometriosis, filmy adhesions, small uterine fibroids, and functional ovarian cysts to be incidental findings.

For these reasons, we do not consider laparoscopy to be a requisite for referral to the pain clinic, although we continue to recommend it in cases in which the examination is abnormal, initial management fails to provide significant resolution of symptoms, or the patient has fixed attributions regarding causality of pain, which may interfere with treatment.

Clinical Evaluation. A thorough physical examination is performed on all patients, which includes attempts to elicit trigonal or urethral tenderness and abdominal trigger points (Slocumb, 1986; Thomson, 1977). Screening laboratory tests include stool guaiac, urinalysis, cervical culture, cytology, and chlamydial antigen. Special studies, including endoscopy and radiographic studies, are obtained only as indicated.

Likely symptom sources (frequently multiple) are identified in approximately 95% of patients: Irritable bowel syndrome and functional bowel disorders, abdominal trigger points, and atypical menstrual cycle pain account for 85% of these diagnoses. Urological diagnoses, such as chronic urethritis, trigonitis, detrusor instability, interstitial cystitis, and recurrent cystitis, are found in 5% to 10% of referrals. A number of unusual diagnoses are observed anecdotally, including inflammatory bowel disease, multiple sclerosis, progressive retroperitoneal fibrosis, interstitial cystitis, reflex sympathetic dystrophy, acute intermittent porphyria, and pelvic neurofibromatosis. No identifiable symptom source is apparent in 2% to 3% of referrals.

Irritable Bowel Syndrome (IBS).   Using standard validated questionnaires, investigators have reported that symptoms consistent with irritable bowel syndrome are evident in from 65% to 79% of referrals for CPP (Hogston, 1987; Walker et al., 1991). We have observed similarly high prevalences of functional bowel disorders in approximately 70% of new referrals for CPP. The diagnosis of IBS is straightforward, using criteria-based self-reported questionnaires, such as those developed by Thompson, Dotevall, and Drossman (1989). Diagnostic criteria include continuous or recurrent abdominal pain of at least 3 months' duration and two or more associated symptoms, including altered stool frequency, altered stool form, altered stool passage, passage of mucus, or abdominal distention and bloating (Thompson et al., 1989).

Abdominal Trigger Points.   Trigger points are discrete (nonmigratory 1–2 cm) hyperpathic foci, the cause of which remains obscure. Impingement of subcutaneous sensory nerves in, or adjacent to, fibrotic surgical incisions has been documented, although many cases are nonincisional (Applegate, 1972). Slocumb (1986) diagnosed trigger points in 74% of patients referred for evaluation of CPP. Although this prevalence undoubtedly reflects some observer bias, our experience has tended to confirm these impressions. We have diagnosed abdominal wall pain syndromes, most commonly trigger points, in 50% to 60% of women referred to our clinic following negative laparoscopy. Interestingly, peripartum onset of pain is reported by approximately 30% of patients diagnosed with abdominal trigger points, suggesting a possible relationship to distention and contraction of the abdominal wall in association with pregnancy.

Menstrual Cycle Pain.   Another sometimes overlooked source of symptoms are several menstrual cycle–specific pain syndromes, including atypical or protracted dysmenorrhea, midcyle ovulatory pain (mittleschmerz), or luteal phase pain (or perimenstrual magnification of pain) associated with late luteal dysphoric disorder (LLDP, or premenstrual syndrome). These disorders may be present in up to 20% of patients referred for evaluation of *noncyclic* CPP (Reiter & Gambone, 1991). Consistent cyclicity of symptoms may not be apparent to the patient or physician until pain calendars are reviewed.

Psychosocial Evaluation

Evaluation of women with CPP requires both a thorough medical examination as well as assessment of the many psychosocial variables noted previously. Relevant data are collected through several modalities, including interviews, questionnaires, and observation. Ideally, information should be obtained from both the patient and her partner or family. The goals of this assessment include the identification of problem areas that can be targets for intervention, the development of a treatment plan, and the establishment of baseline information to allow for evaluation of progress and treatment outcomes. Through the course of assessment, a collaborative process should be developed with the patient who participates in identification of treatment goals.

In our clinic, we use a variety of self-report questionnaires designed to assess the impact of chronic pain on the life of the patient as well as current psychosocial variables that may affect the patient's ability to cope. The 52-item West Haven–Yale Multidimensional Pain Inventory (WHYMPI) developed by Kerns, Turk, and Rudy (1985) assesses perceptions of pain severity, support, control, spouse responses to pain, and impact on health status. We have added a scale assessing frequency of sexual activity to the WHYMPI. A number of additional questionnaires are available to assess a variety of psychosocial aspects of pain (Kerns & Jacob, 1992).

Psychological morbidity, particularly depression, is commonly observed as a consequence of chronic pain and the associated learned helplessness and loss of self-control. We use the Beck Depression Inventory (BDI), a well-validated 21-item self-report questionnaire, to assess the severity of depressive symptoms and to identify symptoms that should be targets for intervention, such as suicidal ideation or intent (Beck, 1991). Marital adjustment has also been shown to be associated with the maintenance of chronic pain and with depression (Turk, Kerns, & Rosenberg, 1992). We use the 15-item Locke–Wallace Marital Adjustment Test (which we have modified to allow for assessment of nonmarried or same sex partners) to assess dyadic adjustment (Locke & Wallace, 1959).

All patients undergo a standard structured intake interview, taking approximately 45 minutes and carried out by a nurse clinician. In addition to providing an excellent medical and pain history, the interview provides information on medical and social history that may represent targets for intervention. The interview also provides an opportunity to present the patient the organization and philosophy of the clinic and to address specific fears or misunderstandings. Finally, the interview establishes a relationship between the patient and the clinic staff, which facilitates motivating the patient to adhere to treatment recommendations and follow-up.

This interview includes a comprehensive history of pain, gynecological and other medical problems, sexuality, past and current physical abuse, and psychosocial assessment. We obtain a detailed pain history, including duration, intensity, and location, including verbal analog scales. We utilize checklists and open-ended questions to ascertain activities that exacerbate or improve pain. We screen for gastroenterological symptoms utilizing a modification of the Thompson et al. (1989) criteria for diagnosis of IBS (such as intermittent diarrhea or constipation), which may suggest a functional bowel disorder; and for urological symptoms, which may suggest detrusor instability or other bladder pathology. A checklist is used to identify previous pain treatments and there efficacy. An open-ended question regarding the patient's attributions about the origins of her pain is designed to provide information about possible misconceptions and fears. The detailed pain history also conveys to the patient the team's interest in her complaints and concerns.

Numerous studies have documented high rates of abuse in CPP populations (Walker et al., 1991; Walling, Reiter et al., 1994). For this reason, the sexual history is of particular importance in the assessment interview (Hameroff, Cook, & Scherer, 1982; Kerns & Jacob, 1992). Previous studies have documented advantages of gathering evidence regarding abuse experience through an interview format rather than through questionnaire, including improved facilitation of disclosure, opportunity to clarify language and interpretations or responses, and an early opportunity to make resources available to the patient. We ask patients directly about experiences of genital trauma (such as straddle injuries) and transition it to questions about abuse experience, including rape, molestation, and/or incest. We attempt to elicit some detail about the experiences, including age, circumstances, whether the perpetrators were known, and previous treatment. Additional sexual issues, such as pain associated with sex, sexual satisfaction, libido, and orgasmic function, are also assessed briefly. Assumptions regarding heterosexuality are avoided and care is taken to use language that is inclusive of heterosexuals, bisexuals, and lesbians. Finally, we also inquire about childhood and adult physical abuse, including age, duration, circumstances, medical injuries and treatment, and any counseling received.

In order to establish a baseline "wellness" profile and facilitate goal setting, we assess general health habits, including nutritional habits and diet, current activity and exercise, and sleep habits. Sleep disorders are commonly associated with chronic pain and are a common sign of associated mood disturbance. Total hours of sleep, sleep latency, and early morning awakening should be assessed. Social history, including substance use, educational attainment, income, and current financial concerns are also reviewed.

Several studies have documented high prevalences of depression, somatization, and anxiety disorders in women with chronic pelvic pain (Walker et al., 1991; Walling, O'Hara et al., 1994). In our experience, approximately 50% of patients are found to have at least one psychological diagnosis, with major depressive disorder, acute situational disturbances, anxiety disorders, and somatization observed in from 10% to 50% of referrals. Less frequently identified diagnoses include posttraumatic stress disorder, eating disorders, obsessive compulsive disorder, and personality disorders, which are diagnosed in 5% or less of patients. Rare diagnoses include multiple personality disorder, psychoses, and malingering (Reiter et al., 1992), accounting for 1% or less of diagnoses.

Clearly, the assessment process is critical to establishing a complete understanding of the myriad complex issues involved in the cause and maintenance of CPP. The time spent in this process is usually rewarded by higher patient satisfaction, the ability to develop individualized treatment plans, and improved communication and collaboration between the patient and the provider team regarding recommended treatments and expectations of outcome.

Treatment

Overview

The composition of the provider team is central to multidisciplinary management of CPP. In our clinic, the team includes a nurse clinician, a gynecologist, and a health psychologist, all of whom have expertise in chronic pain evaluation and management. Additional health professionals may also be included on the provider team, including physical therapists, rehabilitation specialists, and biofeedback technologists.

The nurse clinician performs the assessment interview, administers psychometric tests, and performs certain selected interventions, such as relaxation training and wellness management. The nurse clinician frequently has the most contact with the patient because she handles patient calls. For this reason, the nurse clinician must become skilled in providing reassurance and support to the patient without reinforcing pain behaviors or catastrophic thinking.

The gynecologist is responsible for medical evaluation, medical interventions, and medication management. This individual must devote a significant amount of time to each patient, in order to provide education, support, and reassurance, as well as reeducation regarding the nature of chronic pain and likely causes and treatment. Maladaptive beliefs or attribution regarding pain causes and treatment expectations must also be addressed.

The health psychologist provides psychological assessment and psychotherapy when indicated. Psychological interventions are commonly focused on broadening the patient's conceptionalization of chronic pain and emphasizing personal responsibility for management. For patients who identify current psychosocial issues for which they desire treatment, the psychologist provides psychotherapy, couples therapy, and sex therapy.

The primary goals of treatment of CPP are to relieve suffering by treating identifiable symptoms and concurrent psychological morbidity, to restore normal function, improve quality of life by managing symptoms and minimizing disability, and prevent recurrence of chronic symptoms and disability.

Drug Therapy

Increasingly, surgical treatment of CPP is being replaced by multidisciplinary management emphasizing optimization of symptom control, education, restoration of function, modification of maladaptive behaviors, and cognitive pain management (Gambone & Reiter, 1990; Peters et al., 1991). Although these modalities are primary nonmedical, drug therapy plays an important role in management of CPP.

Psychotropic Medications. Tricyclic antidepressants (TCAs) have been used in the treatment of many chronic pain syndromes, such as arthritis, diabetic neuropathy, headache, back pain, and cancer. In these populations, TCAs have been shown to improve pain tolerance, restore normal sleep, and reduce depressive symptoms (Berlin, 1986; Hameroff et al., 1982; Kvinesdal, Molin, & Froland, 1984; Walsh, 1983; Watson et al., 1982). Several studies have documented pain responses with dosages lower than those typically used to treat depression (Walsh, 1983). A plausible, but unsubstantiated mechanism of action may be repletion of serum endorphins (endogenous morphinelike substance).

TCA therapy for patients with sleep disturbance, mild to moderate mood disturbance, or both, is usually initiated with imipramine, amitriptyline, or doxepin 10–25 mg at bedtime. This dosage is titrated to 50–75 mg as needed. Full antidepressant dosages (up to 200 mg daily) may be utilized for patients with major mood disturbance. Selective serotonin reuptake inhibitors (SSRIs), such as Prozac 20–40 mg or Paxil 10–20 mg every morning, are effective and safe alternatives for patients with moderate to severe depression, or patients with less severe mood disturbance failing TCA therapy. SSRIs may be used alone or in combination with low-dose TCAs.

Oral Analgesics. Optimization of oral analgesic therapy is an obvious initial treatment option for CPP. Therapy should begin with a less expensive prostaglandin synthetase inhibitor, such as ibuprofen, on a *scheduled* rather than "prN" (*pro re nata* or as needed) basis. PRN dosing is discouraged because analgesics are typically more effective when taken for mild to moderate symptoms. PRN dosing also may increase pain, which is an attention-driven phenomenon, by encouraging the patient to focus on symptoms and monitor pain severity.

Narcotic analgesics are not recommended for treatment of CPP. These agents have a potent smooth muscle–relaxing effect that may exacerbate functional dysmotility disorders in women with chronic abdominal pain. In addition, sedation and altered cognition associated with narcotic use may limit restoration of normal function.

Drug Therapy of Functional Bowel Disorders. Functional bowel disorders, including IBS and chronic constipation, are symptomatic manifestations of altered bowel motility. These disorders are amenable to a variety of treatment strategies, including dietary management and psychotherapy, particularly when directed toward stress management (Flor, Fydrich, & Turk, 1992). Oral fiber supplementation in the form of psyllium powder increases stool bulk and water content and decreases transit time, thus relieving painful constipation; it also decreases frequency of bowel movements and encourages formed stools in patients with hyperpredominant motile patterns and diarrhea.

Positive results require consistent long-term psyllium supplementation in adequate dosages of at least 6 grams (1 tablespoon) daily (Drossman & Thompson, 1992). Natural dietary fiber sources, such as bran and cellulose, commonly require unpalatably large quantities in comparison to psyllium supplements. Excellent adherence rates and a symptomatic response rate of approximately 90% can be achieved if the regimen is presented to the patient as an integral part of a comprehensive management plan and with appropriate education about the mechanism of action and potential long-term health benefits of fiber supplementation.

Medical regimens that directly alter bowel motility, such as diphenoxylate/atropine and loperamide, are occasionally useful during severe hypermotile phases, and should be used only after a thorough exclusion work-up.

Local Anesthetics. Abdominal wall pain syndromes, including trigger points, are among the more frequent medical diagnoses in women referred for CPP. They are amenable to treatment with a variety of modalities, including transcutaneous electric nerve stimulation (TENS), acupuncture, and infiltration with a variety of agents. Although injectable steroids are commonly used for this purpose or combined with local anesthetics, we have favored the use of 0.25% bupivicaine 5–10 cc injected at the point of maximal tenderness following needle tip localization. Response rates of from 80% to 90% are observed following three to four injections (Slocumb, 1986).

Ovarian Cycle Suppression. Functional menstrual cycle pain is usually amenable to antiprostaglandin therapy or to cycle suppression. For patients failing antiprostaglandin therapy, the choice of cycle suppression therapy is based on safety, cost, and patient acceptance. For these reasons, oral contraceptives and continuous oral or injectable progestins are favored as primary therapy for cyclic functional pain disorders. Gonadotropin-releasing hormone agonist (GnRH-A) may have a limited (primarily diagnostic) role in refractory cases.

Antibiotics. In a woman with CPP and uterine tenderness, who does not meet standard clinical criteria for the diagnosis of endometritis salpingitis, subacute upper genital tract infection is occasionally suspected on the basis of a positive cervical culture, or an endometrial biopsy suggesting chronic endometritis. Standard antibiotic therapy may alleviate symptoms in this setting. With this exception, however, empiric antibiotic therapy is discouraged in women with CPP, negative cultures, and an absence of supporting clinical criteria. Chronic urethral syndrome characterized by urethral irritative symptoms (urgency, frequency, dysuria, suprapubic pain) without bacteriuria, has been reported in up to 2% to 3% of women with CPP (Hibbard, 1983). In an early placebo-controlled study, Stamm et al. (1981) reported that tetracycline improved symptoms only in women with associated pyuria (without bacteriuria); no benefit was observed in women without pyuria.

Cognitive Behavioral Pain Management

Cognitive behavioral treatments operationalize the biopsychosocial treatment model by applying specific interventions for each dimension of the chronic pain phenomenon, including symptom control, treatment of predisposing psychosocial variables, and interventions to reverse or ameliorate adverse outcomes of pain. The phases of treatment include education, skills acquisition, behavioral rehearsal, and maintenance (Holzman, Turk, & Kerns, 1986).

Specific techniques are taught that increase the patient's coping ability and sense of control. For example, relaxation techniques, such as progressive muscle relaxation, deep breathing, and imagery, decrease generalized myotonia and arousal. These techniques provide opportunities for attention diversion and decreased focus on physical signals (Holzman et al., 1986). Distraction techniques are similarly useful to decrease the patient's preoccupation with pain and the focus on her body. These techniques include both cognitive strategies as well as activity, such as work and recreation. Cognitive techniques can also be used to identify and address maladaptive thoughts (such as with cancer phobia) that may influence pain perception. Patients frequently require some persuasion that attention diversion is a useful and acceptable pain management practice because many believe that pain is a signal of danger and should not be ignored.

Patients with CPP frequently limit their activity in order to avoid possible pain exacerbations. Additional factors that may attribute to physical disability include fear, mood disturbances, deconditioning, and financial pressures such as disability compensation. For this reason, progressive activity programs are initiated to increase physical activity and decrease disability behaviors (Hanson & Gerber, 1990). Return to work is an important outcome goal, as well as an important component of intervention.

Another important aspect of cognitive behavioral pain management is stress management (Hanson & Gerber, 1990). This approach includes the identification of stressful events and training in ways to alter these events, such as problem solving, assertiveness, and time management. Relaxation techniques and exercise also decrease physical effects of stress. Many women with CPP have very poor wellness profiles, many of which perpetuate disability and pain. Specific education regarding nutrition, exercise, sleep, relaxation, and substance use is provided as appropriate.

Patients are seen at a 1- to 2-month interval following their initial evaluation and at 3-month intervals thereafter for the first year. After the first year, patients are scheduled at 6-month intervals unless a change in status necessitates earlier follow-up.

Additional Psychotherapies

Patients with psychiatric diagnoses, such as clinical depression, anxiety, eating disorders, or posttraumatic stress disorders, are referred to the health psychologist for individual psychotherapy or referral to another mental health professional. Women experiencing current distress related to a history of past sexual or physical abuse may benefit from treatment focused on reducing the trauma associated with these events. Direct intervention is offered in all cases involving current domestic violence. Patients with current substance abuse problems are referred to appropriate substance abuse treatment programs. Couples therapy is provided as appropriate, including addressing potentially dysfunctional (e.g., punitive or overly solicitous) spousal responses to pain. Other family members may be included in treatment as indicated. Sexual dysfunction, including inhibited sexual desire and arousal and orgasmic dysfunction are common in the CPP population. Patients are offered sexual therapy when these problems are identified.

Treatment Outcomes

A recently published randomized trial confirmed that multidisciplinary treatment of CPP emphasizing pain management, restoration of function, and optimization of adaptive and coping skills appears to offer the best long-term prognosis for women with CPP (Peters et al., 1991). These authors observed global somatic symptom scores and pain severity scores at 18 months following interdisciplinary management, which were approximately half those observed in women treated with traditional medical management only. Other studies have shown that this approach can significantly reduce the use of hysterectomy for this indication (Reiter, Gambone, & Johnson, 1991). In the latter study, overall rates of hysterectomy declined significantly, and the percentage of hysterectomies performed for CPP decreased from 16% to less than 6% following initiation of a multidisciplinary CPP clinic in a defined population catchment area.

The role of surgery is limited in this setting. Current data suggest that the removal of a normal uterus and adnexa is usually ineffective. Although many patients may report temporary improvement in symptoms lasting from 3 to 6 months postoperatively, recurrence may complicate from 50% to 70% of cases. Furthermore, because surgery does not alter the predisposing psychosocial determinants of chronic pain, recurrences of pain may manifest as disabling nonpelvic symptoms.

Studies evaluating cognitive behavioral pain management for nonpelvic pain populations have demonstrated improvements in coping ability, reduction in pain severity, and a decrease in pain-related physical and psychosocial dysfunction (Caudill, Schnable, & Zuttermeister, 1991). A recent meta-analysis of outcomes of behavioral pain treatment showed that mood and associated distress and disability improved more than pain variables. This suggests that reduced distress and increased health-related quality of life may be a more realistic outcome than total pain relief for some patients (Malone & Strube, 1988). In a separate meta-analysis of 65 studies evaluating the efficacy of multidisciplinary pain management, Flor et al. (1992) found benefits of treatment, including improvements in pain, mood, and interference, as well as increased return to work and decreased health care utilization. These effects appear to be stable over time.

Approximately 25% of patients will experience recurrence of significant symptoms within a few months after completion of treatment. In our experience, these recurrences are usually readily amenable to rapid retreatment and maintenance therapy. We have also observed that relapse rate is reduced if patients themselves initiate discontinuation from maintenance (biannual) follow-up.

Caudill et al. (1991) examined the effect of interdisciplinary pain management on health care utilization and cost. They reported a 36% reduction in clinic visits following a 10-session outpatient program for 109 participants, which was sustained for a second-year follow-up. The authors determined that the cost was not the result of shifting of services and projected a total cost savings of $12,000 for the first year and $23,000 for the second year to the health system. A second study documented a 58% reduction in medical costs and utilization rates as a result of multidisciplinary pain treatment (Simmons, Avant, Demsky, & Parisher, 1988).

Summary

Diagnosis and management of CPP are greatly facilitated by a multidisciplinary approach integrating medical intervention with cognitive behavioral pain strategy and treatment of concurrent psychological morbidity. Available outcomes, including pain severity, health status, and disability, are significantly better following this approach than those observed following isolated medical interventions. Because of the chronicity of many of the underlying psychological and social variables predisposing to chronic symptom formation, care of the patient with CPP must be continuous and longitudinal if recurrent adverse sequelae, including disability, inappropriate health care utilization, and depression, are to be prevented.

REFERENCES

Applegate, W. V. (1972). Abdominal cutaneous nerve entrapment syndrome. *Surgery, 71,* 118–123.

Beck, A. (1991). *Depression inventory.* Philadelphia: Center for Cognitive Therapy.

Berlin, E. V. (1986). Imipramine in the treatment of chronic pelvic pain. *Psychosomatics, 27,* 294–297.

Caudill, M., Schnable, R., & Zuttermeister, P. (1991). Decreased clinic use by chronic pain patients: Responsive to behavioral medicine intervention. *The Clinical Journal of Pain, 7,* 305–311.

Dicker, R. C., Greenspan, J. R., Strauss, L. T., Cowart, M. R., Scally, M. J., Peterson, H. B., DeStefano, F., Rubin, G. L., & Ory, H. W. (1982). Complications of abdominal and vaginal hysterectomy among women of reproductive age in the United States: The collaborative review of sterlization. *American Journal of Obstetrics & Gynecology, 144,* 841–848.

Drossman, D. A., & Thompson, W. G. (1992). The irritable bowel syndrome: Review and a graduate multicomponent treatment approach. *Annals of Internal Medicine, 116,* 1009–1016.

Flor, H., Fydrich, T., & Turk, D. C. (1992). Efficacy of multidisciplinary pain treatment centers: A meta-analytic flow. *Pain, 49,* 221–230.

Fordyce, W. E. (1976). *Behavioral methods of control of chronic pain and illness.* St. Louis, MO: Mosby.

Gambone, J. C., Lench, J. B., Slesinski, M. J., Reiter, R. C., & Moore, J. G. (1989). Validation of hysterectomy indications and the quality assurance process. *Obstetrics and Gynecology, 73,* 1045–1049.

Gambone, J. C., & Reiter, R. C. (1990). Nonsurgical management of chronic pelvic pain: A multidisciplinary approach. *Clinical Obstetrics and Gynecology, 33,* 205–211.

Hameroff, S. R., Cook, R. C., Scherer, K., Cargo, B. R., Neuman, C., Womble, J. R., & Davis, T. P. (1982). Doxepin effects on chronic pain, depression, and plasma opioids. *Journal of Clinical Psychiatry, 43,* 22–27.

Hanson, R. W., & Gerber, K. E. (1990). *Coping with chronic pain: A guide to patient self-management.* New York: Guilford.

Hibbard, L. T. (1983). Chronic pelvic pain. In D. R. Mishell & P. F. Brenner (Eds.), *Management of common problems in obstetrics and gynecology* (p. 173). Oradell, NJ: Medical Economics.

Hogston, P. (1987). Irritable bowel syndrome as a cause of chronic pelvic pain in women attending a gynaecology clinic. *British Medical Journal, 294*, 934–938.

Holzman, A. D., Turk, D. C., & Kerns, R. D. (1986). The cognitive-behavioral approach to the management of chronic pain. In A. D. Holzman & D. C. Turk (Eds.), *Pain management: A handbook of psychological treatment approaches*. New York: Pergamon.

Kerns, R. D., & Jacob, M. C. (1992). Assessment of the psychosocial context of the experience of chronic pain. In D. C. Turk & R. Melzack (Eds.), *Handbook of pain assessment* (pp. 148–169). New York: Guilford.

Kerns, R. D., Turk, D. C., & Rudy, T. E. (1985). The West Haven–Yale Multidimensional Pain Inventory (WHYMPI). *Pain, 23*, 345–350.

Kresch, A. J., Seifer, D. B., Sachs, L. B., & Barrese, I. (1984). Laparoscopy in evaluation of 100 women with chronic pelvic pain. *Obstetrics & Gynecology, 64*, 672–674.

Kvinesdal, B., Molin, J., & Froland, A. (1984). Imipramine treatment of painful diabetic neuropathy. *Journal of the American Medical Association, 251*, 1727–1730.

Locke, H. J., & Wallace, K. M. (1959). Short marital-adjustment and prediction tests: Their reliability and validity. *Marriage and Family Living, 21*, 251–260.

Malone, M. D., Strube, M. J., & Scogin, F. R. (1988). Meta-analysis of non-medical treatments for chronic pain. *Pain, 34*, 231–244.

Melzack, R. (1986). Neurophysiologic foundations of pain. In R. A. Sternbach (Ed.), *The psychology of pain* (pp. 347–365). New York: Raven.

Peters, A. A. W., VanDorst, E., & Jellis, J. (1991). A randomized clinical trial to compare two different approaches in women with chronic pelvic pain. *Obstetrics and Gynecology, 77*, 740–744.

Rapkin, A. J. (1986). Adhesions and pelvic pain. A retrospective study. *Obstet Gynecol, 68*, 13–15.

Rapkin, A. J., Kames, L. D., Darke, L. L., Stampler, F. M., & Naliboff, B. D. (1990). History of physical and sexual abuse in women with chronic pelvic pain. *Obstetrics and Gynecology, 76*, 92–96.

Reiter, R. C., & Gambone, J. C. (1991). Nongynecologic somatic pathology in women with chronic pelvic pain and negative laparoscopy. *Journal of Reproductive Medicine, 3*, 253–259.

Reiter, R. C., Gambone, J. C., & Johnson, S. R. (1991). Availability of a multidisciplinary pain clinic and frequency of hysterectomy for chronic pelvic pain. *Journal of Psychosomatic Obstetrics and Gynecology, 12*(Suppl.), 109–116.

Reiter, R. C., & Milburn, A. (1992). Management of chronic pelvic pain. *Postgraduate Obstetrics and Gynecology, 12*, 1–9.

Simmons, J. W., Avant, W. S., Demski, J., & Parisher, D. (1988). Determine successful pain clinic treatment through validation of cost effectiveness. *Spine, 13*, 342–344.

Slocumb, J. C. (1984). Neurologic factors in chronic pelvic pain: Trigger points and the abdominal pelvic pain syndrome. *American Journal of Obstetrics and Gynecology, 149*, 536–543.

Slocumb, J. C. (1990). Operative management of chronic abdominal pelvic pain. *Clinical Obstetrics and Gynecology, 33*, 196–204.

Stamm, W. E., Running, K., McKevitt, M., Counts, G. W., Turck, M., & Holmes, K. K. (1981). Treatment of the acute urethral syndrome. *New England Journal of Medicine, 304*, 956–958.

Steege, J. F., Stout, A. L., & Somkuti, S. G. (1991). Chronic pelvic pain in women: Toward an integrative model. *Journal of Psychosomatic Obstetrics and Gynecology, 12*, 3–23.

Stenchever, M. A. (1990). Symptomatic retrodisplacement, pelvic congestion, universal joint, and peritoneal defects: Facts or fiction? *Clinical Obstetrics and Gynecology, 33*, 161–167.

Thompson, W. G., Dotevall, G., & Drossman, D. A. (1989). Irritable bowel syndrome: Guidelines for the diagnosis. *Gastroenterology International, 2*, 92–95.

Turk, D. C., Kerns, R. D., & Rosenberg, R. (1992). Effects of marital interaction on chronic pain and disability. Examining the down-side of social support. *Rehabilitation Psychology, 37*, 257–262.

Turk, D. C., Meichenbaum, D., & Genest, M. (1983). *Pain and behavioral medicine: A cognitive-behavioral perspective.* San Diego: Academic Press.

Walker, E., Katon, W., Harrop-Griffiths, J., Holms, L., Russo, J., & Hickok, L. R. (1988). Relationship of chronic pelvic pain to psychiatric diagnosis and childhood sexual abuse. *American Journal of Psychiatry, 145,* 75–80.

Walker, E. A., Katon, W. J., & Jemelka, R. (1991). The prevalence of chronic pain and irritable bowel syndrome in two university clinics. *Journal of Psychosomatic Obstetrics and Gynecology, 12*(Suppl.), 65–70.

Walling, M. K., O'Hara, M. W., Reiter, R. C., Milburn, A., Lily, G., & Vincent, S. (1994). Abuse history and chronic pain in women. II: Multivariate analysis of abuse and psychological morbidity. *Obstet Gynecol, 84,* 200–206.

Walling, M. K., Reiter, R. C., O'Hara, M. W., Milburn, A., Lily, G., & Vincent, S. (1994). Abuse history and chronic pain in women. I: Prevalences of sexual and physical abuse. *Obstetrics and Gynecology, 84,* 193–199.

Walsh, T. D. (1983). Antidepressants in chronic pain. *Clinical Neuropharmacology, 6,* 271–276.

Watson, C. P., Evans, R. J., Reed, K., Merskey, H., Goldsmith, L., & Warsh, J. (1982). Amitriptyline versus placebo in post-herpetic neuralgia. *Neurology, 36,* 671–673.

Chapter 22

Functional Gastrointestinal Pain Syndromes

Michael D. Crowell
Ivan Barofsky
The Johns Hopkins University School of Medicine,
The Johns Hopkins Bayview Medical Center,
Marvin M. Schuster Center for Digestive and Motility Disorders

Functional gastrointestinal pain syndromes may be referred to the esophagus, stomach, small bowel, colon, and/or rectum. Presentation is often complex and symptoms may overlap, but generally include complaints of nausea, vomiting, bloating, altered bowel patterns, and most commonly chronic intermittent pain. Broadly defined, these disorders include noncardiac chest pain (NCCP), nonulcer dyspepsia (NUD), and the irritable bowel syndrome (IBS). Together, these functional pain syndromes constitute the most frequent reasons for consultation with gastroenterologists. Abdominal pain is the defining characteristic and the least understood manifestation of these syndromes. The goal of this chapter is to evaluate the mechanisms responsible for pain complaints in gastrointestinal pain syndromes and to determine if each represents different manifestations of a common altered physiology, or whether each reflects different symptom and pathophysiologic profiles. The biopsychosocial aspects of chronic pain in functional bowel patients are also reviewed to emphasize the complexity of providing care for the patient with chronic visceral pain.

The Physiologic Basis of Chronic Pain

Merskey and Bogduk (1994) defined pain as the sensory and emotional sequelia resulting from insult to tissue. However, most patients with functional bowel disorders experience pain chronically or intermittently without evidence of organic lesions. Chronic pain may, therefore, be defined as that which persists beyond the normal time of healing (Bonica, 1953). This definition implies that persistent tissue damage is not a necessary condition for continued pain reports, suggesting instead that altered physiology, and/or various psychological processes (e.g., pain memory, illness behaviors, etc.) maintain the experience of pain. These mechanisms may be particularly relevant to the evaluation and treatment of patients with chronic abdominal pain.

Visceral pain and cutaneous pain differ functionally and neuroanatomically. Cutaneous pain is generally defined as sharp and well localized, whereas visceral pain is generally perceived as dull, achy, and poorly differentiated in terms of quality and anatomic location (Ness & Gebhart, 1990). Over time pain may become localized and be referred to somatic structures whose afferents converge on the same spinal segment as the visceral afferents. Thus, the clinical picture of visceral pain is complex and may well involve both somatic and visceral structures.

The complexity of chronic pain increases severalfold when the plasticity of the neural substrate is appreciated. Neuronal changes may occur secondary to injury to the nerves, inflammation, and other pathophysiologic processes (Coderre et al., 1993). These changes are reflected in reduced thresholds that may result in pain reports to previously nonpainful stimuli (allodynia), decreased pain thresholds to noxious stimuli (hyperalgesia), increased duration of response to brief stimulation (persistent pain), and a spread of pain and hyperalgesia to adjacent tissue (referred pain and secondary hyperalgesia). These observations imply that *as a person experiences pain, the nature of that pain can change significantly.*

The sensitivity of peripheral receptors to certain types of stimuli may be significantly altered or "up-regulated" and may account for neurally mediated pain (Campbell et al., 1994), and even the peripheral analgesic effects of opioids (Stein, 1995). Chronically irritated afferent nerves may lead to sensitization through a reorganization of dorsal horn cells (Dubner, 1992). Continued stimulation may result in an increase in the number and size of these receptors, and simultaneously lower their threshold. Dorsal root reflexes, initially evoked in response to pain, may also lead to a recurrent cycle of pain and inflammation (Sluka et al., 1995). The plasticity of spinal afferents provides a physiologic explanation for the experience of persistent pain and hyperalgesia (McMahon & Wall, 1984; Menetry & Besson, 1982).

The neurophysiology of learning and memory also offers insight into the development of chronic persistent pain. Recent evidence suggests that n-methyl-d-aspartate (NMDA), a protein found on the cell membrane of some neurons, is involved in the long-term potentiation of pain (Watkins & Collingridge, 1989). Clearly, there are a variety of peripheral, spinal, and even intracellular events that make the neural substrate mediating pain plastic, providing a biological basis for chronic pain.

Chronic pain may also be modulated by a person's illness behavior, emotional state, behavior patterns, and prior learning (Merskey, 1994). This example of centrally mediated chronic pain does not require an organic basis, although it does not preclude concurrent or previous pathophysiology. Chronic pain may evolve as a result of developmental processes or trauma, be classically or instrumentally conditioned, or be a product of life events altering perceptual or cognitive processes. Abnormal illness behavior originating in childhood has been directly associated with chronic pain complaints (Pilowsky & Spence, 1976). Chronic pain may also be conditioned (Linton, 1986). Stimuli originally associated with a painful event can develop the capacity to elicit behavioral and emotional responses that were originally associated with an unconditioned stimulus (pain), but now occur in the absence of the painful event. These altered perceptual processes may result in lowered thresholds to visceral stimuli and provide an explanation for hyperalgesia in the functional bowel patient (Mayer & Gebhart, 1993). Evidence also exists for altered cognitive representations of pain or pain memory (Erskine, Morley, & Pearce, 1990). Strong emotions, such as anger, anxiety, and depression, contribute to or result from the experience of pain (Fernandez & Turk, 1995; Taylor, Lorentzen, & Blank, 1990). An association between a person's history of physical or sexual abuse (and trauma in general) and chronic complaints of pain has also been reported (Drossman et al., 1990). Personality types may significantly influence pain reports and treatment outcomes (e.g., neurotisism, hypochondriasism; Barsky & Klerman, 1983).

These data suggest that the neural systems mediating chronic pain represent the convergence of several overlapping subsystems, and most important, can be modified by the very process whereby painful information is transmitted within this system. The recognition of the diversity of organizational patterns (e.g., visceromotor overlap) and the plasticity of the neural substrates of pain has led to a significant increment in the models available to account for different chronic pain experiences. To such structural diversity must be added the growing awareness that the chronicity of pain can be acquired and that there is a molecular basis for this learning. In addition, a person's behavior pattern and past experiences also contribute to the persistence of pain. Each of these adds an increment of complexity to the task of diagnosing and treating the patient with chronic pain. The magnitude of the task becomes even clearer when the diversity of physiological and pathophysiological factors associated with functional bowel disorders and visceral pain are added to the aforementioned determinants of chronic pain complaints.

THE PHYSIOLOGY OF CHRONIC VISCERAL PAIN

Nociception From the Abdominal Viscera

The gastrointestinal viscera are relatively insensitive to most stimuli compared to cutaneous structures. Abdominal organs are insensitive to light touch, pinching, cutting, and even burning (Bentley, 1948; Hertz, 1911; Ray & Neill, 1947), leading to considerable debate over the traditional definition of a noxious stimulus as one that predicts damage to the integrity of an organ (Sherrington, 1904). The lack of a direct correlation between injury and pain in the abdominal viscera has led to the differentiation of noxious and nociceptive stimuli. Noxious stimuli are those that signal the ". . . relationship between the stimulus and the integrity of the organism" (Cervero, 1994), whereas nociceptive defines the ". . . relationship between the stimulus and the nervous system of the subject" (Cervero & Jänig, 1992, p. 97). Therefore, a noxious stimulus is one that produces actual damage to the organ or tissue and may or may not be associated with the perception of pain, whereas a nociceptive stimulus produces affective and/or autonomic reflex responses and results in pain perception. A stimulus can, consequently, be simultaneously noxious and nociceptive. Therefore, visceral nociceptors can be operationally defined as sensory afferents that encode nociceptive stimuli from the periphery and produce autonomic reflexes or pseudoaffective responses and the perception of pain.

Neuroanatomy of Visceral Nociceptors

Visceral nociceptors consist of small myelinated and unmyelinated afferent fibers terminating in free nerve endings that are sensitive to mechanical and chemical stimulation. These polymodal receptors are located between the smooth muscle layers of hollow organs, on their serosal surface, in the mesentery, and within the mucosa of the gastrointestinal tract. Many additional neurons have cell bodies located in the submucosal and myenteric plexuses and form the enteric nervous system. The enteric neurons are involved in the local control of reflexes, smooth muscle contractile patterns, absorption, and secretion and serve to integrate activity in the gastrointestinal tract. They do not project to the central nervous system (CNS), and therefore, do not appear to play a major role in the sensation and perception of visceral pain, but may modulate the local environment to enhance or inhibit the activation of nociceptors.

Visceral pain derives principally from tension receptors (mechanoreceptors). These mechanosensitive neurons respond to mechanical distortion of the walls of hollow organs and to displacement of the messentery. Presynaptically, first-order neurons travel with the splanchnic nerves to cell bodies in the dorsal root ganglion and into the dorsal horn of the spinal cord. Postsynaptically, second-order neurons in the spinal cord ascend within the contralateral spinothalamic tract and the spinoreticular tract to reach the thalamus and the reticular formation in the brainstem. Third-order afferents carry nociceptive information from the spinothalamic tract to the somato-sensory cortex where discriminative sensory processing occurs. Neurons from the reticular formation nuclei travel to the limbic system and frontal lobe and are thought to be involved in the affective experience of pain (Klein, 1995). These pathways are illustrated in Fig. 22.1.

Mucosal afferents travel via parasympathetic vagal pathways and primarily serve regulatory autonomic functions. These receptors consist of mechanoreceptors that have been shown to respond to light touch, chemoreceptors sensitive to acidity, alkalinity, and nutrients, osmoreceptors, and thermoreceptors that under certain conditions may contribute to nociception. Vagal fibers, however, are thought to have little direct effect on pain or pressure perception under normal conditions (Grundy, 1993; Sengupta, Saha, & Goyal, 1990). Recent data suggest that parasympathetic nerves modulate the transmission of pain from the periphery to the central nervous system, possibly through gating mechanisms.

Gating Mechanisms

Melzack and Wall (1988) proposed the gate control theory of pain transmission and suggested that the perception of pain is dependent on the interaction of first-order neurons from the viscera and second-order neurons in the dorsal horn of the spinal cord. Sensory afferents from the periphery converge on and activate cells in the dorsal horn, thereby opening the gate for the transmission of nociceptive signals to the brain stem. Interneurons from the dorsal horn inhibit the transmission cell neurons and produce analgesic effects (Klein, 1995).

From the CNS, descending inhibitory pathways from the medulla and reticular formation converge in the dorsal horn and interact with the interneurons to inhibit transmission cell neurons and pain perception. Specific descending inhibitory inputs have been identified that are associated with abdominal visceral afferents (Lumb, 1986). The primary neurotransmitters of these descending inhibitory pathways are the endogenous opioids, particularly the enkephalins. These pathways also provide the mechanism of action for exogenous opioid analgesics. A wide variety of central stimulation may also activate these descending neural pathways and produce analgesic effects.

Empiric findings suggest that all spinal cord neurons receiving afferents from the viscera also receive afferents from muscle or cutaneous somatic receptors (Cervero & Tattersall, 1986). No exclusively visceral spinal affer-

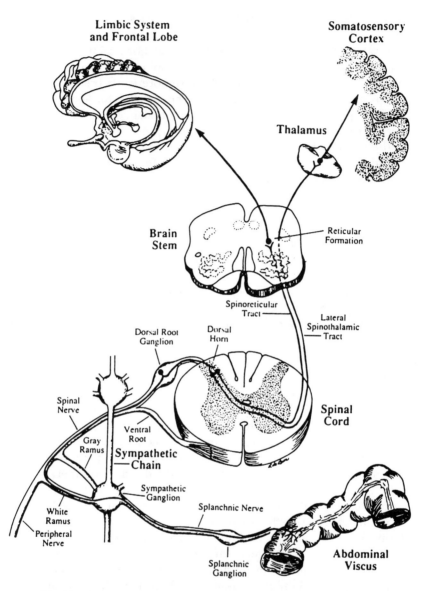

FIG. 22.1. Presynaptically, first-order neurons travel with the splanchnic nerves to cell bodies in the dorsal root ganglion and into the dorsal horn of the spinal cord. Postsynaptically, second-order neurons in the spinal cord ascend within the contralateral spinothalamic tract and the spinoreticular tract to reach the thalamus and the reticular formation in the brainstem. Third-order afferents carry nociceptive information from the spinothalamic tract to the somatosensory cortex where discriminative sensory processing occurs. Neurons from the reticular formation nuclei travel to the limbic system and frontal lobe and are thought to be involved in the affective experience of pain. From Klein (1995). Copyright 1995 by Lippincott-Raven Publishers. Reprinted by permission.

ent pathways have been identified. At the neuronal level, studies have shown both facilitatory and inhibitory effects of cutaneous stimulation on visceral afferents. Simultaneous stimulation of both receptive fields produce a greater response in the spinal neuron, and sequential stimulation produces inhibition in both directions (Gebhart & Randich, 1990).

Thus, pain transmission may be facilitated or inhibited by gating mechanisms at the level of the brain stem or the spinal cord. Recent data have also shown that these inhibitory interneurons can raise the threshold for firing in primary pain afferents (Cervero & Tattersall, 1986). Additionally, stimulation of the cortex can activate these interneurons, and may play a role in central modulation of pain. These observations may help to explain the mechanisms responsible for the modulation of pain thresholds in patients with anxiety and depressive disorders.

Nociceptive Encoding: Intensity Versus Specificity

The two principle theories of encoding nociceptive information from the viscera and the transmission of this information to the central nervous system are the intensity theory and the specificity theory. The intensity theory states that nonspecific afferents respond to both innocuous and noxious stimuli and can be distinguished simply by the frequency of neuronal activity (Jänig & Koltzenburg, 1990). Consequently, the intensity of neuronal stimulation is directly related to the intensity of neuronal firing and sophisticated central processes act to summate and decode incoming signals. The specificity theory proposes that specific populations of afferent fibers exist that respond only to noxious stimulation (Cervero, 1982). Additional factors including central and peripheral convergence and peripheral transduction theories have been proposed to facilitate or inhibit the transmission of sensory information from the viscera.

After years of debate, investigators have begun to make progress at integrating these two theories into more comprehensive models of peripheral encoding. Sengupta et al. (1990) recently identified three types of afferent mechanoreceptors according to their discharge frequency. These afferents were described functionally as (a) low-threshold mechanoreceptors that respond to innocuous stimulation, (b) high-threshold mechanoreceptors that respond only to noxious stimulation, and (c) wide-dynamic range mechanoreceptors that fire to both innocuous and noxious stimuli.

All vagal mechanoreceptors were found to be of the low-threshold type, whereas splanchnic afferents (nociceptors) were found to be a mixture of the wide-dynamic range and the high-threshold fibers. Consequently, these investigators showed that vagal fibers discharged maximally during both peristaltic activity and luminal distention, whereas only a small percentage of splanchnic afferents fired during contractile events, and that maximal firing rates occurred only during luminal distention. It was therefore suggested that the wide-dynamic range of the splanchnic mechanoreceptors supported the hypothesis that a homogeneous population of visceral afferents were responsible for encoding regulatory information, innocuous and noxious stimuli within the gut (Grundy, 1993). To be effective, this hypothesis requires the progressive recruitment of intensity-encoding afferents and a central mechanism responsible for decoding intensity-summation signals from the periphery, which has yet to be identified.

These electrophysiologic data also support the specificity theory by showing the existence of high-threshold intensity populations of afferent fibers that respond only to noxious intensities of stimulation and may represent the recruitment of specific nociceptors. These studies found that approximately 30% of distention-sensitive fibers responded only at distention levels associated with pain (Cervero & Sharkey, 1988; Sengupta et al., 1990). These observations support the existence of high-threshold fibers and silent nociceptors and have prompted investigators to develop more comprehensive integrative theories of pain transmission.

Cervero and Jänig (1992) have proposed a model to account for afferent sensory innervation of visceral organs that again relies on three similar types of nociceptive neurons (Fig. 22.2).

Under normal circumstances, the low-threshold intensity-coding afferent neurons (LTi) relay information about regulatory function and non-painful stimulation through specific second-order spinal neurons. These afferents are of the wide-dynamic range type described by Sengupta et al. (1990) and respond to stimuli from very low to high intensities. It has been suggested that these fibers may provide important information from visceral organs such as the stomach and colon that show gradations in sensation and perception from mild distention, to fullness, to intense pain (Mayer & Gebhart, 1993). If the stimulus intensity in the LTi exceeds a predefined level, these neurons participate in the transmission of nociceptive information to the CNS by activating different second-order neurons in the spinal cord and resulting in the perception of pain. At this set point, dedicated nociceptors or high-threshold intensity-coding neurons (HTi) are also activated and transmit nociceptive information to the CNS.

A third type of neuron, the silent nociceptor, is generally quiet and does not participate in the transmission of either vegetative or nociceptive information to the CNS. These neurons, however, can become activated through injury, inflammation, and central sensitization. Once sensitized, these fibers transmit pain signals to the CNS even during mild stimulation that occurs with normal regulatory activity in the viscera and may provide the physiologic mechanism for persistent or chronic pain in the absence of organic pathophysiology (Jänig & Koltzenburg, 1989, 1991; Mayer & Gebhart, 1994).

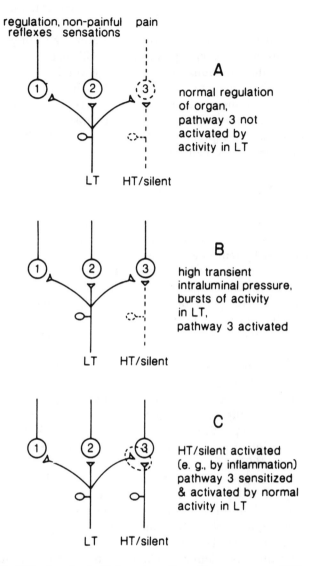

regulation, non-painful   pain
reflexes   sensations

A

normal regulation
of organ,
pathway 3 not
activated by
activity in LT

LT   HT/silent

B

high transient
intraluminal pressure,
bursts of activity
in LT,
pathway 3 activated

LT   HT/silent

C

HT/silent activated
(e. g., by inflammation)
pathway 3 sensitized
& activated by normal
activity in LT

LT   HT/silent

FIG. 22.2. Low-threshold intensity-coding afferent neurons (LTi) relay information about regulatory function and nonpainful stimulation through specific second-order spinal neurons. If the stimulus intensity in the LTi exceeds a predefined level, these neurons participate in the transmission of nociceptive information. At this threshold, dedicated nociceptors or high-threshold intensity-coding neurons (HTi) are also activated. A third type of neuron, the silent nociceptor, is generally quiet, but can become activated through injury, inflammation, and central sensitization. Once sensitized, these fibers transmit pain signals to the CNS even during mild stimulation. From Jänig and Häbler (1995). Copyright 1995 by IASP Press. Reprinted by permission.

In summary, current evidence on visceral afferents and their transmission of innocuous and noxious signals to the CNS suggests the need for a reevaluation of the functional categories of visceral afferents and nociceptors. These data argue for an integration of the intensity and specificity encoding theories into more realistic models of visceral afferents that may account for chronic persistent pain. New models must recognize functional differences in sensory receptors and the coexistence of different neurophysiologic mechanisms in many visceral organs.

Sensitization and Visceral Hyperalgesia

The complexity of sensation and perception of abdominal pain are only partially revealed in the preceding discussion. Chronic visceral pain is directly influenced by temporal changes in both central and peripheral mechanisms. Sensitization, a well-recognized factor influencing somatosensory pain thresholds, also appears to play a significant role in visceral hyperalgesia and referred pain. Mechanisms for both primary (peripheral) and secondary (central) hyperalgesia have been proposed and may be explained through nociceptor sensitization and central plasticity (Cervero, 1994).

Primary hyperalgesia can be defined as a shift in the stimulus-response curve resulting in a decrease in the stimulus intensity required to elicit or maintain nociceptor activation. These observations suggest that primary hyperalgesia could result from changes in the responsiveness of visceral afferent fibers with repetitive stimulation or inflammation (Blumberg, Haupt, Jänig, & Kohler, 1983; Cervero & Sann, 1989; Lamotte, Shain, Simaone, & Tsau, 1991).

Secondary hyperalgesia extends beyond the area of immediate insult and results in referred pain over more diffuse areas including somatic structures. The mechanism of secondary hyperalgesia appears to be continuous afferent input to the CNS from peripherally sensitized neurons (Meller & Gebhart, 1994; Treede, Meyer, Raja, & Campbell, 1992), that may result in activity-dependent synaptic plasticity at the level of the dorsal horn (Cervero, Laird, & Pozo, 1992). Ness, Metcalf, and Gebhart (1990) have shown that noxious visceral stimulation can selectively evoke increases in somatic receptive fields of spinal cord neurons. It has been suggested that both primary and secondary hyperalgesia play a role in chronic pain conditions such as IBS and NUD.

Although many questions remain concerning the mechanisms of pain sensation and perception from the viscera, there is no doubt that the experience of pain is a dynamic process. Clinical investigations have shown that repeated stimulation of the colon and rectum at a constant noxious level results in progressive increases in the perception of pain and increases in the area of pain referral (Crowell et al., 1995; Jänig & Morrison, 1986; Ness et al., 1990).

CHRONIC PAIN IN THE FUNCTIONAL BOWEL PATIENT

As discussed, physiologic activity in the gut is not generally perceived. Perception occurs when individuals become symptomatic with bloating, nausea, vomiting, constipation, diarrhea, or pain. Treatment of the patient with functional bowel disorders focuses on the patient's symptoms because the underlying pathophysiology is generally not evident. The clinical presentation of NCCP, NUD, and even IBS are often similar. As a result, it has been difficult to determine whether the various functional bowel disorders are simply different manifestations of a common altered physiology expressed at different anatomic sites or whether they reflect different pathophysiologies. There is evidence that suggests an overlap in the symptom reports of the various functional bowel disorders (Talley et al., 1991). Trimble, Forouk, Pryde, Douglas, and Heading (1995) have found that IBS and dyspepsia patients both report increased sensitivity to rectal and esophageal distention, which may suggest that the common mechanism is altered visceral sensitivity or perception. However, a consistent feature of patients with functional abdominal pain is psychosocial distress.

Noncardiac Chest Pain

Unexplained chest pain (also called "irritable heart" or "soldier's heart") has long been associated with exposure to extreme stress, such as war (Aisenberg & Castell, 1994). Osler (1892) recognized that emotional factors were often associated with nonspecific complaints of chest pain, which he called pseudo-angina. He was also the first to suggest that such symptoms may be due to esophageal spasms. Recent studies have found 10% to 30% of patients undergoing coronary arteriography following complaints of chest pain to have normal coronary arteries (Kemp et al., 1986), and mortality rates of patients with NCCP are comparable to the general population (Chambers & Bass, 1990). Yet, the NCCP patient resists reassurance and frequently seeks medical care and additional diagnostic tests (Ockene, Shay, Alpert, Weiner, & Dalen, 1980; Richter, Dalton, Bradley, & Castell, 1987). Rao (1995) has estimated that the cost of caring for NCCP patients may have exceeded $1 billion in the United States in the period 1994–1995.

Mechanisms of NCCP may include gastroesophageal reflux (GER), esophageal dysmotility and spasm, esophageal hypersensitivity, and microvascular angina (Aisenberg & Castell, 1994). A review of these mechanisms demonstrates that several may play a role in accounting for patient complaints.

Investigations have shown many patients with NCCP do not report pain during motility and pH studies, and of those who do, only a limited number have reflux or dysmotility (Breumelhof, Nadorp, Akkermans, & Smout, 1990; Ghillebert, Jansens, Vantrappen, Nevens, & Piessens, 1990; Peters et al., 1988; Soffer, Scalabrini, & Wingate, 1989). For example, Breumelhof et al. (1990) found that only 57% of patients reported pain during ambulatory motility and pH-metry studies and that only 32% of those that reported pain had either GER or dysmotility. These studies suggest that GER is more likely to be associated with chest pain than dysmotility, but that a significant proportion of the patient complaints are associated with neither GER nor motility disturbances.

Visceral hypersensitivity or disordered perception may account for symptoms in patients with NCCP. Barish, Castell, and Richter (1986), utilizing balloon distention of the esophagus in patients with NCCP, found that distention caused pain in 56% of patients compared to 20% of normal controls. These observations were confirmed by Deschner, Maher, Cattau, and Benjamin (1990), who found that 68% of their NCCP patients responded to balloon distention with pain complaints. It is of significant interest that only a subset of patients showed hypersensitivity. Further study is needed to evaluate the overlap of motor and sensory responses in these patients.

Nonulcer Dyspepsia

NUD is characterized by persistent or recurrent epigastric pain or discomfort, lasting for 1 month or longer, during which symptoms are present at least 25% of the time and cannot be accounted for by organic disease (Barbara et al., 1989; Heading, 1991; Talley et al., 1991). Talley et al. also pointed out that there can be an overlap in dyspepsia symptoms with IBS, NCCP, GER, and biliary tract disease.

The pathophysiology of NUD is not established, but gastroparesis, small bowel dysmotility, visceral hypersensitivity to distention, gastric acid sensitivity, *Helicobacter pylori* gastritis, and CNS dysfunction have all been implicated (Talley, 1995). Azpiroz (1995) and Malagelada (1993) have suggested that functional gut disorders, such as NUD, are a complex product of altered intraintestinal reflexes leading to altered perception (Azpiroz & Malagelada, 1986). These reflexes appear to be regulated by vagal nonadrenergic, noncholinergic mechanisms (Azpiroz & Malagelada, 1986). Some NUD patients may have a discrete gastric dysfunction, such as postprandial antral hypomotility, and/or impairment of gastric emptying (Camilleri, Malagelada, Kao, & Zinsmeister, 1986; Stanghellini et al., 1992), but in many NUD patients gastric secretion, motility, and emptying are normal before and after a meal (Camilleri et al., 1986; Scott et al., 1993; Tucci et al., 1992).

Distention of the stomach in NUD patients and normal controls with an air-filled balloon demonstrated normal compliance of the stomach, but NUD patients reported perception at lower pressure levels than did normal controls, suggesting that the stomach of the NUD patient may be hypersensitive (Bradette, Pare, Douville, & Morin, 1991; Lemann et al., 1991; Mearin, Cucala, Azpiroz, & Malagelada, 1991). Coffin, Azpiroz, Guarner, and Malagelada (1994) also demonstrated significantly greater sensitivity of the stomach to balloon distention in NUD patients, but showed perception to be normal in the duodenum.

Azpiroz (1995) has shown a dissociation between perception and reflex responses of the gut to distention. Low levels of distention induced gastric relaxation well below the threshold for perception. Additionally, distention of the proximal jejunum produced perception, but no significant gastric relaxation, supporting a dissociation between what patients perceive and intraintestinal reflexes. Azpiroz suggested that enterogastric reflexes occur via vagal pathways, whereas perception is mediated by sympathetic-splanchnic afferents.

Irritable Bowel Syndrome

Over the past two centuries, clinicians have speculated about the origin and nature of IBS (Almy, 1989). IBS has been considered a psychosomatic disorder, a motility disorder, a mechanical and/or chemoreceptor disorder, and a product of nociceptive sensitization (Mayer & Gebhart, 1993). It has also been shown that pain in the IBS patient evolves over time, both in terms of intensity and referral areas (Ness & Gebhart, 1990). What remains unclear is whether IBS is best accounted for by a single cause or whether it should be thought of as multidimensional in nature, much as has been shown for NCCP and NUD.

Early studies of the impact of emotional factors on gut function involved patients who had gastric fistulas (Wolf & Wolff, 1943; Engel, Reischman, & Segal, 1956). The fistula permitted direct observation of the gut during a variety of conditions. With this method, it was possible to observe changes in gastric motility, secretions, and vascularity during emotional events. Almy, Hinkle, and Berle (1949) were able to demonstrate motility changes in the sigmoid colon of normal volunteers in response to stress, and to show both hyper- and hypomotility, depending on the nature of the events, in response to stress by IBS patients (Almy, Kern, & Tulin, 1949). Whitehead and Crowell (1991) summarized the available literature and showed that although emotional and psychiatric factors were associated with IBS they do not appear to be causally linked. Instead, these factors appear to increase the chances that the patient will seek medical care (Drossman, 1991). A recent study showed that 10% to 20% of a random sample of age- and gender-matched community residents reported symptoms consistent with a diagnosis of IBS (Talley, Zinsmeister, & Melton, 1995). However, only 25% of those who reported IBS-like symptoms sought medical care.

Patients with IBS do exhibit lower pain thresholds to distension of the colon (e.g., Whitehead et al., 1990) and small bowel (Accarino, Azpiroz, & Malagelada, 1995; Kellow, Eckersley, & Jones, 1991; Moriarty & Dawson, 1982). One explanation for this hypersensitivity is that the colon's ability to adapt to distention may be reduced and result in increased stimulation of mechanoreceptors (Crowell & Musial, 1994). However, Accarino et al. have shown that intestinal compliance of the small bowel of the IBS patient was within normal limits. IBS patients may misinterpret normal physiologic sensations as painful (Mechanic, 1983). IBS patients are known to show higher thresholds for somatic pain (Cook, VaanEeden, & Collins, 1987) and to perceive intestinal distention over a wider referred area than normal controls (Kingham & Dawson, 1985; Moriarty & Dawson, 1982; Swarbrick, Haggerty, & Bat, 1980). However, direct comparison of mechanical distention and electrical stimulation of the small bowel of the IBS patient has indicated that only mechanical stimulation reflected hypersensitivity (Accarino, et al., 1995). These data imply that hypersensitivity is related to mechanical distortions of the bowel and not to abnormal perceptions. Mayer and Gebhart (1993), however, in their review of this literature suggested that patients with functional bowel disorders may misperceive certain types of visceral sensations.

THE BRAIN-GUT AXIS AND CHRONIC ABDOMINAL PAIN

It is clear from the preceding discussion that a direct relationship between functional pain syndromes and physiologic abnormalities has yet to be identified. This variability may be partially explained by the fact that stress, psychologic traits and states, and prior learning history may directly or indirectly effect patients with functional abdominal pain. Peripheral and central changes may occur that alter the brain-gut axis and result in heightened visceral and somatic afferent input to the spinal cord and central sensitization. Most neurotransmitters found in the brain are also found in the enteric nervous system. These include, but are not limited to, 5-hydroxytryptamine, enkephalins, substance P, and cholecystokinin. Parallel circuits also exist between the central and enteric nervous system that allow bidirectional influences on motor function, perception, mood, and behaviors. Psychosocial factors such as stress may activate an already sensitized bowel and result in symptoms. Conversely, nociceptive stimuli from the viscera may alter perception, mood, and behaviors.

The biopsychosocial model of illness (Fig. 22.3) offers a more comprehensive mind-body approach to the patient with functional abdominal pain. This model recognizes that a patient's symptoms and their behavioral response to symptoms result from complex interactions of early life events, psychosocial factors, and physiology and pathophysiology (Drossman, 1996; Engel, 1977). All of these factors influence symptom expression and treatment outcome. Early life events may establish a predisposition or result in conditioning that may affect a patient's susceptibility to certain chronic pain syndromes. Whitehead et al. (1994) have shown that reinforcement of gastrointestinal symptoms in childhood was specifically associated with IBS symptoms in adulthood. Drossman et al. (1995) have shown that sexual and physical abuse in childhood is associated with the development and severity of gastrointestinal symptoms and negatively influences treatment outcomes without directly altering pain thresholds (see also Whitehead et al., 1997).

Psychosocial factors such as depression and anxiety may influence visceral perception through brain-gut neurotransmitters and modulate descending pathways to increase or decrease pain perception. These psychiatric dysfunctions are common in functional bowel patients and may influence the physiologic response to stressful life events and the interpretation of symp-

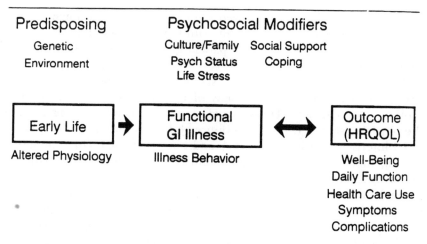

FIG. 22.3. The biopsychosocial model emphasizes the complex interactions that occur between illness, behavior, environment, and clinical outcomes. From Drossman et al. (1994). Copyright 1994 by Degnon Associates. Reprinted by permission.

toms. A lifetime history of psychiatric disturbances has been reported in up to 94% of patients referred to gastroenterologists with IBS (Lydiard, Fossey, Marsh, & Ballenger, 1993). Therefore, these factors strongly influence which patients are seen in tertiary referral centers. Community studies have shown no psychological differences between IBS patients not seeking medical treatment and control groups (Drossman et al., 1988). Psychiatric features, therefore, do not appear to be directly related to functional bowel disorders, but to influence illness behaviors and clinical outcomes and should be addressed within any comprehensive treatment program (Drossman, 1991).

THE BIOPSYCHOSOCIAL APPROACH TO TREATMENT

The preceding data make it clear that it is no longer tenable to separate physiological factors from psychosocial issues in treating the patient with functional gastrointestinal pain syndromes. A comprehensive treatment program should address the physician–patient relationship and follow-up treatments should be based on the severity of symptoms and include pharmacotherapy, behavioral treatments, and potentially psychotherapy (Fullwood & Drossman, 1995). A multinational working team has recently proposed guidelines for treating the patient with functional gastrointestinal disorders, including chronic or intermittent pain (Drossman et al., 1994).

The Physician–Patient Relationship

Drossman et al. (1994) emphasized the importance of the physician–patient relationship in treating patients with functional bowel disorders. Placebo response rates among these patient groups approach 80% in some studies and should be expected to be a significant factor when initiating and evaluating new interventions. Establishing a trusting therapeutic environment is a mutual responsibility of the physician and patient. The Working Team Report (Drossman et al., 1994), therefore, suggests that the physician should (a) obtain a thorough history through a patient-centered interview that is nondirective and nonjudgmental, (b) complete a careful, but cost-effective physical examination, (c) determine the patient's knowledge and concerns about the illness, (d) provide vital information about the disorder (education), (e) identify the expectations of the patient and provide realistic information about outcomes, (f) set consistent limits on patient demands for tests and medications, (g) increase the patient's involvement and responsibility within the treatment program, and (h) establish a long-term relationship with the primary-care provider.

Drossman et al. (1994) also pointed out that because functional gastrointestinal pain syndromes are chronic, the physician should focus on understanding the patient's reason for seeking medical care currently. A number of factors may contribute to the physician visit, including symptom exacerbation, changes in significant life stressors or personal conflict, increased depression or anxiety, changes in quality of life, or secondary gain issues.

Interventions should be based on the severity of physiological and psychological symptoms. Patients with mild symptoms may benefit from educational efforts, reassurance, dietary changes, or medication changes. Patients with moderate symptoms may benefit further from symptom monitoring, pharmacotherapy aimed at specific symptoms, behavioral treatments (relaxation therapy, biofeedback, etc.), and psychotherapy. Patients with more severe or intractable symptoms should be approached by providing psychosocial support, refusing unnecessary tests, setting realistic goals for treatment outcomes, shifting the responsibility for treatment to the patient, and changing the expectations of the patient from cure to coping with chronic illness. Antidepressant therapies are also recommended for patients with chronic pain.

Summary

The preceding discussion makes it clear that although the data are not overwhelming, it is possible to think of functional bowel disorders as reflecting a single disease displayed in different ways at different anatomical sites, with hypersensitivity being the common link. If this is the case, then interventions should be found that would be effective across the different functional bowel disorders. Alternatively, if each disorder reflects an as yet undetermined but unique pathophysiology, then treatment of these disorders should have minimal overlap. Complicating this scenario is the fact that multiconcurrent systems are ordinarily active (local inflammatory responses, motility, neuroplasticity, stress responses, emotional responses, etc.) during treatment, each of which may modify the response, or mask differences in outcomes. The biopsychosocial model appears to offer the most comprehensive treatment approach to these patient populations.

REFERENCES

Accarino, A. M., Azpiroz, F., & Malagelada, J. R. (1995). Selective dysfunction of mechanosensitive intestinal afferents in the irritable bowel syndrome. *Gastroenterology, 108,* 636–643.

Aisenberg, J., & Castell, D. O. (1994). Approach to the patient with unexplained chest pain. *Mt. Sinai Journal of Medicine, 61,* 476–483.

Almy, T. P. (1989). Historical perspectives of functional bowel disease. In W. J. Snape (Ed.), *Pathogenesis of functional bowel disease.* New York: Plenum.

Almy, T. P., Hinkle, L. E., & Berle, B. (1949). Alterations in colonic function in man under stress, III. Experimental production of sigmoid spasm in patients with spastic constipation. *Gastroenterology, 12,* 437–449.

Almy, T. P., Kern, F., & Tulin, M. (1949). Alterations in colonic function in man under stress, II. Experimental production of sigmoid spasm in healthy persons. *Gastroenterology, 12,* 425–436.

Azpiroz, F. (1995). Sensitivity of the stomach and small bowel: Human research and clinical relevance. In G. F. Gebhart (Ed.), *Visceral pain: Progress in pain research and management* (Vol. 5, pp. 391–428). Seattle: IASP Press.

Azpiroz, F., & Malagelada, J. R. (1986). Vagally mediated gastric relaxation induces by intestinal nutrients in the dog. *American Journal of Physiology, 251,* G727–G735.

Barbara, L., Camilleri, M., Corinaldesir, R., Crean, G. T., Heading, R. C., Johnson, A. G., Malagelada, J. R., Stanghellini, V., & Weinbeck, M. (1989). Definition and investigation of dyspepsia: Consensus of an International Ad Hoc Working Party. *Digestive Diseases and Sciences, 34,* 1262–1272.

Barish, C. F., Castell, D. O., & Richter, J. E. (1986). Graded esophageal balloon distention: A new provocative test for noncardiac chest pain. *Digestive Diseases and Sciences, 31,* 1292–1298.

Barsky, A. J., & Klerman, G. L. (1983). Overview: Hypochondriasis, bodily complaints, and somatic styles. *American Journal of Psychiatry, 140,* 273–283.

Bentley, F. H. (1948). Observations on visceral pain. *Annals of Surgery, 128,* 881.

Bonica, J. J. (1953). *The management of pain.* Philadelphia: Lea & Febiger.

Blumberg, H., Haupt, P., Jänig, W., & Kohler, W. (1983). Encoding of visceral noxious stimuli in the discharge patterns of visceral afferent fibers from the colon. *Pfluegers Archives, 33,* 398.

Bradette, M., Pare, P., Douville, P., & Morin, A. (1991). Visceral perception in health and functional dyspepsia. Crossover study of gastric distention with placebo and domperidone. *Digestive Diseases and Sciences, 36,* 52–58.

Breumelhof, R., Nadorp, J. H. S., Akkermans, L. M. A., & Smout, A. J. P. M. (1990). Analysis of 24-hour esophageal pressure and pH data in unselected patients with noncardiac chest pain. *Gastroenterology, 99,* 1257–1264.

Camilleri, M., Malagelada, J-R., Kao, P. C., & Zinsmeister, A. R. (1986). Gastric and autonomic responses to stress in functional dyspepsia. *Digestive Diseases and Sciences, 31,* 1169–1177.

Campbell, J. N., Raja, S. N., Selig, D. K., Belzberg, A. J., & Meyer, R. A. (1994). Diagnosis and management of sympathetically maintained pain. In H. L. Fields & J. C. Liebeskind (Eds.), *Progress in Pain Research and Management Vol 1. Pharmacological Approaches to the Treatment of Chronic Pain: New Concepts and Critical Issues.* (pp. 85–100). Seattle: IASP Press.

Cervero, F. (1982). Afferent activity evoked by natural stimulation of the biliary system in the ferret. *Pain, 13,* 137.

Cervero, F. (1994). Sensory innervation of the visceral: Peripheral basis of visceral pain. *Physiology Review, 74,* 95.

Cervero, F., & Jänig, W. (1992). Visceral nociceptors: A new world order? *Trends in Neurosciences, 15,* 374.

Cervero, F., Laird, J. M., & Pozo, M. A. (1992). Selective changes of receptive field properties of spinal nociceptive neurons induced by noxious visceral stimulation in the cat. *Pain, 51,* 335.

Cervero, F., & Sann, H. (1989). Mechanically evoked responses of afferent fibers innervating this guinea-pig's ureter: An in vitro study. *Journal of Physiology London, 412,* 345.

Cervero, F., & Sharkey, K. A. (1988). An electrophysiological and anatomical study of intestinal afferent fibers in the rat. *Journal of Physiology, 401,* 381–397.

Cervero, F., & Tattersall, J. E. H. (1986). Somatic and visceral sensory integration in the thoracic spinal cord. In F. Cervero & J. F. B. Morrison (Eds.), *Visceral sensation* (p. 189). Amsterdam: Elsevier. *Progress in Brain Research, 67,* Elsevier, Amsterdam, 1986, pp. 189–205.

Chambers, J., & Bass, C. (1990). Chest pain with normal coronary anatomy: A review of natural history and possible etiologic factors. *Progress in Cardiovascular Disease, 33,* 161–184.

Coderre, T. J., Katz, J., Vaccarino, A. L., & Melzack, R. (1993). Contribution of central neuro-plasticity to pathological pain: Review of clinical and experimental evidence. *Pain, 52,* 259–285.

Cook, I. J., VaanEeden, A., & Collins, S. M. (1987). Patients with irritable bowel syndrome have greater tolerance than normal subjects. *Gastroenterology, 93,* 727–733.

Crowell, M. D., Lutz, K., Davidoff, A., & Whitehead, W. E. (1995). Repeated rectal distention leads to perceptual sensitization. *Gastroenterology, 108,* A587.

Crowell, M. D., & Musial, F. (1994). Rectal adaptation to distention is impaired in the irritable bowel syndrome. *American Journal of Gastroenterology, 89,* 1689.

Deschner, W. K., Maher, K., Cattau, E. L., & Benjamin, S. (1990). Intraesophageal balloon distention versus drug provocation in the evaluation of noncardiac chest pain. *American Journal of Gastroenterology, 85,* 938–943.

Drossman, D. A. (1991). Illness behavior in the irritable bowel syndrome. *Gastroenterology International, 4,* 77–81.

Drossman, D. A. (1996). Psychosocial aspects of the functional gastrointestinal disorders. In Corazziari (Ed.), *NeUroGastroenterology* (pp. 34–40). New York: Walter de Gruyter.

Drossman, D. A., Leserman, J., Nachman, G., Li, Z., Gluck, H., Toomey, T. C., & Mitchell, C. M. (1990). Sexual and physical abuse in women with functional organic gastrointestinal disorders. *Ann Intern Med, 113,* 828–833.

Drossman, D. A., McKee, D. C., Sandler, R. S. Mitchell, C. M., Cramer, E. M., Lowman, B. C., & Burger, A. L. (1988). Psychosocial factors in the irritable bowel syndrome. A multivariate study of patients and nonpatients with irritable bowel syndrome. *Gastroenterology, 95,* 701–708.

Drossman, D. A., Richter, J. E., Talley, N. J., Thompson, W. G., Corazziari, E., & Whitehead, W. E. (1994). The functional gastroenterology disorders and their diagnosis: A coming of age. In D. A. Drossman et al. (Eds.), *The functional gastrointestinal disorders: Diagnosis, pathophysiology, and treatment* (pp. 1–23). McLean, VA: Degnon Assoc.

Drossman, D. A., Talley, N. J., Lesserman, J., Olden, K. W., & Barreiro, M. A. (1995). Sexual and physical abuse and gastrointestinal illness: Review and recommendations. *Annals of Internal Medicine, 123,* 782–794.

Dubner, R. (1992). Hyperalgesia and expanded receptive fields. *Pain, 48,* 3–4.

Engel, G. L. (1977). The need for a new medical model: A challenge for biomedicine. *Science, 196,* 129–136.

Engel, G., Reichsman, F., & Segal, H. L. (1956). A study of an infant with gastric fistula. *Psychosomatic Medicine, 18,* 374–398.

Erskine, A., Morley, S., & Pearce, S. (1990). Memory for pain: A review. *Pain, 41,* 255–265.

Fernandez, E., & Turk, D. C. (1995). The scope of significance of anger in the experience of chronic pain. *Pain, 61,* 165–175.

Fullwood, A., & Drossman, D. A. (1995). The relationship of psychiatric illness with gastrointestinal disease. *Annual Review of Medicine, 46,* 483–496.

Gebhart, F. R., & Randich, A. (1990). Brainstem modulation of nociception. In W. R. Klemm & R. P. Vertes (Eds.), *Brainstem mechanisms of behavior* (pp. 315–352). New York: Wiley.

Ghillebert, G., Janssens, J., Vantrappen, G., Nevens, F., & Piessens, J. (1990). Ambulatory 24-hour intraesophageal pH and pressure recordings v provocation tests in the diagnosis of chest pain of esophageal origin. *Gut, 31,* 738–744.

Grundy, D. (1993). Mechanoreceptors in the gastrointestinal tract. *Journal of Smooth Muscle Research, 29,* 37–46.

Heading, R. C. (1991). Definitions of dyspepsia. *Scan J Gastro, 26*(Suppl. 182), 1–6.

Hertz, A. F. (1911). The sensibility of the alimentary canal in health and disease. *Lancet, 1,* 1051.

Jänig, W., & Häbler, J-J. (1995). Visceral-autonomic integration. In G. F. Gebhart (Ed.), *Visceral pain, progress in pain research and management* (Vol. 5, p. 340). Seattle: IASP Press.

Jänig, W., & Koltzenburg, M. (1989). The neural basis of consciously perceived sensations from the gut. In M. V. Singer & H. Goebell (Eds.), *Nerves and the gastrointestinal tract* (pp. 383–398). Dordrecht, The Netherlands: Kluwer.

Jänig, W., & Koltzenburg, M. (1990). On the function of spinal primary afferent fibers supplying colon and urinary bladder. *Journal of the Autonomic Nervous System, 30*(Suppl.), 589–596.

Jänig, W., & Koltzenburg, M. (1991). Receptive properties of sacral primary afferent neurons supplying the colon. *Journal of Neurophysiology, 65,* 1067.

Jänig, W., & Morrison, J. F. B. (1986). Functional properties of spinal visceral afferents supplying abdominal and pelvic organs, with special emphasis on visceral nociception. In F. Cervero & J. F. B. Morrison (Eds.), *Visceral sensation* (p. 189). Amsterdam: Elsevier.

Kellow, J. E., Eckersley, G. M., & Jones, M. P. (1991). Enhanced perception of physiological intestinal motility in the irritable bowel syndrome. *Gastroenterology, 101,* 1621–1627.

Kemp, H. G., Kronmal, R. A., Vliestra, R. E., & Frye, R. L. (1996). Seven year survival of patients with normal or near coronary arteriograms: A CASS registry study. *Journal of American College of Cardiology, 7,* 479–483.

Kingham, J. C. G., & Dawson, A. M. (1985). Origin of chronic right upper quadrant pain. *Gut, 26,* 783–788.

Klein, K. B. (1995). Approach to the patient with abdominal pain. In T. Yamada (Ed.), *Textbook of gastroenterology* (2nd ed., pp. 750–771). Philadelphia: Lippincott.

Lamotte, R. H., Shain, C. N., Simaone, D. A., & Tsau, E-F. P. (1991). Neurogenic hyperalgesia: Psychological studies of underlying mechanisms. *Journal of Neurophysiology, 66,* 190.

Lemann, M., Dederding, J. P., Flourie, B., Franchisseur, C., Rambaud, J., & Jian, R. (1991). Abnormal perception of visceral pain in response to gastric distention in chronic idiopathic dyspepsia: The irritable stomach. *Digestive Diseases and Sciences, 36,* 1249–1254.

Linton, S. J. (1986). Behavioral remediation of chronic pain: A status report. *Pain, 24,* 125–141.

Lumb, B. M. (1986). Brainstem control of visceral afferent pathways in the spinal cord. In F. Cervero & J. F. B. Morrison (Eds.), *Visceral sensation* (p. 279). Amsterdam: Elsevier.

Lydiard, R. B., Fossey, M. D., Marsh, W., & Ballenger, J. C. (1993). Prevalence of psychiatric disorders in patients with irritable bowel syndrome. *Psychosomatic, 34,* 229–234.

Malagelada, J. R. (1993). Altered visceral sensation in functional dyspepsia and related syndromes. In E. A. Mayer & H. E. Raybould (Eds.), *Basic and clinical aspects of chronic abdominal pain. Pain research and clinical management* (Vol. 9, pp. 55–60). Amsterdam: Elsevier.

Mayer, E. A., & Gebhart, G. F. (1993). Functional bowel disorders and the visceral hyperalgesia hypothesis. In E. A. Mayer & H. E. Raybould (Eds.), *Basic and clinical aspects of chronic abdominal pain* (pp. 3–28). Amsterdam: Elsevier.

Mayer, E. A., & Gebhart, G. F. (1994). Basic and clinical aspects of visceral hyperalgesia. *Gastroenterology, 107,* 271–293.

McMahon, S. B. (1984). Receptive fields of rat lamina one projection cells moved to incorporate a nearby region of injury. *Pain, 19,* 235–247.

Mearin, F., Cucala, M., Azpiroz, F., & Malagelada, J-R. (1991). The origin of symptoms on the brain gut axis in functional dyspepsia. *Gastroenterology, 101,* 999–1066.

Mechanic, D. (1983). Adolescent health and illness behavior; review of the literature and a new hypothesis for the study of stress. *Journal of Human Stress, 9,* 4–13.

Meller, S. T., & Gebhart, G. F. (1994). Spinal mediators of hyperalgesia. *Drugs, 47,* 10.

Melzack, R., & Wall, P. D. (1988). Gate-control and other mechanisms. In R. Melzack & P. D. Wall (Eds.), *The challenge of pain* (2nd ed., p. 165). London: Penguin.

Menetry, D., & Besson, J. M. (1982). Electrophysiological characteristics of dorsal horn cells in rats with cutaneous inflammation resulting from chronic arthritis. *Pain, 13,* 343–364.

Merskey, H. (1994). Pain and psychological medicine. In P. D. Wall & R. Melzack (Eds.), *The textbook of pain* (pp. 903–920). Edinborough, Churchill, Livingstone.

Merskey, H., & Bogduk, N. (1994). *Classification of Chronic Pain: Descriptions of Chronic Pain Syndromes and Definition of Pain Terms,* 2nd ed. Seattle: IASP Press.

Moriarty, K. J., & Dawson, A. M. (1982). Functional abdominal pain: Further evidence that the whole gut is affected. *British Medical Journal, 284,* 1670–1672.

Ness, T. J., & Gebhart, G. F. (1990). Visceral pain: A review of experimental studies. *Pain, 41,* 167–234.

Ness, T. J., Metcalf, A. M., & Gebhart, G. F. (1990). A psychophysiological study in humans using phasic colonic distention as a noxious visceral stimulus. *Pain, 43,* 377–386.

Ockene, I. S., Shay, M. J., Alpert, J. S., Weiner, B. H., & Dalen, J. E. (1980). Unexplained chest pain in patients with normal coronary arteriograms: A follow-up study of functional status. *New England Journal of Medicine, 303,* 1249–1252.

Osler, W. (1892). *Principles and practice of medicine.* New York: Appleton.

Peters, L., Maas, L., Petty, D., Dalton, C. B., Penner, J. L., Wu, W. C., Castell, D. O., & Richter, J. E. (1988). Spontaneous noncardiac chest pain: Evaluation by 24-hour ambulatory esophageal motility and pH monitoring. *Gastroenterology, 94,* 878–886.

Pilowsky, I., & Spence, D. N. (1976). Pain and illness behavior: A comparative study. *Journal of Psychosomatic Research, 20,* 131–134.

Rao, S. S. C. (1995). Esophageal (noncardiac) chest pain: Visceral hyperalgesia, motor disorder, or reflux disease? In G. F. Gebhart (Ed.), *Visceral pain: Progress in pain research and management* (Vol. 5, pp. 351–372). Seattle: IASP Press.

Ray, B. S., & Neill, C. L. (1947). Abdominal visceral sensation in man. *Annals of Surgery, 126,* 709.

Richter, J. E., Dalton, C. B., Bradley, L. A., & Castell, D. O. (1987). Oral nifedipine in the treatment of noncardiac chest pain in patients with the nutcracker esophagus. *Gastroenterology, 93,* 21–28.

Scott, A. M., Kellow, J. E., Shuter, B., Cowan, H., Corbett, A. M., Riley, J. W., Lunzer, M. R., Eckstein, R. P., Hoschl, R., Lam, J-K., & Jones, M. P. (1993). Intragastric distribution and gastric emptying of solids and liquids in functional dyspepsia. *Digestive Diseases and Sciences, 38,* 2247–2254.

Sengupta, J. N., Saha, J. K., & Goyal, R. K. (1990). Stimulus-response function studies of esophageal mechanosensitive nociceptors in sympathetic afferents of opossum. *Journal of Neurophysiology, 64,* 796–812.

Sherrington, C. S. (1904). Qualitative difference of spinal reflex corresponding with a qualitative difference of cutaneous stimulus. *Journal of Physiology, London, 30,* 39.

Sluka, K. A., Willis, W. D., & Westlund, K. N. (1995). The role of dorsal root reflexes in neurogenic inflammation. *Pain Forum, 4,* 141–149.

Soffer, E. E., Scalabrini, P., & Wingate, D. L. (1989). Spontaneous noncardiac chest pain: Value of ambulatory esophageal pH and motility monitoring. *Digestive Diseases and Sciences, 34,* 1651–1655.

Stanghellini, V., Ghidini, C., Maccarini, M. R., Paparo, G. F., Corinaldesi, R., & Barbara, L. (1992). Fasting and postprandial gastrointestinal motility in ulcer and non-ulcer dyspepsia. *Gut, 33,* 184–190.

Stein, C. (1995). Control of pain in peripheral tissue by opioid. *New England Journal of Medicine, 332,* 685–690.

Swarbrick, E. T., Haggerty, F. J. E., & Bat, L. (1980). Site of pain from irritable bowel syndrome. *Lancet, ii,* 443–446.

Talley, N. J. (1995). Helicobacter pylori: More than 10 years on and still catchy [editorial]. *Journal of Gastroenterology & Hepatology, 10,* 465–8.

Talley, N. J., Colin-Jones, D., Coch, K. L., Coch, M., Nyre, N. O., & Stanghellini, V. (1991). Functional dyspepsia: A classification with guidelines for diagnosis and management. *Gastroenterology International, 4,* 145–160.

Talley, N. J., Zinmeister, A. R., & Melton, L. J. III. (1995). Irritable bowel syndrome in a community: Symptom subgroups, risk factors, and health care utilization. *American Journal of Epidemiology, 142,* 76–83.

Taylor, A., Lorentzen, L., & Blank, M. (1990). Psychological distress of chronic pain suffers and their spouses. *Journal of Pain Symptom Management, 5,* 6–10.

Treede, R-D., Meyer, R. A., Raja, S. N., & Campbell, J. N. (1992). Peripheral and central mechanisms of cutaneous hyperalgesia. *Progress in Neurobiology, 38,* 397.

Trimble, K. C., Forouk, R., Pryde, A., Douglas, S., & Heading, R. C. (1995). Heightened visceral sensation in functional gastrointestinal disease is not site-specific evidence for a generalized disorder of gut sensitivity. *Digestive Diseases and Sciences, 40*(8), 1607–1613.

Tucci, A., Corinaldesi, R., Stanghellini, V., Tosetti, C., DiFebo, G., Paparo, G. F., Varoli, O., Paganelli, G. M., Labate, A. M. M., Masci, C., Zoccoli, G., Monetti, N., & Barbara, L. (1992). Helicobactor pylori infection and gastric function in patients with chronic idiopathic dyspepsia. *Gastroenterology, 103,* 768–774.

Watkins, J. C., & Collingridge, G. L. (Eds.). (1989). *The NMDA receptor.* Oxford, England: Oxford University Press.

Whitehead, W. E., & Crowell, M. D. (1991). Psychologic considerations in the irritable bowel syndrome. *Gastroenterology Clinics of North America, 20,* 249–267.

Whitehead, W. E., Crowell, M. D., Davidoff, A. L., Palsson, O. S., & Schuster, M. M. (1997). Pain from rectal distention in women with irritable bowel syndrome: Relation to sexual abuse. *Digestive Diseases and Sciences, 42,* 796–804.

Whitehead, W. E., Crowell, M. D., Heller, B. R., Robinson, J. C., Schuster, M. M., & Horn, S. (1994). Modeling and reinforcement of the sick role during childhood predicts adult illness behavior. *Psychosomatic Medicine, 6,* 541–550.

Whitehead, W. E., Holtkotter, B., Enck, P., Hoelzl, R., Holmes, K. D., Anthony, J., Shabsin, H. S., & Schuster, M. M. (1990). Tolerance of rectosigmoid distention in irritable bowel syndrome. *Gastroenterology, 98,* 1187–1192.

Wolf, S., & Wolff, H. G. (1943). *Human gastric function.* London: Oxford University Press.

Part III

SPECIAL POPULATIONS

Chapter 23

Cancer Pain

Randy S. Roth
A. Michael deRosayro
University of Michigan

Pain is a major cause of morbidity and suffering in patients with cancer (Foley, 1985). The World Health Organization (WHO, 1986) has estimated that 4 million people suffer with cancer-related pain and that approximately 90% of these patients can obtain adequate pain control with available medical technologies (Schug, Zech, & Doerr, 1990; Ventafridda, Tamburini, Caraceni, DeConno, & Naldi, 1987). Despite this declaration the undertreatment of pain remains a critical problem in the comprehensive management of the cancer patient (Jacox, Carr, & Payne, 1994; Zenz, Zentz, Tryba, & Strumpf, 1995). Indeed, when physicians who care for cancer patients are surveyed, nearly half express the concern that patients treated within their setting are receiving inadequate pain relief (Von Roenn, Cleeland, Gonin, Hatfield, & Pandya, 1993). Serious and multiple barriers to effective pain control continue to frustrate both patients and their physicians (Cleeland, 1993). Furthermore, the advance of pain symptoms following the diagnosis of cancer may signify for the patient an inevitable and progressive deterioration in health and function, leading to hopelessness and despair. As an increasing number of cancer patients survive their disease or enjoy extended life expectancy due to early diagnosis and advances in cancer therapies, an emphasis on pain management and quality of life has emerged as a major priority for cancer investigators (Portenoy, 1990).

An unforeseen but profound outgrowth from the study of cancer pain has been the reexamination of the risk of analgesic tolerance historically linked to chronic opioid therapy. As Foley (1993) has noted, the cancer pain patient has served as a "natural experiment" in reconsidering long-held and misinformed views that surround long-term opioid use by pain patients. Twycross (1974) was one of the first to observe that cancer patients receiving daily maintenance opioids did not evidence the escalation in dosage levels presumed to be characteristic of chronic opioid therapy. Later studies at the Memorial Sloan-Kettering Cancer Center (Coyle, 1989; Kanner & Foley, 1981; Portenoy, Moulin, Rogers, Inturrisi, & Foley, 1986) and elsewhere (Chapman & Hill, 1989; Schug et al., 1992) confirmed that regardless of whether the cancer pain patient was hospitalized, ambulatory, or suffering far-advanced disease, there was little evidence for the development of analgesic tolerance during a course of maintenance opioid therapy, and when dosage escalation was observed it was generally due to increasing pain severity or progression of disease. As a result of these findings, there has been renewed interest in the application of maintenance opioid therapy for chronic nonmalignant pain, with preliminary findings suggesting clinical promise (Portenoy & Foley, 1986; Zenz, Strumpf, & Tryba, 1992).

Although it is not surprising that the prevalence of cancer pain increases with disease progression, it is now clear that significant cancer pain is not exclusive to the late stages of the disease. Between 5% and 15% of cancer patients with early onset or nonmetastatic disease complain of significant pain, a prevalence that grows to 30% to 40% during the intermediate stage of the disease particularly if metastases has occurred (Cleeland, 1984, 1991; Daut & Cleeland, 1982; Twycross & Lack, 1984). For cancer patients with advanced disease, significant pain is present in 70% to 90% of cases (Foley, 1985; Portenoy, 1989; Twycross, Harcourt, & Bergl, 1996). Of cancer patients with pain, nearly 75% describe it as moderate to very severe (Bonica, 1990). In addition to its prevalence and severity, the mere presence of pain has implications for psychosocial and physical functioning of the cancer patient. Cancer patients with pain are more prone to depression, exhibit greater psychosocial disturbance, and report a lower quality of life compared to cancer patients without pain (Ahles, Blanchard & Ruckdeschel, 1983; Heim & Oei, 1993; Serlin, Mendoza, Nakamura, Edwards, & Cleeland, 1995).

This chapter reviews pertinent issues related to cancer pain management. The discussion describes the prevalence and character of cancer pain, attitudes and beliefs shared by patients and health care providers that contribute to the formation of barriers to more effective cancer pain relief, the measurement of pain in cancer patients, psychosocial factors associated with cancer pain, and both medical and psychological interventions for cancer pain control. This representative review is selective and emphasizes cancer pain management for an adult population. The interested reader is referred to more exhaustive accounts of cancer-related pain management (Arbit, 1993; Chapman & Foley, 1993; Parris, 1997; Patt,

1993) and sources in pediatric oncology (J. R. Hilgard & LeBaron, 1984; Schechter, Altman, & Weisman, 1990; Sutters & Miaskowski, 1992).

CHARACTER AND PREVALENCE OF CANCER PAIN

Cancer-related pain has been categorized by etiology into three broad groups—pain syndromes associated with direct tumor infiltration, pain associated with cancer treatments (e.g., chemotherapy, radiotherapy, surgery), and pain unrelated to tumor growth or cancer therapy (K. Elliott & Foley, 1990; Foley, 1979). Pain that directly results from cancer disease accounts for approximately 75% of all cancer pain and varies based on tumor type and location, the presence of metastases, and the stage of the illness (Coyle & Foley, 1987; Foley, 1985; Kori, Foley, & Posner, 1981). Tumors of bone, breast, prostate, and oral cavity appear to have the highest incidence of pain, estimated between 60% and 85%, whereas patients with lymphoma and leukemia report a lower incidence of pain compared to other cancer syndromes (Ahles, Ruckdeschel, & Blanchard 1984a; Daut & Cleeland, 1982; Foley, 1979; Greenwald, Bonica, & Bergner, 1987). Portenoy et al. (1992) studied the prevalence and characteristics of pain in ambulatory patients with lung and colon cancer. Thirty-nine percent of patients with lung cancer reported a recent history of "persistent and frequent" pain compared to 29% of the colon cancer patients. The average pain intensity for the combined groups was described as moderate. Ahles et al. reported on the prevalence of pain in 208 consecutive ambulatory cancer patients. The authors noted that patients with metastases, particularly to bone, reported the highest prevalence of cancer pain.

Not surprisingly, the prevalence and severity of pain increases as cancer progresses to its end stage. As part of an international collaborative study, Vainio and Auvinen (1996) described the prevalence of pain in over 1,800 cancer patients in hospice care in the United States, Europe, and Australia. Moderate to severe pain was reported by more than half the patients, and the prevalence of pain across cancer syndromes was reported as follows: gynecologic 80%, head/neck 72%, prostate 61%, colorectal 59%, lymphoma 58%, breast 52%, and lung 51%. Comparing these data to the studies by Daut and Cleeland (1982) and Foley (1979), it appears that the prevalence of pain in different cancer syndromes varies based on the stage of illness.

There is some disagreement on the distribution of pathophysiologic mechanisms associated with nociception from direct tumor involvement. Foley (1985) suggested that metastatic bone disease, neuropathy secondary to direct tumor infiltration or nerve compression, and pain associated with the viscera are the most frequent causes of tumor-related pain. However, more recently Banning, Sjogren, and Henriksen (1991) analyzed the pain symptoms of 200 patients attending a specialized cancer pain clinic. Of these,

158 patients had pain attributable specifically to their cancer. Visceral pain was observed in 37% of patients, metastatic bone disease in 34%, soft tissue invasion in 28%, and neuropathic pain in 20% of the study sample. Similarly, Grond, Zech, Diefenbach, Radbruch, and Lehmann (1996) reported on a prospective study of 2,266 cancer patients and classified the nociceptive etiology of their pain. Pain of soft tissue origin was noted to be most common (45%), followed by bone infiltration and metastases (35%), visceral pain (34%), and neuropathies (33%). These discrepancies across studies are likely due to sample differences, measurement methodology, and variability in disease characteristics. What is clear, however, is the pervasive nature of cancer pain symptoms associated with tumor growth.

In general, it is assumed that between 10% and 20% of cancer pain may be related to medical and surgical therapies for cancer (Banning et al., 1991; Foley, 1979; Kanner & Foley, 1981). Portenoy (1989) summarized the numerous pain syndromes related to anticancer interventions. Pain syndromes induced by chemotherapy include polyneuropathies, asceptic necrosis, or painful oral mucositis. Postradiotherapy pain syndromes most commonly result from radiation fibrosis that involve neural structures such as the brachial or lumbosacral plexus. Mucositis, myelopathy, and bone necrosis are further potential sources of pain that result from radiation treatment for cancer. Surgical interventions for tumor control or excision can leave patients with a variety of postsurgical complications. Most common among these are syndromes associated with thoracotomy, mastectomy, and radical neck dissection. In addition, patients who require limb amputation for tumor growth may suffer sequelae that include stump and phantom pain. Little is known regarding the incidence of these unfortunate complications of cancer treatment. Furthermore, many of these pain disorders can be particularly resistant to treatment (e.g., neuropathic pain). Thus, although the prevalence of this second classification of cancer-related pains may be modest, they may be extremely troublesome for the individual patient.

A third class of cancer pain syndromes derives indirectly from the disease itself and its treatment. Cancer pain frequently results in functional impairment and psychological morbidity (Cleeland et al., 1994), both of which can result in disability and disuse, thereby promoting musculoskeletal disorders. For example, Twycross and Fairfield (1982) reported that of 100 patients with advanced cancer, 39 were found to have pain symptoms unrelated to cancer and its treatment. The most common diagnosis was myofascial pain syndrome. Banning et al. (1991) reported that 68 of 200 cancer patients attending a specialty cancer pain clinic were diagnosed with myogenic pain. Whereas previous authors have suggested that cancer pain unrelated to disease process or treatment may account for only 5% to 10% of cancer pain (Foley, 1985), it is evident from the studies of Twycross and Fairfield (1982) and Banning et al. (1991) that the prevalence of this group of cancer-related pain may be underestimated. Further research is necessary to document the prevalence and etiologies for this poorly delineated class of cancer-related pain.

Given the varied sources of cancer pain, it is not surprising that numerous studies have reported the relatively high prevalence of multiple pain syndromes suffered by individual cancer patients (Twycross & Fairfield, 1982). Portenoy et al. (1992) found that approximately one third of patients with lung or colon cancer had more than one source of pain. More recently, Grond et al. (1996) observed that 39% of their sample of cancer patients had two different sources of pain and 31% had at least three or more pain disorders. Twycross et al. (1996) reported an even higher prevalence of multiple pain disorders among cancer patients with far-advanced disease. In their study 85% of patients were found to have multiple pain diagnoses and 40% had four or more pain syndromes.

The diversity of causes for pain in cancer patients raises a serious challenge for the practitioner who cares for this population. The multiplicity of pain syndromes presented by so many cancer patients requires the clinician to utilize a broad armamentarium of intervention strategies. As a result, several writers have emphasized the need for multidisciplinary treatment of chronic cancer pain (Cleeland et al., 1986). Furthermore, there is a need for careful examination of pain symptoms in the cancer patient in order to distinguish alternative sources of nociception beyond the primary cancer site. Two studies illustrate this point. Gonzales, Elliot, Portenoy, and Foley (1991) studied 276 consecutive cancer pain patients seen for neurological consultation at Memorial Sloan-Kettering Cancer Center. The authors identified a previously undiagnosed etiology for pain in 64% of the patients, with metastatic tumor growth the most common source of pain. A new neurological diagnosis was found in 36% of patients and an unsuspected infection was identified in an additional 4%. Based on these findings, 18% of the study sample received further medical treatment for their pain symptoms, including chemotherapy, radiotherapy, and surgery. In a second study conducted at the same institution, Clouston, DeAngelis, and Posner (1992) focused on neurologic symptoms among 851 patients with known systemic cancer. A surprising 45% of patients were found to have evidence for metastases to the nervous system.

ATTITUDES TOWARD CANCER PAIN AND BARRIERS
TO EFFECTIVE CANCER PAIN MANAGEMENT

Cleeland (1993) has emphasized the need to address the numerous barriers that impede the provision of timely and effective interventions for cancer pain. He observed that the administration of pain treatment to cancer patients occurs as a complex interplay between the patient and health care provider within the context of a health care delivery system. As such, each component of this interactional system can serve as a barrier to efforts at pain treatment. Two sources of impediment to cancer pain management concern the practice habits of physicians and nurses and the restrictive scrutiny that medicolegal forces place on the prescription and availability of opioid analgesics for patients with significant pain (Portenoy, 1989). However, of equal importance are the strong, pervasive, and problematic attitudes and beliefs shared by the general population and medical community regarding cancer pain and its control. Data are accumulating that help to elucidate how these belief systems interfere with attempts to achieve adequate analgesia for the cancer pain patient.

A number of studies have documented the perceptions of the public in general, and cancer patients specifically, with regard to cancer pain. Levin, Cleeland, and Dar (1985) surveyed adults in Wisconsin to determine public attitudes toward cancer pain. The results were quite startling in revealing the fear and apprehension that cancer pain and its treatment hold for the average citizen. Forty-eight percent and 79% of respondents believed cancer pain and cancer treatment, respectively, were very or extremely painful. Amazingly, nearly one in five persons indicated that they might delay seeking medical attention for cancer due to fear of pain. Seventy-two percent of the adults interviewed felt that cancer pain can become so grave that a person would consider discontinuing life support measures, 69% felt that the severity of pain might lead to consideration of suicide, and 57% were convinced that cancer patients die a painful death. Half of all respondents expressed concern regarding the use of narcotics for the treatment of cancer pain and the incidence of side effects associated with opioid therapy. In a follow-up study (Doyle, Cleeland, & Joranson, 1991), normal adults continued to express strong fears regarding the gravity of cancer pain and its treatment, but there was some downturn in concerns related to possible side effects of tolerance, addiction, and mental confusion with opioid treatment although nearly half of those surveyed still harbored apprehension.

Fear of addiction, tolerance, and other morbidities presumed to be inherent in opioid therapy is evident in studies of cancer patients as well. Dar, Beach, Barden, and Cleeland (1992) reported that among cancer patients who suffered with significant pain associated with moderate impairment in activities of daily living, a majority of patients believed they should not take opioids on a regular basis but only when pain was most severe. Patient fears of problems with opioid-induced side effects were strongly associated with reports of reluctance to report pain to physicians and willingness to experience pain rather than take analgesics. In a corroborating study, Ward et al. (1993) developed a 31-item Barriers Questionnaire (BQ) and administered it to 270 adults with cancer. Of these patients, 79% believed that a person can become addicted to pain medications, whereas 61% believed it is better to live with pain rather than risk untoward side effects with opioid therapy. Of particular significance for understanding patient underreporting of their pain (Cleeland, 1984), 60% of cancer patients endorsed the belief that complaining of pain would distract their physician from directly treating their cancer, and 45% believed that a "good patient" does not disclose problems with pain. Higher scores on the BQ predicted greater pain interference with daily function. Of those patients reporting pain at the time of the survey, 42% were undermedicated based on the severity of their pain report and in accordance with WHO (1986) guidelines for analgesic use for pain control.

Taken together, these data illustrate formidable patient attitudes that vitiate effective cancer pain management. Patients and potential patients possess misinformation about the controllability of cancer pain and maintain misconceptions regarding the use and morbidity associated with routine opioid therapy. Furthermore, consumers of pain treatment maintain dysfunctional attitudes pertaining to the conduct of a "good patient" who suffers with cancer and the effect of requests for pain treatment on more general management of cancer. Clearly, educational efforts are necessary to alter these maladaptive perceptions (Max 1990; Rimer et al., 1987). In this regard, de Wit et al. (1997) recently demonstrated the efficacy of a pain education program for cancer pain patients that resulted in both an increase in pain knowledge and decrease in pain intensity for the intervention group.

A second potential barrier to adequate cancer pain relief derives from the attitudes and practice habits of clinicians involved in cancer pain management. Vortherms, Ryan, and Ward (1992) surveyed 790 nurses regarding their perceptions of barriers to the provision of adequate treatment of cancer pain. Sixty percent of those interviewed worked with cancer patients. Forty-four percent of respondents believed that cancer patients overreport the severity of their pain. Furthermore, only 56% of nurses could correctly identify practice management guidelines for analgesics. More than 75% expressed the belief that lack of adequate assessment of cancer pain was a significant deterrent to cancer pain management. Lack of clinician knowledge was viewed as another significant barrier for 72% of the sample.

Von Roenn et al. (1993) surveyed 897 physicians who treat cancer patients and participated in the Eastern Cooperative Oncology Group (ECOG) to determine their knowledge and practice habits related to cancer pain. With regard to opioid management of cancer pain, 61% of the study participants expressed reluctance to prescribe strong analgesics due to various concerns regarding side effects and the development of tolerance. Thirty-one percent of the physicians would wait until that patient's prognosis was only 6 months before initiating maximum opioid therapy. Only 60% of the physicians would consider potent analgesics early in cancer treatment. Not surprisingly, only 51% of respondents judged the pain management in their own clinical setting to be good or very good. These physicians cited poor educational preparation in clinical pain medicine as an important obstacle to better cancer pain management. Thus, only 11% and 27% of physicians reported that their medical school and residency training, respectively, provided good or excellent instruction in cancer pain treatment. In over 60% of the sample, poor pain assessment, patient reluctance to report pain, patient reluctance to take opioids, and physician reluctance to prescribe opioids were seen as major barriers to more effective management of cancer pain.

Portenoy (1989) has observed that the threat of government regulation and scrutiny over physician prescription practices may be among the reasons for the underprescription of strong analgesics for pain. Von Roenn et al. (1993) found some support for this concern. Physicians in the ECOG who practiced in states that required triplicate prescription for scheduled pain medications expressed significantly more apprehension about government regulation of opioids, and admitted to significantly greater reluctance to prescribe narcotics compared to their physician counterparts from states where scheduled analgesics were less restricted. Fear of regulatory control and recrimination can have subtle effects on physician prescription practices beyond the simple decision whether to prescribe opioids for pain. For example, physicians may reduce the quantity, potency, and number of refills for a given opioid or choose an analgesic from a weak opioid group (Weissman, Joranson, & Hopwood, 1991). This problem is further reinforced by data suggesting that among members of state medical boards, who are responsible for the licensure and regulation of physicians, there is widespread misinformation and prejudice on the use of opioids in the treatment of pain, including unrealistic estimates on the incidence of dependency and addiction with chronic opioid therapy (Joranson, Cleeland, Weissman, & Gilson, 1992).

Another potential barrier to improved cancer pain management concerns changes in the health care system. The recent and increasing popularity of managed care systems of health care delivery, with their emphasis on reduction of cost through decreased health care utilization, may eventually pose serious obstacles to the multidisciplinary and long-term medical and psychosocial needs of the cancer pain patient. Although managed care systems may be proficient in providing acute medical interventions during the early and intermediate stages of cancer treatment, their ability to address the needs of patients with chronic illness, similar to those of many cancer pain patients, has been called into question (Ware, Bayliss, Rogers, Kosinski, & Tarlov, 1996). Cancer investigators need to develop methodologies to track the treatment course of cancer pain within various models of health care delivery to determine if cancer pain patients receive adequate care through the full extent of their illness.

ASSESSMENT OF THE CANCER PAIN PATIENT

Nearly 75% of clinicians who treat cancer pain agree that accurate pain assessment is a critical determinant of effective cancer pain management (Grossman, Sheidler, Swedeen, Mucenski, & Piantadosi, 1991; Von Roenn et al., 1993). Unfortunately, there is less agreement on who is the best judge of a cancer patient's pain (Slevin, Plant, Lynch, Drinkwater, & Gregory, 1988). Studies have demonstrated that proxy (e.g., physician, nurse, significant other) estimations of pain bear poor relationship with patient self-report of pain intensity, with health care providers underestimating the patient's pain complaint (Peteet, Tay, Cohen, & MacIntyre, 1986; Sprangers & Aaronson, 1992). Cancer pain assessment is also complicated by the variety of pain syndromes that coexist in a cancer patient and the vicissitudes of pain experience that come with recurrent medical interventions and fluctuations in disease. Thus, cancer pain does not neatly categorize into the dichotomous acute versus chronic typology that has proven to be a meaningful clinical distinction for nonmalignant pain (Roth & Kamholz, 1997). This conundrum has led Ahles, Ruckdeschel, and Blanchard (1984b) to characterize some forms of cancer pain as "chronic-acute."

Consistent with a modern conceptualization of pain that acknowledges sensory, affective, and cognitive components of pain experience (Melzack & Casey, 1968), most cancer pain investigators advocate for a multidimensional assessment of cancer pain (Ahles et al., 1983). Typically, cancer pain assessment relies on self-report inventories or scales that examine pain severity, selected psychological variables such as mood or pain beliefs, and the effect of pain on physical and social function. For example, Padilla, Ferrell, Grant, and Rhiner (1990) asked cancer patients with pain several open-ended questions regarding the effect of cancer pain on their life. The responses appeared to identify three dimensions of life satisfaction adversely affected by pain that the authors labeled (a) physical functioning, (b) psychological well-being, and (c) interpersonal relationships. Expanding cancer pain assessment beyond simple measures of pain intensity allows a more broad-based understanding of the variables that impact on and are impacted upon by cancer pain. Such a comprehensive assessment of health-related quality of life for cancer pain patients can aid in the evaluation of cancer pain treatment outcome and identify moderator variables, such as social support or mood, that influence the impact of cancer pain on an individual's health and function (Guyatt, Feeny, & Patrick, 1993; Moinpur, Georidov, Chapman, & Donaldson, 1993).

Jensen and Karoly (1993) reviewed the literature on self-report measures in the evaluation of cancer pain. The authors noted that an assessment of pain can include several aspects including pain intensity, pain behavior and coping, pain beliefs, or affective disturbance attributable to pain. They determined that simple instruments frequently employed in pain studies to assess pain intensity, such as the Visual Analogue Scale, Numerical Rating Scale, and Verbal Rating Scale, have demonstrated adequate psychometric stability and validity and are sensitive to pain treatment effects (DeConno et al., 1994). In addition, these unidimensional scales can be adapted for the assessment of pain-related affect (Ahles et al., 1984b). Their ease of administration and brevity are notable advantages for their use in clinical trials or treatment settings. However, the authors concluded that, given the effect of various contextual factors such as mood or memory on pain report, it is advisable to obtain multiple pain measurements and aggregate them to calculate a single pain severity index. Data point aggregation has been shown to improve the reliability of pain measurements and their sensitivity to treatment effects (Littman, Walker, & Schneider, 1985).

Several inventories have been developed or adapted to assess symptom severity in patients with cancer (Graham, Bond, Gerkovich, & Cook, 1986; Portenoy et al., 1994). Of these, the most thoroughly investigated and specific to cancer pain is the Brief Pain Inventory (BPI) developed by Cleeland and his colleagues (Cleeland, 1989; Daut, Cleeland, & Flannery, 1983). The BPI is a self-report questionnaire that provides a measure of pain intensity and the degree to which pain interferes with various domains of life function (e.g., mood, general activity, walking, normal work, sleep, relationships, and life satisfaction). The scale has been validated in a group of cancer patients (Cleeland et al., 1994) and has been used with patients who are in the terminal stages of the disease (Larue et al., 1994). Chinese, French, and Philippine versions have been developed and employed in cross-cultural studies of cancer pain (Serlin et al., 1995; X. S. Wang, Mendoza, Gao, & Cleeland, 1996). In a recent expansion of the construct validity of the BPI, Serlin et al. compared numerical ratings of pain severity on a 0–10 scale and ratings of pain interference with activity as measured by the BPI. The authors found reliable correspondence between mild (e.g., 1–4), moderate (e.g., 5–6), and severe (e.g., 7–10) levels of pain and discrete categories of increasing pain-related dysfunction. Serlin et al. went on to suggest that this graded schema for pain severity and pain interference may coincide with the WHO (1986) analgesic ladder for the differential treatment of mild, moderate, and severe pain. Also of note, this study found remarkable consistency in the association of pain severity and pain interference reports across French, Philippine, and Chinese cancer patients.

Beyond assessment tools that singly measure cancer pain severity or include a determination of pain-related disability, there has been an expanding interest in the assessment of health-related quality of life for patients with cancer and cancer pain (Cella, 1994; Portenoy, 1991). Health researchers have developed global measures of quality of life in order to assess the pervasive impact of illness and disease on health and function (Guyatt et al., 1993). Comprehensive cancer pain management can no longer be limited to the provision of analgesia but must also address issues of suffering, disability, and impairment that envelop the life experience of many cancer pain patients (Cassell, 1982; Portenoy, 1991). Persistent pain and cancer are inextricably linked for many cancer patients, and it is obvious that pain exerts a significant and deleterious impact on quality of life (Lee & Rowlingson, 1990). Several studies have reported an association between cancer pain and quality-of-life measures. For example, Strang and Qvarner (1990) found that cancer pain intensity correlated positively with depression, mental distractibility, functional disability, and social withdrawal. Tannock et al. (1989) observed improvements in measures of quality of life following treatment-related reduction in metastatic pain from prostate cancer. Coyle, Adelhart, Foley, and Portenoy (1990) observed similar associations between cancer pain and disruption in quality of life in patients with far-advanced disease. A comprehensive review of cancer and quality of life is beyond the purview of the present discussion. The interested reader is directed to studies by Ganz, Schag, Lee, and Sim (1992), Cella et al. (1993), Schipper, Clinch, McMurray, and Levitt (1984), Ferrans (1990), and Padilla et al. (1983) for a description of quality-of-life inventories developed specifically for a cancer population.

PSYCHOSOCIAL FACTORS AND CANCER PAIN

A study of the influence of psychosocial factors on cancer pain is complicated by the nature of cancer and adverse effects associated with its treatment (Massie & Holland, 1987). Previous studies have identified an increased risk of psychological disturbances in patients diagnosed with cancer (Derogatis et al., 1983), although these prevalence rates appear to be similar to other medical populations (Moffic & Paykel, 1975). Symptoms of depression and anxiety have been observed in cancer patients who undergo surgery, radiation, and chemotherapy for tumor infiltration (Davies, Davies, & Delpo, 1986; Gottesman & Lewis, 1982). Furthermore, the increased mood disturbance in cancer pain patients may be related to the disability associated with cancer pain rather than to pain per se (Cleeland, 1984). The etiologic contribution of affective distress to cancer pain is compromised by data suggesting that psychosocial problems resolve when cancer pain is controlled (Bond, 1979; Marks & Sachar, 1973).

There is little doubt that mood disturbance and pain severity are positively related in cancer pain (Glover, Dibble, Dodd, & Miaskowski, 1995;

Spiegel & Bloom, 1983). Studies comparing cancer patients with low levels or no pain to those with complaints of moderate to severe pain consistently document increased symptoms of depression, anxiety, and general affective disturbance associated with more severe pain (Bond, 1979; Glover et al., 1995; Heim & Oei, 1993; Spiegel, Sands, & Koopman, 1994). These studies are important because they allow for the control of cancer as a confounding factor in assessing the association of distress and cancer pain.

Dalton and Feuerstein (1988) reviewed the literature on selected psychological variables and their contribution to cancer pain. They concluded that there was no evidence for the influence of personality factors and only weak or modest support for an association between affective and environmental/social variables and cancer pain. More recently, Syrjala and Chapko (1995) reported on a prospective study of pain in cancer patients receiving bone marrow transplantation. Biomedical factors were found to account for the largest proportion of variance in patient pain report, with affective distress concerning cancer treatment, self-efficacy, and coping style also contributing to pain experience.

Considerable interest has been paid to the coexistence of depression and pain in cancer patients. The coprevalence of pain complaints in depressed patients and depression among chronic pain patients has received extensive study in nonmalignant pain populations (Romano & Turner, 1985). It is generally accepted that the causal relationship between pain and depression is two-way, and that the prevalence of comorbidity for these disorders is significant (Fishbain, Cutler, Rosomoff, & Rosomoff, 1997). For cancer pain, it also appears that, in general, depressive symptoms predict a higher rate and severity of pain (Lansky et al., 1985), whereas the presence of pain is associated with greater depression (Derogatis et al., 1983; Spiegel et al., 1994) although not all studies are in agreement (Cleeland, 1984).

The study of the association between cancer pain and depression is hindered by diagnostic ambiguities regarding depression in cancer patients. Depression rates are highest among cancer patients who are hospitalized or with far-advanced disease and only modest during ambulatory care (Bukberg, Penman, & Holland, 1984; Lansky et al., 1985). Depression may also be underdiagnosed and undertreated in cancer patients due to the expectation that depression is a "normal" psychological sequela of a cancer diagnosis or if somatic symptoms of depression are mistakenly attributed to cancer or its treatment (Massie & Holland, 1984; Rodin & Voshart, 1986).

Suicidal intention and risk are natural concerns for a patient population that endures both pain and the prospect of terminal illness. Interestingly, there appears to be no significant relationship between pain intensity and suicidal ideation (Breitbart, 1993) although uncontrolled pain is generally recognized as a risk factor for suicide in cancer patients (Breitbart, 1987, 1990). The influence of cancer pain on suicide appears to be mediated by a number of comorbid factors including gender (male), age (older), type of cancer (e.g., oral, lung, breast, pharyngeal, urogenital), poor prognosis, and premorbid psychopathology including a history of a suicide attempt (Breitbart, 1993).

Dalton and Feuerstein (1988) noted the paucity of studies assessing cognitive variables that might contribute to pain experience in cancer pain. Turk and colleagues (Turk & Feldman, 1992; Turk & Salovey, 1985) reviewed the theoretical basis for the relevance of cognitive factors for pain experience and extended this discussion to cancer pain. Several studies have provided preliminary evidence to support the relevance of cognitive factors for cancer pain. Cancer patients who attribute the cause of their pain to worsening of their disease complain of increased pain and distress. Spiegel and Bloom (1983) reported that the belief that pain in cancer is an indication of cancer proliferation significantly contributed to the patients' pain report. Others have noted increased affective distress and greater functional disability when pain is attributed to cancer rather then other causes (Ahles et al., 1983; Daut & Cleeland, 1982). Perceived control is another cognitive factor that has been shown to be positively associated with pain tolerance (Thompson, 1981). Loss of perceived control is a common experience for cancer patients who report pain (Dalton & Feuerstein, 1989). Hill, Saeger, and Chapman (1986) found that patients receiving bone marrow transplants and who utilized patient-controlled analgesia for pain control required one third as much morphine, with equivalent pain relief, as patients who depended on nurse administration for their opioids. Similarly, the cognitive factor labeled self-efficacy, where an individual possesses the belief they can perform a particular skill (e.g., control pain), has been found to predict enhanced quality of life in cancer pain patients (Cunningham, Lockwood, & Cunningham, 1981). These data point to the potential role of cognition in determining pain, suffering, and function in cancer pain. Further investigation to explore the interaction of cognitive factors and cancer pain is warranted.

Finally, any discussion of psychological variables associated with cancer should consider its impact on the family system. Ventafridda, Tamburini, et al. (1987) have suggested that the involvement of families is a critical element in the treatment of the cancer pain patient. Mor, Guadagnoli, and Wool (1987) observed that increased severity of cancer pain was associated with more severe emotional and financial burden for the family. Miaskowski, Kragnes, Dibble, and Wallhagen (1997) studied the impact of pain and cancer on family caregivers. When the cancer patient also suffered with pain, family members reported more severe symptoms of tension, depression, and overall mood disturbance. Dar et al. (1992) noted that cancer pain patients appear to underestimate the effect of their disease on spouse adjustment. B. A. Elliot, T. E. Elliot, Murray, Braun, and Johnson (1996) observed that family members tend to overestimate a cancer patient's degree of pain and disability, but the accuracy of this assessment was predicted by the level of knowledge that family members possessed on the nature of cancer pain and opioid therapy.

PHARMACOLOGIC MANAGEMENT

Nonsteroidal Anti-Inflammatory Drugs (NSAIDs). For patients with mild to moderate cancer pain, NSAIDs are recommended in combination with an adjuvant analgesic drug (see later discussion). For patients with moderate to severe pain, NSAIDs are typically combined with opioids and, if necessary, an adjuvant agent to optimize analgesic effect. NSAIDs have been particularly effective in the treatment of bone cancer pain (Kanner, 1987).

Opioids. Opioids are the mainstay of cancer pain management. In 1986 the WHO proposed a step-wise progression from weak to strong opioids depending on the severity of pain—The WHO Ladder (WHO, 1986). When NSAIDs and adjuvant medications, such as antidepressants, anticonvulsants, and steroids, are incorporated into this ladder, it has been shown that up to 90% of cancer pain and over 75% of pain in terminal cancer can be adequately managed (Grond, Zech, Schug, Lynch, & Lehmann, 1991). The main concerns among practitioners regarding the use of opioids have been based on the issues of tolerance, dependence, and side effects. The subjects of tolerance and dependence have been addressed earlier in this chapter. Potential side effects from opioids include respiratory depression, sedation, nausea and vomiting, constipation, urinary retention, and itching. Respiratory depression, the most feared side effect of opioid therapy, has proven to be rare and occurs only with relative overdosage in the opioid naive patient. Constipation is the most common side effect but this can generally be managed with adequate attention paid to diet, prophylactic stool softeners, and mild laxatives. Sedation and nausea and vomiting are more common at the initiation of opioid therapy, and commonly tolerance to these side effects develop and they become less troublesome (Kaplan et al., 1995).

The opioids used most commonly for mild to moderate pain are codeine, hydrocodone, propoxyphene, and oxycodone. These are generally used in combination with aspirin or acetaminophen, which act synergistically to enhance analgesia. Oxycodone, which is a synthetic morphine congener and is about 10 times more potent than oral codeine, is now available in a controlled-release preparation, which allows for twice-a-day dosing (Grandy, Reder, Fitzmartin, Benziger, & Kaiko, 1994; Heiskanen & Kalso, 1997). Its use for chronic cancer and noncancer pain has been recently reviewed by Patt (1996). Morphine remains the gold standard for strong opioids since its introduction into clinical use almost 200 years ago. It is now available for administration not only by the oral route but by rectal, parenteral, and intraspinal routes as well. The introduction of two slow-release preparations of morphine, MS Contin®, and Oramorph SR®, has greatly enhanced the use of opioids in cancer pain by allowing for less frequent dosing. These preparations are particularly useful in reducing sleep disturbance among cancer patients with pain. Several studies have now demonstrated the safety and efficacy of these preparations in controlling cancer pain (Goughnour, Arkinstall, & Stewart, 1989; Heiskanen & Kalso, 1997). An alternative to patients who are intolerant of morphine is methadone, a synthetic opioid with oral bioavailability greater than 85%. It has a long half-life of approximately 24 hours and can therefore be used on a two- to three-times-a-day dosing schedule. A transdermal preparation of a potent opioid agonist, fentanyl, is available for patients unable to swallow pills or who have poor absorption from the gastrointestinal tract (Lehmann & Zech, 1992). Patches are available from 25 micrograms to 100 micrograms and require change once every three days. Titration of fentanyl is somewhat difficult because of uncertain absorption rates and the fact that blood levels are present for several hours after discontinuation of the patch (Payne, Moran, & Southam, 1991). Although the majority of cancer pain patients obtain adequate pain control with standard analgesic management, patients with neuropathic pain, significant psychological distress, pain on movement, or histories of recent analgesic tolerance or premorbid chemical dependency exhibit relatively poor outcome (Bruera et al., 1995). For the interested reader, the American Pain Society has published an excellent handbook on the principles of analgesic use in cancer pain suitable for all clinicians involved in cancer pain management (American Pain Society, 1992).

Intraspinal Opioids. Since the discovery of specific opioid receptors in the spinal cord in the early 1970s by Pert and Snyder (1973), the clinical use of intraspinal opioids has developed quite rapidly (Nehme, 1993). The first report of intrathecal morphine for cancer pain was in 1979 by J. F. Wang at the Mayo Clinic (J. F. Wang, Nauss, & Thomas, 1979) and in the same year its use by the epidural route was also described (Behar, Alshwang, Magora, & Davidson, 1979). Intraspinal opioids are an alternative for those patients who fail to get adequate pain relief despite escalating doses of oral or parenteral opioid preparations and for those who have intolerable side effects from systemic opioids (Waldman, 1990). As the delivery system allows close application of the drug to the active receptor sites, the doses required for intraspinal opioids are considerably less than when used systemically. For short-term use, generally less than 3 months, the use of percutaneous catheters into the epidural space, which also may be tunneled subcutaneously to the chest wall or flank region, are generally adequate (Bruera, 1990). For long-term use, however, implantable systems are more convenient and safer with reduced risk of infection and are the preferred mode (Krames, 1997; Plummer et al., 1991). A recent meta-analysis on the efficacy of intrathecal epidural opiates was reported by Chrubasik and Chrubasik (1997). This review concluded that the success rate of treatment outcome for the use of intrathecal and epidural opiates is somewhat less than previously assumed. Most of the studies included in the review concerned the use of epidurals and spinal opioids for the treatment of chronic nonmalignant pain. Thus, the data for cancer pain alone were more difficult to examine. The authors also found that the complication rate is often as high as 50% and increases with the duration of treatment. Although availability of intraspinal opioid delivery has clearly enhanced the life of many cancer pain patients, particularly those in the terminal stage of illness, it is clear that further prospective study of the efficacy and complication rate of intraspinal opioid intervention is needed.

Adjuvant Agents. Adjuvants are drugs developed primarily for other, nonpain medical conditions that have been found to promote analgesia for certain pain syndromes (Portenoy, 1996). These drugs are viewed as supplementary to opioids and NSAIDs but can provide pain relief beyond that achieved with analgesics alone, particularly for cancer-related pain syndromes involving neuropathic and bone nociception.

The tricyclic antidepressants are the most common adjuvant drugs for use with cancer and nonmalignant chronic pain (Magni, Arsie, & DeLeo, 1987; Watson, 1994). In chronic pain, antidepressants are most often considered for the treatment of neuropathic pain, for which there is considerable evidence supporting their efficacy (Max et al., 1987). Clinical experience suggests that analgesic potency appears to be highest for the tertiary amine (e.g., amitriptyline, nortriptyline) and secondary amine (e.g., desipramine) tricyclic compounds. There is preliminary evidence supporting the analgesic efficacy of the newer selective serotonin reuptake inhibitor antidepressants (e.g., fluoxetine) (Rani, Naidu, Prasad, Rao, & Shobha, 1996) and their more favorable side-effect profile make them an alternative adjuvant antidepressant for some patients. Of particular relevance, antidepressants have been shown to increase the bioavailability of morphine in cancer patients (Ventafridda, Ripamonti, et al., 1987).

Several alternative adjuvants have been clinically useful for the treatment of refractory neuropathic pain in cancer patients, but unfortunately the clinical utility of these agents, apart from the anticonvulsants, has yet to be confirmed in controlled outcome studies. Neuropathic pain is opioid-resistant in many patients (Dubner, 1991). The experimental data are strongest for the use of anticonvulsant drugs for various forms of neuropathy, particularly if the syndrome includes episodes of lancinating and paroxysmal pain (Swerdlow, 1984). The recent availability of gabapentin, a GABAergic anticonvulsant that has demonstrated particular clinical promise in reducing neuropathic pain (Rosner, Rubin, & Kestenbaum, 1996), has expanded the class of traditional anticonvulsants prescribed for the management of neuropathic pain (e.g., phenytoin, carbamazapine, valproate, clonazepam). Other adjuvant analgesics applicable to neuropathic pain in cancer include baclofen, another GABAergic agent; mexilitene, an oral local anesthetic; neuroleptics (Patt, Proper, & Reddy, 1994); calcitonin; clonidine, an alpha-2 adrenergic agonist; and topical preparations such as capsaicin that are presumed to inhibit the release of substance P, a neurotransmitter that is known to facilitate nociception (Portenoy, 1996).

Corticosteroids have been utilized for a variety of cancer-related pain including bowel obstruction, neuropathies, and bone pain (Watanabe & Bruera, 1994). Osteoclast inhibitors (e.g., pamidronate, alendronate), NSAIDs, and calcitonin have also been clinically useful specifically for bone pain. Psychostimulants have been found to potentiate opioid analgesia for cancer pain and have had added benefits in reducing the adverse effects of sedation and cognitive impairment induced by opioid analgesia (Bruera & Watanabe, 1994).

Neurolytic Nerve Blocks. The introduction of intraspinal opioids to pain management has greatly reduced the use of neurolytic nerve blocks for the management of cancer pain. However, a few select procedures are still utilized and have a place in the overall management of cancer pain, especially if the pain is regional in distribution. In particular, celiac plexus blockade for upper abdominal cancer, most often for pancreatic cancer, has a long track record of efficacy and safety (Sharfman & Walsh, 1990). A recent meta-analysis indicates that it is effective in up to 85% of patients, producing good to excellent pain relief with a very low incidence of major complications (Eisenberg, Carr, & Chalmers, 1995). Plancarte, Amescua, Patt, and Aldrete (1990) reported that another type of sympathetic block, the superior hypogastric plexus block, can be effective and safe in patients with intractable pelvic pain. Subarachnoid epidural neurolytic blocks have been described extensively in the older literature (Maher, 1955). However, these techniques are rarely performed today, are associated with considerable risk of neurologic complication, and are unpredictable in their outcome. Nonetheless, they may have limited application when pain relief can be achieved with selective blocking of one or two nerve roots in the cervical, thoracic, lumbar, or sacral areas (Mehta & Duthies, 1993).

The empirical data supporting the clinical efficacy of neurolysis are based on uncontrolled clinical trials and case studies (Jacox et al., 1994). Further study is needed to clarify for whom these procedures are most applicable and how they can be best utilized within a comprehensive management program for treating cancer pain.

PSYCHOLOGICAL TREATMENT OF CANCER PAIN

Psychological approaches to chronic pain treatment have a long and commendable history (Turk, Meichenbaum, & Genest, 1983). Numerous authors have advocated the use of a variety of behavioral and cognitive-behavioral therapies in addressing the pain associated with cancer (Cleeland, 1987; Fishman & Loscalzo, 1987; Turk & Feldman, 1992). Behavioral therapies have proven effective in reducing the incidence of adverse effects (e.g., nausea, vomiting) associated with antitumor treatment (Burish & Tope, 1992) and have shown promise in reducing the pain associated with these procedures (Jay, C. Elliot, & Varni, 1986). In spite of this evidence, there have been surprisingly few controlled outcome studies examining the benefits of psychological and behavioral therapies in the control of cancer pain. This is likely due, in part, to the documented success of the use of analgesics for cancer pain management. In addition, the unequivical pathphysiology of cancer pain has added to the emphasis on a medical solution to cancer pain, in contrast to the suspicion of psychological contributions to pain inferred in a variety of nonmalignant pain disorders (e.g., low back pain, headache, pelvic pain). As a result, psychological interventions for cancer pain management have been relegated to a secondary status. This is readily illustrated by Cleeland's (1987) declaration regarding cancer pain that "should analgesics produce satisfactory relief of pain . . . no further need for therapy exists" (p. S23).

Turk and Fernandez (1990) raised concerns regarding the apparent stepdown status of psychological therapy in the treatment of cancer pain. After reviewing the biopsychosocial nature of pain experience and the large literature on the efficacy of behavioral treatment of pain, the authors argued that psychosocial factors are equally relevant for the study of cancer pain. In fact, given the potentially devastating nature of a cancer diagnosis and the evidence for cognitive and affective disturbance associated with cancer treatment, cancer pain may be distinguished among pain syndromes for the prevalence of reactive psychological distress. Turk and Fernandez appropriately observed that simply because a patient has cancer-related pain does not ensure that the pain report is a veridical representation of nociception, and that psychosocial factors are not contributing to the patient's pain experience.

The application of hypnosis in the treatment of cancer pain has the longest tradition and strongest empirical support among psychologically based interventions. Numerous case studies and clinical reports describe the successful use of hypnotic suggestion in reducing cancer pain (Barber & Gitelson, 1980; Butler, 1954). In an early investigation, Spiegel and Bloom (1983) studied pain and mood disturbance in 54 women with metastatic breast cancer who received group therapy or no treatment for 1 year. Half of the treatment subjects also were instructed in self-hypnosis. At follow-up both treatment conditions reported less pain and distress and hypnosis appeared to provide additive benefits to group therapy in reducing pain severity. In two comparative studies, Syrjala and colleagues have assessed the effect of hypnosis and behavior therapy for controlling oral mucositis pain commonly associated with bone marrow transplantation for neoplastic disease. In the first study (Syrjala, Cummings, & Donaldson, 1992) subjects were randomly assigned to treatment conditions that included instructions in hypnosis or cognitive-behavior coping skills training (CBT), a therapist contact condition, or a no-treatment control group. Only the hypnosis patients reported a significant improvement in oral pain. A second study (Syrjala, Donaldson, Davis, Kippes, & Carr, 1995) also compared hypnosis (relabeled "relaxation and imagery") and CBT in bone marrow transplant patients. Two experimental groups were instructed in hypnotic suggestions with one group receiving additional training in CBT. Standard medical treatment and a therapist contact group served as controls. Again the authors found that only hypnosis was effective in promoting decreased pain, whereas CBT had no additive benefit.

Several uncontrolled studies have assessed the effect of various relaxation modalities on cancer pain. Graffam and Johnson (1987) instructed 30 cancer patients in both guided imagery and progressive muscle relaxation training. Both relaxation exercises were found to reduce pain and affective distress, with subjects expressing preference for the progressive muscle technique. Fotopoulos and colleagues (Fotopoulous et al., 1983; Fotopoulous, Graham, & Cook, 1979) reported two clinical studies that evaluated the impact of combined Electromyogram-Electroencephalogram (EMG-EEG) and Electromyogram (EMG)-Electrodermal biofeedback training on cancer pain. Although several patients demonstrated reduced pain during training sessions, few were able to transfer pain control outside of the treatment setting and the patients with advanced disease had significant difficulty learning the biofeedback task.

In summary, it appears that behavioral strategies such as relaxation and hypnosis hold promise as simple and effective techniques for cancer pain control and deserve further study. It is equally apparent that despite arguments for the suitability of CBT for cancer pain control (Turk & Rennert, 1981; Turk & Salovey, 1985) there is little empirical evidence to date to support its use. Standard CBT interventions for nonmalignant chronic pain may need to be adapted to the specific cognitive dysfunctions of the cancer patient, where increased pain is often attributed to disease progression (Spiegel & Bloom, 1983). Previous attempts to apply attribution theory to cancer pain have been disappointing, however (Nehemkis, Charter, Stampp, & Gerber, 1982–1983). Nonetheless, the potential utility of CBT in cancer pain merits further inquiry given its documented efficacy in the treatment of other chronic pain syndromes.

An additional topic of future research concerns the question of when is it best to consider psychological training for pain control given the emphasis on medical management in cancer pain. Consideration of psychological modalities is typically postponed unless medical measures fail. However, delaying psychological intervention may be inopportune for purposes of behavioral training. Skills in pain control obtained by psychological training such as hypnosis are often less effective for severe pain (E. R. Hilgard & J. R. Hilgard, 1983) and can be more difficult to acquire due to adverse effects of high-dose opioid therapy (e.g., fatigue, distractibility) commonly prescribed for severe or far-advanced cancer pain. This would suggest that behavioral training earlier in the illness course, when pain levels are only mild or moderate, may be advantageous. This approach, if broadened to a wider range of cancer pain patients, may also reduce opioid requirements and associated side effects for a larger population of cancer patients.

SUMMARY AND CONCLUSIONS

Cancer pain is virtually inevitable in patients with metastatic disease and, if left untreated, exerts a negative and profound impact on a patient's quality of life. The assessment and treatment of cancer-related pain syndromes are complicated by the variety of ways a cancer patient may incur pain and the high probability that more than one pain syndrome will come to coexist within an individual patient. Furthermore, it is clear that psychological distress can adversely affect a patient's pain experience and response to cancer pain management. The good news is that the vast majority of cancer patients with pain can obtain adequate pain control through available pharmacologic and medical interventions.

Unfortunately, serious prohibitions still exist in the delivery of these efficacious therapies to a wider population of cancer patients. There is a need for further research that targets clinical, political, and legal restraints on the availability of opioids for cancer pain treatment (Kanner & Portenoy, 1986) and educational efforts that enhance patient and practitioner understanding of cancer pain and opioid therapy (Elliot et al., 1996; T. Elliot, et al., 1997; Rimer et al., 1987). In addition, there is a need for increased study of the role of supplemental pain control strategies, such as neurolysis and adjuvant analgesics, to determine their efficacy and role in the comprehensive management of cancer pain. The examination of the interaction between psychologically based interventions and somatic cancer pain treatments also appears to be an area of needed inquiry (Ahles, 1985). The last 10 years have witnessed a welcomed and expanded interest in cancer pain management with resultant advances in therapeutic outcome. Continued efforts to implement educational and delivery systems that are directed to cancer pain patients and their families will prove critical to assuring effective pain relief for all cancer patients.

REFERENCES

Ahles, T. A. (1985). Psychological approaches to the management of cancer-related pain. *Seminars in Oncology Nursing, 1,* 141–146.

Ahles, T. A., Blanchard, E. B., & Ruckdeschel, J. C. (1983). The multidimensional nature of cancer-related pain. *Pain, 17,* 277–283.

Ahles, T. A., Ruckdeschel, J. S., & Blanchard, E. B. (1984a). Cancer-related pain: I. Prevalence in an outpatient setting as a function of stage of disease and type of cancer. *Journal of Psychosomatic Research, 28,* 115–119.

Ahles, T. A., Ruckdeschel, J. C., & Blanchard, E. B. (1984b). Cancer-related pain: II. Assessment with visual analogue scales. *Journal of Psychosomatic Research, 28,* 121–124.

American Pain Society. (1992). *Principles of analgesic use in the treatment of acute and cancer pain.* Skokie, IL: Author.

Arbit, E. (Ed.). (1993). *Management of cancer-related pain.* Mount Kisco, NY: Futura.

Banning, A., Sjogren, P., & Henriksen, H. (1991). Pain courses in 200 patients referred to a multidisciplinary cancer pain clinic. *Pain, 45,* 45–48.

Barber, J., & Gitelson, J. (1980). Cancer pain: Psychological management using hypnosis. *CA: A Cancer Journal for Clinicians, 30,* 130–136.

Behar, M., Alshwang, D., Magora, F., & Davidson, J. T. (1979). Epidural morphine in treatment of pain. *Lancet, 1,* 527–528.

Bond, M. R. (1979). Psychologic and emotional aspects of cancer pain. In J. J. Bonica & V. Ventrafidda (Eds.), *Advances in pain research and therapy: International Symposium on Pain in Advanced Cancer* (pp. 81–88). New York: Raven.

Bonica, J. J. (1990). Cancer pain. In J. J. Bonica (Ed.), *The management of pain* (2nd ed., pp. 400–460). Philadelphia: Lea & Febiger.

Breitbart, W. (1987). Suicide in cancer patients. *Oncology, 1,* 49–53.

Breitbart, W. (1990). Cancer pain and suicide. In K. Foley, J. J. Bonica, & V. Ventafridda (Eds.), *Advances in pain research and therapy* (Vol. 16, pp. 399–412). New York: Raven.

Breitbart, W. (1993). Suicide risk and pain in cancer and AIDS patients. In C. R. Chapman & K. M. Foley (Eds.), *Current and emerging issues in cancer pain: Research and practice* (pp. 49–65). New York: Raven.

Bruera, E. (1990). Subcutaneous administration of opioids in the management of cancer pain. In K. M. Foley, J. J. Bonica, & V. Ventafridda (Eds.), *Advances in pain research and therapy: Second International Congress on Cancer Pain* (pp. 203–218). New York: Raven.

Bruera, E., Schoeller, T., Wenk, R., MacEachern, T., Marcelino, S., Hanson, J., & Suarez-Almazor, M. (1995). A prospective multicenter assessment of the Edmonton staging system for cancer pain. *Journal of Pain and Symptom Management, 10,* 348–355.

Bruera, E., & Watanabe, S. (1994). Psychostimulants as adjuvant analgesics. *Journal of Pain and Symptom Management, 9,* 412–415.

Bukberg, F., Penman, D., & Holland, J. (1984). Depression in hospitalized cancer patients. *Psychosomatic Medicine, 46,* 199–211.

Burish, T. G., & Tope, D. M. (1992). Psychological techniques for controlling the adverse side effects of cancer chemotherapy: Findings from a decade of research. *Journal of Pain and Symptom Management, 7,* 287–301.

Butler, B. (1954). The use of hypnosis in the care of the cancer patients. *Cancer, 7,* 1–14.

Cassell, E. J. (1982). The nature of suffering and the goals of medicine. *New England Journal of Medicine, 306,* 639–645.

Cella, D. F. (1994). Quality of life: Concepts and definitions. *Journal of Pain and Symptom Management, 9,* 186–192.

Cella, D. F., Tulsky, D. S., Gray, G., Sarafian, B., Linn, E., Bonomi, A., Silberman, M., Yellen, S. B., Winicour, P., & Brannon, J. (1993). The functional assessment of cancer therapy scales: Development and validation of the general measure. *Journal of Clinical Oncology, 11,* 570–579.

Chapman, C. R., & Foley, K. M. (Eds.). (1993). *Current and emerging issues in cancer pain: Research and practice.* New York: Raven.

Chapman, C. R., & Hill, H. F. (1989). Prolonged morphine self-administration and addiction liability. *Cancer, 63,* 1636–1644.

Chrubasik, J., & Chrubasik, S. (1997). Meta-analysis on the efficacy of intrathecal and epidural opiates. In W. C. V. Parris (Ed.), *Cancer pain management: Principles and practice* (pp. 207–214). Boston: Butterworth-Heinemann.

Cleeland, C. S. (1984). The impact of pain on patients with cancer. *Cancer, 54,* 263–267.

Cleeland, C. S. (1987). Nonpharmacologic management of cancer pain. *Journal of Pain and Symptom Management, 2,* 523–528.

Cleeland, C. S. (1989). Measurement of pain by subjective report. In C. R. Chapman & J. D. Loeser (Eds.), *Advances in pain research and therapy. Vol. 12: Issues of pain measurement* (pp. 391–403). New York: Raven.

Cleeland, C. S. (1991). Analgesic trials to clinical practice: When and how does it happen? In M. Max, R. Portenoy, & E. Laska (Eds.), *Advances in pain research and therapy: Design of analgesic clinical trials* (pp. 631–645). New York: Raven.

Cleeland, C. S. (1993). Documenting barriers to cancer pain management. In C. R. Chapman & K. M. Foley (Eds.), *Current and emerging issues in cancer pain: Research and practice* (pp. 321–330). New York: Raven.

Cleeland, C. S., Gonin, R., Hatfield, A. K., Edmunson, J. H., Blum, R. H., Stewart, J. A., & Pandya, K. J. (1994). Pain and its treatment in outpatients with metastatic cancer: The Eastern Cooperative Oncology Group's outpatient study. *New England Journal of Medicine, 330,* 592–596.

Cleeland, C. S., Rotondi, A., Brechner, T., Levin, A., MacDonald, N., Portenoy, R., Schutta, H., & McEniry, M. (1986). A model for the treatment of cancer pain. *Journal of Pain and Symptom Management, 1,* 209–215.

Clouston, P., DeAngelis, L., & Posner, J. B. (1992). The spectrum of neurological disease in patients with systemic cancer. *Annuals of Neurology, 31,* 268–273.

Coyle, N. (1989). Continuity of care for the cancer patient with chronic pain: Management of cancer pain. *Cancer, 63*(Suppl.), 2289–2293.

Coyle, N., Adelhart, J., Foley, K. M., & Portenoy, R. K. (1990). Character of terminal illness in the advanced cancer patient: Pain and other symptoms during the last four weeks of life. *Journal of Pain and Symptom Management, 5,* 83–93.

Coyle, N., & Foley, K. (1987). Prevalence and profile of pain syndromes in cancer pain. In D. B. McGuire & C. H. Yarbro (Eds.), *Cancer pain management* (pp. 21–46). New York: Grune & Stratton.

Cunningham, A. J., Lockwood, G. A., & Cunningham, J. A. (1981). A relationship between perceived self-efficacy and quality of life in cancer patients. *Patient Education and Counseling, 17,* 71–78.

Dalton, J. A., & Feuerstein, M. (1988). Biobehavioral factors in cancer pain. *Pain, 33,* 137–147.

Dalton, J. A., & Feuerstein, M. (1989). Fear, alexithymia and cancer pain. *Pain, 38,* 159–170.

Dar, R., Beach, C. M., Barden, P. C., & Cleeland, C. S. (1992). Cancer pain in the marital system. *Journal of Pain and Symptom Management, 7,* 87–93.

Daut, R. L., & Cleeland, C. S. (1982). The prevalence and severity of pain in cancer. *Cancer, 50,* 1913–1918.

Daut, R. L., Cleeland, C. S., & Flannery, R. C. (1983). Development of the Wisconsin brief pain questionnaire to assess pain in cancer and other diseases. *Pain, 17,* 197–210.

Davies, A. A. M., Davies, C., & Delpo, M. C. (1986). Depression and anxiety in patients undergoing diagnostic investigations for head and neck cancer. *British Journal of Psychiatry, 149,* 491–493.

DeConno, F., Caraceni, A., Gamba, A., Mariani, L., Abbattista, A., Brunelli, C., LaMura, A., & Ventafridda, V. (1994). Pain measurement in cancer patients: A comparison of six methods. *Pain, 57,* 161–166.

Derogatis, L. R., Morrow, G. R., Fetting, J., Penman, D., Piasetsky, S., Schmale, A. M., Heinrichs, M., & Carnicke, C. L. M. (1983). The prevalence of psychiatric disorders among cancer patients. *Journal of the American Medical Association, 249,* 751–757.

de Wit, R., van Dam, F., Zandbelt, L., Buuren, A., van der Heijden, K., Leenhouts, G., & Loonstra, S. (1997). A pain education program for chronic cancer pain patients: Follow-up results from a randomized controlled trial. *Pain, 73,* 55–69.

Doyle, D., Cleeland, C. S., & Joranson, D. (1991, November). *Public survey of cancer pain and its treatment.* Paper presented at the meeting of the American Pain Society, New Orleans.

Dubner, R. (1991). A call for more science, not more rhetoric, regarding opioids and neuropathic pain. *Pain, 33,* 11–23.

Eisenberg, E., Carr, D. B., & Chalmers, T. C. (1995). Neurolytic celiac plexus block for treatment of cancer pain: A meta-analysis. *Anesthesia and Analgesia, 80,* 290–295.

Elliott, B. A., Elliot, T. E., Murray, D. M., Braun, B. L., & Johnson, K. M. (1996). Patients and family members: The role of knowledge and attitudes in cancer pain. *Journal of Pain and Symptom Management, 12,* 209–220.

Elliott, K., & Foley, K. M. (1990). Neurologic pain syndromes in patients with cancer. *Critical Care Clinics, 6,* 393–420.

Elliot, T., Murray, D. M., Oken, M. M., Johnson, K. M., Braun, B. L., Elliot, B. A., & Post-White, J. (1997). Improving cancer pain management in communities: Main results from a randomized controlled trial. *Journal of Pain and Symptom Management, 13,* 191–203.

Ferrans, C. E. (1990). Development of a quality of life index for patients with cancer. *Oncology Nursing Forum, 17,* 15–19.

Fishbain, D. A., Cutler, R., Rosomoff, H. L., & Rosomoff, R. S. (1997). Chronic pain—Associated depression: Antecedent or consequence of chronic pain? A review. *Clinical Journal of Pain, 13,* 116–137.

Fishman, B., & Loscalzo, M. (1987). Cognitive-behavioral interventions in the management of cancer pain: Principles and applications. *Medical Clinics of North America, 71,* 217–286.

Foley, K. M. (1979). Pain syndromes in patients with cancer. In J. J. Bonica & V. Ventafridda (Eds.), *Advances in pain research and therapy: International symposium on pain in advanced cancer* (pp. 59–75). New York: Raven.

Foley, K. M. (1985). The treatment of cancer pain. *New England Journal of Medicine, 313,* 84–95.

Foley, K. M. (1993). Changing concepts of tolerance to opioids: What the cancer patient has taught us. In C. R. Chapman & K. M. Foley (Eds.), *In Current and emerging issues in cancer pain: Research and practice* (pp. 331–350). New York: Raven.

Fotopoulous, S. S., Cook, M. R., Graham, C., Gerkovich, M., Bond, S. S., & Knapp, T. (1983). Cancer pain: Evaluation of electromyographic and electrodermal feedback. *Progress in Clinical and Biological Research, 132D*, 33–53.

Fotopoulos, S. S., Graham, C., & Cook, M. R. (1979). Psychophysiologic control of cancer pain. In J. J. Bonica & V. Ventafridda (Eds.), *Advances in pain research and therapy* (Vol. 2, pp. 231–244). New York: Raven.

Ganz, P. A., Schag, C. A. C., Lee, J. J., & Sim, M-S. (1992). The CARES: A generic measure of health-related quality of life for patients with cancer. *Quality Life Research, 1*, 19–29.

Glover, J., Dibble, S. L., Dodd, M. J., & Miaskowski, C. (1995). Mood states of oncology outpatients: Does pain make a difference. *Journal of Pain and Symptom Management, 10*, 120–128.

Gonzales, G. R., Elliot, K. J., Portenoy, R. K., & Foley, K. M. (1991). Impact of a comprehensive evaluation in the management of cancer pain. *Pain, 47*, 141–144.

Gottesman, D., & Lewis, M. (1982). Differences in crisis reactions among cancer and surgery patients. *Journal of Consulting and Clinical Psychology, 50*, 381–388.

Goughnour, B. R., Arkinstall, W. W., & Stewart, J. H. (1989). Analgesic response to single and multiple doses of controlled—release morphine tablets and morphine oral solution in cancer patients. *Cancer, 63*, 2294–2297.

Graffam, S., & Johnson, A. (1987). A comparison of two relaxation strategies for the relief of pain and its distress. *Journal of Pain and Symptom Management, 2*, 229–231.

Graham, S., Bond, S., Gerkovich, M., & Cook, M. (1986). Use of the MPQ in assessment of cancer pain: Reliability and consistency. *Pain, 8*, 377–387.

Grandy, R. P., Reder, R. F., Fitzmartin, R. D., Benziger, D. P., & Kaiko, R. F. (1994). Steady-state pharmacokinetic comparison of controlled-release oxycodone vs. oxycodone oral liquid. *Journal of Clinical Pharmacology, 34*, 1015.

Greenwald, H. P., Bonica, J. J., & Bergner, M. (1987). The prevalence of pain in four cancers. *Cancer, 60*, 2563–2569.

Grond, S., Zech, D., Diefenbach, C., Radbruch, L., & Lehmann, K. A. (1996). Assessment of cancer pain: A prospective evaluation in 2266 cancer patients referred to a pain service. *Pain, 64*, 107–114.

Grond, S., Zech, D., Schug, S. A., Lynch, J., & Lehmann, K. A. (1991). Validation of WHO guidelines for cancer pain relief during the last days and hours of life. *Journal of Pain and Symptom Management, 6*, 411–422.

Grossman, S. A., Sheidler, V. R., Swedeen, K., Mucenski, J., & Piantadosi, S. (1991). Correlation of patient and caregiver ratings of cancer pain. *Journal of Pain and Symptom Management, 6*, 53–57.

Guyatt, G. H., Feeny, D. H., & Patrick, D. L. (1993). Measuring health-related quality of life. *Annals of Internal Medicine, 118*, 622–629.

Heim, H., & Oei, T. P. S. (1993). Comparison of prostate cancer patients with and without pain. *Pain, 53*, 159–162.

Heiskanen, T., & Kalso, E. (1997). Controlled-release oxycodone and morphine in cancer related pain. *Pain, 73*, 37–45.

Hilgard, E. R., & Hilgard, J. R. (1983). *Hypnosis in the relief of pain*. Los Altos, CA: Kaufmann.

Hilgard, J. R., & LeBaron, S. L. (1984). *Hypnotherapy of pain in children with cancer*. Los Altos, CA: Kaufmann.

Hill, H. F., Saeger, L. C., & Chapman, C. R. (1986). Patient controlled analgesia after bone marrow transplantation for cancer. *Postgraduate Medicine, 79*, 33–40.

Jacox, A., Carr, D. B., & Payne, R. (1994, March). *Management of cancer pain. Clinical practice guideline No. 9* (AHCPR Publication No. 94-0592). Rockville, MD: Agency for Health Care Policy and Research, U. S. Department of Health and Human Services, Public Health Service.

Jay, S. M., Elliot, C., & Varni, J. M. (1986). Acute and chronic pain in adults and children with cancer. *Journal of Consulting and Clinical Psychology, 55,* 601–607.

Jensen, M. P., & Karoly, P. (1993). Measurement of cancer pain via patient self-report. In C. R. Chapman & K. M. Foley (Eds.), *Current and emerging issues in cancer pain: Research and practice* (pp. 193–218). New York: Raven.

Joranson, D. E., Cleeland, C. S., Weissman, D. E., & Gilson, A. M. (1992). Opioids for chronic cancer and non-cancer pain: A survey of state medical board members. *Federation Bulletin: The Journal of Medical Licensure and Discipline, 79,* 15–49.

Kanner, R. M. (1987). Pharmacologic management of pain and symptom control in cancer. *Journal of Pain and Symptom Management, 2,* 519–522.

Kanner, R. M., & Foley, K. M. (1981). Patterns of narcotic drug use in a cancer pain clinic. *Annals of the New York Academy of Sciences, 362,* 161–172.

Kanner, R. M., & Portenoy, R. K. (1986). Unavailability of narcotic analgesics for ambulatory cancer patients in New York City. *Journal of Pain and Symptom Management, 1,* 87–89.

Kaplan, R., Parris, W., Croghan, M., Citron, M., Herbst, L., Rosenbluth, R., Slagle, S., Buckley, B., & Reder, R. (1995). Decrease in opioid-related adverse events during chronic therapy with controlled-release oxycodone in cancer patients. *Proceedings of the American Pain Society,* Los Angeles, A-146.

Kori, S., Foley, K. M., & Posner, J. B. (1981). Brachial plexus lesions in patients with cancer: 100 cases. *Neurology, 31,* 45–50.

Krames, E. S. (1997). Implantable technologies: Spinal cord stimulation or spinally administered opioids. In W. C. V. Parris (Ed.), *Cancer pain management: Principles and practice* (pp. 157–164). Boston: Butterworth-Heinemann.

Lansky, S. B., List, M. A., Hermann, C. A., Ets-Hokin, E. G., DasGupta, T. K., & Wilbanks, G. S. (1985). Absence of major depressive disorder in female cancer patients. *Journal of Clinical Oncology, 3,* 1553–1560.

Larue, L., Brasseur, L., Musseault, H. P., Demeulemeester, R., Bonifassi, L., & Bez, G. (1994). Pain and symptoms in HIV disease: A national survey in France [Abstract]. *Journal of Palliative Care, 10,* 95.

Lee, V. C., & Rowlingson, J. C. (1990). Chronic pain management. In B. Spilker (Ed.), *Quality of life assessments in clinical trials* (pp. 269–293). New York: Raven.

Lehmann, K. A., & Zech, D. (1992). Transdermal fentanyl: Clinical pharmacology. *Journal of Pain and Symptom Management, 7,* S8–S16.

Levin, D. N., Cleeland, C. S., & Dar, R. (1985). Public attitudes toward cancer pain. *Cancer, 56,* 2337–2339.

Littman, G. S., Walker, B. R., & Schneider, B. E. (1985). Reassessment of verbal and visual analog ratings in analgesic studies. *Clinical Pharmacology and Therapeutics, 38,* 16–23.

Magni, G., Arsie, D., & DeLeo, D. (1987). Antidepressants in the treatment of cancer pain: a survey in Italy. *Pain, 29,* 347–353.

Maher, R. M. (1955). Relief of pain in incurable cancer. *Lancet, 1,* 18–20.

Marks, R. M., & Sachar, E. J. (1973). Undertreatment of medical inpatients with narcotic analgesics. *Annals of Internal Medicine, 78,* 173–181.

Massie, M. J., & Holland, J. (1984). Diagnosis and treatment of depression in the cancer patient. *Journal of Clinical Psychiatry, 45,* 25–29.

Massie, M. J., & Holland, J. C. (1987). The cancer patient with pain: Psychiatric complications and their management. *Medical Clinics of North America, 71,* 243–258.

Max, M. B. (1990). Improving outcomes of analgesic treatment: Is education enough? *Annals of Internal Medicine, 113,* 885–889.

Max, M. B., Culnane, M., Schafer, S. C., Gracely, R. H., Walther, D. J., Smoller, B., & Dubner, R. (1987). Amitriptyline relieves diabetic neuropathy pain in patients with normal or depressed mood. *Neurology, 37,* 589–596.

Mehta, M., & Duthies, A. M. (1993). Anesthetic management of cancer pain. In C. A. Warfield (Ed.), *Principles and practice of pain management* (pp. 251–258). New York: McGraw-Hill.

Melzack, R., & Casey, K. L. (1968). Sensory, motivational and central control determinants of pain: A new conceptual model. In D. Kenshalo (Ed.), *The skin senses* (pp. 423–438). Springfield, IL: Thomas.

Miaskowski, C., Kragnes, L., Dibble, S., & Wallhagen, M. (1997). Differences in mood states, health status, and caregiver strain between family caregivers of oncology outpatients with and without pain. *Journal of Pain and Symptom Management, 13,* 138–147.

Moffic, H., & Paykel, E. S. (1975). Depression in medical inpatients. *British Journal of Psychiatry, 126,* 346–353.

Moinpur, C. M., Georidou, F., Chapman, C. R., & Donaldson, G. W. (1993). Cancer pain and quality of life. In C. R. Chapman & K. M. Foley (Eds.), *Current and emerging issues in cancer pain: Research and practice* (pp. 267–282). New York: Raven.

Mor, V., Guadagnoli, E., & Wool, M. (1987). An examination of the concrete service needs of advanced cancer patients. *Journal of Psychosocial Oncology, 5,* 1–17.

Nehemkis, A. M., Charter, R. A., Stampp, M. S., & Gerber, K. S. (1982–1983). Reattribution of cancer pain. *International Journal of Psychiatry in Medicine, 12,* 213–228.

Nehme, A. M. E. (1993). Intraspinal opioid analgesia. In C. A. Warfield (Ed.), *Principles and practice of pain management* (pp. 363–377). New York: McGraw-Hill.

Padilla, G. V., Ferrell, B., Grant, M. M., & Rhiner, M. (1990). Defining the content domain of quality of life for cancer patients with pain. *Cancer Nursing, 13,* 108–115.

Padilla, G. V., Presant, G., Grant, M. M., Metter, G., Lipsett, J., & Heide, F. (1983). Quality of life index for patients with cancer. *Research Nursing Health, 6,* 117–126.

Parris, W. C. V. (1997). *Cancer pain management: Principles and practice.* Boston: Butterworth-Heinemann.

Patt, R. B. (Ed.). (1993). *Cancer pain.* Philadelphia: Lippincott.

Patt, R. B. (1996). Using controlled-release oxycodone for the management of chronic cancer and noncancer pain. *American Pain Society Bulletin, 6,* 1–6.

Patt, R. B., Proper, G., & Reddy, S. (1994). The neuroleptics as adjuvant analgesics. *Journal of Pain and Symptom Management, 9,* 446–453.

Payne, R., Moran, K., & Southam, M. (1991). The role of transdermal fentanyl in the management of cancer pain. In F. G. Estafanous (Ed.), *Opioids in anesthesia* (Vol. 2, p. 215). Boston: Butterworth-Heinemann.

Pert, C. B., & Snyder, S. (1973). Opiate receptors demonstration in nervous tissue. *Science, 179,* 1011–1014.

Peteet, J., Tay, V., Cohen, G., & MacIntyre, J. (1986). Pain characteristics and treatment in an outpatient cancer population. *Cancer, 57,* 1259–1265.

Plancarte, R., Amescua, C., Patt, R. B., & Aldrete, J. A. (1990). Superior hypogastric plexus block for pelvic cancer pain. *Anesthesiology, 73,* 236–239.

Plummer, J. L., Cherry, D. A., Cousins, M. J., Gourlay, G. K., Onley, M. M., & Evans, K. H. A. (1991). Long-term spinal administration of morphine in cancer and non-cancer pain. *Pain, 44,* 215–220.

Portenoy, R. K. (1989). Cancer pain: Epidemiology and syndromes. *Cancer, 63,* 2298–2307.

Portenoy, R. K. (1990). Pain and quality of life: Clinical issues and implications for research. *Oncology, 4,* 172–178.

Portenoy, R. K. (1991). Pain and quality of life: Theoretical issues. In D. Osoba (Ed.), *Effect of cancer on quality of life* (pp. 279–292). Boca Raton, FL: CRC Press.

Portenoy, R. K. (1996). Adjuvant analgesic agents. *Hematology Oncology Clinics of North America, 10,* 103–120.

Portenoy, R. K., & Foley, K. M. (1986). Chronic use of opioid analgesic in nonmalignant pain: Report of 38 cases. *Pain, 25,* 171–186.

Portenoy, R. K., Miransky, J., Thaler, H. T., Hornung, J., Bianchi, C., Cibas-Kong, I., Feldhamer, E., Lewis, F., Matamoros, I., Sugar, M. Z., Oliver, A. P., Kemeny, N. E., & Foley, K. (1992).

Pain in ambulatory patients with lung or colon cancer: Prevalence characteristics, and impact. *Cancer, 70,* 1616–1624.

Portenoy, R. K., Moulin, D. E., Rogers, A. G., Inturrisi, C. E., & Foley, K. M. (1986). Continuous intravenous infusion of opioids in cancer pain: Review of 46 cases and guidelines for use. *Cancer Treatment Reports, 70,* 575–581.

Portenoy, R. K., Thaler, H. T., Kornblith, A. B., Lepore, J. M., Friedlander-Klar, H., Kisau, E., Sobel, K., Coyle, N., Kemeny, N., Norton, L., & Scher, H. (1994). The memorial symptom assessment scale: An instrument for the evaluation of symptom prevalence, characteristics and distress. *European Journal of Cancer, 30A:9,* 1326–1336.

Rani, P. U., Naidu, M. V. R., Prasad, V. B. N., Rao, T. M. K., & Shobha, J. C. (1996). An evaluation of antidepressants in rheumatic pain conditions. *Anesthesia and Analgesia, 83,* 371–375.

Rimer, B., Levy, M. H., Keintz, M. K., Fox, L., Engstrom, P., & MacElwee, N. (1987). Enhancing cancer pain control regiments through patient education. *Patient Education and Counseling, 10,* 267–277.

Rodin, G., & Voshart, K. (1986). Depression in the medically ill: An overview. *American Journal of Psychiatry, 14,* 696–705.

Romano, J. M., & Turner, J. A. (1985). Chronic pain and depression: Does the evidence support a relationship? *Psychological Bulletin, 97,* 18–34.

Rosner, H., Rubin, L., & Kestenbaum, A. (1996). Gabapentin adjunctive therapy in neuropathic pain states. *Clinical Journal of Pain, 12,* 56–58.

Roth, R. S., & Kamholz, B. (1997). Major pain syndromes and chronic pain. In D. Knesper, M. Riba, & T. Schwenk (Eds.), *Guide to psychiatry in primary care and managed settings* (pp. 268–293). Philadelphia: Saunders.

Schecter, N. L., Altman, A., & Weisman, S. (1990). Report of the consensus conference on the management of pain in childhood cancer. *Pediatrics, 86,* 813–817.

Schipper, H., Clinch, J., McMurray, A., & Levitt, M. (1984). Measuring the quality of life of cancer patients'. The Functional Living Index-Cancer: Development and validation. *Journal of Clinical Oncology, 2,* 472–483.

Schug, S. A., Zech, D., & Doerr, V. (1990). Cancer pain management according to WHO analgesic guidelines. *Journal of Pain and Symptom Management, 5,* 27–32.

Schug, S. A., Zech, D., Grond, S., Jung, H., Meuser, T. H., & Stobbe, B. (1992). A long-term survey of morphine in cancer pain patients. *Journal of Pain and Symptom Management, 7,* 259–266.

Serlin, R. C., Mendoza, T. R., Nakamura, Y., Edwards, K. R., & Cleeland, C. S. (1995). When is cancer pain mild, moderate or severe? Grading pain severity by its interference with function. *Pain, 61,* 277–284.

Sharfman, W. H., & Walsh, T. D. (1990). Has the efficacy of celiac plexus block been demonstrated in pancreatic cancer pain? *Pain, 41,* 267–271.

Slevin, M. L., Plant, H., Lynch, D., Drinkwater, J., & Gregory, W. M. (1988). Who should measure quality of life, the doctor or the patient? *British Journal of Cancer, 57,* 109–112.

Spiegel, D., & Bloom, J. R. (1983). Group therapy and hypnosis reduce matastatic breast carcinoma pain. *Psychosomatic Medicine, 45,* 333–339.

Spiegel, D., Sands, S., & Koopman, C. (1994). Pain and depression in patients with cancer. *Cancer, 74,* 2570–2578.

Sprangers, M. A. G., & Aaronson, N. K. (1992). The role of health care providers and significant others in evaluating the quality of life of patients with chronic disease: A review. *Journal of Clinical Epidemiology, 45,* 743–760.

Strang, P., & Qvarner, H. (1990). Cancer-related pain and its influence on quality of life. *Anticancer Research, 10,* 109–112.

Sutters, K. A., & Miaskowski, C. (1992). The problem of pain in children with cancer: A research review. *Oncology Nursing Forum, 19,* 465–471.

Swerdlow, M. (1984). Anticonvulsant drugs and chronic pain. *Clinical Neuropharmacology, 7,* 51–82.

Syrjala, K. L., & Chapko, M. E. (1995). Evidence for a biopsychosocial model of cancer treatment-related pain. *Pain, 61,* 69–79.

Syrjala, K. L., Cummings, C., & Donaldson, G. (1992). Hypnosis or cognitive-behavioral training for the reduction of pain and nausea during cancer treatment: A controlled clinical trial. *Pain, 48,* 137–146.

Syrjala, K. L., Donaldson, G. W., Davis, M. W., Kippes, M., & Carr, J. E. (1995). Relaxation and imagery or cognitive behavioral training reduce pain during marrow transplantation: A controlled clinical trial. *Pain, 48,* 137–146.

Tannock, I., Guspdoarowica, M., Meakin, W., Panzarella, T., Stewart, L., & Rider, W. (1989). Treatment of metastatic prostatic cancer with low-dose prednisone: Evaluation of pain and quality of life as pragmatic indices of response. *Journal of Clinical Oncology, 7,* 590–597.

Thompson, S. C. (1981). Will it hurt less if I can control it? A complex answer to a simple question. *Psychological Bulletin, 90,* 89–101.

Turk, D. C., & Feldman, C. S. (Eds.). (1992). *Noninvasive approaches to pain management in the terminally ill.* Binghamton, NY: Haworth.

Turk, D. C., & Fernandez, E. (1990). On the putative uniqueness of cancer pain: Do psychological principles apply? *Behavior Research and Therapy, 28,* 1–13.

Turk, D. C., Meichenbaum, D., & Genest, M. (1983). *Pain and behavioral medicine: A cognitive behavioral perspective.* New York: Guilford.

Turk, D. C., & Rennert, K. (1981). Pain and the terminally ill cancer patient: A cognitive social-learning perspective. In H. J. Sobel (Ed.), *Behavior therapy in terminal care: A humanistic approach* (pp. 95–123). Cambridge, MA: Ballinger.

Turk, D. C., & Salovey, P. (1985). Toward an understanding of life with cancer: Personal meanings, psychosocial problems, and coping resources. *Hospice Journal, 1,* 78–84.

Twycross, R. G. (1974). Clinical experience with diamorphine in advanced malignant disease. *International Journal of Clinical Pharmacology and Therapeutic Toxicology, 9,* 184–198.

Twycross, R. G., & Fairfield, S. (1982). Pain in far-advanced cancer. *Pain, 14,* 303–310.

Twycross, R., Harcourt, J., & Bergl, S. (1996). A survey of pain in patients with advanced cancer. *Journal of Pain and Symptom Management, 12,* 273–282.

Twycross, R. G., & Lack, S. A. (1984). Symptom control in far advanced cancer. In R. G. Twycross & S. A. Lack (Eds.), *Pain relief* (pp. 100–114). London: Pitman.

Vainio, A., & Auvinen, A. (1996). Prevalence of symptoms among patients with advanced cancer: An international collaborative study. *Journal of Pain and Symptom Management, 12,* 3–10.

Ventafridda, V., Ripamonti, C., DeConno, F., Bianchi, M., Pazzuconi, F., & Panerai, A. E. (1987). Antidepressants increase bioavailability of morphine in cancer patients. *Lancet, 1,* 1204.

Ventafridda, V., Tamburini, M., Caraceni, A., DeConno, F., & Naldi, F. (1987). A validation study of the WHO method for cancer pain relief. *Cancer, 59,* 850–856.

Von Roenn, J. H., Cleeland, C. S., Gonin, R., Hatfield, A., & Pandya, K. J. (1993). Physicians' attitudes towards cancer pain management: Results of the Eastern Cooperative Oncology Group Survey. *Annals of Internal Medicine, 119,* 121–126.

Vortherms, R., Ryan, P., & Ward, S. (1992). Knowledge and attitudes regarding pharmacologic management of cancer pain in a statewide random sample of nurses. *Research Nursing Health, 15,* 459–466.

Waldman, S. D. (1990). The role of spinal opioids in the management of cancer pain. *Journal of Pain and Symptom Management, 5,* 163–168.

Wang, J. F., Nauss, L. A., & Thomas, J. E. (1979). Pain relief by intrathecally applied morphine in man. *Anesthesiology, 50,* 149–151.

Wang, X. S., Mendoza, T. R., Gao, S-Z., & Cleeland, C. S. (1996). The Chinese version of the Brief Pain Inventory (BPI-C): Its development and use in a study of cancer pain. *Pain, 68*, 407–416.

Ward, S. E., Goldberg, N., Miller-McCauley, V., Mueller, C., Nolan, A., Pawlik-Plank, D., Robbins, A., Stormoen, D., & Weissman, D. E. (1993). Patient-related barriers to management of cancer pain. *Pain, 52*, 319–324.

Ware, J. E., Bayliss, M. S., Rogers, W., Kosinski, M., & Tarlov, A. R. (1996). Differences in 4-year health outcomes for elderly and poor, chronically ill patients treated in HMO and fee-for-service systems. *Journal of the American Medical Association, 276*, 1039–1047.

Watanabe, S., & Bruera, E. (1994). Corticosteroids as adjuvant analgesics. *Journal of Pain and Symptom Management, 9*, 442–445.

Watson, C. P. N. (1994). Antidepressant drugs as adjuvant analgesics. *Journal of Pain and Symptom Management, 9*, 392–405.

Weissman, D., Joranson, D., & Hopwood, M. (1991). Wisconsin physicians' knowledge and attitudes about opioid regulations. *Wisconsin Medical Journal, 90*, 671–675.

World Health Organization. (1986). *Cancer pain relief.* Geneva, Switzerland: Author.

Zenz, M., Strumpf, M., & Tryba, M. (1992). Long-term oral opioid therapy in patients with chronic nonmalignant pain. *Journal of Pain and Symptom Management, 7*, 69–77.

Zenz, M., Zentz, T., Tryba, M., & Strumpf, M. (1995). Severe undertreatment of cancer pain: A 3-year survey of the German situation. *Journal of Pain and Symptom Management, 10*, 187–191.

Chapter 24

Chronic and Recurrent Pain in Children

Linda McAlpine
Patrick J. McGrath
Department of Psychology and Pediatric Pain Research Laboratory—
IWK Grace Health Centre and Dalhousie University

Chronic pain can have a profound effect on children, spilling over into every area of a child's life and disrupting not only the child's normal activities but also the functioning of the child's family. Therefore, a comprehensive, multifaceted approach to treatment becomes important. Complete pain relief may not be realistic, but the goal must be to reduce pain to the lowest achievable level and thus permit the maintenance of a good quality of life.

In the past 10 years, great strides have been made in the recognition and better management of children's pain. In particular, physicians are more comfortable with and better equipped to measure and treat acute pain (Shapiro, 1995; Varni & Walco, 1988). Chronic pain has not received as much attention.

Chronic pain is daunting not only for the children but also for parents and health care professionals. A working knowledge of biobehavioral aspects affecting the pain experience, the developmental process of the chronicity, and potentially effective treatments will provide a foundation to manage the majority of chronic pain problems (Shapiro, 1995). This chapter provides an overview of the types of chronic pain, their prevalence and development, a discussion of treatments for chronic pain (pharmacological and nonpharmacological), and psychosocial considerations.

Chronic pain refers to any pain that lasts longer than the normal healing time (usually, 3 to 6 months). Recurrent pain occurs sporadically over an extended period of time. Chronic and recurrent pain can be classified into three categories based on the source of the noxious stimulation: pain from disease or injury, including pain from life-threatening disease, pain from a primary psychological etiology, and pain from an unknown etiology (P. A. McGrath, 1990). Recurrent and chronic pain includes pain accompanied by handicap (interference with social roles) or pain that is not accompanied by handicap.

PREVALENCE

The prevalence of chronic and recurrent pain depends on the type of pain. A complete review of the epidemiology of chronic and recurrent pain in children is beyond the scope of this chapter. A more detailed review is contained in Goodman and P. J. McGrath (1991).

Fortunately some disorders such as cancer and AIDS are rare. However, for those afflicted with these problems, pain is typical. On the other hand, headaches are very common, affecting about one fourth of teenagers (Sillanpää, 1983). Approximately 15% of normal school-age children report musculoskeletal pain (Goodman & P. J. McGrath, 1991) and up to 6% meet the criteria for fibromyalgia (Buskila et al., 1993). In a community-based sample, abdominal pain was noted by 75% of all the students with pain occurring weekly in 13% to 17% of the sample. Irritable bowel symptoms were noted in 17% of the high school sample and 8% of a middle school sample (Hyams, Burke, Davis, Rzepski, & Andrulonis, 1996). There is little research on the prevalence of many other pains such as reflex sympathetic dystrophy and other types of limb pain.

All these conditions can lead to emotional sequelae such as poor self-esteem, anxiety, depression, and externalizing behavior problems (Varni, Rapoff et al., 1996), and can affect daily activities such as school attendance. However, significant handicap affects only a small percentage of those afflicted with chronic and recurrent pain (P. J. McGrath, Unruh, & Branson, 1990). Thus, although pain is common in children and adolescents, they are remarkably resilient and usually not handicapped by pain.

DEVELOPMENTAL PROCESS OF CHRONIC PAIN

Shapiro (1995) described a chain of events that follows the first onset of chronic or recurrent pain. Initially, the child and the family have hope for alleviation of the pain, but this can turn to hopelessness, depression, anger, and apathy as the pain continues to surface in spite of a variety of treatments. Focus on the pain increases and causative links between activity and pain become internalized such that even neutral events become conditioned agents leading to increasing withdrawal from activity. These psychologic and environmental factors modulate the physiologic nociceptive system making it hypersensitive and irritable. Without intervention, the spiral can continue downward while pain increases and family functioning becomes dysfunctional (Shapiro, 1995). Fortunately, there is a growing awareness of this process and implementation of a multifaceted approach to treatment can control pain and increase functioning.

The timing of chronic pain may produce differing effects. For example, pain very early in development such as that which would occur through invasive medical procedures as a neonate may later cause greater sensitization (Taddio, Katz, Ilersich, & Koren, 1997). Pain that occurs during a transition stage in a child's social life, such as when a child begins high school, may have greater impact on socialization than pain at a different time. There has been virtually no research on this topic.

SPECIFIC PAINS

Cancer

Although much of the pain in childhood cancer is acute pain, cancer pain is considered here because it is a serious chronic disease that has repeated incidents of pain. Children with cancer have pain from cancer, pain from procedures (e.g., bone marrow aspirations), and pain from chemotherapy and radiotherapy. The most dramatic improvement in pain management has occurred in hospitals with the use of anesthetic techniques for procedure pain. Miser, Dothage, Wesley, and Miser (1987) found that pain was the presenting symptom in 78% of the children newly diagnosed with cancer. Although studies provide evidence that children with cancer have a variety of pains, pain management remains focused on diagnostic and procedural pain (Bossert, Van Cleeve, & Savedra, 1996). A recent qualitative study (Ferrell, Rhiner, & Shapiro, 1994; Rhiner, Ferrell, & Shapiro, 1994) revealed that parents were concerned that pain other than that from procedures was not taken seriously. Moreover, parents took on the role of managing their children's pain, encouraging them to assess and manage their own pain while remaining concerned about addiction and undesirable side effects of pain medication.

Bossert and colleagues (1996) examined the pain experiences of children with cancer away from health care settings. The most common pain sites were the stomach, joints, legs, and back, with pains described as stabbing, annoying, or terrifying. The source of pain was most frequently identified as chemotherapy. The onset of the chemotherapy-associated pain occurred between 3 days to as late as a month after the treatment.

The most common strategies used to alleviate the pains were rest and analgesics. The children also used many different coping strategies, many of which would be classified as distraction.

Tsanos, Derevensky, and Handman (1995) also examined coping style and found children with cancer to use more adaptive and efficient coping styles than children without cancer. They also were more adaptive at coping with the environment, such as managing challenges, frustrations, and threats. However, all children with cancer in the study had previously undergone some form of psychological intervention such as individual counseling, family therapy, group therapy, and play therapy.

Although pain from cancer seems obvious, parents frequently forget to tell health care professionals about the pain other than procedural pain their children are experiencing at home, because of their concerns about other aspects of the disease (Bossert et al., 1996). They may also forget because the children may not be currently experiencing the pain. Children with cancer should be routinely asked about their pain.

Human Immunodeficiency Virus Infection (HIV)

Relatively few systematic studies of the prevalence or causes of pain in children affected with HIV have been conducted (Schechter, Berde, & Yaster, 1993). Hirschfeld, Moss, Dragisic, Smith, and Pizzo (1996) surveyed 61 families of children with HIV identified by the Pediatric Branch of the National Cancer Institute. They found that the incidence of pain in these children was comparable to that of children with cancer. The source of the pain was attributed to HIV-related infections, joint and muscle inflammation, medical procedures, consequences of therapy, and as a result of leukemia, lymphoma, or solid tumors. Fifty-nine percent of the children in the study stated that their pain was significant enough to have an affect on their daily lives and have a significant effect on their sleeping patterns. Fifty-seven percent treated their pain with medication and 34% also used relaxation, massage, music, or distraction to treat pain. The older children tended to communicate their perception of pain more frequently. The study did not address the nature of the pain or the experiences in children younger than 4 years. Hirschfeld et al. concluded that further work was needed to not only better elucidate the nature and cause of the perceived pain but also to develop rapid pain assessment tools to be integrated into the standard care protocol for these children with HIV.

Yaster and Schechter (1996) voiced further concern that often the focus in the treatment of children with HIV is on prolonging life to the neglect of pain management. They speculated that this may occur because the subspecialists caring for the children are often not trained in pain management. Other issues of concern raised by Yaster and Schechter are related to the

inability of very young children and patients with HIV-related encephalo-
pathy to report their pain, the possibility of having parents who have the
disease and who do not have the energy to advocate for their children, as
well as a technical difficulties with the metabolism of zidovudine, the
principal drug used in the treatment of HIV. Guidelines for the management
of pain in children with HIV are needed.

Sickle Cell Disease

Sickle cell disease is an inherited disease that affects approximately 1 in
600 African Americans (Kolata, 1987). Sickled blood cells aggregate and
occlude blood flow and cause tissue death and severe pain (Shapiro, 1993).
Children with this disease can anticipate painful episodes throughout their
lives. However, until recently, painful episodes in children had not been
described (Walco & Dampier, 1990). Walco and Dampier investigated
painful episodes in children diagnosed with sickle cell disease using the
Varni/Thompson Pediatric Pain Questionnaire (Varni, Thompson, &
Hanson, 1987) and data gathered over the course of hospitalizations for
vaso-occlusive episodes. The pain was frequently described as "aching" and
evaluated very negatively. During hospitalizations there were reports of
high levels of pain intensity. Parents reported a relationship between
emotions such as unhappiness, anger, and upset, and intensity of the pain.
Whereas there was agreement between the physicians' and parents' rating
of pain, the children's descriptors of their pain revealed that the parents
and physicians are not fully aware of the various aspects of their children's
pain experience. This finding, plus the fact that the incidents of pain in
sickle cell disease are not predictable necessitates relying on children's
self-report of their pain.

Van Sciver, D'Angelo, Rappaport, and Woolf (1995) conducted a longitudinal, cross-group comparison to look at treatment compliance, attitudes toward treatment, and family stress. They found that those with sickle
cell disease were compliant with home care (daily penicillin, folate regimens) and precautionary measures such as ophthalmology, orthopaedic,
or haematology appointments and medical tests. However, they were the
least consistent in reporting or seeking treatment for pain that could signify
vaso-occlusive episodes. Family stress tended to be high. They expressed
feelings of increasing hoplessness in the effectiveness of the treatments as
well as their own incompetency and lack of control over treatments. Standard intervention protocol should include education about therapies self-
monitoring of symptoms, and reinforcement for prompt reporting of painful episodes.

Shapiro et al. (1995) had children who had sickle cell disease maintain
home diaries for 10 months. On average 75% of the days each month
were completed. Pain was reported on an average of 30% of the reported

days. School was missed on 41% of the days the children had pain. The majority of painful episodes were managed entirely at home. Pain management was not enough to reduce the absenteeism. More attention should be paid to how pain is managed at home.

Gil et al. (1993) conducted a prospective longitudinal study of children and adolescents with sickle cell disease. She and her colleagues were primarily investigating the use of pain-coping strategies. The coping factors investigated were coping attempts, negative thinking, and passive adherence. They found that children high on coping attempts remained more active in school, social interactions, and household activities during painful episodes and made less frequent health care contacts. Children and adolescents who used passive adherence or who became more negative in their thinking increasingly relied on health care services for their pain management. Coping styles are a significant factor in determining adjustment to sickle cell disease.

Juvenile Rheumatoid Arthritis (JRA)

JRA is a disease of the connective tissue that produces pain, swelling, and stiffness in the small joints of the hands, feet, knees, shoulders, elbows, and cervical spine. As the joints deteriorate, pain and disability increases. Pain is a consistent feature and is predictive of physical and affective adjustment (Walco & Oberlander, 1993). Pain arises from inflammation, chronic changes in the tissues, medication side effects, and affective changes. Varni and his colleagues (Varni, Wilcox, Hanson, & Brik, 1988) developed and empirically tested a model of functional status for children with JRA. They found that psychological adjustment, family psychosocial environment, pain, and disease activity form a complex interrelationship that influences the functional status of the children. In a prospective study using randomized selection of children with JRA, Ross and her colleagues (1993) found the children's and mothers' emotional distress and family functioning accounted for more of the effect on pain levels than did disease severity. As there is no cure for JRA, goals of treatment must address the complex interrelationship of factors, and attempt to control inflammation, preserve joint function, relieve pain, and promote healthy adjustment to the disease. The accepted treatment involves a multidisciplinary approach to treatment that includes pharmacological, physical, and psychosocial interventions (Hackett, Johnson, Parkin, & Southwood, 1996; Southwood & Malleson, 1993). Pharmacological interventions include aspirin, anti-inflammatory drugs, hydroxychloroquine, oral gold, injectable gold, methotrexate, and D-penicillamine (Walco & Oberlander, 1993). Nonpharmacological treatments include physiotherapy and occupational therapy, physical conditioning, and cognitive-behavioural strategies directed at pain perception regulation and pain behaviour regulation. The latter have been taught with significant reduction in pain intensity and increased adaptive functioning (Walco & Oberlander, 1993).

Recently Schanberg and her colleagues (Schanberg, Lefebvre, Keefe, Kredich, & Gil, 1997) examined the pain-coping strategies used by children with JRA to determine their contribution to prediction of pain intensity. Pain-coping strategies, pain control, and rational thinking factors were measured by the Coping Strategies Questionnaire (Rosentiel & Keefe, 1983)—Version for Children (CSQ–C) (Gil, Williams, Thompson, & Kinney, 1991; Schanberg, Keefe, Lefebvre, Kredich, & Gil, 1996). The authors found that these factors in addition to the disease activity accounted for a statistically significant proportion of the variance in measures of pain intensity and pain location. Children who scored higher on the CDQ–C had much lower ratings of pain intensity and reported pain in fewer body areas. These findings provide further support for incorporating the teaching of behavioral and cognitive strategies into the treatment programs of children with JRA.

Lineker, Badley, and Dalby (1996) surveyed families with children with JRA to identify unmet service needs. They found that the delays in diagnosis (from 1–60 months) caused anxiety in the parents and that the parents underestimated their children's pain. They also found that the parents were concerned about school absenteeism. The families identified the need for more information on the disease and its treatment and the need for opportunities to meet through support groups and exercise groups.

As family functioning is also predictive of success (Hagglund et al., 1996) programs have been designed to involve the family as a whole in treatment. In England several training programs taught during summer camps and school holidays and independence training for adolescents have been developed and tried, but no empirical research has been conducted to ascertain their effects (Hackett et al., 1996). However, Hagglund and colleagues did test the efficacy of a 3-day family retreat. The retreat was designed to provide a comprehensive treatment program and as such, was attended by physicians, psychologists, counselors, social workers, occupational and physical therapists, dentists and other health care professionals, as well as the families. The therapeutic program focused on medical management, improving functional capacities, enhancing coping skills, and facilitating family functioning. Children and their caregivers were assessed on behavioral and emotional functioning, pain, strain on the caregivers' work and leisure activities, and caregivers' psychological distress before and 6 months after the family retreat. The results indicated that the children exhibited fewer internalizing behavioral problems and had a moderate reduction in pain intensity. For the families as a whole, there was a reduction of strain on occupational functioning and a reduction of interruption of family leisure activities. However, there were no significant changes in psychological distress of the caregivers. Family retreats for intensive multidisciplinary treatment hold promise.

Fibromyalgia

Children with fibromyalgia have diffuse, often ill-defined aches with accompanying fatigue, disturbed sleep patterns, anxiety, and depression. Yunus and Masi (1985) found that two thirds of the children diagnosed with primary fibromyalgia syndrome had pain and stiffness in the knees and less commonly to other parts of the body. The back was involved in one third of the children. Common features of fibromyalgia include chronic fatigue, irritable bowel syndrome, nonrestorative sleep (Moldofsky & Lue, 1993), and abnormalities of mood (Cassidy, 1994). Pharmacological treatments include anti-inflammatory drugs and tricyclic antidepressants, but the effectiveness of these treatments with children and adolescents has not been studied. Schanberg and her colleagues (Schanberg et al., 1996) examined the coping strategies of 16 children with juvenile primary fibromyalgia syndrome. Their pain behaviour was also observed. In general they found that the children appeared to take an active role in trying to cope with their pain (using strategies such as coping self-statements, praying, hoping, and increasing activity levels) though these children did not perceive themselves as having good control. Schanberg et al. advocated the use of cognitive-behavioral therapy (which teaches strategies to think differently about the pain, as well as strategies such as pacing activities, self-hypnosis, and relaxation and breathing techniques) to add to the strategies they were already using. The authors maintained that cognitive-behavioral therapy would increase the children's perceptions of control over the pain. A small clinical series of cognitive-behavioral therapy with children with fibromyalgia (Walco & Ilowite, 1992) demonstrated its effectiveness, but the study did not use control groups or examine long-term results.

Reid, Lang, and P. J. McGrath (1996) compared 15 children with JRA, 15 children with fibromyalgia, and 15 normal controls. They found that children with fibromyalgia and their families were not significantly psychologically impaired. However, disability in children both with fibromyalgia and with JRA was a function of the child's depression, anxiety, pain, and fatigue. Parents' fatigue and emotion-focused coping also predicted child disability. Parents' participation in the use of cognitive-behavioral therapy might help to reduce the children's disability.

The outcome for children with fibromyalgia is unclear. Buskila et al. (1995) conducted a 30-month follow-up study of 15 children from a community sample who were diagnosed with fibromyalgia. Seventy-three percent no longer had fibromyalgia. However, no long-term follow-up of a sample referred to a clinic has been reported.

Neuropathic Pain

Neuropathic pain implies that the pain is due to damaged functioning of the peripheral or central nervous system rather than because of nociceptive input from an injury. Neuropathic pains include phantom limb pain, reflex sympathetic dystrophy, and pain secondary to cancer treatment. A recent survey (Wilkins, P. J. McGrath, Katz, & Finley, 1997) of 60 children with amputation from surgery or trauma or with congenital amputation found that 16/33 (48.5%) of the children with surgical or traumatic amputation had phantom limb pain and 1/27 (3.7%) of the congenital amputees had phantom pain. Amputees reported that pain was elicited by physical stimuli such as touching the stump or by psychological stimuli such as approaching the stump or by strong emotion. No systematic studies have examined treatment of phantom pain in children and adolescents.

Reflex sympathetic dystrophy (RSD) is a type of neuropathic pain that is not due to major or obvious nerve damage. It is marked by initial, constant, often burning, pain and swelling. Later on there is muscle wasting, skin discoloration, and osteoporosis. The cause is unclear but it arises after a minor injury, apparently not causing nerve damage. There appears to be sympathetic involvement in many cases, although nonsympathetic cases do occur. Typically, the child stops using the injured limb because of pain. The typical pediatric RSD patient is a 12- or 13-year-old girl who has been very active in sports or dance prior to onset (Olsson & Berde, 1993). The reason for the gender and age bias is unclear. Both physiological (overuse) and psychological (a graceful exit from competitive pressure) explanations have been offered for the link with dance and sports (Olsson & Berde, 1993). The clinical outcome is varied. Wilder et al. (1992) in a series of 70 patients in Boston found that although most children had significant benefit, 54% continued to have pain and dysfunction in spite of intensive physical therapy, psychological therapy, use of sympathetic blockade, and tricyclic antidepressants. Olsson, Arner, and Hirsch (1990) in Stockholm found that of 55 children, 33 had complete remission with one intravenous regional block, 14 had significant relief, and 7 were not helped. In reviewing a number of studies, Cassidy (1994) found that the most common form of treatment was intensive physical therapy and that all the reviewed studies questioned the efficacy of any of the published interventions for all children.

Cystic Fibrosis

Treatments such as the aggressive use of antibiotic therapy for pulmonary infection (Fiel, 1993) and recently developed therapies such human recombinant deoxyribonuclease, amiloride, and gene transfer continue to extend the life span and quality of life for children with cystic fibrosis. In these longer-living patients with cystic fibrosis, the incidence of chronic pain increases sharply in later years of life with 84% reporting serious pain—more specifically, 65% reporting chest pain and 61% reporting headaches. Back pain (26%), abdominal pain (39%), and limb pain (26%) were also reported (Ravilly, Robinison, Suresh, Wohl, & Berde, 1996). In a survey of the records of patients who had died between 1984 and 1993 and those using the pain service at a cystic fibrosis center in a large metropolitan city, Ravilly and her colleagues found that the most common cause of headache was either hypercarbia/hypoxia or sinusitis. Both headaches and chest pain were severe enough to require opioid administration. Back pain was caused by compression fractures; abdominal pain was due to ulcers, gastritis, gastroesophgeal reflux, and Barrett's syndrome. Limb pain was caused mainly by arthritis. Other types of pain were cellulitis, muscle aches, and neuropathic pain. Pharmacologic approaches included nonsteroidal anti-inflammatory medications, Ketoralac, tricyclic antidepressants, trazodone, thoracic epidural analgesia, and nerve blocks for headaches. Opioids were used with moderate frequency and no episodes of respiratory depression were related to long-term opiate use. Nonpharmacological treatments included acupuncture, transcutaneous electrical nerve stimulation (TENS), relaxation techniques, and biofeedback. No trials have been published demonstrating effectiveness of any of the suggested treatments.

Ravilly and her colleagues (1996) cautioned that another practice may lead to ineffective pain management in children with cystic fibrosis. The use of chart review can result in underreporting of pain, as physicians may not routinely ask about pain and patients may not volunteer that information. Routine assessment of pain will alleviate this oversight.

Headache

The two major types of nonpathological headache in children and adolescents are migraine and tension headaches. The International Headache Society (IHS) has developed a detailed classification system for headache (The Headache Classification Committee of the International Headache Society, 1988), which is now widely adopted and in common use for research but also very useful for clinical use. There has been some concern that the IHS criteria need some modification for children because attacks are often shorter than with adults (Metsähonkala & Sillanpää, 1994). The criteria for diagnosis of migraine headache include those with and without aura. Other types of migrainous headaches include complicated migraines that have neurological sequelae that last longer than an aura or prodrome. These include confusional migraine in which there are significant disturbances of thinking and hemiplegic migraine in which there are significant motor disturbances. Tension headaches include episodic and chronic varieties.

Recurrent headaches (both migraine and tension headache) increase from a very low rate in the preschool years and become most frequent and most severe in the teenage years. Prior to puberty there is about an equal distribution by gender. However, after puberty, girls are more likely to have headaches and have more severe headaches Bille, 1962). The prevalence of migraine varies from study to study and ranges from 2.5% to 22% (Goodman & P. J. McGrath, 1991). The majority of migraine attacks occur less than once a month in schoolchildren and approximately one third of the migraine sufferers experience an attack once a month or more often (Mortimer, Kay, & Jaron, 1992; Sparks, 1978).

Although the prevalence of migraine headaches has been investigated extensively, surprisingly few well-designed investigations have been conducted on the prevalence of tension-type headaches. Bille (1962) noted that approximately half of the 7- to 15-year-old schoolchildren experienced tension headaches.

The prevalence of headaches has increased during recent decades. In a recent study on children starting school conducted in two Finnish cities by Sillanpää (Sillanpää & Anttila, 1996), a striking increase of the prevalence of migraine as well as unspecified headaches over a 20-year time period was found. The study was carried out not only with the same age group and the same urban population but also with the same assessment methods and an identical design. The highest headache increase was observed in areas with high social instability, suggesting that changes in the psychosocial environment might explain the increase in headache prevalence.

It is very likely that the great variation in prevalence rates of headaches in children in community populations, in particular of the less frequent type, might be attributed to differences between studies in the choice of informant source, assessment methods being used, but also size and characteristics of the samples. The use of the IHS criteria may help to further standardize the assessment of headaches in pediatric populations and reduce the variation in prevalence rates due to different diagnostic sets of criteria.

The short-term as well as the long-term prognosis for childhood migraine seems to be good in at least half of the cases in clinical samples (Hockaday, 1988), and the attacks cease for about a third of the children. The prognosis appears to be better for boys than girls. Over the course of 6 years, Bille (1962) found that approximately 15% of schoolchildren with migraine or pronounced migraine (at least one attack per month) were unimproved and similar rates were found for children with nonmigrainous headaches. However, two thirds of the children in the latter group were headache-free in contrast to about a third in the group with pronounced migraine. In his 30-year follow-up, Bille (1989) noted that 40% of the schoolchildren (in the original study 7–15 years of age) were migraine-free, however, about a third of the sample had suffered from migraine during the whole follow-up period. Although the majority of subjects had been migraine-free during puberty and as young adults, the girls had been migraine-free less often than the boys.

Surprisingly, our knowledge about the prognosis for tension headaches in children and adolescents is much more limited. In a Swedish study, Wänman and Agerberg (1987) found that about 50% of the adolescents suffering from unspecified recurrent headaches (once a week or more often) had improved over a period of 1 year.

There is very limited empirical support for the efficacy of drug treatment, with nonpharmacological treatments offering more promise (Larsson, Melin, & Doberl, 1990). Multiple, well-designed, randomized controlled trials have shown that biofeedback, relaxation, and cognitive therapy are effective with migraine. Although there is less research with children with tension headache, relaxation and biofeedback have been shown to be effective. Therapist-reduced treatments, in which most of the therapy is delivered by means of a manual and a tape with telephone contact, have been shown as effective as therapy face to face with a therapist. Similarly, Larsson and his colleagues have shown that school-based relaxation treatments are effective with tension headache. A summary of this and other randomized trials selected on the basis of their high-quality and rigorous investigations is shown in Table 24.1.

Low Back Pain

Low back pain in adolescents has been underinvestigated as it was thought to be uncommon (F. Balague & Nordin, 1992). However, a school-based survey found a high prevalence with the first episodes occurring at 13–14 years and increasing with age (R. Balague, Dutoit, & Waldburger, 1988; Fairbank, Pynsent, Van Poortvliet, & Phillips, 1984; Salminen, 1984). Salminen, Erkintalo, Laine, and Pentti (1995) found a prevalence of 8% in a survey of 1,377 eighth-grade students. The overall disk degeneration increased from 31% to 42% of those with low back pain at the 3-year follow-up. Low frequency of weekly physical activity was related to an increased occurrence of low back pain and decreased spinal function. It would seem that low activity levels could contribute to low back pain. However, to compare this with the effects of very high levels of physical activity, a prospective study would help determine optimal levels of physical activity to reduce low back pain.

Recurrent Abdominal Pain

Recurrent abdominal pain is a common problem leading to the use of health care resources by a considerable number of students (Hyams et al., 1996). Hyams and colleagues found a prevalence rate of 13% to 17% of a

TABLE 24.1

Selected Randomized Trials of Psychological Treatments of Headache

Study	Headache Type	Treatment/Control	Subjects	Outcome
L'Abbé & Williamson, 1984	Migraine	Autogenic biofeedback/wait-list	28	Biofeedback effective and superior to controls
Richter et al., 1986	Migraine	Relaxation, cognitive therapy, placebo	51	Both treatments superior to controls
P. J. McGrath et al., 1992	Migraine	Therapist-directed and therapist-reduced treatment combined cognitive and relaxation/attention control	94	Both treatments superior to control, therapist reduced less expensive
Larsson & Melin, 1988	Tension (85) and migraine (23)	Therapist and home-based relaxation/attention control	108; Tension (85) and migraine (23)	Both forms of relaxation superior to attention control
Larsson, Daleflod, Hakansson, & Melin, 1987	Primarily tension headaches	Therapist-assisted versus self-help relaxation/attention control	46	Both forms of relaxation superior to control
Larsson et al., (1990)	Tension headache	Self-help versus muscle relaxant drug	48	Self-help relaxation superior to muscle relaxant

community-based middle and high school population had weekly abdominal pain and 14% of the high school and 6% middle school students could be classified as having irritable bowel syndrome (IBS). (IBS results from a disordered and hyperactive gastrointestinal function. It presents in a wide spectrum of symptoms such as diarrhea, constipation, fecal incontinence, vomiting, or abdominal pain.) No gender-based differences in symptoms were found. There was a significant relationship between the presence of IBS and anxiety and depression. Randomized trials have demonstrated that supplementary dietary fiber (Feldman, McGrath, Hodgson, Ritter, & Shipman, 1985) and psychological interventions (Sanders, Shepherd, Cleghorn, & Woolford, 1994) are both effective in treatment of recurrent abdominal pain.

EFFECTS OF PSYCHOSOCIAL FACTORS ON CHRONIC PAIN EXPERIENCE

Prior pain experience, level of social, emotional, and physical development, and cognitive development combine to give meaning to children's pain perception. Situational factors also contribute to the mosaic of the pain experience (P. A. McGrath, 1990; P. J. McGrath et al., 1990). These include the child's understanding of the pain, expectation for obtaining pain relief, perceived control of the pain, and ability to use coping strategies as well as the significance of the pain. Emotions arising from the experience such as anxiety, fear, depression, anger, and sadness can all exacerbate the pain sensation (Varni, Rapoff et al., 1996).

The pain experience is mediated by the environment, the cognitive level of the children, and the culture in which the children experience the pain. Children learn about pain through their own experiences, conditioning, and observing, and modeling their parents, peers, and even the media. These interact with their memory for pain and their cognitive levels of develop to determine the meaning they extract from the experience and how they communicate their perceptions (P. J. McGrath & McAlpine, 1993). Parents seem to have a powerful effect on children's pain behavior (Apley & Naish, 1958; Grunau, Whitfield, Petrie, & Fryer, 1994). Goodman, P. J. McGrath, and Forward (1997), in a prospective survey of a community-based sample, found empirical support for the hypotheses. They found that children whose parents reported numerous painful incidents were also likely to report numerous painful incidents, parents who reported numerous relatively severe incidents during the study period would have children who were also more likely to report numerous severe incidents, and that parents who reported disabling pain incidents would have children who were also more likely to report disabling pain incidents.

Although the influence of the family can readily be seen, the effect of culture is not as clear. A variety of cultural influences have the potential to affect the experience of pain. These influences include the alternative methods used in the treatment of pain (Pachter, 1994), the interpretation of the cause of pain (i.e., wrong-doing) as well as the meaning of pain (i.e., punishment), and the manner of its expression (i.e., culturally specific ailments) (Bernstein & Pachter, 1993), all of which should be considered. However, this is an area that needs more investigation.

It would seem plausible that, with their capacity to pretend and distract themselves, pain intensity in children could be reduced through placebo treatments. A recent investigation of placebo effect on reported pain from venipuncture in children by Goodenough and colleagues (1997) found their hypothesis that application of placebo cream would be associated with a reduction in self-reported pain severity was not supported. The best predictors of reported pain scores were expecting the needle to hurt and feeling anxious. In addition they found that the suggestion of possible benefits rather than the placebo treatment was more effective. Suggestion was effective only with children who were anxious. The investigators postulated that the effect of suggestion served to reduce anxiety for the children expecting significant levels of pain. Empirical studies of the power of suggestion, including through self-hypnosis, have yet to be conducted in the area of chronic pain in children.

ASSESSMENT

It can readily be seen that pain perception is mediated by a myriad of factors and that effective treatment must begin with a comprehensive multifaceted assessment approach (P. J. McGrath, 1996; P. J. McGrath, Mathews, & Pigeon, 1991; Varni, Rapoff et al., 1996). There are a wide variety of instruments available to assess the various factors, such as the familial, biological, emotional, and social influences as well as the level of pain intensity. Varni and his colleagues used a variety of standardized instruments to measure pain intensity, depressive symptoms, state anxiety, general self-esteem, and externalizing and internalizing behavior to investigate emotional distress associated with chronic pain (for a discussion of the instruments used, see Varni et al., 1996). McGrath recently reviewed the multitude of self-report, behavioral, and physiological measures of pain intensity in children. He found that the behavioral and physiological measures useful for acute pain are not as helpful in chronic pain. Self-report measures are more appropriate for assessing chronic and recurrent pain.

Other promising instruments have also been developed to assess and identify coping strategies (e.g. Varni, Waldron et al., 1996).

ALTERNATIVE MEDICINE

An increasing number of parents are turning to alternative medicine to help relieve their children's pain (Spigelblatt, 1995). Some approaches, such as acupuncture (Yee, Lin, & Aubuchon, 1993), hypnosis (Kuttner, 1993), and TENS (Eland, 1993), have been sanctioned by the medical profession and are considered part of the treatment protocol. Carter (1994), in her book on managing child and infant pain, included a chapter on holistic nursing care, which included discussion of massage, touch, therapeutic touch, and aromatherapy. Sawyer, Gannoni, Toogood, Antoniou, and Rice (1994), in a survey of parents of children with cancer, found that whereas 46% had used at least one alternative therapy, only 44% of these discussed them with the child's doctor. The parents subscribed to use of alternative medicines because it gave them a feeling of more control and the children more hope about their prognosis. More books on how to use alternative medicines are appearing on the local booksellers' shelves. It is becoming increasingly important for health care professionals to become familiar with what is being proposed and of the potential dangers (Spigelblatt, 1995). Some, such as the use of massage, appear relatively harmless. Yet even these "safe" alternative treatments warrant well-controlled research (Arnold, 1995).

SUMMARY

Significant strides have been made in the area of recognizing and treating chronic pain in children. Those treating chronic pain have come to realize that the pain perception system in children is more vulnerable than in adults to changes in the pain experience brought about by the effects of biobehavioral and developmental influences. As a result there is a growing appreciation that an interdisciplinary approach to treatment is necessary to address chronic pain in children. There has also been a developing awareness of the value of using nonpharmacological inventions in combination with the traditional medical interventions in order to provide more effective pain management. Although several of the chronic pain conditions such as HIV are still at the descriptive stage, psychological factors such as using coping strategies are increasingly being found to facilitate better pain control and increased functioning in other chronic pain conditions. Promising behavioral strategies have been found to augment the effectiveness of the treatments for musculoskeletal pain, sickle cell disease, headache, and somatization. Although progress is being made, further well-designed studies are needed to determine the contributions of specific nonpharmacological strategies. Once these have been determined, we must move on to more widespread implementation of what we have learned.

ACKNOWLEDGMENTS

We would like to thank Tracy Dobbin for assistance in preparing this manuscript.

REFERENCES

Apley, J., & Naish, N. (1958). Recurrent abdominal pains: A field survey of 1,000 school children. *Archives of Disease in Childhood, 33,* 165–170.

Arnold, E. A. (1995). The nontraditional (unconventional and/or innovative) psychosocial treatments for children and adolescents: Critique and proposed screening principles. *Journal of Abnormal and Child Psychology, 23,* 125–140.

Balague, F., & Nordin, M. (1992). Back pain in children and teenagers. Common low back pain: Prevention of chronicity. *Clinical Rheumatology, 6,* 575–593.

Balague, R., Dutoit, G., & Waldburger, M. (1988). Low back pain in schoolchildren: An epidemiological study. *Scandinavian Journal of Rehabilitation Medicine, 20,* 175–179.

Bernstein, B. A., & Pachter, L. M. (1993). Cultural considerations in children's pain. In N. L. Schechter, C. B. Berde, & M. Yaster (Eds.), *Pain in infants, children, and adolescents* (pp. 113–122). Baltimore: Williams & Wilkins.

Bille, B. (1962). Migraine in school children. *Acta Paediatrica, 51,* 1–150.

Bille, B. (1989). Migraine in childhood: A 30 years follow-up. In G. Lanzi, U. Balottin, & A. Cernibori (Eds.), *Headache in children and adolescents* (pp. 19–26). Amsterdam: Elsevier Science.

Bossert, E. A., Van Cleeve, L., & Savedra, M. C. (1996). Children with cancer: The pain experience away from the health care setting. *Journal of Pediatric Oncology Nursing, 13*(3), 109–120.

Buskila, D., Neumann, L., Hershman, E., Gedalia, A., Press, J., & Sukenik, S. (1995). Fibromyalgia syndrome in children—An outcome study. *Journal of Rheumatology, 22*(3), 525–528.

Buskila, D., Press, J. Gedalia, A., Klein, M., Neumann, l., Boehm, R., & Sukenik, S. (1993). Assessment of nonarticular tenderness and prevalence of fibromalgia in children. *Journal of Rheumatology, 20,* 368–370.

Carter, B. (1994). *Child and infant pain: Principles of nursing care and management.* London: Chapman & Hall.

Cassidy, J. T. (1994). Progress in diagnosing and understanding chronic pain syndromes in children. *Current Opinion in Rheumatology, 6,* 544–546.

Eland, J. (1993). The use of TENS with children. In N. L. Schechter, C. B. Berde, & M. Yaster (Eds.), *Pain in infants, children, and adolescents* (pp. 331–339). Baltimore: Williams & Wilkins.

Fairbank, J. C., Pynsent, P. B., Van Poortvliet, J. A., & Phillips, H. (1984). Influence of anthropometric factors and joint laxity in the incidence of adolescent back pain. *Spine, 9,* 461–464.

Feldman, W., McGrath, P. J., Hodgson, C., Ritter, H., & Shipman, R. T. (1985). The use of dietary fiber in the management of simple, childhood, idiopathic, recurrent, abdominal pain. Results in a prospective, double-blind, randomized, controlled trial. *American Journal of Diseases of Children, 139*, 1216–1218.

Ferrell, B. R., Rhiner, M., & Shapiro, B. (1994). The experience of pediatric cancer pain, part I: Impact of pain on the family. *Journal of Pediatric Nursing, 9*, 368–379.

Fiel, S. B. (1993). Clinical management of pulmonary disease in cystic fibrosis. *Lancet, 341*, 1070–1074.

Gil, K. M., Thompson, R. J., Keith, B. R., Tota-Faucette, M., Noll, S., & Kinney, T. R. (1993). Sickle cell disease pain in chldren and adolescents: Change in pain frequency and coping strategies over time. *Journal of Pediatric Psychology, 18*(5), 621–637.

Gil, K. M., Williams, D. A., Thompson, R. J., & Kinney, T. R. (1991). Sickle cell disease in children and adolescents: The relation of child and parent pain coping strategies to adjustment. *Journal of Pediatric Psychology, 16*, 643–663.

Goodenough, B., Kampel, L., Champion, G. D., Laubreaux, L., Nicholas, M. K., Ziegler, J. B. Ziegler, & McInerney, M. (1997). An investigation of the placebo effect and age-related factors in the report of needle pain from venipuncture in children. *Pain, 72*, 383–391.

Goodman, J. E., & McGrath, P. J. (1991). The epidemiology of pain in children and adolescents: A review. *Pain, 46*, 247–264.

Goodman, J. E., McGrath, P. J., & Forward, S. P. (1997). Aggregation of pain complaints and pain-related disability and handicap in a community sample of families. In T. S. Jensen, J. A. Turner, & Z. Wiesenfeld-Hallin (Eds.), *Proceedings of the 8th World Congress on Pain* (pp. 673–682). Seattle: IASP Press.

Grunau, R. V. E., Whitfield, M. F., Petrie, J. H., & Fryer, E. L. (1994). Early pain experience, child and family factors, as precursors of somatization: A Prospective study of extremely premature and fullterm children. *Pain, 56*, 353–359.

Hackett, J., Johnson, B., Parkin, A., & Southwood, T. (1996). Physiotherapy and occupational therapy for juvenile chronic arthritis: Custom and practice in five centres in the UK, USA and Canada. *British Journal of Rheumatology, 35*, 695–699.

Hagglund, K. J., Doyle, N. M., Clay, D. L., Frank, R. G., Johnson, J. C., & Pressly, T. A. (1996). A family retreat as a comprehensive intervention for children with arthritis and their families. *Arthritis Care and Research, 9*(1), 35–41.

Hirschfeld, S., Moss, H., Dragisic, K., Smith, W., & Pizzo, P. A. (1996). Pain in pediatric human immunodeficiency virus infection: Incidence and characteristics in a single-institution pilot study. *Pediatrics, 98*, 449–452.

Hockaday, J. M. (1988). Definitions, clinical features, and diagnosis of childhood migraine. In J. Hockaday (Ed.), *Migraine in childhood* (p. 16). London: Butterworths.

Hyams, J. S., Burke, G., Davis, P. M., Rzepski, B., & Andrulonis, P. A. (1996). Abdominal pain and irritable bowel syndrome in adolescents: A community-based study. *Journal of Pediatrics, 129*(2), 220–226.

International Headache Society. (1988). Classification and diagnostic criteria for headache disorders, cranial neuralgias, and facial pain. *Cephalalgia, 8(Supplement 7)*, 1–96.

Kolata, G. (1987). Research news: Panel urges newborn sickle cell screening. *Science, 236*, 259–260.

Kuttner, L. (1993). Hypnotic interventions for children in pain. In N. L. Schechter, C. B. Berde, & M. Yaster (Eds.), *Pain in infants, children, and adolescents* (pp. 229–236). Baltimore: Williams & Wilcox.

L'Abbé, E. L., & Williamson, P. A. (1984). Treatment of childhood migraine using autogenic feedback training. *Journal of Consulting and Clinical Psychology, 52*, 968–976.

Larsson, B. S., Daleflod, B., Hakansson, L., & Melin, L. (1987). Therapist-assisted versus self-help relaxation treatment of chronic headaches in adolescents: a school based intervention. *Journal of Child Psychiatry, 28*, 127–136.

Larsson, B. S., & Melin, L. (1988). The psychological treatment of recurrent headache in adolescents—short-term outcome and its predictors. *Headache, 28,* 187–195.

Larsson, B., Melin, L., & Doberl, A. (1990). Recurrent tension headache in adolescents treated with self-help relaxation training and a muscle relaxant drug. *Headache, 30,* 665–671.

Lineker, S. C., Badley, E. M., & Dalby, D. M. (1996). Unmet service needs of children with rheumatic diseases and their parents in a metropolitan area. *Journal of Rheumatology, 23*(6), 1054–1058.

McGrath, P. A. (1990). *Pain in children: Nature, assessment and treatment.* New York: Guilford.

McGrath, P. J. (1996). There is more to pain measurement in children than "ouch." *Canadian Psychology, 37,* 63–75.

McGrath, P. J., Humphreys, P., Keene, D., Goodman, J. T., Lascelles, M. A., Cunningham, S. J., & Firestone, P. (1992). The efficacy and efficiency of self adminstered treatment for adolescent migraine. *Pain, 49,* 321–324.

McGrath, P. J., Mathews, J. R., & Pigeon, H. (1991). Assessment of pain in children: A systematic psychosocial model. In M. R. Bond, J. E. Charlton, & C. J. Woolf (Eds.), *Proceedings of the VIth World Congress on Pain* (pp. 509–526). Amsterdam: Elsevier.

McGrath, P. J., & McAlpine, L. (1993). Psychologic perspectives on pediatric pain. *Journal of Pediatrics, 122,* S2–S8.

McGrath, P. J., Unruh, A., & Branson, S. M. (1990). Chronic nonmalignant pain with disability. In D. C. Tyler & E. J. Krane (Eds.), *Advances in pain research and therapy: Pediatric pain* (Vol. 15, pp. 255–271). New York: Raven.

Metsähonkala, L., & Sillanpää, M. (1994). Migraine in children—an evaluation of the IHS criteria. *Cephalagia, 14,* 285–290.

Miser, A. W., Dothage, J. A., Wesley, R. A., & Miser, J. S. (1987). Pain as a presenting symptom in children and young adults with newly diagnosed malignancy. *Pain, 29,* 85–90.

Moldofsky, H., & Lue, F. A. (1993). Disordered sleep, pain, fatigue and gastrointestinal symptoms in fibromyalgia, chronic fatigue and irritable bowel syndromes. In E. A. Mayer & H. E. Raybold (Eds.), *Basic and clinical aspects of chronic abdominal pain* (pp. 249–255). New York: Elsevier.

Mortimer, M. J., Kay, J., & Jaron, A. (1992). Epidemiology of headache and childhood migraine in an urban general practice using Ad Hoc, Vahlquist and IHS criteria. *Developmental Medicine and Child Neurology, 34,* 1095–1101.

Olsson, G., Arner, S., & Hirsch, G. (1990). Reflex sympathetic dystrophy in children. *Advances in Pain Research and Therapy, 15,* 323–331.

Olsson, G., & Berde, C. B. (1993). Neuropathic pain in children and adolescents. In N. L. Schechter, C. B. Berde, & M. Yaster (Eds.), *Pain in infants, children, and adolescents* (pp. 473–494). Baltimore: Williams & Wilkins.

Pachter, L. M. (1994). Culture and clinical care: Folk illness, beliefs and behaviours and their implications for health care delivery. *Journal of the American Medical Association, 271,* 690–694.

Ravilly, S., Robinison, W., Suresh, S., Wohl, M. E., & Berde, C. B. (1996). Chronic pain in cystic fibrosis. *Pediatrics, 98,* 741–747.

Reid, G. J., Lang, B., & McGrath, P. J. (1996). Primary juvenile fibromyalgia: Psychological adjustment, family functioning, coping and functional disability. *Arthritis and Rheumatism, 40*(4), 752–760.

Rhiner, J., Ferrell, B. R., & Shapiro, B. (1994). The experience of pediatric cancer pain, part II: Management of pain. *Journal of Pediatric Nursing, 9,* 380–387.

Richter, I. L., McGrath, P. J., Humphreys, P., Goodman, J. T., Firestone, P., & Keene, D. (1986). Cognitive and relaxation treatment of paediatric migraine. *Pain, 25,* 195–203.

Rosenstiel, A. K., & Keefe, F. J. (1983). The use of coping strategies in chronic low back pain patients: Relationship to patient characteristics and current adjustment. *Pain, 17,* 33–40.

Ross, C. K., Lavigne, J. V., Hayford, J. R., Berry, S. L., Sinacore, J. M., & Pachman, L. M. (1993). Psychological factors affecting reported pain in juvenile rheumatoid arthritis. *Journal of Pediatric Psychology, 18,* 561–573.

Salminen, J. J. (1984). The adolescent back. A field survey of 370 Finnish schoolchildren. *Acta Paediatrica Scandinavia, 73*(Supp. 315), 1–122.

Salminen, J. J., Erkintalo, M., Laine, M., & Pentti, J. (1995). Low back pain in the young: A prospective three-year follow-up study of subjects with and without low back pain. *Spine, 20,* 2101–2107.

Sanders, M. R., Shepherd, R. W., Cleghorn, G., & Woolford, H. (1994). The treatment of recurrent abdominal pain in children: A controlled comparison of cognitive-behavioral family intervention and standard pediatric care. *Journal of Consulting and Clinical Psychology, 62,* 306–314.

Sawyer, M. G., Gannoni, A. F., Toogood, I. R., Antoniou, G., & Rice, M. (1994). The use of alternative therapies by children with cancer. *Medical Journal of Australia, 160*(6), 320–322.

Schanberg, L. E., Keefe, F. J., Lefebvre, J. C., Kredich, D. W., & Gil, K. M. (1996). Pain coping strategies in children with juvenile primary fibromyalgia syndrome: Correlation with pain, physical function, and psychological distress. *Arthritis Care and Research, 9,* 89–96.

Schanberg, L. E., Lefebvre, J. C., Keefe, F. J., Kredich, D. W., & Gil, K. M. (1997). Pain coping and the pain experience in children with juvenile chronic arthritis. *Pain, 73,* 181–189.

Schechter, N. L., Berde, C. B., & Yaster, M. (Eds.). (1993). *Pain in infants, children, and adolescents.* Baltimore: Williams & Wilcox.

Shapiro, B. S. (1993). Management of painful episodes in sickle cell disease. In N. L. Schechter, C. B. Berde, & M. Yaster (Eds.), *Pain in infants, children, and adolescents* (pp. 385–410). Baltimore: Williams & Wilcox.

Shapiro, B. S. (1995). Treatment of chronic pain in children and adolescents. *Pediatric Annals, 24*(3), 148–156.

Shapiro, B. S., Dinges, D. F., Carota Orne, E., Bauer, N., Reilly, L. B., Whitehouse, W. G., Ohene-Frempong, K., & Orne, M. T. (1995). Home management of sickle cell-related pain in children and adolescents: Natural history and impact on school attendence. *Pain, 61,* 139–144.

Sillanpää, M. (1983). Changes in the prevalence of migraine and other headache during the first seven school years. *Headache, 37,* 15–19.

Sillanpää, M., & Anttila, P. (1996). Increasing prevalence of headache in 7-year-old schoolchildren. *Headache, 36,* 466–470.

Southwood, T. R., & Malleson, P. N. (1993). The team approach. In T. R. Southwood & P. N. Malleson (Eds.), *Arthritis in children* (pp. 729–743). London: Bailliere Tindall.

Sparks, J. P. (1978). The incidence of migraine in schoolchildren. A survey by the medical officers of schools association. *Practitioner, 221,* 407–411.

Spigelblatt, L. S. (1995, July). Alternative medicine: Should it be used by children? *Current Problems in Pediatrics,* pp. 180–188.

Taddio, A., Katz, J., Ilersich, A. L., & Koren, G. (1997). Effect of neonatal circumcision on pain response during subsequent routine vaccination. *The Lancet, 349,* 599–603.

Tsanos, A. P., Derevensky, J. L., & Handman, M. (1995, March). *Childhood cancer patients: An examination of their coping and adaptive behavior.* Paper presented at the Biennial Convention for the Society for Research in Child Development, Indianapolis.

Van Sciver, M. M., D'Angelo, E. J., Rappaport, L., & Woolf, A. O. (1995). Pediatric compliance and the roles of distinct treatment characteristics, treatment attitudes, and family stress: A preliminary report. *Developmental and Behavioral Pediatrics, 16*(5), 350–358.

Varni, J. W., Rapoff, M. A., Waldron, S. A., Gragg, R. A., Bernstein, B. H., & Lindsley, C. B. (1996). Chronic pain and emotional distress in children and adolescents. *Developmental and Behavioral Pediatrics, 17*(3), 154–161.

Varni, J. W., Thompson, K. L., & Hanson, V. (1987). The Varni/Thompson Pediatric Pain Questionnaire: I. Chronic musculoskeletal pain in juvenile rheumatoid arthritis. *Pain, 28,* 27–38.

Varni, J. W., & Walco, G. A. (1988). Chronic and recurrent pain associated with pediatric chronic diseases. *Issues in Comprehensive Pediatric Nursing, 11,* 73–86.

Varni, J. W., Waldron, S. A., Gragg, R. A., Rapoff, M. A., Bernstein, G. H., Lindsley, C. G., & Newcomb, M. D. (1996). Development of the Waldron/Varni Pediatric Pain Coping Inventory. *Pain, 67,* 141–150.

Varni, J. W., Wilcox, K. T., Hanson, V., & Brik, R. (1988). Chroic musculoskeletal pain and functional status in juvenile arthritis: An empirical model. *Pain, 32,* 1–7.

Walco, G. A., & Dampier, C. D. (1990). Pain in children and adolescents with sickle cell disease: A descriptive study. *Journal of Pediatric Psychology, 15*(5), 643–658.

Walco, G. A., & Ilowite, N. T. (1992). Cognitive-behavioral intervention for juvenile primary fibromyalgia syndrome. *Journal of Rheumatolgy, 19,* 1617–1619.

Walco, G. A., & Oberlander, T. F. (1993). Musculoskeletal pain syndromes in childen. In N. L. Schechter, C. B. Berde, & M. Yaster (Eds.), *Pain in infants, children, and adolescents* (pp. 459–471). Baltimore: Williams & Wilcox.

Wänman, A., & Agerberg, G. (1987). Recurrent headaches and craniomandibular disorders in adolescents: A longitudinal study. *Journal of Craniomandibular Disorders, 1,* 229–236.

Wilder, R. T., Berde, C. B., Wolohan, M., Masek, B. J., Vieyra, M. A., & Micheli, M. J. (1992). Reflex sympathetic dystrophy in children and adolescents: Follow up of a cohort of 70 patients and development of a treatment algorithm. *Journal of Bone and Joint Surgery, 74,* 910–919.

Wilkins, K. L., McGrath, P. J., Katz, J., & Finley, A. G. (1997). Phantom sensations and phantom pain in child and adolescent amputees. *Pain Research & Management, 2*(1), 59.

Yaster, M., & Schechter, N. (1996). Pain and human immunodeficiency virus infection in children. *Pediatrics, 98,* 455–456.

Yee, J. D., Lin, Y.-C., & Aubuchon, P. A. (1993). Acupuncture. In N. L. Schechter, C. B. Berde, & M. Yaster (Eds.), *Pain in infants, children, and adolescents* (pp. 341–348). Baltimore: Williams & Wilkins.

Yunus, M. B., & Masi, A. T. (1985). Juvenile primary fibromalgia syndrome: A clinical study of thirty-three patients and matched normal controls. *Arthritis and Rheumatism, 28,* 138–145.

Chapter 25

Geriatric Benign Chronic Pain: An Overview

Ranjan Roy
Faculty of Social Work and Department of Clinical Health Psychology, Faculty of Medicine, University of Manitoba

Michael R. Thomas
Department of Psychology, University of Manitoba

Andrew J. Cook
Pain Clinic, University of Virginia

The topic at hand is very large in scope and there is truly no way of doing justice to its complexity in a short chapter. In this chapter we discuss pain in old age by considering issues of prevalence, psychosocial and psychiatric factors, and some ideas of assessment and treatment.

PREVALENCE

Rate of prevalence of pain in the elderly population reported in a variety of studies varies from 20% to 58% (Farrel, Gibson, & Helm, 1996) and, given the variability of these studies in their design and sampling methods, drawing any firm conclusion is difficult. Although certain chronic pain conditions, such as musculoskeletal pain, are more prevalent in older patients, research has consistently shown declining overall pain complaints with rising age (Anderson et al., 1993; Gibson & Helme, 1995; Moss, Lawton, & Glicksman, 1991; Sternbach, 1986; Thomas & Roy, 1988a).

It is hard to ignore that certain conditions are more common in old age and some are peculiar to that stage of life. It is a generally accepted fact that musculoskeletal pain is most common in the elderly. Joint aches and pains are indeed so common that many elderly persons regard this as part of being old (Roy & Thomas, 1988). The Nuprin Pain Report found that older individuals had more joint pains than any other age group, and incidence and prevalence of joint pain increased with age. Conversely,

551

younger subjects reported more pain in every other category (Louis Harris & Associates, 1985). High prevalence of musculoskeletal pain in old age has been confirmed in several other investigations (Anderson, Ejlertsson, Leden, & Rosenberg, 1993; Demlow, Laing, & Eaton, 1986; Roy, Thomas, & Berger, 1990; Stelian et al., 1992; Valkenberg, 1988; Vanharanta, Sachs, Ohnmeiss, & April, 1989; Von Korff, Dworkin, le Resche, & Kruge, 1988; Warren & O'Brien, 1989).

Demlow and associates (1986) reported that 80% of an elderly population had some form of rheumatic pain. Valkenberg (1988) found with a younger population that 30% of men and 53% of women over the age of 55 years experienced some form of peripheral joint pain. Roy et al. (1990), in a comparative study of community-based healthy elderly and an elderly pain clinic sample, found that back and joint pain accounted for 75% and just over 95% of pain complaints respectively in these two populations. The data also indicated that pain in the community sample was of low intensity, whereas the pain in the clinical sample was in the severe range. This brief review is provided simply to show that musculoskeletal pain is a common phenomenon in the elderly and when this problem is encountered in a pain clinic setting, the pain is usually severe and may have remained unresponsive to treatment.

Herpes zoster (Donahue, Choo, Manson, & Platt, 1995; Guillet & Plantin, 1992) and postherpetic neuralgia (Bowsher, 1992; Robertson & George, 1990) are conditions that tend to afflict the aged, though not exclusively, and are rather disabling conditions requiring active medical intervention, often with limited success.

Prevalence of abdominal pain tends to decline with aging (Sternbach, 1986; Von Korff et al., 1988). On the other hand, one study has shown that abdominal pain may be an important cause of pain in old age (Bugliosi, Meloy, & Vukov, 1990). The authors conducted a 1-year retrospective study of 127 patients with acute abdominal pain who were seen at an emergency department. These patients ranged in age from 68 to 91. Twenty-four percent were diagnosed with intermediate abdominal pain, 12% with biliary tract disease, and another 12% with small bowel obstruction. Four percent of the patients were admitted and of those 22 required surgical intervention. Altogether, 17.3% of the 127 patients required surgery. It must be acknowledged that this was a retrospective, uncontrolled study with an acutely ill group of patients. The fact remains that prevalence of abdominal pain tends to decline with old age.

Headaches are common complaints in the elderly (Lipton, Pfeffer, Newman, & Solomon, 1993; Raskin, 1988; Solomon, Kunkel, & Frame, 1990). However, recent onset of headache is uncommon after age 65 (Ward & Clough, 1995). Incidence and prevalence of migraine decline with age, whereas prevalence of tension headaches either remains the same (Stewart,

Lipton, Celantano, & Reed, 1992) or increases in the over-65 group (Solomon et al., 1990). Hypnic (sleep-inducing) headache syndrome is one headache condition that is peculiar to the elderly (Newman, Lipton, & Solomon, 1991; Raskin, 1988). The age of onset of this painful condition ranges from the mid-60s to the mid-80s.

PSYCHOSOCIAL ISSUES

Many factors complicate the understanding of pain in the elderly. Common parameters that are routinely incorporated into the assessment and treatment of chronic pain are often ignored in this population (Sorkin & Turk, 1995). For example, the social dimension is often not adequately addressed, as the following case vignette of a 68-year-old woman with severe low back pain seen at a pain clinic illustrates. It also highlights the absolute necessity of a multidisciplinary approach to treatment:

> Miss A., age 68 and single, was referred to a pain clinic with an unremitting complaint of low back pain, which commenced some 3 years prior to her arrival at the clinic and had continued unabated. She had had medical, neurological, and orthopedic investigations, which were all inconclusive. She complained that the pain was so severe that she had become housebound almost from the time of onset. She had a sister living nearby, with whom she had enjoyed a close friendship, but now she rarely saw her. She was adamant that her pain was so overwhelming that she had no inclination to socialize. Her other main complaint was lack of sleep, again due to pain. She denied any feelings of sadness or depression.
>
> Her past history was revealing. She owned a very successful business, had numerous business associates, was very active in the chamber of commerce, and was highly regarded by the business community. On the domestic front, she devoted herself to looking after her sick and elderly mother, who lived with her. Six months prior to the onset of her pain problem, she sold her business for a considerable sum of money and a year later her mother died. She decompensated rather rapidly and embarked on a career of a chronic pain patient trying to find a solution to her pain problem.
>
> A critical question raised by Miss A.'s case centered on the psychological and psychiatric issues, which were key issues in the development of a treatment plan. She denied any feelings of sadness and depression. Yet she was dysphoric and had neurovegetative symptoms such as loss of appetite, sleep disturbance, and loss of energy, commonly associated with both chronic pain and depressive disorders. Symptoms of self-deprecation have been noted as of special significance in diagnosing depression in the elderly (Desonville, Reeves, Thompson, & Gallagher, 1985). The question of some kind of somatizing disorder, although uncommon in the elderly, was also considered. These matters are discussed later in the chapter.
>
> The striking feature of her case was the rapid, almost dramatic, disappearance of her support system—the sources that provided her with a sense

of self and purposeful roles. Death of her elderly mother combined with selling of her business at age 65, which both can be viewed as normal developmental events, coincided with the onset of her pain. Support for this relationship between recent life events and onset of pain has received some attention in the literature, as has the role of social support as a mediating or buffering factor.

One plausible explanation is that loss of these two aspects of her life left her in a social vacuum, that is without any meaningful social roles, and she rapidly assumed a new identity as chronically ill. Some understanding of the association of life events perceived to be negative and the buffering role of social support may further explain and illuminate this rather rapid transformation from being a caregiver and a highly effective businessperson to the chronic sick role.

Life Events and Pain

It is within the realms of probability that life events encountered by Miss A. precipitated her back pain. A critical question centers on the nature of this relationship. Does one lead to the other? There is indeed some evidence to suggest such an association. There now exists a reasonable body of research that substantiates a relationship between life events and onset of pain and psychological problems in pain patients (Atkinson et al., 1988; Craig & Brown, 1984; DeBenedittis et al., 1990; Feurstein, Sult, & Houle, 1985; Oosterhuis, 1984; Roll & Theorell, 1987; Smith et al., 1985). A few studies also exist that failed to show any strong relationship (Jensen, 1988; Marbach, Lennon, & Dohrenwend, 1988). The weight of the evidence suggests that undesirable, uncontrollable, and unpredictable events have the capacity to engender morbidity. Despite the evidence in support of a causal relationship between negative life events and morbidity, it would be perilous to view such an association as the only cause. Pain is a complex biopsychosocial phenomenon and any single factor of etiologic merit, however powerful, must be viewed as a partial explanation.

Two studies that may have direct bearing on Miss A.'s case are briefly discussed. Atkinson and colleagues (1988) investigated the influence of life events in the development of depression in patients with chronic low back pain (CLBP). A structured interview elicited life-events data based on both self-report and interview-rated measures of life stress over a 12-month period preceding the evaluation. Thirty-four consecutive male patients attending an orthopedic clinic comprised the CLBP sample. The main finding of this study was that depressed CLBP patients reported significantly more life events, more stressful life events, and more ongoing life difficulties than either the nondepressed CLBP patients or nondepressed, nonpain controls. A key conclusion was that the life events were quite directly related to back pain problems rather than independent events. This study confirmed an earlier investigation of an association between life events and psychological distress in CLBP patients by Smith et al. (1985). Negative life events were clearly associated with depression and social maladjustment emanating from pain conditions.

Social Support

For adequate appreciation of the power of life events, the question of social support must also be examined. The role of social support in general, and spousal support in particular, has been a topic of some controversy (Turk, Kerns, & Rosenberg, 1992). The detractors of social support argue that this support translates into reinforcement of pain behavior, thereby counteracting the positive effects.

There is, however, much empirical evidence demonstrating the positive forces exerted on the well-being of an individual in the throes of distressing life events by the availability of social support. A study that is of particular relevance to Miss A.'s case was reported by Weickginant and colleagues (1993). Disinclination to seek social support when confronted with exacerbation of back pain was a factor that contributed significantly to the general level of distress for chronic pain patients. Jamison and Virts (1990), in an investigation of the role of family members in preventing "maladaptive" behaviors in a group of chronic pain patients, found that patients reporting a high level of family support also reported significantly less pain intensity and higher levels of activity. The final study considered was conducted by Faucett and Levine (1991), in which they assessed the impact of social network and pain complaints in patients with arthritic and myofascial pain disorders. Generalized conflict within the entire social network (not uncommon in chronic pain patients) was more harmful for patients with myofascial pain disorders than with arthritic diseases. Second, cumulative social network stress was more harmful than conflict with intimates, which was more evident in the myofascial group than the arthritics. These three studies did not exclusively study the geriatric population, but the conclusions are perhaps even more relevant to the elderly, who tend to experience shrinking social and family network.

PSYCHOPATHOLOGY OF PAIN IN THE ELDERLY

Psychiatric Diagnoses

Chronic pain in the elderly is not generally viewed as psychogenic. Comparisons of combined psychiatric diagnoses for different age cohorts found that persons over 65 had the lowest prevalence rates. However, the comorbidity of chronic pain syndromes, depression, and anxiety in the elderly is not uncommon (Kramlinger, Swanson, & Maruta, 1983).

In the most recent revision of the *Diagnostic and Statistical Manual of Mental Disorders* (4th ed., *DSM–IV*), the prevalence of chronic pain complaints attributed to the diagnoses of pain disorder associated with psychological factors, and pain disorder associated with both psychological factors and a general medical condition were estimated at an annual rate between 10% and 15% (American Psychiatric Association [APA], 1994). Women reported more headaches and musculoskeletal pain but there was no difference in the rate of prevalence by age.

Somatization disorders have an estimated annual prevalence rate between .02% and 2%, and the onset typically occurs before age 25 and is reported approximately 10 times more frequently in women than men. Although somatization disorder may have early onset according to *DSM–IV* (APA, 1994), Pribor, Smith, and Yutzy (1994), evaluating 353 adult women (ages 18–86) with pain problems, found a prevalence of 24% in patients 55 years or older.

Finally, in the last category in the *DSM–IV* (APA, 1994) relating to chronic pain complaints, hypochondriasis or delusional disorders–somatic type have an estimated annual prevalence rate between 4% and 9%, with an approximately even gender ratio. In a study on hypochondriasis and its relationship to aging, Barsky (1993) found that the elderly were at especially high risk for certain factors likely to foster hypochondriacal (HPC) symptoms including chronic pain. These included social isolation, a high prevalence of psychiatric disorders that commonly had HPC symptoms as secondary features, and increasing medical morbidity and bodily decline. Barsky proposed that because of the long-term psychological features of this disorder in the elderly, the management of the HPC patient was best conceptualized as care, not cure. This approach required a major focus on helping the older patient cope effectively with their symptoms rather than trying to eliminate them or expect them to diminish or cease with treatment and/or time.

Emotional State

It is a commonly held belief among health care professionals that chronic pain complaints in the elderly do not have a strong psychological factor. Such a view is understandable because in the elderly population pain complaints are mostly rooted in organic causes. Furthermore, less than 5% of individuals aged 65 or older attend pain clinics where psychosocial factors are more likely to be considered in assessment and treatment.

However, a link does seem to exist between chronic pain and depression in the elderly, beyond the unhappiness that normally accompanies an illness or pain (Parmelee, Katz, & Lawton, 1989; Roy, Thomas, & Matas, 1984). Parmelee, Katz, and Lawton (1991), in a study of institutionalized elderly subjects diagnosed with major depression, found that these subjects more frequently reported more intense pain, and a greater number of pain locations than did mildly depressed or nondepressed groups. Turk, Okifuji, and Scharff (1995) examined a cognitive-behavioral mediation model in explaining the association between pain and depressed affect in the elderly. A strong association was observed in the older patients between pain severity and depression.

There are many possible explanations for the relationship between pain and depression in the elderly. For example, depression may psychologically sensitize individuals to pain so that their psychological reactions to physical discomfort become intensified to an interpretation of pain (Waddell, 1987). Conversely, chronic pain may lead to multiple significant life changes that affect the individual's sense of self-identity, resulting in development of depression. Other research suggests that, contrary to popular assumption, depression and other psychological distress are less common features of chronic pain in the elderly than in younger chronic pain patients (Harkins & Price, 1992; Kee, Middaugh, & Pawlick, 1996).

Due to gender differences in longevity, women represent over 75% of the elderly population. Thus psychological dimensions of chronic pain in the elderly involve some interaction between gender and age. The relationship between depressive cognitive processes and cognitive processes present during experiences of pain is consistent with the findings that women have more reported depression as well as pain complaints (Peterson & Seligman, 1984) than men throughout their lives (G. Kaplan, Barell, & Lusky, 1988).

Another major psychological factor associated with chronic pain in the elderly is anxiety. Anxiety in the elderly, according to Turnbull (1989), is highly correlated with the experience of chronic pain, chronic ill health, isolation, and facing death. Life changes have an important influence on the self-reported health status of elderly individuals, and anxiety often accompanies these changes. The most common types of anxiety disorders in the elderly are phobias, anxiety states, and adjustment disorders. The prevalence of anxiety disorders in the elderly requires that health care professionals be aware of how these disorders may be manifested in these patients. For example, chest pain and palpitation are strongly associated with panic and general anxiety, but headache and chronic pain are more strongly associated with depression. Another finding regarding anxiety is that functional limitations associated with chronic pain often stabilize after 6 months, but the level of anxiety and psychological disturbance typically continues to increase (Abbott et al., 1992).

Depression, somatoform disorders, anxiety, and hypochondriasis can occur in elderly chronic pain patients. It seems that these conditions, for complex reasons, remain underdiagnosed. At this point we briefly return to our patient, Miss A., and consider the possibility that her pain complaints represent a somatoform pain disorder as defined by *DSM–IV* (APA, 1994). The key criteria for somatoform pain disorder are that pain is the predominant feature of the presentation and is of sufficient severity to warrant clinical attention; the pain must cause significant distress or impairments in social, occupational, or other important areas of functioning; and psychological factors are judged to play a significant role in the onset, severity, exacerbation, or maintenance of the pain.

At this point some of the clinical features of Miss A. are worthy of recall. A fully functioning woman, in a matter of a few months, was transformed into a virtual invalid. Her major focus was on pain and not her mood. Initial diagnosis of depression and a trial of antidepressant therapy proved ineffectual. Her active coping style was almost completely replaced by passivity and withdrawal. Her dependency on the health care system to find a "cure" for her pain was telling. All this was in marked contrast to her past coping style. There is indeed evidence to suggest that Miss A. presented with a somatoform pain disorder.

Melding (1995) cautioned that somatoform pain disorders are too readily diagnosed in elderly pain patients in the absence of pathophysiology. This she viewed as wholly undesirable and suggested that strict adherence to the *DSM–IV* (APA, 1994) diagnostic criteria is desirable.

Judged against the criteria just outlined, Miss A. seemed to meet most of them. Her pain was severe enough to render her disabled and most definitely warranted medical attention. Distress caused by her pain was all-encompassing, not leaving any area of her life intact. Implication of psychological factors, her unexpected or paradoxical reaction to selling of her business combined with mother's death, in the onset of her back pain was discussed earlier and their significance was unmistakable. Therefore, a working hypothesis of somatoform pain disorder was thought to be the most relevant.

ASSESSMENT AND TREATMENT

Because elderly patients are underrepresented at specialty pain clinics, research and clinical recommendations regarding assessment and treatment of this group have not been readily available. This situation has been gradually improving as greater recognition of the problem of chronic pain in the elderly is achieved. The general consensus from the literature appears to be that the similarities between older and younger chronic pain patients are more important than the differences (Sorkin, Rudy, Hanlon, Turk, & Steig, 1990), although there are a number of issues that deserve special consideration in assessment and treatment of elderly pain patients.

There is a solid body of literature demonstrating that elderly patients do benefit from multidisciplinary pain treatments (Gibson, Farrell, Katz, & Helme, 1996), and they benefit as much as do younger patients (Cutler, Fishbain, Rosomoff, & Rosomoff, 1994; Kee et al., 1996). They also benefit from psychosocial and behavioral treatments such as cognitive-behavioral pain programs (Cook, in press; Puder, 1988), biofeedback (Middaugh, Woods, Kee, Harden, & Peters, 1991), and relaxation training (Arena, Hightower, & Chang, 1988). Kee and colleagues (1996) surveyed 96 chronic pain programs and found that age biases continue to restrict admission to some programs for elderly patients. Some clinicians suggest that elderly patients may benefit more by participating in programs with other patients in their age group (Gibson et al., 1996). Specialty pain clinics for elderly pain patients have started to evolve and initial outcome data are promising (Sandin, 1993).

Sorkin et al. (1990) and others have reported similar clinical presentations for older and younger pain patients, including similar pain severity ratings, emotional reactions, reported interference from pain, and acceptance of treatments. However, there is evidence that older patients may differ on some of these dimensions, and in general their assessment warrants special consideration to issues such as cognitive status, comorbid conditions, social support, and medication use. Thus, as with all chronic pain patients, thorough multidimensional assessment is essential.

Assessment Issues

The cognitive-behavioral perspective offers a good framework for assessment of the older pain patient. Keefe, Beaupre, Weiner, and Seigler (1996) offered a three-factor model that includes biomedical, psychological, and socio-environmental variables. These three factors are viewed as influencing the experience of chronic pain and the resultant pain behavior. Biomedical variables include painful medical conditions, other medical comorbidity, and cognitive, sensory, and physical functioning. A physician with geriatric medicine specialization is an important participant in the assessment of the elderly pain patient, to ensure adequate consideration of comorbidity and medication issues (Gibson et al., 1996). Medical conditions affecting physical functioning must be considered in the development of a treatment program that includes increasing activity level and improving strength, flexibility, and/or cardiovascular fitness.

Cognitive impairment is an important issue to consider in both assessment and treatment, but should not be regarded as a barrier unless the patient has substantial deficits in cognitive functioning (e.g., attention, comprehension, memory, orientation). The incidence of moderate to severe dementia is approximately 5% to 7% between age 65 and 80, and 20% for those over 80. There is conflicting evidence on the influence of cognitive impairment on reports of pain among the elderly. Yet it is clear that a serious risk of overinterpreting mild cognitive impairment is unnecessary exclusion of patients from treatment (Kee et al., 1996). Elderly individuals with mild to moderate impairment can complete and benefit from many forms of treatment, including psychologically based ones (e.g., Cook, 1998). Deficits may also be reversible, especially if they are the result of a delirium or medication side effect. Kee et al. noted the high use among older pain patients of benzodiazepines, which can produce impairments in concentration and memory. Even if a patient has been withdrawn from the medication, the cognitive deficits can continue for days or weeks.

A brief screening for cognitive impairment should be a standard component of assessment with older pain patients. Screening tools such as the Mini-Mental Status Examination (Folstein, Folstein, & McHugh, 1975) or Short Portable Mental Status Questionnaire (Pfeiffer, 1975) can serve this purpose and are easily administered. Results should be interpreted in conjunction with medical conditions, current medications, and level of emotional distress. If moderate to severe impairment or a sudden change in cognitive status is suggested, referral for neuropsychological or neurological assessment should be considered. With regard to pain assessment and treatment, the willingness of the patient to report pain and the method of assessment or intervention are more important than cognitive status for patients with mild to moderate impairment. Effective and acceptable forms for communicating or implementing interventions can generally be worked out with patients (and caregivers where appropriate) once adequate rapport has been established.

Psychological variables in the three-factor model of assessment include (a) current pain-coping strategies, (b) emotional distress (i.e., depression, anxiety, frustration/anger), and (c) beliefs and personality factors. Elderly individuals with chronic pain usually have developed a repertoire of personally effective coping strategies such as capacity to conduct daily routines despite periodic severe pain (Cook & Thomas, 1994), and these should be assessed for incorporation into planned interventions. The previous discussion of depression in older pain patients indicates that assumptions regarding emotional reactions to pain should be avoided. It is preferable to use assessment instruments that have been developed and standardized with elderly patients, such as the Geriatric Depression Scale (Yesavage et al., 1983), but results should not be interpreted in the absence of other clinical data.

Regarding beliefs that may influence pain interpretation or behavior, it is especially important when working with older patients to be sensitive to potential cohort or generational differences in beliefs regarding pain, coping, and acceptable treatments (Cook & Roy, 1995). The source of the beliefs and strength of conviction may need to be considered in assessing current behavior and openness to change. For example, one 70-year-old man, with CLBP treated at our clinic, was strongly resistant to the concept of pacing of physical activities because he had grown up watching several generations of his family doing hard physical labor despite pain because "they had no choice." Similarly, "tried and true" home remedies may provide an important source of comfort, and can often be effectively incorporated into a self-management program for chronic pain.

Socio-environmental variables in the three-factor model include (a) social support, (b) patterns of interaction with spouses and family members, (c) life stressors, and (d) involvement with the health care system. The literature relating to these issues has been reviewed, and the importance of incorporating a thorough psychosocial history in the assessment of the elderly pain patient has been illustrated through the case example of Miss A.

Treatment Issues

Although it has been established that the elderly benefit from the same approaches to chronic pain management as younger patients, Sorkin and Turk (1995) concluded from their review of the treatment outcome literature that older patients had better outcomes when treatment was modified to specifically address their needs. The foundation for effective treatment is thorough assessment, allowing matching and tailoring of interventions with patient needs and characteristics. This appears to be the most effective approach with elderly pain patients (Cook, 1998).

Special Needs. Sensitivity and creativity are often all that is required for effective tailoring of interventions to the needs of the elderly patient. Some common sense, absent of ageism and gerontophobia, is also very helpful (Butler & Gastel, 1980). Asking patients to repeat the rationale and instructions for the treatment (Arena, Hannah, Bruno, & Meador, 1991) is an effective way of addressing concerns regarding attention, hearing, or comprehension. Hearing problems can often be overcome by minor modifications such as sitting closer to the patient, making good eye contact, and speaking slowly (Kee et al., 1996). Written information can also be used to supplement verbal education or instruction. Kee et al. suggested using written scripts in conjunction with the audiotapes commonly used for relaxation training.

Modifications can also be made to treatment programs to make them more attractive or compatible for older patients. For example, a preferred music selection can be incorporated in a relaxation-training program, large print can be used on written educational materials, and walking can be the focus of a cardiovascular exercise routine. It is also important to recognize that expectations and/or standards may need to be adjusted. With physical therapy components, steady progress is possible for older patients but generally occurs at a slower rate and with a lower ceiling. With bio-feedback training, the elderly can learn self-regulation skills and make equivalent changes as compared to younger patients, but can have different baselines for physiological processes such as higher average respiration rates (Kee et al., 1996).

Beliefs. As with pain patients of all ages, beliefs and expectations re-garding treatments and outcomes need to be assessed and incorporated into treatment. With the elderly, it is especially important to consider the patient's belief in his or her ability to complete tasks. Goals for various components of a pain management program (e.g., medication reduction, activity level increase) may seem straightforward to the therapist but com-pletely unrealistic for the elderly patient (Gibson et al., 1996). Beliefs about the etiology of pain and its relationship to the aging process, on the part of both patients and health care professionals, are also important (Cook & Roy, 1995). Cook and Thomas (1994) found that 38% of elderly indi-viduals reporting chronic pain stated that their physicians had attributed their pain to aging. Discussion of these types of beliefs with patients is a valuable component of intervention, as research has established that pa-tient–physician agreement contributes to better treatment outcomes, greater compliance with prescribed regimens, and greater patient satisfaction (Cook & Roy, 1995).

Compliance. Richardson (1986) provided suggestions for enhancing com-pliance with medical regimens for elderly patients, and these can apply equally to all types of pain management intervention. These include (a) pacing the presentation, task relevance, and difficult level to the elderly patient's ability, (b) increasing time for the patient to study visual material and to respond, (c) slowing speech pace, (d) providing additional organi-zation assistance to assist memory, (e) nurturing the patient's hope in their care and treatment, and (f) ensuring that support is available. Re-garding the latter, the involvement of family members and other caregivers in treatment is crucial with elderly patients (Gibson et al., 1996; Roy et al., 1996). Sessions with members of the support network should be a standard treatment component to ensure that both patients and family members/caregivers understand the components of treatment and can work together to maximize follow-through. If adequate support is not avail-able, then arrangements should be made for home care visits, support group participation, involvement in a community center, and so on.

Education is a crucial component of pain management therapy for patients of all ages, including the elderly. Ferrell (1996) and her colleagues have developed a pain education program for elderly cancer patients, encompassing 19 nondrug interventions across five areas including heat, cold, massage, and relaxation/distraction. Written instructions are provided for each of the interventions, printed in larger type with illustrations. Caregivers are included in the program, and information on economical sources of equipment (e.g., heating pads, electric massagers) is provided. Ferrell provided a useful list of teaching principles for pain education, with tips such as keeping education sessions brief and reinforcing written material with audiotapes that can be replayed as often as necessary.

Drug Therapy. This method of therapy is an important component of pain management in the elderly, but special considerations apply as elderly patients have different sensitivities to medications than do younger patients and are at increased risk for adverse effects. These differences are due to changes in drug metabolism, absorption, distribution, and elimination resulting from physiological changes associated with aging, such as decreases in kidney function, serum albumin levels, intestinal motility, intestinal blood flow, and gastric secretion (Morris & Goli, 1994; Popp & Portenoy, 1996). The details of pharmacology relevant to elderly pain patients are summarized elsewhere (e.g., Popp & Portenoy, 1996) and are not repeated here. Harkins and Price (1992) provided a good summary of considerations regarding dosage, adverse effects, and special characteristics for the various classes of medications used in pain therapy. It is worthy of note that older patients can decrease their use of medications and health services as effectively as younger patients through interdisciplinary pain management programs (Kee et al., 1996).

Institutional Care. For elderly individuals in long-term care facilities, there may be additional considerations for treatment planning. A higher incidence of cognitive impairment is typical and should be considered in the assessment process, as previously noted. Herr and Mobily (1996) discussed other considerations such as the common knowledge deficits among caregivers regarding chronic pain. However, these issues need not be barriers to effective treatment. Cook (1998) evaluated a cognitive-behavioral pain management program for elderly nursing home residents against an attention/support control treatment. Results revealed that residents who received the cognitive-behavioral training reported less pain and pain-related disability, and that these effects were maintained at 4-month follow-up. Residents participating in the program ranged in age from 61 to 98, and included individuals with mild cognitive impairment.

Treatment Evaluation. The measures and criteria for evaluating treatment success with elderly pain patients often need to be different than those applied for younger patients. Vocational issues are less relevant to some older patients than involvement in social and community activities. When productive activity is used as an outcome measure for treatment evaluation, it can be broadly defined to include paid employment, housework, volunteer work, yardwork, and training/education (Kee et al., 1996). Generally, evaluation of treatment efficacy should be based on success at achieving individually established goals that are specified during the assessment process. The same measures as used with younger patients are usually applicable, though criterion levels may need to be adjusted. The earlier noted examples regarding physical therapy and biofeedback illustrate the value of considering all dimensions of changes including magnitude, proportion, and rate. Involving the patient in monitoring of various aspects of pain and functioning provides a means of ongoing monitoring of treatment effects and can enhance interest and compliance with interventions.

A commonly held assumption is that older patients are more difficult to treat in some way, such as requiring more therapist time or highly specialized treatment programs. Kee et al. (1996) evaluated this assumption as part of an outcome study of their multidisciplinary chronic pain reha- bilitation program. Clinician ratings on compliance, amount of time and attention required, need for modification of treatment protocols, and ex- tent of improvement indicated that older patients responded well and were not harder to treat. No treatment components were identified as providing special problems for them. These findings are consistent with our experi- ence in working with older pain patients in various settings. A blend of standard chronic pain management interventions with application of some gerontological knowledge/experience will generally provide an effective treatment program.

SUMMARY

In this chapter, we have presented an overview of some of the critical issues confronting the elderly person suffering from chronic pain. That chronic pain is endemic in the elderly population is beyond debate. What, however, remains ominous is underestimation of pain combined with overmedicalization to the exclusion of critical psychosocial factors. Our effort here has been to propose a more complete approach to the assessment and treatment, which includes social and psychological factors, in addition to the medical, in the assessment and treatment of the elderly chronic pain sufferer.

REFERENCES

Abbott, F., Gray-Donald, K., Sewitch, M., Johnston, C., Edgar, L., & Jeans, M. (1992). The prevalence of pain in hospitalized patients and resolution over six months. *Pain, 50,* 15–28.
American Psychiatric Association. (1992). *Diagnostic and statistical manual of mental disorders* (3rd ed., rev.). Washington, DC: Author.

American Psychiatric Association. (1994). Diagnostic and statistical manual of mental disorders (4th ed., rev.). Washington, DC: Author.

Anderson, J., Kaplan, M., & Falsenthal, G. (1992). Brain injury obscured by chronic pain. *Archives of Physical and Rehabilitation Medicine, 71,* 703–708.

Anderson, H., Ejlertsson, G., Leden, I., & Rosenberg, C. (1993). Chronic pain in a geographically defined population: Studies of differences in age, gender, social class, and pain localization. *The Clinical Journal of Pain, 9,* 174–182.

Arena, J., Hightower, N., & Chang, G. (1988). Relaxation therapy for tension headache in the elderly: A prospective study. *Psychology and Aging, 3,* 96–98.

Arena, J., Hannah, S., Bruno, G., & Meador, K. (1991). Electromyographic biofeedback training for tension headache in the elderly: A prospective study. *Biofeedback and Self-Regulation, 16,* 379–390.

Atkinson, J., Slater, M., Grant, I., Patterson, I., et al. (1988). Depressed mood in chronic low pain: Relationship with stressful events. *Pain, 35,* 47–55.

Barsky, A. (1993). The diagnosis and management of hypochondriacal concerns in the elderly. *Journal of Geriatric Psychiatry, 26,* 129–141.

Bowsher, D. (1992). Post-herpetic neuralgia in older patients: Incidence and optimal treatment. *Drugs & Aging, 5,* 411–418.

Buglosi, T., Meloy, T., & Vukow, L. (1990). Acute abdominal pain in the elderly. *Annals of Emergency Medicine, 19,* 1383–1396.

Butler, R., & Gastel, B. (1980). Care of the aged: Perspectives on pain and discomfort. In L. Ng & J. Bonica (Eds.), *Pain and Discomfort* (pp. 20–37). Amsterdam: Elsevier.

Cook, A., & Roy, R. (1995). Attitudes, beliefs, and illness behavior. In R. Roy (Ed.), *Chronic pain in old age: An integrated biopsychosocial perspective* (pp. 20–37). Toronto: University of Toronto Press.

Cook, A. (1998). Cognitive-behavioral pain management for elderly nursing home residents. *Journal of Gerontology: Psychological Sciences, 53B,* 51–59.

Cook, A., & Thomas, M. (1994). Pain and the use of health services among the elderly. *Journal of Aging and Health.*

Craig, I., & Brown, G. (1984). Goal frustration and life-events in the etiology of painful gastrointestinal disorder. *Journal of Psychosomatic Research, 28,* 411–421.

Crook, J., Rideout, F., & Browne, G. (1984). The prevalence of pain complaints in a general population. *Pain, 18,* 299–314.

Cutler, R., Fishbain, D., Rosomoff, R., & Rosomoff, H. (1994). Outcomes in treatment of pain in geriatric and younger age groups. *Archives of Physical Medicine and Rehabilitation, 75,* 457–464.

DeBennedittis, G., Lovevenzetti, A., & Pieri, A. (1990). The role of life-events in the onset of primary headaches. *Pain, 40,* 65–75.

Demlow, M., Liang, M., & Eaton, H. (1986). Impact of chronic arthritis in the elderly. *Clinics in Rheumatic Diseases, 12,* 329–335.

Desonville, C., Reeves, J., Thompson, I., & Gallagher, D. (1985). The pattern of depressive symptomatology in geriatric normals, depressives and chronic pain patients. *Pain,* (Suppl.) *2,* S210.

Donahue, J., Choo, P., Manson, J., & Platt, R. (1995). Incidence of herpes zoster. *Archive of Internal Medicine, 155,* 1005–1009.

Farrel, M., Gibson, S., & Helme, R. (1996). Chronic non-malignant pain in older patients. In B. R. Ferrel & B. A. Ferrel (Eds.), *Pain in the elderly.* Seattle, WA: IASP Press.

Faucett, J., & Levine, J. (1991). The contribution of interpersonal conflict to chronic pain in the presence or absence of organic pathology. *Pain, 44,* 35–43.

Ferrell, B. A. (1991). Pain management in elderly people. *Journal of the American Geriatric Society, 39,* 64–73.

Ferrell, B. R. (1996). Patient education and non-drug interventions. In B. R. Ferrell & B. A. Ferrell (Eds.), *Pain in the elderly* (pp. 35–44). Seattle, WA: IASP Press.

Feurstein, M., Sult, S., & Houle, M. (1985). Environmental stressors and chronic low back pain: Life-events, family and work environment. *Pain, 22,* 295–307.

Folstein, M., Folstein, S., & McHugh, P. (1975). Mini-Mental State: A practical method for grading the cognitive state of patients for the clinician. *Journal of Psychiatric Research, 12,* 189–198.

Gibson, S., & Helme, R. (1995). Age differences in pain-perception and report: A review of physiological, laboratory and clinical studies. *Pain Reviews, 2,* 111–137.

Gibson, S., Farrell, M., Katz, B., & Helme, R. (1996). Multidisciplinary management of chronic nonmalignant pain in older adults. In B. R. Ferrell & B. A. Ferrell (Eds.), *Pain in the elderly* (pp. 91–100). Seattle, WA: IASP Press.

Guillet, P., & Plantin, P. (1992). Herpes zoster: Epidemiology, physiopathology, diagnosis and treatment. *Review Practitioner, 42,* 2495–2497.

Haley, W., & Dolce, J. (1986). Assessment and management of chronic pain in the elderly. *Clinical Gerontologist, 5,* 435–455.

Harkins, S., & Price, D. (1992). Assessment of pain in the elderly. In D. Turk & R. Melzack (Eds.), *Handbook of pain assessment* (pp. 315–331). New York: Guilford Press.

Harris, L., & Associates. (1985). *The Nuprin Report.* New York: Louis Harris Associates.

Herr, K., & Mobily, P. (1996). Pain management for the elderly in alternate care settings. In B. R. Ferrell & B. S. Ferrell (Eds.), *Pain in the elderly* (pp. 101–110). Seattle, WA: IASP Press.

Jamison, R., & Virts, K. (1990). The influence of social support on chronic pain. *Behavior, Research & Therapy, 28,* 283–287.

Jensen, J. (1988). Life events in neurologic patients with headache and low back pain in relation to diagnosis and persistence of pain. *Pain, 32,* 47–53.

Kaplan, G., Barell, V., & Lusky, A. (1988). Subjective state of health and survival in elderly adults. *Journal of Gerontology: Social Sciences, 43,* S114–121.

Kaplan, H., & Sadock, B. (1989). *Comprehensive textbook of psychiatry* (pp. 2014–2015). Baltimore, MD: Williams & Wilkins.

Kee, W., Middaugh, S., & Pawlick, K. (1996). Persisitent pain in the older patient: Evaluation and treatment. In R. Gatchel & D. Turk (Eds.), *Psychological approaches to pain management* (pp. 371–402). New York: Guilford Press.

Keefe, F., Beaupre, P., Weiner, D., & Siegler, I. (1996). Pain in older adults: A cognitive behavioral perspective. In B. R. Ferrell & B. F. Ferrell (Eds.), *Pain in the elderly* (pp. 11–20). Seattle, WA: IASP Press.

Kramlinger, K., Swanson, D., & Maruta, T. (1983). Are patients with chronic pain depressed? *American Journal of Psychiatry, 140,* 747–749.

Lipton, R., Pfeffer, D., Newman, I., & Solomon, S. (1993). Headaches in the elderly. *Journal Pain & Symptom Management, 8,* 87–97.

Marbach, J., Lennon, M., & Dohrenwend, B. (1988). Candidate risk-factor for temporomandibular pain and dysfunction syndrome: Psychosocial, health behavior, physical illness and injury. *Pain, 34,* 139–151.

Melding, P. (1995). Psychiatric aspects of chronic pain in the elderly. In R. Roy (Ed.), *Chronic pain in old age: An integrated biopsychosocial approach* (pp. 190–210). Toronto: University of Toronto Press.

Middaugh, S., Woods, E., Kee, W., Harden, R., & Peters, J. (1991). Biofeedback assisted relaxation training for the aging chronic pain patient. *Biofeedback and Self-Regulation, 16,* 362–377.

Morris, C., & Goli, V. (1994). The physiology and biomedical aspects of chronic pain in later life. In K. Roberto (Ed.), *Older women with chronic pain* (pp. 9–24). New York: Haworth Press.

Moss, M., Lawton, M., & Glicksman, A. (1991). The role of pain in the last year of life in the older persons. *Journal of Gerontology, 42*, 51–57.

Newman, L., Lipton, R., & Solomon, S. (1991). The hypnic headache syndrome. In F. C. Rose (Ed.), *New advances in headache research* (2nd ed.). London: Smith-Gordon.

Oosterhuis, W. (1984). Early screening of pain to prevent it from becoming intractable. *Pain, 20*, 193–200.

Parmelee, P. A., Katz, I. R., & Lawton, M. P. (1991). The relation of pain to depression among institutionalized aged. *Journal of Gerontology: Psychological Sciences, 46*(1), P15–P21.

Parmelee, P. A., Katz, I. R., & Lawton, M. P. (1989). Depression among institutionalized aged: Assessment and prevalence estimation. *Journal of Gerontology: Medical Sciences, 44*, M22–M29.

Peterson, C., & Seligman, M. E. P. (1984). Causal explanations as a risk factor for depression: Theory and evidence. *Psychological Review, 91*, 347–374.

Pfeiffer, E. (1975). A short portable mental state questionnaire for the assessment of organic brain deficit in elderly patients. *Journal of the American Geriatric Society, 23*, 433–441.

Popp, B., & Portnoy, R. (1996). Management of chronic pain in the elderly: Pharmacology of opioids and other analgesic drugs. In B. R. Ferrell & B. S. Ferrell (Eds.), *Pain in the elderly* (pp. 21–34). Seattle, WA: IASP Press.

Pribor, E., Smith, D., & Yutzy, S. (1994). Somatization disorders in elderly patients. *American Journal of Geriatric Psychiatry, 2*, 109–117.

Puder, R. (1988). Age analyses of cognitive-behavioral group therapy for chronic pain outpatients. *Psychology and Aging, 3*, 204–207.

Raskin, M. (1988). *Headache* (2nd ed.). New York: Churchill-Livingstone.

Richardson, J. (1986). Perspectives on compliance with drug regimens among the elderly. *Journal of Compliance in Health Care, 1*, 33–46.

Robertson, D., & George, F. (1990). Treatment of post herpetic neuralgia in the elderly. *British Medical Bulletin, 46*, 113–123.

Roll, M., & Theorell, T. (1987). Acute chest pain without obvious organic cause before age 40: Personality and recent life events. *Journal of Psychosomatic Research, 31*, 215–221.

Rowe, J. W., & Besdine, R. W. (Eds.). (1982). *Health and disease in old age*. Boston: Little, Brown.

Roy, R., Thomas, M., & Matas, M. (1984). Chronic pain and clinical depression: A review. *Comprehensive Psychiatry, 25*(1), 96–105.

Roy, R., & Thomas, M. (1986). A survey of chronic pain in an elderly population. *Canadian Family Physicians, 31*, 513–516.

Roy, R., & Thomas, M. (1988). Pain, depression and illness behavior in a group of community based elderly persons (part 2). *The Clinical Journal of Pain, 3*, 207–211.

Roy, R., Thomas, M., & Berger, S. (1990). A comparative study of Canadian non-clinical and British pain clinic subjects. *The Clinical Journal of Pain, 3*, 213–222.

Roy, R., Thomas, M., & Cook, A. (1996). Social context of elderly chronic pain patients. In B. R. Ferrell & B. S. Ferrell (Eds.), *Pain in the elderly* (pp. 111–118). Seattle, WA: IASP Press.

Sandin, K. (1993). Specialized pain treatment for geriatric patients. *The Clinical Journal of Pain, 9*, 60.

Smith, T., Follick, M., & Ahern, D. (1985). Life events and psychological disturbance in chronic low back pain. *British Journal of Clinical Psychology, 24*, 207–208.

Solomon, G., Kunkel, R., & Frame, J. (1990). Demographics of headache in elderly patients. *Headache, 30*, 273–276.

Sorkin, B., & Turk, D. (1995). Pain management in the elderly. In R. Roy (Ed.), *Chronic pain in old age: A biopsychosocial perspective*. Toronto: University of Toronto Press.

Sorkin, B., Rudy, T., Hanlon, R., Turk, D., & Steig, R. (1990). Chronic pain in old and young patients: Differences appear less important than similarities. *Journal of Gerontology, 45*, 64–68.

Stelian, J., Gil, I., Habot, B., Rosenthal, M., et al. (1992). Improvement of pain and disability in elderly patients with degenerative arthritis of the knee treated with narrow band light therapy. *Journal of Geriatric Society, 40,* 23–26.

Sternbach, R. (1986). Survey of pain in the United States: The Nuprin pain report. *The Clinical Journal of Pain, 2,* 49–53.

Stewart, W., Lipton, R., Celentano, D., & Reed, M. (1992). Prevalence of migraine headache in the United States. *Journal of American Medical Association, 267,* 64–69.

Thomas, M., & Roy, R. (1988). Age and pain: A comparative study of younger vs. older elderly persons. *Journal of Pain Management Practice, 4,* 174–179.

Thomas, M., & Roy, R. (1988). Age and pain: A comparative study of younger and older elderly. *Pain Management, 1,* 174–179.

Turk, D., Kerns, R., & Rosneberg, R. (1992). Effects of marital interaction on chronic pain and disability: Examining the down side of social support. *Rehabilitation Psychology, 37,* 259–274.

Turnbull, J. M. (1989). Anxiety and physical illness in the elderly. Symposium: Anxiety: The silent partner. *Journal of Clinical Psychiatry, 50*(Suppl. 11), 40–45.

Valkenberg, H. (1988). Epidemiologic considerations of the geriatric population. *Gerontology, 34*(Suppl.), 2–10.

Van Korff, M., Dworkin, S., le Resche, L., & Kruger, A. (1988). An epidemiologic comparison of pain complaints. *Pain, 32,* 173–183.

Vanaranta, H., Sachs, B., Ohnmeiss, M., & April, C. (1989). Pain provocation and disc denegation by age. *Spine, 14,* 420–423.

Waddell, G. (1987). A new clinical model for the treatment of low-back pain. *Spine, 12,* 632–644.

Ward, N., & Clough, C. (1995). Headache and headpain. *Reviews in Clinical Gerontology, 5,* 143–153.

Warren, R., & O'Brien, S. (1989). Shoulder pain in the geriatric patient: Approaches to senior care. *Orthopedic Review, 18,* 129–135.

Weickgenant, A., Slater, M., Patterson, T., Atkinson, J., et al. (1993). Coping activities in chronic low-back pain: Relationship with depression. *Pain, 53,* 95–103.

Yesavage, J., Brink, T., Rose, T., Lum, O., et al. (1983). Development and validation of a geriatric depression screening scale: A preliminary report. *Journal of Psychiatric Research, 17,* 37–39.

Chapter 26

Sickle Cell Disease

Jennifer J. Wilson Schaeffer
University of Kentucky

Karen M. Gil
Laura S. Porter
University of North Carolina at Chapel Hill

Sickle cell disease (SCD) is an inherited disorder affecting 1 in 500 African Americans, in which the most common complication is variable and unpredictable episodic pain (Weisman & Schechter, 1992). Since the 1980s, there have been exciting advances made in the medical management and prevention of these painful episodes. Recent studies have demonstrated that the antimetabolite medication, hydroxyurea, is effective in reducing painful episodes in adults and children (Charache et al., 1995; Scott, Hillery, Brown, Misiewicz, & Labotka, 1996). In addition, medical centers are exploring the use of bone marrow transplant to treat patients with SCD who have multiple medical complications (Walters et al., 1996). Despite these improvements, there is still no cure for SCD. Children and adults with SCD cope with both acute and chronic complications including painful episodes.

The purpose of this chapter is to present a biopsychosocial perspective on coping with SCD pain. We first describe the clinical features of SCD and outline the current medical approaches to SCD pain. Second, we discuss the relevant psychosocial factors. In the third and fourth sections, we review the research on the assessment and the psychological and cognitive-behavioral treatment of SCD pain. In these two final sections, suggestions for clinical practice are highlighted.

CLINICAL FEATURES

SCD is characterized by the production of primarily hemogloblin S (HbS), which is structurally different from normal hemoglobin (HbA) by the substitution of a single amino acid in the beta chain of the molecule. Because of this amino acid substitution, the solubility of deoxygenated HbS within the red blood cell is altered. This alteration subsequently leads to the sickling of the red blood cell (Vichinsky & Lubin, 1980). SCD includes sickle cell anemia (Hb SS), sickle hemoglobin SC disease (Hb SC), and sickle beta-thalassemia (Rucknagel, 1974). Hb SS occurs when both inherited beta globin genes have the sickle mutation. Sickle beta-thalassemia and Hb SC occur when a sickle beta globin gene is inherited from one parent and another abnormal beta globin gene is inherited from the other parent. There are data that suggest that Hb SS is associated with more severe pain than Hb SC or sickle beta-thalassemia (Platt et al., 1991).

The sickling of red blood cells leads to two common pathophysiologic characteristics of SCD—hemolytic anemia and vascular occlusion (Holbrook & Phillips, 1994). Because of the sickling, the red blood cells are fragile, which leads to destruction of the cells (hemolysis) and subsequently produces anemia. Sickled cells are sticky and rigid and obstruct blood flow when they stick to the lining of small blood vessels. This vaso-occlusion can result in acute and chronic problems. Patients with SCD may experience acute and chronic symptoms affecting multiple organ systems (see Table 26.1). Many of these symptoms are progressive in nature and some can lead to end organ system failure as the patient ages. Mortality rates for patients with SCD peak during two periods, the first 5 years of life due to infections and between ages 20 and 24 because of multiple organ system failure (Serjeant, 1985).

The most common and disabling complication of SCD is recurrent and unpredictable episodes of severe pain (Shapiro & Ballas, 1994). Pain is often located in the abdomen, joints, low back, knees, and extremities and is believed to be due to ischemic tissue injury secondary to the vascular occlusion. The frequency, severity, and intensity of painful episodes is variable. Some individuals experience one or two episodes a month, whereas others only have one a year (Shapiro & Ballas, 1994). The duration of the painful episodes can last from a few hours to several weeks, although the average length is about 4 to 6 days (Platt et al., 1991; Shapiro & Ballas, 1994).

Although medical researchers have studied hemoglobin parameters such as the concentration of irreversible sickled cells, high density red cells, elevations in plasma levels of fibrinogen, fetal hemoglobin levels, and high hematocrit levels (Fabry, Benjamin, Lawrence, & Nagel, 1984; Westerman & Bacus, 1983; Wrath & Rucknagel, 1984), there is no agreed on objective, physiological indicator of painful episodes. Health care professionals remain dependent on patients to determine the severity and course of the SCD painful episode.

TABLE 26.1
Complications of Sickle Cell Disease

Complications	Symptoms	Probable Cause (if known)	Typical Treatments
Acute Problems			
Acute chest syndrome	Chest pain, fever, may result in hypoxemia	Adults: Sickling in pulmonary microvascular Children: Bacterial or viral infection	Hospitalization to treat pain, infection, and hypoxemia strokes
Priapism	Acute or chronic painful or nonpainful enlargement of penis	Not well understood	Acute priapism: Frequent emptying of bladder, taking warm baths, increasing hydration, and exercising. If persists for 3 hours, emergency room visit
Strokes	Subtle to extreme neurological deficits	Adults: Subarachnoid and intracerebral hemorrhages Children: Cerebral infarction	Medical treatment may involve ventilation and medications to decrease swelling of the cerebrum. Blood transfusion may be used to prevent reoccurrence

(Continued)

TABLE 26.1
(Continued)

Complications	Symptoms	Probable Cause (if known)	Typical Treatments
Chronic Problems			
Kidney dysfunction	Children: Kidneys have difficulty concentrating urine, leading to greater urine output (hyposthenuria), which leads to increased fluid intake Adults: Chronic asymptomatic and symptomatic urinary tract infections Chronic renal failure	Sickling in kidney Renal failure: Increase macroscopic papillary necrosis, interstitial nephritis, decreased renal flow, and hypertension	Children: Treat hyposthenuria with blood transfusion. After age 15 condition becomes irreversible Adults: Renal failure: Conservative treatment such as medication and low protein diet. Dialyses may become necessary if condition persists
Leg ulcers	Elevated, crusting sores usually on lower third of leg, extremely painful	More likely to occur in patients with lower steady-state hemoglobin, and lower fetal hemoglobin	Active involvement of patient in washing, dressing, and care. If ulcer persists, blood transfusion or skin grafts may be used
Aseptic necrosis	Femoral Head: Pain in the buttocks or groin Shoulder: Pain in the shoulder	Sickling	Avoid weight-bearing activities, use braces, use local heat and analgesics Patients: Severe pain associated with disability may be candidates for surgery; yearly eye exams
Sickle retinopathy	Vitreous hemorrhage, retinal detachment, blindness		

Note. Information from Brown, Armstrong, and Eckman (1993); Charache, Lubin, and Reid (1992); and Holbrook and Phillips (1994).

MEDICAL MANAGEMENT

Although there is still no universal therapy for SCD, recent advances in biomedical treatment of SCD have led to more effective prevention and treatment of many of these complications. Patients with SCD survive longer than they did in the past (Platt et al., 1994). Blood transfusion regimens, which are used in acute circumstances such as severe anemia, sepsis, pneumonia, stroke, preparation for surgery, and pregnancy, lead to a reduction in total hospitalization rate, hospitalization for painful episodes, bacterial infection, and cases of acute chest syndrome (Styles & Vichinsky, 1994). The antimetabolite medication, hydroxyurea, is effective in reducing report of pain and the incidence of acute chest syndrome in adults with SCD (Charache et al., 1995). Moreover, preliminary work examining the effects of hydroxyurea on children found that hydroxyurea led to improvement on hematologic measures and demonstrated a trend toward reduced hospitalization with acceptable toxic effects. Double blind controlled studies are presently being conducted (Scott et al., 1996). Finally, multicenter trials are assessing the efficacy of bone marrow transplant for patients with a history of stroke, recurrent acute chest syndrome, and recurrent painful episodes. A recent study found that the survival rate at 4 years of 22 children who received bone marrow transplant was 91% and the event-free rate was 73% (Walters et al., 1996).

Although these advances are exciting, there are limitations to these treatments. For example, not all patients with SCD respond to hydroxyurea and the long-term side effects of this medication are not yet well understood. Furthermore, bone marrow transplant is associated with many risks. Graft versus host disease is a known complication and the long-term outcome of bone marrow transplantation is not yet known.

The primary biomedical treatment of SCD pain involves the active involvement of the patient in managing painful episodes. This treatment consists of encouraging preventative behaviors such as increasing fluid intake and avoiding activities that lead to deoxygenation of the blood. Individuals with SCD are encouraged to maintain a daily intake of 4 to 6 quarts of fluid (Charache et al., 1992). When painful episodes do occur, treatment at home with increased hydration (6 to 8 quarts of fluid) and over-the-counter analgesic medication such as acetaminophen and ibuprofen are occasionally successful (Charache et al., 1992). For moderate pain, oral administration of narcotics such as Demerol or Percodan may be needed. Thus, the patient plays a very active role in the prevention (i.e., maintaining hydration, avoiding deoxygenating activities) and treatment (increasing hydration, taking pain medication) of painful episodes.

Pain of severe intensity usually requires emergency room treatment or hospitalization for intravenous fluid and aggressive intramuscular or intravenous administration of narcotics such as Morphine, Demerol, or Dilaudid (Charache et al., 1992). Narcotic medication should be administered on a fixed-time schedule to maintain a steady serum drug level (Charache et al., 1992). Unfortunately, health care professionals often under use narcotic medication when treating an SCD painful episode due to fear of patient addiction (Charache et al., 1992). During an emergency room visit, the patient receives hydration and medication to break the painful episode (Rosse, 1983). Hospitalization is occasionally needed for severe painful episodes. Hospitalization involves continual hydration and a gradual tapering off of medications as the painful episode subsides (Rosse, 1983).

In summary, SCD is a chronic and unpredictable illness. A primary complication of SCD is pain due to vaso-occlusion of the blood vessels by sickled cells. Patients with SCD may also experience pain secondary to other medical complications of SCD such as aseptic necrosis, priapism, leg ulcers, and acute chest syndrome. Although advances in treatment have been made, the primary medical treatment for patients with SCD includes their active involvement in the prevention of sickled episodes as well as managing pain once it occurs. Thus, an understanding of both the impact of SCD on psychological functioning as well as how psychological factors influence illness processes is essential in the effective treatment of individuals with SCD.

RELEVANT PSYCHOLOGICAL FACTORS

Psychological Adjustment in Children

Since the late 1980s, increasing attention has been given to the issue of psychological adjustment of children with SCD (Brown, Buchanan, et al., 1993; Brown, Kaslow, et al., 1993; Hurtig, Koepke, & Park, 1989; Hurtig & White, 1986; Thompson, Gil, Burbach, Keith, & Kinney, 1993). Researchers have found that children and adolescents with SCD are at risk for emotional and behavioral problems (Hurtig & Park, 1989), poor psychological adjustment (Thompson et al., 1993), and disturbances in body image and sexuality (Morgan & Jackson, 1986). Evidence suggests that poor psychological adjustment is not directly related to illness severity (Hurtig et al., 1989; Thompson et al., 1993). Socioeconomic status (SES), gender, age, coping skills, and family functioning have been identified as factors that may mediate the relation between psychological adjustment and illness severity (Hurtig et al., 1989; Thompson et al., 1993).

The effect of SCD on the psychological adjustment of the developing child can perhaps be seen most clearly when the child enters school. School-aged children with SCD have more academic difficulties than their siblings and healthy peers (Brown, Buchanan, et al., 1993; Treiber, Mabe, & Wilson, 1987). Academic difficulties seem to be specific deficits in attention and concentration and reading decoding (Brown, Buchanan, et al., 1993). These significant, yet subtle neurological deficits may be secondary to chronic hypoxemia of the brain at an early age (Brown, Buchanan, et al., 1993). SES and frequent school absences have been identified as possible contributors to poor academic functioning (Brown, Buchanan, et al., 1993; Morgan & Jackson, 1986).

Age has been identified as a factor associated with poor academic performance and adaptive functioning. Older school-aged children have lower reading and spelling achievement scores; are more likely to require additional help for reading or math; and display impaired visual motor, reading, and attention skills when compared to younger children with SCD. However, these findings are not associated with disease severity, rather they are associated with SES, maternal education, and gender of the child (with boys having more problems; Fowler et al., 1988; Hurtig et al., 1989). In addition, as children with SCD age they are at more risk for adjustment problems, especially if they are boys (Brown, Kaslow, et al., 1993; Hurtig et al., 1989).

As Morgan and Jackson (1986) noted, it is probably not surprising that more academic and behavioral problems occur in adolescents with SCD. Adolescence is a difficult time in which forming peer relationships and the developmental task of identity formation is heavily influenced by a sense of physical and sexual competence. The secondary effects of SCD, that is, small stature, delayed puberty, and limited physical activities, may interfere with both peer relationships and identity formation, and may be more damaging to boys than girls (Hurtig et al., 1989). Frequent medical complications may impede the adolescent in becoming independent and prevent the parents from encouraging independence (Morgan & Jackson, 1986).

Family functioning has received much attention as a factor that may contribute to the overall adjustment of children with SCD (Midence, McManus, Fuggle, & Davies, 1996; Thompson et al., 1993). Several studies have found that poor maternal adjustment is associated with poor adjustment in children with SCD (Brown, Kaslow, et al., 1993; Midence et al., 1996; Thompson et al., 1993). Specifically, poor maternal adjustment was associated with the use of palliative coping methods and high levels of daily stress in children with SCD. A factor associated with poor maternal adjustment is low levels of social support (Hurtig, 1994; Thompson et al., 1993). Interestingly, although anecdotal evidence suggests that siblings of children with SCD are at risk for adjustment difficulties, a recent study examining peer relationships of siblings found no differences between the siblings and peers who were matched for age (Noll et al., 1995).

Psychological Adjustment in Adults

Examination of psychosocial problems in adults with SCD have shown that many are at risk for poor psychological adjustment (Midence & Elander, 1996; Thompson, Gil, Abrams, & Phillips, 1992; Vichinsky, Johnson, & Lubin, 1982), depression (Belgrave & Molock, 1991), employment difficulties (Barrett et al., 1988), and psychiatric morbidity (Damlouji, Kevess-Cohen, Charache, Georgopoulos, & Folstein, 1982). As many as 50% of adults with SCD meet criteria for depression, anxiety, or other psychological disturbances (Belgrave & Molock, 1991; Thompson et al., 1992). However, some individuals with SCD display good adjustment (Thompson et al., 1992). Furthermore, recent studies suggest there is considerable variability in adjustment over a 20-month period (Thompson, Gil, Abrams, & Phillips, 1996).

Psychological maladjustment exhibited through addiction to narcotics is often a concern of health care professionals. Surveys of health care professionals find that medical residents have perhaps an unwarranted fear about the risk of narcotic addiction in patients with SCD (Vichinsky et al., 1982). However, most health care professionals who regularly treat patients with SCD find that narcotic addiction is uncommon (Rosse, 1983). A review of studies assessing addiction in patients with SCD being treated with narcotic medications found that rates of addiction varied from 0 of 610 patients to 7 of 101 (Elander & Midence, 1996). These rates are low considering the frequency of use of narcotic medication in treating SCD. Addiction to narcotics is usually related to psychological and social factors such as anxiety (Charache et al., 1992). Some patients may become overly concerned with having available narcotics for the next painful episode. However, even when addiction is a problem for patients with SCD it is important to remember that they still experience painful episodes that need to receive adequate treatment (Charache et al., 1992).

Recent efforts have been directed toward identifying processes that are associated with good and poor adjustment to SCD (Gil, Abrams, Phillips, & Keefe, 1989; Midence & Elander, 1996; Thompson et al., 1992, Thompson et al., 1996). Originally, it was assumed that adults with more severe disease would display more significant psychological disturbances. However, research has determined that factors such as family support, general coping strategies as well as pain coping, daily stressors, and psychological factors are more predictive of poor psychological adjustment than are disease severity variables (Thompson et al., 1992). In fact, as with children, adults with good psychological adjustment do not differ from individuals with poor psychological adjustment on measures of disease severity such as phenotype of SCD, number of complications, and pain report. Moreover, these disease severity variables only account for a small portion of the variance in psychological adjustment (Thompson et al., 1992).

Thompson and colleagues (1992, 1996) used a transactional stress and coping model to elucidate factors that contribute to overall psychological adjustment in adults and children with SCD. In this model, SCD is seen as a potential stressor to which the individual and the family have to adapt. Psychological adjustment is thought to be influenced by illness factors (e.g., phenotype of SCD, complications, frequency of painful episodes), demographic factors (gender, age, SES), and adaptational processes. This model helps focus on the adaptational processes that might affect psychological functioning over and above disease severity and demographic factors. The adaptational processes include cognitive processes (appraisal of stress, daily hassles, and illness tasks), coping methods (palliative, adaptive, and pain coping strategies), and family functioning (supportive, conflicted, controlling; Thompson et al., 1992, 1996). Good psychological adjustment is associated with lower levels of perceived daily stress and stress related to SCD illness tasks, higher efficacy expectations, less reliance on palliative coping, lower report of negative thinking and illness-focused pain coping strategies, and families characterized by high levels of support and low levels of conflict and control (Thompson et al., 1992). Stability of good adjustment over a 20-month period is associated with lower levels of daily and illness-related stress, less reliance on palliative means of coping with stress, and less reliance on negative thinking and illness-focused pain coping strategies (Thompson et al., 1996).

Taken together, the evidence suggests that poor psychological adjustment cannot be explained by illness severity alone. In children demographic factors such as SES, age, and gender influence psychological adjustment over and above disease severity (Hurtig et al., 1989; Thompson et al., 1993). In both adults and children, lower levels of daily and illness-related stress as well as less reliance on negative thoughts were related to good psychological adjustment. In terms of the influence of family on psychological adjustment, in children with SCD psychological adjustment is related to maternal adjustment (Brown, Buchanan, et al., 1993; Midence et al., 1996; Thomp-son et al., 1993). Less research has been done on the influence of family variables on the psychological adjustment of adults with SCD.

Demographic and Psychological Factors Related to SCD Pain

Recognition that pain severity and adjustment varies widely across people has led some researchers to focus specifically on the demographic and psychological factors that might predict or influence pain frequency, severity, and adjustment.

Demographic Variables. Both gender and age are related to the frequency of SCD painful episodes. Studies have demonstrated that the frequency of painful episodes increases as individuals age (from 0 to 30) and decreases thereafter (Platt et al., 1991). Thus, adolescents have longer painful episodes than younger children (Gil, Williams, Thompson, & Kinney, 1991) and younger adults (younger than 35) report more severe pain (Gil et al., 1989) and have more frequent emergency room visits for painful episodes than older adults (Belgrave & Molock, 1991; Gil et al., 1989). Moreover, young men (20–35 years old) have more frequent clinic visits and hospitalizations for painful episodes than same-age females (Platt et al., 1991; Powars, Chan, & Schroeder, 1990). It is not clear whether there are age-related physiological mechanisms for more severe disease expression, whether the psychological demands of this age period lead to less effective coping, or whether with age comes more effective coping strategies to deal with pain (Gil et al., 1989).

The influence of SES on frequency of painful episodes has been demonstrated in Nigeria. Individuals who ranked at a lower SES had more frequent painful episodes than those at a higher SES (Okany & Akinyanju, 1993). However, additional studies on the influence of SES are needed before conclusions can be drawn.

Stress and SCD Pain. Psychological stress may play a role in the onset of painful episodes (Midence & Elander, 1994; Nash, 1994). However, few studies have examined this assumption empirically. A retrospective study on a small sample found that 50% of patients with SCD reported that episodes were preceded by stressful and depressing life events, especially when stressful life events led to feelings of hopelessness, helplessness, and dependency (Nadel & Portadin, 1977). In a prospective longitudinal study, Leavell and Ford (1983) found that adults with SCD who reported more life change as measured by the Schedule of Recent Events life change list at baseline, were more likely to have painful episodes requiring hospitalization at the 6-month follow-up. Thus, although not conclusive, these studies suggest that stress may lead to an increased likelihood of painful episodes.

Cognitive Coping Strategies and Pain. Research has examined how cognitive and behavioral coping strategies impact the frequency, duration, and severity of painful episodes as well as psychological adjustment.

A series of studies (Gil et al., 1989; Gil, Abrams, Phillips, & Williams, 1992; Gil et al., 1993; Gil et al., 1991) has demonstrated that cognitive coping strategies and negative thought patterns accounted for significant portions of the variance in pain report in adults and children with SCD even after controlling for frequency of episodes, disease severity variables, and demographics. Specifically, adults who reported more negative thoughts (e.g., catastrophizing) and illness-focused coping (e.g., using only physiological strategies such as increasing fluids and resting) had more severe painful episodes, were less active during painful episodes, had higher levels of psychological distress, and more frequent hospitalizations and emergency room visits (Gil et al., 1989). Although use of active coping (e.g., imagining a pleasant scene) was not associated with less severe pain, it was significantly associated with being more active during painful episodes (Gil et al., 1989).

A 9-month follow-up study of these participants found that adults with SCD who relied on negative thinking and illness-focused strategies during the baseline had greater reductions in housework, work, and social activity; less uptime; and longer hospitalizations during painful episodes. Relying on active coping was not related to psychological adjustment at follow-up. This study found that coping strategies remain fairly stable over time. However, individuals who relied more on negative thinking and illness-focused strategies over the 9-month period showed greater reductions in uptime (i.e., the time they spent out of a reclining position) during painful episodes (Gil et al., 1992).

Similar studies have been conducted with children. Although coping strategies did not predict pain intensity, duration, or frequency in children with SCD, their use was significantly related to how well children adjusted to their painful episodes. A cross-sectional study found that children who relied on illness-focused coping had more frequent emergency room visits and were less active during painful episodes. Moreover, children who relied on negative thoughts were less active during painful episodes and more psychologically distressed as rated by their parents. Children who relied on active cognitive and behavioral coping strategies such as diverting attention, calming self-statements, and reinterpreting pain sensations had less frequent emergency room visits and were more active during painful episodes (Gil et al., 1991). A 9-month follow-up of these children demonstrated that those who relied on active cognitive and behavioral coping strategies were more active in school, household, and social areas during painful episodes, whereas those who relied on illness-focused strategies had more frequent health care contacts. Finally, the study demonstrated that increases in use of negative thinking were associated with an increase in health care contacts in children (Gil et al., 1993).

In an attempt to assess how negative thoughts might influence pain and pain report, Gil and her colleagues (1995) assessed the relation of negative thoughts to the likelihood of reporting pain (i.e., report criterion) and the ability to discriminate different levels of painful stimulation (i.e., sensory discrimination) using laboratory pain induction (a finger pressure task) and sensory decision theory analyses. In this study, adults with SCD completed the Inventory of Negative Thoughts in Response to Pain (INTRP), the laboratory pain-induction task, and clinical measures of pain.

The study demonstrated that the laboratory pain was somewhat similar in quality to SCD pain and to the magnitude of mild clinical pain. Moreover, adults with SCD who reported frequent negative thoughts were more likely to report pain in response to painful stimulation, even very slight stimulation. These results suggest that report of more severe pain may be associated with negative thoughts even during mild painful stimulation (Gil et al., 1995).

Similar results have been found using sensory decision theory and laboratory pain stimulation in children and adolescents with SCD. Children who reported more use of active cognitive and behavioral strategies on the Coping Strategies Questionnaire (CSQ; Gil et al., 1991) reported less pain (higher report criterion) in response to laboratory-induced stimulation (Gil et al., 1997). In other words, children who relied on active measures of coping were more stoic in response to laboratory pain stimulation. No association was found for frequency of negative thoughts and report criterion (Gil et al., 1997).

Taken together, these studies suggest children who relied on active coping strategies and adults who reported less frequent negative thoughts reported less pain to noxious stimulation in a laboratory pain procedure (Gil et al., 1997). Adults who reported more frequent negative thoughts had more severe SCD painful episodes, were less active during these episodes, and had more frequent emergency room and hospital admissions (Gil et al., 1991).

Given the involvement of psychological and cognitive factors in the frequency, severity, and duration of painful episodes, the evaluation of these factors through the use of the aforementioned assessments (INTRP, CSQ) is often useful when conceptualizing a case and formulating a treatment plan for a patient with SCD. The following two sections of this chapter focus more specifically on the issues of assessment and treatment of SCD pain. First, we focus on methods of assessing SCD pain. The assessments reviewed here can be used in conjunction with assessments of cognitive coping styles to help conceptualize how a patient is managing SCD pain.

ASSESSMENT OF SCD PAIN

There has been increased attention to the assessment of SCD pain in recent years (Gil et al., 1989; Gil, 1994; Gil, Phillips, Abrams, & Williams, 1990; Gil, Phillips, Edens, Martin, & Abrams, 1994; Walco & Dampier, 1990). Specifically, there have been attempts to develop more objective measures of pain perception and report and attempts to assess overt pain behaviors. Little research has been conducted on which method of assessment is more useful. Thus, Table 26.2 presents a brief description of each method of assessing

TABLE 26.2

Summary of Assessments of Pain Used With SCD

Assessment	Description	Usefulness	Citations
Pain Ratings			
Numerical scales	Rate pain on a 0 to 10 scale	Provides estimate of pain level that can be compared to patient's ratings before and after treatment	Gil (1994), Gil et al. (1989), Gil et al. (1992), Walco and Dampier (1990)
Visual Analogue Scales	Rate pain mild, moderate, or severe		
Word Descriptor Scales			
Pain Activity Ratings	• Measure of uptime versus downtime	Views pain as a behavior, provides estimate of how much patient is reducing activity secondary to painful episodes	Gil (1989), Gil et al. (1992), Gil (1994), Gil et al. (1996)
	• Estimate percent of reduction in household, social, and work activities from 0 (none) to 100% (complete)		
Health Care Utilization in Response to Pain	• Estimate number of emergency room visits for pain	Provides estimate of how frequently patient is seeking treatment for painful episodes	Gil et al. (1989), Gil et al. (1992), Gil (1994)
	• Estimate number of hospitalizations for pain		
	• Estimate duration of hospitalizations		
Varni and Thompson body maps	On body chart, patient shades in area of body in which they experience pain	Assesses how consistent patient's pattern of pain is to typical SCD pain	Gil (1994)
Observation of pain behavior	Observe pain behavior such as guarding, bracing, grimacing	Provides indicant of pain that does not rely on patient self-report	Gil et al. (1994)
Laboratory pain-induction methods and sensory decision theory	Lucite edge is applied at a continuous pressure to the finger. Can vary amount of pressure by using different weights	Helps train patient in pain coping skills and assesses patient's response to treatment. Data can be used to assess sensory discrimination (how accurate patient is at distinguishing between different weights) and report criterion (how likely the participant is to report pain)	Gil et al. (1995), Gil et al. (1997)

SCD pain, a description of the usefulness of each assessment, and citations for further information concerning each assessment.

PSYCHOLOGICAL TREATMENT

Studies evaluating the psychological treatment of SCD pain can be grouped into three separate categories: uncontrolled studies, studies evaluating psychological treatment within the context of a multidisciplinary program to manage SCD pain, and controlled outcome studies.

Studies Evaluating One Psychological Treatment

The first intervention studies evaluated the efficacy of teaching behavioral skills such as progressive relaxation, biofeedback, hypnosis, and cognitive strategies to individuals or small samples of adults or children with SCD (Hall, Chiarucci, & Berman, 1992; Thomas, Koshy, Patterson, Dorn, & Thomas, 1984; Zeltzer, Dash, & Holland, 1979). Several case studies examined the use of behavioral techniques thought to provide both psychological and physiological benefits by increasing vaso-dilation (Hall et al., 1992; Zeltzer et al., 1979). Such training led to marked reductions in outpatient visits, hospitalizations, and duration of hospital stays for adults (Zeltzer et al., 1979) and to decreased school absences and medication use in children (Hall et al., 1992).

Small group studies assessing pre- and postcomparisons after treatment have shown positive, yet less dramatic findings. In one study, 15 adults with histories of frequent painful episodes were trained in self-hypnosis, thermal biofeedback, progressive relaxation, and cognitive strategies (Thomas et al., 1984). The results showed a 50% reduction in duration of hospital stay, 38% reduction in emergency room visits, and 31% reduction in number of hospital admissions. Another study assessed pre- and postintervention effects of 12 weekly sessions of electromyographic and thermal biofeedback training for children and adolescents ages 10 to 20 years (Cozzi, Tryon, & Sedlacek, 1987). Significant pre–post reductions were found for anxiety, number of headaches reported, number of days medication was taken, and in pain intensity ratings. A 6-month follow-up assessment revealed that although the patients viewed the technique as effective, there was not a subsequent reduction in hospitalization admissions or emergency room visits.

Studies Evaluating Multidisciplinary Approaches

A second approach to the treatment of SCD pain involves multidisciplinary programs. A multidisciplinary approach to SCD pain that includes medical treatment plus a family conference, individual and family counseling, and patient education is described by Vavasseur (1977). However, no data on the effectiveness of the program is presented. Vichinsky et al. (1982) described a comprehensive program with fixed-time delivery of medication, use of positive reinforcement and extinction to shape appropriate pain-coping behavior, and counseling to patients and their families. Data from 10 patients who participated in the program demonstrate a decrease in the number of emergency room visits and hospital admissions.

Controlled Outcome Studies

Recently, controlled outcome studies have been conducted to evaluate the effectiveness of training in coping skills strategies on SCD pain (Gil et al., 1996; Gil et al., 1997). In a randomly assigned controlled outcome study, Gil et al. (1996) compared adults with SCD who participated in three, 45-minute, weekly training sessions in coping skills (e.g., breathing relaxation, counting backward slowly, pleasant imagery, reinterpretation of painful sensation, and focus on physical surroundings) to adults who participated in three, 45-minute, weekly disease education sessions. Pain sensitivity, as measured by response to laboratory pain stimulation (described earlier in this chapter), use of cognitive coping strategies, clinical pain, and pain behaviors were measured at pre- and posttesting. The results indicated that adults who received training in coping skills demonstrated an increase in positive coping attempts, a decrease in negative thoughts, and a reduction in tendency to report pain during laboratory pain stimulation. There were no significant effects on clinical outcome measures (SCD pain frequency, duration, and severity and health care use variables; Gil et al., 1996). This lack of effect may be due to the short period between pre- and posttesting (1 month).

A similar study has been conducted with children and adolescents (Gil et al., 1997). Children and adolescents with SCD were randomly assigned to either two, 45-minute training sessions in coping skills (breathing relaxation and counting, pleasant imagery, and focus on physical surroundings) or a standard care control group (standard medical care). Similar to the adult study, sensory decision theory was used to determine report criterion and sensory discrimination from children's response to laboratory pain stimulation. The participants in the coping skills condition displayed significantly lower levels of negative thinking compared to their peers in the standard care control condition. Moreover, children and adolescents in the coping skills treatment were less likely to report pain during low levels of painful stimulation at posttesting compared to the control participants. These results suggest that brief training in coping skills may reduce reliance on negative thinking and reduce report of pain to low levels of painful stimulation in children.

Taken together, these studies suggest that psychological treatment involving training in behavioral strategies such as relaxation, biofeedback, hypnosis, and positive reinforcement and extinction may be effective in helping both children and adults cope with SCD. Psychological intervention led to decreases in pain report, reduction of medication usage, and decreases in emergency room visits and hospital admissions.

CONCLUSIONS

SCD is an inherited chronic illness of genetic origin and as such, people who inherit the two recessive genes from their parents will have the disease from birth. Thus, across the life span, psychological factors interact with biomedical factors in determining adjustment to the illness. It is only recently that behavioral scientists have begun to study the psychosocial and behavioral factors that contribute to the course of the disease and its effective management. In particular, researchers have recently made major contributions to the understanding of the complexities of SCD pain and its management.

Empirical data indicate that individuals with SCD are at risk for poor psychological adjustment and that this risk is accounted for by factors other than illness severity. Psychological factors, such as stress, coping strategies, and family support, have been identified as significant predictors of overall adjustment to SCD and to the report of pain in particular. Good psychological adjustment is associated with lower levels of daily stress and illness-related stress, less reliance on palliative means of coping, and less reliance on negative thinking (Thompson et al., 1996). On the other hand, depression and other psychological problems are associated with high levels of daily stress, passive coping strategies, and conflict in the family. Patients who take an active approach to pain management participate in more vocational and recreational activities and are often able to manage pain effectively at home; whereas those who are more passive and engage in negative thinking have higher pain ratings and more frequent health care use. Clearly, an assessment of daily stress and illness-related stress levels, type of coping strategies, and family support would be useful in treating patients who are having problems managing their disease or exhibiting poor psychological adjustment.

REFERENCES

Barrett, D. H., Wisotzek, I. E., Abel, G. G., Rouleau, J. L., Platt, A. F., Pollard, W. E., & Eckman, J. R. (1988). Assessment of psychosocial functioning of patients with sickle cell disease. *Southern Medical Journal, 81*, 745–750.

Belgrave, F. Z., & Molock, S. D. (1991). The role of depression in hospital admissions and emergency treatment of patients with sickle cell disease. *Journal of the National Medical Association, 83*, 771–781.

Brown, R. T., Armstrong, F. D., & Eckman, J. R. (1993). Neurocognitive aspects of pediatric sickle cell disease. *Journal of Learning Disabilities, 26,* 33–45.

Brown, R. T., Buchanan, I., Doepke, K., Eckman, J. R., Baldwin, K., Goonan, B., & Schoenherr, S. (1993). Cognitive and academic functioning in children with sickle-cell disease. *Journal of Clinical Child Psychology, 22,* 207–218.

Brown, R. T., Kaslow, N. J., Doepke, K., Buchanan, I., Eckman, J., Baldwin, K., & Goonan, B. (1993). Psychosocial and family functioning in children with sickle cell syndromes and their mothers. *Journal of American Academy of Child and Adolescent Psychiatry, 32,* 545–553.

Charache, S., Lubin, B., & Reid, C. D. (1992). *Management and therapy of sickle cell disease* (NIH Pub. No. 92-2117). Washington, DC: U.S. Government Printing Office.

Charache, S., Terrin, M. L., Moore, R. D., Dover, G. J. Barton, F. B., Eckert, S. V., McMahon, R. P., & Bonds, D. R. (1995). Effect of hydroxyruea on the frequency of painful crises in sickle cell anemia. Investigators of the Multicenter Study of Hydroxyurea in Sickle Cell Anemia. *The New England Journal of Medicine, 332,* 1317–1322.

Cozzi, L., Tryon, W. W., & Sedlacek, K. (1987). The effectiveness of biofeedback-assisted relaxation in modifying sickle cell crises. *Biofeedback and Self-Regulation, 12,* 51–61.

Damlouji, N. F., Kevess-Cohen, R., Charache, S., Georgopoulos, A., & Folstein, M. F. (1982). Social disability and psychiatric morbidity in sickle cell anemia and diabetes patients. *Psychosomatics, 23,* 925–931.

Elander, J., & Midence, K. (1996). A review about factors affecting quality of pain management in sickle cell disease. *The Clinical Journal of Pain, 12,* 180–193.

Fabry, M. E., Benjamin, L., Lawrence, C., & Nagel, R. L. (1984). An objective sign in painful crisis in sickle cell anemia: The concomitant reduction of high density red cells. *Blood, 64,* 559–563.

Forgione, A. G., & Barber, T. X. (1971). A strain gauge pain stimulator. *Psychophysiology, 8,* 102–106.

Fowler, M. G., Whitt, J. K., Lallinger, R. R., Nash, K. B., Atkinson, S., Wells, R. J., & McMillan, C. (1988). Neuropsychologic and academic functioning of children with sickle cell anemia. *Developmental and Behavioral Pediatrics, 9,* 213–230.

Gil, K. M. (1994). Psychosocial aspects of sickle cell disease. *Journal of Health and Social Policy, 5,* 19–38.

Gil, K. M., Abrams, M. R., Phillips, G., & Keefe, F. J. (1989). Sickle cell disease pain: Relation of coping strategies to adjustment. *Journal of Consulting and Clinical Psychology, 57,* 725–731.

Gil, K. M., Abrams, M. R., Phillips, G., & Williams, D. A. (1992). Sickle cell disease: 2. Predicting health care use and activity level at 9-month follow-up. *Journal of Consulting and Clinical Psychology, 60,* 267–273.

Gil, K. M., Edens, J. L., Wilson, J. J., Raezer, L. B., Kinney, T. R., Schultz, W. H., & Daeschner, C. (1997). Coping strategies and laboratory pain in children with sickle cell disease. *Annals of Behavioral Medicine, 19,* 1–8.

Gil, K. M., Phillips, G., Abrams, M. R., & Williams, D. A. (1990). Pain drawing and sickle cell disease pain. *The Clinical Journal of Pain, 6,* 105–109.

Gil, K. M., Phillips, G., Edens, J., Martin, N. J., & Abrams, M. (1994). Observation of pain behaviors during episodes of sickle cell disease pain. *The Clinical Journal of Pain, 10,* 128–132.

Gil, K. M., Phillips, G., Webster, D. A., Martin, N. J., Abrams, M., Grant M., Clark, W. C., & Janal, M. N. (1995). Experimental pain sensitivity and reports of negative thoughts in adults with sickle cell disease. *Behavior Therapy, 26,* 273–294.

Gil, K. M., Thompson, R. J., Keith, B. R., Tota-Faucette, M., Noll, S., & Kinney, T. (1993). Sickle cell disease pain in children and adolescents: Change in pain frequency and coping strategies over time. *Journal of Pediatric Psychology, 18,* 621–637.

Gil, K. M., Williams, D. A., Thompson, R. J., & Kinney, T. R. (1991). Sickle cell disease in children and adolescents: The relation of child and parent pain coping strategies to adjustment. *Journal of Pediatric Psychology, 16,* 643–663.

Gil, K. M., Wilson, J. J., Edens, J. L., Webster, D. A., Abrams, M. A., Orringer, E., Grant, M., Clark, W. C., & Janal, M. N. (1996). Effects of cognitive coping skills training on coping strategies and experimental pain sensitivity in African American adults with sickle cell disease. *Health Psychology, 15,* 3–10.

Gil, K. M., Wilson, J. J., Edens, J. L., Workman, E., Ready, J., Sedway, J., Reading-Lallinger, R., & Daeschner, C. (1997). Cognitive coping skills training in children with sickle cell disease pain. *International Journal of Behavioral Medicine, 4,* 365–378.

Hall, H., Chiarucci, K., & Berman, B. (1992). Self-regulation and assessment approaches for vaso-occlusive pain management for pediatric sickle cell anemia patients. *International Journal of Psychosomatics, 39,* 28–33.

Holbrook, C. T., & Phillips, G. (1994). Natural history of sickle cell disease and the effects on biopsychological development. *Journal of Health and Social Policy, 5,* 7–18.

Hurtig, A. L. (1994). Relationships in families of children and adolescents with sickle cell disease. In K. B. Nash (Ed.), *Psychosocial aspects of sickle cell disease: Past, present, and future directions of research.* New York: Haworth Press.

Hurtig, A. L., Koepke, D., & Park, K. B. (1989). Relation between severity of chronic illness and adjustment in children and adolescents with sickle cell disease. *Journal of Pediatric Psychology, 14,* 117–132.

Hurtig, A. L., & Park, K. B. (1989). Adjustment and coping in adolescents with sickle cell disease. *Annals of New York Academy of Science, 565,* 172–182.

Hurtig, A. L., & White, L. S. (1986). Psychological adjustment in children and adolescents with sickle cell disease. *Journal of Pediatric Psychology, 11,* 411–427.

Leavell, S. R., & Ford, C. V. (1983). Psychopathology in patients with sickle cell disease. *Psychosomatics, 24,* 23–37.

Midence, K., & Elander, J. (1994). *Sickle cell disease: A psychosocial approach.* Oxford: Radcliff Medical Press.

Midence, K., & Elander, J. (1996). Adjustment and coping in adults with sickle cell disease: An assessment of research evidence. *British Journal of Health Psychology, 1,* 95–111.

Midence, K., McManus, C., Fuggle, P., & Davies, S. (1996). Psychological adjustment and family functioning in a group of British children with sickle disease: Preliminary empirical findings and a meta-analysis. *British Journal of Clinical Psychology, 35,* 439–450.

Morgan, S. A., & Jackson, J. (1986). Psychological and social concomitants of sickle cell anemia in adolescents. *Journal of Pediatric Psychology, 11,* 429–440.

Nadel, C., & Portadin, G. (1977). Sickle cell crises: Psychological factors associated with onset. *New York State Journal of Medicine, 77,* 1075–1078.

Nash, K. B. (1994). Introduction: Psychological aspects of sickle cell disease: Past, present, and future directions of research. *Journal of Health and Social Policy, 5,* 1–6.

Noll, R. B., Yosua, L. A., Vannatta, K., Kalinyak, K., Bukowski, W. M., & Davies, W. H. (1995). Social competence of siblings of children with sickle cell anemia. *Journal of Pediatric Psychology, 20,* 165–172.

Okany, C. C., & Akinyanju, O. O. (1993). The influence of socio-economic status on the severity of sickle cell disease. *African Journal of Medical Science, 22,* 57–60.

Platt, O. S., Brambilla, D. J., Rosse, W. F., Milner, P. F., Castro, O., Steinberg, M. H., & Klug, P. P. (1994). Mortality in sickle cell disease. Life expectancy and risk factors for early death. *The New England Journal of Medicine, 331,* 1639–1644.

Platt, O. S., Thornington, B. D., Brambilla, D. J., Milner, P. F., Rosse, W. F., Vichinsky, E., & Kinney, T. R. (1991). Pain in sickle cell disease: Rates and risk factors. *The New England Journal of Medicine, 325,* 11–16.

Powars, D., Chan, L. S., & Schroeder, W. A. (1990). The variable expression of sickle cell disease is genetically determined. *Seminal Hematology, 27,* 360–376.

Rosse, W. (1983). Diagnosis and treatment of painful episodes in sickle cell disease. *North Carolina Medical Journal, 44,* 419–420.

Rucknagel, D. L. (1974). The genetics of sickle cell anemia and related syndromes. *Archives of Internal Medicine, 133,* 595–606.

Scott, J. P., Hillery, C. A., Brown, E. R., Misiewicz, V., & Labotka, R. J. (1996). Hydroxyurea therapy in children severely affected with sickle cell disease. *Journal of Pediatrics, 128,* 820–828.

Serjeant, G. R. (1985). *Sickle cell disease.* New York: Oxford University Press.

Shapiro, B. S., & Ballas, S. K. (1994). The acute painful episode. In S. H. Embury, R. P. Hebbel, N. Mohandas, & M. H. Steinberg (Eds.), *Sickle cell disease: Basic principles and clinical practice* (pp. 531–543). New York: Raven Press.

Styles, L. A., & Vichinsky, E. (1994). Effects of a long-term transfusion regimen on sickle cell-related illness. *Journal of Pediatrics, 125,* 909–911.

Thomas, J. E., Koshy, M., Patterson, L., Dorn, L., & Thomas, K. (1984). Management of pain in sickle cell disease using biofeedback therapy: A preliminary study. *Biofeedback and Self-Regulation, 9,* 413–420.

Thompson, R. J., Jr., Gil, K. M., Abrams, M. R., & Phillips, G. (1992). Stress, coping, and psychological adjustment of adults with sickle cell disease. *Journal of Clinical and Counseling Psychology, 60,* 433–440.

Thompson, R. J., Jr., Gil, K. M., Abrams, M. R., & Phillips, G. (1996). Psychological adjustment of adults with sickle cell anemia: Stability over 20 months, correlates, and predictors. *Journal of Clinical Psychology, 52,* 253–261.

Thompson, R. J., Jr., Gil, K. M., Burbach, D. J., Keith, B. R., & Kinney, T. R. (1993). Role of child and maternal processes in the psychological adjustment of children with sickle cell disease. *Journal of Clinical and Counseling Psychology, 61,* 468–474.

Treiber, G. A., Mabe, P., & Wilson, G. (1987). Psychological adjustment of sickle cell children and their siblings. *Children's Health Care, 16,* 82–88.

Varni, J. W., & Thompson, K. L. (1985). *The Varni/Thompson pediatric pain questionnaire.* Unpublished manuscript.

Vavasseur, J. (1977). A comprehensive program for meeting psychosocial needs of sickle cell anemia patients. *Journal of the National Medical Association, 69,* 335–339.

Vichinsky, E. P., Johnson, R., & Lubin, B. H. (1982). Multidisciplinary approach to pain management in sickle cell disease. *The American Journal of Pediatric Hematology/Oncology, 4,* 328–333.

Vichinsky, E. P., & Lubin, B. H. (1980). Sickle cell anemia and related hemoglobinopathies. *Pediatric Clinics of North America, 27,* 429–447.

Walco, G. A., & Dampier, C. D. (1990). Pain in children and adolescents with sickle cell disease: A descriptive study. *Journal of Pediatric Psychology, 15,* 643–658.

Walters, M. C., Patience, M., Leisenring, W., Eckman, J. R., Scott, J. P., Mentzer, W. C., Davies, S. C., Ohene-Fremong, K., Bernaudin, F., Matthews, D. C., Storb, R., & Sullivan, K. M. (1996). Bone marrow transplantation for sickle cell disease. *The New England Journal of Medicine, 335,* 369–376.

Weisman, S. J., & Schechter, N. L. (1992). Sickle cell anemia: Pain management. In R. S. Sinatra, A. H. Hord, B. Ginsberg, & L. M. Prebles (Eds.), *Acute pain: Mechanism and management* (pp. 508–516). St. Louis, MO: Mosby Yearbook.

Westerman, M. P., & Bacus, J. W. (1983). Red blood cell morphology in sickle cell anemia as determined by image processing analysis: The relationship to painful crises. *American Journal of Clinical Pathology, 79,* 667–672.

Wrath, J. A., & Rucknagel, D. L. (1984). Density ultracentrifugation of sickle cell anemia as determined by image processing analysis: Increased dense echinocytes in crisis. *Blood, 64,* 507–515.

Zeltzer, L., Dash, J., & Holland, J. P. (1979). Hypnotically induced pain control in sickle cell anemia. *Pediatrics, 64,* 533–536.

Chapter 27

Burn Pain

David R. Patterson
University of Washington School of Medicine

Jason N. Doctor
University of Washington School of Medicine

Sam R. Sharar
University of Washington School of Medicine

A substantial portion of the world's population experiences severe burn injury. In the United States alone, burn injuries are thought to account for approximately 500,000 emergency room visits, 54,000 hospital admissions, and 5,500 deaths annually (Brigham & McLoughin, 1996). Patients in such circumstances will typically experience pain greater than or equal to that produced by almost any other etiology. The pain associated with the initial injury is often incomparable; yet, the pain experienced during treatment for burn injury is frequently worse. Further, painful burn treatments are seldom a one-time occurrence, and patients must often experience such suffering on a daily basis until the wound is healed. Because burn pain is intense, repeated, and unpredictable, its treatment represents a formidable challenge for clinicians working in this area of trauma care. The extent and severity of burn pain, however, also provides a valuable setting for studying acute pain relevant to a variety of other etiologies. The ensuing discussion addresses burn pain with respect to (a) medical and psychological conditions, (b) quantitative and qualitative aspects of burn pain, (c) pathophysiology, and (d) treatment.

MEDICAL AND PSYCHOLOGICAL FACTORS

Sufficiently large and/or severe burn injuries, without appropriate treatment, can result in severe disfigurement, amputation, or death. Modern burn care has done much to improve survival after such injuries through the use of topical antibacterial agents, skin substitutes, and early excision and grafting (Caldwell, Wallace, & Cone, 1996). Such interventions allow the burn wound to close and heal as soon as possible, thus minimizing the risk of infection. A number of other interventions are important to treat the complications and impact of the initial burn trauma, including sophisticated cardiovascular and respiratory support, nutritional therapy, and intravascular fluid resuscitation (Patterson et al., 1993a). Because the quality of such interventions has improved dramatically over past decades (Currerie, Braun, & Shires, 1980), survival rates have improved for every age group of burn patient (Currerie et al., 1980; Nguyen, Gilpin, Meyer, & Herndon, 1996).

Despite these advances, improving in burn pain management has proven more difficult. When one considers the typical course of a hospitalized burn patient, it is not surprising to discover that severe pain is virtually a universal experience. The depth and severity of the burn wound is often not easy to determine immediately after burn injury, thus complicating decisions about excision and grafting. Consequently the practice of many burn centers is to change burn wound dressings on a once- or twice-daily basis, each time debriding necrotic skin from the wound. This practice is repeated for days, weeks, or even months until the need for surgical intervention is indicated, or the wound is healed. Even with the use of potent opioid analgesics (e.g., morphine), the pain from such wound care is seldom completely managed (Choiniere, Melzack, Girard, Rondeau, & Paquin, 1990). To complicate matters, many patients undergo several surgeries over their course of hospitalization. Further, pain from wound care is exacerbated by that of physical therapies necessary to preserve and improve joint range of motion, overall mobility, and performance of daily activities. Rather than becoming easier to patients with time, these repeated, intrusive, and painful procedures tend to exacerbate anxiety and overwhelm patients' coping mechanisms.

In understanding the psychology of burn pain it is important to understand that many people who are hospitalized for such injuries experience suboptimal psychologic health prior to their injury. The estimated rates of previous psychiatric illness in patients with burn injuries range from 28% to 75% (Patterson et al., 1993b). The most prevalent psychiatric diagnoses include depression, character disorder, and alcohol and drug abuse (Patterson et al., 1993b). Because of such factors, patients are thought to stay in the burn unit longer (Berry, Wachtel, & Frank, 1982; Brezel, Kassenbrock, & Stein, 1988) and develop more serious psychiatric complications after the injury (Steiner & Clark, 1977). There are other unfavorable factors associated with burn hospitalizations. Suicide attempts, adult battery, child abuse, and child neglect are often problems associated with such trauma (Patterson et al., 1993a). Thus, burn victims cared for in the hospital setting very often have one or more severe psychosocial stressors and accompanying psychiatric diagnoses that complicate their recovery from trauma.

Additional psychological complications can occur as a result of the burn injury and its care. In order to understand such complications in the context of burn pain, it is useful to delineate the three typical stages of burn hospitalization. Patients with very severe burns are typically hospitalized in intensive care units where care is focused on both the burn wound and critical life support issues. Once their care is stabilized, they are then treated in acute care units where care is focused primarily on the burn wound. The final stage of burn care is centered on rehabilitation, which may occur in the hospital, the rehabilitation setting, or at home. When patients are in the intensive care unit, delirium and other psychotic reactions are common (Andreasen & Norris, 1972; Steiner & Clark, 1977). Infections, alcohol withdrawal, and metabolic complications are frequent etiologies for such transient psychosis (Perry & Blank, 1984). As such, pain control is often complicated in this setting by the patient's altered mental status. When patients are in acute care units, depression and anxiety are the most frequently reported psychological complications (Patterson et al., 1993a). Anxiety may be generalized or may be consistent with the *DSM–IV* (*Diagnostic and Statistical Manual of Mental Disorders*, 4th ed.; American Psychiatric Association, 1994) criteria for acute stress disorder. During the rehabilitation phase, pain reports usually decrease; however, the presence of depression and possible posttraumatic stress disorder may complicate treatment. As such, pain management during all phases of burn care must take into account these associated psychological problems.

BURN PAIN PATHOPHYSIOLOGY

Very little has been written on the pathophysiology of burn pain. This is, in part, the result of a greater focus in the burn literature on clinical pain issues, as well as ongoing controversies with regard to the validity of particular neurobiological pain models (Craig, Zhang, Bushnell, & Blomqvist, 1995; Wall, 1995). This section is intended to briefly expose the reader to some of the broader findings of the pain and neurobiology literature and how they may relate to burn pain. We caution the reader that this section is only a brief overview and does not represent the entire "neurobiological picture." The experience of burn pain is the result of the integrated activity of several central and peripheral neuroanatomic structures. A basic understanding of the anatomical structures and physiological mechanisms involved in pain is useful for evaluating how burns lead to the experience of pain.

Peripheral Pain Mechanisms

Physical information that results in painful sensation is transduced by free nerve endings. After a serious burn, nerve endings are both excited and damaged by the injury. Additionally, regeneration of nerve endings and mechanical stimulation during wound care can lead to additional excitement of primary afferent fibers. These primary afferent pain neurons have cell bodies located in the dorsal root ganglia of the spinal cord. Primary afferents respond to a variety of noxious stimulation (e.g., mechanical injury, chemical irritation, heat energy, ischemia, electrical stimulation). Pain appears to be mediated by two distinct populations of nociceptive peripheral afferent fibers (Kelly, 1985). The first type of fiber consists of small, thinly myelinated A-δ (A-delta) fibers that are activated primarily by noxious mechanical and thermal stimulation. Such fibers are likely stimulated during the initial burn injury, as well as during procedural (wound debridement) procedures. The A-δ fibers conduct rapidly (5 to 30 m/sec) and are associated with a fast, sharp, localized painful sensation. With repeated stimulation of A-δ fibers, reports of pain tend to decrease. The second type of nociceptive fibers are the unmyelinated C fibers. These fibers can also be activated by several types of physical energy including mechanical, chemical, and thermal energy. The C fibers are slow in conducting (0.5 to 2 m/sec) and the stimulation of C fibers is associated with what is described as a burning or dull aching pain. C fibers are also known as polymodal nociceptors and can be found in skin, deep tissue, muscle tissue, joints, and tendons (Chapman, 1986). These two types of fibers represent the peripheral nerve fibers that are activated in painful stimulation.

Ascending Transmission Pathways

The A-δ and the C fibers enter the spinal cord in the lateral portion of the dorsal root. After separating in the dorsal root, the fibers both ascend and descend before synapsing on neurons in the dorsal horn. The dorsal horn is divided into six laminae. A-δ and C fibers terminate primarily in the outermost laminae, laminae I and the substantia gelatinosa (laminae II and III). Some of the A-δ fibers, however, do terminate on lamina V. The dendrites from cell bodies in lamina V extend to the outermost layers of the dorsal horn. This allows for excitation from nociceptive fibers that do not travel beyond laminae I, II or III. Neurons in laminae I and V (second-order neurons) receive input from A-δ and C fibers through interneurons in the substantia gelatinosa.

Information from second-order neurons is transmitted by ascending fiber projections that cross the gray matter of the spinal cord to the lateral spinal thalamic tracts in the white matter of the spinal cord. There are two major nociceptive projection pathways, the neospinothalamic (NS) tract and the paleospinothalamic (PS) tract. These tracts make up what is called the anterolateral system. The NS carries signals from the largest and fastest second-order nociceptive neurons located in lamina I. These neurons are activated by noxious thermal and mechanical stimulation. However, they are not affected by touch (Perl, 1985). The axons from NS neurons ascend the lateral portion of the spinal cord, and extend to the ventroposterolateral and posterior thalamus where they synapse. There is, however, not a direct connection of neurons from the spinal cord to the thalamus. Axons from the spinal cord first synapse in the reticular formation before the information reaches the thalamus (Chapman, 1986).

The PS tract begins with cells in laminae I and V that receive input from both noxious and non-noxious stimulation. Because of this, nociceptors of the PS tract are referred to as wide dynamic range nociceptors. The PS tract is not somatotopically organized and tends to produce a report of diffuse burning or dull aching pain. Activity of the PS tract may be instrumental in the experience of "background pain" often reported by hospitalized burn patients during rest.

Pain Systems in the Brain

Most of the fibers of the anterolateral system synapse at the brainstem nuclei such as the reticular formation, below the thalamus. From here a group of fibers project to, and end at the level of the midbrain in the superior and inferior colliculi. A larger number of fibers enter the periaqueductal gray (PAG) that surrounds the cerebral aqueduct. The PAG has strong connections with the periventricular region of the diencephalon and the limbic system.

A small number of fibers from the NS tract terminate in the thalamus. Specifically, these fibers terminate in three nuclei of the posterior thalamus: the ventrobasal complex, the ventrocaudal parvocellular nucleus, and the posterior nuclear group. A small number of cells in the posterior nuclei respond to noxious stimulation. The ventrocaudal parvocellular nucleus, however, appears to be the most important area related to localized pain in humans (Kelly, 1985). Bushnell, Duncan, and Tremblay (1993a) have also found that the medial thalamus plays an important role in discriminating sensory aspects of pain.

Currently, the role of cortical structures in pain processing is not well understood. Recent studies, however, utilizing positron emission tomography (PET) have shed some light on this issue (Jones, Brown, Friston, Qi, & Frackowiak, 1991; Talbot et al., 1991). The posterior nuclei of the thalamus projects strongly to somatosensory cortex (S1 and S2) and direct electrical stimulation of S1 and S2 is known to elicit painful sensations in humans (Bonica, 1990). However, PET studies suggest that S1 and S2 seem to be primarily involved in processing tactile and positional changes in painful stimulation (Talbot et al., 1991). PET research has revealed that the most active cortical structure in pain perception is the cingulate cortex (Jones et al., 1991; Talbot et al., 1991). Primate research suggests that the cingulate cortex receives information from two specific thalamic areas: the central medial region (CM) and the parafiscular nuclei (Pf). Both of these areas have been shown to have remarkable pain intensity discrimination properties in monkeys (Bushnell, Duncan, & Tremblay, 1993). Cm and Pf connections with the cingulate cortex are thought to be involved in the appraisal of the intensity of painful stimulation (Talbot et al., 1991). After processing sensory information, the cingulate cortex may project to other areas (e.g., limbic structures) responsible for generating affective responses to painful stimulation. Establishing the connections between the cingulate cortex and limbic structures will be important for understanding the relationship between pain and emotion and may have implications for understanding how anxiety influences the pain response in burn patients. It has indeed been established that burn pain and state anxiety are closely associated (Patterson, Ptacek, Carrougher, & Sharar, 1997).

Descending Pathways of Pain Inhibition

The physiology of analgesic mechanisms is important for understanding the activity of opioid agents used in burn pain management. Since Melzack and Wall's (1965) seminal work on the gate-control theory, pain research has undergone a marked shift in theory. There is substantial evidence that the perception of pain can be inhibited at several different physiological levels (Basbaum & Fields, 1984; Melzack & Wall, 1965; Shibutani, 1990). The integrated activity of neurons at these different levels is collectively known as the descending pain system. The following is a brief review of the anatomical structures and physiological mechanisms that are known to be involved in pain inhibition.

Current understanding of pain inhibition suggests that it occurs at four levels in the central nervous system. The first level involves the cortex and diencephalon (the cortex may be active in hypnotic analgesia or other psychological burn pain reduction strategies). The second includes the PAG. At the third level is the rostroventral medulla. Within the rostroventral medulla is the nucleus raphe magnus (NRM), which serves an important inhibition function. The fourth level of the descending system is the dorsal horn of the spinal cord (Basbaum & Fields, 1984; Bonica, 1990).

Neuronal inputs in the somatosensory cortex (S1 and S2) are known to project to the midbrain PAG. Electrical stimulation of neurons in S1 and S2 has been shown to inhibit the activity of wide dynamic range somatosensory neurons, suggesting that relays to the PAG may inhibit prolonged activity with cortical stimulation (Bonica, 1990). The periventricular gray, located in the hypothalamus, also projects to the PAG and is an effective site for pain inhibition (Hosobuchi, Adams, & Linchitz, 1977).

The PAG of the midbrain is known to incite analgesia with stimulation and plays a crucial role in the pain inhibition circuit (Bonica, 1990). The PAG receives inputs from cortex, limbic structures, and, as previously mentioned, the hypothalamus (Basbaum & Fields, 1984). Injections of morphine into the PAG produce analgesia, suggesting that opiate receptors within this structure play a role in pain inhibition (Bennett & Mayer, 1979). Although some PAG neurons project directly to the dorsal horn where they have inhibitory effects on ascending transmission pathways, the majority of PAG neurons involved in the descending system project to the rostroventral medulla (RVM) (Bonica, 1990). Many of the interneurons within the PAG are enkephalinergic, but most of the neurons that project to the RVM are serotonergic (Basbaum & Fields, 1984).

The RVM represents the third level of the descending pain system. Like the PAG, stimulation of, or morphine injection into the RVM results in inhibition of painful response (Basbaum & Fields, 1984). The most important structure within the RVM is the NRM. Serotonergic neurons within the NRM project to the dorsal horn via the dorsolateral funiculus (DLF). The DLF has inputs from other structures involved in pain inhibition. For example, the locus coeruleus, a pontine structure, receives input from the PAG and sends axons to the dorsal horn via the DLF (Ruda, Bennett, & Dubner, 1986). The locus coeruleus also sends axons to the dorsal horn, the final level of the descending pathway, through the ventrolateral and ventral funiculi (Ruda et al., 1986).

Although the inhibition of nociceptive transmission clearly occurs at the dorsal horn, the exact mechanisms are not entirely understood. Descending serotonergic and noradrenergic neurons may postsynaptically inhibit nociceptive transmission directly in the spinothalamic tract. Another possible mechanism of inhibition may involve the activation of dorsal horn enkephalinergic and GABA-containing neurons by descending axons projecting from the DLF. Activation of these dorsal horn interneurons would presynaptically inhibit primary nociceptive neurons, or postsynaptically inhibit spinothalamic tract neurons (Basbaum, 1985; Ruda et al., 1986). Although the exact route of inhibition is not known, there is substantial evidence to suggest that the aforementioned structures are active during clinical pain management of burn patients with opioid medications.

Molecular Biological Factors That Influence Pain Perception

There is mounting evidence that noxious stimulation may have long-standing influences on genetic factors responsible for the production and release of pain excitatory and inhibitory neurochemicals (see Coderre, Katz, Vaccarino, & Melzack, 1993, for a review). These discoveries have called for the recent utilization of immunocytochemical methods in pain research (Basbaum, 1991). Of recent interest has been the proto-onco-gene cellular fos (c-fos). C-fos is of interest in pain research because it may be involved in modulating the experience of pain. C-fos is expressed in neurons that are active during painful stimulation. The messenger Ribonucleic Acid (mRNA) for the c-fos gene is observable within 10 minutes of stimulation and its protein, the fos protein, is expressed in the nuclei of neurons within 30 minutes of stimulation (Basbaum, 1991). Therefore, c-fos in and of itself may be a useful tool for learning about which neurons are firing during painful stimulation. However, c-fos has also been shown to be involved in producing long-term neurochemical changes (Morgan & Curran, 1986). C-fos may play a role in mediating pain and nociceptive thresholds. The expression of c-fos seems to depend on an interaction between Ca^{++} influx through N-methyl-D-aspartate (NMDA) receptor-operated Ca^{++} channels and the stimulation of second messengers. Because c-fos participates in the regulation of mRNA encoding, it may ultimately influence the amount of neuropeptide that is released. For instance, c-fos is thought to be involved in the transcriptional control of dynorphin and enkephalin, and its expression following noxious stimulation leads to an increased synthesis of dynorphin and enkephalin. Enkephalin typically produces inhibitory or antinociceptive effects (Vaught, Rothman, & Westfall, 1982). Dynorphin, however, has been shown to have dual effects. Dynorphin has been found to produce expanded receptive fields and a facilitation of the responses of approximately one third of the superficial dorsal horn cells, while producing an inhibition of responses in another third of the cells (Coderre et al., 1993; Hylden, Nahin, Traub, & Dubner, 1991). This has led some researchers to conclude that whereas dynorphin may produce direct excitatory effects on spinal cord projection neurons, it may also produce inhibition by a negative feedback mechanism on dynorphin-containing neurons (Dubner & Ruda, 1992). In summary, enkephalin, whose production may be mediated by c-fos, may provide a mechanism that minimalizes hyperalgesia (decreased threshold for nociception), whereas dynorphin, also thought to be mediated by c-fos, may have more complex effects in modulating hyperalgesia. Such activity and modulation of nociceptive input at the molecular level undoubtedly have complex effects on the pain experience of burn patients; however, at this stage of pain research the clinical implications of these effects are unclear.

In summary, the burn injury itself represents only a small part of the physiological activity involved in a burn patients' experience of pain. Central processing and the integrated activity of several brain structures, as well as changes in neuroplasticity act to place strong constraints on nociceptive input. Only through the understanding of broader pain systems in the body can we hope to better manage burn pain.

Just as psychological factors can impact burn pain, pain might have much to do with a patient's emotional reaction to this form of trauma. Ptacek, Patterson, Montgomery, Ordonez, and Heimbach (1995) recently reported that pain may be one of the most powerful variables in accounting for postburn adjustment. The authors found that the pain patients experienced during hospitalization was a stronger predictor of measures of psychological well-being after follow-up than was the size of the burn or length of hospitalization. Adequate pain control might facilitate both physical (Chapman & Bonica, 1983) and psychological recovery.

QUANTITATIVE AND QUALITATIVE ASPECTS OF BURN PAIN

One well-known component of burn pain that is relevant to treatment is the distinction among procedural, background, and breakthrough pain. Procedural pain refers to that which occurs during medical interventions, dressing changes, or therapies, and almost always involves some type of intrusion to, or movement of, the body. Understandably, pain during procedures is acute, intense, of short duration, and associated with significant suffering in patients. Procedural pain typically offers the greatest challenge for clinicians. In contrast, background pain occurs between procedures while the patients are immobile, and, although lasting longer, is almost always of a more tolerable intensity (Patterson & Sharar, 1997). Breakthrough pain refers to those instances when episodic pain occurring at rest reaches levels of substantial discomfort for the patient.

Burn pain occurs repeatedly over the duration of care, but there has been little study of its course over time. Choiniere et al. (1990) assessed burn pain over hospitalization and found that pain (a) varies both across and within patients, (b) intensity is worst and is poorly controlled during procedures, and (c) is not well predicted by sociodemographic variables or burn size. Ptacek, Patterson, and Doctor (1998) administered Visual Analogue Scales and McGill Pain Questionnaires to 47 patients over at least 10 days of hospital burn care. They found widely divergent patterns of pain between patients but also noted that pain decreased with time. Patients with more severe burns reported higher levels of affective components to their pain, and patients with high scores on trait anxiety measures reported more pain overall.

What is clear from this preliminary work is that the burn pain pattern for any given patient is extremely difficult to predict and staff should be wary of assuming that they can anticipate the amount of suffering that will be experienced based merely on the size of the burn injury. The fluctuating nature of burn pain indicates there is no substitute for ongoing assessment of both background and procedural pain, with interventional strategies that are flexible enough to meet individual patient needs.

TREATING BURN PAIN

Pharmacologic Approaches

As stated previously, the pain experienced by burn victims can vary widely and somewhat unpredictably, both from patient to patient and over the course of hospitalization. In considering pharmacologic approaches for burn analgesia, however, three consistent observations can be made. First, for patients with injuries extensive enough to require hospitalization, pain from the burn itself is severe. In addition, the nature of burn wound care (daily wound debridement, intermittent surgical excision and grafting) results in highly variable pain reports. For these reasons, potent opioids and occasionally potent anesthetics form the cornerstones of pharmacologic pain control for these patients, leaving few indications for the mild to moderate analgesia provided by nonsteroidal anti-inflammatory drugs (NSAIDs). Second, because burn pain has two well-defined components— background and procedural pain—pharmacologic choices for analgesia should target each pain pattern individually. Finally, because burn pain will vary somewhat unpredictably throughout hospitalization due to surgical intervention, activity levels, and so forth, analgesic regimens should be continuously evaluated and reassessed to avoid problems of under- or overmedication. Pain assessment is facilitated by the regular use of standardized, self-report scales for patients and observational scoring systems for care providers, the latter being particularly useful in young children or patients with other cognitive abnormalities (Chapman & Syrjala, 1990). In addition to aiding both pain assessment and communication between patients and staff, these standardized tools also facilitate communication between the various care providers by indicating success or failure in burn pain treatment.

Because the potent opioids and anesthetics used frequently for procedural analgesia in these patients carry uncommon, but potential risks of life-threatening side effects (e.g., respiratory depression and inadequate ventilation, depressed level of consciousness), use of these agents should occur only in settings with adequate monitoring, personnel, and resuscitation equipment appropriate for the degree of sedation anticipated. For most wound debridement procedures opioid analgesia with minimal sedation is sufficient, and no special monitoring is required. Larger or more potent doses of opioids, or the concurrent use of anxiolytic sedatives (e.g., benzodiazipines) may produce more pronounced sedation ("conscious sedation"), but can progress to "deep sedation" where patient-staff communication and/or consciousness are lost. Current guidelines of the Joint Commission on Accreditation of Healthcare Organizations (JCAHO) (1993), as well as physician specialty professional organizations (Drugs, 1992), dictate both general and specific levels of monitoring (e.g., continuous pulse oximetry, presence of an independent observer specifically responsible for monitoring ventilation and vital signs) for patients requiring this level of analgesia/sedation. Finally, for those occasional wound care procedures that may require brief general anesthesia, the requirement for comprehensive monitoring and management by an anesthesiologist is obvious (Dimick et al., 1993; Powers, Cruse, Daniels, & Stevens, 1993).

Opioids. Opioid agonists are the most commonly used analgesics in the treatment of burn pain, in part because (a) they are potent analgesics, (b) the benefits and risks of their use are familiar to the majority of care providers, and (c) they provide some dose-dependent degree of sedation that can be advantageous to both burn patients and staff, particularly during burn wound care procedures. Opioid interactions with opiate receptors concentrated primarily in the PAG (as described earlier) mediate analgesia, with these same interactions also being responsible for a long list of side effects including nausea, pruritis, urinary retention, constipation, sedation, and respiratory depression. The wide spectrum of opioids available for clinical use (Benedetti & Butler, 1990) provides dosing flexibility (i.e., variable routes of administration, variable duration of action) that is ideal for the targeted treatment of both background and procedural pain in burn patients. The opioids commonly used in these settings are listed in Table 27.1.

TABLE 27.1
Opioids Commonly Used in Burn Pain Management

Drug	Route[a]	Peak Effect (hr)[b]	Plasma t1/2 (hr)	Duration (hr)
morphine	PO, IV	0.2–1.5	2–3	3–5
hydromorphone	PO, IV	0.5–2.0	2–3	4–5
methadone	PO, IV	0.5–2.0	15–30	4–12
meperidine	PO, IV	0.5–2.0	3–4	2–3
codeine	PO	0.5–1.0	2–3	3–4
oxycodone	PO	1.0	—	4–6
fentanyl	IV	0.1	3–4	1–2

[a]Preferred routes of administration are shown (PO = oral, IV = intravenous), although other routes (intramucosal, transmucosal, transcutaneous) are possible with specific drugs. Dosing is variable and dependent on route of administration (see text).

[b]Peak effect occurs rapidly with IV administration, but is more delayed with PO administration.

The route of opioid administration is an important issue in burn patients, with the choice between intravenous (IV) or oral administration dictated by the severity of burn (critically ill patients require IV access and may have abnormal gut function) and the high risk for developing intravascular catheter-related sepsis among burn patients (hence, physician reluctance to maintain long-term IV access) (Franceschi, Gerding, Phillips, & Fratianne, 1989). For patients capable of taking oral medications, background pain is treated with either long-acting agents administered orally (e.g., oral methadone or sustained-released morphine) or regularly scheduled (as opposed to "as needed" or "prn") dosing of short-acting agents (e.g., oral oxycodone) that offer mild to moderate analgesia. Because most intravenously administered opioids have a short duration of action, background analgesia in patients unable to take oral medications is often achieved by continuous IV infusion of a short-acting agent (e.g., continuous IV morphine infusion). Procedural pain is generally treated with highly potent, short-acting opioids. Opioids that can be administered intravenously (e.g., morphine, fentanyl) have the distinct advantages of (a) rapid onset of action, (b) short duration of action, and (c) the potential safety of rapidly titrating dose to desired effect. However, orally administered opioids with relatively short durations of action (e.g., oxycodone, hydromorphone) are frequently used for procedural analgesia in patients without IV access.

Because even background pain is variable in intensity and subject to changes with activities (e.g., physical and occupational therapy) or sleep, flexibility in opioid use can be advantageous and is usually accomplished by the patient's request for more drug (*prn* dosing). In some cases where articulation of pain is limited (e.g., children) nursing staff assume a greater responsibility for determining the need for additional analgesia. This reliance upon nurse assessment of burn patient pain can be problematic, however, as it is well documented that nurses' and patients' assessment of burn pain and analgesia are not always comparable (Choiniere et al., 1990; Iafrati, 1986). Patient-controlled analgesia (PCA) with IV opioids offers the burn patient a safe and efficient method of achieving more flexible analgesia. PCA also offers the patient some degree of control over his or her medical care, this issue often being a major one for burn patients whose waking hours are often completely scheduled with care activities ranging from wound care to physical and rehabilitation therapy. Studies comparing PCA opioid use to other routes of administration in the burn population, however, have shown positive, but limited benefits of PCA (Choiniere, Grenier, & Paquette, 1992; Kinsella, Glavin, & Reid, 1988). The PCA administration of potent, short-acting opioids (e.g., alfentanil, remifentanil) for procedural analgesia may also have a useful role in burn analgesic management.

It should be noted that opioid analgesics are often under used for the treatment of burn pain, just as they are for acute pain of other etiologies (Melzack, 1990). Unwarranted fears of addiction often drive such poor practice, even though reports of addiction among burn patients are negligible (Porter & Jick, 1980). Perry (1984) reported that burn staff tendencies to undertreat with opioids unfortunately persist, even after educational programming to the contrary.

Nonopioids. The list of nonopioid analgesics in widespread use for the treatment of burn pain is currently limited, although not without potential benefit. NSAIDs, as outlined previously, are only mild analgesics that exhibit a ceiling effect in their dose-response relationship, rendering them unsuitable in most cases for the inpatient treatment of burn pain. The opioid agonist-antagonist drugs (e.g., nalbuphine, butorphanol) produce "mixed" actions at the opiate receptor level, theoretically providing analgesia (agonist property) with lesser side effects (antagonist properties). Although studies have shown this class of drugs to be effective in treating burn pain (Lee, Marvin, & Heimbach, 1989), experience with them is both limited and suggests efficacy in patients with only relatively mild burn pain.

Inhaled nitrous oxide is an analgesic agent safe for administration by nonanesthesia personnel, carries an established track record in providing safe and effective analgesia for moderately painful procedures in dentistry (Dworkin, Chen, Schubert, & Clark, 1984), obstetrical labor (Carstoniu et al., 1994; Westling, Milson, Zetterstrom, & Ekstrom-Jodal, 1992), and other medical specialties, and is also a commonly used, though less well studied agent for the treatment of burn pain (Filkins, Cosgrav, & Marvin, 1981). It is typically used as a 50% mixture in 50% oxygen, and is self-administered by an awake, cooperative, spontaneously breathing patient. A secondary benefit of nitrous oxide use, like that of PCA opioid administration, is the element of control given to the patient for his or her care, albeit a small portion of their overall care. Nitrous oxide is of less use in critically ill or uncooperative patients. Finally, although not in the setting of burn pain treatment, it has also been implicated in a very small, but measurable incidence of toxicity issues (e.g., spontaneous abortion, bone marrow suppression) involving patients or staff exposed for prolonged periods (Anesthesiologists, 1974; Nunn, Chanarin, & Tanner, 1986).

It is widely understood that acute pain is exacerbated by anxiety (Chapman, 1986; Egan, 1989), although the mechanisms by which this occurs are poorly understood. Anxiolysis or sedation, therefore, may be of benefit in treating burn pain syndromes. In one survey, benzodiazepines were reported to be used in burn pain management in 40% of U.S. burn centers (Perry & Heidrich, 1982). Although the sedative side effects of potent opioid analgesics can provide some limited degree of anxiolysis, benzodiazepines are the most commonly used pharmacologic anxiolytics in the treatment of acute pain, and have been reported to attenuate anxiety relative to nonburn procedures (Egan, Ready, Nessly, & Greer, 1992). It is recently reported that lorazepam administration results in improved analgesic effect of opioids in the burn-injured population, and that anxiety reduction likely contributes to this analgesic effect (Patterson, Ptacek et al., 1997).

Anesthetics. It is obvious that general anesthesia would be required for the excision and grafting of deep burn wounds. There is, however, a small population of patients who require specific wound care procedures on a scale well below that of surgical burn care, but nonetheless difficult to perform on a conscious patient. These procedures include (a) the removal of hundreds of skin staples from recently grafted wounds, (b) meticulous wound care of recently grafted, and often, tenuous skin on the face or neck, and (c) wound care procedures in variably cooperative children. Historically, IV or intramuscular ketamine has been used for these procedures (Demfling, Ellerbe, & Jarrett, 1978; Ward & Diamond, 1976), but its use is limited by the potential risk of emergence delirium reactions (5% to 30% incidence) associated with its use. More recently, the extension of full anesthetic care capabilities outside of the operating room and into the burn unit has been implemented in some specialized burn centers with apparent success (Dimick et al., 1993; Powers et al., 1993). This has been facilitated by the recent introduction into clinical anesthetic practice of a variety of drugs with a rapid onset and short duration of action, a more rapid awakening/recovery, and fewer associated side effects—ideal qualities for agents to be used for procedural burn wound care. These agents include IV propofol and remifentanil, and inhaled sevoflurane. Propofol is particularly advantageous, and can be titrated to effect both in terms of level of consciousness and duration of action using continuous IV infusion techniques. The provision of brief, dense analgesia/anesthesia in a comprehensively monitored setting by individuals specifically trained to provide the service appears safe and efficient, both in terms of allowing wound care to proceed rapidly under ideal conditions for patient and nursing staff, and in terms of cost-effective use of the operating room for only true surgical burn care procedures.

Nonpharmacologic Approaches

Hypnosis. Despite controversy surrounding hypnosis as a treatment, it has probably received more empirical attention with burn pain than any other type of psychological interventions. Over a dozen reports have appeared in the literature on the use of this technique with burn pain. Patterson, Questad, and Boltwood (1987) have reported success not only with analgesia, but with a number of other complications from burns. The research on the use of hypnosis with burn pain, however, is generally of poor quality. Only a handful of controlled studies have been reported and these are limited by other shortcomings, such as lack of measurement and failure to report pain medications.

Pioneering work on treating burn pain with hypnosis was done by Crasilneck, Stirman, and Wilson (1955), who reported dramatic analgesic effects in six out of eight patients. Wakeman and Kaplan (1978) reported a well-controlled study in which burn patients using hypnosis needed less pain medication than control subjects. In our own series of studies, we have also noted that patients receiving hypnosis report lower levels of pain than do controls. However, we have also found that the patients who seem to respond well to hypnosis are those with higher initial levels of pain (Patterson, Everett, Burns, & Marvin, 1992; Patterson & Ptacek, 1997). Practically, it appears that hypnosis may be more useful for patients with high levels of pain, or who are having a poor response to opioid analgesics.

It is important to specify the type of burn pain that will be treated with hypnosis. Hypnosis is generally less suited for the prolonged duration of background pain but can be quite useful for patients experiencing procedural pain. One advantage of treating procedural pain is that it is predictable in onset and duration. It is possible to prepare patients for a scheduled procedure with behavioral techniques, and, in our own work, we typically apply hypnosis to the patient the morning before they receive their dressing change. Patients receive posthypnotic cues that are tied to events associated with the procedural pain. Thus, if patients are aware that they will be sitting in a hydrotherapy tub, this will become the cue that subsequently elicits relaxation and analgesia. This approach is based on Barber's (1977) Rapid Induction Analgesia, which relies on techniques such as indirect suggestion, anchoring, and posthypnotic suggestions.

We have identified a number of factors that suggest the utility of hypnosis with patients experiencing burn pain (Patterson, Adcock, & Bombardier, 1997). Specifically, we have postulated that the factors of motivation, hypnotizability, dissociation, and regression may influence hypnotic receptivity at various points in burn care. Certainly the motivation to reduce burn pain can be a strong incentive for a patient to participate in a psychologically based approach. Hypnotizability has long been shown to influence analgesic response, particularly in the laboratory setting (Hilgard & Hilgard, 1975). Burn injuries cause high rates of acute stress disorder (Patterson, 1992) and the dissociation that is often a component of this anxiety reaction may facilitate hypnotic response. Finally, the emotional regression that is often a natural response to trauma and its medical care may lead patients to be more compliant with the clinician providing hypnosis (Patterson, Adcock et al., 1997).

Hypnosis represents a promising form of psychologically based pain control in the burn unit. It can be quickly administered, which suits the rapid pace of the burn unit environment. This intervention can be used at any phase during burn care, although the nature of the intervention will vary dramatically between what might be seen in the intensive care unit and in long-term rehabilitation (Patterson, Goldberg, & Ehde, 1996).

Cognitive-Behavioral Interventions. There are few reports on the use of cognitive-behavioral interventions with burn pain. The application of such techniques is more typically reported with patients with chronic pain (Holzman & Turk, 1986; Turk, Meichenbaum, & Genest, 1983). Nevertheless, a number of studies have reported the use of such interventions with acute pain from etiologies such as rectal examinations, surgery, and dental work (Everett, Patterson, & Chen, 1990).

A particularly useful distinction is whether patients respond to a painful event with avoidant or reappraisal strategies (Tan, 1982). Because it is well established that people vary in their cognitive style, it is important to tailor cognitive-behavioral approaches to the individual characteristics of the patient. Avoidant cognitive-behavioral techniques will likely be more effective with patients who cope with acute pain by distracting or dissociating themselves. For those patients who excessively rely on an information-gathering approach, or are hypervigilant during procedures, reappraisal techniques might be more beneficial.

Avoidant techniques operate by distracting the patient away from pain during the acute procedure. Essentially, the greater the probability that a distraction will capture the patient's attention, the more effective it will likely be. For example, we are currently investigating the use of virtual reality as a means of distracting patients, particularly children, during painful procedures (Hoffman, Doctor, Patterson, Weghorst, & Furness, 1998). Typically, avoidance strategies involve teaching the patient to envision a relaxing place, such as the beach, and to use that imagery during the procedure. Distraction techniques can be as simple as providing conversation during the procedure or other means of diverting the patient's attention. Again, the more the staff is able to capture the patient's attention and match avoidance strategies to the patient's interest, the more successful such interventions will be. Using avoidance or distraction techniques will often be hindered if the patient fears that the procedures will in some way be harmful to them. Consequently, it is often a prerequisite that the patient receive education as to what the procedure will involve, and that it will not make their condition worse. Distraction techniques necessitate a certain amount of trust from the patient. When this trust has not been established, the patient is often compelled to monitor the staff during whatever procedure occurs, and avoidant/distraction techniques are often futile under such circumstances.

For those patients who are not able to remove themselves mentally, reappraisal techniques may be beneficial. In essence, such strategies take advantage of the patient's hypervigilance during the procedure. Thus, rather than being encouraged to focus away from the painful sensation, the patient is encouraged to pay attention to what they are experiencing. In essence, by focusing on the sensation, the patients are cognitively able to shift away from the notion of pain and replace it with other sensations. To a certain degree, reappraisal techniques can teach patients to differentiate between sensory and affective components of pain. Thus, the patient may acknowledge that the pain is "burning," which would be a sensory interpretation of the pain, while at the same time giving up the notion that the pain is "unbearable," which would be an affective appraisal of the pain. For example, it is quite typical for burn wounds to become more sensitive as they heal over the course of burn care. With increased healing, skin buds begin to appear that are often quite sensitive to touch. If a patient is warned about this early in his or her care, they can essentially be encouraged to develop reappraisal techniques. In other words, patients can be taught that when they feel more sensitivity in their burn area, this is actually a sign that they are healing.

A final form of cognitive-behavioral intervention involves the provision of education and preparatory information. Preparatory information with acute pain simply refers to letting the patient know what they can expect during a potentially painful procedure. This can be in the form of sensory preparatory information (what they can expect to feel as they go through a procedure) or procedural preparatory information (what they can expect will actually occur during a procedure). There is substantial evidence that providing preparatory information reduces both pain and anxiety during medical procedures (Tan, 1982). We are unable to find any studies on preparatory information in the context of burn pain. The studies reported in the literature for the use of preparatory information with acute pain typically are done with one-time procedures. A particular problem with burn pain is that procedures are often repeated several times. It is unknown how preparatory information affects patient response over a multitude of procedures.

Operant Approaches. It is particularly useful to attend to operant behavioral principle when considering the scheduling of pain medication. Burn pain is frequently medicated through as needed or prn schedules. Medication is administered through this approach based on expressed patient need, typically in response to pain complaints. Pharmacologically, a prn schedule may result in varying levels of blood opioid levels, with patients fluctuating between suboptimal analgesia and oversedation (Melzack, 1990). Learning theory would suggest that this strategy for opioid administration is essential for reinforcing pain behavior and increasing the potential for chronic problems. Time-contingent schedules of medications provide a simple means for avoiding such problems. Medications administered at regular time intervals provide stable blood plasma levels and remove the problem of staff attention to pain complaints.

A second application of operant principles is with those patients that demonstrate pain behaviors that are modulated by factors other than the nociception from their wound. Occasionally, burn patients will fail to respond to a pharmacologically based regimen for pain. The pain behaviors in such patients may be mediated by psychological factors such as dependency needs, somatoform disorders, or addictive tendencies. In such instances, it is important to establish time-contingent schedules of medication, for the reasons discussed earlier. It is further useful to convince patients that they are receiving optimal biomedical treatments for their pain (e.g., they are at the upper limit of opioid analgesic doses). Having accomplished these prerequisites, patients can then be taught principles of operant chronic pain management, particularly the advantages of being distracted from pain. Teaching burn unit staff members to ignore patient pain behaviors and distract attention to other topics can be challenging, as they are typically trained to attend to patients' complaints.

A third potential application of operant principles is training staff not to reward escape behavior during adversive procedures, when such avoidance will only serve to exacerbate the patient's pain. This can particularly be the case with pediatric burn care. It is unacceptable clinical practice to provide suboptimal pharmacologic analgesia for children undergoing wound care. However, most children will dislike undergoing burn care procedures, no matter how well their analgesic needs are being met. Conditioning factors as well as the basically unpleasant nature of burn wound care will lead many children to attempt to escape such adversive procedures. If children are allowed to avoid procedures, at will, their behavior may escalate to the point where they refuse all wound care procedures. Once staff members have adequately medicated children, they can minimize such escape behavior by providing firm limits as to what is expected from the patient, and making the wound care environment as enjoyable as possible. For children, this may involve integrating games, play, and reinforcement (e.g., token economies) into wound care procedures.

A final application of operant principles has to do with enhancing therapy performance in burn rehabilitation. Burn patients are forced to cope with a series of invasive therapies throughout their care. Often the pain associated with procedures may act as the stimulus for patients to stop an activity; in essence, patients are learning to let "pain be their guide" with respect to therapy compliance (Fordyce, 1976). Therapy performance can be greatly enhanced by having patients use rest as a reward for activity, rather than a response to pain. The quota system can provide useful guidelines for gradually building patient activity by using rest as a reinforcer. This system provides a formula for establishing a baseline of activity and gradually increasing demands within a patient's capacity. The use of the quota system with particularly overwhelmed and depressed patients is discussed in Ehde, Patterson, and Fordyce (in press).

SUMMARY

Aggressive care approaches for severe burn injuries have led to increased survival rates, but also have contributed to substantial patient suffering. Neurophysiologically, burn pain is likely mediated in a fashion similar to other forms of nociception. Burn pain is relatively unique, however, in that its care necessitates exposure to repeated, intrusive, and painful procedures. Such pain is complicated by psychological/psychiatric issues associated with burn injuries and their care. We advocate an approach to burn pain that involves initial aggressive stabilization of patients on a regimen of opioid analgesics. As individual cases warrant, other forms of pharmacologic (e.g., anesthetics, nonsteroidal agents, inhalants) or nonpharmacologic (hypnosis, cognitive-behavioral, operant) interventions should then be added. Because burn pain is so severe, it is seldom controlled by opioid analgesics alone, and the use of such supplemental techniques are often warranted.

REFERENCES

American Psychiatric Association. (1994). Diagnostic and Statistical Manual of Mental Disorders (4th ed.). Washington, DC: American Psychiatric Association.

Andreasen, N. J. C., & Norris, A. S. (1972). Long-term adjustment and adaptation mechanisms in severely burned adults. *Journal of Nervous and Mental Disease, 154*, 352–362.

Anesthesiologists, A. S. A. (1974). Report of an ad hoc committee on the effect of trace anesthetics on the health of operating room personnel. Occupational disease among operating room personnel: A national study. *Anesthesiology, 41*, 32–47.

Barber, J. (1977). Rapid induction analgesia: A clinical report. *American Journal of Clinical Hypnosis, 19*, 138–147.

Basbaum, A. I. (1985). Functional analysis of the cytochemistry of the spinal cord. In H. L. Fields, R. Dubner, & F. Gervero (Eds.), *Advances in pain research and therapy* (Vol. 9, pp. 149–175). New York: Raven.

Basbaum, A. I. (1991). *The central nervous system substrates for the transmission of "pain" messages.* Paper presented at the Western USA Pain Society meeting, Oxnard, CA.

Basbaum, A. I., & Fields, H. L. (1984). Endogenous pain control systems: Brainstem spinal pathways and endorphin circuitry. *Annual Review of Neuroscience, 7*, 309–338.

Benedetti, C., & Butler, S. H. (1990). Systemic analgesics. In J. J. Bonica (Ed.), *The management of pain* (pp. 1640–1674). Philadelphia: Lea & Febiger.

Bennett, G. J., & Mayer, D. J. (1979). Inhibition of spinal cord interneurons by narcotic microinjection and focal electric stimulation in the periaqueductal gray matter. *Brain Research, 172*, 243–257.

Berry, C. C., Wachtel, T. L., & Frank, H. A. (1982). An analysis of factors which predict mortality in hospitalized burn patients. *Burns, 9*, 38.

Bonica, J. J. E. (1990). *The management of pain* (Vols. 1–2). Philadelphia: Lea & Febiger.

Brezel, B. S., Kassenbrock, J. M., & Stein, J. M. (1988). Burns in substance abusers and in neurologically and mentally impaired patients. *Journal of Burn Care and Rehabilitation, 9*, 169–171.

Brigham, P. A., & McLoughin, E. (1996). Burn incidence and medical care use in the United States: Estimates, trends and data sources. *Journal of Burn Care and Rehabilitation, 17*(3), 95–107.

Bushnell, M. C., Duncan, G. H., & Tremblay, N. (1993). Thalamic VPM nucleus in the behaving monkey. I. Multimodal and discriminative properties of thermosensitive neurons. *Journal of Neurophysiology, 69*(3), 739–752.

Caldwell, F. T. J., Wallace, B. H., & Cone, J. B. (1996). Sequential excision and grafting of the burn injuries of 1507 patients treated between 1967 and 1986: End results and the determinants of death. *Journal of Burn Care and Rehabilitation, 17*(2), 137–146.

Carstoniu, J., Levytam, S., Norman, P., Daley, D., Katz, J., & Sandler, A. N. (1994). Nitrous oxide in early labor: Safety and analgesic efficacy assessed by a double-blind, placebo-controlled study. *Anesthesiology, 80*, 30–35.

Chapman, C. R. (1986). Pain, perception and illusion. In R. A. Sternbach (Ed.), *The psychology of pain* (pp.). New York: Raven.

Chapman, C. R., & Bonica, J. J. (1983). *Acute pain.* Kalamazoo: The Upjohn Company.

Chapman, C. R., & Syrjala, K. L. (1990). Measurement of pain. In J. J. Bonica (Ed.), *The management of pain* (pp. 580–594). Philadelphia: Lea & Febiger.

Choiniere, M., Grenier, R., & Paquette, C. (1992). Patient-controlled analgesia: A double blind study in burn patients. *Anaesthesia, 47*, 467–472.

Choiniere, M., Melzack, R., Girard, N., Rondeau, J., & Paquin, M-J. (1990). Comparisons between patients' and nurses' assessment of pain and medication efficacy in severe burn injuries. *Pain, 40*, 143–152.

Coderre, T. J., Katz, J., Vaccarino, A. L., & Melzack, R. (1993). Contributions of central neuroplasticity to pathological pain: Review of a clinical and experimental evidence. *Pain, 55*, 259–285.

Commission on Accreditation of Healthcare Organizations. (1993). *Accreditation manual for hospitals.* St. Louis, MO: Mosby Yearbook.

Craig, A. D., Zhang, E. T., Bushnell, M. C., & Blomqvist, A. (1995). Reply to P. D. Wall. *Pain, 62*, 391–393.

Crasilneck, H. B., Stirman, J. A., & Wilson, B. J. (1955). Use of hypnosis in the management of patients with burns. *Journal of the American Medical Association, 158*, 103–106.

Currerie, P. W., Braun, D. W., & Shires, G. T. (1980). Burn injury: Analysis of survival and hospitalization time for 937 patients. *Annals of Surgery, 192*, 472.

Demling, R. H., Ellerbe, S., & Jarrett, F. (1978). Ketamine anesthesia for tangential excision of burn eschar: A burn unit procedure. *Journal of Trauma, 18*(4), 269–270.

Dimick, P., Helvig, E., Heimbach, D., Marvin, J., Coda, B., & Edwards, W. T. (1993). Anesthesia-assisted procedures in a burn intensive care unit procedure room: Benefits and complications. *Journal of Burn Care and Rehabilitation, 14*, 446–449.

Drugs, C. O. (1992). Guidelines for monitoring and management of pediatric patients during and after sedation for diagnostic, dental, and therapeutic procedures. *Pediatrics, 89*, 1110–1115.

Dubner, R., & Ruda, M. A. (1992). Activity-dependent neuronal plasticity following tissue injury and inflammation. *Trends in Neuroscience, 15*, 96–103.

Dworkin, S. F., Chen, A. C., Schubert, M. M., & Clark, D. W. (1984). Cognitive modification of pain: Information in combination with N2O. *Pain, 19,* 339–351.

Egan, K. J. (1989). Psychological issues in postoperative pain. In R. V. Oden (Ed.), *Anesthesia clinics of North America* (pp. 183–192). Philadelphia: Saunders.

Egan, K. J., Ready, L. B., Nessly, M., & Greer, B. E. (1992). Self-administration of midazolam for postoperative anxiety: A double blinded study. *Pain, 49,* 3–8.

Ehde, D. M., Patterson, D. R., & Fordyce, W. E. (in press). The quota system in burn rehabilitation. *Journal of Burn Care and Rehabilitation.*

Everett, J. J., Patterson, D. R., & Chen, A. C. N. (1990). Cognitive and behavioral treatments for burn pain. *The Pain Clinic, 3*(3), 133–145.

Filkins, S. A., Cosgrav, P., & Marvin, J. A. (1981). Self-administered anesthesia: A method of pain control. *Journal of Burn Care and Rehabilitation, 2,* 33–34.

Fordyce, W. E. (1976). *Behavioral methods for chronic pain and illness.* St. Louis, MO: Mosby Yearbook.

Franceschi, D., Gerding, R. L., Phillips, G., & Fratianne, R. B. (1989). Risk factors associated with intravascular catheter infections in burned patients: A prospective, randomized study. *Journal of Trauma, 29,* 811–816.

Hilgard, E. R., & Hilgard, J. R. (1975). *Hypnosis in the relief of pain.* Los Altos, CA: William Kaufmann.

Hoffman, H. G., Doctor, J. N., Patterson, D. R., Weghorst, S., & Furness, T. (1998). *Use of virtual reality for adjunctive treatment of pediatric and adolescent burn pain: A case report.* Manuscript under review.

Holzman, A. D., & Turk, D. C. (1986). *Pain management.* Oxford, England: Pergamon.

Hosobuchi, Y., Adams, J. E., & Linchitz, R. (1977). Pain relief by electrical stimulation of the central gray matter in humans and its reversal by naloxone. *Science, 196,* 183–186.

Hylden, J. K. L., Nahin, R. L., Traub, R. J., & Dubner, R. (1991). Effects of spinal kappa-opioid receptor agonists on the responsiveness of nociceptive superficial dorsal horn neurons. *Pain, 44,* 187–193.

Iafrati, N. S. (1986). Pain on burn unit: Patient vs. nurse perceptions. *Journal of Burn Care and Rehabilitation, 7*(5), 413–416.

Jones, A. K. P., Brown, W. D., Friston, L. Y., Qi, R. S., & Frackowiak, J. (1991). *Cortical and subcortical localization of response to pain in man using positron emission tomography.* Proceedings of the Royal Society of London. Series B: Biological Sciences. Vol. 244 (1301) pp. 39–44.

Kelly, D. D. (1985). Central representations of pain and analgesia. In E. R. Kandel & J. H. Schwartz (Eds.), *Principles of Neural Science,* 2nd Edition (pp. 331–343). New York: Elsevier.

Kinsella, J., Glavin, R., & Reid, W. H. (1988). Patient-controlled analgesia for burn patients: A preliminary report. *Burns, 14,* 500–503.

Lee, J. J., Marvin, J. A., & Heimbach, D. M. (1989). Effectiveness of nalbuphine for relief of burn debridement pain. *Journal of Burn Care and Rehabilitation, 10,* 241–246.

Melzack, R. (1990). The tragedy of needless pain. *Scientific American, 262,* 27–33.

Melzack, R., & Wall, P. D. (1965). Pain mechanisms: A new theory. *Science, 150,* 971–979.

Morgan, J. I., & Curran, T. (1986). Role of ion flux in the control of c-fos expression. *Nature, 322,* 552–555.

Nguyen, T. T., Gilpin, D. D., Meyer, N. A., & Herndon, D. N. (1996). Current treatment of severely burned patients. *Annals of Surgery, 223*(1), 12–25.

Nunn, J. F., Chanarin, I., & Tanner, A. G. (1986). Megaloblastic bone marrow changes after repeated nitrous oxide anaesthesia. *British Journal of Anaesthesiology, 58,* 1469–1473.

Patterson, D. R. (1992). Practical applications of psychological techniques in controlling burn pain. *Journal of Burn Care and Rehabilitation, 13,* 13–18.

Patterson, D. R., Adcock, R. J., & Bombardier, C. H. (1997). Factors predicting hypnotic analgesia in clinical burn pain. *International Journal of Clinical and Experimental Hypnosis, 45,* 377–395.

Patterson, D. R., Everett, J. J., Bombardier, C. H., Questad, K. A., Lee, V. K., & Marvin, J. A. (1993b). Psychological effects of severe burn injuries. *Psychological Bulletin, 113*(2), 362–378.
Patterson, D. R., Everett, J. J., Burns, G. L., & Marvin, J. A. (1992). Hypnosis for the treatment of burn pain. *Journal of Consulting and Clinical Psychology, 60*(5), 713–717.
Patterson, D. R., Goldberg, M. L., & Ehde, D. M. (1996). Hypnosis in the treatment of patients with severe burns. *American Journal of Clinical Hypnosis, 38*(3), 200–212.
Patterson, D. R., & Ptacek, J. T. (1997). Baseline pain as a moderator of hypnotic analgesia for burn injury treatment. *Journal of Consulting and Clinical Psychology, 65*(1), 60–67.
Patterson, D. R., Ptacek, J. T., Carrougher, G. J., & Sharar, S. (1997). Lorazepam as an adjunct to opioid analgesics in the treatment of burn pain. *Pain, 72,* 367–374.
Patterson, D. R., Questad, K. A., & Boltwood, M. D. (1987). Hypnotherapy as a treatment for pain in patients with burns: Research and clinical considerations. *Journal of Burn Care and Rehabilitation, 8*(3), 263–268.
Patterson, D. R., & Sharar, S. (1997). Treating pain from severe burn injuries. *Advances in Medical Psychotherapy, 9,* 55–71.
Perl, E. (1985). Pain and pain management. In L. T. Silver (Ed.), *Research briefings, National Academy of Sciences* (pp. 20–32). Washington, DC: National Academy Press.
Perry, S. W. (1984). Undermedication for pain on a burn unit. *General Hospital Psychiatry, 6,* 308–316.
Perry, S., & Blank, K. (1984). Relationship of psychological processes during delirium to outcome. *American Journal of Psychiatry, 141,* 843–847.
Perry, S., & Heidrich, G. (1982). Management of pain during debridement: A survey of U.S. burn units. *Pain, 13,* 267–280.
Porter, J., & Jick, H. (1980). Addiction rare in patients treated with narcotics. *New England Journal of Medicine, 302,* 123–124.
Powers, P. S., Cruse, C. W., Daniels, S., & Stevens, B. A. (1993). Safety and efficacy of debridement under anesthesia in patients with burns. *Journal of Burn Care and Rehabilitation, 14,* 176–180.
Ptacek, J. T., Patterson, D. R., & Doctor, J. (1998). *Describing and predicting the nature of procedural pain following thermal injury.* Manuscript under review.
Ptacek, J. T., Patterson, D. R., Montgomery, B. K., Ordonez, N. A., & Heimbach, D. M. (1995). Pain, coping, and adjustment in patients with severe burns: Preliminary findings from a prospective study. *Journal of Pain and Symptom Management, 10,* 446–455.
Ruda, M. A., Bennett, G. J., & Dubner, R. (1986). Neurochemistry and neurocircuitry in the dorsal horn. *Progress in Brain Research, 66,* 219.
Shibutani, T. (1990). Mechanisms of the modulation of pain transmission at the subnucleus caudalis of the trigeminal sensory nuclear complex in rabbits. *Journal of Osaka University Dental Society, 35*(2), 594–608.
Steiner, H., & Clark, W. R. (1977). Psychiatric complications of burned adults: A classification. *Journal of Trauma, 17,* 134–143.
Talbot, J. D., Marett, S., Evans, A. C., Meyer, E., Bushnell, M. C., & Duncan, G. H. (1991). Multiple representations of pain in the human cortex. *Science, 251*(4999), 1355–1358.
Tan, S. (1982). Cognitive and cognitive-behavioural methods for pain control: A selective review. *Pain, 12,* 201–228.
Turk, D. C., Meichenbaum, D., & Genest, M. (1983). *Pain and behavioral medicine: A cognitive-behavioral perspective.* New York: Guilford.
Vaught, J. L., Rothman, R. B., & Westfall, T. C. (1982). Mu and delta receptors: Their role in analgesia and in the differential effects of opioid peptides on analgesia. *Life Sciences, 30,* 1443–1455.
Wakeman, R. J., & Kaplan, J. Z. (1978). An experimental study of hypnosis in painful burns. *American Journal of Clinical Hypnosis, 21,* 3–12.
Wall, P. D. (1995). Pain in the brain and lower parts of the anatomy. *Pain, 62,* 389–391.

Ward, C. M., & Diamond, A. W. (1976). An appraisal of ketamine in the dressing of burns. *Journal of Postgraduate Medicine, 5,* 222–223.

Westling, F., Milson, I., Zetterstrom, H., & Ekstrom-Jodal, B. (1992). Effects of nitrous oxide/oxygen inhalation on the maternal circulation during vaginal delivery. *Acta Anaesthesiologica Scandinavica, 36,* 175–181.

Chapter 28

Somatization, Hypochondriasis, and Related Conditions

Stefan Lautenbacher
University of Marburg, Germany

Gary B. Rollman
University of Western Ontario, Canada

DESCRIPTION OF THE DISORDERS

General Considerations

Medical patients often present with physical symptoms, including pain, that have no apparent somatic cause. The complaints are frequently accompanied by anxiety, depression, and denial of psychological problems (Dworkin, 1994; Dworkin, Wilson, & Massoth, 1994). In such cases, subclinical or clinical forms of somatoform disorders should be considered. These are conditions in which psychological conflicts and problems have taken the form of a somatic illness (Ford, 1995).

According to the *Diagnostic and Statistical Manual of Mental Disorders* (4th ed., *DSM–IV*) (American Psychiatric Association [APA], 1994), somatoform disorders are subdivided into five specific conditions: body dysmorphic phobia, hypochondriasis, somatization disorder, conversion disorder, and pain disorder. As well, there are two residual diagnostic categories: undifferentiated somatoform disorder and somatoform disorder not otherwise specified. Many other labels, such as hysteria, functional complaints, vegetative dystonia, and Briquet's syndrome, have previously been used to describe similar conditions. Not infrequently, disorders such as asthma, peptic ulcer, esophageal motility disorder, or nonulcer dyspepsia have been erroneously mixed with somatoform disorders; the former have a clearly more distinct psychophysiological basis (Kellner, 1994; Salkovskis, 1996).

613

Although somatoform disorders have been of interest for a long time, sound scientific approaches to these conditions have been rare (Rief, 1996). Consequently, these diagnostic terms fail to offer straightforward explanations for the pain problems of the afflicted patients or to lead to conspicuous success in pain management. Hence, the first part of this chapter emphasizes the description of those somatoform disorders that focus on pain problems, particularly somatization disorder, pain disorder, conversion disorder, and hypochondriasis. Later sections deal with speculations on the cause of these conditions and on the implications of concepts such as hypervigilance and somatosensory amplification.

Somatization Disorder and Pain Disorder

Somatization disorder and (somatoform) pain disorder have much in common, because pain is a prime component of both. A somatization disorder has to be considered if, after careful investigation, investigators have failed to find an organic basis for pain and other somatic complaints, and yet the patient's worries have increased instead of decreased. A somatization disorder is also likely if the complaints are grossly beyond the level that can be explained by organic pathology. Patients are very often demanding and complain in a dramatic and emotional fashion (Ford, 1995; Kaplan, Sadock, & Grebb, 1994; Rief, 1996).

The process of somatization is considered "the selective perception and focus on the somatic manifestations of depression" (Katon, A. Kleinman, & Rosen, 1982) or "an idiom of distress in which patients with psychosocial and emotional problems articulate their distress primarily through physical symptomatology" (Katon, A. Kleinman, & Rosen, 1982, p. 127). Somatic complaints without known organic etiology are not necessarily due to somatization, because patients suffering from such conditions may acknowledge psychological problems. Somatizers, however, see themselves as markedly and exclusively vulnerable to bodily problems and downplay their emotional and psychological difficulties (Bass & Benjamin, 1993; Dworkin, 1994; Salkovskis, 1996).

Multiple pains are characteristic and mandatory criteria (at least four pain problems in *DSM–IV*; APA, 1994; see Table 28.1) for a somatization disorder (Dworkin, 1994). Among these are headache, abdominal pain, back pain, articular pain, pain in the extremities, chest pain, anal or genital pain, menstrual pain, or pain during intercourse or micturition (Rief, 1996). In a population-based study, Fink (1992) observed that abdominal pain was the most frequent reason for admission of somatizers to nonpsychiatric health facilities. Rief, Hiller, and Fichter (1997) found back pain and headache to be the most frequent somatoform symptoms among psychosomatic patients. Swartz, Blazer, Woodbury, George, and Landerman

TABLE 28.1

Diagnostic Criteria for Somatization Disorder According to *DSM–IV*

A. Onset before age of 30 years; chronic course; repeated requests for treatment; severe functional disability.
B. At least eight symptoms, four of them being pain symptoms, two gastrointestinal symptoms, one a sexual symptom, and one a pseudo-neurological symptom.
C. No or no sufficient medical explanation for the symptoms in criterion B.
D. No factitious disorder, no malingering.

(1986) described individuals from the general population who suffered from at least three somatization symptoms. Five of their top 10 symptoms were pain related (headache, menstrual pain, chest pain, abdominal pain, and pain in the extremities).

Dworkin, Von Korff, and LeResche (1990) found that the tendency to suffer from somatization symptoms (not including pain) was strongly associated with the number of painful sites. In other words, somatizers tend to have multiple pains or show considerable pain dispersion. Furthermore, they present with strong pain-related disability and interference with daily living (Dworkin et al., 1994).

In addition to pain problems, a diagnosis of a somatization disorder in *DSM–IV* (APA, 1994) requires the presence of psychosexual problems (at least one) and gastrointestinal (at least two) and pseudo-neurological symptoms (at least one), all of which cannot be explained by an organic disorder, as well as a chronic course (episodic with a duration of several years in most cases) and an onset before the third decade. The multiplicity of the complaints helps to distinguish somatization disorder from the other somatoform disorders. However, the high number of complaints has been subject to criticism, because it excludes many individuals, with an apparently similar psychopathology but somewhat fewer symptoms, from this diagnostic category (Dworkin, 1994; Eisendrath, 1995; Ford, 1995; Kaplan et al., 1994; Rief, 1996).

Below the level of a full-blown syndrome, somatization occurs very frequently in a diminished form, but still showing widespread and strongly troubling symptoms. It has become increasingly evident that even such "subclinical" conditions are serious enough to require diagnostic acknowledgment and intervention. Therefore, such categories as undifferentiated somatoform disorder and somatoform disorder not otherwise specified have been introduced into the *DSM–IV* (APA, 1994) classification system. Prevalence estimates for the subsyndromal forms range from 4% to 17 % and can reach 40% (e.g., in neurology), but they are below 1% for a full-blown somatization disorder. Women suffer much more frequently from these conditions than men (with a ratio of about 10 to 1). Whether an increased frequency in some families points to a genetic etiology remains to established

(Bass & Benjamin, 1993; Dworkin, 1994; Dworkin et al., 1994, Eisendrath, 1995; Ford, 1995; Kellner, 1994; Rief, 1996; Rief et al., 1997; Salkovskis, 1996).

The comorbidity with panic disorder is extremely high (up to 100%), and also appreciable for major depression (up to 90%), agoraphobia, substance abuse, and personality disorders (Dworkin et al., 1994; Ford, 1995; Lipowski, 1990). There may be a history of physical and sexual abuse. Consequently, unexplained somatic complaints may be part of a posttraumatic stress disorder (Ford, 1995). The strong overlap with other pathological conditions has led to the conclusion that somatization disorder is a strong aggregation of physical and psychiatric syndromes (Lipowski, 1990).

If pain is the predominant symptom, the diagnosis of a pain disorder is to be preferred (Rief et al., 1997). This condition requires that psychological factors play a central but not necessarily an exclusive role in initiating and maintaining the pain (see Table 28.2). Pathognomic type or location of pain is absent. Pain disorder often develops after an injury or a somatic illness associated with pain. The pain in a pain disorder is real; it is not claimed as part of malingering or a factitious disorder. Women are more likely than men to suffer from such a somatoform pain disorder, although the reasons for this difference are unclear (Comer, 1995; Eisendrath, 1995; Ford, 1995; Kaplan et al., 1994).

This definition of a pain disorder seems to describe a large number of chronic pain patients. Many individuals with specific syndromes suffer not only from pain but also from numerous nonspecific somatic symptoms. The diagnostic concept of a somatoform pain disorder is misused, however, if it is employed in addition to the diagnosis of a specific chronic pain syndrome. If the location of pain, the organ affected by pain, the subjective spatial and temporal characteristics of pain, and the course of pain allow the diagnosis of a specific chronic pain syndrome as described, for example, by the IASP classification system (Merskey & Bogduk, 1994), the understanding and the treatment of the pain are based on more solid ground than if the clinician must rely upon vague speculations about the causes and cures of a somatoform pain disorder.

TABLE 28.2
Diagnostic Criteria for Pain Disorder According to *DSM–IV*

A. Pain in one or more sites as predominant symptom, severe enough to warrant clinical attention.
B. Significant distress and impairment of psychosocial and occupational functioning caused by the pain.
C. Onset, severity, exacerbation, or maintenance of the pain are crucially influenced by psychological factors.
D. No factitious disorder, no malingering.
E. The pain cannot accounted for by mood, anxiety, or psychotic disorder and is not a dyspareunia.

The interaction between somatization and chronic pain is complex. This is especially true when the interaction occurs, as it frequently does, within a depressive disorder. There, pain is often thought to be a symptom of depression and depression to be a consequence of chronic pain (Lipowski, 1990). Despite this puzzling situation, somatization seems to be both an important risk factor for and a symptom of chronic pain conditions (Dworkin et al., 1994). The level of somatization appears to determine how limiting and disabling a pain disorder turns out to be in the long run. This, in turn, is a major influence on number of treatment attempts and on costs for the health care system (Dworkin et al., 1994).

Descriptions of somatization disorder and pain disorder make it clear that these conditions are similar to psychosomatic syndromes. Thus, many symptoms of somatoform disorders can be caused by conditions, which might be called psychosomatic in another context. Furthermore, in both groups of disorders there is a clustering of multiple complaints, a substantial number of which can be triggered by stress (Kellner, 1994).

Conversion Syndrome

If there are one or more neurological symptoms that cannot be explained by a known neurological disorder and that can be related to psychological problems (but not to intentional malingering or feigning), the diagnosis of a conversion disorder should be considered (Kaplan et al., 1994; Rief et al., 1997; see Table 28.3). In contrast to the other somatoform disorders, objective functional deficits are required instead of only subjective ones. These are paralysis, blindness, seizures, aphonia, anesthesia, and others. Anesthesia is important in the present context because of its relation to the perception of pain. Nevertheless, almost nothing is known about the clinical consequences of this problem. However, patients with conversion syndrome do also present with pain (Merskey, 1994).

TABLE 28.3
Diagnostic Criteria for Conversion Disorder According to *DSM–IV*

A. Deficits of voluntary motor and sensory function suggesting a neurological or other general medical condition.

B. Psychological factors associated with the symptoms (initiation or exacerbation after conflict or other stressor).

C. No factitious disorder, no malingering.

D. No sufficient explanation of the symptom by a general medical condition, by substance effects, or as culturally sanctioned behavior or experience.

E. Significant distress and impairment of psychosocial and occupational functioning caused by the symptoms; symptoms severe enough to warrant medical evaluation.

F. Not merely pain or sexual dysfunction as the symptom; the symptom is not exclusively part of a somatization disorder or better explained by another mental disorder.

The difficulty in differentiating objective and subjective dysfunctions for diagnosis, plus the still-influential psychodynamic history of this notion, have led some authors to question the validity of the concept of conversion disorder. This situation is made even more troublesome by the fact that neurological signs often become evident at later stages of the disorder (Comer, 1995; Ford, 1995; Salkovskis, 1996). In addition, as Merskey (1994) has noted, chronic pain patients often keep their limbs immobile or use them in an awkward fashion to avoid discomfort, but this misuse or disuse should not be taken as a sign of conversion.

The prevalence of a comprehensive conversion disorder has been estimated to be low and becoming increasingly rare. However, reliable estimates are difficult to obtain because of sizable differences between various health care settings. Furthermore, it is possible that instead of disappearing, conversion disorder has changed its appearance in more medically knowledgeable Western societies. It has been argued that syndromes involving pain, similar to the somatoform pain disorder described earlier, have become more frequent, replacing the classical forms of conversion syndrome. However, at least among female adolescents and young adults with little education, low intelligence, and low socioeconomic status, conversion symptoms are still felt to be common (Comer, 1995; Ford, 1995; Kaplan et al., 1994; Pilowsky, 1994; Salkovskis, 1996).

Interestingly, even pain patients with physical diagnoses can be classified as suffering from a conversion disorder. Fishbain, Goldberg, Meagher, Steele, and Rosomoff (1986) found that 38% of their patients with organic pain fit the diagnosis of a conversion disorder. This diagnosis was based mainly on the finding of "non-anatomical sensory losses." However, the authors questioned the validity of this label because of the lack of knowledge about the characteristics of that term.

Hypochondriasis

Despite being a syndrome with somewhat different characteristics, hypochondriasis is nevertheless thought to be related to the other somatoform disorders. Contrary to the syndromes described earlier, the outstanding feature is a strong fear or conviction of having a serious illness, maintained despite intensive attempts at correction (see Table 28.4). Somatic complaints may be present and disproportionate, but they are not the hallmarks. The multiplicity of somatic problems seen in somatization disorder is not present in hypochondriasis. Rather, hypochondriacal patients focus on one or two symptoms. The precise relationship between somatization and hypochondriasis is still unclear and there may be some overlap between the two conditions. The situation becomes even more complicated by the fact, discussed later, that the term hypochondriasis is used not only to

TABLE 28.4
Diagnostic Criteria for Hypochondriasis According to *DSM–IV*

A. Preoccupation with fear or conviction of having a serious disease because of the misinterpretation of bodily symptoms.
B. Preoccupation despite appropriate medical evaluation and reassurance.
C. Criterion A is not delusional in nature and restricted to a circumscribed concern about appearance (as in body dysmorphic disorder).
D. Significant distress and impairment of psychosocial and occupational functioning caused by the preoccupation.
E. Disturbance more than 6 months.
F. The preoccupation is not better accounted for by generalized anxiety disorder, obsessive-compulsive disorder, panic disorder, a major depressive episode, separation anxiety, or another somatoform disorder.

---

describe a syndrome but also to name behaviors and attitudes as well as cognitive and affective styles (Barsky & Klerman, 1983; Dworkin et al., 1994; Rief et al., 1997; Salkovskis, 1996).

Pain can be present if a hypochondriacal individual amplifies normal somatic sensations, which is often the case. However, pain is not a necessary criterion for hypochondriasis. The pain in hypochondriasis—like all of the other complaints—is often vague, variable, and generalized. Most frequent locations are the head, neck, chest, and abdomen (Barsky & Klerman, 1983; Dworkin et al., 1994; Eisendrath, 1995).

There has been considerable discussion as to whether hypochondriasis is a discrete and cohesive psychopathological condition in its own right, whether it is mainly secondary to other psychological problems, particularly to depression, or whether it is a cluster of attitudes and behaviors, which are not closely related to any disorders. Primary hypochondriasis is said to exist if hypochondriacal behavior exceeds a critical duration (6 months in *DSM–IV*; APA, 1994) and is not clearly tied to other psychiatric problems. Transient and symptomatic forms exist in patients with major depression, panic disorder, and schizophrenia (Barsky & Klerman, 1983; Ford, 1995; Salkovskis, 1996).

There are several components of hypochondriasis. On an affective level, it appears as body-related phobia and an obsessive preoccupation with one's own body; on a cognitive level, it presents as a rigid conviction that one is ill or is threatened by illness, with sometimes almost delusional character. The cognitive distortion often includes the unrealistic perspective that true health does not permit any bodily discomfort (Barsky & Klerman, 1983; Rief, 1996; Salkovskis, 1996).

Because of their somatic bias, hypochondriacal individuals rarely visit psychiatrists and psychologists. Rather, they look for help from "somatic experts," that is, family physicians or pain specialists, although they often fail to trust medical authorities. In primary-care settings, 3% to 14% of patients may be classified as hypochondriacs and may have extensive histories of previous medical care. In contrast to somatization disorder, men are affected equally often as women. Hypochondriasis starts later in life than somatization disorder (Barsky & Klerman, 1983; Comer, 1995; Eisendrath, 1995; Ford, 1995; Salkovskis, 1996).

CAUSAL FACTORS

Exaggerated Stress Responses

Although, in general, there seems to be no straightforward causal relationship between stress and chronic pain, some findings suggest that exaggerated stress-related responses in the striated muscles form the basis of regional pain in some pain patients (Flor & Birbaumer, 1994; Merskey, 1994). Correspondingly, some authors assume that a more generalized pattern of hyperreactivity to stress affecting various organ systems might be seen in psychosomatic disorders or somatoform disorders. The hypothesized stress responses in both types of disorders may include endocrine changes, striated muscle tension, smooth muscle activity, and hyperventilation (Kellner, 1994).

Augmentation, Amplification, and Hypervigilance

When awareness is reached during processing of bodily signals, perceptual mechanisms become relevant. It is at this stage when amplification, augmentation, and hypervigilance, which are perceptual distortions of potential relevance for somatoform disorders, can occur (Dworkin, 1994). Barsky and Klerman (1983) assumed that hypochondriacal patients experience normal bodily sensation as painful because they augment and amplify bodily sensations, are less stoical, and have low thresholds for discomfort. Such a nonspecific perceptual enhancement of distressing events was labeled by Barsky (1992) as *somatosensory amplification*. However, Spinhoven and van der Does (1997) provided some evidence that somatosensory amplification may not explain the process of somatization particularly well. An even more important causal factor for somatization in their study appeared to be anxiety.

Because there is no direct evidence, from longitudinal studies, that somatosensory amplification, augmentation, or hypervigilance are indeed risk factors for somatoform disorders (Rief, 1996), there are many unanswered questions about the influence of perceptual mechanisms in their genesis. Patients with hypochondriasis and disease phobia have exhibited lowered pain thresholds (Kellner, 1994; Merskey & Evans, 1975), although contrary findings also exist (Lautenbacher, Pauli, Zaudig, & Birbaumer, 1998). Moreover, a lowered pain threshold might be the result or the cause of a somatoform disorder.

Barsky and Klerman (1983) speculated that besides perceptual distortions, hypochondriacal patients misinterpret normal bodily sensations as signals for serious diseases. Such a cognitive distortion may enhance each small discomfort to life-threatening proportions. This phenomenon is also related to catastrophizing, an exaggerated style of cognitive and emotional appraisal (Dworkin, 1994).

Abnormal Illness Behavior

Abnormal illness behavior represents an inappropriate and maladaptive mode of perceiving, evaluating, and acting despite appropriate management of a disease by health care providers and relatives. Illness behavior depends strongly on contingencies determined by the "sick role" in a society. If, for example, it seems more favorable for an individual to present with physical problems instead of depression because the former, but not the latter, leads to sympathy, encouragement, attention, support, and compensation, a somatic masking of psychological problems or, more simply, somatization may occur (Barsky & Klerman, 1983). More attractive contingencies for physical than for psychological complaints appear to be part of our highly "medicalized" Western society (Dworkin et al., 1994). Furthermore, abnormal illness behavior may include the conviction that true health excludes any somatic discomfort. Consequently, the patient is likely to take each sign of discomfort as symptomatic of a disease (Rief, 1996).

Commonly, patients are given reinforcement (e.g., avoidance of responsibilities and increased caring responses from those close to them) for their somatization. Even physicians tend to direct their attention to their patients' somatic symptoms instead of their psychological ones (Bass & Benjamin, 1993; Ford, 1995; Salkovskis, 1996). It is not surprising, then, that increased somatic focus occurs and that patients become preoccupied with monitoring and reporting their physical complaints.

Some authors believe that the concept of abnormal illness behavior provides a theoretical framework for all somatoform disorders (Pilowsky, 1994). Eisendrath (1995) argued that the type of somatoform disorder attributable to abnormal illness behavior depends mainly on whether the patient's motivation is conscious or not.

A result obtained by Dworkin et al. (1994) is of special interest for the management of chronic pain. The authors reported that whether chronic pain patients attributed the cause of their pain to physical or behavioral factors was dependent on their individual level of somatization as measured by the SCL–90. Hence, somatization is associated with a belief system that blames organic factors for chronic pain. Consequently, it is very likely that somatizers will also look for a "somatic expert" to cure their pain problem.

Phobic and Obsessive-Compulsive Response Pattern

Hypochondriasis shares several cognitive features with phobic and obsessive-compulsive disorders. The similarity with obsessive-compulsive disorders involves mainly the narrowing and automatization of thinking that focuses on the threat of a serious illness, that tends to catastrophize, and that withstands all attempts of correction. Not surprisingly, some hypochondriacal patients meet the criteria for obsessive-compulsive disorders. The emotional similarity with anxiety disorder is also obvious because of the constant worry and concern about health status. Therefore, some authors prefer to group hypochondriasis with anxiety disorders and treat it accordingly, often with considerable success (Dworkin et al., 1994; Ford, 1995; Merskey, 1994).

TREATMENT CONSIDERATIONS

Most patients with somatoform disorders are seen and treated first by family physicians (Rief et al., 1997). When the somatoform disorder is finally diagnosed, a therapeutic nihilism often results, because even psychotherapists consider somatizers as extremely difficult patients. Somatoform disorders have been thought to be extremely resistant to change, a view that needs correction, at least in the case of hypochondriasis, which can be treated with some success (Rief, 1996; Salkovskis, 1996).

Physicians' usual emphasis on seeking evidence of a physical disorder is understandable, but it is often detrimental to patients suffering from somatoform disorders. Contact with many medical personnel merely increases the patient's opportunity to demonstrate various somatic complaints. The major aim of therapy should be a gradual replacement of a patient's physical perspective by a psychosocial one, using regularly timed appointments rather than ones scheduled in response to somatic complaints. This approach may include training in various psychological coping strategies and in expressing emotions in a nonsomatic fashion. Such psychological treatments are most likely to be effective if they can decrease the patient's catastrophizing and increase her or his self-efficacy. A major reason for dropping out of therapy and for paradoxical exacerbations of symptoms is a management style that pushes a patient too hard and too early toward a psychological perspective and that consequently challenges the "sick role" of the patient without sufficient preparation (Barsky &

Klerman, 1983; Bass & Benjamin, 1993; Dworkin et al., 1994; Kaplan et al., 1994; Pilowsky, 1994, 1995; Rief, 1996).

Many patients with somatoform disorders have unrealistic ideas: that a healthy person does not experience any kind of bodily discomfort and that bodily discomfort can be caused only by a somatic disease and not by psychological problems or stress. The offer of alternative explanations can be very beneficial and can help to prepare patients for "coping not curing." However, somatic beliefs are deeply rooted and often withstand vigorous attempts at modification. Nevertheless, treatment of somatizers can hardly be successful without a change in cognitions, because the patient's conceptions of his or her illness determines what type of help is asked for, from whom, when, and where. A purely physical perspective and an overly aggressive psychological one can each prove ineffective. The former reinforces the patient's inappropriate somatic convictions, whereas the latter shatters the patient's system of illness beliefs. Strong dysfunctional illness beliefs and too many contacts with health care providers are both predictive of chronic courses of an illness (Bass & Benjamin, 1993; Dworkin et al.; 1994; Pilowsky, 1995; Rief et al., 1997).

Despite the pharmacological emphasis of contemporary psychiatry, it is still doubtful whether there are indications for using drugs to treat patients with somatoform disorders. Systematic treatment attempts have been rare. The use of antidepressants has the best empirical basis (Pilowsky, 1994; Rief et al., 1997). It is noteworthy that the so-called "psychogenic" pain of somatoform disorders does not respond any better than do "somatic" pains to antidepressive medication (Volz, Stieglietz, Menges, & Möller, 1994).

SOMATIZATION, HYPOCHONDRIASIS, AND HYPERVIGILANCE IN OTHER PAIN DISORDERS

Questions about somatization, hypochondriasis, and related matters arise in attempts to understand pain syndromes whose symptoms are clear but whose underlying processes remain murky. Consider, for example, fibromyalgia. This disorder, characterized by widespread bodily pain, multiple tender points, fatigue, sleep disturbances, stiffness, and attentional difficulties, has no evident pathophysiological basis.

Numerous investigators have reported that fibromyalgia patients score high on scales of depression, anxiety, and hypochondriasis (e.g., Ahles, Yunus, & Riley, 1984; Goldenberg, 1987; Payne et al., 1982; Wolfe, Cathey, & Kleinheksel, 1984; Yunus, Ahles, Aldag, & Masi, 1991). Interpretations of such findings, however, must be made with caution. The Minnesota Multiphasic Personality Inventory (MMPI) has often been used as the personality questionnaire in these studies. The MMPI has been deemed inappropriate for use with pain patients by some specialists (e.g., Merskey et al., 1985; Smythe, 1984) because individuals suffering from painful disorders will almost inevitably affirm health-related items, such as "I feel weak all over much of the time," or answer in the negative to "I am about as able to work as I ever was," both of which raise their scores on psychopathological scales. Patients suffering from disorders that have an identifiable organic pathology will also, not surprisingly, answer in the same way and, consequently, show scale elevations.

Scudds, Rollman, Harth, and McCain (1987) examined personality measures for fibromyalgia and arthritis patients, as well as normal controls, on the Basic Personality Inventory, an instrument designed with strong psychometric criteria. They eliminated items that might be included among the symptomatic features of the two disorders. Fibromyalgia patients scored markedly higher than controls on the hypochondriasis scale, but those scores were only slightly higher than those obtained for rheumatoid arthritis sufferers. It is inappropriate to conclude from personality tests such as these, which fail to appropriately assess all of the necessary diagnostic criteria, that fibromyalgia is a hypochondriacal disorder.

Fibromyalgia patients were also elevated on measures of depression and anxiety when compared to normals, but this is not surprising given that they are suffering from a disorder that is painful, troubling, and difficult for the patients, their families, and their physicians to understand. Still, it does not rule out a common pathopsychophysiology of affective disorders, anxiety disorder, and fibromyalgia. Related findings, also using the Basic Personality Inventory, were obtained by Schnurr, Brooke, and Rollman (1990). They compared individuals with temporomandibular pain and dysfunction syndrome (TMPDS), who have intense pain in the masticatory muscles, with patients who had painful conditions arising from injury and with a group of pain-free controls. TMPDS patients also suffer from a disorder whose pathophysiology is unknown and that has been linked to stress. As well, they, too, have been reported to show abnormal elevations in a variety of personality characteristics (e.g., Gale, 1978; Merskey et al., 1987). Schnurr et al. found that the hypochondriasis scores of TMPDS patients were strikingly elevated compared to pain-free subjects but were essentially identical to those of the patients with pain due to injury. Again, one cannot conclude that hypochondriacal traits are the root of their disorder. However, they may well serve as a risk factor for the transition from acute to chronic pain.

At least three contrasting possibilities can be suggested by findings such as these. First, traditional psychological scales that assess psychological distress and bodily complaints, often developed and normed for psychiatric patients, are not applicable to the study of medical patients, especially for those suffering from serious pain. Second, hypochondriacal traits may be seen in syndromes with pain that has an organic basis as well as with pain of unknown origin. Third, elevated levels of hypochondriasis, as well as anxiety and depression, might be a consequence of pain and not necessarily its cause. Similar considerations apply when looking at the relation between somatization and various pain syndromes (McKinney, Londeen, Turner, & Levitt, 1990). More investigations, using instruments for assessing psychological distress and bodily complaints that are normed on pain patients and that look also at individuals suffering from chronic illnesses that are not marked by pain, are needed to help distinguish among these alternatives.

Clues about factors that contribute to disorders such as fibromyalgia and TMPDS have come from a series of perceptual studies. It is a given that fibromyalgia patients will have exquisite sensitivity at 11 or more of the 18 tender points specified in the American College of Rheumatology criteria for the disorder (Wolfe et al., 1990). Scudds et al. (1987), among others, found that they also show much lower pain threshold and pain tolerance to pressure applied at control sites. Whatever differentiates the pain reaction of fibromyalgia patients and controls is not limited to specific loci. Nor is the difference to be found only for pain involving the muscles. Lautenbacher, Rollman, and McCain (1994) showed that fibromyalgia patients had significantly lower pain thresholds when the noxious stimulus was heat (delivered to the arm and the trapezius by means of a Peltier thermode system) or a train of electrical pulses (presented to a pressure-sensitive point on the trapezius through a pair of silver electrodes). At the least, fibromyalgia patients generally show a considerable degree of responsiveness to noxious stimuli, whatever the origin.

McDermid, Rollman, and McCain (1996) demonstrated that this hypersensitivity extends beyond the traditional pain domain. Fibromyalgia patients, when presented with 3-second bursts of white noise through a headset, had a tolerance level of about 66 dB, an intensity that would sound only moderately loud to control subjects (whose noise tolerance was 100 dB). Rheumatoid arthritis patients also showed a diminished noise tolerance, but to a lesser extent (76 dB). Fibromyalgia patients stood out from both of the other two groups in their scores on the Noise Sensitivity Scale (Weinstein, 1978), a questionnaire designed to elicit information about the disturbance and interference elicited by environmental sounds.

More recent studies have employed psychophysical methods to look at possible deficiencies of pain modulation in fibromyalgia patients. Using the diffuse noxious inhibitory control paradigm, in which a tonic noxious stimulus (such as a tourniquet or a long-lasting intense heat stimulus) at one site on the body, such as the arm, suppresses the pain threshold or rated painfulness of a noxious phasic stimulus (such as electrical shock) applied to a distant body part, both Kosek and Hansson (1997) and Lautenbacher and Rollman (1997) found less suppression of pain in patients than in controls. It remains to be determined whether this reflects a dysfunction of physiological inhibition or an attentional disorder in which the fibromyalgia sufferers concentrate on all noxious inputs whereas pain-free individuals channel their attentional capacity to the more lasting and noxious input.

The hyper-responsiveness and the lack of inhibitory capacities in fibromyalgia patients may explain why it is associated with such a wide range of bodily symptoms and complaints including headache, irritable bowel, dysmenorrhea, light sensitivity, temporomandibular dysfunction, and paresthesias (Waylonis & Heck, 1992; Yunus et al., 1991). Smythe (1986), in observing their response to both internal and external stimuli, has described fibromyalgia patients as suffering from the "irritable everything syndrome" (p. 2). McDermid et al. (1996) found confirmatory evidence through the Pennebaker Inventory for Limbic Languidness (Pennebaker, 1982), a checklist that assesses the frequency of occurrence of 54 common physical symptoms and sensations. Scores for the fibromyalgia patients were considerably greater than for the controls. The arthritis patient scores were also elevated, but to a much smaller degree.

A host of factors may contribute to the hyper-responsiveness seen in chronic, multisymptom pain disorders such as fibromyalgia and TMPDS. Recent studies on fibromyalgia have tended to emphasize biological rather than psychosocial mechanisms, concentrating on muscles, substance P, serotonin, neuroendocrine agents, central processing of pain as revealed by positron emission tomography scans, and others. Alterations have been seen in many of these, but McDermid et al. (1996) cautioned, "while some of these factors may be of primary importance in the pathophysiology of the disease, most must be secondary influences and thus should be viewed as correlates rather than causes of the disorder" (p. 140). Hence, there is no reason to stop the quest for causal factors or to exclude explanations on a psychological level.

Such perceptual studies on pain thresholds or pain inhibition in pain patients provide insights into some of the mechanisms that underlie their disorders. Rollman and Lautenbacher (1993), examining evidence from a number of investigations, suggested that fibromyalgia involves a generalized pattern of hyper-responsiveness to internal and external discomfort that could be characterized under the heading of *hypervigilance*. They noted that hypervigilance is a more focused concept than hypochondriasis. As Barsky, Wyshak, and Klerman (1990) observed, "hypochondriacal symptoms can be thought of as the product of psychodynamic forces, interpersonal miscommunication, formative learning experiences, or an amplifying cognitive and perceptual style" (p. 323). Most notions of hypochondriasis imply a psychopathological process. Hypervigilance emphasizes a perceptual and cognitive one.

Barsky, Wyshak, and Klerman (1986) found that disease fear, disease conviction, bodily preoccupation, and somatic symptoms, all of which are compatible with the *DSM–IV* (APA, 1994) diagnosis of hypochondriasis, also cluster together in many medical patients. Consequently, it is important to distinguish individuals who have hypochondriacal attitudes and beliefs that are distinct and severe enough for a diagnosis of hypochondriasis from those who do not suffer from a psychiatric disorder but who do demonstrate heightened awareness and sensitivity to bodily events. The latter might be characterized by some as somatosensory amplification (Barsky & Wyshak, 1990) and by others as hypervigilance. Somatosensory amplification is measured by means of questionnaires whose items are similar to those that are used to assess hypochondriasis. Hypervigilance is typically determined through examination of perceptual performance. It remains to be established whether the two tap into common behavioral and cognitive elements.

We prefer to use the term hypervigilance when dealing with disorders such as fibromyalgia and TMPDS. This is partly for historical reasons, because Naliboff, Cohen, Schandler, and Heinrich (1981) contrasted Chapman's (1978) model of hypervigilance with Rollman's (1979) model of adaptation level in examining the threshold for noxious input in pain patients. The first suggests that pain patients have diminished pain threshold and tolerance levels, hyper-responding to both internal and external stimuli. In contrast. the adaptation level model suggests that pain patients compare external stimuli to their endogenous pain, rating the stimuli as less intense than they would if they did not have a high level of pain as an internal anchor or comparison point. Both models have received support (Naliboff & Cohen, 1989; Rollman, 1992), but for different populations of pain patients.

Kellner (1994) suggested that many of the phenomena of disorders such as fibromyalgia, chronic fatigue, irritable bowel, nonulcer dyspepsia, urethral syndrome, and others are caused by clustering of psychosomatic syndromes and a low sensation threshold. Naliboff et al. (1997) found that patients with irritable bowel syndrome showed Ahypervigilance for visceral stimuli, manifested as lowered response criteria for using the descriptor 'discomfort' " (p. 505).

Hypervigilance, as a descriptive term, has tended to focus attention on perceptual performance. The differences in pain thresholds, tolerance values, or ratings between certain groups of pain patients and other pain patients or pain-free controls, have often been substantial. However, it would be premature to suggest that this simply reflects a difference in transduction or transmission of noxious signals. Hypervigilance may be associated with a series of processes, beyond the perceptual ones, that have potentially pathogenic relevance (Rollman, 1998).

Those who are hypervigilant may be more likely to (a) show greater sensitivity to stimuli (although this may turn out not to be an integral characteristic), (b) monitor internal and external events, (c) attribute bodily signs to physiological causes rather than to environmental or psychological ones, (d) demonstrate a cognitive pattern of catastrophizing in attempting to cope with their situation, and (e) react to negative events and cognitions with one or more of a number of bodily reactions such as localized or widespread muscle tension, altered gastric motility, or marked autonomic or cardiovascular function.

In a recent study, McDermid and Rollman (1996) were able to discriminate among fibromyalgia patients, TMPDS patients, arthritis patients, and pain-free controls on measures of monitoring, symptom attribution, anxiety, and coping response. In a discriminant function analysis, fibromyalgia patients stood out from the other pain groups on a dimension characterized as monitoring and both the fibromyalgia and TMPDS groups had significantly higher scores than the arthritis patients on a second dimension related to symptom anxiety.

Issues concerning the interplay of biological and psychosocial factors in pain remain both fascinating and controversial. To stress the importance of one is not to negate the other; nor should it be seen, by patient or physician, as either favorable or pejorative to emphasize a particular predisposing or contributing factor. Monitoring of somatic signals, interpretation of bodily symptoms, evaluation of symptoms, and the marshaling of coping responses (Dworkin, 1990; Mechanic, 1985) occur to varying degrees in all individuals. Moreover, much as one might wish to see concepts such as hypochondriasis, somatization, illness behavior, and hypervigilance as independent constructs, the evidence indicates that they are closely related to one another (Spekens, Spinhoven, Sloekers, Bolk, & van Hemert, 1996).

A host of questions remain unanswered concerning the underpinnings of various painful disorders: the leap from correlation to causation, the role of various psychological and pharmacological approaches in dealing with psychological manifestations of pain, the reasons why many of the pain disorders marked by hypervigilant behavior are found strikingly more often in women than in men (Berkley, 1997; Rollman, 1995; Unruh, 1996), and the distinction between behavioral and physiological manifestations of stress (Jones, Rollman, & Brooke, 1997). Longitudinal studies are badly needed to determine the predictors of various psychologically linked pain disorders, the determinants of good and bad outcomes relating to their pain problem, and the incidence of comorbid psychiatric disorders (Walker et al., 1997). We need a better understanding of why some patients with disorders such as fibromyalgia (Aaron et al., 1996; Wolfe, Ross, Anderson, Russell, & Hebert, 1995) and irritable bowel syndrome (Drossman et al., 1988) meet all criteria for the disorder but feel no need to seek medical treatment. Finally, we need to identify the mechanisms that determine why a somatic presentation occurs at a particular system or site (Robbins, Kirmayer, & Hemami, 1997) and why, when there is an overlap of symptoms (e.g., Hudson, Goldenberg, Pope, Keck, & Schlesinger, 1992), a patient often chooses to report one to a physician (say, pain rather than fatigue), thereby possibly affecting both the diagnosis and the treatment that follow.

ACKNOWLEDGMENTS

Preparation of the manuscript was aided by a grant to both authors from the TransCoop Program of the German-American Academic Council Foundation and by grants to Gary B. Rollman from the Agnes Cole Dark Fund, Faculty of Social Science, University of Western Ontario and the Natural Sciences and Engineering Research Council of Canada.

REFERENCES

Aaron, L. A., Bradley, L. A., Alarcón, G. S., Alexander, R. W., Triana-Alexander, M., Martin, M. Y., & Alberts, K. R. (1996). Psychiatric diagnoses in patients with fibromyalgia are related to health care-seeking behavior rather than to illness. *Arthritis and Rheumatism, 39,* 436–445.

Ahles, T. A., Yunus, M. B., & Riley, S. D. (1984). Psychological factors associated with primary fibromyalgia syndrome. *Arthritis and Rheumatism, 27,* 1101–1105.

American Psychiatric Association. (1994). *Diagnostic and statistical manual of mental disorders* (4th ed.). Washington, DC: Author.

Barsky, A. J. (1992). Amplification, somatization, and the somatoform disorders. *Psychosomatics, 33,* 28–34.

Barsky, A. J., & Klerman, G. L. (1983). Overview: Hypochondriasis, bodily complaints, and somatic styles. *American Journal of Psychiatry, 140,* 273–283.

Barsky, A. J., & Wyshak, G. (1990). Hypochondriasis and somatosensory amplification. *British Journal of Psychiatry, 157,* 404–409.

Barsky, A. J., Wyshak, G., & Klerman, G. L. (1986). Hypochondriasis: An evaluation of the *DSM–III* criteria in medical outpatients. *Archives of General Psychiatry, 43,* 493–500.

Barsky, A. J., Wyshak, G., & Klerman, G. L. (1990). The Somatosensory Amplification Scale and its relationship to hypochondriasis. *Journal of Psychiatric Research, 24,* 323–334.

Bass, C., & Benjamin, S. (1993). The management of chronic somatisation. *British Journal of Psychiatry, 162,* 472–480.

Berkley, K. J. (1997). Sex differences in pain. *Behavioral and Brain Sciences, 20,* 371–380.

Chapman, C. R. (1978). The perception of noxious events. In R. A. Sternbach (Ed.), *The psychology of pain* (pp. 169–203). New York: Raven.

Comer, R. J. (1995). *Abnormal psychology* (2nd ed.). New York: Freeman.

Drossman, D. A., McKee, D. C., Sandler, R. S., Mitchell, C. M., Cramer, E. M., Lowman, B. C., & Burger, A. L. (1988). Psychosocial factors in the irritable bowel syndrome. *Gastroenterology, 95,* 701–708.

Dworkin, S. F. (1990). Illness behavior and dysfunction: Review of concepts and application to chronic pain. *Canadian Journal of Physiology and Pharmacology, 69*, 662–671.

Dworkin, S. F. (1994). Somatization, distress and chronic pain. *Quality of Life Research, 3*, 77–83.

Dworkin, S. F., Von Korff, M., & LeResche, L. (1990). Multiple pains and psychiatric disturbance. *Archives of General Psychiatry, 47*, 239–244.

Dworkin, S. F., Wilson, L., & Massoth, D. L. (1994). Somatizing as a risk factor for chronic pain. In R. C. Grzesiak & D. S. Ciccone (Eds.), *Psychological vulnerability to chronic pain* (pp. 28–54). New York: Springer-Verlag.

Eisendrath, S. J. (1995). Psychiatric aspects of chronic pain. *Neurology, 45*(Suppl. 9), 26–34.

Fink, P. (1992). Physical complaints and symptoms of somatizing patients. *Journal of Psychosomatic Research, 36*, 125–136.

Fishbain, D. A., Goldberg, M., Meagher, B. R., Steele, R., & Rosomoff, H. (1986). Male and female chronic pain patients categorized by *DSM–III* psychiatric diagnostic criteria. *Pain, 26*, 181–197.

Flor, H., & Birbaumer, N. (1994). Basic issues in the psychobiology of pain. In G. F. Gebhart, D. L. Hammond, & T. S. Jensen (Eds.), *Proceedings of the 7th World Congress on Pain* (pp. 113–125). Seattle: IASP Press.

Ford, C. V. (1995). Dimensions of somatization and hypochondriasis. *Neurologic Clinics, 13*, 241–253.

Gale, E. N. (1978). Psychological characteristics of long-term female temporomandibular joint pain patients. *Journal of Dental Research, 57*, 481–483.

Goldenberg, D. L. (1987). Fibromyalgia syndrome: An emerging but controversial condition. *Journal of the American Medical Association, 257*, 2782–2787.

Hudson, J. I., Goldenberg, D. L., Pope, H. G., Jr., Keck, P. E., Jr., & Schlesinger, L. (1992). Comorbidity of fibromyalgia with medical and psychiatric disorders. *American Journal of Medicine, 92*, 363–367.

Jones, D. A., Rollman, G. B., & Brooke, R. A. (1997). The cortisol response to psychological stress in temporomandibular dysfunction. *Pain, 72*, 171–182.

Kaplan, H. I., Sadock, B. J., & Grebb, J. A. (1994). *Kaplan and Sadock's synopsis of psychiatry: Behavioral sciences, clinical psychiatry* (7th ed.). Baltimore: Williams & Wilkins.

Katon, W., Kleinman, A., & Rosen, G. (1982). Depression and somatization: A review (part I). *American Journal of Medicine, 72*, 127–135.

Kellner, R. (1994). Psychosomatic syndromes, somatization and somatoform disorders. *Psychotherapy and Psychosomatics, 61*, 4–24.

Kleinman, A., & Kleinman, J. (1986). Somatization: The interconnections among culture, depression experiences, and the meaning of pain. In A. Kleinman & B. Good (Eds.), *Culture and depression* (pp. 429–490). Berkeley: University of California Press.

Kosek, E., & Hansson, P. (1997). Modulatory influence on somatosensory perception from vibration and heterotopic noxious conditioning stimulation (HNCS) in fibromyalgia patients and healthy subjects. *Pain, 70*, 41–51.

Lautenbacher, S., Pauli, P., Zaudig, M., & Birbaumer, N. (1998). Attentional control of pain perception: The role of hypochondriasis. *Journal of Psychosomatic Research, 44*, 251–259.

Lautenbacher, S., & Rollman, G. B. (1997). Possible deficiencies of pain modulation in fibromyalgia. *Clinical Journal of Pain, 13*, 189–196.

Lautenbacher, S., Rollman, G. B., & McCain, G. A. (1994). Multi-method assessment of experimental and clinical pain in patients with fibromyalgia. *Pain, 59*, 45–53.

Lipowski, Z. J. (1990). Somatization and depression. *Psychosomatics, 31*, 13–21.

McDermid, A. J., & Rollman, G. B. (1996). Generalized hypervigilance in chronic pain patients: An examination of contributing factors. In *Abstracts of the Eighth World Congress on Pain* (p. 62). Seattle: IASP Press.

McDermid, A. J., Rollman, G. B., & McCain, G. A. (1996). Generalized hypervigilance in fibromyalgia: Evidence of perceptual amplification. *Pain, 66,* 133–144.

McKinney, M. W., Londeen, T. F., Turner, S. P., & Levitt, S. R. (1990). Chronic TM disorder and non-TM disorder pain: A comparison of behavioral and psychological characteristics. *Cranio, 8,* 40–46.

Mechanic, D. (1985). Illness behavior: An overview. In S. McHugh & T. M. Vallis (Eds.), *Illness behavior: A multidisciplinary model* (pp. 101–109). New York: Plenum.

Merskey, H. (1994). Pain and psychological medicine. In P. D. Wall & R. Melzack (Eds.), *Textbook of pain* (3rd ed., pp. 903–920). Edinburgh: Churchill Livingstone.

Merskey, H., & Bodguk, N. (1994). *Classification of chronic pain: Descriptions of chronic pain syndromes and definitions of pain terms* (2nd ed.). Seattle: IASP Press.

Merskey, H., Brown, J., Brown, A., Malhotra, L., Morrison, D., & Ripley, C. (1985). Psychological normality and abnormality in persistent headache patients. *Pain, 23,* 35–48.

Merskey, H., & Evans, P. R. (1975). Variations in pain complaint threshold in psychiatric and neurological patients with pain. *Pain, 1,* 73–79.

Merskey, H., Lau, C. L., Russell, E. S., Brooke, R. I., James, M., Lappano, S., Neilsen, J., & Tilsworth, R. H. (1987). Screening for psychiatric morbidity: The pattern of psychological illness and premorbid characteristics in four chronic pain populations. *Pain, 30,* 141–157.

Naliboff, B. D., & Cohen, M. J. (1989). Psychophysical laboratory methods applied to clinical pain patients. In C. R. Chapman & J. D. Loeser (Eds.), *Issues in pain measurement: Advances in pain research and therapy* (Vol. 12, pp. 365–386). New York: Raven.

Naliboff, B. D., Cohen, M. J., Schandler, S. L., & Heinrich, R. L. (1981). Signal detection and threshold measures for chronic back pain patients, chronic illness patients, and cohort controls to radiant heat stimuli. *Journal of Abnormal Psychology, 3,* 271–274.

Naliboff, B. D., Munakata, J., Fullerton, S., Gracely, R. H., Kodner, A., Harraf, F., & Mayer, E. A. (1997). Evidence for two distinct perceptual alterations in irritable bowel syndrome. *Gut, 41,* 505–512.

Payne, T. C., Leavitt, F., Garron, D. C., Katz, R. S., Golden, H. E., Glickman, P. B., & Vanderplate, C. (1982). Fibrositis and psychologic disturbance. *Arthritis and Rheumatism, 25,* 213–217.

Pennebaker, J. W. (1982). *The psychology of physical symptoms.* New York: Springer-Verlag.

Pilowsky, I. (1994). Pain and illness behavior: Assessment and management. In P. D. Wall & R. Melzack (Eds.), *Textbook of pain* (3rd ed., pp. 1309–1319). Edinburgh: Churchill Livingstone.

Pilowsky, I. (1995). Low back pain and illness behavior (inappropriate, maladaptive, or abnormal). *Spine, 20,* 1522–1524.

Rief, W. (1996). Die somatoformen Störungen: Großes unbekanntes Land zwischen Psychologie und Medizin [Somatoform disorders: A large unknown territory between psychology and medicine]. *Zeitschrift für Klinische Psychologie, 25,* 173–189.

Rief, W., Hiller, W., & Fichter, M. M. (1997). Somatoforme Störungen [Somatoform disorders]. *Nervenheilkunde, 16,* 25–29.

Robbins, J. M., Kirmayer, L. J., & Hemami, S. (1997). Latent variable models of functional somatic distress. *Journal of Nervous and Mental Disease, 185,* 606–615.

Rollman, G. B. (1979). Signal detection theory pain measures: Empirical validation studies and adaptation-level effects. *Pain, 6,* 9–21.

Rollman, G. B. (1992). Cognitive variables in pain and pain judgments. In D. Algom (Ed.), *Psychophysical approaches to cognition* (pp. 515–574). Amsterdam: North-Holland.

Rollman, G. B. (1995). Gender differences in pain: The role of anxiety. *Pain Forum, 4,* 331–334.

Rollman, G. B. (1998). Culture and pain. In S. S. Kazarian & D. R. Evans (Eds.), *Cultural clinical psychology: Theory, research, and practice* (pp. 267–286). New York: Oxford University Press.

Rollman, G. B., & Lautenbacher, S. (1993). Hypervigilance effects in fibromyalgia: Pain experience and pain perception. In H. Vaeroy & H. Merskey (Eds.), *Progress in fibromyalgia and myofascial pain* (pp. 149–159). Amsterdam: Elsevier.

Salkovskis, P. M. (1996). Somatoforme Störungen [Somatoform disorders]. In J. Margraf (Ed.), *Lehrbuch der Verhaltenstherapie, Band 2: Störungen—Glossar [Handbook of Behavior Therapy Volume 2: Disturbances—Glossary]* (pp. 163–183). Berlin: Springer-Verlag.

Schnurr, R. F., Brooke, R. I., & Rollman, G. B. (1990). Psychosocial correlates of temporomandibular joint pain and dysfunction. *Pain, 42,* 153–165.

Scudds, R. A., Rollman, G. B., Harth, M., & McCain, G. A. (1987). Pain perception and personality measures as discriminators in the classification of fibrositis. *Journal of Rheumatology, 14,* 563–569.

Smythe, H. A. (1984). Problems with the MMPI. *Journal of Rheumatology, 11,* 417–418.

Smythe, H. A. (1986). Tender points: Evolution of concepts of the fibrositis/fibromyalgia syndrome. *American Journal of Medicine, 81*(Suppl. 3A), 2–5.

Spekens, A. E. M., Spinhoven, P., Sloekers, P. P. A., Bolk, J. H., & van Hemert, A. M. (1996). A validation study of the Whitely Index, the Illness Attitudes Scales, and the Somatosensory Amplification Scale in general medical and general practice patients. *Journal of Psychosomatic Research, 40,* 95–104.

Spinhoven, P., & van der Does, A. J. W. (1997). Somatization and somatosensory amplification in psychiatric outpatients: An explorative study. *Comprehensive Psychiatry, 38,* 93–97.

Swartz, M., Blazer, D., Woodbury, M., George, L., & Landerman, R. (1986). Somatization disorder in a US southern community: Use of a new procedure for analysis of medical classification. *Psychological Medicine, 16,* 595–609.

Unruh, A. M. (1996). Gender variations in clinical pain experience. *Pain, 65,* 123–167.

Volz, H.-P., Stieglitz, R.-D., Menges, K., & Möller, H.-J. (1994). Somatoform disorders: Diagnostic concept, controlled clinical trials, and methodological issues. *Pharmacopsychiatry, 27,* 231–237.

Walker, E. A., Keegan, D., Gardner, G., Sullivan, M., Katon, W. J., & Bernstein, D. (1997). Psychosocial factors in fibromyalgia compared with rheumatoid arthritis: I. Psychiatric diagnoses and functional disability. *Psychosomatic Medicine, 59,* 565–571.

Waylonis, G. W., & Heck, W. (1992). Fibromyalgia syndrome: New associations. *American Journal of Physical Medicine and Rehabilitation, 71,* 343–348.

Weinstein, N. D. (1978). Individual differences in reaction to noise: A longitudinal study in a college dormitory. *Journal of Applied Psychology, 63,* 458–466.

Wolfe, F., Cathey, M. A., & Kleinheksel, S. M. (1984). Fibrositis (fibromyalgia) in rheumatoid arthritis. *Journal of Rheumatology, 11,* 814–818.

Wolfe, F., Ross, K., Anderson, J., Russell, I. J., & Hebert, L. (1995). The prevalence and characteristics of fibromyalgia in the general population. *Arthritis and Rheumatism, 38,* 19–28.

Wolfe, F., Smythe, H. A., Yunus, M. B., Bennett, R. M., Bombardier, C., Goldenberg, D. L., Tugwell, P., Campbell, S. M., Abeles, M., Clark, P., Fam, A. G., Farber, S. J., Fiechtner, J. J., Franklin, C. M., Gatter, R. A., Hamaty, D., Lessard, J., Lichtbroun, A. S., Masi, A. T., McCain, G., Reynolds, W. J., Romano, T. J., Russell, I. J., & Sheon, R. P. (1990). The American College of Rheumatology 1990: Criteria for the classification of fibromyalgia. *Arthritis and Rheumatism, 33,* 160–172.

Yunus, M. B., Ahles, T. A., Aldag, J. C., & Masi, A. T. (1991). Relationship of clinical features with psychological status in primary fibromyalgia. *Arthritis and Rheumatism, 34,* 15–21.

Author Index

A

Aaron, L. A., 261, 263, 264, 268, 275, 276, 278, 628, 629
Aaronson, N. K., 507, 525
Abbattista, A., 508, 521
Abbott, F., 557, 564
Abbott, K. H., 240, 255
Abdelmoumene, M., 25, 37
Abel, G. G., 576, 584
Abeles, M., 15, 22, 625, 632
Abelson, J. L., 327, 343
Abraham, N., 266, 278
Abram, S. E., 173, 174, 184, 186, 329, 336, 344
Abrams, D. B., 109, 121
Abrams, M. A., 578, 583, 586
Abrams, M. R., 576, 577, 579, 580, 581, 584, 585, 587
Abramson, A. S., 413, 428
Aburatani, H., 357, 366
Accarino, A. M., 488, 491
Acland, R. H., 421, 429
Adams, C. B. T., 445, 450
Adams, J. E., 595, 609
Adams, L. E., 329, 336, 344
Adams, S., 341, 347
Adcock, R. J., 603, 609
Adelhart, J., 509, 520
Adelman, A. M., 13, 14, 19
Adriaensen, H. F., 389, 397
Affleck, G., 130, 143, 262, 264, 265, 266, 268, 276, 278, 279
Afifi, J., 44, 55
Agambar, L., 249, 256

Agerberg, G., 540, 549
Agnoli, A., 288, 301
Agre, J. C., 174, 188
Agreus, L., 13, 14, 20
Agudelo, C. A., 269, 270, 273, 277
Ahern, D., 554, 555, 567
Ahles, T. A., 261, 276, 500, 501, 507, 508, 511, 519, 519, 623, 626, 629, 632
Ahles, T. M., 289, 300
Ahlgren, P., 379, 400
Ahlin, J. H., 314, 315
Ahmad, S., 406, 428
Ahrens, S., 199, 202, 204, 210
Aisen, P. S., 378, 394
Aisenberg, J., 485, 491
Akarasereenont, P., 151, 163
Akinyanju, O. O., 578, 586
Akkermans, L. M. A., 486, 492
Aksmanovic, V. M., 362, 363, 366
Alarcón, G. S., 261, 262, 263, 264, 265, 266, 268, 274, 275, 276, 278, 279, 280, 628, 629
Albert, M., 130, 144
Alberts, K. R., 261, 263, 264, 268, 274, 275, 276, 278, 279, 628, 629
Alburger, G. W., 307, 319
Aldag, J. C., 623, 626, 632
Aldam, C. F., 175, 187
Alderman, M. M., 219, 231
Alders, E. E. A., 10, 20
Aldrete, J. A., 515, 524
Alexander, E. J., 389, 400
Alexander, J. I., 385, 394
Alexander, M. P., 303, 315
Alexander, M. T., 263, 264, 276

633

Subject Index